1001

TAROT
SPREADS

**THE COMPLETE BOOK OF TAROT SPREADS
FOR EVERY PURPOSE**

CASSANDRA EASON

STERLING ETHOS
New York

STERLING ETHOS
New York

An Imprint of Sterling Publishing Co., Inc.

Text © 2021 Cassandra Eason
Cover © 2021 Sterling Publishing Co., Inc.

ISBN 978-1-4549-4215-3 (print format)
ISBN 978-1-4549-4216-0 (e-book)

Distributed in Canada by Sterling Publishing Co., Inc.
C/o Canadian Manda Group, 664 Annette Street
Toronto, Ontario M6S 2C8, Canada
Distributed in the United Kingdom by GMC Distribution Services
Castle Place, 166 High Street, Lewes, East Sussex BN7 1XU, England
Distributed in Australia by NewSouth Books
University of New South Wales, Sydney, NSW 2052, Australia

For information about custom editions, special sales, and premium and corporate purchases,
please contact Sterling Special Sales at 800-805-5489 or specialsales@sterlingpublishing.com.

Manufactured in India

2 4 6 8 10 9 7 5 3

sterlingpublishing.com

Cover design by Igor Satanovsky
Interior design by Christine Heun

Image Credits:

Depositphotos.com: ©Akini: 423, 445
Dreamstime.com: ©Lestyan (sun/moon): cover, 1
Getty Images: DigitalVisons Vectors: ET-ARTWORKS:
462; ulimi: 179, 253,456, 507; iStock/Getty Images Plus:
-Albachiaraa-: 374, 377; Art-Digital-Illustration: 469;
bsd555: 500; Hathairuth: 46; kolb art: 487; LironPeer:
425; Mashot: 390, 407, 408, 409, 410, 411; Alona
Savchuk: 414, 420; Suesse: 206

Shutterstock.com: 4LUCK: 331, 337, 407, 409, 411, 434;
Arcady: 383; AV-Art: 30; bluepencil (dividers): cover, 1;
Olha Bocharova: 388, 389, 394, 408, 410, 412, 524;
Dualororua: 513; lineartestpilot: 384; Olkita: 395;
Oleksandr Panasovskyi: 405, 455, 456; Photology1971
(cards): cover, 4; Pixejoo: 338; ray.e: 425; Sudowoodo:
462; Svetsol: 275, 380; Vertyr: 391

CONTENTS

INTRODUCTION TO
1001 TAROT SPREADS

**Welcome to this book of 1001 Tarot Spreads,
also called Tarot Layouts.**

Tarot cards, seventy-eight highly illustrated cards signifying love, happiness, travel, making your own money, long-term security, new beginnings, and many other themes, are as relevant to our lives today as when they were first created in medieval times. In this book, you will discover everything you need in order to read Tarot cards. This includes the basic meanings of each card, and methods of dealing or laying out the cards and interpreting them. You will be able to use this information to try any of the 1001 different ways of instantly laying out the cards, even if you are a total Tarot-card beginner.

Why read the Tarot?

Tarot is the most exciting, versatile, and portable form of divination, or discovering and deciding, your own destiny. For Tarot is much more than fortune-telling. The cards offer guidance to assist you in making *your own* decisions about your future or the future of those for whom you are reading. As well as reading for yourself, you can read the Tarot during a fun evening with friends, in a heart-to-heart with someone who is distressed or anxious, or even to take up Tarot reading professionally. If you are already a professional Tarot reader or teacher of the Tarot, this book will offer you source material and new ideas for developing your existing good practice.

For, whether reading for ourselves or others, Tarot reading provides the chance to look over the horizon to the possibilities that are on offer if we follow a certain path rather than another, and also alerts us to challenges along the way with suggestions on how to overcome them and even to turn an obstacle into an advantage. Sometimes the cards may indicate a totally unexpected factor that can help us make wise choices, so we steer *our own* destiny, rather than going along with what life or others offer. A Spread or Layout of cards chosen seemingly at random from a facedown deck may suggest new approaches in love, career, health, money, travel, family, workplace issues, and social life—or alternatives to an existing problem or dilemma.

A Tarot deck also forms the focus for many divinatory and psychic activities and can be used—as well as in Spreads or indeed as an extension of a card Layout—as a basis for meditation, creative thinking, discovering past lives, mediumship, magick spells, or manifestation of needs and desires. A Tarot reading can even incorporate crystals and pendulums in more detailed decision-making following on from—or as part of—a reading.

Why do we need 1001 Spreads or Layouts?

If you read Tarot cards, you may already have several favorite Layouts. Even if you are new to Tarot, you will soon—as you either dip into this book or rapidly work your way through it—discover that some methods work better for you than others. There are no definite set-in-stone rights and wrongs in laying out and indeed in interpreting cards: just ways that people have found helpful when using Tarot cards. If any order of cards or card meaning doesn't feel right, change it and note your changes. Tarot is a living, growing art, and every one of us brings to it our unique insights and intuition.

All the Spreads/Layouts in this book are ones that I have created and have been tried and tested by me in thousands of readings over forty years or more. Some I have adapted by watching the way other Tarot readers in different countries I have visited set out their cards. Others are inspired by various folk, magical, and psychic traditions. For Tarot Layouts, like the Spread positions themselves, belong to no one—and everyone—who reads Tarot cards, because they are a living and constantly evolving tradition. Frequently I will modify a Tarot Spread when someone points out to me an alternative I had not considered, but which on reflection offers a new dimension to the reading. You will probably eventually have perhaps twenty favorite Spreads that fit all occasions, some of which you will have created yourself once you see the way it all works. Some of you experienced readers will already have your special Spreads but may find that some of mine inspire you to new ways of interpreting and setting out the cards.

Use both the Spread card positions and the suggested Layouts in the way that's most helpful to you on your personal Tarot journey, whether for self-assessment, for advising friends and family, or in professional practice. Experiment/adapt and replace my ideas where they aren't quite right for you. For you will discover that the more you make the Tarot your own, the more you tap into its true inner magick. Tarot cards are an ever-evolving science, one about which I am learning more and more every day.

Different Tarot Spreads are suited to particular themes and areas of life, with each card position in the Layout representing a different aspect of the question asked. In this way, the overall answer can be clearly built up and seen as answering a daily life problem or a major life issue.

Some Spreads will need only one card to answer a straightforward question, or two cards set side by side to choose between options. At the other end of the spectrum, I have listed Spreads using all seventy-eight cards as a life review or to answer really complex matters.

You will find Layouts to suit every purpose—for example: based around your zodiac signs, around angels, the days of the week, a wheel of the year to predict the key issues in the twelve months ahead, or an eight-stage reading linked with the eight phases of the moon. There are Spreads for every special occasion, from a baby-naming ceremony, a birthday, a graduation, a wedding or handfasting, an anniversary, Christmas and Thanksgiving,

retirement, moving home, and dealing positively with the problems when someone dies, especially if there are inheritance disputes.

How do we choose the right cards to answer our questions?

The cards, chosen from a facedown deck in response to a certain question, will invariably pinpoint what needs to be discovered to find a solution to the question asked.

We cannot precisely explain the way this happens time after time, only that it does. At one time not a lot more than a hundred years ago, electricity would have been considered magick. It may be that one day the power behind choosing the right Tarot cards or the movement of a pendulum will be explained in terms of energies that can be scientifically measured. Until then, the process is described as psychokinesis or psychic touch. This is the ability to draw to us by touch, as we shuffle or mix a deck of cards and then select from a facedown deck, what we most need to know to resolve a seemingly tangled issue. The more you relax as you choose your cards by psychic touch, the easier the energies flow. This is the reason it is important, if you are reading for others, that they handle the cards as well.

How and when to read the Tarot

You can do readings any time, anywhere, with just your Tarot deck. On special occasions, when you have plenty of time, you can add the right colored candles and the best days of the week for specific issues. You can also add the use of a pendulum and writing guided by your guardian angels, spirit guides, or your own wise self to expand the message of the cards. You can even use chosen cards for Spreads to bring the desired result or person as foretold in the cards into your life.

Tarot and everyday life

However, this is far more than a book of instructions. Some of the Layouts include the stories of people who chose certain Spreads, why they needed the reading, the cards they selected, and how they interpreted the Spreads. There is also a brief account of the results of following the advice of the reading in the everyday world of the questioner.

Choosing the right deck

There is a seemingly endless choice of Tarot decks on the market. There are Cats, Celts, Viking heroes and heroines, and Ancient Egyptians. You will find decks showing medieval knights in armor on white chargers, or up-to-date sets with guys and gals catching or even piloting a plane.

It's best to start with a straightforward deck, with seventy-eight cards, including twenty-two Major or keynote cards. Some decks do have a different number of cards, and this can be confusing.

You'll also need a deck in which what are called the Minor or number cards, the Aces to Tens, forty in all, have pictures and not just—for example—six cups or chalices sitting in a row.

Excellent decks for your 1001 Spreads are the Golden Waite, Universal Waite, or Radiant Waite. These are brightly colored forms of the basic Rider Waite deck. You'll find that the meanings in most 78-card decks are based on the famous Rider Waite deck. These also have pictures that show you the characters of what we call the Court, Royalty or Personality cards, the Pages/Princesses, Knights/Princes, and Queens and Kings.

Most bookstores and New Age stores sell Tarot decks. Expect to be able to see the cards in a sample deck. That way, you can decide if they are for you. If you are not sure, go back another day or try somewhere else.

You can also buy your cards off the Internet. Choose a site where sample cards from each set can be seen before buying. In my experience, one of the best online sites for viewing individual cards within sets is www. aeclectic.net/tarot/cards—although there are many other sites from which you can purchase Tarot cards. Just google "tarot cards," and you'll find more choices than you thought existed.

The book has two main sections. Chapters 1 to 9 show effective different Spread formats for reading with between one and nine cards and Layouts that work well with each specific number of cards. These contain examples of Tarot Spreads for different purposes that work especially well with the different number of cards: for example, five-card readings for change, or for communicating needs and revealing talents, for speculation and risk-taking, for travel plans, and for salvaging what is good from situations that didn't work out and so moving forward positively. This method will enable you to work confidently with Tarot Spreads from the beginning, even if you are new to Tarot.

The remaining chapters are devoted to Spreads for many hundreds of different questions you may ask, divided into different themes.

For all Spreads used in the book, deal the cards facedown. Turn over and read each card in numerical order, faceup, one at a time. Finish reading the card you have turned before turning the next card faceup and reading that. Continue until you have read every card in the Spread. If you decide to add an extra card for clarity, deal it facedown as before.

So, let us begin.

CHAPTER 1

ONE-CARD SPREADS

One-card Spreads are ideal for an almost instant reading or when you have a single question requiring a relatively straightforward answer. *Yes/no, should I go/stay, speak/remain silent, act/wait* all work well with one-card Spreads. One-card readings are also effective for date/time-specific questions asking *when will I/should I/can I.* If you use your 40 Minor cards for time readings, the number of the card will give you days/weeks/months according to a realistic time frame and how you should proceed according to the suit. The nature of the card selected often suggests how a negative can be turned into a positive.

You can also ask an *Is/will be/what* question about a person or situation to offer the clarity needed when you have been overthinking an issue or the outer evidence is at odds with your gut feeling.

You can add a second card if necessary. Set your second card to the right of the first. There is also the option to use a single card reading as the first card in a reading that you build up with three, six, or even nine cards.

1
CARD OF THE DAY

Purpose and background information:
You can use this Spread every day to alert you to what you need to know about the day ahead. If the answer is not clear, or if it is a particularly significant day, add a second card.

You may find it useful to note in your Tarot journal the card you pick each day. If the same card appears regularly or occurs on the same day each week, ask yourself what or who in your everyday life is connected with that day, and the relationship that might exist with that card.

If necessary, add a more extensive reading when you have time, using the repeated card as Card 1 in the Spread.

What you should use:
A full deck of seventy-eight cards. Choose one card at random from anywhere in the facedown deck.

When:
Every morning, soon after you have woken up. If you are still somewhat sleepy, you will be relaxed enough to interpret the chosen card with your intuition, rather than trying to make sense of the card with your logical mind.

2
ONE QUESTION

Purpose and background information:
Any single uncomplicated question that requires a straightforward *yes or no* answer.

What you should use:
A single card from the full deck of seventy-eight cards. Choose one card taken at random from anywhere in the facedown deck. If the answer is not clear, add a second card.

When:
Whenever a quick answer is needed to an uncomplicated question.

3
IS THIS A FAVORABLE TIME TO ACT/ SPEAK OUT/GO FOR IT?

Purpose and background information:
When you are not sure whether or how to act/react but need to decide the best approach.

What you should use:
The twenty-two Major cards. Choose a single card at random.

When:
The evening before you need to act/speak out/go for it.

4
WHAT STRATEGY SHOULD I USE?

Purpose and background information:
Whenever you have an issue that you need to solve and are unsure how to tackle it.

What you should use:
Forty cards: the four suits, Ace to Ten. Choose a single card. Note the suit of the chosen card and the number on the card to help you make sense of the meaning.

When:
Early morning, if you need the right strategy for the day ahead.

Example:
Paul had to find money fast to pay for his vacation. He picked the **Eight of Pentacles,** showing the person making their own golden coins. Paul had hoped that his brother might lend him the money, but this card suggested otherwise.

Paul therefore decided to take a second evening job for a few weeks to boost his income. His brother subsequently did refuse to loan him the money, but Paul was able to earn enough himself for the vacation.

5
WHAT IS MY GREATEST STRENGTH IN THIS SITUATION?

Purpose and background information:
If you encounter or anticipate a situation where you know there is an opportunity. You have the option of combining this with Spread 6 if you suspect (or know) there will also be opposition.

What you should use:
A single card picked at random from the twenty-two Major cards and the sixteen Court cards. These will enable you to see the broader picture and determine who is a potential ally or what strength you possess to win the day.

When:
Before reaching out for the opportunity.

6
WHAT IS MY GREATEST CHALLENGE IN THIS SITUATION?

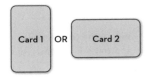

Purpose and background information:
A single card can be chosen entirely independently of Spread 5 if there is known or suspected opposition from a person or organization to an opportunity you seek.

However, you may wish to combine this with Spread 5. If so, choose Card 1 to determine what the opposition is/obstacles are. Then choose a second card to see what allies/strengths you have to overcome the opposition.

What you should use:
The Major Arcana (this is another term for the twenty-two Major or trump cards). Do not replace the first card in the deck before choosing the second.

When:
If you suspect or know of opposition to your plans.

7
WILL I PASS MY EXAMINATION/ DRIVING TEST/INTERVIEW?

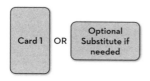

Purpose and background information:
To gain from the card a positive or negative answer plus, depending upon the chosen card, what could make things work better if the answer is negative.

What you should use:
The Minor Arcana (the fifty-six suit cards: four suits, fourteen cards in each suit), but only using the Ace to Ten from each suit. Choose a single card. If the answer is not clear, return the card to the deck, reshuffle, and pick a substitute rather than picking an extra card. Combine the information.

When:
In the days or weeks before the test/examination/interview so you can modify your approach or increase your efforts.

Example:
Christina was due to take a major exam in mathematics that she needed for college entrance, in three weeks' time. She hadn't been studying, as she had been out every night with her new boyfriend, so she expected a negative result in the card.

However, the chosen card, **The Three of Pentacles,** showing the person building a wall by hard work, said that she could pass if she worked really hard between the Tarot reading and the examination. She stayed home every night, studying, and just got the necessary grades to gain her college place.

8
IS THIS PERSON/SITUATION TRUSTWORTHY?

Purpose and background information:
If your intuition/gut feeling is warning you to look below the surface of a person or situation, especially regarding an investment.

What you should use:
If a person, then use the 16 Court cards; if a situation, use the 40 Minor cards. Choose a single card.

When:
A Thursday, traditionally a day of truth.

Example:
Paolo had been asked to invest some money in a project that promised great dividends, along with what he was told was nineteen other investors. But it seemed too good to be true. He picked the **Seven of Swords,** suggesting behind-the-scenes trickery. When he dug deeper, Paolo found he was in fact the only investor, and so the promises of rich returns were unlikely to come true.

9

HOW LONG BEFORE I SELL MY HOME/BUSINESS?

Purpose and background information:
When your home or business has been on the market for a while and isn't moving.

What you should use:
Decide a realistic time scale—days, weeks, or months—and use the forty Minor cards, Aces to Tens. Choose a single card.

When:
Before trying a new agent or tactic.

10

HAS (NAME OF PERSON) LEFT MY LIFE FOREVER?

Purpose and background information:
If someone close has broken off contact, and all your attempts to mend the situation have been ignored or rejected.

What you should use:
All 78 cards. Choose a single card.

When:
If you do not want to give up, but do not know what more to do.

11

SHOULD I MOVE TO WHERE I REALLY WANT TO LIVE, ALTHOUGH IT MEANS LEAVING THE PLACE WHERE I HAVE LIVED ALL MY LIFE?

Purpose and background information:
When a chance comes to live in a desired location.

What you should use:
The 22 Major cards. Choose a single card.

When:
A Tuesday, the day of change.

12

WILL MY NEW DIET/FITNESS REGIME GIVE PERMANENT GOOD RESULTS?

Purpose and background information:
When you have tried a lot of different methods and none seems to work.

What you should use:
The full deck. Choose a single card.

When:
The beginning of the week or month, or for a New Year's resolution.

Example:
Edgar had a cupboard full of the latest sports equipment and membership to countless fitness clubs. He also had a cupboard crammed with health shakes, but nothing worked. Now he had joined a jogging club, but was afraid his enthusiasm would go the way of all the others.

He picked the **Ace of Pentacles,** the new-beginning and slow-but-sure card, above all indicating the need to stick with a project when enthusiasm waned. Edgar had a high-powered job and was always rushing and tired. So he decided to delegate his work and actually take weekends off. He found that he started to enjoy the jogging club and the social side, as well as the exercise itself. He met a really nice guy whom he is now dating. Edgar is relaxed, and his fitness is slowly improving instead of the usual: a mad burst of activity, followed by exhaustion, followed by giving up.

The next chapter explains how to use two-card readings for anywhere there are choices or alternatives that may not be so clear-cut.

CHAPTER 2

TWO-CARD SPREADS

Spreads using just two cards are ideal when you are in a hurry or want to cut through indecision and get instant clarity. There are many times when we need to make a fast but important decision in our daily lives. If you are bogged down with detail and find your-self going in circles, a two-card Spread will often cut through indecision.

You can also use two cards if you are asking a question about the next two days, weeks, or months. They can pinpoint which of two dates or times is the best for a special occasion or interview, or even which of two places is the best location for a vacation. Best of all, they help you to decide between two options, people, or situations, as an *either/or*.

If neither option card seems right, maybe the answer is "wait," as neither choice will make you happy at present. But first of all, try adding a third card to the right of the second card to see if an alternative comes up. On the other hand, both options might be right and just involve compromise, if you then allow the two meanings to merge.

13
SHOULD YOU CONTINUE SAVING FOR A HOUSE, OR TAKE A BREAK AND HAVE A LONGED-FOR VACATION OVERSEAS?

Purpose and background information:
If you are saving hard for your first home or to upsize, but feel you just aren't having any fun anymore.

What you should use:
The full deck. Choose, before turning the cards over, one card for each option and read left to right.

When:
Everyone is going on vacation and you feel left out.

Example:
John and Julie have been saving for their first house for five years; but getting on the housing ladder just seems to get further away with house prices constantly rising.

The first card, suggesting pressing on with the saving, is the **Seven of Pentacles,** slowly building up and growing their savings, which they know is a sensible option.

The second card is the **World** card, showing the World expanding, their desired option. But must it be one or the other, or are both possible?

On closer examination the **Seven of Pentacles** shows a person *growing* their Pentacles, which can indicate growing/improving property as well as money. John has been talking to a friend whose grandfather was moving into a retirement village and selling his unmodernized home cheaply. John and Julie realized that they could just afford that house now and still have sufficient money to go camping around Europe before moving in.

14

SHOULD YOU GO FOR A MAJOR PROMOTION, OR FOCUS ON HAPPINESS IN YOUR OUT-OF-WORK LIFE?

Purpose and background information:
If you are offered a promotion or extra training that will involve long hours and working weekends, but it promises great prospects for the future.

What you should use:
The full deck.

When:
Before you apply for a promotion or go for an interview for that higher position you have been offered.

15

SHOULD YOU STICK WITH YOUR PREDICTABLE BUT RELIABLE BOYFRIEND/GIRLFRIEND, OR ACCEPT A DATE WITH AN EXCITING NEW PERSON WHO HAS A BIT OF A REPUTATION AS A FLIRT?

Purpose and background information:
If you are feeling restless in a longstanding relationship and want some excitement, but do not want to lose your present boyfriend/girlfriend.

What you should use:
The 22 Major cards and the 16 Court cards.

When:
If you are tempted to cheat.

Example:
Jodie has been dating her boyfriend Steve for two years. But a new guy, Alexander, has started coming into the office once a week and always takes her out for lunch. Now he has asked her to go for a weekend out of town, no strings attached, and she is tempted.

Her first card, for sticking with Steve, is the **Knight of Pentacles**. Steve is a typical Knight of Pentacles, kind and reliable, but she is getting bored watching Sky Sports in the evenings and going for Sunday lunch with his family. Though she has tried, Steve is resistant to change in his routine.

Alexander's card is the **Knight of Swords**, fun but unreliable and a warning that she could get hurt. Nether card felt right. Jodie then picked a third card, **The High Priestess**, which stands for independence. Jodie then realized that Steve wasn't right for her and she wasn't ready to settle down with anyone yet.

16

WHAT DO THE NEXT TWO DAYS/WEEKS/MONTHS HOLD FOR YOU?

Purpose and background information:
If you are coming up to a major change/opportunity/challenge in the next two days/weeks/months.

What you should use:
The 22 Major cards and the 40 Court cards.

When:
Immediately before the two-week/month period begins.

17
SHOULD YOU GO IT ALONE IN BUSINESS, OR WORK WITH A PARTNER?

Purpose and background information:
If you are planning on starting a solo business, but a colleague, friend, or family member wants you to go in with them.

What you should use:
The full deck.

When:
A Sunday, day of new beginnings.

18
WHICH SHOULD YOU GO FOR: THE PRESTIGIOUS STUDY CHOICE, OR THE ONE WITH PRACTICAL ON-THE-JOB TRAINING?

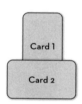

Purpose and background information:
When you have to decide between two educational/further education choices. If you have more than two choices, add an extra card for each additional one, moving left to right.

What you should use:
The full deck.

When:
A Wednesday, a good study/training decision day.

19
IF YOU HAVE MAJOR FINANCIAL PROBLEMS, SHOULD YOU NEGOTIATE, OR IGNORE THEM?

Purpose and background information:
When you are getting threatening phone calls or letters from creditors.

What you should use:
The 22 Major cards.

When:
Before contacting your creditors.

Example:
Phil had lost his job when the company he worked for folded. The town he lives in has high unemployment due to the closure of the steel works and its suppliers.

Phil picks **The World** card, showing the world expanding. But he doesn't feel that this indicates running away. The World suggests traveling to a new destination or job in a new location. He knew he owed so much that he would never get out of debt, even if creditors agreed to reduce interest on the debts.

His second card, the **Eight of Pentacles**, shows someone making their own gold coins. Phil found this interesting because that same day, he had seen an advertisement to teach welding at a college in Saudi Arabia, with a large tax-free salary. The card showing working with metal he considers a good omen.

So Phil applied for and got the job in Saudi Arabia and is making inroads into his debts.

20
IF YOU CANNOT DECIDE BETWEEN TWO VENUES FOR A FAMILY CELEBRATION

Purpose and background information:
When prices and facilities are similar.

What you should use:
The 22 Major cards.

When:
After you have visited and narrowed it down to two venues.

21
TO DECIDE BETWEEN TWO DATES FOR YOUR WEDDING OR A FAMILY CELEBRATION.

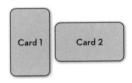

Purpose and background information:
If two dates are available.

What you should use:
The forty Minor cards.

When:
When both dates have merits and drawbacks. You can add a third card to the right if there is a third possible date. See which card is the better omen.

22
SHOULD YOU TAKE UP ART/CREATIVE WRITING AS A PROFESSION, OR KEEP YOUR DAY JOB UNTIL YOU ARE ESTABLISHED?

Purpose and background information:
If it would be a financial struggle to support yourself, but you fear that if you do not devote time to your creativity, you will never launch it.

What you should use:
The full deck.

When:
When you are uncertain as to whether your talents will take you where you want to go.

23
IF YOUR PARTNER IS UNWILLING TO TRAVEL, SHOULD YOU GO BY YOURSELF, OR PERSIST IN PERSUADING HIM/HER?

Purpose and background information:
When you have found the right vacation, but your partner will not commit to the trip even though money is not a problem.

What you should use:
The full deck.

When:
When you are in a quandary about your travel plans.

24
SHOULD YOU QUIT, OR COMPLAIN, BECAUSE YOU ARE CONSTANTLY BEING PICKED ON AT WORK BY A GROUP OF WORKPLACE BULLIES?

Purpose and background information:
When you dread going to work, but the Human Resources team, in spite of official policy, has no interest in finding out why.

What you should use:
The 22 Major cards and the 16 Court cards.

When:
When matters just seem to get worse, no matter what you do.

Example:
Tom is new in a huge industrial workplace, and though he is a highly skilled worker, the others, including the manager, give him the worst jobs and constantly criticize him in front of customers so that he becomes flustered and is starting to make mistakes.

The first card he picked was the **Tower,** which looks very fearsome with thunder and lightning and people falling out of a splitting tower. However, it is not predicting disaster, as the situation couldn't get worse, but it is advising Tom to break the conspiracy of silence in which even Human Resources is playing down the problem. The second card, **Judgment,** showing the people rising up in rebirth as Michael the Archangel blows his trumpet, tells Tom that if he takes his complaints high enough, he will get the desired results.

So Tom went back to Human Resources and said he was going to make an official complaint to a tribunal. The department didn't want a fuss, as other people had left because of bullying; so, with some strategic movement of people, Tom was able to work freely in a new department and indeed got a promotion.

In the following chapter, I will describe Spreads using three cards that offer greater flexibility than one- or two-card Spreads, but also will enable you to focus on key issues that may not be so easy with Spreads that use larger numbers.

CHAPTER 3

THREE-CARD SPREADS

Three-card Spreads extend the scope of a reading, offering more detail for individual position meanings than one- or two-card Spreads. However, they also provide a clear focus when issues are specific or involve choices that are reasonably straightforward.

Three cards extend the two-card option Spread in the previous chapter, showing which of three choices, for example vacations or venues for a special occasion, is best.

You can also—when choosing between two people, two jobs, two alternative new homes you are considering buying, or two study courses—use a third card to consider an extra choice if neither option feels right. This third card will reveal an unexpected—or maybe previously rejected or unthought-of—path.

Past, present, and future considerations also work well. Use the first card representing what is moving out of your life, the second representing the present situation and influences, and the third card for what is just over the horizon.

Above all, a three-carder allows you to do an entirely unstructured Spread. In this case, the three cards do not have assigned position meanings. Rather, they open up like an evolving story of your life as you add each card, building up by Card 3 to the solution to the question. This enables you to focus on the significance of each picture and what you feel.

Unless stated otherwise in a Spread, use a horizontal-row formation. Deal all three cards and turn them over one at a time, reading each before turning the next. Read left to right, turning over all the cards before beginning your reading.

If you get one of those gloomy Swords, remember it is not *predicting* disaster, rather reflecting the fears we all have. Replace a fear card with a substitute card so you can see what will happen when you replace that fear. If you get another fear card, substitute another until those fears have blown away.

25
A THREE-CARD UNSTRUCTURED READING TO ANSWER ANY QUESTION ON ANY TOPIC

Purpose and background information:
This Spread can answer any question.

Consider what you feel about each card, and combine the information once you have read all three. If in doubt, add a fourth card directly above **Card 2** to act as the **Crown** or summary of the reading.

What you should use:
A full deck of 78 cards.

When:
Any time you will not be disturbed, so you can allow the ideas to form.

26
PAST, PRESENT, AND FUTURE

Purpose and background information:
Useful if you are planning changes based on what has previously happened in your life.

Card 1: What you need to leave behind to make the change or what is already moving out of your life. **Card 2:** The present influences and factors already emerging affecting your decision. **Card 3:** The results of taking action and what lies over the horizon if you do.

What you should use:
The full seventy-eight-card deck.

When:
Once you have all the facts and figures, but still hesitate.

Example:
Petra has been asked by her fiancé to move overseas from the UK for two years once they marry, where they will both have the chance of major promotion. But her ex-husband Simon, who never sees their teenage children, has said he will oppose the move and threatens her with a court order. What can she do?

Card 1: What is moving out of your life, the Past:

The Emperor
Petra's ex-husband Simon has always been controlling and has used the children as a weapon, so she will not ask for any money for them, although he is wealthy. But it has been several years since he has seen or contacted the children.

Card 2: The Present Influences:

Justice
Petra takes the initiative and says she will go to court herself. Before the case went ahead, Simon said he would let her take the children overseas if she continued not to claim any money from him for their upbringing.

Card 3: The Future as a result of taking the action:

The World
Petra agreed to bring the children back home four times a year and allow phone and Skype contact with Simon whenever he wanted. He phoned only once in the two years.

27
WHAT LIES AHEAD
AN OVERVIEW OF THE NEXT THREE DAYS, WEEKS, OR MONTHS

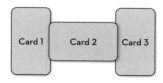

Purpose and background information:

If the next three days, weeks, or months are of significance, but there are unknown factors.

Card 1: Will represent factors or people who will be helpful.
Card 2: Will signify factors or people who may stand in your way. And the all-important **Card 3** represents what *you* can do to achieve the desired result by the end of the period.

What you should use:

The forty Number cards, Ace to Ten, and the sixteen Court or Personality cards.

When:

The day before the selected period begins.

28
OVERCOMING CONFLICT IN AN OTHERWISE LOVING RELATIONSHIP

Purpose and background information:

When you keep arguing about the same issues and never resolving them.

Card 1: Reveals the real underlying problem. **Card 2:** Shows what keeps it simmering. **Card 3:** Shows how it can be overcome.

What you should use:

The full seventy-eight cards.

When:

If you are just going around in circles arguing, but you want to be together.

29
MOVING TO A NEW HOME AND/OR AREA

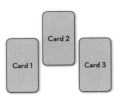

Purpose and background information:

When the right move isn't clear-cut.

Card 1: Is for moving home locally. **Card 2:** Is for a total relocation. **Card 3:** Is for staying put in your present home.

What you should use:

The full deck.

When:

When you have had enough of indecision.

30
IMPROVING FINANCES

Purpose and background information:

If you need an urgent money review because of major expenditure, or if the books just do not balance.

Card 1: Is your biggest money drain. **Card 2:** Is your most lucrative financial asset. **Card 3:** Is the way to balance the finances.

What you should use:

The forty number cards, Aces to Tens.

When:

At a time of financial crisis or before a big outlay.

31
MAKING A MAJOR LEISURE EXPENDITURE

Purpose and background information:
When you have a chance to invest in your leisure time but there are options. You may have choices of your own and so can substitute your dreams for my suggestions.

CARD 1: Could be a fun camper van. **CARD 2:** Could be a boat. **CARD 3:** Could be long-distance travel. If you have more choices, for example a retreat in the wilderness or by the shore, add extra cards. The method is the same.

What you should use:
The full deck.

When:
Once you have priced your different options.

32
THE HEALING SPREAD

Purpose and background information:
When you have tried most options but feel constantly unwell and exhausted, although there seems nothing medically wrong.

CARD 1: Involves necessary lifestyle changes. **CARD 2:** Involves reducing emotional pressures. **CARD 3:** Involves unexpected positive resources/input that will turn things around health-wise.

What you should use:
The full deck.

When:
Any Sunday or Wednesday, days associated with improving health.

33
WHAT STANDS IN YOUR WAY OF FULFILLMENT

Purpose and background information:
When you have a plan or ambition, but it always fails at the first hurdle.

CARD 1: Your ambition. **CARD 2:** Represents what or who stands in the way. **CARD 3:** Represents the way to get around the obstacle.

What you should use:
The twenty-two Major cards and the Court cards.

When:
Before trying again after a major setback.

34
THE UNITY SPREAD FOR BRINGING TWO FAMILIES TOGETHER

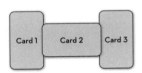

Purpose and background information:
When there are two sets of children involved in a new relationship. You can also use this Spread if there are in-laws, grandparents, and exes who are going to be part of the scene.

CARD 1: Your family. **CARD 2:** Your partner's family. **CARD 3:** How to unite the family as one.

What you should use:
The full deck.

When:
Before you all get together for a major event.

35
TO ACHIEVE THE BEST POSSIBLE OUTCOME

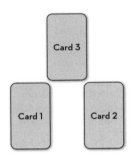

Purpose and background information:
When you know there is an inevitable change coming.

CARD 1: Represents the best possible outcome of the change. **CARD 2:** Represents the worst that can happen as a result of the change. **CARD 3:** Shows how to mitigate any possible bad effects, to make the best possible outcome likely.

What you should use:
The full deck.

When:
As soon as you become aware of the inevitable change.

36
THE STARTING-AT-A-NEW-WORKPLACE SPREAD

Purpose and background information:
To understand the way a new workplace functions and who holds the power.

CARD 1: Who is my ally? **CARD 2:** Of whom should I be wary?
CARD 3: How should I act/react initially?

What you should use:
The whole deck.

When:
After your first day.

In the following chapter, you will meet four-card Spreads that are especially helpful for all questions about security, stability, property, finances, practical matters, and protection.

CHAPTER 4

FOUR-CARD SPREADS

Four is a very solid number. Four-card Spreads work well for offering insights into practical matters and questions about security, stability, property, finances, family, the home, and protection. Unless stated specifically in a Spread, for four-card readings deal your cards in a horizontal row of four, turn them over one at a time, and afterward read them in the order dealt, left to right.

37
AN UNSTRUCTURED READING OF FOUR CARDS

Purpose and background information:
For absolutely any question, to build up an answer without assigning specific meanings. You can extend any unstructured three-card reading (see p. 18) into a four-card reading to summarize the solution offered in the three main cards.

After reading **CARDS 1, 2,** and **3,** the fourth card, the **CROWN,** will complete the answer and bring the other three cards together.

What you should use:
Any combination of the seventy-eight cards that fits with your question.

When:
Whenever you need extra information about your three-card reading.

38
SPREAD FOR BREAKING THROUGH THE BARRIERS OF FEAR

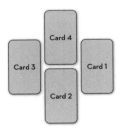

Purpose and background information:
When fears or phobias are restricting your lifestyle.

CARD 1: What is the real cause of my fear? **CARD 2:** Is this bad thing actually likely to happen, or is it just fear? **CARD 3:** What triggers/makes the fear worse? **CARD 4:** What action can I take to prevent or overcome my fear?

What you should use:
The full deck.

When:
A Tuesday, the day of courage.

39
GETTING ON THE PROPERTY OR BUSINESS LADDER

Purpose and background information:
When you are getting impatient, but do not have the finances for your dream home or business venture.

CARD 1: What you cannot or will not compromise on. **CARD 2:** What you will/can compromise on. **CARD 3:** The breakthrough card. **CARD 4:** How to fulfil at least part of the dream sooner rather than later.

What you should use:
The full deck.

When:
The beginning of a new month.

Example:
Rick and his partner Paula wanted to own and run a horse stud and training business, but the goal seemed just to get further away.

CARD 1 showed the **Six of Wands,** the person riding on a horse to victory, so the horse business was their priority. The card also suggested that something was possible within six months.

CARD 2 was the **Four of Wands** and, though this card showed a couple, land, and a house in the background, they cannot compromise on the land, but they *could* compromise on their living accommodation. How?

Card 3 showed the **Seven of Wands.** The person was putting down the wands on which the leaves were growing, marking out their territory. Rick said they had enough money for the land with basic stables and could initially train and breed horses for others. But the house has disappeared from the card.

Card 4 was the **Three of Pentacles**, building step by step over three years. Paula's family members were builders and had volunteered, as the money came in, to help with a self-built house on the land.

Rick and Paula found land with good grazing with a derelict house and run-down stables. Paula's family helped to get the stables and training ring into good order. They moved into a trailer on the land and are building up the business.

40
THE LIFE JOURNEY SPREAD

Purpose and background information:
When you are trying to unravel a longer-term life path.

Card 1: Who/where you are now. **Card 2**: Who/what will help you on your life journey. **Card 3**: Who/what will hinder you on your life journey. **Card 4**: Who/what you will or can become.

What you should use:
The sixteen Court cards

When:
At one of life's crossroads. You could redo the reading every three months if they are significant times.

41
THE MONTH AHEAD

Purpose and background information:
When you need to assess the four weeks ahead in terms of opportunities, challenges, and tactics.

Card 1 is Week 1, **Card 2** Week 2, **Card 3** Week 3, and **Card 4** Week 4. Some weeks, according to the cards dealt, will focus on opportunity, others on challenges, and this will help you develop the best strategy for maximizing your chances and minimizing conflict. Read each card at the beginning of its own week, returning all cards to the deck (you may get the same card two weeks running), noting what you previously picked.

What you should use:
The forty Minor cards, Aces to Tens, and the 16 Court cards.

When:
Ideally before the month begins, but you can start the reading at any time in the month and simply do four consecutive weeks.

42
A 24-HOUR PREDICTION

Purpose and background information:
If there is a particularly significant day ahead.

The Spread runs from dawn (or when you wake), until midnight (or the time you go to sleep). Ideally you will read each card at its own time of day. Take your deck with you during the day, having returned all the cards to the deck after reading them. You may get a repeat card. Note the previous cards dealt.

CARD 1: You will pick when you wake, traditionally at dawn to alert you of what lies ahead during the morning. **CARD 2:** Is noon or when you break, however briefly, in the middle of the day, to show what you still have to strive for and any warnings. **CARD 3:** Is dusk/late afternoon or when you go home, indicating what you have achieved. **CARD 4:** Before you go to bed, traditionally read at midnight, offers an overall assessment of the day.

What you should use:
The twenty-two Major cards.

When:
As soon as you wake on the big day.

43
THE FOUR-POINT ANTI-DEBT SPREAD

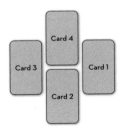

Purpose and background information:
This Spread is for when debts and pressure to repay them are building up.

CARD 1: What is the main drain on your finances right now? **CARD 2:** What sources of help are available to reduce payments? **CARD 3:** How can you earn more money in the short term? **CARD 4:** How can you prevent the problem from recurring?

What you should use:
The forty Minor cards and the sixteen Court cards.

When:
Any Saturday, the anti-debt day.

44
THE SPREAD FOR OVERCOMING BAD LUCK

Purpose and background information:
When you seem to be locked in a cycle of one misfortune after another.

CARD 1: What caused the original bad luck? **CARD 2:** How can the bad-luck cycle be broken? **CARD 3:** How can good fortune be attracted in its place? **CARD 4:** What unexpected factor will continue the new good fortune?

What you should use:
The forty Minor cards and the sixteen Court cards.

When:
Any Saturday, the anti-debt day.

45
THE FOUR CORNERS OF THE WORLD TRAVEL SPREAD

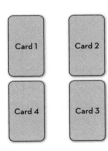

Purpose and background information:
When you are planning a major trip around the world or to a new continent.

    CARD 1: Am I ready for this major adventure? **CARD 2:** Should I go alone or with a companion? **CARD 3:** Shall I just travel, or will I need to earn as I go? **CARD 4:** What is totally unmissable on my journey?

What you should use:
The twenty-two Major cards and the sixteen Court cards.

When:
Before finalizing your plans.

46
FOR FAME AND FORTUNE

Purpose and background information:
    When you have a dream of fame and know you have talent but are afraid of failure.

    CARD 1: What is my special talent? **CARD 2:** Should I go all out to develop it? **CARD 3:** What must I do to get the necessary training? **CARD 4:** Where/how can I launch myself publicly?

What you should use:
The twenty-two Major cards.

When:
When an opportunity arises, preferably when you are alone in your Tarot space.

Card 4
Card 3
Card 2
Card 1

In the following chapter you will further extend your readings by working with Spreads with five cards that are especially useful for all changes and progressions.

CHAPTER 5

FIVE-CARD SPREADS

Five-card Spreads form a transition between fast, focused Spreads and more complex detailed Layouts. They are especially useful for questions concerning change, communicating needs and revealing talents, overcoming deception, bullying, and spite. Five cards also work well with finances, especially involving financial recovery, speculation and risk-taking, and travel plans, and for salvaging what is good from situations that did not work out and so moving forward positively.

47
THE HORSESHOE SPREAD

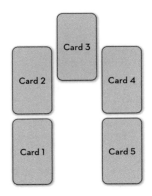

Purpose and background information:
You can use this Spread for absolutely any question.

CARD 1: Your choice, dilemma or predominant question.
CARD 2: Present influences, people, and circumstances that affect your present position. **CARD 3:** Hidden influences, both the messages in our heads from the past and what is just beyond the horizon. **CARD 4:** Suggested action, whether to change or preserve the status quo. **CARD 5:** Likely outcome, of either acting or waiting according to **CARD 4**.

What you should use:
The full deck.

When:
When there are several background factors in play.

48
DEALING WITH CLIQUES AND PETTY BULLYING

Purpose and background information:
When you are suffering at work or socially from being excluded, and from sarcasm or put-downs.

CARD 1: Who/what is excluding me most. **CARD 2:** What the motive is. **CARD 3:** Can or should I ignore it? **CARD 4:** Should I complain/tackle it head on? **CARD 5:** Should I cut my losses and leave?

What you should use:
The full deck.

When:
A Wednesday, day of protection against human snakes.

49
THE FIVE-YEAR PLAN

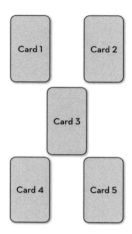

Purpose and background information:
When you are making long-term plans for any aspect of your life.

Card 1: Where I am now. **Card 2:** Where I would like to be in five years' time. **Card 3:** What extra resources/training/practice do I need? **Card 4:** Any possible challenges to overcome? **Card 5:** To achieve this long-term goal, do I need to expand/move on now, or stay where I am?

What you should use:
The full deck.

When:
At a time when you need to make decisions about your future, rather than letting life decide.

50
THE FIVE-POINTED STAR FOR RAISING YOUR PROFILE AT WORK OR CREATIVELY

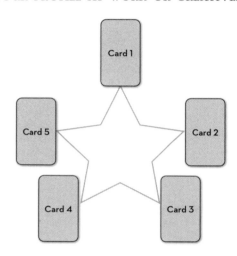

Purpose and background information:
Whether you want a major promotion or to showcase a talent.

Card 1: Your ultimate goal. **Card 2:** How to bring yourself/your work to the notice of those who can offer the most help in raising your profile. **Card 3:** The next step in gaining momentum. **Card 4:** Making a bid for the top. **Card 5:** What is the unknown factor?

What you should use:
The full deck.

When:
When you are feeling lucky.

51
FIVE STEPS TO DEVELOPING PSYCHIC POWERS

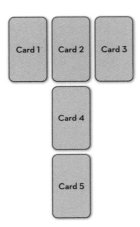

Purpose and background information:

When people tell you that you are psychic, but you feel blocked. **CARD 1:** How does your psychic gift appear in your life now? **CARD 2:** What is stopping you from developing your psychic gift? **CARD 3:** Do you need help to develop this power, reading books, classes? **CARD 4:** How far do you want your psychic powers to develop? **CARD 5:** Do you want to turn professional, help others, or use your gifts to improve your own life?

What should you use:
The full deck.

When:
A full-moon night.

Example:
Shelley had been psychic as a child and teenager, but gradually her abilities faded. However, recently she has been experiencing random accurate premonitions, and this is worrying her.

CARD 1: THE EIGHT OF WANDS, showing the growing wands flying everywhere. Shelley finds that her psychic powers aren't under her control and are often about travel disasters she cannot prevent. The premonitions are becoming more frequent.

CARD 2: The **Nine of Swords,** portraying a woman in bed having had a nightmare. Shelley says she is afraid of her growing powers, but admits that it is mainly because she cannot control them.

CARD 3: THE THREE OF PENTACLES, illustrating a person building a solid stone wall step by step. A slow learning guided approach such as going to sit in a mediumship and healing circle and taking courses, maybe using focused methods such as the Tarot to make it seem less scary.

CARD 4: THE SUN, showing a child riding a white horse into the sunlight. Shelley says once she feels confident in her powers, she is happy to let them emerge in her daily life as far as possible.

CARD 5: THE EIGHT OF PENTACLES, the person making their own gold through using their gifts. Shelley admits she has always wanted to work professionally as a clairvoyant and healer.

Shelley's frightening premonitions have stopped, as she is developing her psychic gifts formally.

52
THE COMPANY TAKEOVER FIVE-CARD SPREAD

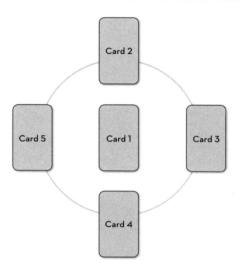

Purpose and background information:
When a takeover seems inevitable, to see how it will affect you and so how you should act. **CARD 1:** Will this takeover be of benefit to me and, if so, how? **CARD 2:** Should I be looking for another position, even as a precaution? **CARD 3:** How can I best secure my own position/my department when the takeover comes? **CARD 4:** What new skills should I be developing to secure a good position or to advantageously move on? **CARD 5:** Is there any information I am missing?

What you should use:
The full deck.

When:
Sunday for new beginnings.

53
FIVE-CARD RELOCATION SPREAD

Purpose and background information:
When you are being relocated because of work or because a close family member or partner is being relocated, but you do not really want to go.

CARD 1: Is there any positive way to avoid the relocation? **CARD 2:** What are the drawbacks of relocation, and can they be minimized? **CARD 3:** What are the benefits of relocation for you/the family? **CARD 4:** What can you not compromise on in the future location? **CARD 5:** What can you compromise on?

What you should use:
The full deck.

When:
The crescent moon or soon after, on any Monday, day of the moon.

54
THE FIVE-DAY-WORKING-WEEK SPREAD

Purpose and background information:
Useful for planning the week ahead, if you work a five-day week for a company or in your own business.

CARD 1: What you aim to achieve in the week ahead. **CARD 2:** Any anticipated challenges or pitfalls to avoid. **CARD 3:** Any new opportunities that may or will arise. **CARD 4:** Whom you need to impress. **CARD 5:** What can you build on for the following week as a result of your achievements this week?

What you should use:
The whole deck.

When:
The evening before your work week starts.

55
SEEKING ALTERNATIVE SOURCES OF FUNDING IF YOUR USUAL SUPPORT/ FINANCE IS NOT AVAILABLE

Purpose and background information:
When you need to resolve a cash flow/resource crisis.

CARD 1: Who/what will help you resolve this? **CARD 2:** Can you go it alone and, if so, how? **CARD 3:** Is there a new official source, and is it viable? **CARD 4:** Is there an unofficial source, and is it reliable? **CARD 5:** The ideal outcome.

What you should use:
The whole deck.

When:
A Wednesday, the day of ingenuity.

In the next chapter, you will meet six-card Layouts that offer even more detail of the different positions and are particularly helpful for love and relationship issues.

CHAPTER 6

SIX-CARD SPREADS

Six-card Spreads allow a question to be explored in detail to build up, step-by-step, a structured solution. They are sufficiently flexible if the dilemma or opportunity under consideration has different aspects which are closely related and interdependent.

Use six-card Spreads for any question, especially for harmony, negotiations and reconciliation, family matters, love, marriage, fidelity, fertility, friendship, self-image, health and fitness, confidence, or for anything concerning growth and the environment. They can also be used for assessing the next six days, weeks, or months.

56
AN UNSTRUCTURED SIX-CARD SPREAD TO ANSWER ANY QUESTION ON ANY TOPIC

Purpose and background information:
An extremely versatile Spread suitable for answering questions on any topic.

A natural progression from the three-card unstructured reading on page 18.

As you read the cards, consider what you feel about each card from its picture. Combine the information like a story, card by card, until by **CARD 6** the answer falls into place. Almost always the person shown in each card represents you—or, if not, then the person/people who affect the question.

What you should use:
A full deck of seventy-eight cards.

When:
Any time when you are unlikely to be disturbed.

57
THE NEXT SIX WEEKS/MONTHS SPREAD

Purpose and background information:
A predictive view of the six weeks or months directly ahead, so you can plan strategies, meet challenges, and avoid pitfalls.

CARD 1: What do you hope to achieve in the next six weeks/months? **CARD 2:** What specific opportunities are you seeking? **CARD 3:** What challenges are you worried about? **CARD 4:** What would you like to remain unchanged? **CARD 5:** What/who would you like to change? **CARD 6:** What do you seek in the longer term?

What you should use:
The full deck.

When:
The evening before the chosen period.

58
WILL I EVER FIND MY SOUL MATE?

Purpose and background information:
If you despair of finding the right love.

This is a heart-shaped Spread. **CARD 1:** Should I give up looking and just wait for it to happen? **CARD 2:** Should I try an online dating site/friendship group? **CARD 3:** Should I join a face-to-face/singles group? **CARD 4:** Should I join new activities? **CARD 5:** Should I relocate/change my job? **CARD 6:** Will I meet my Twin Soul, or settle for someone nice?

What you should use:
The whole deck.

When:
A Friday, the day of love.

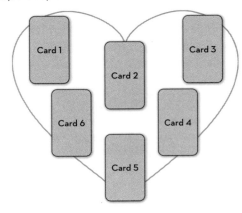

59
HOW CAN I OVERCOME MY SHYNESS AND BECOME MORE POPULAR?

Purpose and background information:

If you want friends but are too shy to approach people.

CARD 1: Is shyness ruining my social/working life, or am I happy to remain a private person? **CARD 2:** What do I fear most that stops me from approaching people or responding when people speak to me? **CARD 3:** Do I need professional help, or can I overcome my shyness myself? **CARD 4:** What first steps can I take to be more sociable that will not stress me out? **CARD 5:** With whom am I most comfortable? **CARD 6:** What environment/situation do I relax in to practice socializing?

What you should use:

The twenty-two Major cards and sixteen Court cards.

When:

A Wednesday, day of clear communication.

60
THE NEGOTIATION AND PEACE-MAKING SPREAD

Purpose and background information:

When there has been a quarrel in the family or among your friends. You can also adapt it for mending a love argument with a partner.

CARD 1: What/who is the sticking point that prevents the quarrel being resolved? **CARD 2:** Do I have all the facts, or am I seeing this too emotionally/making assumptions? **CARD 3:** Are others/is the other person prepared to compromise? **CARD 4:** Am I willing to compromise/suggest a compromise? **CARD 5:** What cannot be overlooked/accepted? **CARD 6:** What can be resolved/put aside as insoluble?

What you should use:

The forty Minor cards, Aces to Tens, and the sixteen Court cards

When:

The end of the day or week.

61
IS (NAME PERSON) A TRUE FRIEND OR A FALSE ONE?

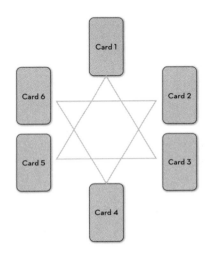

Purpose and background information:
Good for uncovering a person's true self as well as Spreads for love, success, fortune, and fame.

Card 1: What makes me question his/her loyalty? **Card 2:** Are the doubts within me due to my fear that I am unlovable? **Card 3:** Does . . . make me feel uncomfortable/excluded when we are with other people? **Card 4:** Has . . . ever betrayed a confidence to others? **Card 5:** Do I give more in the relationship than I receive? **Card 6:** Would . . . help me if I were in trouble?

What you should use:
The whole deck.

When:
A Wednesday, day for discovering deception.

Example:
Maria was a young mother. Recently Annie, a mother of two, moved next door. Maria invited her along to the local mother-and-baby events. Soon they were best friends. But recently Maria noticed that at the social events, Annie would make jokes and be sarcastic at Maria's expense. Maria had confided in Annie about her marriage problems, and she realized the others in the group were gossiping about her. Maria had thought Annie was her best friend, but. . . .

Card 1: Five of Cups, which Maria saw as Annie walking away from her, leaving spilled cups (broken confidences?). **Card 2: The Two of Pentacles;** Maria said she always tried to keep everyone happy, as she did not have much confidence that people would like her. **Card 3: The Hermit;** Annie was fine when it was just the two of them, but she had taken over the mother/baby group and would arrange events without telling Maria. **Card 4: The Five of Swords,** a betrayal card; Maria knew the only person to whom she had told her troubles was Annie. **Card 5: The Six of Cups,** the person giving to those with hands outstretched; Maria did a lot of babysitting for Annie at short notice, as Annie frequently went off for hours for trivial reasons. **Card 6: The Five of Pentacles;** whenever Maria asked for help in emergencies, Annie always had an excuse as to why she was too busy.

Maria withdrew from Annie and heard that there had been a major argument at the mother-and-baby group over Annie's causing trouble. Annie moved away not long after that.

62
COPING WITH A LONG-DISTANCE RELATIONSHIP

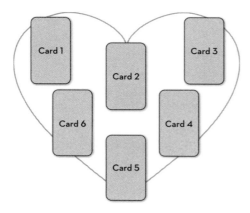

Purpose and background information:
When you or your partner work away from home or have to temporarily live apart because of circumstances.

CARD 1: Is there sufficient trust/a strong enough relationship between us for this to work? **CARD 2:** Do we have definite plans for being together permanently as soon as possible? **CARD 3:** Can we share the difficult journeys/rearrange our schedules to see each other as often as possible? **CARD 4:** Have/can we set up mutual times for daily communication through cyberspace/phone, etc? **CARD 5:** Have we agreed in advance how to talk through/put right any inevitable misunderstandings/lack of communication to avoid growing apart? **CARD 6:** Do we both have sufficient separate interests and safe social networks to avoid the dangers of loneliness?

What you should use:
The full deck.

When:
Before you part—or, if already working apart, any Monday for long-distance connections.

63
DEALING WITH A DIFFICULT FAMILY MEMBER OR CLOSE COLLEAGUE AT WORK

Purpose and background information:
What to do about a difficult person.

CARD 1: What is the main trigger of trouble between us? **CARD 2:** Is this person difficult with everyone, or does s/he mainly take out frustrations on me? **CARD 3:** How can I avoid playing their mind games/manipulation? **CARD 4:** What positive feelings/activities can help build a more positive relationship? **CARD 5:** Should I be tougher and less tolerant? **CARD 6:** Should I cut off contact?

What you should use:
The twenty-two Major cards and the sixteen Court cards.

When:
Before you meet/have contact.

In the next chapter, you will meet Spreads using seven cards that are especially good for making choices about every aspect of your life, finding good fortune, seeing through illusion, protection against paranormal events or psychic attack, and turning challenges into opportunities.

CHAPTER 7

SEVEN-CARD SPREADS

Seven is a special number in many mystical traditions. It is equally special in Tarot Spreads as a number that gives depth to a reading about core issues that affect us, without overloading the Layout with information.

Seven is found as the key to the seven ancient planets, the seven colors of the rainbow, the seven main chakra or psychic energy centers in the body, and as a measure of time as the seven days of the week. Seven-card Spreads work especially well for making choices of all kinds, including overseas or long-distance travel, because of its connection with the moon, for good fortune, for fertility, especially where there have been difficulties, for all mystical and psychic questions, life reviews, and questions of what is real and attainable and what are unrealistic dreams.

64
THE OPTIONS SPREAD

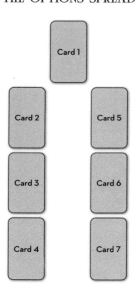

Purpose and background information:
When you have two main options and wish to discover which is the most advantageous choice (if there are more than two options).

You decide, or ask the questioner, which option will represent which choice before dealing the cards.

CARD 1: The choice to be made which may be different from the conscious question. **CARD 2:** (Option 1) The suggested action to carry out **Option 1,** the left-hand row. **CARD 4:** Unforeseen consequences, good or challenging, that result from carrying through **Option 1**. **CARD 6:** The likely outcome of following the path of **Option 1**.

Now read **Option 2. CARD 3:** The suggested action. **CARD 5:** The unforeseen consequences. **CARD 7:** The likely outcome of **Option 2**.

What you should use:
The whole deck.

When:
Whenever you have time to study the options in depth.

65
THE MYSTICAL SEVEN SPREAD

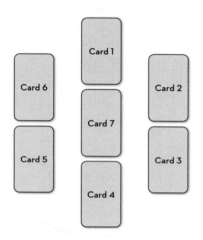

Purpose and background information:
An unstructured Spread for spiritual or psychic questions, or wherever an outcome depends on information not yet accessible or which is being deliberately concealed.

The last card you turn over, **CARD 7,** will reveal what is just over the horizon or being hidden and the answer to your dilemma.

What you should use:
The twenty-two Major cards or the full deck.

When:
A good full-moon night or any Monday evening, day of the moon.

66
THE GOOD-LUCK SPREAD

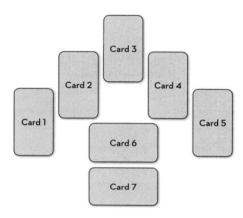

Purpose and background information:
If you have a venture that depends partly on good luck, or you need a lucky break in any part of your life, to see if fortune is with you.

CARD 1: For what do I need good fortune the most, in order to make this venture/life stage work? **CARD 2:** When will good luck come, and from what source? **CARD 3:** What or who is holding me back from/delaying good fortune? **CARD 4:** In which part of my life will it come, and how? **CARD 5:** Can I/how can I hasten good fortune? **CARD 6:** Who or what will help me? **CARD 7:** What is the hidden secret to my future good fortune?

What you should use:
The twenty-two Major cards and the sixteen Court cards.

When:
Crescent or full-moon night, or a Monday.

67
SEVEN-CARD CHAKRA OR ENERGY-CENTER SPREAD FOR A MAJOR LIFE REVIEW

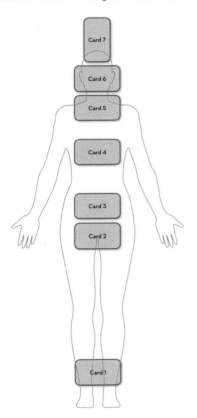

Purpose and background information:
To reassess your life path. Draw on thin card or visualize the outline of the front of the body.

CARD 1: ROOT where I am now. **CARD 2: SACRAL,** what I most desire. **CARD 3: SOLAR,** my greatest power/strength. **CARD 4: HEART.** What does my heart advise? **CARD 5: THROAT.** What do I most want to share with/say to the world/significant people in my life? **CARD 6: BROW/THIRD EYE.** What are my hidden gifts, especially spiritual ones? **CARD 7: CROWN.** Where do I want to be? What do I want to attain?

What you should use:
The full deck.

When:
When events shake your certainty.

68
THE SEVEN DAYS SPREAD FOR PLANNING A SIGNIFICANT WEEK AHEAD

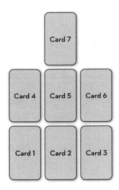

Purpose and background information:
To make a plan to ensure that the week ahead gives you the results you need and desire.

You can also use this Spread as a substitute for picking a card each day if you want an overview of what lies ahead for the next seven days.

CARD 1: SUNDAY. Clearing the decks/what needs to be prepared. **CARD 2: MONDAY.** Underlying currents/factors to watch out for. **CARD 3: TUESDAY.** What strengths you will need/issues to push for. **CARD 4: WEDNESDAY.** Checking facts and figures/watching for possible double-dealing in others. **CARD 5: THURSDAY.** Showing your leadership authority/revealing your expertise. **CARD 6: FRIDAY.** Dealing with others' emotions/negotiating. **CARD 7: SATURDAY.** Consolidating gains/assessing and minimizing any loss.

What you should use:
The full deck.

When:
The Saturday night immediately before the significant week.

69
THE LONG-VACATION/SABBATICAL/ LONG-SERVICE-LEAVE SPREAD

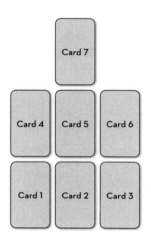

Purpose and background information:

When you are planning a major trip away but are worried about leaving your current life for so long.

Card 1: Is this the right time and circumstance to embark on my big adventure? **Card 2:** How will I finance it/do I need to work while away? **Card 3:** Can I put my future on hold without damaging my career? **Card 4:** Do I want to make definite itinerary plans before I go, or wait and see what opportunities arise as I travel? **Card 5:** How can I keep in touch with those I care for? Will anyone come along with me? **Card 6:** What is my real purpose: to see new places, or to take time out from my present life? **Card 7:** Is this a major change point, so when I come back I will follow a different life path?

What you should use:

The full deck.

When:

A Monday if overseas travel, or a Thursday for interstate travel.

Example:

Bella was due for six months' long-service leave. She no longer enjoyed her job, and her husband had left her for a younger woman after thirty years of marriage. Bella wanted to travel around the world and had saved enough, but her real aim was to take photographs to sell and maybe change careers upon her return.

Card 1: The Five of Cups, showing three spilled cups as the person walked away, with two intact. Bella saw this as herself and her new photographic interest. **Card 2: Seven of Pentacles.** She had saved enough money but also intended to see if she could get a commission for a future project for over-fifties solo travel. **Card 3: The Nine of Cups,** showing the person surrounded by cups of fulfillment; Bella said she had lost interest in her career and wanted to work for herself. **Card 4: The World.** Apart from her initial destination of India, Bella wanted to keep the trip open, but had worried that this was irresponsible. This card reassured her that she could be spontaneous: the world was open to her, as long as she was careful. **Card 5: The Hermit.** Bella had no family and had focused 100% on her marriage, so she was looking forward to the trip as a way of discovering herself. **Card 6: The Tower of Freedom.** Bella's aim was to put her life back together and rediscover herself. **Card 7: The Eight of Pentacles.** Bella intended to focus on photography to see if she could make at least a part-time career in that field.

Bella has been offered a commission by an over-fifties lifestyle magazine who saw her online blog, to write about/photograph her experiences, and she hopes this may lead to a book.

In the next chapter, you will meet the all-powerful eight-card Spreads for major transformations, success, fame, fortune, business, and self-generated enterprises, and for going places in every way.

CHAPTER 8

EIGHT-CARD SPREADS

Eight-card Spreads are the big players for major matters, both in terms of significance and complexity, and so should not be hurried. They can be used for absolutely any question, but especially for major transformations, life changes and life reviews, success, fame, fortune, business, self-generated enterprises, for going places, freedom, and widening horizons in every way. Use also for when you are being intimidated by someone with power over you or an inflexible organization or official body, and against aggressiveness from neighbors and in your community (see also the nine-card Spreads).

70
MOVING TOWARD FULFILLING YOUR GREATEST AMBITION OR DREAM

Purpose and background information:
When a chance, however small, opens a door toward a longed-for opportunity, but you know it will bring disruption.

CARD 1: Is this the window of opportunity for which I have been waiting? **CARD 2:** Is this step that I am contemplating realistic? **CARD 3:** Am I ready—and, if not, when will I be? **CARD 4:** Who/what will help me? **CARD 5:** Who/what will oppose me/disapprove? **CARD 6:** Should I modify/compromise my dream to make the step less disruptive? **CARD 7:** The short-term outcome of taking the step, the next six months. **CARD 8:** The longer-term outcome, the next five years.

What you should use:
The full deck.

When:
A Tuesday for major change, sometimes involving disruption.

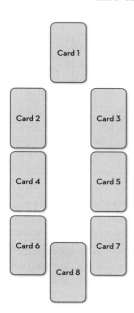

When:

A Friday, the day of fertility and families.

Example:

Joanna was forty and feared that she was leaving it too late to start a family. She and her partner Chris have a comfortable lifestyle, a luxurious city-center apartment, and enjoy frequent exotic holidays. Chris is worried that they might resent losing their freedom.

CARD 1: THE EMPRESS, the mother card; Joanna comes from a large happy family and wants the same. **CARD 2: THE WHEEL OF FORTUNE**; she fears time running out unless they try for a baby soon. **CARD 3: THE PRINCE OF WANDS.** This is Chris, an only child who enjoys their spontaneous lifestyle with no money worries, but also hates responsibility. **CARD 4: THE EMPEROR.** Joanna felt Chris couldn't go on with his prolonged childhood and that a family would help him to become less selfish. **CARD 5: TEN OF CUPS,** showing the long-term happiness of a man, woman, and children under a rainbow. **CARD 6: TEMPERANCE.** Joanna admitted they both drank and partied too much. **CARD 7: THE FOUR OF WANDS,** showing a man and woman with a house in the countryside. Joanna said they had talked of moving and working from home together but had never put the idea into practice. **CARD 8: THE EIGHT OF SWORDS.** Joanna said unless they tried soon, it would be too late and that there was something holding Chris back.

After the reading, the couple talked deeply. Chris admitted that his unhappy childhood, which he had always denied, made him afraid of having a family. They have bought their house in the country for their business, and Joanna and Chris are now trying for a baby.

Purpose and background information:

When the biological clock is ticking and you and your partner are deciding the pros and cons of having a baby, which you both realize is a major lifestyle change. This Spread can also be used for any question where there are significant pros and cons.

CARD 1: Do we want a child/children now or in the future? **CARD 2:** If we try, how soon can we conceive? **CARD 3:** What will we lose most in terms of freedom/finances if we have a baby? **CARD 4:** What will we gain most by having a family? **CARD 5:** Can we/how can we keep the special magic alive between us if we have a baby? **CARD 6:** How best can I/ my partner improve our health to maximize our chances of conceiving? **CARD 7:** What practical lifestyle changes would a new baby bring about? **CARD 8:** Should we leave nature to take its course, or will this reduce our chances of having a baby?

What you should use:

The whole deck.

72
SEVEN DAYS OF THE WEEK PLUS ONE TO DISCOVER LONGER-TERM RESULTS

Purpose and background information:
Finding a daily strategy to ensure that the week ahead will give you the results you need and desire, adding an eighth card to show what the following weeks will bring as a result of the strategies adopted.

Card 1: Sunday, developing new strategies. **Card 2: Monday,** anticipating the reactions/actions of others. **Card 3: Tuesday,** putting your action plan in place. **Card 4: Wednesday,** checking details and finding whom you can trust. **Card 5: Thursday,** taking the initiative/lead in adopting strategies. **Card 6: Friday,** making compromises/ negotiating. **Card 7: Saturday,** assessing what worked and what should be retried/abandoned. **Card 8:** What are the opportunities that will open/be retrievable in the coming weeks as a result of following these strategies?

What you should use:
The full deck.

When:
The Saturday night before the significant week.

73
EIGHT STEPS TO OVERCOMING MAJOR INTIMIDATION BY A POWERFUL INDIVIDUAL OR ORGANIZATION

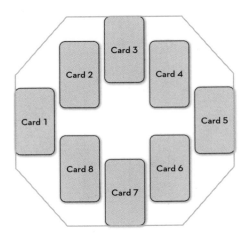

Purpose and background information:
When the odds are stacked against you and you fear being crushed.

Use an octagonal (eight-sided) formation with each card in the center of one of the visualized eight sides.

Card 1: Who/what seeks to crush you? **Card 2:** What is the motive/real power behind the perpetrator? **Card 3:** What evidence do you have on your side? **Card 4:** Who will support you? **Card 5:** Can you/should you walk away, or fight on? **Card 6:** What is the weakness/flaw of the person/ organization intimidating you? **Card 7:** What positive publicity/exposure can you get to strengthen your cause? **Card 8:** What is the ideal outcome?

What you should use:
The forty Minor cards, Aces to Tens, and the sixteen Court cards.

When:
A Tuesday, day of fierce power and protection.

74
FOR MAKING AN ALL-OR-NOTHING DECISION

Purpose and background information:
Any major or complex decision where the answer must be yes/no, act/wait, go/stay, or speak/be silent.

Card 1: Is this what I really want? **Card 2:** Are there serious drawbacks to saying yes? **Card 3:** Am I prepared to put everything into it? **Card 4:** What about my other priorities/commitments? **Card 5:** Will saying yes give me a better lifestyle? **Card 6:** Can I have/do this without hurting anyone/leaving anyone I care for behind? **Card 7:** What is the best outcome of saying yes? **Card 8:** What is the worst outcome of saying yes?

What you should use:
The forty Minor cards, Aces to Tens, and the sixteen Court cards.

When:
Any early morning for extra clarity.

75
FOR LAUNCHING OR EXPANDING AN AMBITIOUS BUSINESS VENTURE

Purpose and background information:
When you have plans ready to go but are hesitant.

Card 1: Are the energies/time right to go for it now, or should I wait? **Card 2:** Are my plans really cast-iron, or are there risks I need to consider? **Card 3:** Should I go it alone/with existing partners/seek wider input? **Card 4:** What is its greatest strength that makes it viable? **Card 5:** Are there any rivals/similar businesses I need to consider? **Card 6:** If I go for it now, what lies ahead for the next three to six months? **Card 7:** If I go for it now, what lies ahead in the next twelve months and beyond? **Card 8:** What do not I know that I need to be aware of?

What you should use:
The full deck.

When:
A Wednesday, the day of commercial/creative ventures.

In the following chapter, you will meet the nine-card Spreads for answering even more complex questions. Nine-card readings are good for matters of justice, completing or ending situations, for matters of principle and ethics, for global issues, physical and emotional strength, and for resolving seemingly impossible situations.

CHAPTER 9

NINE-CARD SPREADS

Nine-card Spreads offer the opportunity for studying, in depth and in quiet reflection, everything from a full lifepath review to justice, whether through the legal or official system or personal ethics. Nines also work well for disputes over inheritance, completing projects, ending unsatisfactory situations, for finding a way through seemingly impossible situations, for global issues, or where there is a serious or chronic illness.

76
AN UNSTRUCTURED NINE-CARD READING

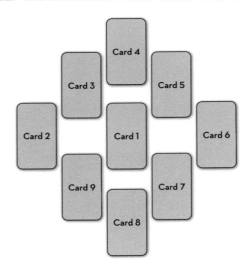

Purpose and background information:
The nine-card unstructured reading will answer absolutely any question as you build up a whole picture step by step. You can add a tenth card as the Crown of the reading if it hasn't all come together by **Card 9**.

What you should use:
The full deck.

When:
Any leisurely evening. Afterward, scribble in your Tarot journal any extra ideas for each card before clearing the cards away.

THE PATHWAY TO JUSTICE

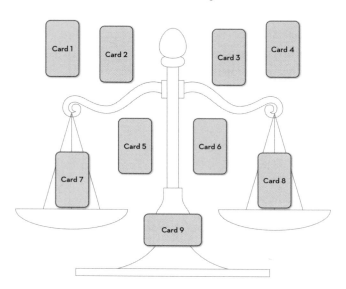

Purpose and background information:

For any official, legal, or compensation matter, especially where there has been unfairness, corruption, or lies blocking your path.

CARD 1: What/who is causing the injustice? **CARD 2:** What/who is in the way of revealing the truth? **CARD 3:** What is the weakness of your opponent? **CARD 4:** What is the greatest strength/in your favor? **CARD 5:** What unexpected new facts/evidence will come to light to benefit you? **CARD 6:** Can you do more, or should you wait? **CARD 7:** Are you well represented/need new representation? **CARD 8:** Can/should you settle out of court/through mediation? **CARD 9:** What is the ideal outcome?

What you should use:

The full deck.

When:

A Thursday, the day of justice and truth.

Example:

Flynn had been falsely accused by his ex-wife of threatening and attacking her and their six-year-old child. He had been officially banned from seeing his son. **CARD 1: The Queen of Swords.** His ex-wife would stop at nothing to deprive Flynn of his child. **CARD 2: The Page of Cups.** Flynn was unwilling to have his son questioned, as it would be too distressing for the young boy. **CARD 3: The Five of Wands.** Flynn suspected that his ex-wife would be unable to resist boasting that she had tricked him. **CARD 4: The Five of Swords**. Flynn's ex-wife was a very convincing liar. **CARD 5: Seven of Pentacles.** Flynn knew that her motive was to extract a large sum of money from him in return for her dropping the charges. **CARD 6: Strength** advised him to wait and let things unfold. **CARD 7: The Hermit.** Flynn represented himself, as he could not afford a lawyer. **CARD 8: Temperance**. Achieving justice by entirely avoiding the court system. **CARD 9: The Six of Cups.** To be reunited with his son was his only desire.

Shortly after the reading, his ex-wife boasted to a mutual friend that she had made it all up to blackmail Flynn. The friend offered to be a witness for Flynn. The ex-wife dropped the charges. Flynn now regularly sees his son.

78
THE FORTUNE-TELLING ORACLE

Purpose and background information:
This is an especially good formula for a general life review or for major career and love questions. Sometimes used with playing cards, this nine-card Spread is credited to nomadic people who practiced divinatory arts. The cards form three rows of three and each row has a different overall theme.

First, turn over and read **Row 1, Cards 1–3, the cards of your current life path, relationship, or career.**

Card 1: Past events moving away and lessons learned. **Card 2:** Present sticking points or doubts. **Card 3:** What you most want to preserve from your life/relationship/career.

Now, turn over and then read **Row 2, Cards 4–6, the Cards of Outside Influences.**

Card 4: Positive aspects and people who affect your life. **Card 5:** Hidden opposition. **Card 6:** What must be overcome to make positive changes/find lasting happiness/success.

Finally, deal, turn, and read **Row 3, Cards 7–9, the Cards of Action and Outcome.**

Card 7: Suggested action. **Card 8:** Short-term outcome. **Card 9:** Long-term outcome.

What you should use:
The full deck.

When:
Full moon or any Monday night.

79
TO ESCAPE FROM AN ABUSIVE OR DESTRUCTIVE SITUATION

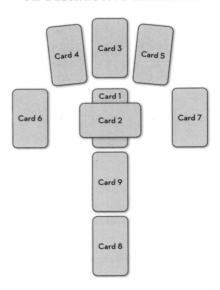

Purpose and background information:
When you feel powerless but know you need to leave.

This Spread is also useful for any life-changing event, a major life review, or where a minor miracle is needed.

Card 1: The card of the self and what is at stake. **Card 2:** Deals with fears relating to the destructive/abusive situation/person that holds you back. **Card 3:** Action you can take. **Card 4:** Who will rescue/help you? **Card 5:** What makes you hesitate? **Card 6:** The first step. **Card 7:** The dangers of taking this first step. **Card 8:** Who else must you consider/rescue? **Card 9:** The beginning of your new life.

What you should use:
The full deck.

When:
A Saturday, day of protection and endings.

80
OVERCOMING/COPING WITH A SERIOUS OR CHRONIC ILLNESS

Purpose and background information:
When results are slow or there is a deterioration.

CARD 1: What is the worst/hardest aspect of the condition? **CARD 2:** What extra/new conventional treatment can be offered? **CARD 3:** Would alternative medicine/energy therapies provide extra relief? **CARD 4:** What new research is around, and where can it be found/accessed? **CARD 5:** What practical methods exist in order to ease your/the patient's life? **CARD 6:** How can stress be minimized? **CARD 7:** What unknown positive factors will come into play? **CARD 8:** What extra resources can be applied for/accessed? **CARD 9:** What is the best possible outcome?

What you should use:
The forty Minor cards, Aces to Tens, and the sixteen Court cards.

When:
A Wednesday, day of healing.

81
THE TOWER OF FREEDOM FOR BREAKING FREE OF RESTRICTIONS TO ENABLE YOU TO LIVE BY YOUR OWN RULES

Purpose and background information:
When you want to shake off what no longer makes you happy, but are scared to do so.

Angle the position of the nine cards as they ascend, so each is above and slightly to the right of the previous card, so it looks like a leaning tower.

CARD 1: What freedom/independence do you seek, and in what way? **CARD 2:** What/who restricts you from having this? **CARD 3:** Is now the right time, or should you wait? **CARD 4:** What is the first step to freedom/independence? **CARD 5:** What will be the immediate positive effects of attaining freedom/independence on yourself/others? **CARD 6:** What objections/obstacles to be overcome will be put in your path in the early days? **CARD 7:** What must be sacrificed to attain freedom/independence? **CARD 8:** What will be the longer-term positive effects of the new freedom/independence in six to twelve months? **CARD 9:** Where you will be in five years if you follow this path?

What you will use:
The full deck.

When:
The beginning of a new month or year.

In the next chapter, we will work with even larger numbers of card positions and identify some of the more detailed classic Spreads that have stood the test of time.

CHAPTER 10

MULTI-CARD SPREADS

In this chapter is a selection of Spreads using ten cards or more. They include the classic eleven-card Celtic Cross broken down into manageable sections, and a Wheel of the Year Spread so that you can look at the twelve months ahead in detail. For Spreads with larger numbers of cards, you have the option of using two identical decks, picking cards alternately from each facedown deck. There are other longer Spreads throughout the book in the themed chapters.

82
AN UNSTRUCTURED
TWELVE-CARD SPREAD

Purpose and background information:
For absolutely any question where you need more detail, or where there are many different aspects.

What you should use:
The full deck.

When:
You have time to contemplate each card and allow the answer to form.

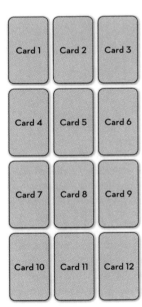

83
A WHEEL OF THE YEAR
TWELVE-MONTHS-AHEAD SPREAD

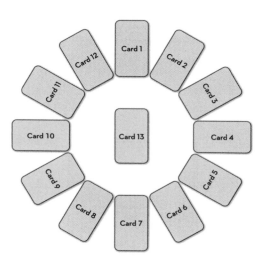

Purpose and background information:
If you want to know what the year ahead has in store.

Pick a card from the deck for each month ahead and set the cards in a circle clockwise, starting with the month following the reading.

Start at any time in the year, especially a birthday month, new year, or personal change points, anniversaries, engagements, a wedding, or the birth of a child—or even after a break-up.

Name the month that each card represents, with **CARD 1** being the month following the reading. Record the opportunities or challenges each card suggests during a particular month. As a rule, Major Arcana cards indicate major events or where outside circumstances play a big part. Minor cards refer to more ordinary but nevertheless significant happenings occurring in the period you are measuring. Court cards indicate dominant personalities—or a new love or pregnancy. Finally, choose a card to sum up the twelve months ahead and put this in the center of the circle. You can pick two cards for each month if you wish.

What you should use:
One or two full decks.

When:
During the current month. If the month is nearly over, begin on the following one.

84
THE MONTH AHEAD, 28–31 DAYS IN DETAIL

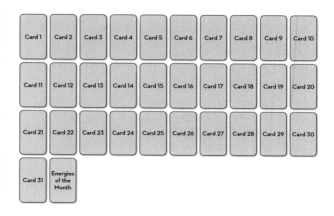

Purpose and background information:
For a crucial month ahead.

Pick separate cards for the daily opportunities and challenges for each of the 28, 29, 30, or 31 days ahead. Your Card of the Day will supplement this as to the best strategy to use (see Spread 1).

What you should use:
One or two whole decks.

When:
The last day of the previous month.

85
A 24-CARD SPREAD FOR PAST, PRESENT, AND FUTURE

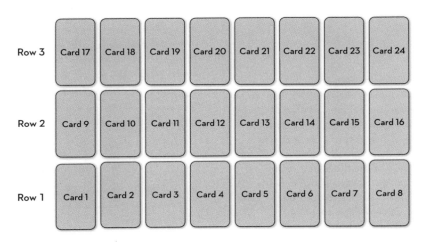

Row 3: Card 17, Card 18, Card 19, Card 20, Card 21, Card 22, Card 23, Card 24

Row 2: Card 9, Card 10, Card 11, Card 12, Card 13, Card 14, Card 15, Card 16

Row 1: Card 1, Card 2, Card 3, Card 4, Card 5, Card 6, Card 7, Card 8

What you should use:
Full deck.

When:
Once every six months.

Purpose and background information:
To see the interconnections in your life and how the past can unconsciously influence the future.

Use the Spread once every six months as different influences from the past and present will come into play with changing circumstances. There is a more complex version of this Spread, adding eight strategy cards, which I describe on page 443.

Pay particular attention to the ends and beginning of rows. Even at the beginning of **Row 1, The Past**, some childhood trauma or unfair criticism may be influencing the present and, unless resolved, the future.

Row 1: The Past
The nearest row to you, the bottom row of the Spread, will represent what has passed and is passing out of your life. The cards nearest the beginning of the row (to the left) will refer to childhood and become more recent toward the right of the row. This row may contain several unresolved issues; but, more

positively, also those talents that can be revived or developed in the present or future and people who have contributed to present success or happiness.

Row 2: The Present
The middle row, **Present Influences,** should also be read left to right. In the present will reside current relationships, home and work opportunities and challenges, current goals, achievements, wishes, and as-yet-unfulfilled dreams and ambitions. Toward the beginning of the row, you may find lingering issues from the past that need to be acknowledged and so overcome.

Row 3: The Future
The top row (remember, we're reading the rows from bottom to top) looks not at a set future, but potential paths. The immediate future will be to the left of the row, and the distant future up to ten years away is to the right. The actions and plan cards at the end of the **Present** row may kickstart or hold back the immediate future in the left-hand **Future** row cards. You can, if you wish, add a 25th card, dealt facedown, that will give you the unexpected factor that will help your future success. Place this at the top of the reading, above the third **(Future)** row.

THE CELTIC CROSS FOR ANY MAJOR QUESTION

What you should use:
One or two full decks.

When:
A quiet evening.

Purpose and background information:
This is one popular version of the ultimate Tarot Layout in terms of complexity, named after the shape of the Celtic Cross.

The Celtic Cross is excellent for resolving very complex issues, whether challenge or opportunity or an in-depth life review.

I have divided the Celtic Cross into three sections and therefore it is not as hard as it first looks to learn. I would recommend drawing the positions on thin cardboard at first and setting the cards on each position while you practice.

Firstly, look at the whole Spread and see how the Spread progresses from **CARD 1** to **CARD 11** through different stages.

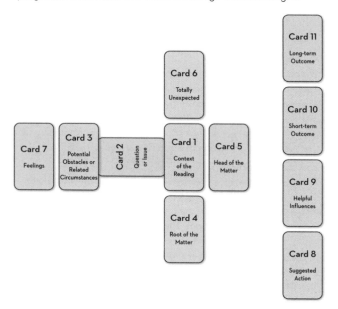

Deal **CARDS 1–11** and turn over each **SECTION 1–3** shown below in turn. Read that section before turning over the next section. When you have turned over all three sections and interpreted them, see how the individual sections fit together to give an overall picture and answer.

Section 1: The Center or Heart of the Reading, Cards 1–3
These cards set the scene and help to expand the context and purpose of the reading.

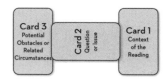

CARD 1, which partly covers **CARD 2,** is the **Context** of the reading, the reason you are asking the question and the underlying issues that led you to the reading.

CARD 2, lying beneath **CARDS 1** and **3,** is the actual here-and-now **Question** or **Issue** to be resolved by the reading.

CARD 3, which also partly obscures **CARD 2,** represents **Potential Obstacles** or **Related Circumstances**. These could be personal reluctance to change the status quo, or other people who make the present situation or life difficult, or people whose lives would be affected by change—any or all of which prompted and shaped the question.

Section 2: The Surrounding Square, Cards 4–7

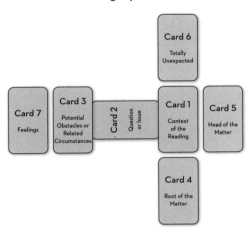

CARDS 4–7 enclose the Heart of the reading and refer to **strengths and weaknesses** of those involved in the question. These assist in determining what can be resolved or incorporated into the future path and what must be left behind.

CARD 4: Practical Considerations, the Root of the matter. This card refers to the nuts and bolts of your life or those of the questioner, the financial, domestic, or day-to-day matters or responsibilities and how they affect or could affect the issue.

CARD 5: Reality versus Illusion, the Head of the matter. This card separates wish fulfillment and illusion from achievable dreams: what can be attained given any constraints but also potentials.

CARD 6: The **Totally Unexpected,** which can transform a seemingly impossible situation into real possibility. The good-fairy card and the most predictive card of the Spread.

CARD 7: The **Feelings** card, both your own true desires and dreams and the perhaps confusing messages from those around you.

Pathway to Happiness Cards, Cards 8–11

These are the action and decision cards that will lead you to the desired result, even if it wasn't quite the result you consciously expected when you began the reading. These develop and resolve the themes of the earlier sections.

CARD 8: Suggested Action. This involves any action you decide to take to resolve the question, or at least to take the first steps to resolution.

CARD 9: Helpful Influences. This is the counterbalance to **CARD 3, the Obstacles in your path**. This card refers to people or circumstances that can make the action or decision more likely to succeed. These influences may be unexpected and involve those you thought would oppose you, whether individuals or institutions.

CARD 10: Short-Term Outcome. This card highlights the initial results of setting a plan or decision in motion that may be different and sometimes involve a struggle.

CARD 11: Long-Term Outcome. This card gives you the most likely end result and—hopefully—resolution of the matter.

The next chapter forms the first of the themed chapters, offering Spreads for every aspect of love and commitment, varying from quick readings with three cards to more complex Spreads with seven or more cards.

CHAPTER 11

LOVE AND COMMITMENT SPREADS

Cards particularly lucky to pick in love and commitment Spreads:

Minor Cards: Ace of Cups, Two of Cups, Three of Cups, Six of Cups, Ten of Cups, Four of Wands, Ten of Pentacles.

Major Cards: The Emperor, the Empress, the Lovers, the Wheel of Fortune, the Sun, the Moon, the Star.

The Court Cards: The Page/Princess of Cups, the Knight of Cups, the Queen of Cups, the King of Cups, and the Page/Princess, Knight, Queen, and King of Pentacles.

About Love Spreads:

SIX-CARD SPREADS, the number of love and the planet of love goddess Venus are especially associated with love, marriage, and commitment. But you can use any number of cards, from the simple two-card options through to a full-blown nine-card review of the relationship. The following Spreads work well for all matters of love. I will direct you to diagrams in earlier chapters with Layouts you have met before.

87
HAVE I FOUND MY SOULMATE FROM A PAST WORLD?

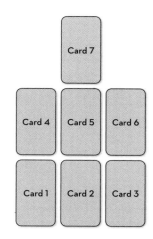

Purpose and background information:
When you are with a partner/have met someone special.

CARD 1: Is (name) my Soul mate? **CARD 2:** When and how were we together in past worlds? **CARD 3:** What do we share from past worlds that brings us even closer in this life? **CARD 4:** What or who divides us in this life? **CARD 5:** What is unfinished from earlier worlds? **CARD 6:** What is our karmic destiny together? **CARD 7:** Will we stay forever together in this life?

What you should use:
The forty Minor cards and the sixteen Court cards.

When:
A Friday, the day of love.

88
CAN IT BE TRUE I HAVE MET MY TWIN SOUL AT LAST?

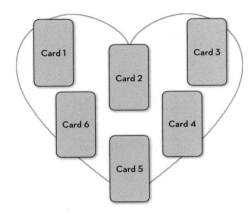

Purpose and background information:
When deep sudden love feels right.

CARD 1: Do you feel you have known each other forever?
CARD 2: Was there instant recognition/connection at the first meeting? **CARD 3:** Does s/he fit totally with your family/friends/interests? **CARD 4:** Is the relationship fast-moving but quite natural-feeling? **CARD 5:** Is a missing part of your life now complete? **CARD 6:** Do you have constant déjà vu and telepathic links?

What you should use:
The full deck.

When:
On the same day of the week and at the same time you met/reconnected.

89
IF YOU MEET OR RECONNECT WITH AN OLD FLAME MANY YEARS LATER

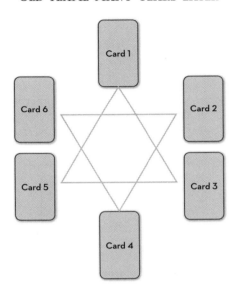

Purpose and background information:
When the years disappear as if you never were apart.

CARD 1: Do you feel you have never been apart? **CARD 2:** Have your lives followed parallel paths? **CARD 3:** Are you free to be together, or are there difficulties be overcome? **CARD 4:** Can/how can you meet/spend time together? **CARD 5:** Is a long-term future possible and how? **CARD 6:** Now that you have reconnected, will you always stay in touch regardless?

What you should use:
The full deck.

When:
A full moon, or any Monday.

90
THE SOUL-MATE SPREAD IF ONE OR BOTH OF YOU IS ALREADY COMMITTED

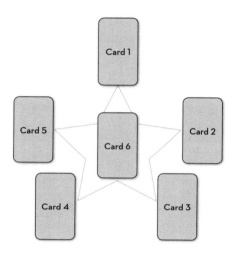

Purpose and background information:

When you either meet someone new who is very special, or reconnect with an old flame.

A five-star formation, but with an extra **CARD 6** in the middle,

CARD 1: Have I met/reconnected with my twin soul? **CARD 2:** Is the feeling mutual and noticeable to others? **CARD 3:** Are we each unhappy in our present relationships? **CARD 4:** Am I/ are we willing to make sacrifices/cause disruption in order to be together? **CARD 5:** Will what we have now be enough until we can be together more easily, or must we part? **CARD 6:** Can there be a "happy ever after"?

What you should use:

The full deck.

When:

The end of the week/month

91
WILL WE BE HAPPY TOGETHER FOREVER?

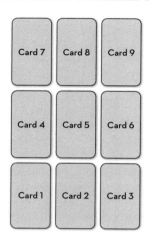

Purpose and background information:

When you are considering marriage or living together.

ROW 1: Cards of compatibility.

CARD 1: Previous negative life experiences to be shed. **CARD 2:** What unites you? **CARD 3:** Are you both ready for the next stage?

ROW 2: Cards of outside influences.

CARD 4: Who will support your future together? **CARD 5:** Who will oppose the relationship? **CARD 6:** External factors causing pressures or acting in your favor.

ROW 3: Cards of action and outcome.

CARD 7: Future plans and time scale. **CARD 8:** Short-term outcome. **CARD 9:** Long-term outcome.

What you should use:

The full deck.

When:

A full moon, or any Monday night.

92
SHOULD I ASK HIM/HER ON A DATE?

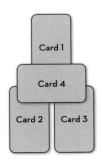

Purpose and background information:

When you really like someone but are scared s/he will reject you.

CARD 1: Does s/he like me enough to say yes? **CARD 2:** What makes me doubt s/he will agree? **CARD 3:** Do we need more time getting to know each other, or is now the right time? **CARD 4:** Am I hoping for a longer-term relationship, or just fun?

What you should use:

The forty Minor cards, Aces to Tens, and the sixteen Court cards.

When:

The night before you plan to ask for the date.

93
WHEN YOU REALIZE YOU ARE FALLING IN LOVE WITH YOUR BEST FRIEND

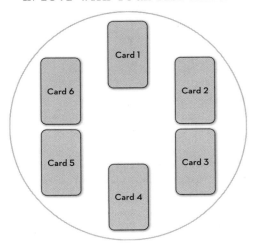

Purpose and background information:

When a long-standing friendship suddenly seems something more.

Deal six cards at regular intervals clockwise around a circle, starting with **CARD 1** at the top.

CARD 1: Has your friend shown signs of wanting something more? **CARD 2:** Would you welcome/encourage this growing feeling? **CARD 3:** Can you get more time alone together to explore/develop this awareness? **CARD 4:** Are you both ready for a physical relationship, or should you take it slowly? **CARD 5:** Can you/how can you move the relationship up a notch without spoiling the friendship? **CARD 6:** What is the ideal outcome?

What you should use:

The forty Minor cards, Aces to Tens, and the sixteen Court cards.

When:

The beginning of a week or month.

94
WHEN WILL MY PARTNER COMMIT?

Purpose and background information:
When you have been together a while, and you are ready to move to the next stage.

Card 1: Are you prepared to wait a while, or is this starting to cause resentment in you? **Card 2:** The real reason that holds him/her back from commitment. **Card 3:** Can/how can this reluctance be overcome?

What you should use:
The twenty-two Major cards.

When:
At a full moon.

95
SHOULD WE MOVE IN TOGETHER?

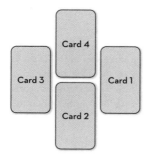

Purpose and background information:
When you want confirmation that this is the right time.

Card 1: Is this the right time, or should we wait a while?
Card 2: What are the advantages of living together?

Card 3: What are potential drawbacks? **Card 4:** Is this the next step to spending the rest of our lives together?

What you should use:
The twenty-two Major cards and the sixteen Court cards.

When:
A Sunday, for new beginnings.

96
WILL WE BECOME ENGAGED SOON?

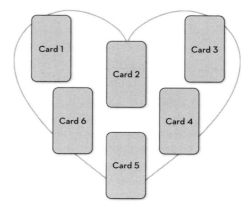

Purpose and background information:
When you feel ready to tell the world you are an "item."

Card 1: Should I wait for him/her to propose, or initiate it myself? **Card 2:** Do we want a ring/rings/official announcement? **Card 3:** Do we want a big celebration, or more low-key? **Card 4:** Are we setting a wedding date, or leaving this open for now? **Card 5:** Will becoming engaged improve/stabilize our relationship? **Card 6:** How can we avoid/deal with unexpected pressures?

What you should use:
The full deck.

When:
Valentine's Day, New Year's Day, or any significant anniversary in your relationship.

97

IF YOU WANT A QUIET WEDDING, BUT YOUR FAMILY IS PLANNING A BIG CELEBRATION

Purpose and background information:
When wedding arrangements are getting out of control.

CARD 1: What/who is causing the unwanted escalation?
CARD 2: What lies behind this? **CARD 3:** Can there be a compromise? **CARD 4:** Where and how do you want your wedding to take place? **CARD 5:** Who do you want to come?
CARD 6: Strategy to take control of arrangements.

What you should use:
The twenty-two Major cards and the forty Minor cards, Aces to Tens.

When:
Before the event is irrevocably booked.

Example:

CARD 1: The Empress. Flora's mother has been saving for years for a big white wedding for her daughter. **CARD 2: The Five of Pentacles.** Flora's mother had a rushed small wedding herself, as she was pregnant with Flora. **CARD 3: Temperance.** Flora plans on suggesting a quiet beautiful wedding followed by a big party when they come home from their honeymoon. **CARD 4: The Six of Swords,** showing a boat on the water. Flora and her fiancé want a quiet beach wedding in an exotic location. **CARD 5: The Ten of Pentacles,** picturing the generations of immediate family, all happy together. **CARD 6: The Two of Cups.** Flora will wear a flowing white dress to please her mother so they can both have their dream.

98

WE'RE ENGAGED, SO WHY WILL S/HE NOT SET A DEFINITE DATE?

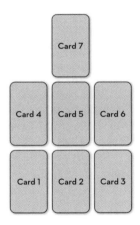

Purpose and background information:
When time is ticking by.

CARD 1: Is this a sticking point in our relationship? **CARD 2:** What is the real cause of my partner's reluctance to set a date? **CARD 3:** Are finances/fears of the wedding ceremony causing problems? **CARD 4:** Does my partner have unresolved past-commitment issues? **CARD 5:** Would marrying affect the relationship for better or worse? **CARD 6:** Are we right for each other? **CARD 7:** Can I accept the relationship as it is?

What you should use:
The full deck.

When:
A Thursday, day of commitment.

99
THE RIGHT HONEYMOON

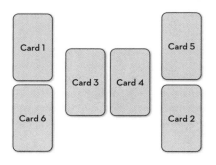

Purpose and background information:

Card 1: Do we want a honeymoon, or do we prefer to save the money for the future? **Card 2:** Simple or exotic, home or overseas? **Card 3:** Should the honeymoon be in the wedding setting if an exotic one? **Card 4:** What kind of honeymoon do you want, action adventure/romantic? **Card 5:** Do you want it right after the wedding, or to wait a while? **Card 6:** Can you/how can you compromise so you are both happy?

What you should use:
The full deck.

When:
The beginning of a week or month.

100
THE UNREQUITED LOVE SPREAD

Purpose and background information:
When you cannot think of anyone else.

Card 1: Do I want this love at any cost? **Card 2:** Am I prepared to persist? **Card 3:** Will s/he return my feelings? **Card 4:** What is the main obstacle to this love? **Card 5:** Are existing or former relationships causing hesitation? **Card 6:** Should I make a move now, or hold back? **Card 7:** Should I put a time limit on waiting? **Card 8:** Is anyone new coming into my life?

What you should use:
The forty Minor cards, Aces to Tens, and the sixteen Court cards.

When:
Sunset.

101
IF IT IS THE FIRST LOVE OR A NEW RELATIONSHIP AFTER BETRAYAL

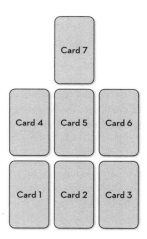

Purpose and background information:
When you are scared of its going wrong.

Card 1: What qualities do you love in your new partner? **Card 2:** What makes you happiest about the relationship? **Card 3:** What does your partner say s/he loves most about you? **Card 4:** What do you fear? **Card 5:** What joint dreams/

interests do you share? **CARD 6:** How would you like the relationship to progress in the months ahead? **CARD 7:** How do you ideally see the relationship twelve months from now?

What you should use:
The forty Minor cards, Aces to Tens, and the sixteen Court cards.

When:
During the crescent or waxing moon.

102
WHEN YOU OR YOUR PARTNER FIND IT HARD TO EXPRESS YOUR FEELINGS OR TRUST

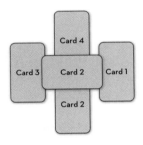

Purpose and background information:
If you want more open communication/trust between you.

CARD 1: Is the relationship strong between you, or are there underlying trust issues? **CARD 2:** Are there unresolved problems from childhood/previous hurts that make it hard for you/your partner to openly show love? **CARD 3:** Are there other ways you can show love? **CARD 4:** Can you accept this situation if it doesn't improve? **CARD 5:** What strategies can you adopt to open communication?

What you should use:
The forty Minor cards, Aces to Tens, and the sixteen Court cards.

When:
A Wednesday, day of clear communication.

103
SHOULD I DATE ONLINE?

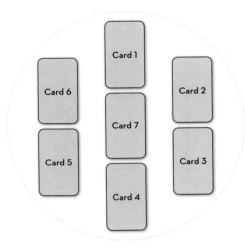

Purpose and background information:
When it's hard to meet potential partners because of location or circumstances.

CARD 1: Will online dating open your life to love? **CARD 2:** Would you be happier building up a relationship online instead of face-to-face, dating agencies, or other activities? **CARD 3:** Do you want to develop this into phone/Skype/face-to-face relationship? **CARD 4:** Would you prefer formal online dating agencies, or social media/interest groups? **CARD 5:** What scares you most about online dating? **CARD 6:** How will you know if a profile is genuine? **CARD 7:** Will you meet your twin soul online?

What you should use:
The full deck.

When:
A Wednesday, cyber contact day.

WHEN YOU HAVEN'T YET MET YOUR ONLINE LOVE IN PERSON

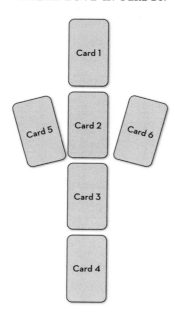

105

MARRYING OR LIVING TOGETHER IF ONE OR BOTH OF YOU ALREADY HAVE CHILDREN

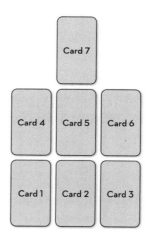

Purpose and background information:
When you are trying to make everything work.

Card 1: What most unites you in spite of difficulties?
Card 2: What/who causes divisions in the new family?
Card 3: What financial/child access burdens do you need to resolve/incorporate? **Card 4:** What reconciliation from the past is needed? **Card 5:** How can you bring everyone together? **Card 6:** Do you need practical changes/new joint living arrangements? **Card 7:** What is the ideal state of the relationship in five years?

What you should use:
The twenty-two Major cards and the sixteen Court cards.

When:
At any crisis point.

Purpose and background information:
When you plan to meet but it never happens.

Card 1: Do you enjoy regular loving phone and messaging contact without the other person asking for anything?
Card 2: Is the reason why you meet online a question of logistics and distance? **Card 3:** Do you have any doubts about the person/their authenticity? **Card 4:** Can you arrange to meet at a location halfway between where you both live? **Card 5:** How long are you prepared to wait before meeting in person? **Card 6:** If a meeting doesn't happen, will you end the relationship?

What you should use:
The full deck.

When:
Before an online contact.

106
IF YOU LOVE SOMEONE WHO EVERYONE SAYS IS WRONG FOR YOU

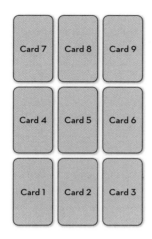

Purpose and background information:
When you know this is the only love for you.

CARD 1: What is the main opposition to your love? **CARD 2:** Do you have doubts to resolve? **CARD 3:** Can this opposition be overcome with love and goodwill, or is it too deep-seated in social/religious/cultural differences? **CARD 4:** Who can help you mediate/bridge the gap? **CARD 5:** Will time and going slowly help? **CARD 6:** What steps can you take to be together, with or without support? **CARD 7:** Do you have the resources and the desire to move away together? **CARD 8:** Are you prepared to give up friends/family/community? **CARD 9:** Will this relationship last forever?

What you should use:
The full deck.

When:
The waning moon.

107
SHOULD YOU GO BACK TO YOUR EX-PARTNER, OR CARRY ON WITH YOUR NEW LOVE AND LIFE?

Purpose and background information:
When you are moving to a new life with a new partner, but your ex-partner, whom you formerly believed was the love of your life, asks for another chance.

A two-card Spread to cut through the emotional confusion. Set the left-hand **CARD 1** for take him/her back and the right-hand **CARD 2** for stay in your present relationship. If neither card seems satisfactory, add a third card to the right for waiting for the right person.

What you should use:
The twenty-two Major cards and the sixteen Court cards.

When:
Sunset.

CHAPTER 12

SPREADS FOR OVERCOMING DIFFICULTIES IN LOVE, RECONCILIATION, AND ENDING DESTRUCTIVE RELATIONSHIPS

Cards that are lucky include:

Major Cards: Strength, Temperance, Chariot, High Priest/Hierophant and High Priestess, the Sun, the Moon.

Minor Cards: The Ace of Wands, Five of Wands, Ten of Wands, Ace of Cups, Two of Cups, Six of Cups, Ten of Cups, Ace of Pentacles, Three of Pentacles, Ten of Pentacles, Six of Swords.

Court Cards: The Pages/Princesses, Queens and Kings of Pentacles and Wands.

About the difficulties in love Spreads:

Six-card Spreads are especially good for all matters of reconciliation in love, fives for questions about fidelity, and nines for justice, sticking points, and endings. You can also use four-card Spreads for questions about security and stability and sevens for options and matters that are not clear. Three-cards will focus matters.

108
THE LOVE QUARREL

Purpose and background information:
When neither of you will back down.

BOTTOM ROW: CARD 1: What is the outward cause of the disagreement? **CARD 2:** What is the underlying issue for you? **CARD 3:** What is the underlying issue for your partner?

MIDDLE ROW: CARD 4: Is there a compromise? If so, what? **CARD 5:** Are there principles on which you cannot/will not back down? **CARD 6:** Are there issues on which your partner cannot/will not back down?

TOP ROW: CARD 7: Do you want the relationship to continue even without resolution? **CARD 8:** Is anyone outside fueling the fire? **CARD 9:** What is the best outcome?

What you should use:
The full deck.

When:
A Friday, day of peace.

109
THE IMMATURE PARTNER

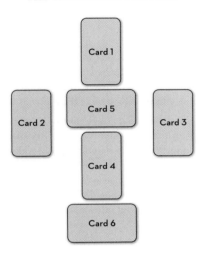

Purpose and background information:
When your partner's childish behavior is impacting on the relationship.

CARD 1: How is this most adversely affecting the relationship? **CARD 2:** Will s/he change, given time? **CARD 3:** How can change come about? **CARD 4:** If s/he doesn't grow up, should I stick with the relationship? **CARD 5:** What can I do to make things better? **CARD 6:** Who/what bad influences need to be removed from his/her life?

What you should use:
The forty Minor cards, Aces to Tens, and the sixteen Court cards.

When:
The waning moon.

110
THE CONTROLLING PARTNER

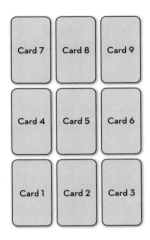

Purpose and background information:
When your partner constantly undermines you.

CARD 1: What is the underlying cause of your partner's negative behavior? **CARD 2:** What makes you accept this? **CARD 3:** Does your partner have compensatory good qualities? **CARD 4:** Can/should you accept/ignore his/her behavior, or is it eating away at your confidence? **CARD 5:** Can you/how can you change the pattern? **CARD 6:** Should you walk away? **CARD 7:** Is outside interference making the problem worse? **CARD 8:** Can you change your own reactions to deal better with the problem? **CARD 9:** The ideal outcome.

What you should use:
The full deck.

When:
A Saturday, day of imposing boundaries.

111
THE INTERFERING RELATIVE OR FRIEND

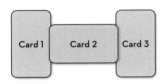

Purpose and background information:
When a relative or friend is causing trouble, but your partner cannot/will not see it.

CARD 1: The motives of the interfering person. **CARD 2:** The tactics they use to fool your partner. **CARD 3:** How to deal with the problem.

Deal all the cards and turn them all over before reading.

What you should use:
The twenty-two Major cards and the sixteen Court cards

When:
When you know s/he/they are next expected.

112
THE RIVALS

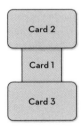

Purpose and background information:
When someone is trying to steal your partner.

CARD 1 is your partner, **CARD 2** the love rival, and **CARD 3** your relationship and what you can do to overcome the rivalry.

What you should use:
The twenty-two Major cards and the sixteen Court cards.

When:
When you know there is going to be contact between them.

Example:
Leo's girlfriend Sophie travels a lot with her job. Recently a new young male colleague, Greg, joined her Events team. Sophie has become very defensive and refuses to talk about work anymore, and her phone is often switched off in the evenings while away.

CARD 1 showed not a Cups/love card, as might be expected if an affair was occurring, but a **Princess of Wands,** suggesting work-related. **CARD 2** for the rival is the **Magician,** the powerful businessman. Leo felt there was an aspect of the con man in Greg, again no direct link with love, though Greg was no doubt flirting with Sophie. **CARD 3:** The all-important relationship card, **Two of Cups,** showed Leo and Sophie as twin souls. So Leo tried to be supportive. Sophie arrived home one weekend in tears. Greg had stolen her best contract. She said he had been oh, so charming and admitted she was flattered. Others had warned her that he was ruthless. Sometimes the cards can reveal a completely different problem from the one the outward signs suggest.

113
IF YOU ARE TEMPTED TO STRAY

Purpose and background information:
When a long-lasting relationship hits a down or dull period.

Card 1: What is lacking in the relationship that makes you want to stray? **Card 2:** Does your partner's behavior/ indifference justify this? **Card 3:** Can you stray without getting emotionally burned? **Card 4:** Can you stray without being discovered? **Card 5:** Are you bored with life generally and want changes?

What you should use:
The forty Minor cards, Aces to Tens, and the sixteen Court cards.

When:
At a waning moon.

114
CAN THIS RELATIONSHIP BE SALVAGED?

Purpose and background information:
When it all goes wrong, but you are reluctant to let go.

Card 1: Is there love/goodwill left? **Card 2:** What you are prepared to concede. **Card 3:** What can you *not* concede? **Card 4:** Would counseling/mediation help? **Card 5:** Would temporary time apart help? **Card 6:** Would a change of scene/lifestyle mend the situation?

What you should use:
The forty Minor cards, Aces to Tens, and the sixteen Court cards.

When:
A Friday, day of good will and hope.

115
IF YOUR PARTNER IS A SERIAL FLIRT

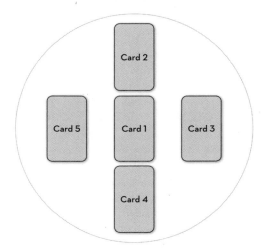

Purpose and background information:
When you worry about potential infidelity.

Card 1: Do/should you trust your partner when you aren't around? **Card 2:** Does your partner initiate attention, or only respond when others flirt with him/her? **Card 3:** Is your partner defensive/accusing you of jealousy, so you doubt yourself? **Card 4:** Are you afraid/suspect s/he may have affairs? **Card 5:** If s/he doesn't change, can you accept this behavior?

What you should use:
The full deck.

When:
After another argument about his/her flirting.

116
SHOULD YOU WALK AWAY FROM YOUR RELATIONSHIP?

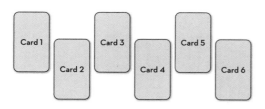

Purpose and background information:
When the relationship is destructive or going nowhere.

CARD 1: Should you leave the relationship even if you do not want to? **CARD 2:** Do you need help/support to give you the strength to walk away? **CARD 3:** If you walk away, what do you gain? **CARD 4:** If you walk away, what will you lose? **CARD 5:** Where/to what do you walk away? **CARD 6:** What/who will prevent you from weakening/going back?

What you should use:
The forty minor cards, Aces to Tens, and the sixteen Court cards.

When:
The end of a week or month.

117
MOVING ON FROM ESTRANGEMENT OR SEPARATION

Purpose and background information:
If you cannot forget, even if you feel it's over.

CARD 1: Is there any hope of reconciliation? **CARD 2:** If there is still hope, or you are trying to maintain communication, will this work? **CARD 3:** What have you gained as a result of the separation? **CARD 4:** What have you lost that you most regret? **CARD 5:** An action plan for moving forward.

What you should use:
The forty Minor cards and the sixteen Court cards.

When:
The end of a week or month.

118
WHEN A FRIEND SAYS YOUR PARTNER IS CHEATING

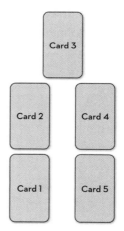

Purpose and background information:
When you do not know what to believe.

CARD 1: Could your friend have reasons to try to break you up? **CARD 2:** Is there evidence/past problems with your partner to justify your doubts? **CARD 3:** Should you do some behind-the-scenes investigation? **CARD 4:** Can/do you trust your partner not to lie when confronted? **CARD 5:** Will you stick with your partner regardless of what unfolds?

What you should use:
The forty Minor cards, Aces to Tens, and the sixteen Court cards.

When:
A Thursday, the day of truth.

119
IF YOUR PARTNER LEAVES WITHOUT EXPLANATION AND WILL NOT ANSWER YOUR CALLS

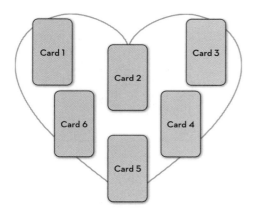

Purpose and background information:

When you do not know whether to wait or give up.

CARD 1: Has your partner been depressed/stressed with work/family/exes? **CARD 2:** Is your partner generally secretive, or is this out of character? **CARD 3:** Are there unresolved problems between you? **CARD 4:** Do you trust your partner? **CARD 5:** Is there any way to get in touch to resolve things one way or the other? **CARD 6:** Do you want him/her back regardless?

What you should use:

The full deck.

When:

When you wake.

120
IF YOUR PARTNER IS ROMANTIC AND FULL OF GRANDIOSE PLANS, BUT WANTS FREEDOM AS WELL

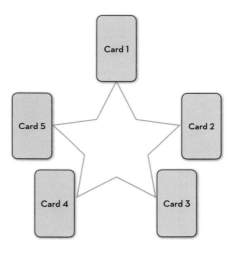

Purpose and background information:

If your partner wants the best of both worlds.

CARD 1: Is your partner a dreamer who never grew up? **CARD 2:** Are your partner's uncommitted friends a major part of his/her life? **CARD 3:** Can/do you trust your partner when you are not together? **CARD 4:** Can/how can you steer the relationship towards realistic future plans? **CARD 5:** If your partner cannot/will not change, is this enough for you now/in the future?

What you should use:

The twenty-two Major cards and the sixteen Court cards.

When:

On a significant anniversary in your relationship.

121
HOW TO KEEP A RELATIONSHIP UNITED IF EXES OR STEPCHILDREN CAUSE TROUBLE

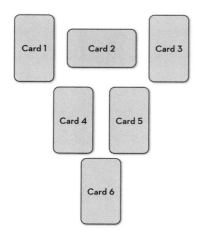

Purpose and background information:
When the only time you quarrel is over each other's children/exes.

CARD 1: Who/what is/what are the main trigger/s that cause arguments? **CARD 2:** Can you/how can you avoid any children's becoming pawns/any financial levers by exes. **CARD 3:** What strategies can you develop to avoid/deal with the main flash points? **CARD 4:** Do you need mediation/official intervention to resolve unfair custody/access/financial problems? **CARD 5:** What can you do to build happy times with your new family? **CARD 6:** What is the main unifying factor that unites you when the situation/others try to split you?

What you should use:
The full deck.

When:
A waxing Moon, or any Monday.

122
IF YOU ARE IN A RELATIONSHIP THAT IS GOING TOO FAST

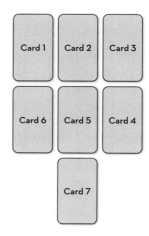

Purpose and background information:
If you feel you are being railroaded into a forever relationship before you are ready.

CARD 1: Is your partner naturally impatient, all or nothing? **CARD 2:** Are you normally cautious, or is your partner's pressure causing anxiety? **CARD 3:** Does your partner feel insecure/afraid of losing you if s/he takes it slowly? **CARD 4:** Is your partner pressurized if everyone s/he knows is settling down/having a family? **CARD 5:** Do you want to stay together, just at a slower pace? **CARD 6:** What strategies will slow things down? **CARD 7:** If s/he will not back off a little, will you walk away?

What you should use:
The full deck.

When:
A waning moon.

123
IF YOUR PARTNER IS UNFAITHFUL

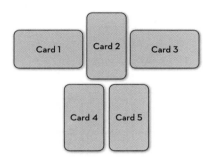

Purpose and background information:
What should you do?

CARD 1: Is this infidelity linked to a mid-life/personal crisis in your partner's life that is totally out of character? **CARD 2:** Has someone deliberately set out to seduce him/her, or was it a moment of madness? **CARD 3:** Is this a fling, or something more serious? **CARD 4:** Are you prepared to fight and/or wait for it to burn out? **CARD 5:** Has this happened before/ shattered your trust so you are ready to leave regardless?

What you should use:
The twenty-two Major cards and the sixteen Court cards.

When:
A Wednesday, day of unraveling deception.

124
IS THIS INFATUATION, OR THE REAL THING?

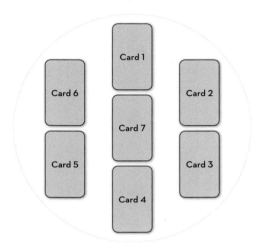

Purpose and background information:
When you *must* be with someone, regardless of consequences.

CARD 1: Does this love fill every moment of your waking life dreams? **CARD 2:** Are your feelings returned? **CARD 3:** Is something missing in your life/your present relationship? **CARD 4:** Are you/the other person free to love? **CARD 5:** Are you prepared to give up everything/do anything to have this love? **CARD 6:** If it doesn't work, are there major life changes you want/need to make? **CARD 7:** Can you take time to develop this or let it go?

What you should use:
The full deck.

When:
Mid-morning for clarity.

125
IF JEALOUSY IS AN ISSUE

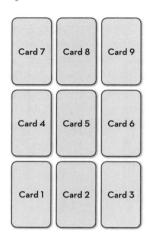

Purpose and background information:
When your partner is constantly suspicious or checking up on you.

Card 1: Are there betrayal/issues from your partner's past/childhood? **Card 2:** Does the problem interfere with your social/work life/freedom? **Card 3:** Does it occur when you pay attention to family members/friends who pose no threat? **Card 4:** Can you persuade your partner to get counseling? **Card 5:** Are there triggers that escalate the jealousy? **Card 6:** Can the problem get better with patience and reassurance? **Card 7:** If it continues, will you accept, or leave? **Card 8:** What outcome do you fear? **Card 9:** What is the best outcome?

What you should use:
The forty Minor cards, Aces to Tens, and the sixteen Court cards.

When:
A waning moon.

126
IF ONE OF YOU WANTS CHILDREN, BUT THE OTHER SAYS "NEVER"

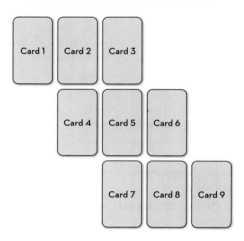

Purpose and background information:
When the matter becomes a problem.

Card 1: Was the reaction expected/a new reaction? **Card 2:** Are there underlying issues causing the unwillingness? **Card 3:** Is the reason financial/a desire for freedom/travel? **Card 4:** What merits are there in not having a family? **Card 5:** What would be lost by remaining childless? **Card 6:** Will the unwilling partner change their mind? **Card 7:** Is the relationship more important than a family? **Card 8:** Is now not the right time for a family? **Card 9:** Will/should the person wanting children find someone else/have a child alone?

What you should use:
The whole deck.

When:
Beginning of a new month or year.

127
HOW TO GET OVER A BROKEN HEART WHEN YOU HAVE BEEN DUMPED

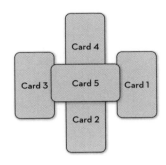

Purpose and background information:
When you are finding it difficult getting over a past relationship.

CARD 1: Could you still be/want to be reconciled? **CARD 2:** Do you know what/who caused the breakup? **CARD 3:** What coping strategies will help in the weeks ahead? **CARD 4:** Who will help you to get over this? **CARD 5:** What new person will come into your life to mend your broken heart if s/he doesn't come back?

What you should use:
The forty Minor cards, Aces to Tens, and the sixteen Court cards.

When:
A Sunday, for new beginnings.

128
IF YOU WANT TO TRAVEL AROUND THE WORLD, BUT YOUR PARTNER WANTS TO BUY A HOUSE INSTEAD

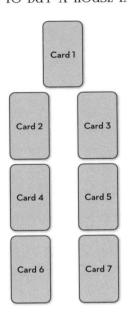

Purpose and background information:
When disagreement occurs.

CARD 1: What underlies the question? **CARD 2:** Advantages of traveling financially unburdened. **CARD 3:** Practical benefits to the relationship of traveling. **CARD 4:** Negative results of waiting to buy a house. **CARD 5:** Practical benefits of buying a house now. **CARD 6:** Benefits to the relationship of postponing travel. **CARD 7:** Negative results of postponing/modifying travel.

What you should use:
The whole deck.

When:
A Monday.

CHAPTER 13

PROSPERITY AND MONEY-MAKING SPREADS

Cards that are lucky include:

Major Cards: The Magician, Justice, Wheel of Fortune, the Sun, the Star.

Minor Cards: Ace of Pentacles, Three of Pentacles, Seven of Pentacles, Eight of Pentacles, Nine of Pentacles, Ten of Pentacles.

Court Cards: Queen and King of Pentacles.

About Prosperity and Money-Making Spreads:

Money-acquiring Spreads vary in number according to the complexity of the question and the different factors. They span through a basic three-card Spread, a relatively straightforward four-carder where security or property is involved, the speculating five-carders, seven for the intuitive rather than logical approach, eight and nine for complex issues, and even twelve-card Spreads where you are looking at the year ahead month by month financially. You can of course, as with the other theme chapters, adapt any of the Spreads introduced in the earlier chapters and repeated in Appendix 4.

129
TO MAKE MONEY FAST AND URGENTLY

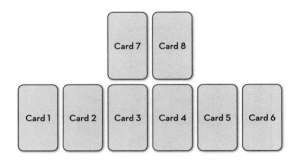

Purpose and background information:
Making an informed decision as to the best way forward.

CARD 1: Who will/can help; what are the strings? **CARD 2:** What existing assets/resources can you release? **CARD 3:** What talents/skills can generate more income fast? **CARD 4:** What will temporarily stop/reverse the outflow? **CARD 5:** What official/unofficial borrowing sources are there? **CARD 6:** Are there unpaid money/favors owing to you? **CARD 7:** The hidden obstacle. **CARD 8:** The as-yet-unrevealed rescue/rescuer.

What you should use:
The full deck.

When:
A Wednesday, day for financial maneuverability.

130
IF YOU ARE OFFERED AN OVERSEAS/OFFSHORE JOB WITH A HUGE TAX-FREE SALARY

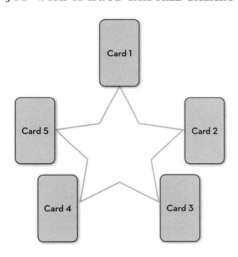

Purpose and background information:
When you would be set up for life financially, but other factors intrude.

CARD 1: What benefits of taking the offer short-term might outweigh other considerations? **CARD 2:** What longer-term advantages would occur if you stayed in the job indefinitely? **CARD 3:** What emotional/lifestyle problems might arise, and can they be overcome? **CARD 4:** What are the hidden drawbacks? **CARD 5:** Yes or no, taking the other four cards into account.

What you should use:
The twenty-two Major cards.

When:
Any morning, as soon as you wake.

131
MINIMIZING THE FINANCIAL RISK IN SPECULATION/GAMBLING

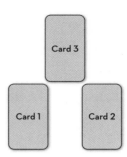

Purpose and background information:
To build from what is known and certain for a leap into the unknown with a minimum of risk.

CARD 1 tells your skills and intuitive ability to step into the financial unknown, **CARD 2** shows what you have in terms of resources/a viable system/insider knowledge, **CARD 3** shows the direction and nature of the leap you should/can take.

What you should use:
The twenty-two Major cards.

When:
A Wednesday, day of speculation

132
FOUR WEEKS TO PAYDAY

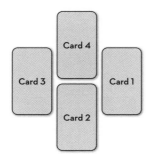

Purpose and background information:
If you are juggling your finances so they last the month.

CARD 1: What anticipated and unavoidable monthly expenses exist for the month ahead? **CARD 2:** What anticipated finances will come in during the month, and will they suffice? **CARD 3:** What/who can be postponed until next month? **CARD 4:** What can tip the balance in your favor financially?

What to use:
The forty minor cards, Aces to Tens.

When:
The first days of the new pay period, if it's looking difficult.

133
CAN YOU MAKE SERIOUS MONEY FROM YOUR TALENTS?

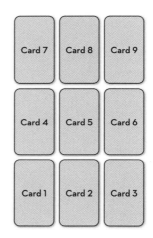

Purpose and background information:
Considering the implications of an uncertain path.

Bottom Row, CARDS 1–2–3, Cards of your current position.

CARD 1: Do people say you should go professional? **CARD 2:** What extra resources/training do you need? **CARD 3:** Is this a lucrative or oversubscribed market?

Middle Row, CARDS 4–5–6, Cards of opportunities and challenges.

CARD 4: What makes you unique? **CARD 5:** Should you invest in publicity/start small? **CARD 6:** Should you take a financial risk?

Top Row, CARDS 7–8–9, Cards of action and outcome.

CARD 7: Should you keep your job until established? **CARD 8:** Should you go all out for your dream? **CARD 9:** What unexpected good fortune waits?

What you should use:
The full deck.

When:
A Sunday, to raise your profile.

134
A TWELVE-MONTH-AHEAD CALENDAR FINANCIAL ASSESSMENT

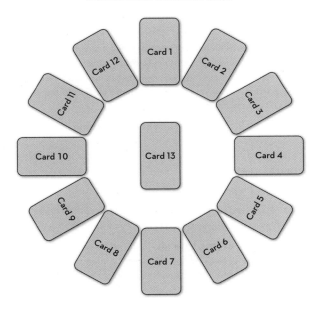

Purpose and background information:
When you need to predict your financial position for the year ahead.

Start at any time in the year. Make a clockwise circle of cards starting with the current month. Turn and read each card before turning over the next, naming each for a month. Record the financial opportunities or challenges each card suggests during a particular month.

Finally, choose a card to sum up the twelve months ahead and put this in the center of the circle. You can pick two cards for each month if you wish.

What you should use:
One or two full decks.

When:
The current month—or, if nearly through a month, the following one.

135
IF YOUR FUTURE IN-LAWS OR FAMILY OFFER TO BUY YOU THE HOUSE NEXT DOOR TO GET YOU ON THE PROPERTY LADDER.

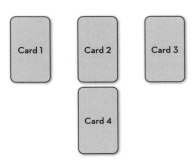

Purpose and background information:
If it's the only way you can get on the property market, but you feel your life will not be your own.

CARD 1: Do financial benefits outweigh other considerations? **CARD 2:** Will longer-term obligations, if you take the offer, be hard to break? **CARD 3:** Are there potential relationship problems between you and your partner in accepting the gift? **CARD 4:** What alternative options do you have for housing?

What to use:
The forty Minor cards, Aces to Tens, and the Court cards.

When:
A Monday, day of the moon when emotional pulls are strong.

SHOULD YOU BUY PROPERTY OR INVEST IN STOCKS?

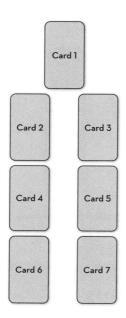

Card 1

Card 2 Card 3

Card 4 Card 5

Card 6 Card 7

Example:

Paul was left a sizable inheritance by his mother. He has been studying the stock market and making minor investments for several years. Now he has a chance to make a major investment that, if successful, would allow him to retire early from his paid job and start a business in the money market, his real passion. But his partner, who is more cautious, thinks he should buy two condos as an investment for their future.

FOR CARD 1, Paul picks **the Wheel of Fortune,** indicating this is a lucky time for him to invest. Since it is associated with good fortune rather than security, it leans toward stocks.

OPTION 1 is property.

CARD 2, The Ten of Pentacles, shows the settled home, the play-safe card, acquiring property through the years.

CARD 3, The Eight of Wands. Paul and his partner are only in their forties and children aren't in their plans, but traveling is (the traditional meaning of this card). So speculating could be good right now while their future is open.

CARD 4, The Four of Pentacles, the guy holding on to his gold, property as a safe investment but restricting freedom. **Card 5, Nine of Swords,** showing the person having a nightmare—and Paul's partner will need some reassurance, as he is naturally cautious and anxious.

CARD 6, Page of Pentacles, not spreading their wings or exploring life if they are tied to property. **CARD 7, The Three of Wands,** the world opening up, rapid movement and leaves growing, which augurs well for speculation.

The Spread seems to be saying *Go for it.*

Purpose and background information:

If you are deciding whether to invest in property or take a risk on the stock market.

Use the seven-card Options Spread.

CARD 1: Should you buy or invest, save your money or do something completely different?

OPTION 1 (property) **CARDS 2, 4,** and **6, then Option 2,** (speculate) **CARDS 3, 5,** and **7.**

DEAL AND READ CARD 1, then **Option 1** and **Option 2.**

CARDS 2 AND 3: The main advantage of the chosen option.
CARDS 4 AND 5: The main drawback of the chosen option.
CARDS 6 AND 7: The outcome of each option.

What you should use:

The full deck of seventy-eight cards.

When:

A Wednesday, day of speculation.

137
IF YOU HAVE WON OR INHERITED UNEXPECTED MONEY

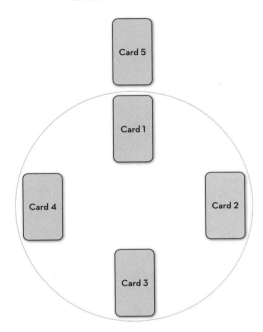

Purpose and background information:
When you need to decide how to use your good fortune.

Card 1: Do you save your money for a rainy day? **Card 2:** Do you invest it? **Card 3:** Do you spend it on something special? **Card 4:** Do you spend part/save or invest part? **Card 5:** Do you use it to bring into reality the first steps of a long-held dream?

What you should use:
The forty Minor cards, Aces to Tens.

When:
Any time from the crescent through the waxing moon.

138
HOW CAN YOU MAKE MONEY THROUGH PROPERTY?

Purpose and background information:
When considering property options.

Card 1: Should you buy property as a renovator/renovate your own property to sell? **Card 2:** Should you buy to rent one or more properties? **Card 3:** Should you wait until you have necessary resources/re-mortgage/borrow? **Card 4:** Should you speculate on property in a rundown area? **Card 5:** Should you extend borrowing to buy in an up-and-coming district? **Card 6:** Should you purchase land for a self-build? **Card 7:** Should you consider commercial property? **Card 8:** Is property expansion/investment the way forward for you?

What you should use:
The forty Minor cards.

When:
A Saturday, for successful property deals.

139
IS THIS THE TIME TO SPREAD MY WINGS FINANCIALLY?

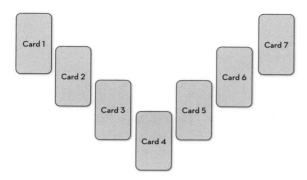

Purpose and Background information:

When you seek financial expansion/freedom; also for travel and adventure Spreads.

We call this the Bird Wing Spread.

Card 1: Financial situation to be changed. **Card 2:** Desired financial freedom. **Card 3:** Financial obligations to be shed. **Card 4:** Achieving a new freer way to earn/acquire money. **Card 5:** Who/what are potential obstacles? **Card 6:** Do you need to relocate/walk away? If so, where? **Card 7:** Attaining financial freedom without sacrificing the happiness of self/others.

What you should use:

The full deck.

When:

The beginning of a month.

140
IF YOU HAVE A MONEY-SPINNING IDEA YOU WANT TO DEVELOP

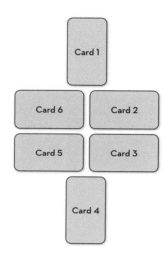

Purpose and background information:

If you are ready to go, but others say no.

Card 1: Is the idea commercially viable? **Card 2:** How is it sufficiently original to set it apart from others? **Card 3:** Do you need financial backing initially/is this available/attainable? **Card 4:** Do you have a ready market/existing/potential sales outlets? **Card 5:** Is now the time/should you wait? **Card 6:** What known obstacles/opposition do you face?

What you should use:

The full deck.

When:

A Sunday, for fresh approaches.

141
IF YOU ARE OFFERED WHAT IS APPARENTLY THE CHANCE OF A LIFETIME FINANCIALLY

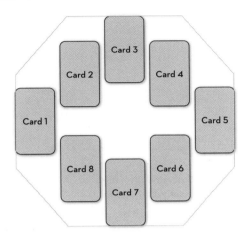

Purpose and background information:
Your heart says yes, your head says *slow down*.

Card 1: Is this too good to be true/am I being overly cautious? **Card 2:** Do the people involved have good financial track records? **Card 3:** Are you being pressured into a fast decision? **Card 4:** If you say no, will you regret it? **Card 5:** Should you explore other options? **Card 6:** Are short-term returns assured? **Card 7:** What safeguards are in place if results fall short of promises? **Card 8:** What is your intuition saying?

What you should use:
The full deck.

When:
A Wednesday morning.

142
SHOULD YOU REINVEST YOUR PENSION OR SAVINGS, OR STAY AS YOU ARE?

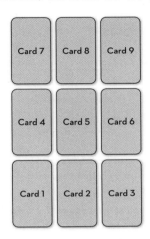

Purpose and background information:
When you are being pushed toward schemes with seemingly better returns.

Card 1: Is the alternative accredited and established? **Card 2:** Does it offer realistic returns? **Card 3:** What hidden difficulties of changing? **Card 4:** What hidden difficulties of staying where I am? **Card 5:** Do I need impartial advice? **Card 6:** Are there other options/schemes I haven't considered? **Card 7:** What immediate benefits of changing to the favored scheme? **Card 8:** What long-term advantages of changing? **Card 9:** Do I actually need/want to move my money?

What you should use:
The full deck.

When:
A Saturday, for caution in money.

143
SAVING FOR THE FUTURE

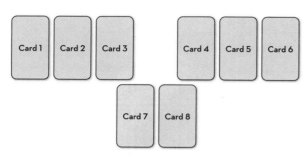

Purpose and background information:
Assessing your position, whether beginning savings or building up savings through the years.

CARD 1: Should you save for something special? **CARD 2:** Should you save for a rainy day? **CARD 3:** Are you satisfied with your present saving scheme, short-term profit-wise? **CARD 4:** Are you satisfied with your scheme, longer-term? **CARD 5:** Do you want/need to make money faster? **CARD 6:** What or who inhibits your savings capacity/how can this be remedied? **CARD 7:** Do your savings get in the way of/ enhance personal happiness? **CARD 8:** What unexpected boosts or bonuses are waiting?

What you should use:
The forty Minor cards, Aces to Tens.

When:
A Thursday, day of increasing prosperity

144
THE SUCCESSFUL JUGGLER

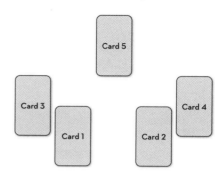

Purpose and background information:
When you are constantly juggling money.

CARD 1: What priorities must be balanced? **CARD 2:** What/ who causes imbalance? **CARD 3:** What financial demands can/should be temporarily/permanently shed to restore balance? **CARD 4:** What resources/sources of money can be accessed to adjust imbalance? **CARD 5:** How can permanent financial stability be attained?

What you should use:
The forty Minor cards, Aces to Tens, and the sixteen Court cards.

When:
Before doing your accounts.

145
SHARING FINANCIAL RESOURCES WHEN MARRYING OR MOVING IN WITH A PARTNER

Purpose and background information:
If your new partner wants to pool finances.

Card 1: Is this a central issue to resolve from the start? **Card 2:** Will your independence be compromised if you pool everything? **Card 3:** Should there be separate accounts plus a joint expenses account? **Card 4:** Do my partner and I differ in attitudes to money? **Card 5:** Do you want to share everything, regardless? **Card 6:** Is there an underlying emotional issue regarding money? **Card 7:** Should you have a formal/informal agreement? **Card 8:** What is the best way forward?

What you should use:
The forty Minor cards, Aces to Tens.

When:
A Saturday.

146
SHOULD YOU PURCHASE SOMETHING SPECIAL?

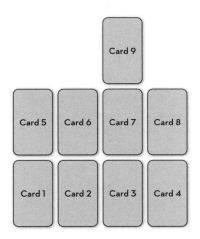

Purpose and background information:
When considering alternative sources of funding.

Card 1: Do I really need/want this? **Card 2:** Do I want/need it sufficiently to go all out for it now? **Card 3:** Have I checked all sources for the best price? **Card 4:** If I need a loan, shall I borrow officially, or from family/friends? **Card 5:** Will buying it leave me short of money? **Card 6:** If I borrow, can I pay it back? **Card 7:** Will the pleasure outweigh disadvantages?

Card 8: Should I use my money in a different way? **Card 9:** Yes or no.

What you should use:
The full deck.

When:
Before committing yourself.

147
SHOULD YOU INVEST IN A TRAINING COURSE TO IMPROVE YOUR FUTURE?

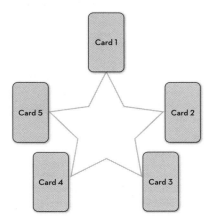

Purpose and background information:
When you have an opportunity to improve your qualifications, but wonder if the outlay is worthwhile.

Card 1: Will this course provide the missing link/the next major step in your career? **Card 2:** Will the investment of money and time prove worthwhile financially? **Card 3:** Is this the right time to spend on the course, or should you wait? **Card 4:** Is there similar on-the-job training/moving to a new job that will save the outlay? **Card 5:** Do you want to take the course, regardless of short/long term profitability?

What you should use:
The twenty-two Major cards.

When:
A Wednesday, day of study and training.

148
IS BARGAIN-HUNTING A POTENTIAL SOURCE OF INCOME?

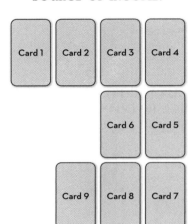

Purpose and background information:
When you have an eye for a bargain.

CARD 1: Can I find good sources online for buying and selling? **CARD 2:** Should I rely on local sources/go further afield? **CARD 3:** Should I stick to tried and tested sources/branch out? **CARD 4:** Can I develop my hobby into a lucrative business? **CARD 5:** Is there hidden treasure waiting? **CARD 6:** How soon can I begin trading? **CARD 7:** Will trading bring satisfaction as well as profit? **CARD 8:** What avoidable pitfalls await? **CARD 9:** Do I want a store, online trading, a market stall, or all three?

What you should use:
The whole deck.

When:
A waxing moon.

CHAPTER 14

SPREADS FOR SOLVING DIFFICULTIES WITH MONEY

Cards that are lucky for solving money difficulties:

Major Cards: The Magician, The Chariot, Justice, Judgment, Wheel of Fortune, Temperance, the Sun.

Minor Cards: Ace of Pentacles, Three of Pentacles, Four of Pentacles, Seven of Pentacles, Eight of Pentacles, Nine of Pentacles, Ten of Pentacles, Ace of Wands, Three of Wands, Six of Swords.

Court Cards: Knight, Queen, and King of Pentacles.

All the money Spreads described in the previous chapter work equally well when considering money problems, four-carders being good for anti-debt Spreads and where security or property is involved. Five cards assist with any potential fraud, scamming, or unwise investments, or where speculation is involved. Six-carders also appear, as money problems do often have emotional implications, as do seven-card Spreads for family or love partnership issues caused or made worse by money worries. For more complicated matters, eight, nine, or even longer card Spreads may be helpful in untangling matters that are unclear.

149
WHY DOES MONEY DRAIN OUT, NO MATTER HOW HARD YOU TRY?

xPurpose and background information:
When you are constantly juggling your finances and it doesn't add up.

CARD 1: What/who causes the financial drain?
CARD 2: The emotional payback of the drain.
CARD 3: Stopping the drain in the short-term.
CARD 4: Resolving the problem in the longer term. **CARD 5:** Would outside assistance/advice/a change of tactic reduce the shortfall?

What you should use:
The forty Minor cards, Aces to Tens, and the sixteen Court cards.

When:
A Wednesday for money dilemmas.

Example:
Sue and Andy had run up huge loans and credit card payments and were borrowing from one card to pay another. Creditors were piling on interest.

CARD 1: The **Princess of Swords,** their daughter Virginia. She had gone from one disastrous relationship to another, had five children by three different fathers, and was now home again, destitute, with the children. **CARD 2:** The **Two of Pentacles**, trying to balance the needs of their daughter and grandchildren with spiraling interest payments. **CARD 3:** The **Princess of Pentacles.** Their daughter was at home smoking and sleeping, even though the children were at school and she could work. **CARD 4:** The **Five of Pentacles,** their daughter looking for help from another source. She wasn't claiming welfare benefits or support from the fathers. Andy and Sue showed their daughter their debts and sent her job-hunting and to find out about social housing and standing on her own two feet. **CARD 5:** The **High Priest.** Andy and Sue contacted a debt charity and are negotiating reasonable repayments.

Card 5
Card 4
Card 3
Card 2
Card 1

150
WHY DO PEOPLE TAKE ADVANTAGE OF YOU FINANCIALLY?

Card 4 | Card 5 | Card 6
Card 1 | Card 2 | Card 3

Purpose and background information:
When you realize you are always paying and are made to feel guilty if you do not.

CARD 1: What stops you from saying no? **CARD 2:** Who takes advantage of you the most? **CARD 3:** How will you cope with the resentment/pressure if you start saying no? **CARD 4:** What do you gain by being overly generous? **CARD 5:** Who will resist/protest/use emotional blackmail if you say no? **CARD 6:** Are you with the wrong people?

What you should use:
The twenty-two Major cards and the sixteen Court cards.

When:
A Tuesday, the day of courage.

151
FOR FINANCIAL RESTORATION AFTER LOSS

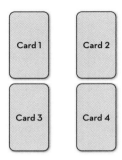

Purpose and background information:
When a sudden business, job, or financial loss causes a major crisis.

Card 1: What can be salvaged? **Card 2:** What economies/downsizing can help you get back on your feet? **Card 3:** What new opportunities are just over the horizon? **Card 4:** Who or what will come to the rescue?

What you should use:
The forty Minor cards and the sixteen Court cards.

When:
A Sunday, day of new beginnings.

152
WHEN PLANS GO AWRY AND YOUR USUAL MONEY SOURCE DRIES UP

Purpose and background information:
When time is not on your side and you are under pressure to find money fast.

Turn all the cards over except **Card 4,** which you will turn over after reading the others.

Card 1: Is it worth one more try to revive the former money source, and how? **Card 2:** What is your first port in the storm? **Card 3:** How can you avoid disaster? **Card 4:** What unexpected positive factor/input/rescuer will intervene?

What you should use:
The twenty-two Major cards.

When:
As soon as possible after the bad news hits.

153
SHOULD YOU STRUGGLE ON FINANCIALLY?

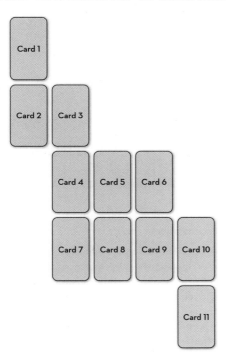

Purpose and background information:
When no option seems right.

CARD 1: Where you are now. **CARD 2:** Your strengths/assets. **CARD 3:** Your weaknesses/obstacles. **CARD 4:** How to buy time. **CARD 5:** What must you give up to survive? **CARD 6:** What to avoid in order to survive. **CARD 7:** Could you start again? **CARD 8:** Should you start again? And, if so, what actions should you take? **CARD 9:** Who throws a lifeline? **CARD 10:** Who/what pushes you under? **CARD 11:** Should you walk away?

What to use:
The whole deck.

When:
At the beginning of a month.

154
IF YOU ARE LEFT WITH DEBT AFTER A BREAKUP OR A BETRAYAL

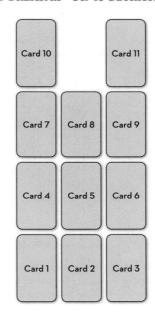

Purpose and background information:

CARD 1: Can you regain money through direct personal negotiation? **CARD 2:** Will official channels help? **CARD 3:** What joint assets can you access? **CARD 4:** Can you obtain breathing space to negotiate? **CARD 5:** Can you negotiate a reasonable settlement with creditors? **CARD 6:** Can you refuse to accept liability? **CARD 7:** Should you walk away? **CARD 8:** Can you find urgent extra income? **CARD 9:** What decisive major step can you take? **CARD 10:** Next twelve-month prospects. **CARD 11:** Longer-term prospects.

What you should use:
The whole deck.

When:
A waning moon.

155
OBTAINING FINANCIAL COMPENSATION FOR AN ACCIDENT OR CLAIM

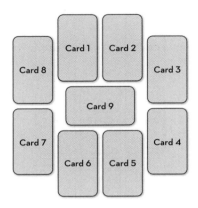

Purpose and background information:
When what is rightfully yours is being withheld.

CARD 1: What should be paid to you under a just system?
CARD 2: Is injustice or corruption involved? **CARD 3:** Why it is officially being withheld/delayed? **CARD 4:** Who/what can move the situation along? **CARD 5:** What is going on behind the scenes? **CARD 6:** What facts/truths will emerge? **CARD 7:** Who/what do you need to watch for preventing/slowing justice? **CARD 8:** Short-term resolution. **CARD 9:** Long-term resolution.

What you should use:
The twenty-two Major Arcana and the sixteen Court cards.

When:
A Thursday, day of justice.

156
SHOULD YOU REINVEST/DRAW ON YOUR PENSION FUND IF YOU HAVE RECEIVED A SEEMINGLY BETTER OFFER?

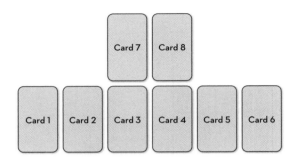

Purpose and background information:
If you are uncertain about change.

CARD 1: Is the offer from an accredited source? **CARD 2:** Does it offer reasonable—rather than miraculous—returns? **CARD 3:** What are the hidden difficulties or disadvantages? **CARD 4:** Do you actually need/want to reinvest? **CARD 5:** Should you take impartial advice? **CARD 6:** Are there other options? **CARD 7:** What are the immediate benefits? **CARD 8:** What are the longer-term advantages?

What you should use:
The full deck.

When:
Early morning, for clarity.

157
SHOULD YOU TAKE A LOAN TO CONSOLIDATE FINANCES?

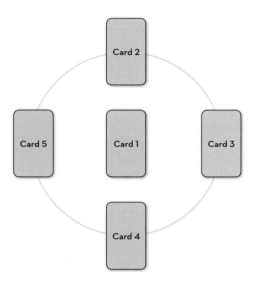

Purpose and background information:
When you need to rearrange your debt situation.

CARD 1: Do I need a loan, or can I economize? **CARD 2:** What loan options do I have? **CARD 3:** Is a loan the best way to consolidate? **CARD 4:** Would other options such as re-mortgaging/credit cards be better? **CARD 5:** Should I borrow from friends/family, or official sources?

What you should use:
The forty Minor cards, Aces to Tens.

When:
A Wednesday, day of rebalancing funds.

158
WHEN YOU ARE PRESSURED FOR REPAYMENT AND YOU DO NOT HAVE THE FUNDS

Purpose and background information:
If you are feeling intimidated or worried by a creditor/creditors.

CARD 1: Should/could you offer partial repayment? **CARD 2:** Can you negotiate for more time/better terms? **CARD 3:** Is there a reputable organization to negotiate on your behalf? **CARD 4:** Can/should you use avoidance tactics until you get financially straight? **CARD 5:** Can you tough it out? **CARD 6:** Are there any extra ways of earning money fast? **CARD 7:** Can you consolidate what you owe? **CARD 8:** Can you sell off any assets? **CARD 9:** What is the longer-term outlook?

What you should use:
The full deck.

When:
A Saturday, for containing out-of-control finances.

159
IF YOU ARE NOT CERTAIN THE PERSON OR COMPANY OFFERING TO FIX YOUR FINANCIAL PROBLEMS IS GENUINE

Purpose and background information:
When the solution seems almost too easy.

A quick three cards in a row to cut through detail.

CARD 1: Is this person/company's offer genuine? **CARD 2:** Even if genuine, is this person/company able to deliver a solution? **CARD 3:** Should you look elsewhere first before making a decision?

What you should use:
The twenty-two Major cards.

When:
Early morning, for clarity.

160
WHEN MONEY BURNS A HOLE IN YOUR PARTNER'S POCKET

Purpose and background information:
If every time money comes in, it is spent.

CARD 1: What is/are the main extravagances? **CARD 2:** Is your partner willing to tackle the problem? **CARD 3:** Is this an emotional issue, or a power issue? **CARD 4:** Can you impose reasonable spending limits? **CARD 5:** Can you increase income to plug the outflow? **CARD 6:** Is the problem increasing? **CARD 7:** Should you separate your finances? **CARD 8:** If it gets worse, would you think about leaving?

What you should use:
The forty Minor cards, Aces to Tens, and the sixteen Court cards.

When:
A Wednesday, for curbing extravagance.

161
IF YOU ARE DISPUTING A PAYMENT WITH THE IRS OR ANOTHER OFFICIAL ORGANIZATION

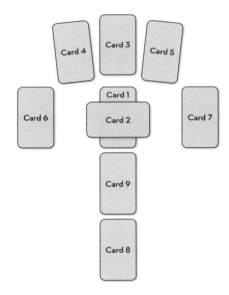

Purpose and background information:
When they will not see reason.

CARD 1: Can you dispute this through an ombudsman/public advocate or similar procedure? **CARD 2:** What unfair tactics is the organization using? **CARD 3:** How can you reschedule until resolved? **CARD 4:** If they are insisting on immediate payment what funds can you temporarily divert? **CARD 5:** Can you offer assets as temporary surety? **CARD 6:** Can you put other plans/demands on hold to give yourself breathing space? **CARD 7:** The short-term outcome. **CARD 8:** The longer-term outcome. **CARD 9:** How to avoid similar problems in the future.

What you should use:
The full deck.

When:
A Saturday, for resolving official matters.

162
IF YOU HAVE SUFFERED FINANCIAL LOSS THAT WASN'T YOUR FAULT

Purpose and background information:
When you are trying to recover financially.

Use the slanting nine-card ladder. **CARD 1:** The current position to be remedied. **CARD 2:** What can be salvaged? **CARD 3:** What can be abandoned? **CARD 4:** The key to recovery. **CARD 5:** What potential financial help is available from friends and family? **CARD 6:** What official funding sources are available? **CARD 7:** Is there possible compensation from the person/organization that caused the loss? **CARD 8:** Should you rebuild/make a complete change? **CARD 9:** How swift is recovery?

What you should use:
The forty Minor cards, Aces to Tens, and the sixteen Court cards.

When:
A Sunday, for new beginnings.

163
IF A FRIEND OR RELATIVE BORROWS MONEY BUT NEVER REPAYS

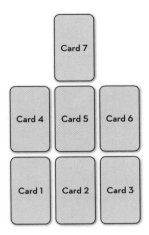

Purpose and background information:
When you are asked yet again for a loan.

CARD 1: Will the money be repaid this time? **CARD 2:** Are there always plausible excuses for not repaying? **CARD 3:** Why do you feel you have to say yes? **CARD 4:** Does the person ever give money to you? **CARD 5:** If you refuse, what will be the emotional consequences? **CARD 6:** Is there non-financial support you could offer? **CARD 7:** Do you want this person in your life?

What you should use:
The forty Minor cards, Aces to Tens, and the sixteen Court cards.

When:
A Friday, for resolving emotional pressure.

164
IF AN EX-PARTNER IS ALWAYS DEMANDING MORE MONEY

Purpose and background information:
When financial and emotional pressures make it hard to go forward.

CARD 1: Is this an ongoing problem that needs final resolution? **CARD 2:** Is this an emotional guilt game to control you? **CARD 3:** Do you/why do you feel obliged to pay whatever is asked? **CARD 4:** Is there room for compromise? **CARD 5:** Are these demands causing problems in a new relationship/fulfilling other financial needs? **CARD 6:** Do you need official closure to avoid personal confrontation?

What you should use:
The twenty-two Major cards and sixteen Court cards.

When:
Before responding to the latest demand.

165
A MAJOR FINANCIAL VIEW TO FIND THE WAY TO SOLVENCY

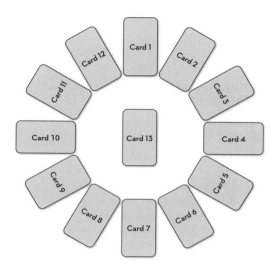

Purpose and background information:
To rationalize your finances before seeing your accountant or the bank.

Read the circle cards, leaving the thirteenth for the last.

CARD 1: Where you are financially. **CARD 2:** Unavoidable people and circumstances affecting solvency. **CARD 3:** Avoidable people and circumstances affecting solvency. **CARD 4:** Short-term actions to improve finances. **CARD 5:** Longer-term strategies. **CARD 6:** Hidden obstacles/challenges. **CARD 7:** Hidden advantages. **CARD 8:** Financial goals for the next twelve months. **CARD 9:** Potential expansion of income. **CARD 10:** Potential economies and the viability of borrowing or financial consolidation. **CARD 11:** Cutting potential losses. **CARD 12:** Preserving what is working financially. **CARD 13:** The ideal outcome.

What you should use:
The full deck.

When:
When any major financial crisis or opportunity arises.

166

IF YOU ARE OFFERED THE CHANCE TO INVEST IN A SYNDICATE WITH SEEMINGLY GOOD RETURNS

Purpose and background information:
When everyone seems to be making fast money and you are offered a way in.

CARD 1: Should you leap in and worry afterward? **CARD 2:** What guarantees are there that you will not lose all your money? **CARD 3:** Are the people involved generally sound in investments? **CARD 4:** Can you make independent inquiries to confirm viability/answer questions? **CARD 5:** Should you make a partial investment, or walk away?

What you should use:
The forty Minor cards, Aces to Tens.

When:
Any transition hour of the day, such as dawn or sunset.

167

IF YOU WANT TO HELP AN ADULT CHILD WITH A MAJOR PURCHASE THAT WILL EAT INTO YOUR SAVINGS

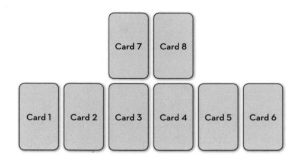

Purpose and background information:
When your heart says yes, but your head questions.

CARD 1: What are the implications of giving money? **CARD 2:** Is it worth the sacrifice? **CARD 3:** What conditions are you imposing? **CARD 4:** Is it a loan, or a gift? **CARD 5:** What are the emotional implications of refusing? **CARD 6:** If you agree, can you still fund your own plans? **CARD 7:** Will you need to modify/postpone your future plans? **CARD 8:** Are there non-financial ways to help?

What you should use:
The whole deck.

When:
The beginning of the month.

168
THE SHOPAHOLIC SPREAD

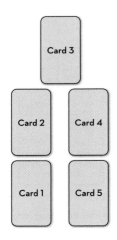

Purpose and background information:
When you or your partner wastefully spends money on items that are never used or opened.

CARD 1: Is the problem increasing and causing real financial worries? **CARD 2:** What is the underlying cause of the problem? **CARD 3:** What is the short-term payoff of the shopaholic behavior? **CARD 4:** Can the problem be curbed informally? **CARD 5:** Is professional help necessary/advisable?

What you should use:
The forty Minor cards, Aces to Tens.

When:
The waning moon.

CHAPTER 15

CAREER SPREADS

Lucky cards for Career Spreads:

Major Arcana: The Magician, The Emperor/Empress, The Chariot, The Wheel of Fortune, Strength, The Sun, The Star, The World.

Minor Cards: Ace of Pentacles, Ace of Wands, Three of Pentacles, Three of Wands, Six of Wands, Seven of Pentacles, Eight and Nine of Pentacles, Eight of Wands, Nine and Ten of Pentacles.

Court Cards: King and Queen of Pentacles, King and Queen of Wands.

About Career Spreads:

If an either/or question, a two-card reading will cut to the heart of the matter. Use three for considering alternatives, six where emotional issues are linked, and nine-card readings for expansion or conflict. Four- and eight-carders assist in matters of stability and security, five for interviews, presentations, and where there are questions of honesty and integrity. Seven-carders are good where dreams and ambitions are central.

169
WILL YOU GET THE JOB YOU ARE APPLYING FOR?

Purpose and background information:
When you aren't certain about your prospects.

CARD 1: Are there more indications in your favor? **CARD 2:** Are there more indications that you may not get this job?

What you should use:
The twenty-two Major cards.

When:
After submitting your application.

170
WHEN YOU ARE CONSTANTLY IN CONFLICT WITH A COLLEAGUE OR MANAGER

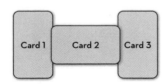

Purpose and background information:
If whatever you do is considered wrong, but you do not want to leave your job.

CARD 1: The open cause of the conflict. **CARD 2:** The hidden cause of the conflict. **CARD 3:** The solution.

What you should use:
The forty Minor cards, Aces to Tens.

When:
The beginning of the work week.

171
WHICH SHOULD TAKE PRIORITY RIGHT NOW YOUR DAY JOB, OR YOUR ON-THE-SIDE BUSINESS?

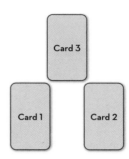

Purpose and background information:
If you are finding it hard to balance the two.

After reading **CARD 1** and **CARD 2** and neither seems definite, add a third card above and between **CARDS 1 AND 2.**

What you should use:
The twenty-two Major cards.

When:
At a crisis point in your working world.

172

WILL YOU MAKE A SUCCESS OF YOUR NEW JOB?

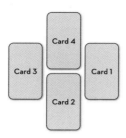

Purpose and background information:
When you are worried about starting in a new challenging workplace.

CARD 1: What expertise do you take to your new job that will ensure success? **CARD 2:** What do you especially like about your new workplace? **CARD 3:** What positive changes can you make to ensure that your presence is felt? **CARD 4:** How can/ must you compromise/learn new methods in order to fit in?

What you should use:
The forty Minor cards, Aces to Tens.

When:
The evening before you start.

173

IF YOU NEED MORE DETAILED SOLUTIONS TO RESOLVE CONFLICT WITH A COLLEAGUE OR MANAGER

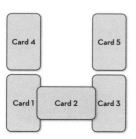

Purpose and background information:
If, having done the previous Spread, you need more information, deal and turn the three-card Spread as before. Then add **CARD 4** above **CARD 1** and **CARD 5** above **CARD 3.** Turn the final two cards over and read them.

CARD 1: The open cause of the conflict. **CARD 2:** The hidden cause of the conflict. **CARD 3:** Should you negotiate officially through a mediator/union representative? **CARD 4:** Should you tackle and confront directly**? CARD 5:** Should you just do your job and try to ignore the conflict?

What you should use:
The forty Minor cards, Aces to Tens.

When:
The beginning of the work week.

174

A TRIANGLE THREE-STEP TO SUCCESS WITHIN YOUR PRESENT WORKPLACE

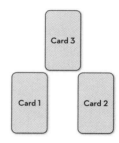

Purpose and background information:
When advancement is slow in your workplace, but you know you are ready.

CARD 1: The first step to take if you are to succeed.
CARD 2: The second step that may involve the support/ recommendation of others. **CARD 3:** How and when success will be manifested.

What you should use:
The full deck.

When:
You see an opportunity.

175
WILL YOU FIND A JOB IF IT IS YOUR FIRST OR AFTER A JOB LOSS?

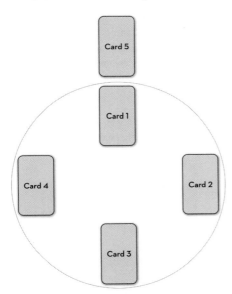

Purpose and background information:
If you have been looking for a job for a while.

CARD 1: Are you looking everywhere, including the Internet? **CARD 2:** Would you relocate to get a foothold on the market? **CARD 3:** Would you apply for a job in a similar field, if retraining would be necessary? **CARD 4:** Would you learn something completely different in order to get a job? **CARD 5:** What unknown factor will positively affect your prospects?

What you should use:
The forty Minor cards, Aces to Tens, and the sixteen Court cards.

When:
Before sending out a batch of new applications.

176
CAN YOU REACH THE TOP OF YOUR PROFESSION?

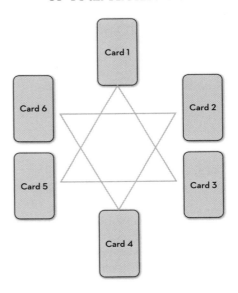

Purpose and background information:
When you have ambitions to go as far as you can.

CARD 1: Will you put 100% effort into advancing your career? **CARD 2:** Are you prepared to face jealousy and resentment from rivals? **CARD 3:** Will you succeed at networking to gain the right support for your upward journey? **CARD 4:** Should you change companies/relocate frequently for increasing promotion? **CARD 5:** Would it be better to work your way up in your current organization/making as few moves as possible? **CARD 6:** What good-luck factor will aid you?

What you should use:
The full deck.

When:
A Tuesday, day of power and action.

177

THERE IS SOMETHING GOING ON AT WORK THAT IS DISHONEST OR BAD PRACTICE, AND YOU WONDER WHETHER TO SPEAK OUT

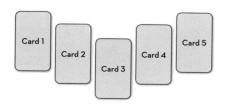

Purpose and background information:
If you are worried that you will be implicated when the dishonesty is discovered.

CARD 1: The nature/extent of the dishonesty. **CARD 2:** Is there a major cover-up conspiracy? **CARD 3:** Is there any way you could be implicated if you speak out? **CARD 4:** Can you/ should you speak out while holding your present position? **CARD 5:** Should you get another job and speak out when you leave?

What you should use:
The full deck.

When:
A waning moon.

Example:
Josie is an accounts manager for a big company and has recently noticed that money is regularly missing from a major account. But her senior manager says she is mistaken and should focus on her own part of the job. Now an even larger sum has gone missing from a different account, and Josie has been warned that if she makes a fuss, she may be implicated in the loss.

Her first card is the **Seven of Swords,** showing the person stealing away with the swords. This confirms that something deliberately dishonest is going on. It also warns Josie to beware of backstabbing and make sure she collects proof before acting.

The second card is the **Six of Pentacles,** money going out and not seeing the hands taking it. Her manager has warned her

more than once that it is not her business to question. **CARD 3** is the **Four of Swords,** the defensive card with swords sticking outward, which suggests maintaining the status quo. Josie needs to collect facts and figures in case she is implicated. **CARD 4** is the **Five of Swords,** another card suggesting there are sneaky dealings afoot. Josie feels her manager will stop her from speaking out by any means. **CARD 5** is the **Eight of Cups**, Josie walking away with all her cups of integrity upright. So, the time to speak out and produce her evidence is when, and only when, she has another job and is away from the fallout.

178

A MAJOR WORKING LIFE REVIEW

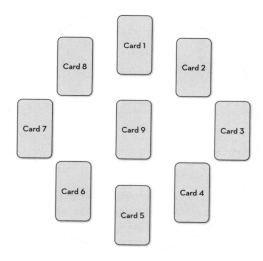

Purpose and background information:
When you have lost direction.

Deal the cards clockwise in a circle formation.

CARD 1: What is missing from my working life? **CARD 2:** What can easily be changed? **CARD 3:** What major changes should I make? **CARD 4:** What major changes would cause disruption? **CARD 5:** Can I progress within my present company? **CARD 6:** Should I change jobs? **CARD 7:** Should I relocate to advance my career? **CARD 8:** Short-term results, 6–12 months' results of change. **CARD 9:** Five-year prognosis of change.

1001 TAROT SPREADS

What you should use:

The twenty-two Major cards and sixteen Court cards—or, if you prefer, the whole deck.

When:

New Year's, a birthday, or the change of a season.

179
HOW TO OVERCOME FIERCE COMPETITION AND OPPOSITION TO A PROMOTION/ CAREER MOVE THAT YOU WANT

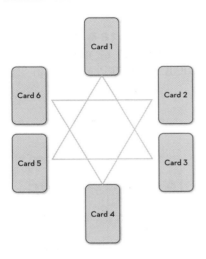

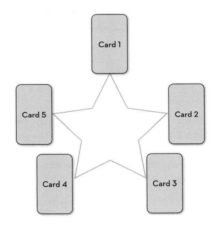

Purpose and background information:

If you are nervous about forgetting your words or saying the wrong thing.

CARD 1: What specific impression/message do you aim to give? **CARD 2:** What challenges do you expect from your audience/interview panel? **CARD 3:** What special skills/ abilities do you want to reveal? **CARD 4:** What strategy can ensure success? **CARD 5:** What is the best result that can be expected from this interview/presentation?

What you should use:

The twenty-two Major cards and the sixteen Court cards.

When:

The evening before the presentation/interview.

Purpose and background information:

When you know there is stiff opposition or favoritism working against you.

CARD 1: Who/what is your main competition/rival? **CARD 2:** Is it a fair competition/are there hidden factors against you? **CARD 3:** How to attract the extra support/resources you need? **CARD 4:** How can you avoid/overcome factors against you? **CARD 5:** Why you deserve to win. **CARD 6:** The winning strategy/tactic to ensure success.

What you should use:

The full deck.

When:

The week before the interview/decision.

181

WHO OR WHAT IS YOUR MAIN OPPOSITION FOR PROMOTION OR ADVANCEMENT?

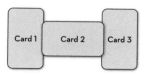

Purpose and background information:

If you are worried that there is a favored candidate or someone influential who opposes you.

Card 1: To the left, the reasons you deserve the new position. **Card 2,** Crossing **Cards 1** and **3:** The actual—as opposed to perceived—threat of the person or situation standing in your way. **Card 3:** For new tactics or strategies to get what you want.

What you should use:

The twenty-two Major Arcana and the sixteen Court cards.

When:

The day before the interview, test, or major application.

182

WILL YOU BE ABLE TO GET A PERMANENT JOB IF YOU CURRENTLY HAVE A TEMPORARY ONE OR A CONTRACT?

Purpose and background information:

If you want security at your present workplace.

Card 1: Do you feel, based on your performance, you should be offered permanent work? **Card 2:** Who/what will help with your application within the organization? **Card 3:** What expertise do you have that makes you valuable to the organization? **Card 4:** Should you consider a permanent contract/job in a similar organization? **Card 5:** What unknown factors are in your favor?

What you will need:

The forty Minor cards, Aces to Tens.

When:

The beginning of a month.

183

SHOULD I QUIT MY GOING-NOWHERE JOB, ALTHOUGH MY CURRENT JOB IS SECURE?

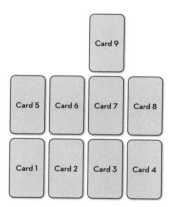

Purpose and background information:

When you are bored at work.

Card 1: Should you resign, taking a chance you'll find something quickly? **Card 2:** Should you stay while you find something new? **Card 3:** Should you stay and make a good life outside work? **Card 4:** Could you get opportunities where you are? **Card 5:** Should you go freelance? **Card 6:** Do you want a change in your career? **Card 7:** Do you want a change in your life? **Card 8:** What will happen in six months if you make changes? **Card 9:** What will happen in six months if you do not make changes?

What you should use:
The full deck.

When:
A waxing moon.

184
WORKPLACE MAJOR CONFLICT

Purpose and background information:
When the atmosphere at work is causing major stress.

CARD 1: Is the conflict new, or longstanding? **CARD 2:** Is it affecting other people as well? **CARD 3:** Who or what is the main outer cause? **CARD 4:** What is the underlying cause? **CARD 5:** Can the stress be ignored/avoided? **CARD 6:** Would mediation/outside intervention help the situation? **CARD 7:** What is the best strategy? **CARD 8:** Could you work from home? **CARD 9:** Are there conflict-free departments to which you could transfer? **CARD 10:** Should you move to another workplace? **CARD 11:** Is there any support within the company?

What you should use:
The full deck.

When:
Before the start of a work week.

185
IF YOUR CAREER IS BEING BLOCKED BY PREJUDICE OR INEQUALITY

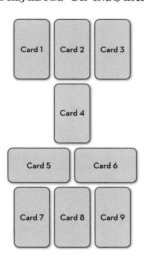

Purpose and background information:
When prejudice and inequality are rife, but everyone denies it.

CARD 1: Is there a particular source of the prejudice/inequality? **CARD 2:** Is it an unspoken attitude/unofficial policy? **CARD 3:** Is there an internal complaint route/is there a conspiracy of silence? **CARD 4:** Do you need outside/union help? **CARD 5:** Is the problem so deep-seated that you should move on? **CARD 6:** If you move on, should you take legal action? **CARD 7:** Would you stay there if the problem was resolved? **CARD 8:** If you stay, what is your next six-months' outlook? **CARD 9:** If you move on, what is your outlook six months after that?

What you should use:
The twenty-two Major cards.

When:
A waning moon.

186
IF YOU WORK FROM HOME FOR AN ORGANIZATION

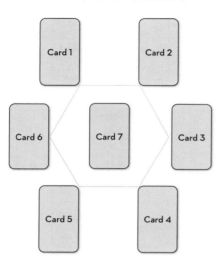

Purpose and background information:

When it's not going well.

Deal cards in a hexagram (six-sided shape). Turn over the first six cards, reading them all, then turn over and read **CARD 7.**

CARD 1: What/who makes it hard to work uninterrupted? **CARD 2:** What are the main problems communicating remotely with the company HQ? **CARD 3:** Is isolation from colleagues a problem? **CARD 4:** Could you work part-time at HQ? **CARD 5:** How can you improve online conferencing, etc.? **CARD 6:** How can you work only official hours/have breaks? **CARD 7:** How can you get uninterrupted time/space?

What you should use:

The forty Minor cards, Aces to Tens, and the sixteen Court cards

When:

In the morning before work.

187
WILL YOUR CONTRACT BE RENEWED?

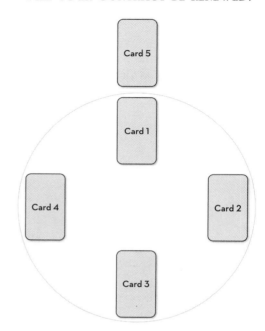

Purpose and background information:

When you are waiting anxiously to find out if your position will remain secure.

CARD 1: Has your performance been well-rated during the contract? **CARD 2:** Is there any informal interest in your staying? **CARD 3:** Is now a good time/situation for you to make a formal application for renewal? **CARD 4:** Who/what is in your favor for having the contract renewed? **CARD 5:** If you don't get the new contract, what good unexpected new offer is waiting?

What you should use:

The twenty-two Major cards.

When:

The month before your contract is up for renewal.

188
WILL YOU ATTAIN YOUR DREAM JOB IN THE FORESEEABLE FUTURE?

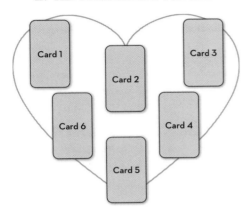

Purpose and background information:
When you know your ultimate goal, but there is a long road ahead.

CARD 1: How can you shape the path to your dream job?
CARD 2: What steps must you take toward attaining it?
CARD 3: What skills and talents must you work on to reach the goal? **CARD 4:** Who/what organization/networks can speed your way? **CARD 5:** Should you start slowly/leap right in? **CARD 6:** Will you make it? How soon?

What you should use:
The full deck.

When:
The beginning of a new month.

189
WILL YOU SURVIVE A TAKEOVER OR MERGER?

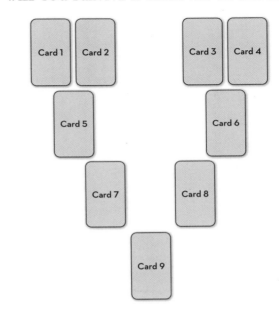

Purpose and background information:
When rumors are flying around and you fear the worst.

CARD 1: Are the rumors exaggerated/unnecessarily negative? **CARD 2:** Does what is known have positive aspects? **CARD 3:** What strengths/attributes assure you a place in the new organization? **CARD 4:** What new skills do you need to acquire for a smooth transition? **CARD 5:** What are your main fears/how can you resolve them? **CARD 6:** What opportunities might lie outside the current organization? **CARD 7:** What changes in work practice would you welcome? **CARD 8:** What compromises can you not/will you not make? **CARD 9:** Your situation nine months ahead.

What you should use:
The whole deck.

When:
A waxing moon.

190
CAN YOU MANAGE A MAJOR PROJECT SUCCESSFULLY?

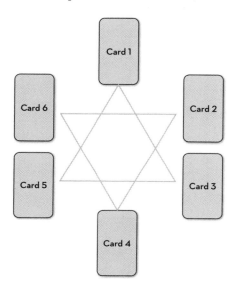

Purpose and background information:
When you are offered a big chance but are scared you will not succeed.

CARD 1: What will you gain most from this challenge?
CARD 2: What qualities do you need in order to lead this project? **CARD 3:** What qualities of compromise do you need to bring a team together so everyone feels valued? **CARD 4:** What difficulties/difficult people do you anticipate standing in your way? **CARD 5:** What are the short-term advantages of succeeding? **CARD 6:** What is the next step after the successful completion of the project?

What you should use:
The full deck.

When:
The full moon, or any Monday for dreams fulfilled.

CHAPTER 16
BUSINESS SPREADS

Lucky cards for business Spreads:

Major Cards: The Magician, the High Priestess, the Emperor and Empress, the Hermit, Justice, Strength, the Wheel of Fortune, the Sun, the Star, Judgment, the World.

The Minor Cards: Ace of Pentacles, Ace of Wands, Ace of Swords, Two of Wands, Three of Pentacles, Three of Wands, Four of Pentacles, Four of Wands, Five of Wands, Six of Wands, Six of Swords, Seven of Pentacles, Eight of Pentacles, Nine of Pentacles, Ten of Pentacles.

The Court Cards: The King and Queen of Pentacles, the King and Queen of Wands, the King and Queen of Swords.

About the business Spreads:

Two- and three-card Spreads can be used for fast decisions, especially for clear-cut options and partnerships; four-carder formats for security or financial stability; fives for launching businesses and anything to do with risks, speculation, or dubious dealings. Six-carders are good for questions where emotions are involved; sevens for dreams and talents; eights and nines for major questions; and ten-plus cards for business reviews/major expansion.

191
STARTING YOUR OWN BUSINESS

Purpose and background information:
If you want to give your business idea a try after years of employment/looking after the home.

CARD 1: Are you ready to launch your business? **CARD 2:** Should you launch it 100%, or run it part-time until established? **CARD 3:** Is there an existing market for your business, or do you need to create one? **CARD 4:** Are the premises/equipment you have/will obtain adequate? **CARD 5:** What expansion plans will be viable over the next twelve months?

What you should use:
The twenty-two Major cards.

When:
A Wednesday, day of enterprise.

192
SHOULD YOU TRADE YOUR PRODUCTS OR SERVICES LOCALLY, OR ONLINE?

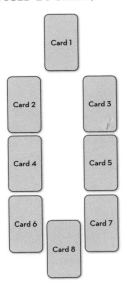

Purpose and background information:
When you are not sure how to maximize sales.

CARD 1: Should you find/develop the right premises locally? **CARD 2:** Is there sufficient local trade to support you/should you aim wider? **CARD 3:** Should you travel to different venues/locations with your goods/services? **CARD 4:** How can you achieve maximum publicity for the least cost? **CARD 5:** Should/how should you incorporate Internet sales outlets into your business? **CARD 6:** Should you focus almost entirely on offering online sales and services? **CARD 7:** Would it be more effective to combine both methods equally? **CARD 8:** Should you franchise or offer your goods/services through other stores/websites?

What you should use:
The full deck.

When:
A Thursday, for secure business ventures.

LAUNCHING OR DEVELOPING A PSYCHIC OR HEALING BUSINESS

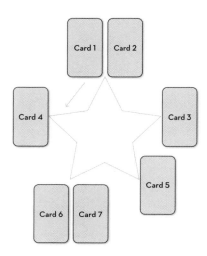

Purpose and background information:

When you know you have the gifts but worry about your marketability. Use the five-pointed mystical pentagram shape.

CARD 1: Should you first practice within an organization/phone line? **CARD 2:** Should you first practice from home or at local events to gain confidence? **CARD 3:** Should you establish your own online/phone readings outlets? **CARD 4:** What anticipated problems may be encountered? **CARD 5:** What will work to your advantage? **CARD 6:** Should you find a regular New Age store where you can do readings? **CARD 7:** How can you raise your profile on- and offline?

What you should use:

The full deck.

When:

At a full moon.

Example:

Liz had always been psychic but worked in real estate, which no longer satisfied her. The company offered her redundancy, so it was now or never.

CARD 1: The Hermit, following your own star. Liz realized that she didn't want to fit into any organization's criteria, even a psychic one. **CARD 2: The Three of Pentacles,** showing someone building a stone pillar, suggesting gradually building up clientele and confidence through personal contacts, as Liz had money to cushion her. **CARD 3: The Two of Wands,** connected with the previous card. Liz thought, once established, of offering live Internet readings as a second source of income. Two friends from a psychic group would help her run a mini personalized phone service. **CARD 4: The Princess of Swords.** While most people encouraged her, Liz was wary of a former psychic group member whom she suspected was behind negative comments on social media. Only a Princess, so no threat. **CARD 5: The Five of Wands.** Media connections. Liz had been asked several times by local radio to answer questions on air, but had always refused. **CARD 6: Queen of Pentacles.** A crystal store in the local town was advertising for psychics to rent a room once a week. This would enable Liz to network. **CARD 7: The Chariot.** Liz had already created a psychic podcast based on workshops she was planning to give in her converted garden chalet.

194

IF YOU WORK FOR YOUR PARENTS AND FEEL YOUR IDEAS AND INITIATIVES ARE DISREGARDED

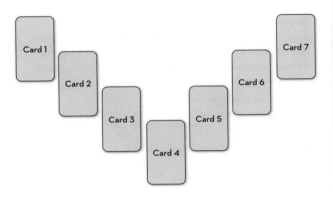

Purpose and background information:
When the family business holds you back.

CARD 1: Do your parents treat you as a child, although you are well qualified? **CARD 2:** Could you focus on one part of the business where there is flexibility? **CARD 3:** Should you present a business plan for the next five years suggesting the growing role for you? **CARD 4:** Can you persuade your parents to take more holidays? **CARD 5:** Can you persuade one parent to offer you more responsibility? **CARD 6:** Is there a major project you can work on alone? **CARD 7:** Should you leave and get another job?

What you should use:
The twenty-two Major cards and the sixteen Court cards.

When:
Sunset on the last day of the work week.

195

IF YOU WANT TO START A NEW BUSINESS AFTER EARLY RETIREMENT OR REDUNDANCY

Purpose and background information:
If you have spare money to invest.

CARD 1: Should you use your funds toward launching your new career? **CARD 2:** Do you want/need to be profitable, or is it for pleasure? **CARD 3:** Do you need any extra study/ training? **CARD 4:** Are you ready to launch, or do you want/ need to start gradually? **CARD 5:** Is there a niche in the market, or is it oversubscribed? **CARD 6:** What is your unique marketing/selling point? **CARD 7:** Do you have sufficient outlets to start, or do you need to work on this before launch? **CARD 8:** Will you go it alone, or network with/involve others? **CARD 9:** Your twelve-month aim. **CARD 10:** Your five-year plan.

What you should use:
The full deck.

When:
A Saturday, day of solid ventures after change.

196

IF YOUR BUSINESS PARTNER IS ALSO YOUR LOVE PARTNER AND YOU ARE BLOCKED AT EVERY TURN

Purpose and background information:

When you feel as if whatever you say or do is overridden by your partner businesswise.

Card 1: Is this symptomatic of your emotional relationship? **Card 2:** Is it the situation/structure of the business causing the issue? **Card 3:** Will your partner compromise/listen to reason? **Card 4:** Are there issues on which you cannot/will not compromise? **Card 5:** Is there an obvious intermediary? **Card 6:** Is there an alternative role in this business you could fulfill? **Card 7:** Are you essential to the business, or could you find another job? **Card 8:** Could/should you run your own business in tandem, or separately?

What you should use:

The full deck.

When:

The last day of the month.

197

SHOULD YOU ALLOW A RELATIVE OR CLOSE FRIEND TO INVEST OR BECOME A PARTNER IN YOUR BUSINESS?

Purpose and background information:

When your heart says yes but you wonder if it's a good business move.

Card 1: Would you allow your relative/friend to participate if they were a stranger? **Card 2:** How far will you share responsibility/hand over the reins? **Card 3:** If a dispute/disagreement occurs, can you both stay emotionally impartial? **Card 4:** Will you feel safe delegating in order to take more time off? **Card 5:** Should you have a trial period working together? **Card 6:** Would you sooner work alone/choose a partner less emotionally connected?

What you should use:

The twenty-two Major cards and the sixteen Court cards.

When:

A Friday, day of emotional connections.

198

A BUSINESS PLAN FOR THE MONTH AHEAD

Purpose and background information:

If you have a significant month ahead, set four cards left to right, one for each week, turning them all over before reading to see the whole month view.

Card 1: Represents opportunities emerging by the end of the four weeks. **Card 2:** The additional resources/input you need by the end of the four weeks. **Card 3:** Hindrances/unhelpful influences you need to overcome during the four weeks. **Card 4:** The unexpected factor of luck or fate. **Card 5:** The overall prognosis for the four-week period.

What you should use:

The whole deck

When:

The evening before your chosen monthly period.

199
SIX WEEKS OR MONTHS TO MAKE OR BREAK IN BUSINESS

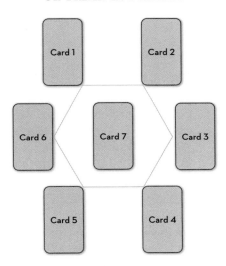

Purpose and background information:
To look ahead to discover the right tactics and wrong moves at a decisive period.

CARD 1: What must be initiated to achieve the goal (specify goal) for the six weeks/months ahead. **CARD 2:** What must be built on/adjusted during the weeks/months ahead for progress. **CARD 3:** What existing strengths can overcome setbacks/obstacles? **CARD 4:** What needs changing/abandoning to stay on course/achieve goal? **CARD 5:** What/who can be most helpful? **CARD 6:** What/who is the hidden enemy to progress? **CARD 7:** The make-or-break factor.

What you should use:
The whole deck.

When:
The night before the six-week/month period.

200
FIVE STEPS TO REVIVING OR IMPROVING A BUSINESS

Purpose and background information:
If business is not going as well as anticipated.

CARD 1: Is the economy/market forces causing the problem and will the situation improve? **CARD 2:** Is it a problem within the company/someone working against you that needs immediate action? **CARD 3:** Should you seek external help/advice? **CARD 4:** Should you launch a major publicity/sales initiative? **CARD 5:** What are the long-term prospects, depending on following the steps of this Spread?

What you should use:
The twenty-two Major cards and the forty Minor cards, Aces to Tens in each suit.

When:
The end of the week or month.

201
TWELVE MONTHS TO SUCCESS

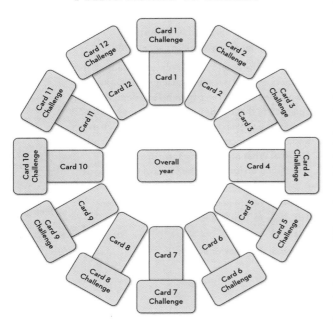

202
TURNING CREATIVITY INTO SELF-EMPLOYMENT

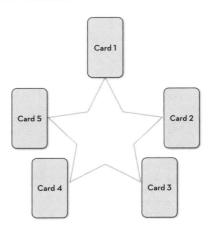

Purpose and background information:
For a month-by-month assessment of opportunities and challenges for twelve months ahead.

Deal twelve cards in a clockwise circle with **CARD 1** at the top of the Spread, for the first month under consideration. These twelve cards detail the monthly opportunities. Turn and read each in turn.

Now deal a second card for each month again starting with **CARD 1,** placing each horizontally over its month card. Turn each over and read it to give the *challenge* for each month. Now deal and turn a twenty-fifth card in the center for the overall year's prognosis.

What you should use:
The full deck.

When:
The day before the first day of the first month under consideration.

Purpose and background information:
When you want to use your talents to make a viable business.

CARD 1: Can your creativity, whether as products or services, form a saleable commodity? **CARD 2:** Do you want to make a full-time career, or to supplement your present income? **CARD 3:** What sacrifices are you prepared to make to attain success and recognition? **CARD 4:** Do you need to add/learn any new techniques/expertise before turning professional? **CARD 5:** What unexpected factors will help you on your way?

If you wish, you can afterward add a sixth card to the center, asking when you can realistically expect success.

What you should use:
The forty Minor cards, Aces to Tens, and the sixteen Court cards.

When:
When the Moon enters your star sign, which it does every month.

203
IF YOUR BUSINESS PARTNER OR EMPLOYEES SERIOUSLY LACK EFFORT AND ENTHUSIASM

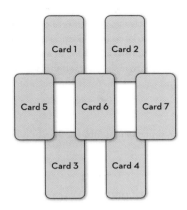

Purpose and background information:

When whatever you suggest or try is met with inertia or negativity.

Use the seven-card overlapping Spread. Turn over **CARDS 1–4 AND** read them, and then **CARDS 5, 6,** and **7.**

CARD 1: Who or what is the underlying cause of the inertia/negativity? **CARD 2:** Is there a particular person/group fueling the problem? **CARD 3:** Should you intervene/confront? **CARD 4:** What is your best strategy for improving the situation? **CARD 5:** Should you introduce a new keen key player to change the power base? **CARD 6:** Should you make major changes of direction to inject new enthusiasm? **CARD 7:** Should you change the structure of the workplace, if necessary letting go of dead wood?

What you should use:

The full deck.

When:

Before the first day of the work week.

204
IF YOU SUSPECT THAT AN EMPLOYEE OR SUPPLIER IS CHEATING YOU

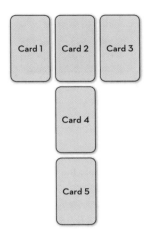

Purpose and background information:

When you notice discrepancies but wonder if you are being overly suspicious.

CARD 1: Is a particular person always around/supplier involved when discrepancies occur? **CARD 2:** If you question them, is the person/supplier overly defensive/secretive? **CARD 3:** Does your instinct tell you something is wrong? **CARD 4:** Should you confront, or watch till you have more proof? **CARD 5:** Is it just one person/supplier, or should you check everything/everyone more closely?

What you should use:

The forty Minor cards, Aces to Tens, and the sixteen Court cards.

When:

A Wednesday, the day for detecting trickery.

205
IF YOUR BUSINESS IS NOT TAKING OFF AS FAST AS YOU HAD HOPED

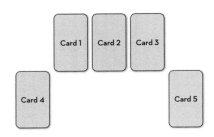

Purpose and background information:
When you are putting 100% into the business and do not understand why it's not flourishing.

CARD 1: Are there outside forces/slow economy holding you back? **CARD 2:** What missing factor within the business could be causing the slowdown? **CARD 3:** Should you be patient and persevere? **CARD 4:** Should you have a massive publicity/advertising push? **CARD 5:** Should you have an overhaul of direction/outlets?

What you should use:
The Major twenty-two cards.

When:
The day before a full moon.

206
IF A NEW SIMILAR BUSINESS OPENS UP IN COMPETITION

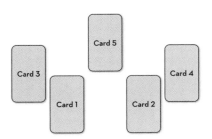

Purpose and background information:
When the new business is using every trick in the book to attract your business.

CARD 1: What main rival tactic must you overcome? **CARD 2:** What unique selling points do you have for your products/services? **CARD 3:** How can you attract new customers? **CARD 4:** How can you keep your existing customers in the face of this competition? **CARD 5:** What extra/different service can you offer to make yourself the preferred option?

What you should use:
The full deck.

When:
When one zodiac sign changes into another, or any Wednesday.

207
SHOULD YOU RISK ALL TO GIVE YOUR BUSINESS A NECESSARY BOOST?

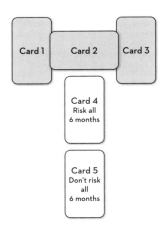

Purpose and background information:
If you believe that what you are doing could develop into something big.

CARD 1: Your ultimate ambition. **CARD 2:** What holds the business back that you may not be fully aware of? **CARD 3:** Should you risk all to get the business where you want it to be?

If **Card 3** isn't clear, add a **Card 4,** vertical, below **Card 2** for the results in six months if you risk all, and a **Card 5** below that for six months' time if you do not risk all.

What you should use:
The twenty-two Major cards.

When:
A Sunday midday.

208
IF YOU WANT TO STEP BACK FROM THE FAMILY BUSINESS, BUT YOUR PARTNER DOES NOT WISH TO

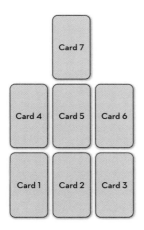

Purpose and background information:
When you want to spend more time traveling or relaxing, but your partner is a workaholic.

Card 1: Should you gradually withdraw, or all at once? **Card 2:** Is there someone trustworthy to take over, part- or full-time, without your totally handing over the reins? **Card 3:** Should you contemplate selling/handing over the business permanently to a family member? **Card 4:** Is this unwillingness to step back caused by uncertainty about the reliability of other family members involved? **Card 5:** Is it a symptom of deeper emotional problems within your partner/relationship? **Card 6:** If necessary, should *you* withdraw to

free your time for other things? **Card 7:** Should you plan some joint trips now and build up from there?

What you should use:
The twenty-two Major cards and the sixteen Court cards.

When:
At the waning moon.

209
IF YOU CANNOT SELL YOUR BUSINESS, WHAT SHOULD YOU DO?

Purpose and background information:
When your business has been on the market for a long time with no viable offers.

Card 1: Is there a slow market/economic downturn that in time will ease? **Card 2:** Should you change your agent/advertise nationally, even internationally? **Card 3:** Should you sell the goodwill/business and any premises separately? **Card 4:** What assets/unique benefits does your business have that, if promoted, might sell it? **Card 5:** Have you used online marketing to its fullest potential? **Card 6:** Should you consider dropping the price? **Card 7:** Could you lease or rent it temporarily in order to free yourself? **Card 8:** Would you contemplate cutting your losses in order to be free of the business?

What you should use:
The full deck.

When:
Any significant date for the business.

210
IF YOU WANT TO RELOCATE AND EXPAND YOUR BUSINESS INTERESTS, INTERSTATE OR OVERSEAS

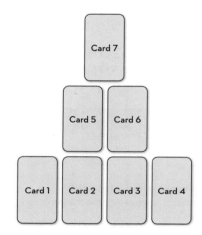

Purpose and background information:
When you are ready for a major relocation and/or business expansion.

Card 1: Should you physically relocate and/or expand by taking the business online? **Card 2:** How much expansion can you handle within your present business capacity?
Card 3: Do you anticipate/need to increase personnel/size of premises? **Card 4:** Is this is a stage-by-stage expansion, or a major leap? **Card 5:** Is this a business-based change, or do you want to relocate anyway? **Card 6:** Do you have a location in mind/is this viable? **Card 7:** Do you have/can you obtain the financial resources to carry out your plans in the near future?

What you should use:
The full deck.

When:
A full moon.

CHAPTER 17

SPREADS FOR FAME AND FORTUNE

Lucky cards for fame and fortune Spreads:

Major Arcana: The Magician, the Chariot, Strength, the Wheel of Fortune, the Hermit, especially when accompanied by the Star, the Moon, the Sun, the Star, the World.

The Minor Cards: Ace of Wands, Three of Wands, Four of Wands, Seven of Wands, Eight of Pentacles, Eight of Wands, Nine of Pentacles, Ten of Pentacles.

The Court Cards: The Knight of Wands, the Queen of Wands, the King of Wands.

About the Fame and Fortune Spreads

Fives are useful for Spreads involving taking a chance and communication via media, sixes for strong wishes and desires, sevens for fulfilling major dreams, eights for consolidating progress, nines for supreme effort, tens for achievement, and one- and two-carders for instant answers.

211
WHAT SHOULD YOU DO TO GET THROUGH TO THE FINALS OF A MAJOR TALENT CONTEST?

Purpose and background information:
A two-carder when you need some no-frills guidance.

CARD 1: What do you need to know to get into the final?
CARD 2: How can you best overcome the competition of other entrants?

What you should use:
The twenty-two Major cards.

When:
The night before the contest.

212
IF YOU WANT TO WIN A TV TALENT SHOW

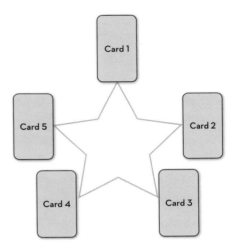

Purpose and background information:
If people say you should enter a TV talent contest, but you lack confidence.

CARD 1: Do you have an act that will make you stand out?
CARD 2: Are you used to showcasing your talents in public?
CARD 3: Do you want to practice more in front of strangers before applying? **CARD 4:** Are you prepared to enter, even if you do not win this time? **CARD 5:** Will/should you keep trying until you win?

What you should use:
The twenty-two Major cards.

When:
When you discover auditions are coming to your area.

213
IF YOU WANT TO STAR IN A TV REALITY SHOW

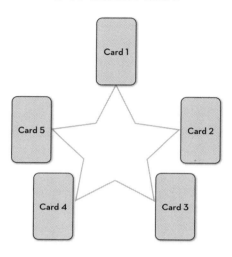

Purpose and background information:
If you want to become a media celebrity overnight.

CARD 1: Do you enjoy being the center of attention and speaking your mind? **CARD 2:** Are you happy sacrificing privacy/media digging up your past, for potential fame? **CARD 3:** How will your friends/family cope with your being recorded 24/7? **CARD 4:** Have you already/can you develop a powerful social media presence/sample video to impress the selectors? **CARD 5:** Can you cope with other would-be celebrities on and off air who may use dirty tactics to discredit you?

What you should use:
The twenty-two Major cards and the sixteen Court cards.

When:
A Sunday at noon.

214
TO BE DISCOVERED BY A TALENT SCOUT OR PRODUCER

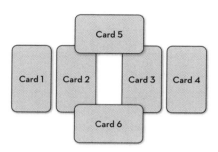

Purpose and background information:
If you want to become famous in a performing career.

CARD 1: Should you up the game by seeking more exclusive venues? **CARD 2:** Should you use social media/YouTube more to get your name/performance out there? **CARD 3:** Should you write original material, as well as performing popular material? **CARD 4:** Should you go to absolutely every audition/talent contest available? **CARD 5:** Do you need to raise money to fund your enterprises? **CARD 6:** Should you contact agencies/producers with your sample video, or let it happen naturally?

What you should use:
The twenty-two Major cards and the sixteen Court cards.

When:
When you feel a strong desire to become famous.

215
IF YOU WANT TO BE AN ACTOR OR PRODUCER IN THE THEATER OR MOVIES

Purpose and background information:
When no other career will satisfy you.

CARD 1: Are you/can you pursue every acting and producing opportunity available, however modest? **CARD 2:** Should you study at theater school/go directly into theater and work your way up? **CARD 3:** Are you prepared to travel anywhere, any time, for auditions/professional opportunities? **CARD 4:** Will you sacrifice financial security for fulfillment, doing anything between gigs to support yourself? **CARD 5:** Should you relocate to famous film/theater centers, or go to more obscure places where it may be easier to get a break? **CARD 6:** Will you succeed/how far will you succeed in the next five years?

What you should use:
The full deck.

When:
New Year's or the beginning of a month.

216
SHOULD YOU GO TO HOLLYWOOD TO ACHIEVE YOUR AMBITION IN THE MOVIE INDUSTRY?

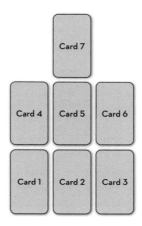

Purpose and background information:
When you are desperate to get your big break.

CARD 1: Should you be prepared to take any kind of work just to be in Hollywood? **CARD 2:** Should you take any kind of acting/dance/beauty work in Hollywood to network? **CARD 3:** Should you go now/soon and work out the details when you get there? **CARD 4:** Should you sign up for absolutely any extra's work, or have a specific game plan? **CARD 5:** Should you hang out where the producers/celebrities go in the hope of being noticed? **CARD 6:** Should you try to find an agency to get work, however modest? **CARD 7:** Is Hollywood where you *have* to be right now, or should you wait?

What you should use:
The forty Minor cards, Aces to Tens.

When:
When the moon is in your zodiac sign during the month.

217
IF YOU WANT TO BECOME A MAKEUP ARTIST/THERAPIST TO CELEBRITIES

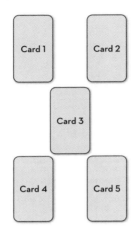

Purpose and background information:
When you have the talent but lack the opportunity.

Turn all cards over and read in order of dealing.

Card 1: Do you need to learn any special skills/acquire extra qualifications before trying? **Card 2:** Should you get work in upmarket salons/therapy centers in order to get the right experience/references? **Card 3:** Should you get media/therapy exposure on local television stations, or go for the big time? **Card 4:** Do you need an agency, or should you apply directly for casual work at first? **Card 5:** Are you prepared/should you relocate to be where the action is?

What you should use:
The twenty-two Major cards.

When:
When the moon is in Taurus during the month.

218
IF YOU WANT TO BE A SUCCESSFUL MUSICIAN OR RECORDING ARTIST

Purpose and background information:
When you are asking what comes next, as you play local gigs for peanuts.

Turn cards over and read row by row.

Card 1: Are your dreams of reaching the top attainable? **Card 2:** Can you/do you fit in the daily practice necessary to reach the top? **Card 3:** Do you need extra training, or just more experience performing in public at more ambitious venues? **Card 4:** Can/should you record your work/find an agent? **Card 5:** Should you enter competitions/more auditions/go on the road as a backup singer/musician, or concentrate on online exposure? **Card 6:** Can you make sufficient money from music to give up the day job/run them in tandem for a time within a year?

What you should use:
The full deck.

When:
A full moon.

219
IF YOU WANT TO BECOME A SUCCESSFUL SONGWRITER OR CREATE A BROADWAY MUSICAL

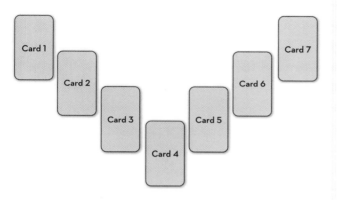

Purpose and background information:
When you are creating but not marketing your efforts.

CARD 1: Are you confident in your musical ability, or do you feel you need more training/practice? **CARD 2:** Can you use the Internet/YouTube to market individual songs/collections? **CARD 3:** Is there a local venue/theater company you can try out? **CARD 4:** Can you get into the music/theater industry through networking? **CARD 5:** Do you need an agent, or will you try the direct approach to lesser known/overseas theater companies? **CARD 6:** Should you record and market your work, even if not 100% satisfied? **CARD 7:** Where will you be success-wise in five years?

What you should use:
The full deck.

When:
The first Sunday in the month.

220
IF YOU WANT TO SECURE A PLACE IN A TOP ORCHESTRA

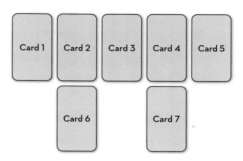

Purpose and background information:
If you dream of playing classical music for a living.

CARD 1: Should you study/are you studying at a formal music academy? **CARD 2:** Can you pass the necessary examinations, formally or informally? **CARD 3:** Should you establish your own solo, duo, trio, or quartet to perform publicly/make YouTube videos to raise your profile? **CARD 4:** Are you ready to audition for any orchestra, even if this means relocating or traveling overseas? **CARD 5:** Do you attend master classes/study live/online performances of your chosen orchestra? **CARD 6:** Should you audition for your chosen orchestra even if initially you are turned down? **CARD 7:** Should you persist until you succeed, or put a time limit on your ambitions?

What you should use:
The twenty-two Major cards and the forty Minor cards, Aces to Tens

When:
When you need to decide whether to go all out for a classical musical career or opt for a safe teaching post.

221
IF YOU WANT TO FIND FAME AS A DANCER

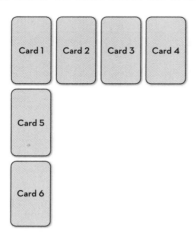

Purpose and background information:

If you need to decide whether to focus on a dancing career or keep it as a fun activity.

CARD 1: Do you love all kinds of dance, or are you dedicated to a particular dance genre? **CARD 2:** Should you focus on formal training, or go to a stage school and learn all kinds of dance? **CARD 3:** Are you prepared to take any kind of chorus work in any production anywhere to gain a reputation? **CARD 4:** Do you have gifts in choreography/production that might get you into a dance company/musical production? **CARD 5:** Are you willing to dedicate yourself to hours of practice each day, even if you have to work to support yourself? **CARD 6:** Could dance remain a pleasurable hobby, or do you want to go all out to reach the top?

What you should use:

The full deck.

When:

When you see a chance to audition as a dancer, even if not your preferred option.

222
BECOMING A PROFESSIONAL ATHLETE

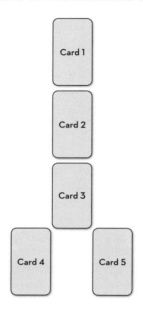

Purpose and background information:

When you have set your heart on a particular sport as a career.

CARD 1: Have you won a number of field events at different levels? **CARD 2:** Do you need/should you apply for a new coach/sponsor/sports scholarship? **CARD 3:** Are you prepared for 100% dedication? **CARD 4:** Would you train/play/compete overseas if advantageous? **CARD 5:** Can you cope with the pressure of competing at the top level, or would you prefer to compete at a less pressurized level/train as an athletic coach for other top athletes?

What you should use:

The forty Minor cards, Aces to Tens, and the sixteen Court cards.

When:

Before applying for a major sporting position.

223
IF YOU ARE LIVING SOMEONE ELSE'S DREAM OF FAME

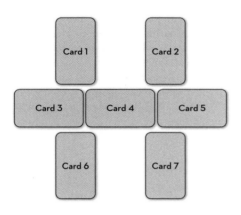

Purpose and background information:
When the path toward success makes you unhappy.

Card 1: What is the prize for persevering? **Card 2:** What is the cost of persevering? **Card 3:** Who and what are pushing you down this track? **Card 4:** What is it that *you* really want? **Card 5:** How can you attain it? **Card 6:** Are you prepared for the disruption of opting out? **Card 7:** What is your long-term aim if you opt out?

What you should use:
The whole deck.

When:
The end of a waning moon cycle.

Example:
Ellie's father, who had been junior tennis champion for his state until injury forced him to give up, has been coaching Ellie since she was five. Already she is junior state champion, aiming for the top. But she is increasingly resentful, practicing for hours every day and spending weekends traveling to matches, instead of being with her friends. Ellie loves animals and wants to have a wildlife preservation career, but her father is pressuring her to become an international tennis star. Ellie loves him but feels railroaded.

Card 1: The Eight of Swords, showing the woman, Ellie, who is tied but could escape, hardly a willing tennis champion card. **Card 2:** The Two of Swords, showing another bound woman, Ellie, who with crossed swords isn't using her real power. **Card 3:** The King of Cups, her father, who with the best intentions is pushing Ellie to fulfill *his* dreams. **Card 4:** The Six of Wands, the person riding to victory, but Ellie wants to be free to pursue her own dreams. **Card 5:** The Chariot, movement; but Ellie wants to take an apprenticeship with a forestry organization that specializes in animal habitats. **Card 6:** The Tower of Freedom. Ellie knows quitting will shatter her father's dreams but that ultimately it will free them both. **Card 7:** The Four of Wands, showing a house surrounded by flowers and open air. Ellie's dream is to live in the wilderness, as opposed to the city as she does currently, and to rescue injured wild animals.

224
HOW TO WIN A SCHOLARSHIP TO THE BEST COLLEGE TO GIVE YOU A FLYING START IN YOUR CHOSEN FIELD OF EXPERTISE

Purpose and background information:
A two-card reading. **Card 1:** How best to shine in the examination/written presentation, and **Card 2:** How to create a positive impression at the interview/spoken presentation.

What you should use:
The twenty-two Major cards and the sixteen Court cards.

When:
Before the first examination/written presentation. If you wish, you can repeat the reading before the interview, using both cards to ask for what it's helpful to know prior to the interview/spoken presentation.

225
WINNING A PLACE ON A MAJOR SOCCER, BASEBALL, OR BASKETBALL TEAM

Purpose and background information:
When you want to be part of a prestigious team.

CARD 1: Are you satisfied with your current sport's scholarship/team membership, or it is holding you back? **CARD 2:** Are you a natural team member or captain material? **CARD 3:** How can you get noticed/a higher profile? **CARD 4:** Can you progress where/as you are, or should you be looking to move upward? **CARD 5:** Are you playing/training at full capacity, or can you achieve more? **CARD 6:** Are you ready for the crowd/media pressures of becoming higher profile? **CARD 7:** Should you/are you free to move interstate/overseas to reach the heights you desire? **CARD 8:** Can you overcome every obstacle/competition to reach the top?

What you should use:
The full deck.

When:
The first Tuesday of the month for action.

226
SEVEN STEPS TO A PLACE IN THE NEXT OLYMPIC GAMES

Purpose and background information:
When you know you are good in your field but want to reach the dizzying heights.

CARD 1: Do/will you have access to sponsorship/top-rate coaching? **CARD 2:** Do you have sufficient funds to devote the necessary time to training? **CARD 3:** Are you competing/able to compete regularly against the best in your field? **CARD 4:** Should you move to where you can access the best training facilities? **CARD 5:** Do you/will you have the right connections/compete in the right events for selection? **CARD 6:** If you succeed in getting a place, what are your plans after the Games? **CARD 7:** If you do not get a place, what next?

What you should use:
The full deck.

When:
The first day of the month.

227
IF YOU WANT TO BE A BEST-SELLING AUTHOR

Purpose and background information:
When you have a brilliant idea for a book, or have written your novel and want to see it published.

CARD 1: Is your idea or novel a commercially viable idea, or does it need adapting for the popular market? **CARD 2:** Can you see/find an immediate gap in a specific market that your book will fill? **CARD 3:** Are you prepared for a long haul with many setbacks if you do not have an instant hit? **CARD 4:** Should you find an agent, or go directly to a publisher? **CARD 5:** Would it be best initially for you to publish online or self-publish? **CARD 6:** Will you succeed, and, if so, how soon?

What you should use:
The Minor cards, Aces to Tens, and the sixteen Court cards.

When:
When the moon is passing through Sagittarius in any month, or any Thursday.

229
IF YOU WANT TO BECOME A FAMOUS FASHION DESIGNER

Purpose and background information:
When you constantly make clothes for friends and family for special occasions and decide you have the talent to make a living out of design.

Card 1: Do your designs/clothes have a unique quality? **Card 2:** Do you have a specialty (wedding dresses, for instance) that you could develop as a brand? **Card 3:** Do you need training in fashion design at college/apprenticeship to a fashion house, or can you remain self-taught? **Card 4:** Should you take commissions on and offline/sell your creations to a store? **Card 5:** Are you ready to work 100% freelance, making and mending everything while developing your business? **Card 6:** How can you attract media interest through YouTube/a stall at festivals and shows/offering distinctive off-the-peg fashions? **Card 7:** Should you initially send your designs to lesser-known fashion houses? **Card 8:** What lucky break can you expect in the next year?

What you should use:
The full deck.

When:
At a crescent moon.

228
IF YOU WANT TO BE A SUCCESSFUL ARTIST, CRAFTSPERSON, OR SCULPTOR

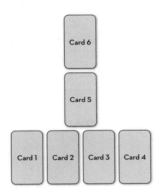

Purpose and background information:
If you want to transform your passionate interest into a successful career.

Card 1: Do you feel ready to start exhibiting/selling your creations, either in a gallery/online or both? **Card 2:** Do you initially need to supplement your income with art classes/ working in a gallery/craft store? **Card 3:** Do you have/where will you find the right gallery/store/online marketplace/ network for your creations? **Card 4:** How can you make sufficient time to create and market your work until you are fully established? **Card 5:** What unique quality sets your work apart from others? **Card 6:** Will you be living off your creativity within five years if you begin now?

What you should use:
The full deck.

When:
The start of a new month.

230
IF YOU WANT TO BECOME A SUCCESSFUL INTERNATIONAL JOURNALIST OR DOCUMENTARY MAKER

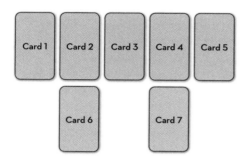

Purpose and background information:
When you truly believe you have a talent for journalism, but don't know where to begin.

CARD 1: Do you already have an online blog/YouTube mini documentaries with growing audiences? **CARD 2:** Have you/should you train through media studies/through starting at the bottom in TV journalism and working your way up? **CARD 3:** Do/will you go anywhere any time for a freelance story/documentary idea you can sell on? **CARD 4:** Are you 24/7 ahead of the news wherever you are/always looking for a good story/angle? **CARD 5:** Are you prepared to work in local media initially, doing anything, however dull or dangerous? **CARD 6:** Should you be/are you working on your own major projects at the same time? **CARD 7:** When/how will you get your lucky national/international break?

What you should use:
The full deck.

When:
When you feel lucky career-wise.

231
TO OBTAIN FAME AND FORTUNE THROUGH THE INTERNET

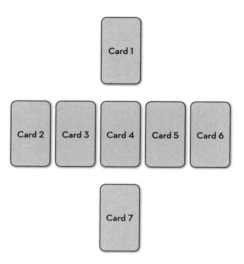

Purpose and background information:
When you have started to get hits with your online presence.

CARD 1: Do you have brilliant ideas for major podcasts/an online radio station or new social media forum? **CARD 2:** Do you need extra expertise, and, if so, where can you find it? **CARD 3:** Do you need a sponsor, or are you able/willing to go it alone? **CARD 4:** What competition/negativity will you face? **CARD 5:** Can you link different online ventures to raise your profile? **CARD 6:** What is your greatest strength/asset? **CARD 7:** Do you anticipate overnight impact, or gradual growth?

What you should use:
The forty Minor cards, Aces to Tens, and the sixteen Court cards.

When:
A Wednesday, for technological success.

232
IF YOU WANT TO BECOME A SUCCESSFUL POLITICIAN, OR EVEN PRESIDENT

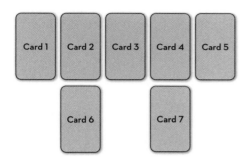

Purpose and background information:
If it is your dream, but you are not moneyed or are lacking the right connections.

CARD 1: Is this your 100% dream no matter how hard or long the road? **CARD 2:** Do you have/can you gain any college/political/legal/business affiliations to gain a foothold? **CARD 3:** Do you have particular beliefs/causes/unique qualities that you champion which will make you popular with sponsors/the electorate? **CARD 4:** Are you creating an increasing media profile by speaking at rallies/peaceful protests/writing articles in journals/participating in TV debates? **CARD 5:** Can you make your modest beginnings an asset as a representative of ordinary people? **CARD 6:** Will you go anywhere/accept any candidacy to get a foot on the ladder? **CARD 7:** When/how will you get your lucky break?

What you should use:
The full deck.

When:
When you are ready to join the campaign trail in any capacity.

233
IF YOU WANT TO MAKE YOUR FORTUNE IN REAL ESTATE

Purpose and background information:
If you are striving for a foothold into the market or already have your first property.

CARD 1: Do you have/trust strong intuition as to good bargains when attending auctions/making offers on repossessions? **CARD 2:** Can you/how can you access fast funds to seal deals? **CARD 3:** Can you renovate/obtain the services of reasonably priced efficient renovators to turn property around fast? **CARD 4:** Are you prepared/able to make your own home part of the sales equation? **CARD 5:** Are you willing/able to recognize bargains in up-and-coming areas? **CARD 6:** Do you have/can you gain access to self-building on land that will increase in value? **CARD 7:** Can you/should you invest in commercial property/land even if not immediately of value? **CARD 8:** Can you hold your nerve in bargaining and know when to press for advantage?

What you should use:
The forty Minor cards, Aces to Tens.

When:
When an apparent property acquisition is within reach.

234
IF YOU WANT TO MAKE A FORTUNE OUT OF STOCKS

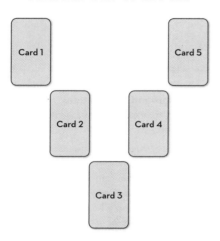

Purpose and background information:
When you have a chance to speculate but are lacking confidence.

CARD 1: Are you sufficiently well-researched in speculation and the ever-changing current world markets to make the right decisions quickly? **CARD 2:** Do you have an instinctive flair for what will be profitable at different times, long-/short-term? **CARD 3:** Should you take financial advice, or can you trust yourself? **CARD 4:** Should you make a swift all-or-nothing investment right now, taking a chance for big returns? **CARD 5:** Should you wait/go slowly and build up profits gradually by accumulating steady returns?

What you should use:
The forty Minor cards, Aces to Tens, and the sixteen Court cards

When:
When you need to make a fast decision on whether to go for it or hold back.

235
IF YOU WANT TO DATE A CELEBRITY, SINGER, MILLIONAIRE, OR SPORTS STAR

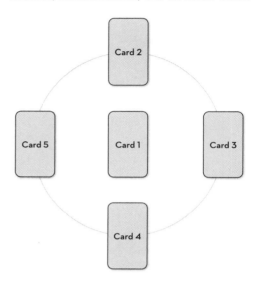

Purpose and background information:
When you want to share the high life.

CARD 1: Do you have/can you gain/maintain access to the places where the rich and famous socialize? **CARD 2:** Do you have the time/money/desire to maintain the clothes/hair/body toning necessary for initial attraction? **CARD 3:** Can you easily blend into their networks, lifestyle, and life priorities? **CARD 4:** Are you prepared to make the sacrifices as well as accept the perks to share this lifestyle? **CARD 5:** If you do not feel love/emotional security, will you settle just for the lifestyle?

What you should use:
The forty Minor cards, Aces to Tens, and the sixteen Court cards.

When:
You get an invitation or a chance to go to an event where the high flyers will be in attendance.

CHAPTER 18

SPREADS FOR MAKING YOUR DEAREST WISHES AND DREAMS COME TRUE

Lucky cards for making personal wishes and dreams come true:

The Major Cards: The Fool/essential self, the Magician, the Empress, the High Priestess and Hierophant/High Priest, Temperance, the Moon, the Star, the World.

The Minor Cards: Ace of Cups, Two of Cups, Three of Cups, Seven of Cups, Ten of Cups.

The Court Cards: The Knight of Cups, the Queen of Cups, the King of Cups.

About wishes and dreams-fulfilled Spreads

One- and two-card Spreads are helpful for straightforward questions, three cards for gradual growth of happiness, four-carders where security/stability is involved, five cards for adventure and pursuing new ideas or reviving old ones, six cards for happiness, love, and fulfillment, seven for choices and unexpectedly positive results, eight for reclaiming your power, and nine and above for the fulfillment of dreams, especially involving performing good deeds for humanity.

236
WILL THE PERSON OF YOUR DREAMS AGREE TO GO ON A DATE WITH YOU IF YOU ASK NOW?

Purpose and background information:
A one-carder to discover if now is the right time to speak. If the answer is negative, you can deal a second card to ask if the person will say yes in the future.

What you should use:
The twenty-two Major cards and the sixteen Court cards.

When:
The morning before you intend to ask.

237
SHOULD YOU SPEND SOME OF THE FAMILY'S FUTURE INHERITANCE ON AN AROUND-THE-WORLD TRIP OR MAJOR HOLIDAY FOR YOURSELF?

Purpose and background information:
When your adult children say you are selfish to spend your money on fulfilling a personal dream rather than saving it.

CARD 1: Are you entitled to spend your own money any way you wish? **CARD 2:** Should you feel guilty if you follow your dream? **CARD 3:** Will you regret it if you do not follow your dream?

What you should use:
The twenty-two Major cards and the sixteen Court cards.

When:
When you are thinking about planning for an adventure.

238
REVIVING YOUR SECRET DREAM IF IT HAS LONG BEEN BURIED

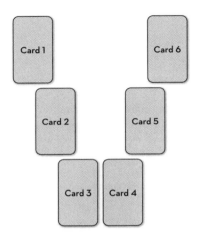

Purpose and background information:
When you suddenly remember what you really wanted but never spoke of and are wondering if it is too late.

CARD 1: Why were you never able to reveal your secret dream? **CARD 2:** What stopped you from trying to attain it? **CARD 3:** Do you have the incentive/motivation to revive it now? **CARD 4:** What is against you? **CARD 5:** What spurs you on? **CARD 6:** How, when, and where will you launch the dream?

What you should use:
The full deck.

When:
On your birthday or another significant date.

239
ATTAINING A CHILDHOOD AMBITION THAT WAS PUT ASIDE BECAUSE OF WORK OR FAMILY COMMITMENTS

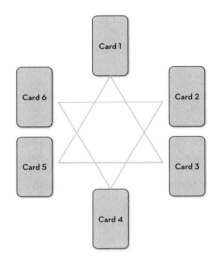

Purpose and background information:
As the years pass and you realize that it is now or never.

CARD 1: Do you still have the same dream, or has it changed? **CARD 2:** How can it still be attained, given the years that have passed? **CARD 3:** What steps have you taken/should you take to manifest the dream now? **CARD 4:** Who/what known factor will support you in attaining your dream? **CARD 5:** Will/how will changing your lifestyle bring the dream closer? **CARD 6:** What unexpected factor/opportunity will make your dream come true?

What you should use:
The forty Minor cards, Aces to Tens, and the sixteen Court cards.

When:
On a starry night.

240
THE SEVEN COLORS OF THE RAINBOW FOR DISCOVERING IF A DREAM OR AMBITION IS REALISTIC

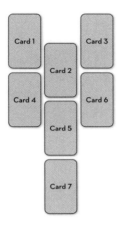

Purpose and background information:

When you need to decide whether to go all out for a dream or wait/modify your plans. If you wish, color a rainbow ladder on thin cardboard, setting one card on each color, with **CARD 1** on red. Turn and read each card in ascending order before turning the next.

CARD 1: Red. How determined are you to succeed whatever the cost? **CARD 2: Orange.** Is the fulfillment of this dream what you truly desire? **CARD 3: Yellow.** Do the facts and figures for success add up? **CARD 4: Green.** Should you let this dream grow slowly, or follow your heart and go all out? **CARD 5: Blue.** Do you have the confidence, knowledge, and experience to pursue your dream? **CARD 6: Indigo/purple.** What hidden resources/gifts will emerge if you go ahead? **CARD 7: Violet/White.** Even if you do not succeed in material terms, do you still want to go ahead?

What you should use:

The whole deck.

When:

When there is a rainbow in the sky/reflected in the room from a sun catcher.

241
DO YOU WANT SUCCESS AT THE COST OF FULFILLMENT IN YOUR LIFE AND CAREER?

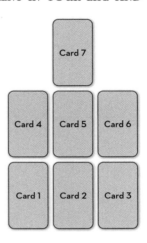

Purpose and background information:

When you are offered a chance to fulfill a career ambition but realize you will lose out in terms of personal happiness.

CARD 1: What is the price you must pay for success? **CARD 2:** What must you give up/leave behind in terms of home/social life if you go for the top? **CARD 3:** Are you prepared to be single-minded, or would you prefer to enjoy a good quality of life outside work? **CARD 4:** What are the long-term advantages of wholeheartedly embracing opportunity? **CARD 5:** What are the long-term advantages of refusing this offer? **CARD 6:** Is there a middle way to have both? **CARD 7:** What is your ultimate dream?

What you should use:

The full deck.

When:

A Thursday, day of contemplating major upward steps.

242
THE CROSSROADS SPREAD

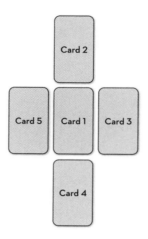

Purpose and background information:

When you know that if you want to attain a dream, you must take another path.

Use the Crossroads Spread. **CARD 1:** What will be gained: the advantages of change to follow your dream. **CARD 2:** What will be lost: the disadvantages of change. **CARD 3:** Should you try to maintain your present position while moving slowly toward change? **CARD 4:** All or nothing: will you regret it if you make the change? **CARD 5:** All or nothing: will you regret it if you do *not* make the change?

What you should use:

The full deck.

When:

When you are at a crossroads in your life.

Example:

Linda has for a long time wanted to take a counseling course and work with women in a shelter. But if she does, she will reduce her pension prospects and sacrifice a good salary in her current high-flying job.

CARD 1: The Seven of Pentacles, showing a person building up the seven pentacles, so gaining job satisfaction by the change and over the years being able to build a secure new career. Linda has been building up savings so could manage financially while she trains.

CARD 2: The Six of Pentacles, showing a person giving out money, which Linda interpreted as losing her longer-term pension rights. But linked to **Card 1,** what she would gain as a counselor, is giving gold of a different kind. That, she said, would make her happy in a way her current job as a *highly paid paper-pusher* (her words) does not.

CARD 3: The Two of Pentacles, showing the person juggling the pentacles. Linda says she feels she needs to focus 100% on the counseling training if she is to succeed.

CARD 4: The Four of Pentacles. So many pentacles indicate that practical concerns are important. This shows the person holding on to what they have, and the steady salary is important, but the picture of the person being unable to move limits Linda's dream.

CARD 5: The Six of Cups, the all-important happiness and fulfillment factor, and Linda reviving a dream she has never stopped wanting to achieve.

243
TO FULFILL THE DREAM OF LIVING SELF-SUFFICIENTLY

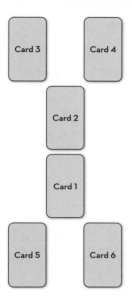

Purpose and background information:
When you want to live close to—and sustained by—the land.

Card 1: Are you ready to take this step now, or should you wait? **Card 2:** Can you/do you want to live more sustainably by adapting your present lifestyle without major change? **Card 3:** Is it possible to lease or rent, if not buy, suitable premises and land soon to fulfill your dream? **Card 4:** Should you keep your present employment/work part-time while setting up your dream? **Card 5:** Can you eventually earn extra money from the land by selling produce/running courses/taking in tourists, etc.? **Card 6:** Is this a sufficiently ultimate lifestyle for you and your loved ones that you are willing to go all out for the dream?

What you should use:
The forty Minor cards, Aces to Tens, and the sixteen Court cards.

When:
At a seasonal change point.

244
IF YOU WANT TO OPEN A NEW AGE OR CRYSTAL STORE

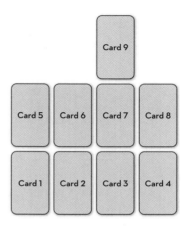

Purpose and background information:
When you want to earn money through fulfilling a longstanding vision.

Card 1: Should/will you open an actual brick-and-mortar store, or begin with an online store? **Card 2:** Can you/have you found premises in a popular town or tourist location for a ready supply of customers? **Card 3:** Have you researched/can you establish reliable local/overseas suppliers before opening? **Card 4:** Do you need resources to stock your store/to build up initially through offering services such as Tarot readings? **Card 5:** What services and unusual products will establish your niche in the market? **Card 6:** Have you/can you build up potential customers through social media/podcasts/festivals, etc.? **Card 7:** Should you work alone, or with family members/friends as partners/employees? **Card 8:** What competition will you need to overcome? **Card 9:** Will you need to supplement your income by keeping your present job/with remote freelance work, etc., initially?

What you should use:
The full deck.

When:
Any waxing-moon day or evening.

245
IF YOUR DREAM IS TO OPEN A SPIRITUAL CENTER

or ceremonies to increase income? **Card 9:** What will you offer that makes you unique among other centers? **Card 10:** Will you start in a small way, using the premises/land for additional purposes until established? **Card 11:** How will your dream progress over five years?

What you should use:
The full deck.

When:
When you set your clocks forward/backward.

246
REALIZING WISHES AND BLESSINGS BY SHEDDING BURDENS

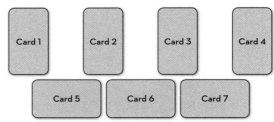

Purpose and background information:

When you want to turn your spiritual vision into reality and make enough to live on, rather than a fortune.

Card 1: Can your personal spiritual visions form the basis for a financially viable enterprise? **Card 2:** Do you have/can you find the right premises/land for your venture? **Card 3:** Should/can you buy/lease/rent your own place, or would initially managing an existing spiritual center be better? **Card 4:** Can/will you self-build/adapt existing premises/land to create your unique vision? **Card 5:** Are there new skills/ therapies you need to acquire before opening? **Card 6:** Will/should you run it yourself/with a partner/family/ bring in experts/therapists to teach/lead different areas? **Card 7:** If residential, what accommodation will you offer: luxury, back to nature, or simple but comfortable? **Card 8:** Do you anticipate incorporating festivals, musical events,

Purpose and background information:

If you need to shed emotional or actual burdens or redundant life baggage in order to realize your wishes.

Card 1: Do I have more burdens than blessings, or more blessings than burdens, in my life right now? **Card 2:** What is my main blessing/advantage to bring about my wishes? **Card 3:** What is the main burden that keeps me from fulfilling my wishes? **Card 4:** How can I increase my blessings/advantages? **Card 5:** How can I best overcome my burdens/disadvantages? **Card 6:** what I would wish for most? **Card 7:** How/when will this wish be achieved?

What you should use:
The forty Minor cards, Aces to Tens, and the sixteen Court cards.

When:
Any evening, with soft music playing in the background.

247
IF YOUR DREAM IS TO TRAVEL THE WORLD

Purpose and background information:

When you have itchy feet and you long to break free.

CARD 1: Is this dream right to fulfill at this stage of your life, or should you wait? **CARD 2:** Would you be content with an exotic trip each year instead? **CARD 3:** Do you have/could you/should you raise the resources to go sooner rather than later? **CARD 4:** How can you support yourself on the road if funds get short? **CARD 5:** Do you need to leave anyone behind, or will the person come with you/meet you on the way/wait for you? **CARD 6:** Should/can you keep a blog/photographic record/make a documentary of your travels for family or to sell? **CARD 7:** Do you have/need a definite itinerary, or is it better to go wherever your fancy takes you? **CARD 8:** If you do not go soon, will you regret it?

What you should use:

The full deck.

When:

A full moon.

248
IF YOU WANT TO PERMANENTLY MOVE OVERSEAS

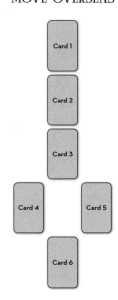

Purpose and background information:

When you crave a different long-term cultural/geographical location.

CARD 1: Do you have family/ancestral links with the desired location/a personal desire to live there based on happy vacations? **CARD 2:** Do you have sufficient skills/income/resources to survive financially? **CARD 3:** Will you open a business, take up a creative money-spinner, or just enjoy the lifestyle? **CARD 4:** Are there cultural/language barriers you will need to overcome? **CARD 5:** Will/should you merge with local lifestyle/culture, or live close to an expat/international community? **CARD 6:** Could you settle for a holiday home, or is this forever?

What you should use:

The forty Minor cards, Aces to Tens, and the sixteen Court cards.

When:

New Year's Day, or the beginning of any new month.

249
IF YOU ALREADY HAVE YOUR DREAM LIFE, BUT EVERYONE KEEPS SAYING YOU ARE SMART ENOUGH TO GO TO THE TOP

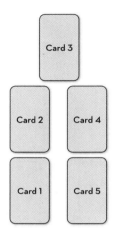

Purpose and background information:
When you are totally happy with your job, home, and relationships, but others believe you are capable of greater achievement.

CARD 1: Is there anything *you* want to change about your present life? **CARD 2:** What are the hidden reasons that others push you to greater achievement? **CARD 3:** What are the benefits of your life as it is? **CARD 4:** Should/do you need to convince others of the rightness of your life, or just ignore them? **CARD 5:** What is your greatest source of happiness now/in the future?

What you should use:
The twenty-two Major cards.

When:
When opportunities arise that you do not want or need to take.

250
THE COMPASS SPREAD IF YOU WANT TO WORK FOR A MAJOR PEACE ORGANIZATION OR INTERNATIONAL CHARITY

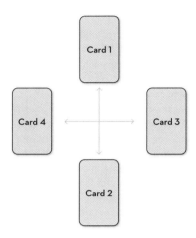

Purpose and background information:
If you want to make a difference to the world's problems rather than making lots of money.

CARD 1: Are you passionate about your cause by raising money/going to events whenever possible? **CARD 2:** Do you have/can you acquire all the necessary expertise to make you eligible for a post? **CARD 3:** Are you initially prepared to do voluntary work to add to your experience? **CARD 4:** Will you go under any conditions/do anything to gain a foothold?

What you should use:
The twenty-two Major cards.

When:
Whenever you see an opening in any capacity.

251
THE DIAMOND SPREAD IF YOU WANT TO BECOME A MEDICAL RESEARCHER AND DISCOVER CURES FOR FATAL DISEASES

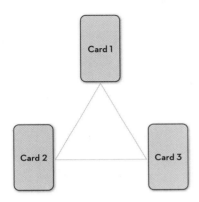

Purpose and background information:
If you are interested in making a difference rather than gaining a lucrative medical post.

CARD 1: Are you passionate about a particular medical field/already making yourself an expert? **CARD 2:** Are you prepared for long, arduous training and time necessarily spent in other fields? **CARD 3:** Will you/how and when will you make a real difference and discover that cure?

What you should use:
The forty Minor cards, Aces to Tens, and the sixteen Court cards.

When:
When you first wake up in the morning.

252
IF YOU WANT TO BE AN ASTRONOMER, OR GO INTO SPACE SCIENCE AND DISCOVER NEW GALAXIES

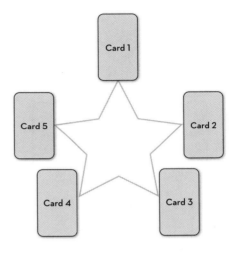

Purpose and background information:
If space discovery is and has always been your passion.

CARD 1: Is there really no other path for you? **CARD 2:** Do you want to study/practice astronomy as a profession, or are you content for it to be a hobby? **CARD 3:** Are you open to whoever and whatever is out there and prepared to be intuitive as well as logical? **CARD 4:** Will you do whatever it takes/go wherever necessary to work your way to the position you want? **CARD 5:** How/when will you get your lucky break?

What you should use:
The full deck.

When:
During an astronomical phenomenon such as a meteor shower.

253
IF YOU ARE BEING RAILROADED INTO ENTERING OR REMAINING IN A FAMILY BUSINESS OR PROFESSION, BUT YOU WANT SOMETHING DIFFERENT

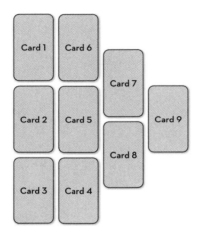

Purpose and background information:
When you know you should take a stand, but are scared of the reaction.

CARD 1: What do you really want? **CARD 2:** What is the underlying cause of opposition to change? **CARD 3:** Do you have support for change within/beyond the company/family? **CARD 4:** Are you ready to take up your new career/sports venture/study now, or do you need more preparation? **CARD 5:** Can you negotiate/withdraw gradually? **CARD 6:** Is it an all-or-nothing? **CARD 7:** Can you/how can you deal with the fallout? **CARD 8:** Can you stay within the family, or do you need to go away for a time to fulfill your dream? **CARD 9:** What is the ideal longer-term outcome?

What you should use:
The full deck.

When:
The end of a month.

254
IF YOUR FOLKS OR COMMUNITY ARE TRYING TO PERSUADE YOU TO MARRY THE BOY/GIRL NEXT DOOR, BUT YOU DO NOT WANT TO BE TIED DOWN

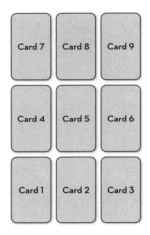

Purpose and background information:
When there is talk of engagements/weddings; but it's your folks' dream, not yours.

CARD 1: Do your folks/the boy/girl next door/your community really know how you feel? **CARD 2:** Will they ever listen/do you need to be more assertive/give up trying? **CARD 3:** Do you feel emotionally pressured to go along with it all, to avoid a major fuss/letting the family/community down? **CARD 4:** What is the price of complying? **CARD 5:** What is the cost of speaking out? **CARD 6:** Should you go away for a while until the dust settles? **CARD 7:** Is there someone else for you, or do you want independence? **CARD 8:** Do you have anyone in or beyond the family/community who will support you? **CARD 9:** Is this a symptom of greater emotional pressure placed on you by your family/community to conform?

What you should use:
The full deck

When:
Before your family starts sending out the invitations.

255
CROSS OF REMEMBRANCE SPREAD FOR LAUNCHING A CHARITY FOLLOWING THE LOSS OF A LOVED ONE

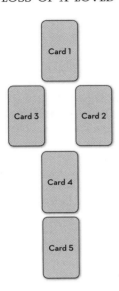

Purpose and background information:
When you want to collect and administer funds for research and financial support for relatives and patients of sufferers.

CARD 1: Is there an existing charity you could join forces with? **CARD 2:** Do you want to keep the charity small and beautiful, or make it an increasingly major initiative in your loved one's name? **CARD 3:** Do you have/can you gain the expertise to fulfill all the legal/official red tape, or do you need someone expert to do this? **CARD 4:** Will you have a strong online presence to raise the profile of your charity? **CARD 5:** Is there a book to be written/media interest in your loved one's life to give the charity a personal presence?

What you should use:
The forty Minor cards, Aces to Tens, and the sixteen Court cards.

When:
You feel ready to express your grief in a tangible way to help others similarly afflicted.

256
IF YOU WANT TO INVENT SOMETHING WORTHWHILE

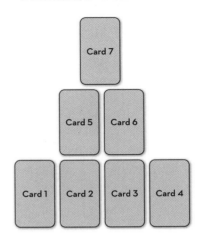

Purpose and background information:
When you are fascinated by inventions and want to develop this gift.

CARD 1: Do you have a naturally creative mind that sees alternative approaches/solutions to problems? **CARD 2:** Are there any particular issues you would like to create an invention to solve? **CARD 3:** Would you be interested in patenting and selling your inventions, or are they for a specific person/known group in need? **CARD 4:** Is this a hobby, or do you want to invent as a living? **CARD 5:** Will you/how will you find/do you need a sponsor to back your work so you can devote yourself to it? **CARD 6:** How do you want/see your inventing developing over the next five years? **CARD 7:** Will you invent something that will change many people's lives for the better?

What you should use:
The forty Minor cards, Aces to Tens.

When:
When the full moon is in Gemini.

257

IF YOU WANT TO MEET YOUR TRUE LOVE WHEN YOU ARE NO LONGER YOUNG, OR AFTER LOSS

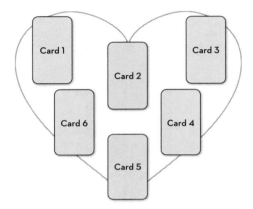

Purpose and background information:

When you long for a lasting loving companion to share your life.

CARD 1: Are you open to the right love when s/he comes along, or do you need longer for hurts to heal? **CARD 2:** Will this love grow slowly from friendship, or be love at first sight? **CARD 3:** When/where will you find this love? **CARD 4:** Will you know/how will you know s/he is the one? **CARD 5:** Will this love last forever? **CARD 6:** Can/how can you avoid/ignore the disapproval/interference of those who will not welcome a new love in your life?

What you should use:

The full deck.

When:

Valentine's Day, or any full moon.

258

IF YOU WANT TO MOVE FROM THE CITY TO THE OCEAN OR COUNTRYSIDE

Purpose and background information:

When you need fresh air/water and a slower more natural lifestyle.

CARD 1: Do you know exactly where you want to go, or are you open to finding the right location? **CARD 2:** Do you want to go sooner rather than later and worry about the logistics later? **CARD 3:** Will you experience any significant opposition to your decision? **CARD 4:** Should you/will you compromise, or is it an all-or-nothing life change? **CARD 5:** Should you/will you start a new career/buy a business/ work from home, enjoying the lifestyle and juggling finances? **CARD 6:** What will be the ideal outcome/ best results of making the change?

What you should use:

The twenty-two Major cards and the sixteen Court cards.

When:

At the end of a vacation when you do not want to return to the city.

259
IF YOU WANT TO STUDY OR GO TO COLLEGE LATER IN LIFE

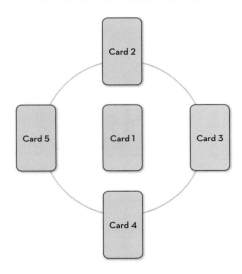

Purpose and background information:

When you increasingly regret not studying/that you were not able to go to college/finish your degree when you were young.

CARD 1: Will study make you happy, even if the road ahead will be hard? **CARD 2:** Do you need/should you start with a short course/part-time study to become familiar with learning again? **CARD 3:** Do you still want to study the same courses as when you were younger, or have your preferences changed in the light of experience? **CARD 4:** Are you studying for pleasure, or for a major career change? **CARD 5:** If you go all out for your dream, will you succeed?

What you should use:

The full deck.

When:

The week before the college applications are due.

260
IF YOU WANT TO OPEN AN ANIMAL-RESCUE CENTER

Purpose and background information:

If you have a passion for rescuing and helping lost, abused, and injured creatures.

CARD 1: Do you want to turn your passion for animal rescue into a full-time occupation, or keep it as a hobby? **CARD 2:** Would working at an existing animal charity as a volunteer or training in animal care satisfy you instead? **CARD 3:** Do you have/can you acquire suitable land/premises and obtain charitable status to help with expenses? **CARD 4:** Will you need to do other animal-related work to initially supplement your income? **CARD 5:** Will you be entirely self-funding within a year/five years? **CARD 6:** Should you/can you organize events to raise the profile of your center through media interest?

What you should use:

The forty Minor cards, Aces to Tens, and the sixteen Court cards.

When:

St Francis Assisi Day (October 4), or any Saturday, day of animal protection.

261

IF YOU WANT TO VOLUNTEER FOR A CHARITY PROJECT OVERSEAS OR WITHIN A COMMUNITY IN NEED

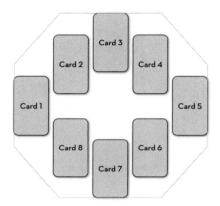

Purpose and background information:
When you are raising money for Third World charities but know you could do more.

CARD 1: Are you prepared to volunteer, even if you have responsibilities/people who say you shouldn't go? **CARD 2:** Do you need extra training/voluntary vacation projects to become familiar with the requirements? **CARD 3:** Are you committed to one country/age group/community, or are you willing to go anywhere to gain a foothold? **CARD 4:** Do you have the resources to initially support yourself before you are paid expenses/fares, etc.? **CARD 5:** Are you prepared to deal with bureaucracy, red tape/petty dictators who may make life hard as you get established? **CARD 6:** Is this all or nothing, regardless of tough conditions and dangers? **CARD 7:** Will you/should you go with a partner/friend, or do you want to go it alone? **CARD 8:** Is this a permanent life change, or will you take it project by project?

What you should use:
The full deck.

When:
When you see something in the news that reminds you of your desire.

262

IF YOU WANT TO CONTACT AN OLD LOVE YOU HAVE NEVER FORGOTTEN

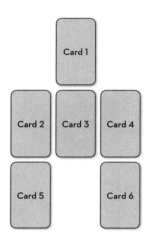

Purpose and background information:
If you cannot get an old love out of your mind.

CARD 1: Are you dreaming of him/her/unexpectedly hearing songs you shared, etc., that would suggest a telepathic link? **CARD 2:** Can/should you try to find him/her on social media/through old contacts in order to assess if s/he is free? **CARD 3:** Even if not free, should you/do you still want to make contact? **CARD 4:** Whether free or not, do you want to develop/revive the friendship? **CARD 5:** Do you want more intimate connection by phone or even in person? **CARD 6:** If it doesn't work out, is it still going to be worthwhile pursuing to put the relationship to rest?

What you should use:
The twenty-two Major cards and the sixteen Court cards

When:
Just after a full-moon phase.

263
IF YOU WANT TO TAKE UP AN ADVENTURE SPORT LATER IN LIFE

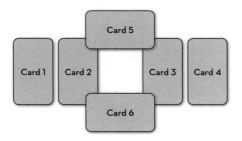

Purpose and background information:

When you feel like you are twenty years younger than you are and crave adventure.

CARD 1: Is adventure sport what you really want, or more excitement generally in your life? **CARD 2:** Is there a particular extreme sport you crave, or any sport in which thrills are involved? **CARD 3:** Is this the beginning of a new/revived fitness/adventure drive? **CARD 4:** Do you have friends/a partner who will share the activity, or are you going it alone? **CARD 5:** Will you enjoy it for its own sake, or is it the beginning of a more radical life change? **CARD 6:** What is the next stage for you/will you return to your old life?

What you should use:

The forty Minor cards, Aces to Tens, and the sixteen Court cards.

When:

New Year's Day, or at the beginning of any new month.

264
IF YOU WANT TO STAY HOME AND ENJOY A RELAXED RETIREMENT, BUT EVERYONE SAYS YOU MUST FIND NEW INTERESTS

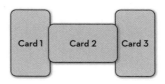

Purpose and background information:

When you are looking forward to stepping back, enjoying house and garden, but everyone around you is pushing you to fill your days with new interests.

CARD 1: What do *you* want to do when you retire? **CARD 2:** What are the motives of those encouraging you to take up new activities? **CARD 3:** Can you resist pressures of others telling you what you ought to do and want, and give yourself time and space without unwarranted guilt?

What you should use:

The twenty-two Major cards.

When:

The day you retire.

CHAPTER 19

FAMILY SPREADS

Lucky cards for family Spreads:

Major Cards: The Empress, the Emperor, Strength, Temperance, the Sun, the Moon.

Minor Cards: Ace of Pentacles, Ace of Cups, Three of Pentacles, Three of Cups, Four of Wands, Six of Cups, Six of Swords, Seven of Pentacles, Nine of Pentacles, Ten of Pentacles, Ten of Cups.

Court Cards: The Pages/Princesses and Knights/Princes of Pentacles and Cups; the Queens and Kings of Pentacles and Cups.

About the Family Spreads

One- and two-carders to answer straightforward questions; three cards for celebrations and the growth of family happiness, also for additions to the family; four cards for security and stability; fives for communication between members and generations; six-carders for family love and mending quarrels; Spreads with nine-plus cards for more complex questions and resolving difficulties.

265
WILL YOU LIKE A NEW PROSPECTIVE FAMILY MEMBER WHEN YOU MEET FOR THE FIRST TIME?

Purpose and background information:
Deal and turn over one card for a yes/no result.

If a positive card, you will like the person instantly and this liking will grow. If the card meaning holds doubts, you will not warm to the person instantly; you have the option of picking a second card and asking how/when this can be improved.

What you should use:
The twenty-two Major cards and the sixteen Court cards.

When:
The morning of the meeting.

266
SHOULD YOU INVITE A PARTICULAR RELATIVE TO A FAMILY GATHERING?

Purpose and background information:
When you know the person's presence will cause difficulties, but you do not want to offend.

Deal two cards. Turn over the first one, read before turning the second. Which card has the strongest message, positive or negative?

Card 1: Will the invitation lead to more trouble than it is worth? **Card 2:** If you do not invite the person, will it cause more problems than it is worth?

If the message is not clear, add a third card after **Card 2** as a tiebreaker.

What you should use:
The twenty-two Major cards and the sixteen Court cards.

When:
When you are planning the guest list.

267
ADDING TO THE FAMILY

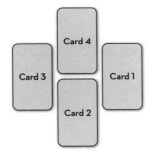

Purpose and background information:
When new family members come on the scene, whether in-laws, grandparents and children through a remarriage, a new baby later in life, or a foster or adopted child.

Card 1: Who will be most resistant to the newcomer/s?
Card 2: What unexpected problems may occur with new family member/s? **Card 3:** What is the best way of integrating the newcomer/s? **Card 4:** How do you retain present family unity/identity while welcoming the new member/s?

What you should use:
The twenty-two Major cards and the sixteen Court cards.

When:
Before a significant event.

268
WILL THIS CELEBRATION BE PEACEFUL?

Purpose and background information:
If you are worried about a family gathering revealing divisions/tensions on what should be a happy occasion.

Card 1: The people/topics that may cause difficulty. **Card 2:** The strengths/good aspects of the occasion/helpful people present to mitigate problems. **Card 3:** The key strategy to ensure that the occasion passes peacefully.

What you should use:
The forty Minor cards, Aces to Tens, and the sixteen Court cards.

When:
Before sending out the invitations.

269
A CIRCLE FOR RESTORING FAMILY UNITY

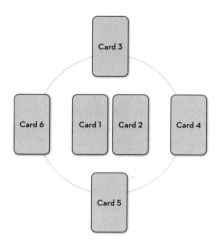

Purpose and background information:
When you have a large family and there are arguments every time you meet.

Card 1: What causes most disagreements? **Card 2:** Who is largely responsible for stirring up the trouble? **Card 3:** Who can best create peace and harmony? **Card 4:** How can trouble be averted beforehand? **Card 5:** The action plan if disagreements break out. **Card 6:** How to resolve the underlying issue long-term.

What you should use:
The twenty-two Major cards and the sixteen Court cards

When:
Toward the end of a waning moon cycle.

270
PRESERVING THE HAPPY FAMILY

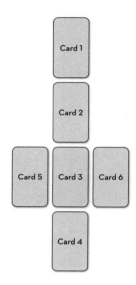

Purpose and background information:
If your immediate family has every reason to be happy, but there is simmering jealousy and resentment. This is another circle Spread as in the previous Spread.

Card 1: Has there always been underlying resentment, or is this caused by a recent event? **Card 2:** Who is playing favorites/power games, and why? **Card 3:** Should you ignore this/refuse to get involved? **Card 4:** Can you/should you tackle family members individually beforehand to draw up rules for socializing? **Card 5:** Would action/intervention at the time improve the situation? **Card 6:** Will/how will the situation improve naturally in time?

What you should use:
The full deck.

When:
A Friday, day of peacemaking.

271
PRESERVING HARMONY BETWEEN GENERATIONS

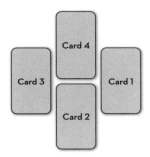

Purpose and background information:
When two or more generations share a home, or work or regularly holiday together.

CARD 1: The issues, actual and underlying, that need to be resolved to create harmony. **CARD 2:** How can everyone's needs be met without sacrificing your own peace of mind? **CARD 3:** How can the shared space/priorities of each member be most peacefully divided? **CARD 4:** What benefits can a multi-generational setting and lifestyle offer to all?

What you should use:
The twenty-two Major cards and the sixteen Court cards.

When:
When you are being the referee too often.

272
IF YOUR IN-LAWS ARE CONSTANTLY CAUSING TROUBLE IN YOUR FAMILY, AND YOUR PARTNER WILL NOT BACK YOU

Purpose and background information:
When the interference and lack of support is threatening your marriage/family life. A two-card reading, to cut through the power plays.

CARD 1: Make or break, insisting that your partner backs you in a confrontation. **CARD 2:** finding a way around the problem, through carefully thought-out strategies without your partner realizing. If the answer is not clear, add **CARD 3** to the right of **CARD 2,** avoidance tactics and refusal to take the bait.

What you should use:
The twenty Major cards and sixteen Court cards.

When:
The morning of a visit.

273
THE SCAPEGOAT SPREAD

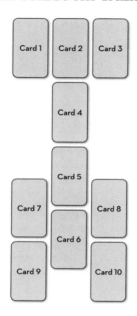

Purpose and background information:
If you have always been blamed for everything by your family.

CARD 1: Have you been the family scapegoat from childhood? **CARD 2:** Who benefits most from making you the scapegoat, and why? **CARD 3:** Will it improve? **CARD 4:** Who will support you within/outside of the family? **CARD 5:** Is the pattern of blame continuing with new members of the family? **CARD 6:** How can you break the pattern? **CARD 7:** Does your family deny the problem? **CARD 8:** Would counseling/outside emotional support help you cope? **CARD 9:** Should you confront individual family members? **CARD 10:** Should you distance yourself from your family and make a life of your own?

What you should use:
The twenty-two Major cards and the sixteen Court cards.

When:
When you are blamed one time too many for problems not of your making.

274
TO GET DIFFICULT IN-LAWS OR STEPFAMILIES TO ACCEPT YOU

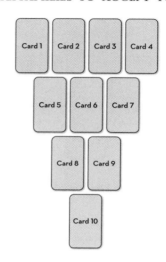

Purpose and background information:
When you have tried the charm offensive and are still Public Enemy Number 1.

CARD 1: What is the main problem that you experience? **CARD 2:** Who is most rejecting/critical of you, and what is their motive? **CARD 3:** Is there a more amenable person within or close to the family to support you? **CARD 4:** Are there areas of compromise/injustices being overlooked? **CARD 5:** What can't/shouldn't you compromise on? **CARD 6:** Is your partner emotionally manipulated by those causing the problem? **CARD 7:** How can you break the stranglehold/guilt factor used against you/your partner? **CARD 8:** Can/how can you reduce contact/confrontational issues? **CARD 9:** Can you ignore the problem and hope it goes away? **CARD 10:** Should you confront the worst offender, letting it be known that you will not back down?

What you should use:
The full deck.

When:
The night before a full moon.

275
IF YOU WANT A QUIET FAMILY OCCASION
TO INTRODUCE YOUR NEW PARTNER

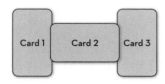

Purpose and background information:
If a relative insists on bringing noisy children/teenagers/boisterous animals along whom s/he never controls.

CARD 1: The problem as it stands. **CARD 2:** The consequences of not dealing with the problem beforehand. **CARD 3:** The solution/compromise that will keep everyone happy.

What you should use:
The forty Minor cards.

When:
Before planning the dinner.

Example:
Billy was really scared about introducing his new partner to the family at dinner, as she is very shy and his sister's five boisterous children wreak havoc at every family occasion.

CARD 1: The Five of Wands, showing the five people (representing the children) not fighting but certainly arguing and jostling, which they constantly do in public.

CARD 2: The Hermit. Billy's worst fears, his partner not coping and so not really getting to know his parents. **CARD 3: The Four of Wands,** showing a happy couple standing in a garden. Is there a compromise? **CARD 3** suggested to Billy meeting his sister and the children outdoors with a playground where they could run around while the adults talk (the **Five of Wands**).

He added a **CARD 4,** upright next to **CARD 3, Temperance,** Billy and his partner going out for a civilized dinner with the adults in the evening, everyone happy.

276
TO REUNITE A FAMILY DIVIDED
BY A POINTLESS QUARREL

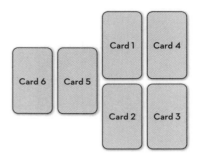

Purpose and background information:
When some family members are not speaking to one another, and no one is prepared to make the first move.

CARD 1: Who/what was the outward cause of the original quarrel? **CARD 2:** Does this reflect existing underlying family tensions/resentments? **CARD 3:** Who is keeping the quarrel going/will not let the matter lie? **CARD 4:** Could/how could there be a compromise? **CARD 5:** Who can best act as peacemaker, and how will this be achieved? **CARD 6:** Can/how can future conflict be avoided?

What you should use:
The twenty-two Major cards and the sixteen Court cards

When:
Sunrise.

277

WHEN ONE MEMBER OF THE FAMILY ALWAYS CAUSES TROUBLE AMONG THE OTHERS

Purpose and background information:

When an otherwise happy family atmosphere is marred by one person's troublemaking.

CARD 1: Has this trouble always existed/has the troublemaker recently suffered a trauma or setback? **CARD 2:** Does the troublemaker target a particular/certain family member/s, or is s/he just generally unpleasant? **CARD 3:** What triggers potentially confrontational situations? **CARD 4:** Can any family member positively influence the troublemaker? **CARD 5:** Do any family members make the situation worse, either deliberately or unconsciously? **CARD 6:** Should the troublemaker be warned and, if necessary, excluded from certain events for the sake of family harmony?

What you should use:

The forty Minor cards, Aces to Tens, and the sixteen Court cards.

When:

Toward the end of a waning moon.

278

IF YOUR FAMILY TAKES YOU FOR GRANTED

Purpose and background information:

When you are regarded as room service/on-tap babysitter/ever-open financier.

CARD 1: Is your family simply thoughtless, rather than deliberately selfish? **CARD 2:** Did you grow up always being expected to help others? **CARD 3:** What makes you say yes when you want to say no? **CARD 4:** Do you get a bad reaction when you do say no? **CARD 5:** Do you *need* to do so much for the family? **CARD 6:** Who will back you up if you start saying no? **CARD 7:** Could you become less available to the needs of others generally? **CARD 8:** What requests you cannot or do not want to refuse. **CARD 9:** Would you be happier if you fulfilled necessary requests when, how, and with thanks? **CARD 10:** Who helps you/could help you more? **CARD 11:** Do you find it hard to ask for/accept help, and why? **CARD 12:** What is the ideal outcome for you?

What you should use:

The full deck.

When:

When you never have time for yourself.

279
IF YOU WANT TO RESEARCH YOUR FAMILY ROOTS IN-DEPTH TO FIND MISSING GENERATIONS

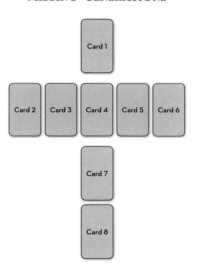

Purpose and background information:
When, in spite of modern technology, you are drawing a blank once you reach a certain date or place.

CARD 1: Have you/should you exhaust every online ancestry/DNA search for the missing link? **CARD 2:** Should you go to the last known location where your family lived, even if overseas? **CARD 3:** Should you study church records online and in records offices to see misspelled/mis-recorded dates or names? **CARD 4:** Should you consult a psychic/use your pendulum over a series of possible locations? **CARD 5:** Should you search workhouse/orphanage lists of servants and old military records? **CARD 6:** When you go back to what was last known, will you intuit a concealed relationship? **CARD 7:** Can you bypass the missing link, going back through another branch? **CARD 8:** Will you succeed? When, and how?

What you should use:
The twenty-two Major cards and the sixteen Court cards.

When:
A Saturday, for uncovering secrets.

280
IF YOU WANT TO UNCOVER A FAMILY SECRET THAT AFFECTS YOU

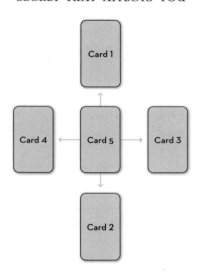

Purpose and background information:
When there is a conspiracy of silence within the family. Deal the *Compass* Spread.

CARD 1: Can anyone connected with the family past offer any clues? **CARD 2:** Should you search every record, on and offline, linked with the missing period/secret? **CARD 3:** Should/can you use social media/pay visits to locate people/places from the missing time? **CARD 4:** Will you uncover the secret? **CARD 5:** Will doing so make you happy?

What you should use:
The twenty-two Major cards.

When:
The night before a crescent moon.

281

WHEN A PARENT OR GRANDPARENT IS AGING BUT WILL NOT GIVE UP THEIR INDEPENDENCE

Purpose and background information:

When you know that they cannot live alone for much longer, but also that it wouldn't work moving in with you.

CARD 1: Can you put daily help in place, overseen by you, so that your relative can stay in their own home? **CARD 2:** Could/should you/another relative do a conversion/extension to your/their home so the older person can have independence with protection? **CARD 3:** Should you/another relative suggest alternative forms of sheltered accommodation which, even if rejected now, sows the seeds? **CARD 4:** Is there anyone the older person listens to who can discuss the future? **CARD 5:** If you have always done everything, maybe with little thanks, should you call on other relatives/social care to step up their input? **CARD 6:** If the older person is very demanding, should you temporarily step back/be less available? **CARD 7:** What is the best possible outcome for everyone concerned?

What you should use:

The twenty-two Major cards and the sixteen Court cards.

When:

When the moon is passing through Capricorn during the month, or a Saturday, day of older people.

282

FOR A SUCCESSFUL MAJOR FAMILY REUNION OR LARGE-SCALE FAMILY HOLIDAY

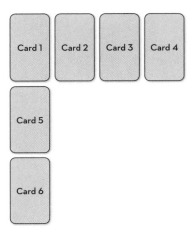

Purpose and background information:

When you are organizing a major family reunion and want it to go well.

CARD 1: Can you/should you delegate some of the responsibility for organizing the event? **CARD 2:** Do/will you have the right mix of relatives sharing accommodation/sitting around the table to avoid pitfalls? **CARD 3:** Can you dilute difficult souls with cheerful thick-skinned family members? **CARD 4:** Have you built your own leisure/pleasure into the master plan? **CARD 5:** Are you organizing a schedule for chore share so it's not left up to you? **CARD 6:** The secret ingredient for making this a resounding success.

What you should use:

The forty Minor cards, Aces to Tens, and the sixteen Court cards.

When:

Before finalizing plans.

283
A FIRST HOLIDAY WITHOUT THE FAMILY

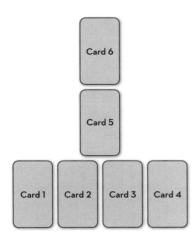

Purpose and background information:
When you/you and your partner are vacationing without the family.

CARD 1: Are you 100% confident that everything is in order at home so you will not worry? **CARD 2:** Have you made a pact not to talk/think about family, bills, plumbing/work? **CARD 3:** Are all mobile devices disabled except for emergencies, so you enjoy peace/talk to each other? **CARD 4:** Does everyone, including your workplace, know that you are only to be contacted in a dire emergency? **CARD 5:** Are you/should you stay in an adult-only venue/plan activities the children would hate? **CARD 6:** Are you prepared to get to know yourself/your partner again/no mom/dad/grandma/grandpa labels?

What you should use:
The twenty-two Major cards, Aces to Tens, and the sixteen Court cards.

When:
Just prior to going on holiday.

284
WHEN FAMILY MEALTIMES ARE EITHER A BATTLEGROUND OR A NONEXISTENT EVENT

Purpose and background information:
When you feel you are running a carry-out food service for your family.

CARD 1: Can you/how can you prevent your family's constantly grazing, instead sharing a meal together? **CARD 2:** Can you/how can you prevent electronic devices dominating mealtimes? **CARD 3:** Can you/how can you institute an inviolable family meal once or twice a week with shared cooking/preparation? **CARD 4:** Alternatively, do you want to let everyone sort out their own food requirements? **CARD 5:** Is the lack of togetherness at mealtimes a symptom of a growing emotional family gap, or is it just lack of time/circumstances? **CARD 6:** Could you/should you make a regular family date to eat out together once a week/go instead with friends/partner?

What you should use:
The full deck.

When:
A Friday, day of family togetherness.

285
WHEN A FAMILY MEMBER'S ADDICTION OR LIFESTYLE IS ADVERSELY AFFECTING THE FAMILY

Purpose and background information:
When one member is destructively dominating family life.

CARD 1: Is this a new problem, or is it ongoing? and is it getting worse? **CARD 2:** Is the family member oblivious to/uncaring of the negative effects on the family? **CARD 3:** Can/should you press for treatment/intervention by outside sources, if necessary trying one more time? **CARD 4:** Can you/should you seek/persevere with outside help for the rest of the family to cope? **CARD 5:** Should/must you harden your heart/protect family finances/safety/peace of mind by distancing the troublesome relative? **CARD 6:** Should you need proof that the relative is trying/has changed before letting down your guard? **CARD 7:** What support can you offer without risking yourself/the rest of the family? **CARD 8:** Can you/should you keep offering access to the right treatment at regular intervals, or step back entirely? **CARD 9:** What unexpected factor/approach will improve the situation within six to twelve months?

What you should use:
The full deck.

When:
When you are let down by false promises yet again.

286
IF A DIFFICULT FAMILY MEMBER IS ESTRANGED BUT YOU DO NOT WANT TO GIVE UP ON THEM

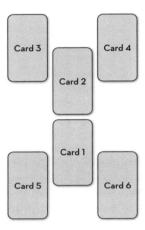

Purpose and background information:
When you worry about the estranged person, but they reject any attempts at reconciliation.

CARD 1: Is this behavior typical, or is it caused by a recent trauma? **CARD 2:** Is the family member unfairly blaming the family for their problems? **CARD 3:** Have you done everything you can to resolve the situation, or is it worth one more try? **CARD 4:** Could anyone outside the family make the person see reason? **CARD 5:** Should you step back and keep an eye out from a distance? **CARD 6:** Will/can this be resolved in the future without adversely affecting the family?

What you should use:
The forty Minor cards, Aces to Tens, and the sixteen Court cards.

When:
After yet another bid for reconciliation has been thrown back in your face.

287
OVERCOMING FAVORITISM OR ADULT SIBLING RIVALRY IN A FAMILY

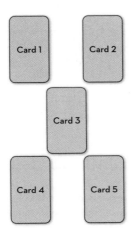

Purpose and background information:
When you are always the one to offer practical help to a parent/grandparent, but a sibling who does nothing is given all the praise.

CARD 1: Has this family favoritism always existed from childhood and, if so, is it getting worse? **CARD 2:** Does the favored child/children encourage this rivalry? **CARD 3:** Can you ask the favored child to do more to justify the praise? **CARD 4:** If you told the older relative how hurtful it was, would they deny it/accuse you of jealousy? **CARD 5:** Should you step back temporarily/permanently/inform all parties you will not be available?

What you should use:
The twenty-two Major cards and the sixteen Court cards.

When:
When you have inconvenienced yourself and received ingratitude once too often.

288
TO RESIST PRESSURE TO CONFORM TO FAMILY BELIEFS OR A SITUATION THAT YOU KNOW IS WRONG FOR YOU

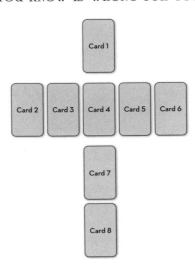

Purpose and background information:
If your beliefs/lifestyle/principles are very different from those of your family.

CARD 1: Have you always felt different from the rest of your family? **CARD 2:** What is the main difference/problem that makes it hard for you to conform? **CARD 3:** Would anyone in your family/community speak up for you? **CARD 4:** Can you live within the family and keep your own beliefs? **CARD 5:** Are there areas on which you can compromise? **CARD 6:** Are there areas on which you cannot compromise? **CARD 7:** Do you need to temporarily/permanently move away from the family?

Add a **CARD 8** if you wish, below **CARD 7:** Can/how can this be resolved?

What you should use:
The twenty-two Major cards and the sixteen Court cards.

When:
On a significant family day.

289
WHEN YOUR FAMILY WILL NOT LET YOU LIVE YOUR OWN LIFE

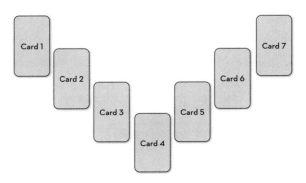

Purpose and background information:
When your family is loving, but possessive and over-involved in your life.

CARD 1: Has your family always been over-protective/trying to influence your life, relationships, and choices? **CARD 2:** Does this represent underlying relationship issues between your parents? **CARD 3:** Can you negotiate more freedom by reassuring them you know what you are doing? **CARD 4:** Do you need to start expressing your independence in small ways? **CARD 5:** Should you get someone close to the family/a family therapist to work with you and the family? **CARD 6:** Should you move away/reduce contact for a while? **CARD 7:** Can this be resolved amicably so you can live your own way without undue struggle?

What you should use:
The full deck.

When:
When the moon is in Aquarius.

290
FOR RESTORING BALANCE WHEN TWO FRIENDS OR FAMILY MEMBERS ARE PULLING YOU IN OPPOSITE DIRECTIONS

Purpose and background information:
When you cannot please both parties involved and are in danger of being blamed by both.

CARD 1: Have you ever been asked to choose by the same people? **CARD 2:** Can you see rights and wrongs on both sides, so a verdict is not clear-cut? **CARD 3:** Are the parties prepared to compromise at all? **CARD 4:** If it's all or nothing, will you be blamed by the party you do not support? **CARD 5:** Should you step back and refuse to choose? **CARD 6:** Will this matter be resolved with or without your intervention?

What you should use:
The twenty-two Major cards and the sixteen Court cards.

When:
Any twilight.

291
FOR OVERCOMING PREJUDICE WITHIN YOUR FAMILY IF YOU ARE IN A SINGLE-SEX RELATIONSHIP OR ARE TRANSGENDER OR GENDER-FLUID

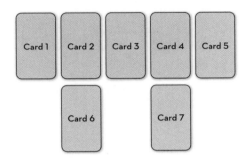

Purpose and background information:

CARD 1: Have you recently come out, or has this been a growing awareness by family members which they have chosen to ignore? **CARD 2:** Is there a sympathetic family member who could help your family understand? **CARD 3:** Do you need outside support to formulate strategies to deal with your family's attitude? **CARD 4:** Should you bring a partner/ friend home to show your family you are serious? **CARD 5:** Should you involve your family in discussions/decisions regarding lifestyle choices/your body/future children? **CARD 6:** If your family will not accept you right now, are you prepared to walk away? **CARD 7:** If/when/how will they accept that you are the same person you have always been?

What you should use:
The twenty-two Major cards and the sixteen Court cards.

When:
Before what you believe will be a family confrontation.

292
IF YOU ARE TRYING TO COMBINE RAISING A FAMILY WITH PAID WORK OR STUDY

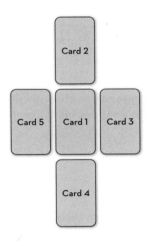

Purpose and background information:
When you appear to be doing it all and having the worst of both worlds.

CARD 1: Are you doing too much so that you need to cut down/prioritize? **CARD 2:** Are you not getting the backup from family? How can this be remedied? **CARD 3:** Do you feel you should be more assertive and demand help? **CARD 4:** How can your burden be eased? **CARD 5:** When and how will your life come into happy balance?

What you should use:
The forty Major cards, Aces to Tens, and the sixteen Court cards

When:
Before the start of another work week.

CHAPTER 20

SPREADS FOR BABIES, CHILDREN, AND GRANDCHILDREN OF ALL AGES

There are separate chapters on babies, fertility, and Spreads for teenagers.

Lucky cards for Spreads concerning babies, children, and grandchildren:

Major Arcana: The Fool, the Empress, the Emperor, Temperance, the Moon, the Sun, the Star, the World.

Minor Cards: Aces of Pentacles, Cups, and Wands; Three of Pentacles, Cups, and Wands; Four of Wands, Six of Cups, Six of Wands, Seven of Cups, Eight of Wands, Ten of Pentacles, Ten of Cups.

The Court Cards: Pages/Princesses and Knights/Princes of Pentacles, Cups, and Wands; Queens and Kings of Pentacles and Cups.

About Spreads for children and grandchildren

One- and two-carders for straightforward questions, threes for growth and happiness, fours for home and stability, fives for health, travel, communication, and education, sixes for family, sevens for dreams and overcoming fears and difficulties, eights for progress, and nines for anti-bullying; and even higher numbers of cards for complex issues involving several members of the family.

293
IF YOUR CHILD OR TEENAGER IS BEING BULLIED AT SCHOOL

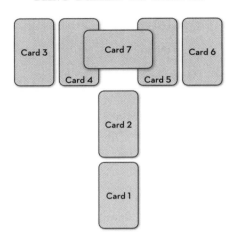

Purpose and background information:
When your child is afraid to go to school, but the school will not listen.

CARD 1: Who are the main bullies? Are they generally regarded as challenging children? **CARD 2:** What is the main reason given for bullying your child? **CARD 3:** Do they bully other children? Can you contact other parents for support? **CARD 4:** Can you discover the official bullying policy and insist it is followed? **CARD 5:** Can you avoid being intimidated by the school, which may blame your child in order to defend the school's reputation? **CARD 6:** Can you/should you go higher than the principal to resolve this? **CARD 7:** Whatever happens, do you want to move your child into a different school?

What you should use:
The full deck:

When:
A Tuesday, the day of courage.

294
IF YOUR CHILD OR TEENAGER IS
BEING BULLIED ON SOCIAL MEDIA

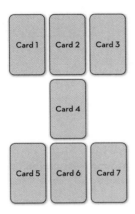

Purpose and background information:

If your child becomes upset by text messages/is unduly secretive about social media contacts.

CARD 1: Is your child receiving an unusual number of text messages/does s/he appear upset after reading text messages? **CARD 2:** Does your child come straight home after school instead of hanging out with friends? **CARD 3:** Does your child look anxious and is s/he constantly checking their phone for messages? **CARD 4:** Should you make a quiet time to talk about cyber bullying? **CARD 5:** Would one of your child's friends talk to you regarding what may be happening to your child? **CARD 6:** Can/should you contact a school counselor/leave a teenage helpline number around where it can be seen by your child? **CARD 7:** Can/should you offer your child a new phone/number/social media page with strict privacy settings?

What you should use:

The full deck

When:

A Wednesday, day for overcoming human snakes.

295
IF AN OLDER CHILD OR TEENAGER IS
OBSESSED WITH COMPUTER GAMES
OR SOCIAL NETWORKS, TO THE
EXCLUSION OF EVERYTHING ELSE

Purpose and background information:

When your child is spending an inordinate amount of time online/gaming.

CARD 1: Is this a new problem/due to a setback and is increasing? **CARD 2:** Is this more time than the average teenager spends online? **CARD 3:** Is your child depressed/anxious/being bullied? **CARD 4:** Should you recheck sites your child is accessing/chat room contacts? **CARD 5:** Are there local computer courses/clubs/festivals/conventions where your child could socialize? **CARD 6:** Should you insist that the child join family outings/meals? **CARD 7:** Should you take a more active interest in your child's online activities, even if your child is resistant? **CARD 8:** Should you encourage your child toward a career in technology/computers/designing game software?

What you should use:

The forty Minor cards, Aces to Tens.

When:

A Wednesday, day of technology.

296
FOR FINDING THE RIGHT SCHOOL FOR YOUR CHILD/REN

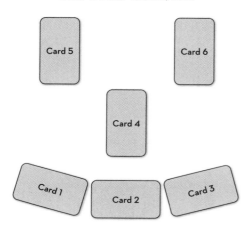

Purpose and background information:

When you have a choice and are undecided.

CARD 1: Would your child benefit from a challenging, lively atmosphere? **CARD 2:** Should you find a quiet, small, unhurried school? **CARD 3:** Is academic excellence important/would your child benefit from informal self-motivated teaching? **CARD 4:** How important are sports/after-school clubs? **CARD 5:** Is the journey to your ideal school relatively easy for you/your child? **CARD 6:** How will the chosen school positively affect further education/university/apprenticeships?

Once you have read all six cards in the Spread, add a card for each school to which you are contemplating sending your child, naming a school for each card.

What you should use:

The forty Minor cards, Aces to Tens, and the sixteen Court cards.

When:

You have visited suitable schools in the area.

297
IF YOUR CHILD IS TERRIFIED OF THE DARK

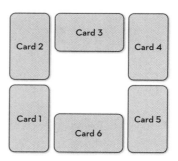

Purpose and background information:

When your child is afraid to sleep alone unless a light is on.

CARD 1: Is this sensitivity an ongoing problem? If so, does it occur in other areas of life? **CARD 2:** Are there background tensions at home/school/socially that may be contributing to fears? **CARD 3:** Are there new television programs, books, or computer games that have unsettled your child? **CARD 4:** Could you make practical changes to bedroom/lighting, etc. to lessen the fears? **CARD 5:** Should you let the child change rooms? **CARD 6:** Does the room feel spooky/do you need to smudge/give the child a crystal or crystal angel for reassurance? (Smudging, a native American Indian tradition, is done by burning dried herbs and letting the smoke float around the house as a means of cleansing.)

What you should use:

The twenty-two Major cards.

When:

At sunset.

298
IF YOU HAVE A PSYCHIC CHILD WHO IS FRIGHTENED OF GHOSTS

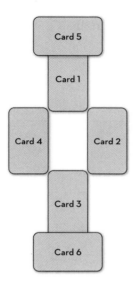

Purpose and background information:

If your child talks about ghosts/refuses to stay alone in certain rooms.

Card 1: Has your child seen departed relatives before/talked to angels/fairies? **Card 2:** Have any family members recently died/anyone died in the house before you moved in? **Card 3:** If the problem is getting worse, have any friends/siblings told scary stories/shown a ghost movie? **Card 4:** Even if you do not believe in ghosts, can you reassure your child that nothing can harm them? **Card 5:** Can you create a bedtime ritual if fears are worse at night involving angels/prayers, etc? **Card 6:** Would you be prepared to invite a reputable medium to visit to check for and/or clear any negative energies?

What you should use:

The full deck.

When:

A Monday, day of Gabriel, protector of children.

299
WHEN YOUR NEW PARTNER AND CHILDREN AREN'T GETTING ALONG

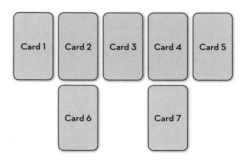

Purpose and background information:

Card 1: Are they worse when you are around to intervene? **Card 2:** Are both parties playing power games competing for your love? **Card 3:** Is anyone stirring the pot, one of the children/one or both exes? **Card 4:** Can you and your partner agree on a joint united strategy? **Card 5:** Can you both spend time with your own child/ren so they do not feel pushed out? **Card 6:** Can you beg/borrow/steal regular time with your partner to focus on yourselves? **Card 7:** When and how will you all come together in harmony?

What you should use:

The forty Minor cards, Aces to Tens, and the sixteen Court cards.

When:

A Friday, day of family harmony.

300
IF THERE IS INTENSE JEALOUSY TOWARD A SIBLING OR NEW BABY

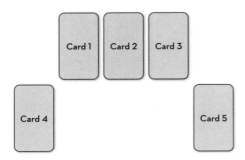

Purpose and background information:

When jealousy is causing constant arguments and bad behavior, whatever you say and do.

CARD 1: Is the jealousy longstanding if a sibling/new if a baby, but escalating? **CARD 2:** Does a particular relative/older sibling fuel the jealousy? **CARD 3:** How can you deal with the antisocial aspects while still supporting the jealous child? **CARD 4:** Can a family member spend time with the jealous child, building up their confidence? **CARD 5:** Can you build up a relationship between the children by making sure that there is equality of treatment?

What you should use:

The forty Minor cards, Aces to Tens, and the sixteen Court cards.

When:

Any late waning-moon day.

301
IF YOUR CHILD OR CHILDREN ARE BRIBED BY AN ABSENT PARENT AND THREATEN TO LIVE WITH THE OTHER PARENT IF YOU DO NOT PAY UP

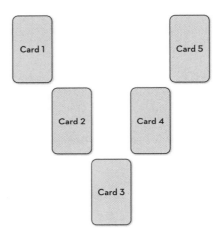

Purpose and background information:

If the absent parent is acting like Santa/Mrs. Claus and you cannot compete materially.

CARD 1: Can you try one more time to explain to your ex the problem/use mediation? **CARD 2:** Can you counteract this power ploy by giving your children fulfilling and inexpensive outings/experiences? **CARD 3:** Can you insist officially, or unofficially, that you be given sufficient money by the ex-partner so you are not struggling? **CARD 4:** Should/can you step back from the competition and refuse to fall for this emotional blackmail? **CARD 5:** If they carry out their threat, are you confident that before long they will realize that money is not the same as loving care?

What you should use:

The full deck.

When:

During a visit to the other parent.

302

IF YOUR CHILD IS HAVING PROBLEMS KEEPING UP WITH SCHOOLWORK, AND THE SCHOOL WILL NOT HELP

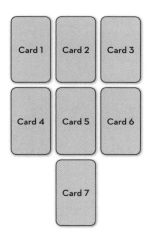

Purpose and background information:
When you know that with extra school input/specialist help, your child can develop their potential.

CARD 1: Should you try more assertively for a specialist assessment via the school so your child gets the help s/he needs? **CARD 2:** Is a particular class/subject teacher making problems for your child? **CARD 3:** If the school is unresponsive to students' needs, should you find a more sympathetic school environment? **CARD 4:** Would extra out-of-school help during the holidays assist your child in catching up? **CARD 5:** Are unrecognized physical problems/known disabilities responsible for your child's difficulties? **CARD 6:** Are emotional issues/bullying/lack of friends causing issues? **CARD 7:** Does your child have other gifts to build confidence and express talents in other ways?

What you should use:
The full deck

When:
The beginning of a month.

303

SHOULD YOU HOMESCHOOL YOUR CHILD OR TEENAGER?

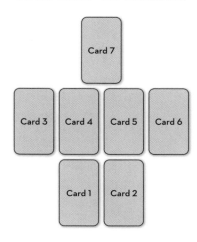

Purpose and background information:
When your child dislikes school.

CARD 1: Is it the school/the other students/lack of confidence/excess shyness, or all of these? **CARD 2:** If the school cannot/will not help, should you consider an alternative school, or is the problem schooling generally? **CARD 3:** What would be the advantages/disadvantages of homeschooling for your child? **CARD 4:** What would be the advantages/disadvantages of homeschooling for you? **CARD 5:** Would homeschooling give you the benefit of long-term/long-distance traveling/holidays to suit you? **CARD 6:** How/can you ensure that your teen still socializes with peers? **CARD 7:** Does your teen have special gifts that would come to the fore from alternative education/extra non-academic training?

What you should use:
The full deck.

When:
The beginning of a new month.

304

WILL YOUR TEENAGER GET THE COLLEGE OR UNIVERSITY PLACEMENT THEY WANT?

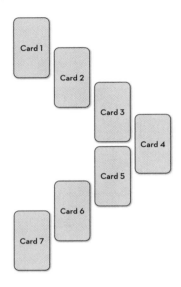

Purpose and background information:

You know they have worked hard, but the competition is fierce.

CARD 1: Is there a relaxed atmosphere at home about study/exams/success? **CARD 2:** Can you make sure your teen doesn't stay up all night studying/give up outside interests? **CARD 3:** Should you explore alternatives, both colleges and alternative careers, should they not get into the coveted school? **CARD 4:** Can you make sure other relatives/the current educational establishment aren't exerting undue pressure? **CARD 5:** Can you make the whole process from application to interview as stress-free and supported as possible? **CARD 6:** Will they succeed with this particular venture this time around? **CARD 7:** In your opinion, will they succeed longer-term in life?

What you should use:

The twenty-two Major cards and the sixteen Court cards.

When:

When studying gets intense.

305

HOW CAN YOU HELP YOUR TEENAGER DEAL WITH ANXIETY OVER ASSIGNMENTS AND EXAMINATIONS?

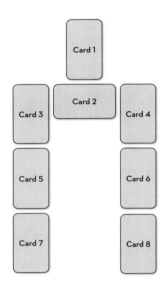

Purpose and background information:

If your teenager gets overly stressed about failing.

CARD 1: What is the chief pressure to be alleviated, from the current educational establishment/competitive peers/pushy relatives? **CARD 2:** What outside interests/gifts can be encouraged/developed to lessen anxiety about academic success? **CARD 3:** Is the teen a natural perfectionist, a trait that can be gently modified? **CARD 4:** Does the teen struggle academically, maybe needing extra help educationally/counseling? **CARD 5:** Does the current educational establishment put too much emphasis on academic success/would your teen benefit from a less intense educational establishment? **CARD 6:** What is your child's ultimate dream/are there different routes and time frames for that? **CARD 7:** Are there other emotional issues expressed through anxiety caused by study? **CARD 8:** Will the anxiety lessen naturally/can be modified but will always be present?

What you should use:

The twenty-two Major cards and the sixteen Court cards.

When:

Before a new school term.

306
IF YOUR TEEN HAS QUIT SCHOOL AND WILL NOT APPLY FOR COLLEGE OR GET A JOB

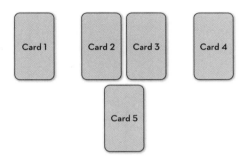

Purpose and background information:

If your teen sleeps in, stays in his/her room, or hangs around with friends all day and night.

CARD 1: Should you restrict finances until they co-operate/ would this cause them to take drastic measures for money?
CARD 2: Should you insist that they get a job, however basic/ voluntary work, until they decide what they want to do?
CARD 3: Should you devote time every day directing job hunting/researching college courses/sending applications?
CARD 4: Should you restrict room service/insist they carry out daily chores to earn their keep? **CARD 5:** Are they depressed/in with the wrong crowd and need counselling, or are they just lazy?

What you should use:

The forty Minor cards, Aces to Tens.

When:

Between a crescent and a waxing moon.

307
IF YOUR TEENAGER IS NOT DOING THEIR SCHOOLWORK BUT FOCUSING ENTIRELY ON FRIENDS AND SOCIAL LIFE

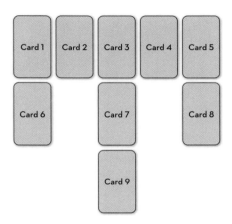

Purpose and background information:

When there has been a total change in attitude and your teen is out almost every night.

CARD 1: Is this more serious than ordinary teenage rebelliousness? **CARD 2:** Has your teenager met new influential pleasure-seeking friends? **CARD 3:** Has the school noticed a falling-off in interest/will they offer extra support/ encouragement? **CARD 4:** Is your teen depressed/drinking alcohol/experimenting with drugs? **CARD 5:** How can you intervene without causing further rebellion if you suspect your teen may be keeping bad company? **CARD 6:** Even if you are busy, can you make more time to do activities as a family/spend weekends away from the friends? **CARD 7:** Can/should you encourage taking up interests/former friends that have been abandoned? **CARD 8:** Does your child want different things now from life/a different kind of future? How can you steer this? **CARD 9:** Will this phase end if you do not intervene?

What you should use:

The twenty-two Major cards and the sixteen Court cards.

When:

The last day of a month.

IF YOUR TEEN IS OBSESSIVELY IN LOVE WITH A USER OR LOSER, AND WANTS TO MOVE OUT

Purpose and background information:

If your teen has turned their back on friends, family, study, and interests for this love.

Card 1: Should you forbid your child to see this person/if necessary, keep them home except when at school? **Card 2:** Is there anyone they will listen to? **Card 3:** Should you invite the boy/girlfriend to visit your home or, if necessary, invite them to move in to keep the lid on the situation? **Card 4:** Should you avoid giving any criticism, whatever you are feeling? **Card 5:** If you keep the situation contained, will your child grow out of the relationship and/or will the relationship end naturally?

What you should use:
The full deck.

When:
The last day of a month.

Example:
Sue is sixteen and madly in love with an older college dropout who has already fathered a child. Whatever her parents say, Sue insists on spending all her time with him, neglecting studies,

staying out half the night with him, sometimes not coming home at all. She says if her parents keep her from seeing him, they will run away together.

Card 1: The Eight of Wands, suggesting if her parents ground Sue, she will most likely run away out of sheer defiance. **Card 2: The Hierophant.** Sue has always been close to her maternal grandfather, who has lived an adventurous life but is very wise. So far, her parents have kept him out of it to keep him from worrying. **Card 3: The Ten of Pentacles.** Bringing her boyfriend home may not only influence him for the better, but might help Sue to see him in the context of her formerly happy united family. **Card 4: Temperance.** So far, any criticism has proven counter-productive, with Sue rushing to her beloved's defense; so moderation and gentle questioning of what she feels about some of his antisocial behavior may help. **Card 5: The Ten of Wands,** the person staggering up the hill with all the wands. Once opposition has dropped, Sue will most likely cool her feelings as, she is very ambitious and wants to go to medical school.

IF YOUR TEENAGER SPENDS ALL THEIR TIME IN THEIR ROOM AND WILL NOT COME OUT, EVEN FOR MEALS

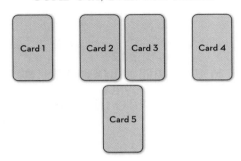

Purpose and background information:

When your normally sociable teen has become a recluse.

CARD 1: Can you pinpoint any love/school/emotional traumas to trigger this? **CARD 2:** Can you monitor/block undue all-night contact on the Internet/social media on unsuitable sites/chat rooms? **CARD 3:** Is your teen depressed/suffering from a phobia needing assessment/treatment? **CARD 4:** Should you insist on access to clean the room/check that food is not being hidden/signs of drug use? **CARD 5:** Is this an antisocial phase that will pass without pressure?

What you should use:

The forty Minor cards, Aces to Tens, and the sixteen Court cards.

When:

A Sunday morning, for clarity.

IF YOUR TEEN WANTS TO GO BACKPACKING AROUND THE WORLD AFTER COLLEGE, BUT YOU WORRY THEY WILL NOT COPE

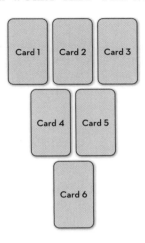

Purpose and background information:

If your teen has a vague plan for a gap year traveling with friends.

CARD 1: Is this a dream that will not get off the ground? **CARD 2:** Is your teen independent and resourceful/totally dependent on room service? **CARD 3:** With the right safeguards, could this be the making of your teen? **CARD 4:** Should you get involved with planning so you won't worry so much? **CARD 5:** Should you explore, with your child, applying for student visas for a working holiday/voluntary work? **CARD 6:** Do you have friends/relatives overseas to act as safe havens/can you arrange an organized exchange visit?

What you should use:

The forty Minor cards, Aces to Tens, and the sixteen Court cards.

When:

When the moon is in Sagittarius, it's time for adventure.

311

IF YOUR TEEN HAS DREAMS OF FAME AND FORTUNE TO THE EXCLUSION OF EVERYTHING ELSE

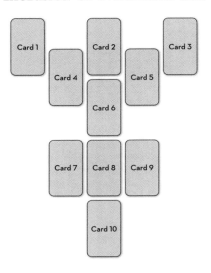

Purpose and background information:

When your teen is obsessed with celebrity/becoming a TV reality-show star or winning a TV talent show.

CARD 1: Without shattering dreams, can you suggest alternative high-profile moneymaking careers? **CARD 2:** Should you watch reality and TV talent shows with your teenager, gently highlighting negativity, jealousy, and lack of privacy on air and afterward? **CARD 3:** Should you help your teen to develop the necessary skills to enter a talent show/reality show, so they see how hard it is to get the break? **CARD 4:** Should you together explore practicalities/how to make sample videos/apply? **CARD 5:** Can you find details of celebrities/talent-show winners who faded after their fifteen minutes of fame? **CARD 6:** Should you introduce exciting activities in sport/theatre/dance groups, etc., to counteract the boredom-with-life factor? **CARD 7:** Should you barter tickets to concerts in return for school results achieved? **CARD 8:** Can you offer training in the performing arts/beauty fields to direct this passion in a more realistic way? **CARD 9:**

Will your teen succeed as a celebrity? **CARD 10:** Will the desire fade away naturally?

What you should use:

The full deck.

When:

When a particular reality/talent show blots out real life.

312

IF YOUR ADULT CHILDREN WILL NOT LEAVE HOME, OR HAVE RETURNED AFTER HAVING LEFT HOME

Purpose and background information:

When you hoped to be free, you find yourself subsidizing and servicing overgrown baby birds.

CARD 1: Are you willing to forgo rent so your child/ren can save for their own home? **CARD 2:** How can you impose limits on room service/suggest a sensible payment for food/extra utilities? **CARD 3:** Should/how can you insist on a fair division of chores/household responsibilities? **CARD 4:** Should you impose a time limit or suggest alternatives such as flat-sharing/house-sitting? **CARD 5:** How can you maintain privacy so you can share the space amicably?

What you should use:

The forty Minor cards, Aces to Tens, and the sixteen Court cards.

When:

When tensions are rising.

313

IF A SPITEFUL OR NEEDY ADULT STEPCHILD IS EMOTIONALLY AND FINANCIALLY BLACKMAILING YOUR PARTNER

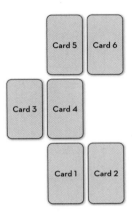

Purpose and background information:
When the adult stepchild drives a wedge between you and your partner/drains their finances.

CARD 1: Has this always been an issue/is it worsening because of a change in the stepchild's life? **CARD 2:** Does the other birth parent cause trouble/encourage this greediness/neediness? **CARD 3:** Why does your partner feel obliged to respond to demands, however unreasonable? **CARD 4:** Can you present a united front/deal with the stepchild yourself? **CARD 5:** Should the stepchild be actively encouraged to become financially and emotionally more independent? **CARD 6:** Can/will this be resolved sooner rather than later?

What you should use:
The twenty-two Major cards and the sixteen Court cards.

When:
At a waning moon.

314

IF YOUR GRANDCHILDREN LIVE FAR AWAY AND YOU ARE MISSING THEIR GROWING-UP

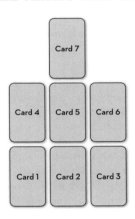

Purpose and background information:
If you aren't getting enough close contact.

CARD 1: Is there a gap in the rest of your life you need to fill that makes this loss seem worse? **CARD 2:** Is there a chance they/you may move nearer soon? **CARD 3:** Can/should you regularly book accommodations near the grandchildren/buy a camper van so you can entertain them? **CARD 4:** As they get older, can you fix trips with your grandchildren/for them to spend part of the holiday with you? **CARD 5:** Can you make even greater use of social media/Skype/emails? **CARD 6:** Can/should you create a separate life/new activities/quality time with your partner/friends? **CARD 7:** Should you focus on the benefits of quality time with grandchildren as something precious to be celebrated, not as a loss?

What you should use:
The full deck.

When:
On a significant date when you cannot be together.

315
IF YOU ARE DENIED ACCESS TO GRANDCHILDREN BY A VINDICTIVE FAMILY MEMBER

Purpose and background information:
When a relationship breakup/hostile new partner prevents contact.

CARD 1: Should you try one more time for peace? **CARD 2:** What is the motive for depriving you of contact? **CARD 3:** Should you try official mediation? **CARD 4:** Should you explore legal channels? **CARD 5:** Should you challenge the partner head-on? **CARD 6:** Should you wait for a resolution? **CARD 7:** Should you go along to school events uninvited? **CARD 8:** If lies are being told/gifts returned, could other family members/friends intervene? **CARD 9:** Will the situation soon improve?

What you should use:
The full deck.

When:
On a special birthday/anniversary.

316
IF YOUR CHILDREN AND GRANDCHILDREN ARE TOO BUSY TO CONTACT YOU

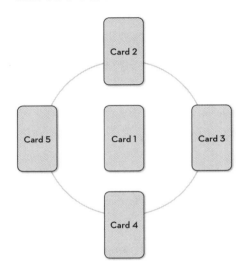

Purpose and background information:
When you hardly ever hear from your grandchildren/get invited by your children.

CARD 1: Should you send more invitations, even if rejected or ignored? **CARD 2:** Can you take emotion out of the situation, avoiding guilt/blame, however justifiable? **CARD 3:** Should you be less available for last-minute requests for babysitting/money, etc.? **CARD 4:** Should you make your life rich and fulfilling so the family is a welcome bonus/not the center of your world? **CARD 5:** Should you use social media to send news to the grandchildren, no matter how unresponsive they are?

What you should use:
The twenty-two Major cards and the sixteen Court cards.

When:
When you are let down at the last minute.

317
IF YOUR LONGED-FOR RETIREMENT IS SEEN AS FREE BABYSITTING FOR GRANDCHILDREN 24/7 BY ADULT CHILDREN

Purpose and background information:
When you adore your grandchildren but have your own plans for retirement.

Card 1: How can you avoid the guilt/obligation trap?
Card 2: Can/should you state what you can offer without the need to justify or explain? **Card 3:** Can you fix your timetable to be available for emergencies? **Card 4:** Should you plan a major holiday/home move to set the scene from the start? **Card 5:** Should you dispel assumptions by other relatives/partner that you will step into babysitting 24/7? **Card 6:** Should you sometimes see your children/son- and daughter-in-law without the grandchildren?

What you should use:
The forty Minor cards, Aces to Tens, and the sixteen Court cards.

When:
Well before your retirement.

318
TO STAY INDEPENDENTLY IN YOUR OWN HOME IF YOUR ADULT CHILDREN ARE PRESSURIZING YOU TO MOVE IN WITH THEM AND INVEST IN THEIR PROPERTY

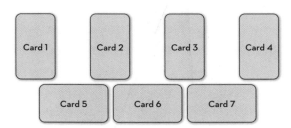

Purpose and background information:
When your life and independence are being taken over, although you are hale and hearty.

Card 1: What would be the advantages for you of moving in with your child? **Card 2:** What would be the disadvantages for you? **Card 3:** What would be the advantages for your children having you invest/living so close? **Card 4:** Have you considered future strategies/support for independent living should you/your partner become frail? **Card 5:** Should you, if you accept, insist on an entirely self-contained annex/part of the home? **Card 6:** Could you retain privacy from resident children and grandchildren? **Card 7:** Are there emotional pressures on you to accept that might blind you to financial implications of investing in their home?

What you should use:
The full deck.

When:
A Wednesday, for a clear head.

319

IF YOU WANT TO MOVE OVERSEAS OR TO THE OTHER END OF THE COUNTRY, BUT YOUR ADULT CHILDREN WANT YOU TO STAY CLOSE

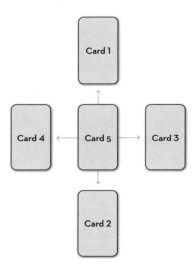

Purpose and background information:

If it is time for you/and your partner to fulfil a lifetime dream.

CARD 1: How can you avoid guilt/reproaches if you are not around so much? **CARD 2:** Can you find a property with sufficient room for the family to come and stay regularly when you move? **CARD 3:** Should you postpone your move, and do you want to? **CARD 4:** How can you reassure your family that you will always hop on a plane in an emergency? **CARD 5:** If you give up your dream, will you always regret it?

What you should use:

The forty Minor cards, Aces to Tens.

When:

When you are making plans for the future.

320

IF YOU ARE CAUGHT BETWEEN CARING FOR GRANDCHILDREN AND ELDERLY PARENTS AND WANT SOME TIME FOR YOURSELF AND YOUR PARTNER

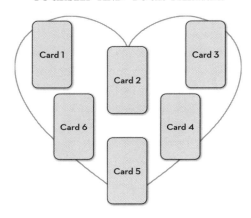

Purpose and background information:

When you feel you are disappearing underneath the needs of others.

CARD 1: Why do/should you feel obliged to fulfill everyone's needs? **CARD 2:** Can/should any of the people you care for do more for themselves? **CARD 3:** Can you identify which are priorities/necessities and which aren't? **CARD 4:** Can/should you consider more social care/sheltered housing for your parents/ask your children to fix outside childcare for the grandchildren? **CARD 5:** Should/can you prioritize yourself/yourself and your partner more as essentials to keep the family wheel turning? **CARD 6:** Should you plan regular breaks, making other relatives/social care help more while you are away?

What you should use:

The full deck.

When:

When you are getting stressed and unwell.

CHAPTER 21

HEALTH AND HEALING SPREADS

Lucky cards for health and healing Spreads:

Major Cards: The Magician, the High Priestess, the Hierophant, Strength, Temperance, the Sun, the Moon, the Star, Judgment/Rebirth.

Minor Cards: All the Aces; Ace of Swords is good for successful surgery; Two of Wands; Threes of Pentacles, Cups, and Wands; Three of Swords for overcoming fears and phobias; Four of Swords for saying the worst will not happen; Five of Pentacles; Five of Wands; Sixes of Wands and Swords; Sevens of Pentacles and Wands; Eight of Cups; Nine and Ten of Wands.

Court Cards: All the Pages/Princesses and Knights/ Princes for recovery; Page and Knight of Swords for recovery from surgery.

About the Health and Healing Spreads:

Ones and twos for quick answers and options. Threes for growth of health, fours for stability, five for healing, surgery, and alternative remedies, sixes for emotional issues, sevens for unhoped-for results, nines and above for major illnesses and complex questions.

321
THE OVERCOMING-ANXIETY SPREAD

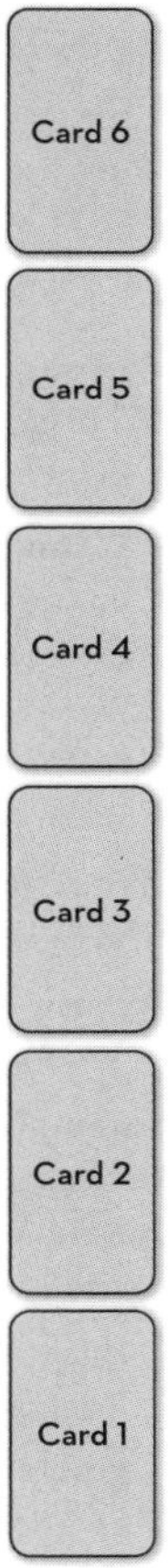

Purpose and background information:
When you are constantly anxious, but do not want to take calming pills.

CARD 1: Is your anxiety triggered by external circumstances, or does it come from within?
CARD 2: Who or what situation makes it worse? Can you avoid these? **CARD 3:** Who or what helps to calm the anxiety? **CARD 4:** What instant strategies can you develop when you feel anxiety rising?
CARD 5: Would a change of lifestyle/location/ career/relationship relieve the problem? **CARD 6:** What new activity/desired situation suddenly becomes possible without the anxiety?

What you should use:
The forty Minor cards, Aces to Tens, and the six Court cards.

When:
Any time during the waning moon.

Card 6

Card 5

Card 4

Card 3

Card 2

Card 1

322
WILL YOUR HEALTH IMPROVE?

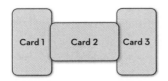

Purpose and background information:
When you are chronically ill, but no organic or medical solution can be found.

CARD 1: Is there anything in your life/lifestyle causing undue stress? **CARD 2:** Should you explore alternative energy therapies such as acupuncture, acupressure, reiki, kinesiology, or meditation classes to release blocks and restore energy? **CARD 3:** Will your health improve naturally when your life is in balance?

What you should use:
The twenty-two Major cards.

When:
A Wednesday, day of health and healing.

Example:
Sandra suffers from an energy-deficit syndrome that has been getting worse since her mother's death. Physicians could find no cause.

CARD 1: The Death card, which didn't mean she was going to die, but rather her mother's death had triggered a physical problem, understandable grief, but maybe something additional connected with the death holding her back. **CARD 2:** The Two of Pentacles. What was Sandra trying to keep in balance? She said whatever alternative energy therapy she tried was marred by constantly bubbling resentment against her sister, who had always bullied her. On the death of their mother, her sister had taken all the jewelry, half of which had been promised to Sandra. **CARD 3:** Strength, which showed a woman closing the jaws of the lion rather than attacking it. Strength is a good sign for improved health. All Sandra wanted was her late grandmother's engagement ring and wedding ring. Sandra is getting

married and really wants to wear them at the ceremony. So she stood up to her sister, saying her sister could have the pick of the valuable items but the wedding and engagement rings were Sandra's. Her sister handed them over and Sandra's health began to improve almost instantly.

323
WHEN YOUR ANXIETY IS MANIFESTED AS A PHOBIA THAT SERIOUSLY LIMITS YOUR LIFE

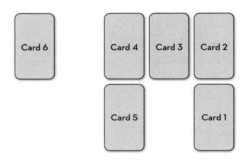

Purpose and background information:
When claustrophobia, agoraphobia, or fear of eating in public, etc., are affecting your work, family, and/or social life

CARD 1: Who or what is the hidden cause of this life-crippling phobia? **CARD 2:** Does a particular person, situation, or place trigger a bad attack? **CARD 3:** What practical lifestyle changes/strategies would reduce the intensity of the fear? **CARD 4:** What emotional/spiritual life changes/therapies would alleviate the occurrence? **CARD 5:** Should you seek (more) professional help/counseling/cognitive behavioral or past life therapy, or should you work on the problem yourself? **CARD 6:** What is your greatest present quality/strength that will move you toward a happy life/prevent the problem recurring?

What you should use:
The full deck.

When:
When you have an invitation that you really want to accept.

324
THE FOUR ANGELS SPREAD FOR HEALING

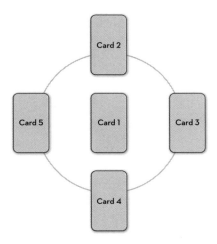

Purpose and background information:

When you are seeking healing remedies or progress in an acute or ongoing illness, whether of the body or the mind.

CARD 1 (in the center): Yourself, where you want to be health-wise within the next six months to a year. **CARD 2:** Zadkiel, Archangel of gentleness, with sky-blue wings, revealing what positive life changes will remove obstacles to healing and health. **CARD 3:** Raphael, with his yellow halo and green healing ray, for helpful people/better responses to existing treatment that will aid healing. **CARD 4:** Mumiah, shimmering white angel of medicine and medical research, conventional and alternative, for a new kind of intervention or treatment. **CARD 5:** Green-winged Rehael, Angel of health, for naturally occurring immune system/metabolic improvements.

What you should use:

The twenty-two Major cards.

When:

A Sunday morning for Michael, Archangel of the Sun and new beginnings.

325
TO OVERCOME FOOD ISSUES

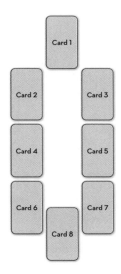

Purpose and background information:

When bingeing/excessive dieting or food disorders are badly affecting your life.

CARD 1: What triggers food issues in daily life? **CARD 2:** What/who has made you feel bad about yourself by insensitive words/teasing/bullying? **CARD 3:** Are you/ should you be daunted by impossible media images of body perfection? **CARD 4:** Have feast and famine/weight issues/yoyo dieting affected you all your life? **CARD 5:** Can/ should you overcome the problem alone, or should you seek counseling/healthful-eating organizations? **CARD 6:** Do you exercise excessively to counteract overeating/perceived image problems? **CARD 7:** Should you jettison people or situations from your life where you are made to feel bad about yourself? **CARD 8:** What would make you happy, regardless of your shape and size, and how can you attain it?

What you should use:

The full deck.

When:

After the failure of yet another diet.

326
HOW CAN YOU SUCCESSFULLY GIVE UP SMOKING?

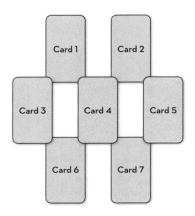

Purpose and background information:
When you need to stop smoking but struggle to do so.

Card 1: If you have tried and failed before, what caused the lapse? **Card 2:** What stresses/triggers in your life prompt you to smoke/keep you smoking? **Card 3:** Do you need a cigarette substitute, electronic cigarettes, or nicotine patches, or should you go cold turkey? **Card 4:** Do you need/want help/support from a clinic or counselor/group? **Card 5:** How to overcome relapses on the way. **Card 6:** Will you succeed this time/how long will it take? **Card 7:** How to make quitting permanent.

What you should use:
The forty Minor cards, Aces to Tens.

When:
When your health is suffering in small ways.

327
SHOULD YOU GO FOR SURGERY, OR TRY OTHER WAYS OF DEALING WITH A HEALTH PROBLEM?

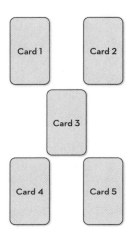

Purpose and background information:
When surgery is advised but there are lots of risks and side effects.

Card 1: Do you need treatment soon, or do you want to let time take its course? **Card 2:** What are the advantages of surgery? **Card 3:** Are these potentially outweighed by the risks of surgical intervention? **Card 4:** Can/should you get independent advice as to the best course? **Card 5:** Do you want to set a time limit on the effectiveness of non-surgical intervention before considering surgery?

What you should use:
The twenty-two Major cards.

When:
The beginning of a month.

328
WILL YOUR OPERATION BE A SUCCESS?

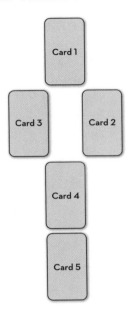

Purpose and background information:
When you are scheduled for surgery but are worried about the results.

CARD 1: Do the potential benefits outweigh the disadvantages/risks? **CARD 2:** Have you talked/should you discuss the operation, recovery, and longer-term prognosis with a medical expert? **CARD 3:** Are you confident in the surgeon/hospital/after-care you will be experiencing, or do you need to explore other hospitals? **CARD 4:** Are you/can you become as fit mentally, emotionally, and physically for the best chance of success? **CARD 5:** Will your operation be a total, or only a partial success? And will your recovery be swift, or will it take time?

What you should use:
The forty Minor cards, Aces to Tens, and the sixteen Court cards.

When:
A Wednesday, for successful surgery.

329
IF YOU CATCH ONE MINOR ILLNESS AFTER ANOTHER

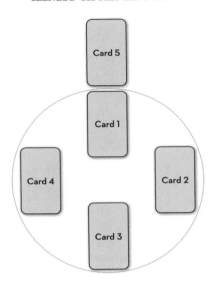

Purpose and background information:
If you frequently feel unwell.

CARD 1: Is there ongoing stress or an emotional drain in your life? **CARD 2:** Have you/should you be tested for allergies? **CARD 3:** Are you depressed or anxious, such that illness enables you to opt out for a time? **CARD 4:** Should you be taking extra dietary supplements/more exercise to boost your immune system? **CARD 5:** Should you consider getting more sunshine, artificial or actual, to boost your immune system or energy-boosting therapies/crystals/reiki, etc., to put body, mind, and spirit in balance?

What you should use:
The twenty-two Major cards.

When:
The beginning of a month.

330
IS YOUR CURRENT TREATMENT OR HEALING THERAPY RIGHT FOR YOU?

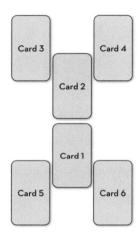

Purpose and background information:
If you have been having the same treatment for a while and it has declined in effectiveness.

CARD 1: Should you go for a reassessment with your physician/alternative practitioner to see why your body is no longer responding like it was? **CARD 2:** If your physician/ alternative practitioner is indifferent or not interested in new research or methods, is it time for a change of practitioner? **CARD 3:** Have you/should you research the Internet for the latest proven treatments and then ask your doctor for them? **CARD 4:** Do you need additional boosts to stimulate your metabolism, exercise/a more healthful diet/regular meditation/a new form of energy therapy? **CARD 5:** Do you need a lifestyle improvement/more time focusing on your needs rather than the needs of others? **CARD 6:** Is there an online/local group for people with your condition to exchange ideas/practical suggestions?

What you should use:
The full deck.

When:
The beginning of a month, in the early morning.

331
IF YOU ARE PLANNING COSMETIC SURGERY OR DENTISTRY BUT WONDER IF THE SURGICAL INTERVENTION WILL HARM YOU

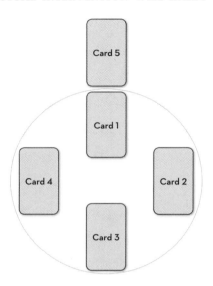

Purpose and background information:
When you are torn between improving your looks and fears of the process.

CARD 1: Will having the procedure give you sufficient new confidence that will outweigh any negative aspects? **CARD 2:** Are you seriously worried about the surgery and after- effects? **CARD 3:** Will you regret it if you do not go ahead? **CARD 4:** Should you wait until you are more certain? **CARD 5:** Is it now or never?

What you should use:
The twenty-two Major cards.

When:
When a possible date for surgery is offered.

332

IF YOU HAVE AN ENERGY-DEPLETING CONDITION SUCH AS FIBROMYALGIA AND PEOPLE SAY YOU ARE JUST LAZY

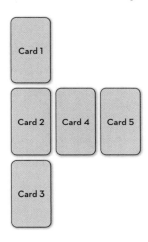

Purpose and background information:

When you have a debilitating condition with few visible symptoms.

CARD 1: Does the negative attitude of some people make your condition worse? **CARD 2:** Do you have understanding clinicians, or are they part of the problem? **CARD 3:** Are you able to work so you aren't under pressure to perform on bad days, or should you seek the right work at any cost? **CARD 4:** Should you use alternative remedies/practitioners to balance your body/energize you? **CARD 5:** Can you see an end to your problems? How soon will you find natural relief?

What you should use:

The forty Minor cards, Aces to Tens, and the sixteen Court cards.

When:

After unfair criticism.

333

IF YOU HAVE EXPERIENCED A LIFE-CHANGING INJURY OR ILLNESS

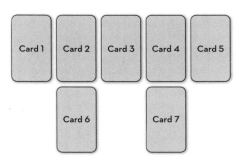

Purpose and background information:

When life cannot go back to what it was, what is the way forward?

CARD 1: Should/can you claim/fight for compensation/special allowances to make life easier? **CARD 2:** What extra help should/can you access to enable you to live as independently as possible? **CARD 3:** Is this a chance to start a new career/study path that can use as-yet-untapped abilities? **CARD 4:** What has been lost that cannot be replaced? **CARD 5:** What new strengths do you have to build a new different but fulfilling life? **CARD 6:** What is the short-term aim that can be attained? **CARD 7:** What is the longer-term goal to be striven for?

What you should use:

The full deck.

When:

As dawn breaks.

334
IF YOU HAVE A CHRONIC CONDITION THAT FREQUENTLY FLARES UP

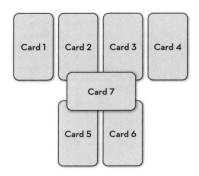

Purpose and background information:
When you can never be certain whether you will be well enough to function satisfactorily at work or socially.

CARD 1: Are there certain stressful situations or people who make the condition worse? **CARD 2:** Are there allergies that throw your system out of balance? **CARD 3:** Can you rearrange your everyday life to avoid stress and allergic reactions? **CARD 4:** Do you/have you tried and tested medication/therapies you can call on when a flare-up is imminent, or do you need more help with this from physicians/therapists? **CARD 5:** Can/should you consider moving and adopting a more natural lifestyle? **CARD 6:** Are there new treatments/preventatives you should request? **CARD 7:** Is there a center of excellence for treating your condition in another state or overseas?

What you should use:
The full deck.

When:
Any evening after sunset.

335
CAN YOU HELP A LOVED ONE TO OVERCOME ALCOHOL OR SUBSTANCE ABUSE?

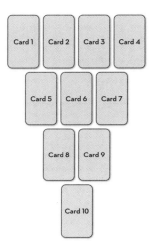

Purpose and background information:
When your loved one's addiction is of great concern to you.

CARD 1: Does the person want to be helped, or is any aid rejected/just a temporary fix? **CARD 2:** Is the abuse seriously affecting family life and finances? If so, what should you do? **CARD 3:** Is the abuse preventing the person from working/living a normal life? **CARD 4:** Are there counterproductive undesirable friends/pushers with undue influence? **CARD 5:** Can you get more help for yourself/the family to cope? **CARD 6:** Is it time for tough love/putting limits on the effects of antisocial behavior? **CARD 7:** Should you/the person stay away from people until the problem is resolved/help is accepted? **CARD 8:** Is the relationship/trust too far fractured to mend? **CARD 9:** What is the realistic prognosis in six months? **CARD 10:** What is the realistic prognosis in twelve months?

What you should use:
The full deck.

When:
After continued promises to stop the abuse prove worthless.

TO HELP A CHILD WITH COMMUNICATION OR SOCIAL DIFFICULTIES, SUCH AS AUTISM, ASPERGER'S, OR ADHD

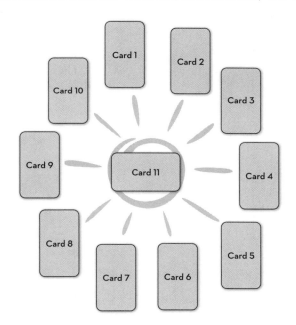

Purpose and background information:

When you are feeling isolated and tired of outsiders criticizing you and your child.

CARD 1: Are you satisfied with the diagnosis you have received, or do you want a second opinion, even if this is resisted by the experts? **CARD 2:** Are you getting the best possible educational/social resources, or do you need to fight even harder? **CARD 3:** Are you unhappy with being offered medication/fobbed off with glorified childminding? Do you need to research and demand alternatives? **CARD 4:** Should you move to a new location if necessary to get the best treatment/facilities for your child? **CARD 5:** Are there clubs/holiday activities for other children with similar issues? **CARD 6:** Can you at the same time insist on integration/

involvement in community activities? **CARD 7:** Can you ignore the critics/spread awareness to those who say it's down to your own bad childrearing? **CARD 8:** Do you have/can you insist on a long-term educational/social program so your child can live an integrated life as s/he grows up? **CARD 9** Can you insist that your child be treated as a whole person/not a condition/label with limitations? **CARD 10:** Can you fix activities so your child's unique talents can be developed? **CARD 11:** Are there any receptive family members/close friends to give you a break?

What you should use:

The full deck.

When:

You become desperate for answers.

337
TO ENCOURAGE A CHILD WITH PHYSICAL DISABILITIES OR A DEBILITATING ILLNESS TO REACH THEIR FULL POTENTIAL

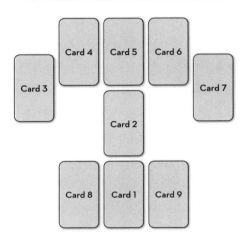

Purpose and background information:

If your child or teenager is limited by facilities or resources.

Card 1: What limitations physically, educationally, and socially are holding your child back? **Card 2:** What are your child's special gifts that—with the right resources/access to facilities—would lead to a fulfilling future/career? **Card 3:** What legal/official guidelines are being ignored where you can press for action? **Card 4:** Is there a website/local group of parents with similar issues? If not, can you organize one? **Card 5:** What holiday activities/residential events can be arranged for your child if necessary, involving additional pressure on providers? **Card 6:** Are you getting adequate backup from family/social and disability services so you can enjoy your child as well as physically care for him/her? **Card 7:** Are there any extra desired resources/facilities you could spearhead a campaign to obtain? **Card 8:** What is the main short-term improvement you are seeking? **Card 9:** What is the long-term aim for an independent and fulfilling future for your child?

What you should use:

The forty Minor cards, Aces to Tens, and the sixteen Court cards.

When:

When you hit a barrier and are told it cannot be fixed.

338
TO GET HELP FOR YOUR OWN PHYSICAL CHALLENGES TO WHICH YOU FEEL ENTITLED IN ORDER TO LIVE A MORE FULFILLING LIFE

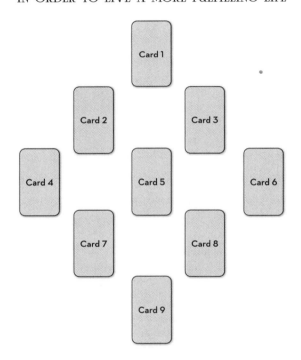

Purpose and background information:

If your career/travels/social life are being hindered by lack of facilities even though legislated for.

Card 1: What is the main physical obstacle or unspoken prejudice in your working life that holds you back? **Card 2:** How can this be overcome, using both official means and dialog? **Card 3:** What is the main obstacle in your home because of lack of access and appropriate technology? **Card 4:** What are the main obstacles in your social life and travel plans? **Card 5:** What resources/funding is available given pressure by you? **Card 6:** How can obstacles be conquered to benefit you and others similarly physically afflicted? **Card 7:** Can you/should you be campaigning for improvements in attitudes and facilities? **Card 8:** What is your main plan for the year ahead in every aspect of your life? **Card 9:** What is your ultimate dream for the next five years?

What you should use:
The full deck.

When:
The beginning of a significant week for you, good or bad.

339
WHEN AN OLDER PERSON'S MEMORY IS FADING

Purpose and background information:
When deterioration can no longer be ignored.

Card 1: Is the problem causing safety/mobility issues if the person lives alone/with a partner of similar age? **Card 2:** Is daily care/supervision now proving a strain on you/the main family carer? **Card 3:** Are there other relatives who can/should help out so it's not left to you/an aging partner? **Card 4:** Is it possible to get, however hard to ask for/insist upon, respite care/additional social services input? **Card 5:** Are there other physical problems/issues, such as falls, that are making independent living unsafe? **Card 6:** Should sheltered housing/residential care be considered, perhaps where a couple can still live together if desired? **Card 7:** Can you be tough with any family members who are opting out of the issue? **Card 8:** Can you put aside any guilt/blame issues offloaded on you to look at the situation practically? **Card 9:** If residential care is needed, can you find a place where memory is stimulated/there is loving individual care? **Card 10:** How should/can residential care be financed without the burden falling on one person? **Card 11:** Can you gradually prepare the family/the partner to make a life for what may be a long road?

What to use:
The whole deck.

When:
When alarm bells are ringing about near accidents/the relative wandering off.

340
IF YOU ARE UNDERGOING INVASIVE TREATMENT AND DO NOT KNOW IF YOU SHOULD CONTINUE

Purpose and background information:

When the treatment and side effects sometimes seem worse than the illness.

CARD 1: Will the treatment offer a cure/major remission, or are lasting results uncertain? **CARD 2:** Do negative side effects last between treatments, or do you get periods of welcome relief? **CARD 3:** Have you/should you talk to different clinicians/surgeons for a second opinion as to the best way forward? **CARD 4:** Is there a center of excellence in another state/overseas where you could get better advice/treatment? **CARD 5:** What are the predicted effects of stopping the treatment? **CARD 6:** Would you sooner have a good quality of life now and reconsider treatment later? **CARD 7:** What is your preferred option for treatment/non-treatment, regardless of the pressures from medics/family, etc.? **CARD 8:** Are you trying to get keep fit/eating healthfully/adding alternative non-contraindicated treatments to strengthen your immune system?

What you should use:

The forty Minor cards, Aces to Tens, and the sixteen Court cards.

When:

At a decision point.

341
IF YOU ARE CONSTANTLY IN PHYSICAL PAIN.

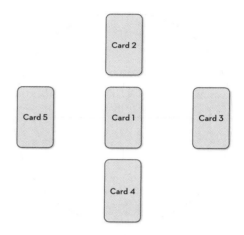

Purpose and background information:

When life is a constant round of painkillers.

CARD 1: Can the cause of the pain be resolved by surgery/treatment or managed effectively? **CARD 2:** Are you receiving effective pain control from a monitoring pain clinic, or just given ever-stronger painkillers? **CARD 3:** What extra/better pain management can you find interstate/via new research on the Internet? **CARD 4:** Will alternative methods such as acupuncture/acupressure/authentic energy therapies provide relief? **CARD 5:** Would meditation/visualization/mindfulness methods/Reiki, etc., help?

What to use:

The twenty-two Major cards.

When:

The end of a month.

342
FOR DEALING WITH EMOTIONAL PAIN AFTER ABUSE OR TRAUMA

Purpose and background information:
When life goes on, but you cannot move forward.

CARD 1: Is there any justice/recompense that would make you feel that you were being taken seriously? **CARD 2:** Are loved ones/colleagues trying to move you forward before you are ready/should you take more time out? **CARD 3:** Do you still see the person/are reminded of the trauma? If so, should you move away, or outface them? **CARD 4:** Are there support groups/expert counselors who can help you work through the trauma? **CARD 5:** Can you use your experience to help/counsel others in future? **CARD 6:** Though life cannot be the same, what good things lie ahead for you?

What you should use:
The twenty-two Major cards and the sixteen Court cards.

When:
A reminder of what you have endured occurs.

343
IF YOU ARE SERIOUSLY DEPRESSED

Purpose and background information:
When everything seems hopeless.

CARD 1: Have you always suffered from depression, or has this been triggered/made worse by recent trauma/major betrayal or setback? **CARD 2:** Are you seeing/can you find a psychologist/physician you trust who doesn't fob you off with a prescription? **CARD 3:** Are you contented with the support you are receiving, counseling/support groups on- and offline/good friends or family, or do you need to look elsewhere? **CARD 4:** Do you have emergency numbers, whether a help line/friends or family you can turn to 24/7? **CARD 5:** Are there people/situations who make you feel worse/contribute to the problem? **CARD 6:** How can you remove them from your life? **CARD 7:** Can you find something good in your life to develop/cling to in bad times? **CARD 8:** What is your goal within six months that you can work toward in good times and bad? **CARD 9:** What major changes in study/career/general health/fitness could turn your life around?

What you should use:
The full deck.

When:
When the moon is growing in the sky.

344

IF YOU ARE A HEALER BUT ARE ALWAYS EXHAUSTED

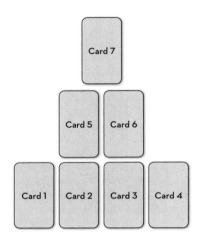

Purpose and background information:

If you take on your clients' pain and sorrows.

CARD 1: Are there particular clients with whom you become overwhelmed? If so, why? **CARD 2:** Are you protecting yourself sufficiently before healing/cleansing your energies afterward, or do you have such a busy schedule that you never have time? **CARD 3:** Should you use different kinds of healing with an inbuilt shield, such as crystals? **CARD 4:** Should you cut back/step away from healing for a time until your energies are fully restored? **CARD 5:** Should you combine healing with counseling/divination to reduce the intensity of sessions? **CARD 6:** Should you fill your everyday life with pleasurable interests and activities? **CARD 7:** Should you learn to receive as well as give healing?

What you should use:

The twenty-two Major cards.

When:

When healing becomes a burden, not a blessing.

345

IF YOU ARE TOLD YOU ARE A NATURAL HEALER BUT DON'T KNOW HOW TO DEVELOP YOUR GIFTS

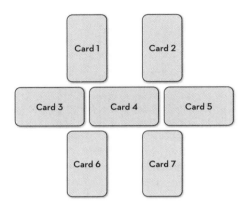

Purpose and background information:

When your healing powers seem random and sometimes disturbing.

CARD 1: From when you were young, have you soothed people and animals by touch or by talking to them? **CARD 2:** Do you want to develop your powers professionally, or to use them in your everyday life? **CARD 3:** Would you like to join classes/a healing circle, or let your own healing powers develop naturally? **CARD 4:** Are your greatest gifts with children/animals/people who are physically sick/emotionally distressed, or all of these? **CARD 5:** At what point would you consider offering healing/advertising and working professionally? **CARD 6:** Do you believe your healing powers come from God/the Goddess, angels/your spirit guides/past lives/the universal life force? **CARD 7:** What protection do/should you draw around yourself: angelic light, prayer/crystals, or calling on your guides?

What you should use:

The twenty-two Major cards.

When:

When you can no longer ignore the healing powers flowing through you.

346
SHOULD YOU CHARGE FOR HEALING?

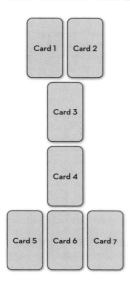

Purpose and background information:
When people say you should give your spiritual gifts without payment, but you still have to pay the grocery bills.

Card 1: Do you plan/want to make a career/business involving healing? **Card 2:** Would you treat anyone in need without payment if they needed it but were unable to afford it? **Card 3:** Should you put a monetary value on your time and resources to give your time/energy for healing without trying to hold a paid job as well? **Card 4:** Would your detractors work without payment at their profession? **Card 5:** Will people value your gifts more because they offer money in exchange? **Card 6:** Can you also make money through teaching/sales of crystals, etc., to supplement your income? **Card 7:** Should you ignore those jealous of your growing success and reputation?

What you should use:
The forty Minor cards, Aces to Tens.

When:
A Wednesday, day for overcoming jealousy.

347
IF YOU KNOW YOU CAN HEAL OTHERS, BUT FIND THAT CLASSES JUST AREN'T WORKING

Purpose and background information:
When you are trying to learn accepted healing techniques, but they are blocking your gifts.

Card 1: Do you know what to do without being told consciously? **Card 2:** Do you sense that your healing wisdom is coming from past lives/spirit guides/angels? **Card 3:** If none of the methods you have learned feels quite right, should you establish your own way of healing? **Card 4:** If your unique way of healing is producing good results, should you trust yourself? **Card 5:** Should you create, over time, your own unique system that you can teach to others? **Card 6:** Should you ask for guidance from your angels, guides, and ancestors, some of whom were probably healers?

What you should use:
The full deck.

When:
When you feel the presence of your angels and guides.

348
IF YOU ARE SUFFERING FROM OBSESSIVE-COMPULSIVE DISORDER

Purpose and background information:
If you feel locked into a cycle of repetitive actions that are spoiling your life.

CARD 1: What is most out of control in your life that you need to try to regain control over? **CARD 2:** Are there special triggers/people/situations you could avoid? **CARD 3:** Do you have good support from the medical profession/a sympathetic counselor? If not, can you seek support that works for you? **CARD 4:** Would meditation/mindfulness/cognitive behavioral techniques minimize compulsions in daily situations? **CARD 5:** Do you belong to a good on- and off-line support group? If not, can you create one? **CARD 6:** Can you develop practical coping strategies that work for you? **CARD 7:** Can you divert the feelings into fixing chaos and problems in others' lives?

What you should use:
The twenty-two Major cards.

When:
When you know you will be facing a trigger situation in the near future.

349
WHEN YOU HAVE AN INVISIBLE HEALTH/EMOTIONAL PROBLEM

Purpose and background information:
When no one believes that you are ill or you have a challenging health problem.

CARD 1: Should you explain to significant people/colleagues/managers/friends, etc., and not worry what the rest of the world says/thinks? **CARD 2:** Are there any special cards/badges you can obtain from your clinician/an official support group to show when you need to access facilities urgently? **CARD 3:** Can you raise awareness of invisible conditions through the media/social media so others are aware of the problem? **CARD 4:** Can you organize a local/statewide/national campaign on- or offline for the necessary facilities for other sufferers as well as yourself? **CARD 5:** Should you raise your own sense of entitlement so you do not feel self-conscious about asking for assistance/access to resources? **CARD 6:** Can you develop coping strategies for most contingencies so the problem doesn't interfere excessively with travel/social/working life? **CARD 7:** Is there any alternative new/conventional treatment/dietary change that can alleviate your condition?

What you should use:
The full deck.

When:
When you are tired of explaining to an unhelpful world.

350
IF YOU ARE BEING CHARGED AN EXCESSIVE AMOUNT FOR AN ALTERNATIVE THERAPY OR MEDICATION, BUT ARE TOLD THAT YOU NEED IT

Purpose and background information:

When the costs are mounting, but there seems no end in sight for the treatment.

CARD 1: Should you question the practitioner about how long the treatment needs to continue, not being fobbed off with vague promises? **CARD 2:** Should you contact the practitioner's association/go online in order to compare costs? **CARD 3:** Is your therapist encouraging emotional dependency on them/the treatments? **CARD 4:** Should you go for a second opinion in the same area of therapy? **CARD 5:** Should you take a relative/friend with you if you intend to terminate treatment, in case of undue pressure? **CARD 6:** Should you check online to see if similar treatment would be covered by insurance or if conventional medicine could help? **CARD 7:** Should you gradually reduce the frequency of treatment/medication, especially if you are being sold a lot of pills and potions (checking with another professional for possible side effects)?

What you should use:
The full deck.

When:
A Thursday, for truth and transparency.

351
IF YOU OR A CHILD HAVE A VERY RARE CONDITION AND YOU FEEL UNSUPPORTED

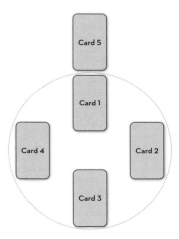

Purpose and background information:
When you keep drawing a blank on help and support.

CARD 1: Have you found any treatment center in any state/country that does specialize in this condition, with which you can make closer associations? **CARD 2:** Can you find a worldwide online group for the condition/start an online group? **CARD 3:** Can you raise awareness of the condition through media interest/writing a book on the human aspect of the illness? **CARD 4:** Can you obtain a grant/raise money locally so you/your child can visit the center of excellence for advice/treatment? **CARD 5:** Can you present all the facts/research to the main doctor treating you so they can offer the best-informed treatment available locally?

What you should use:
The fifty Minor cards, Aces to Tens, and the sixteen Court cards.

When:
When the moon is passing through Aquarius.

352
IF YOU HAVE MENTAL-HEALTH ISSUES

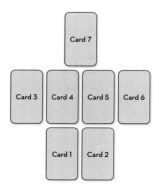

Purpose and background information:
When you are aware of the stigma still attached by some people to mental health.

CARD 1: Are you content with the present medical support/ medication/counseling you are receiving, or should you ask for more appropriate assistance? **CARD 2:** Are techniques such as meditation/mindfulness/cognitive behavioral therapy available? Do they help? Do you need new teachers/extra support? **CARD 3:** Are people who need to know, such as managers/colleagues/friends and family, there for you? **CARD 4:** Are any less-than-helpful people in your life from whom you need distancing, or seeking recourse if at work/ in education to official support against bullying? **CARD 5:** Are you obtaining all the resources/allowances you are entitled to? If not, who will help you fight for them? **CARD 6:** Are you raising awareness of mental-health issues through social media/the media to reduce stigma/fears by the uninitiated? **CARD 7:** Should you use your own experiences to train in counseling/psychology/psychotherapy, whether professionally or voluntarily?

What you should use:
The full deck.

When:
At the beginning of a month.

353
IF YOU SUFFER FROM ALLERGIES THAT SERIOUSLY RESTRICT YOUR LIFE

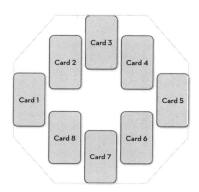

Purpose and background information:
If you have a major allergy or multiple allergies that seriously affect your life.

CARD 1: Have you/should you receive adequate testing for allergens to be identified? **CARD 2:** Do others in your working/social and home life know the antidotes/how to use them if an allergy becomes life-threatening? **CARD 3:** Do you have a safe diet/workable travel arrangements so you can still participate in life? **CARD 4:** Do you have access to a good specialist allergy clinic? If not, is one with an excellent reputation accessible for diagnosis/initial treatment? **CARD 5:** Are there emotional triggers/difficult people to avoid who trigger bad reactions/make an attack worse? **CARD 6:** Should you consider an alternative location/lifestyle away from pollutants and stress? **CARD 7:** Will you find the right alternative treatments/natural remedies/new research that will bring serious relief within the next year? **CARD 8:** Will new research/treatments bring a dramatic improvement within five years?

What you should use:
The full deck.

When:
After a bad attack.

CHAPTER 22

SPREADS FOR GOOD LUCK

Good cards for your good-luck Spreads:

Major Arcana: The Fool (taking a chance), the Magician, The Wheel of Fortune, the Sun, the Star.

Minor Arcana: Ace of Wands, Ace of Cups, Three of Cups, Seven of Pentacles, Eight of Pentacles, Eight of Wands, Nine of Pentacles, Ten of Pentacles, Ten of Cups.

Court Cards: Any Wands.

Remember, the Death card doesn't indicate bad luck, merely new beginnings; the Tower, freedom from restrictions; the Devil, that you're suppressing the desire for change; and the Swords cards represent facing and overcoming fears.

About good-luck Spreads:

Use one- to three-carders for quick questions; fours for stabilizing fortunes; fives for lucky speculation, being in the right place at the right time, and avoiding being tricked; sixes for emotional matters and increasing good fortune; sevens for changing bad luck and unexpected or desired good fortune; eight and above for seeking turning fortunes completely around and more complicated questions involving deciding one's own fate.

354
BRINGING GOOD LUCK INTO YOUR LIFE

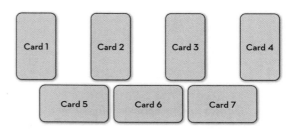

Purpose and background information:
If you need more good luck in your life.

CARD 1: In what area of your life do you most need good luck? **CARD 2:** How soon will this good luck come? **CARD 3:** What or who is holding you back from good fortune? **CARD 4:** In which part of your life will good fortune first come? **CARD 5:** How can you hasten good fortune? **CARD 6:** Who or what will help you attain good fortune? **CARD 7:** What is the hidden secret to your good fortune?

What you should use:
The twenty-two Major cards and the sixteen Court cards.

When:
At the crescent or waxing moon.

355
WILL YOUR BAD LUCK CHANGE SOON?

Purpose and background information:

When one thing after another goes wrong, making you feel jinxed.

CARD 1: Do you believe you are in the hands of fate? If so, is this true, or a perception? **CARD 2:** Is anyone causing your misfortune? **CARD 3:** Can you/how can you change your luck?

What you should use:

The twenty-two Major cards.

When:

A Friday or Saturday, both days of good fortune.

Example:

Murray had one disaster after another, losing his phone and his only set of car keys. Then his dog got sick and he had forgotten to renew the pet medical insurance. When running because he was late for work, having taken his dog to the vet, he slipped and hurt his ankle. He feels totally jinxed.

Murray picked the **Wheel of Fortune** for **CARD 1**, and that indicates a change in fortune for the better. More importantly, it says that we have to make efforts to avoid situations where things can go wrong.

CARD 2: Two of Pentacles. Murray realized he had been so busy that he was creating his own misfortune by not keeping an eye on his possessions, and not having backup car keys and ignoring the renewal notice for the pet insurance.

CARD 3: Ace of Pentacles. Murray needed to slow down and keep a check on the details of his life. Once he did this, his bad luck disappeared.

356
WHY ARE YOU ALWAYS UNLUCKY IN LOVE?

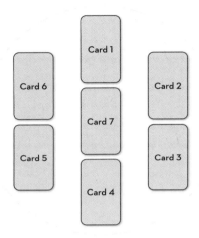

Purpose and background information:

If every relationship fails after a promising start.

CARD 1: Do you instantly fall in love and become as rapidly disillusioned? **CARD 2:** Should you focus on friendship and shared values/interests and allow a relationship to slowly grow? **CARD 3:** Have you simply not met the right person/ your twin soul and are settling for second best? **CARD 4:** Do you always go for the same kind of partner who checks all the boxes, rather than someone who makes you happy? **CARD 5:** Should you stop looking for love and just let it happen when it will? **CARD 6:** Will you be lucky and find love within the next year? **CARD 7:** Will it last forever?

What you should use:

The forty Minor cards, Aces to Tens, and the sixteen Court cards.

When:

A Friday, day of lasting love.

357
IF YOU EXPERIENCE ONE PIECE OF BAD LUCK
AFTER ANOTHER AND FEAR YOU ARE JINXED

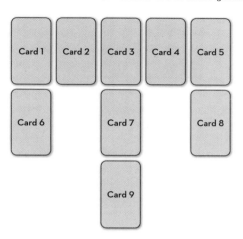

Purpose and background information:
When you are feeling spooked about your ongoing misfortune.

CARD 1: Was the original misfortune that started the cycle a miscalculation, the actions of someone else, or a random event? **CARD 2:** Did that make you lose confidence in your own judgment, leading to impulsive actions? **CARD 3:** Is there someone malicious/jealous of you who you fear has jinxed you? **CARD 4:** How can you practically deal with any detractors/critics/malicious people who make you feel jittery? **CARD 5:** Should you carry crystals/smudge your home/workplace/surround yourself with light/carry a lucky charm? (Smudging, a native American Indian tradition, is done by burning dried herbs and letting the smoke float around the house as a means of cleansing.) **CARD 6:** Should/can you take expert/impartial advice on future life/financial matters? **CARD 7:** Should you avoid any foreseeable risks/get-rich schemes/unwise temptations in love and life? **CARD 8:** What good luck will occur in the next six months to reverse the trend? **CARD 9:** Can you cultivate lucky/happy people and remove any negative influences in your life?

What you should use:
The full deck.

When:
After dark on the last day of the month.

358
WHY ARE YOU ALWAYS
UNLUCKY WITH MONEY?

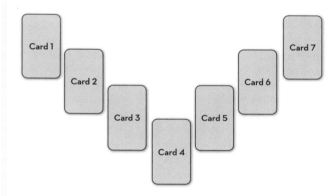

Purpose and background information:
If money seems to flow out the minute it comes in.

CARD 1: Are you simply overcommitted financially, rather than unlucky? **CARD 2:** Do you fall for hard-luck stories/are over-generous with friends and family? **CARD 3:** Do you invest/make major purchases of seeming bargains without checking facts and figures? **CARD 4:** If you have suffered a major loss/losses, was it explicable in terms of an economic downturn/betrayal/fraud rather than random ill-fortune? **CARD 5:** Should you urgently get a good accountant or financial adviser to set your finances back on track? **CARD 6:** Is better financial luck coming in the next six months? **CARD 7:** Will your money luck, once restored, hold in the foreseeable future?

What you should use:
The forty Minor cards, Aces to Tens.

When:
A Saturday, for wise financial caution.

359
TO AVOID JINXING YOURSELF
BEFORE COMPETING OR GOING
FOR WHAT YOU WANT

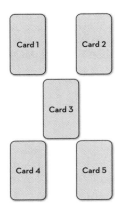

Purpose and background information:
If you are afraid you will suffer from nerves and it will all go wrong.

CARD 1: What is your skill/expertise that will bring success in spite of nerves? **CARD 2:** Do you have past successes/ successful training you can call upon? **CARD 3:** Are there people you should avoid who make you doubt yourself? **CARD 4:** Do you have/could you create a lucky charm/routine to draw good luck around you? **CARD 5:** Will good luck be with you on this occasion?

What you should use:
The twenty-two Major cards.

When:
The day before the event.

360
WILL YOU BE LUCKY IN WINNING THE
LOTTERY OR A MAJOR RAFFLE?

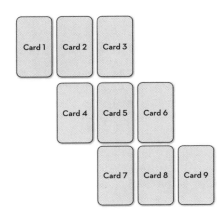

Purpose and background information:
When you've been playing games of chance for years with no luck.

CARD 1: Is winning the lottery your top priority right now to solve all your problems/make dreams come true? **CARD 2:** Is there another way you could reach the same goals? **CARD 3:** Are you generally lucky in raffles/draws/have had minor lottery wins? **CARD 4:** Should you increase your chances by adopting a system/joining a syndicate? **CARD 5:** Should you choose the same lucky numbers every week/base choices on family dates, etc.? **CARD 6:** Should you only enter when you feel lucky/picking different random numbers? **CARD 7:** Would you be content with a modest win/want to go for the jackpot? **CARD 8:** Do you believe you will win soon? **CARD 9:** This week, enter or wait?

What you should use:
The twenty-two Major cards and the forty Minor cards, Aces to Tens.

When:
Before buying your ticket.

361
WILL YOU WIN A COMPETITION YOU HAVE ENTERED?

Purpose and background information:
When you are competing for a prize that would greatly improve your life.

Card 1: Are you generally lucky in competitions? **Card 2:** Is there skill involved as well, or is this one 100% luck? **Card 3:** Do you have a special system/lucky numbers that might tip the odds your way? **Card 4:** Should you submit multiple entries/join a syndicate? **Card 5:** Is there any other legal way you could obtain similar results even it if takes longer to attain? **Card 6:** Will you win the competition this time? **Card 7:** If you do not win this time/win a lesser prize, will you be luckier next time you enter? **Card 8:** If you do not win, should you give up this avenue of potential gain, or keep trying?

What you should use:
The full deck.

When:
Before entering.

362
IS TODAY YOUR LUCKY DAY?

Purpose and Background Information:
When you are determining whether to make a major decision on a given day.

Card 1: The positive or challenging aspect of the card will give you your answer. If in doubt, pick a second card and set it to the right.

What you should use:
The twenty-two Major cards.

When:
When you wake.

363
WILL THE WEEK AHEAD BE LUCKY?

Purpose and background information:
When it's a significant week of opportunity or challenge. Note the results in your journal.

Card 1: Sunday/the first day of the working or significant week, seeing if it is more positive or challenging, which will indicate the luck for that day. Do the same for the subsequent days.

Calculate if it's a lucky week overall, according to whether there are more positive than negative cards for the seven-day period as a whole, noting any days that are particularly lucky.

What you should use:
The full deck.

When:
The day before the relevant period.

364
WILL YOU BE LUCKY IN AN INTERVIEW?

Purpose and background information:
When you have been offered an interview for a new job.

CARD 1: Will the person/people interviewing you be on your wavelength? **CARD 2:** Are you confident you are right for the job/right experience/qualifications? **CARD 3:** Will you get all the right questions? **CARD 4:** Will you say exactly the right thing/hit the right note? **CARD 5:** Is Lady Luck with you in this interview? **CARD 6:** Will you get the job even if there is a lot of competition?

What you should use:
The twenty-two Major cards and the sixteen Court cards.

When:
The evening before the interview.

365
IS TODAY A GOOD DAY TO ASK THE BOSS FOR A PAY INCREASE, PROMOTION, OR EXTRA HOLIDAY?

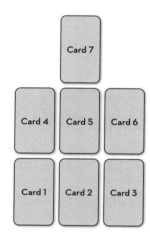

Purpose and background information:
When timing is crucial, as your boss's mood can be changeable.

CARD 1: Are good-luck energies with me today? **CARD 2:** Will my day go smoothly from the moment I reach work? **CARD 3:** Is my boss in a good or bad mood today? **CARD 4:** Will I know the right time to ask? **CARD 5:** Will a good report/result of something I did previously come to their notice today? **CARD 6:** Will I say the right thing? **CARD 7:** Should I wait until tomorrow?

What you should use:
The forty Minor cards, Aces to Tens, and the sixteen Court cards.

When:
Before work.

366
WILL TODAY BE A LUCKY DAY
FOR JOB HUNTING?

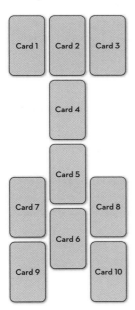

Purpose and background information:

When you have been job hunting for a while.

CARD 1: Is today a lucky day for job hunting? **CARD 2:** Should you have a major push in applications/job agencies today? **CARD 3:** Has someone left suddenly/gone on unexpected leave, creating an unexpected vacancy where you have already applied? **CARD 4:** Will your application be read favorably at the right time? **CARD 5:** Can you expect an interview soon? **CARD 6:** Will your qualifications/experience exactly match an opportunity on the horizon? **CARD 7:** Will you be given a chance to step into a vacancy almost immediately? **CARD 8:** Is there anything you need to know right now about where to look? **CARD 9:** Will you need to relocate for the vacancy/a longer daily commute? **CARD 10:** Do you need to wait for that lucky break a little longer?

What you should use:

The full deck.

When:

When you wake.

367
WILL THE YEAR AHEAD BE LUCKY?

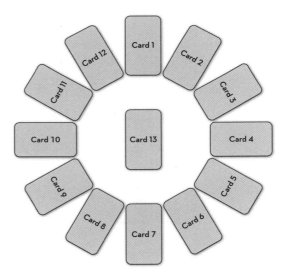

For each of **CARDS 1-12** reading clockwise, ask if this a lucky or unlucky month. Be guided by the meaning of the card as to the area in which it will be especially lucky or challenging each month. If it's not strongly lucky, it simply means it's a month to put in more effort in the area of life highlighted by the card. Note the results in your journal and see whether as a whole the year is lucky or one where you have to work hard for results. **CARD 13** in the center will reveal an unexpected piece of good fortune, whether you get it easily (positive meaning) or have to work for it to materialize once it is revealed.

What you should use:

The full deck.

When:

The first day of any month, or New Year's Day.

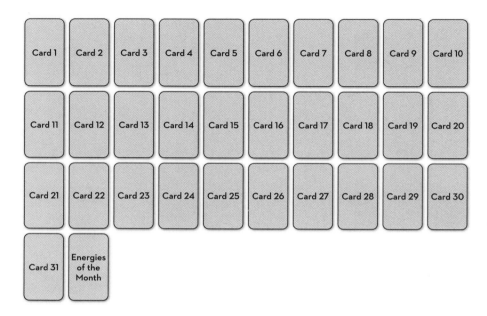

Purpose and background information:

When it's a significant month ahead, but you will need some luck. Record the results in your journal to study during the month ahead.

Deal a card for each day of the month according to whether there are 28, 29, 30, or 31 days in the month, starting with **CARD 1** for the first day being studied, then **CARD 2, CARD 3,** etc. As with the previous Spread, see whether the daily cards have more positive than challenging aspects. Count how many lucky days are in the month and whether overall it is a month to go for it or to be cautious.

What you should use:

The full deck, or two decks mixed.

When:

The last day of the previous month.

WHICH QUARTER OF THE YEAR WILL BE LUCKIEST TO MAKE A NEW VENTURE GO WELL?

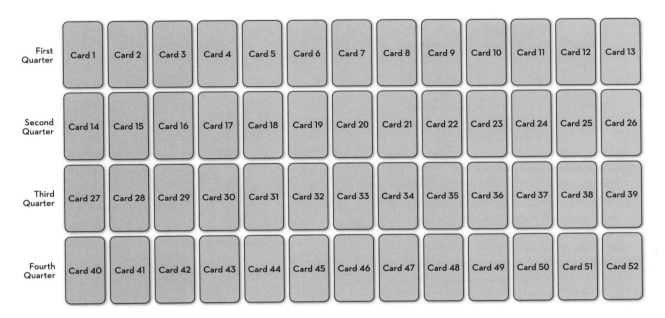

Purpose and background information:

Divide your year into four three-month periods, from the first day of the first month to the last day of the third month.

Pick one card for each day for each quarter, starting with **Card 1** for Day 1. See if you have more lucky or more challenging days in each quarter. Note the results for each day in your journal and highlight any especially lucky days as a chance for major opportunity.

Be guided by the meaning of each card as to the area in which it will be especially lucky.

See which quarter has the largest number of lucky or positive cards. Note which has the least.

What you should use:

The full deck or two mixed decks.

When:

New Year's Day, or the beginning of any quarter.

370

WILL YOU HAVE BAD LUCK IF YOU HAVE LOST OR BROKEN YOUR LUCKY CHARM?

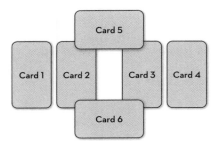

Purpose and background information:

When you are spooked by not having your special lucky talisman.

CARD 1: Should you replace it with a replica, or choose something completely different? **CARD 2:** Should you put your new charm with something that is known to be lucky, a Buddha/Kuan Yin/a lucky elephant, to restart your good luck? **CARD 3:** Should you take your replacement charm somewhere you are always happy/lucky, and will that restart your luck? **CARD 4:** In fact, is your luck within you so just by holding a new talisman you can fill it with all the good luck you have accumulated? **CARD 5:** Is losing or breaking your charm telling you it's time to explore new places and activities/attract new different luck? **CARD 6:** Had your old charm run out of energy, telling you that you need to take more care/make wiser choices to attract new good fortune?

What you should use:

The twenty-two Major cards.

When:

A full moon, Midsummer, or any Sunday.

371

CAN YOU AVERT BAD LUCK IF YOUR PERSONAL ASTROLOGICAL CHART IS AGAINST YOU RIGHT NOW OR MERCURY IS RETROGRADE?

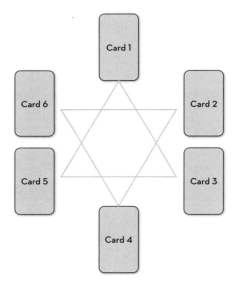

Purpose and background information:

If the stars are saying no, but you need some good luck.

CARD 1: If possible, should you postpone any major decisions or plans till the stars improve? **CARD 2:** Should you check your chart for any counterbalancing positive influences to the present general negative outlook? **CARD 3:** Should you consult a general astrology prediction online or in a daily/weekly journal to see a more positive spin, taking everything about your sign and the day/week/month more generally into account? **CARD 4:** Should you use extra lucky charms/rituals to strengthen the good-fortune odds in your favor? **CARD 5:** Should you go ahead anyway with plans in the belief that actions and determination can put you more in control, in spite of less-than-helpful stellar trends? **CARD 6:** Will you be lucky anyway, in spite of the stars?

What you should use:
The full deck.

When:
A cloudy evening when you cannot see the stars/Saturday for good luck.

372

WILL YOU HAVE SEVEN YEARS' BAD LUCK FOR BREAKING A MIRROR?

Purpose and background information:
When you have broken a mirror and fear the worst.

CARD 1: Should you ignore old superstitions as just that, outworn beliefs of a bygone age? **CARD 2:** Were you brought up in a superstitious household and still hold the beliefs subconsciously? **CARD 3:** If you have ever had bad luck as a result of breaking a superstition, did you jinx yourself by believing you would have bad luck? **CARD 4:** Should you wrap the old mirror in cloth, bury it very deep, and replace it with a beautiful new one to make yourself feel better and reverse any bad luck? **CARD 5:** Should you polish your new mirror in bright sunlight to put good luck into it? **CARD 6:** Should you go out with friends who make you feel good and have a good time, so filling yourself with extra good luck vibes?

What you should use:
The full deck.

When:
When you are feeling seriously spooked.

373

IS THIS A LUCKY NIGHT FOR MEETING SOMEONE NEW WHO IS SPECIAL?

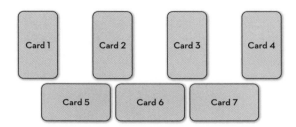

Purpose and background information:
When you are uncertain whether or not to accept an invitation.

CARD 1: Is this a lucky time for me socially? **CARD 2:** Will a special person be where I am going/should I go somewhere different? **CARD 3:** Will I say and do the right things to impress? **CARD 4:** Will the person be unattached or, if in a relationship, planning to leave it? **CARD 5:** Will my luck hold if I ask them out? **CARD 6:** If this isn't the right time to meet someone, should I go and have a good time anyway? **CARD 7:** Will this occasion open new doors socially to lead me to the right person soon, if not tonight?

What you should use:
The forty Minor cards, Aces to Tens, and the sixteen Court cards.

When:
Soon after you receive the invitation.

374
IS THIS A GOOD NIGHT TO TRY ONLINE DATING?

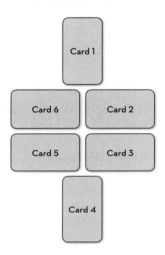

Purpose and background information:
When you have had no luck on dating sites.

CARD 1: Does tonight/today feel especially lucky for love? **CARD 2:** Should you try a new site, or go back to one that you know well? **CARD 3:** Should you trust yourself to know the right time to log in tonight, or try the usual time? **CARD 4:** Will the right person also be logging in/joining for the first time at the time you log in? **CARD 5:** Will you know instantly if this connection is right? **CARD 6:** For your luck to be at its maximum, should you try tonight, or wait until tomorrow?

What you should use:
The twenty-two Major cards.

When:
Just before planning to log in.

375
IS THIS A LUCKY TIME TO GAMBLE?

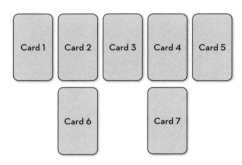

Purpose and background information:
If you are not certain whether to take a risk or hold back.

CARD 1: Are lucky energies around me right now? **CARD 2:** Will the method/place that I am planning be the right one at this time? **CARD 3:** Will my luck hold for the desired win? **CARD 4:** Will I know if and when to stop while I'm ahead? **CARD 5:** If my luck does run out, would any losses be catastrophic? **CARD 6:** Should I test my luck by trying a small gamble first, or go for broke? **CARD 7:** Is tonight the night, or not the night?

What you should use:
The full deck.

When:
Before gambling, whether online or going out.

376
IF YOU HAVE BEEN UNLUCKY FOR MOST OF YOUR LIFE

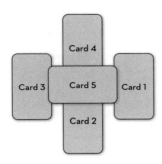

Purpose and background information:
If family members say you have always been unlucky.

CARD 1: Is this generally true, or is it a negative perception you have been given that you have applied to events?
CARD 2: Did your family use you as a scapegoat whenever things went wrong/are they generally pessimistic people?
CARD 3: What success/good fortune have you experienced because of your own efforts rather than pure luck? **CARD 4:** What strengths/qualities do you have you can use to bring good fortune? **CARD 5:** Should you surround yourself with happy, fortunate people, avoiding those who bring/talk you down?

What you should use:
The twenty-two Major cards and the sixteen Court Cards.

When:
You decide that it's time you faced life more positively.

377
WILL LUCK BE WITH YOU WHEN YOU TAKE YOUR EXAMINATION?

Purpose and background information:
If you are feeling nervous, although you have done your best to prepare.

CARD 1: Is this a naturally lucky day? **CARD 2:** Will you get asked the right questions? **CARD 3:** Will you remember all the right information when needed? **CARD 4:** Will you have a sympathetic examiner/assessor? **CARD 5:** Will you pass your examination? **CARD 6:** Is there anything of which you should be aware before taking the exam?

What you should use:
The full deck.

When:
The evening before the examination/the first examination.

378
WILL YOU PASS YOUR DRIVING TEST OR PRACTICAL EXAMINATION?

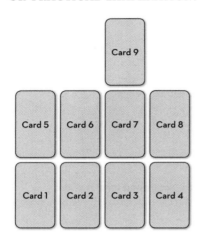

Purpose and background information:
If you are feeling nervous and do not want to let nerves spoil your chances.

CARD 1: Are you ready as you will ever be, or should you delay? **CARD 2:** Is there anything you need to be aware of about the test day/conditions? **CARD 3:** Is the test day lucky energy-wise? **CARD 4:** Will the examiner/assessor be in a good mood? **CARD 5:** Will the traffic/test conditions be right? **CARD 6:** What special skills would you like to get the chance to show? **CARD 7:** What worries you the most about being tested? **CARD 8:** What, if any, missing expertise is needed to succeed? **CARD 9:** Will you pass/your efforts be well received?

What you should use:
The forty Minor cards, Aces to Tens, and the sixteen Court cards.

When:
When you receive your test date.

379
IS THIS A LUCKY INVESTMENT?

Purpose and background information:
When you know investing could potentially bring big gains.

CARD 1: Are you generally lucky in investments/speculation? **CARD 2:** Does this particular investment intuitively feel right? **CARD 3:** Have/should you back up this intuitive feeling with as much information/expert advice as possible? **CARD 4:** Should you wait, or would this lose the opportunity? Wait anyway? **CARD 5:** Will this investment be lucky and bring promised returns?

What you should use:
The twenty-two Major cards.

When:
When you have almost decided to go ahead.

380
WILL YOU BE LUCKY IN AN AUCTION OR BIDDING ON THE INTERNET?

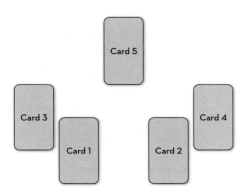

Purpose and background information:
When you need to make decisions fast.

CARD 1: Do you have an intuitive feel for when and how much to bid? Has this intuition previously worked? **CARD 2:** Should you hold back/put in a lower bid until you feel sure of the right moment? **CARD 3:** Do you want the item/property badly enough to pay more than you intended if necessary? **CARD 4:** Should you be prepared, if necessary, to pull out/wait for a similar item/property to be available at a cheaper price? **CARD 5:** Is luck with you to win on your terms?

What you should use:
The forty Minor cards, Aces to Tens.

When:
Just before the item/property is going up for auction.

381
WILL YOU SOON GET YOUR LUCKY BREAK IN YOUR CHOSEN FIELD?

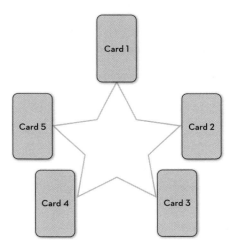

Purpose and background information:
When you have explored every avenue, but the big break eludes you.

CARD 1: Can you feel the luck energies around you changing for the better? **CARD 2:** Can you feel anticipation/excitement building around you? **CARD 3:** Should you re-explore old avenues/expand your horizons of possibility/more distant locations to trigger those luck energies? **CARD 4:** Will you make that right contact in the very near future? **CARD 5:** Will your lucky break come really soon if you persevere?

What you should use:
The forty Minor cards, Aces to Tens, and the sixteen Court cards.

When:
A Sunday, really early.

CHAPTER 23

SPREADS FOR THE HOME AND PROPERTY

Lucky cards for home and property Spreads:

Major Arcana: The Emperor and Empress, the Hierophant, the Chariot, the Wheel of Fortune, Justice, Temperance, the Sun, Judgment, the World.

Minor Arcana: Aces of Pentacles, Cups, and Wands, Two of Cups, Three of Pentacles, Three of Wands, Four of Pentacles, Four of Wands, Six of Cups, Six of Wands, Seven of Pentacles, Eight of Cups, Eight of Wands, Ten of Pentacles, Ten of Cups.

Court Cards: The Queens and Kings of Pentacles, Cups, and Wands.

About home and property Spreads:

One-, two-, and three-carders for straightforward questions; four-card Spreads for finances and property/renovation questions; fives for getting bargains and negotiations; sixes for happiness at home; sevens for dreams, renting, and finding the right home; eights for moving and relocating; nines and above for major questions and buying and selling homes in a difficult market.

382
WILL YOUR NEW HOME BE LUCKY FOR YOU?

Purpose and background information:
When you have rented or purchased a new home or are about to do so.

Card 1: Did you feel when you first saw it that it was meant to be yours and that that was a valid feeling? **Card 2:** Will everything progress smoothly in negotiations/finance, etc., right through to the move? **Card 3:** Is this going to be a place of health, happiness, and prosperity? **Card 4:** Do you have any worries about the house/location and how can these be resolved?

What you should use:
The forty Minor cards, Aces to Tens.

When:
A Sunday for new beginnings.

383
WILL YOU EVER SELL YOUR HOME?

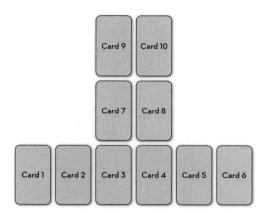

Purpose and background information:

When your home has been on the market for a while without any serious offers.

CARD 1: Are there good reasons for the lack of serious offers, such as economic downturn/time of year, etc.? **CARD 2:** If you are patient, will the sale come naturally eventually? **CARD 3:** Are you being unrealistic about your price in relation to similar properties? **CARD 4:** What is it about your home that, if emphasized, makes it particularly salable? **CARD 5:** Should you change the target market at which it is aimed/family wanting a large place to renovate, etc.? **CARD 6:** Should you get a new agent? **CARD 7:** Should you advertise more on the Internet/advertise further afield? **CARD 8:** Will the buyer be local, or from interstate or overseas? **CARD 9:** Will the home sell within three to six months, or take up to a year? **CARD 10:** Is there anything you should know that would speed the sale, such as price reduction/auction?

What you should use:

The full deck.

When:

A Wednesday for speeding up sales.

384
SHOULD YOU RENOVATE YOUR HOME, OR SELL IT AS IT IS?

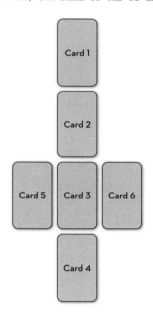

Purpose and background information:

When you are not sure whether to invest time and expense on renovations in order to sell for more money.

CARD 1: Is it marketable for a reasonable price as it is? **CARD 2:** If you renovate, will you recoup the expense and time by achieving a better sale price? **CARD 3:** Should you accept less money to save time and effort that could be used in other ways? **CARD 4:** Should you settle for partially renovating to make it easier to sell? **CARD 5:** Should you totally renovate it to maximize the sale price? **CARD 6:** Should you keep the home and not sell it at all?

What you should use:

The forty Minor cards, Aces to Tens.

When:

Before making major decisions about marketing your property.

385
CAN YOU MAKE MONEY THROUGH PROPERTY RENOVATION?

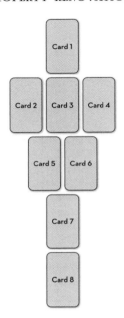

Purpose and background information:
If you are wondering if this could be a good money spinner.

CARD 1: Do you have a good eye for a bargain and its future selling potential? **CARD 2:** Do you have/can you easily access the necessary funds to launch yourself? **CARD 3:** Do you have skills in renovation/access to those who will do it cheaply? **CARD 4:** Should you start with one property and build up slowly? **CARD 5:** Should you work with a partner/syndicate on multiple renovation projects? **CARD 6:** Do you intend to make a business of house renovation, or is it just a sideline? **CARD 7:** Are there any unforeseen hazards you should be aware of? **CARD 8:** Will house renovation prove a success for you?

What you should use:
The whole deck.

When:
The beginning of a month.

386
WILL YOUR NEXT MOVE BE INTERIM OR LONG-TERM?

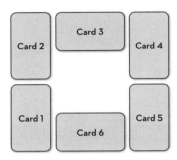

Purpose and background information:
When you are contemplating putting down roots but aren't sure this is the right place and time.

CARD 1: Does this new home/potential new home offer everything you want for the long-term future? **CARD 2:** Is it in the "right forever" location/right for now? **CARD 3:** Is there room for extension/adapting for future requirements if you make it a permanent home? **CARD 4:** Is this move a compromise dictated by circumstances? **CARD 5:** Is it a stepping-stone to your forever home? **CARD 6:** If it doesn't feel right even as an interim, should you look around until you see exactly what you want?

What you should use:
The forty Minor cards, Aces to Tens.

When:
Before signing a contract.

387
IS THE PROPERTY YOU ARE BUYING A GOOD INVESTMENT?

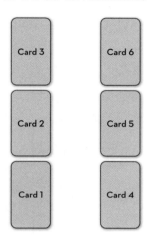

Purpose and background information:

If you wonder if your purchase will be a money-spinner, a happy home, or both.

CARD 1: Will this purchase be a happy home to buy, regardless of future profit? **CARD 2:** Are there special reasons this property may increase in value more than expected/an area that will become more upmarket/new industry coming to the area/undiscovered mineral finds? **CARD 3:** Would renovation/extension prove profitable? **CARD 4:** Would knocking it down and rebuilding/selling the land prove unexpectedly profitable? **CARD 5:** Is this a longer-term investment? **CARD 6:** Should you regard this as a fast-yielding turnover?

What you should use:

The forty Minor cards, Aces to Tens.

When:

When you want to invest money in something solid.

388
SHOULD YOU RELOCATE NOW?

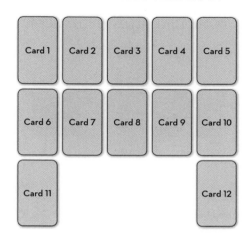

Purpose and background information:

CARD 1: Do you definitely know the place/the home to which you want to move? **CARD 2:** Is this a vague idea prompted by feelings of restlessness in your life? **CARD 3:** Do you actively dislike where you are living/regard it as an interim home? **CARD 4:** Will moving make you happy? **CARD 5:** Should you move now, or wait a few months (or longer)? **CARD 6:** What is the main advantage of moving soon? **CARD 7:** What are the drawbacks of moving? **CARD 8:** Is it financially viable/is that not a consideration? **CARD 9:** Do you want a move to a better home in your present area, or a major location shift? **CARD 10:** Will it be easy/swift to move? **CARD 11:** Will you have moved within twelve months? **CARD 12:** Should you improve your present life/home where you are now, rather than moving?

What you should use:

The whole deck.

When:

You find yourself studying real estate for a suitable future home.

389
DECIDING WHETHER TO RENOVATE, BUILD YOUR OWN HOME, OR BUY AN EXISTING HOME THAT NEEDS LITTLE WORK

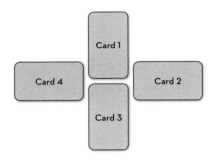

Purpose and background information:
If you want to change your home for something better but are not sure how best to spend your money.

CARD 1: Should you do renovations to extend your present home? **CARD 2:** Should you build your own home, or have a custom-made home built on land you acquire/own? **CARD 3:** Should you purchase an existing property that is ready to move into? **CARD 4:** Should you stay where you are, as you are?

What you should use:
The forty number cards, Aces to Tens.

When:
At the end of a month.

390
SHOULD YOU RELOCATE TO WHERE YOU REALLY WANT TO LIVE, ALTHOUGH IT MEANS LEAVING THE PLACE WHERE YOU HAVE LIVED ALL YOUR LIFE?

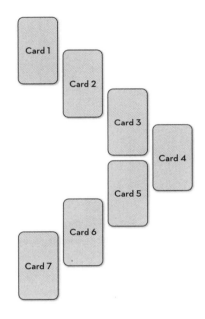

Purpose and background information:
When a chance comes to live in a desired location.

CARD 1: Is it viable economically/relationship/career-wise right now? **CARD 2:** Would any sacrifices be worthwhile in terms of personal happiness? **CARD 3:** Is now the right time emotionally to go for it? **CARD 4:** Should you wait until a more suitable time, taking all factors into account? **CARD 5:** Will you need/should you make a fast decision to move? **CARD 6:** Can/should it be more gradual, getting everything in place first? **CARD 7:** Will you regret it if you delay/decline?

What you should use:
The twenty-two Major cards.

When:
At a full moon, or any Monday for fulfilling dreams.

WHERE TO LIVE ON RETIREMENT OR IF YOU ARE PLANNING A NEW LIFESTYLE

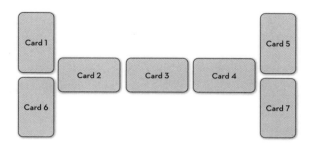

Purpose and background information:

When you are making a major life change with different factors/a partner's wishes to build in.

CARD 1: Should you move to the city? **CARD 2:** Should you move to the ocean? **CARD 3:** Should you move to a small town/established community? **CARD 4:** Should you go rural? **CARD 5:** Should you stay where you are? **CARD 6:** Should you move locally? **CARD 7:** Should you move overseas/interstate?

You can of course add additional cards to the Spread for extra options.

What you should use:

The forty Minor cards, Aces to Tens, and the twenty-two Major cards.

When:

At the beginning of a month, or on New Year's Day for new beginnings.

Example:

Lucy was a city woman and didn't want to retire in the wilderness. She loves concerts and the theater, runs a flourishing art group, and hopes to sell paintings in retirement. Her husband Sam craves the ocean, where he could fish and walk every morning on the beach and add to his collection of minerals.

CARD 1: The Sun, a full-on card, bright, filled with life. Sam, who shared the reading, pointed out that there was no water on the card and he wanted a quieter lifestyle away from the city where it wouldn't be too hot.

CARD 2: The Eight of Cups, masses of water, and the person on the card with all the cups of happiness. This shows that nothing would be lost by a move to the ocean. But how could Lucy be happy?

CARD 3: The Two of Wands, creativity and perfectly balanced, both Sam and Lucy happy. Is this possible in a small-town community?

CARD 4: The Eight of Swords, showing a woman tied. Lucy said she would go mad out in the countryside, which to Sam was his second choice where he could river-fish.

CARD 5: The Four of Swords, Sam feeling stuck as he has outgrown city life.

CARD 6: The Two of Pentacles, trying to balance their different needs within the current environment and neither of them fully happy, because Sam would be restless in the city and Lucy not happy if Sam wasn't happy. So staying where they were was a compromise that wouldn't work.

CARD 7: The Ten of Cups. While they didn't want to go overseas, a new state might offer everything they wanted.

Supposing, Sam suggested, they found a small town near the ocean where there was a good cultural life and a center for artists for Lucy. They could live near the beach for him, but close enough to the town for Lucy to develop her work and even run courses for tourists. Lucy was happy with that decision, and they are exploring small cultural towns on or near the coast.

392
SHOULD YOU BUY THE HOUSE THAT YOU LOVE, ALTHOUGH IT IS AT A HIGHER PRICE THAN YOU WANTED TO PAY?

Purpose and background information:

If your heart says yes but your mind talks in terms of financial caution.

Card 1: Is this the property of your dreams? **Card 2:** Should you hold out for a lower price? **Card 3:** Will a lower offer be accepted straightaway, after negotiations, or not at all? **Card 4:** Is there any way you can make more money from your sale/borrow extra to make the move possible? **Card 5:** If you lose the house through hesitating, would you be prepared to look/wait for one similar? **Card 6:** Is this an all-or-nothing decision? **Card 7:** Are you confident that you can recoup the extra outlay as a result of living in a better place?

What you should use:

The whole deck.

When:

The day before you need to make an offer to secure the desired property.

393
IS YOUR HOME CURSED WITH BAD LUCK?

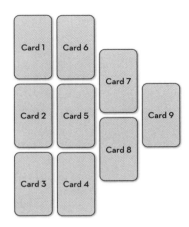

Purpose and background information:

If your home feels spooky or has heavy energies.

Card 1: Did your bad luck start when you moved in? **Card 2:** Did some recent misfortune trigger it/make it worse? **Card 3:** Can any of the bad luck be linked to external circumstances/bad decisions that would have occurred anyway? **Card 4:** Does the home have a spooky/heavy feeling no matter how much you smudge, etc.? (Smudging, a native American Indian tradition, is done by burning dried herbs and letting the smoke float around the house as a means of cleansing.) **Card 5:** Did unhappy events happen in the house before you moved in/does the land have a bad reputation from the past? **Card 6:** Should you ask a priest/medium to cleanse your home, especially if you sense paranormal activity? **Card 7:** Should you fill your home with good-luck symbols/get an expert to feng shui the house and land? **Card 8:** Should you consider your own lifestyle/relationships to see whether that is the problem? **Card 9:** Should you move anyway when you are able?

What you should use:

The full deck.

When:

When you feel especially unsettled or spooked.

394
IF YOUR HOME IS TOO BIG NOW THAT THE CHILDREN HAVE LEFT, BUT YOU DON'T WANT TO SELL

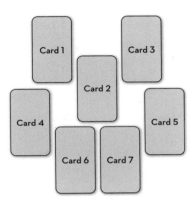

Purpose and background information:
If you are being pressured by others to downsize.

CARD 1: Are there any valid urgent reasons, such as finances, that suggest you should sell? **CARD 2:** Will you be happier staying there, especially as the children will come to stay/someday there may be grandchildren? **CARD 3:** Would you consider renting out a room/starting a business from home? **CARD 4:** Will you enjoy having more space and peace for yourself/your partner? **CARD 5:** Is this a time when you are considering changing your lifestyle? If so, would your current home suit this? **CARD 6:** Do you want to relocate now, later, or never? **CARD 7:** Should you do nothing and re-examine the question in a few years' time?

What you should use:
The forty Minor cards, Aces to Tens, and the 16 Court cards.

When:
When you are home alone.

395
IF YOU WANT TO DOWNSIZE YOUR HOME

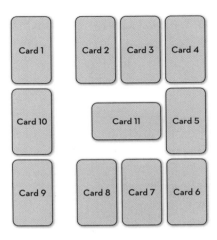

Purpose and background information:
At a crossroads time.

CARD 1: Would postponing the decision make it harder, or do you need more time to decide? **CARD 2:** Is this a head-or-heart decision to fulfill a better lifestyle/economic necessity/both? **CARD 3:** Can your head and your heart be matched? **CARD 4:** Do you know where/when/how you want to downsize? **CARD 5:** Is this still an idea to fulfill a dream you/your partner have always had to release some of the equity in your home? **CARD 6:** Can/should you take time exploring options, so downsizing means an upsizing in quality of life? **CARD 7:** What are the advantages of downsizing? **CARD 8:** What are the disadvantages of downsizing? **CARD 9:** Should you go all out for the dream, regardless of obstacles? **CARD 10:** Will you be happy? **CARD 11:** If you don't downsize now, will you feel you have missed the moment?

What you should use:
The full deck.

When:
A Tuesday, day of the pioneer.

396
IF YOUR HOME IS IN A BEAUTIFUL PLACE AND IS USED AS A FREE HOLIDAY BASE BY RELATIVES AND FRIENDS

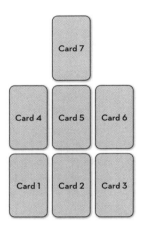

Purpose and background information:

If you would like a weekend by yourself/with your partner/family without visitors.

Card 1: Are you naturally hospitable but feel you are being taken advantage of? **Card 2:** Do you/why do you feel guilty about saying *no* without explanation/putting limits on their length of stay? **Card 3:** Should you discriminate between real friends and those wanting a free holiday at your expense, at the risk of losing a few hangers-on? **Card 4:** Can you use social media to say friends are always welcome if they let you know in advance/offer a list of local bed-and-breakfasts/suggest they consider using Airbnb? **Card 5:** Should you claim some weekends as your own/your family's because that is why you chose to live there? **Card 6:** If it's not convenient when people arrive unannounced, should you be brave enough to say so? **Card 7:** Should you be tougher with users and those who take advantage of you?

What you should use:

The forty Minor cards, Aces to Tens, and the sixteen Court cards.

When:

When you dread weekends and public holidays.

397
SHOULD YOU CONSIDER GOING INTO THE BUY-TO-RENT MARKET?

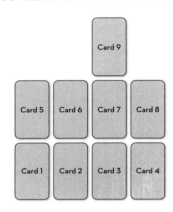

Purpose and background information:

When you have some spare money/borrowing potential.

Card 1: Should/do you want to invest in upgrading your own home/moving upmarket rather than going into the rental market? **Card 2:** Is this a good time for you to invest in the rental market? **Card 3:** In which area should you buy to attract the kind of tenants you want: students/professionals/house sharers, etc.? **Card 4:** Will your investment pay off if you buy cheap and renovate? **Card 5:** Will your investment be better if you buy up to your limit, or move tenants in right away? **Card 6:** Should you get a reliable rental agent, or keep your eye on the ball yourself? **Card 7:** Should you/can you use a single rental property as a long-term nest egg? **Card 8:** Should you aim to buy more than one property when you have the funds available in order to build up a good portfolio? **Card 9:** Will this be a successful venture for you?

What you should use:

The full deck.

When:

A Wednesday, the day of speculation.

398
FOR BUYING A VACATION HOME

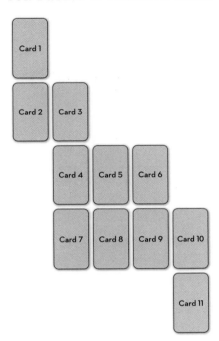

Purpose and background information:

When you are considering a more permanent vacation base.

CARD 1: Is there a special area where you would like to buy your vacation home? **CARD 2:** Do you want the home to be for yourself, or for friends and family? **CARD 3:** Do you think you will instantly know the right property when you see it? **CARD 4:** Should you make a choice based on head as well as heart, or on its rental potential? **CARD 5:** Should/could you rent it out for part of the year so it pays some of the expenses? **CARD 6:** Do you want a basic fun vacation base where you can hang out? **CARD 7:** Do you want somewhere more elaborate where you could live permanently in the future? **CARD 8:** Would/should you consider a large fun camper vehicle instead and keep vacations mobile? **CARD 9:** Will the happiness of your future vacations outweigh the costs involved in the purchase? **CARD 10:** Should you go ahead when you find the right one, even if a strain? **CARD 11:** Should you continue to search using head and heart and financial caution until it comes together?

What you should use:

The twenty-two Major cards.

When:

You truly believe it's time you put more thought into leisure.

399
IF YOU NEED A WORK BASE AT HOME

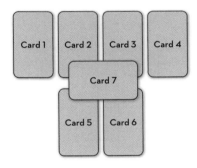

Purpose and background information:

When you are commencing working/operating a business or studying from home.

CARD 1: What are the advantages of working from home? **CARD 2:** What are the disadvantages of working from home? **CARD 3:** Should you/would you prefer to rent a room somewhere else? **CARD 4:** Do you have/can you make a space in your home away from everyone else? **CARD 5:** Can/should you create uninterrupted work time entirely separate from demands of family/friends? **CARD 6:** If you have/take on other employees, can you find/create the extra space/need to extend/move? **CARD 7:** Should/will you be able to keep to working hours to avoid work encroaching on your home life?

What you should use:

The full deck.

When:

On Thursdays, the day of working successfully for yourself.

400
IF YOU ARE CONSIDERING ADAPTING YOUR HOME TO ACCOMMODATE ELDERLY RELATIVES

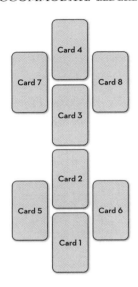

Purpose and background information:

When you are juggling your domestic life to fit in with family needs.

CARD 1: Will having your elderly relatives living with you be workable for all of you? **CARD 2:** Will the adjustments you need to make to the home/home life be worthwhile in terms of less worry for you? **CARD 3:** Can you arrange the accommodation to give you privacy and separate facilities? **CARD 4:** Can you arrange the finances so the burden doesn't fall on you but is shared by all involved? **CARD 5:** Should you/can you arrange care packages/domestic help for your relatives/arrange for other relatives to help so you are still able to have your own life? **CARD 6:** Should you move to larger premises if yours aren't easily adaptable? **CARD 7:** Do you have built-in safeguards if your relatives need to go into assisted living? **CARD 8:** Do you have legal safeguards in place in case it goes wrong/for the more distant future when other relatives may make claims on your investments?

What you should use:

The forty Minor cards, Aces to Tens, and the sixteen Court cards.

When:

A Saturday for property matters.

401
IF YOUR GRANDCHILDREN MOVE INTO YOUR HOME

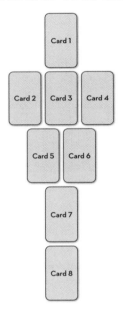

Purpose and background information:

When one of your children moves into your home with a grandchild/grandchildren after a relationship breakup or as a single parent.

CARD 1: Will this be/do you want this to be a temporary arrangement while your adult child gets back on their feet? **CARD 2:** Can you adapt the accommodation so you each have your privacy? **CARD 3:** Can you avoid taking over domestic chores and 24/7 babysitting? **CARD 4:** What are the advantages of having members of the family living with you? **CARD 5:** How can you minimize the problems? **CARD 6:** Can you ensure that your house rules are respected/avoid your home being taken over by the needs of the young? **CARD 7:** If the arrangement is to be more permanent, should you consider moving to a place with separate accommodations/a larger home with space? **CARD 8:** Will it all work out?

What you should use:
The full deck.

When:
A Friday, family and children day.

402
IF YOU ARE LIVING WHERE YOU DO NOT WANT TO BE

Purpose and background information:
When you intensely dislike where you live.

CARD 1: Is it possible to move somewhere you feel happier, even if this involves major life adjustments/financial loss? **CARD 2:** While you are living where you are, can you make improvements to your home and lifestyle to make it more bearable? **CARD 3:** Is there an end in sight when it will be easier to move? **CARD 4:** Can you speed up a future move? **CARD 5:** Can you spend weekends away/plan events to give yourself a better life balance? **CARD 6:** Are there any advantages to living in your present home that you can maximize?

What you should use:
The twenty-two Major cards.

When:
The first day of the month.

403
IF YOU ARE SEEKING RENTAL ACCOMMODATION IN A VERY CROWDED MARKET

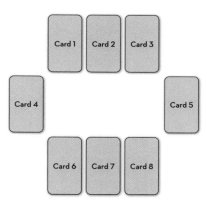

Purpose and background information:
When everything you apply for is gone before you get there.

CARD 1: Are you connected to absolutely every agency/online source, even ones that seem unlikely? Is there one you are missing? **CARD 2:** Are you using social media contacts/advertising to let it be known what you want? **CARD 3:** Should/would you consider widening your search to involve longer commutes/less popular areas? **CARD 4:** Should/could you set up an apartment/house-sitting service taking care of pets/precious plants, etc., to make you a more desirable tenant? **CARD 5:** Should/could you offer babysitting services/companionship for an older person in return for accommodation? **CARD 6:** Should/could you pool resources with friends to rent a larger/more expensive place? **CARD 7:** Should/would you consider buying a place in need of renovation with friends? **CARD 8:** Would/should you consider a live-in job temporarily?

What you should use:
The full deck.

When:
A Wednesday, for swift transactions.

404
IF YOU ARE HAVING TO FIND A NEW HOME AFTER A SEPARATION, DIVORCE, OR BEREAVEMENT

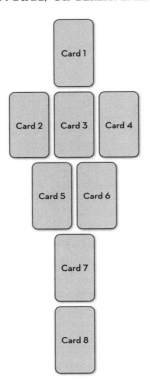

Purpose and background information:
When you are relocating out of necessity or because of unhappy circumstances.

Card 1: Should/can you insist that this move occur when right for you, not on someone else's agenda? **Card 2:** Do you have/can you gather all the resources to which you are entitled, if necessary getting tougher? **Card 3:** Is this a chance to start over/move to where/what you want to be? **Card 4:** Who/what will help you to resettle/remain an unchanging part of your new world? **Card 5:** Who do you want to/should you leave behind/ignore if making life hard?

Card 6: What do you most want for your happy future? **Card 7:** Can you be single-minded, in spite of sorrow, to make your future home right for yourself, irrespective of the advice/opinions of others? **Card 8:** Will your new home open a completely new chapter of happiness for you?

What you should use:
The whole deck.

When:
When you feel that your wants and needs are being forgotten.

405
IF YOU DESPERATELY WANT A HOME OF YOUR OWN, BUT IT SEEMS IMPOSSIBLE

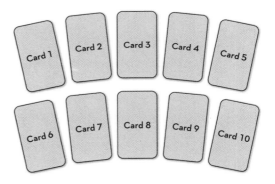

Purpose and background information:
When the chance of owning your own home never seems to get nearer.

Card 1: What is the main obstacle to saving money? **Card 2:** Is there any way you can improve your credit scores/get a more lucrative job for a more substantial home loan? **Card 3:** Are there any affordable home/lease-purchase schemes available that would work for you? **Card 4:** Could you buy a home that needs major renovations? **Card 5:** Would you consider something small/in a less desirable area to get a foothold on the ladder? **Card 6:** Are there relatives you could persuade to invest/temporarily help out? **Card 7:** Should you relocate to a cheaper area/a different State/ overseas to make a home more affordable? **Card 8:** What

unexpected good luck will come along within 12/18 months?
Card 9: Will you be in your own home in 12/18 months?
Card 10: In the meantime, how can you make sure you/your partner still enjoy a good if modest quality of life?

What you should use:
The forty Minor cards, Aces to Tens, and the sixteen Court cards.

When:
At the crescent or increasing moon period.

406
IF YOU HAVE HAD TO MOVE TO LIVE WITH YOUR PARENTS AFTER HAVING HAD YOUR OWN HOME

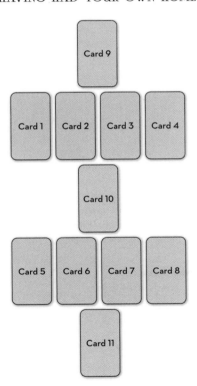

Purpose and background information:
When you are sharing living space between jobs/after a relationship breakup or after studying when you are not going to be earning much initially.

Card 1: Is there anywhere else/anyone else you could stay with while you get on your feet if you do not want to move home? **Card 2:** If you go home, do you want to put realistic time limits on your stay? **Card 3:** Are you able to save extra toward your new home/life by living at home? **Card 4:** Are you able to have good privacy arrangements, so you all have your separate spaces and lives? **Card 5:** Can you/how can you avoid being cast back into the role of child/slipping into this role? **Card 6:** Have you explored every option for apartment shares/house-sitting/buying a property jointly with friends to restore your independence? **Card 7:** Do you have agreed strategies if irritations spill over? **Card 8:** Can you borrow from family to finance a move, however modest? **Card 9:** Would it suit you all to stay indefinitely until you are fully on your feet careerwise/in a new permanent relationship? **Card 10:** If the arrangement suits you all, would you contemplate buying/splitting a large home/buying land to share with parents permanently? **Card 11:** Will you be back living independently within six to nine months if you so choose?

What you should use:
The full deck.

When:
A Saturday for working within the boundaries of possibility.

407
IF YOU HAVE TO LIVE IN STAFF HOUSING

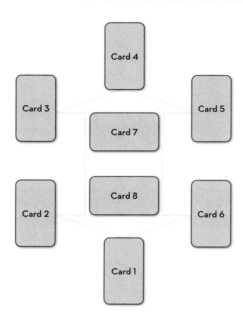

Purpose and background information:

When you are feeling very restricted without a home to call your own.

CARD 1: Is it worth accepting limitations on freedom while you save/earn a promotion to be able to get your own place? **CARD 2:** Should/can you impose boundaries around your personal living space so you aren't constantly being invaded by others, even at the risk of appearing unsociable? **CARD 3:** Can/should you acquire a camper van/spend time off with family/friends so you have a life outside? **CARD 4:** Can you impose limits on your employment so you cannot just be called in at a moment's notice because you live on-site?

CARD 5: Are the drawbacks of living on-site compensated for by benefits/no travel to work/subsidized food/rent? **CARD 6:** If drawbacks seriously outweigh benefits, should you be looking for accommodations close to work? **CARD 7:** Should you look for a new live-out job with more money? **CARD 8:** Will you see/get an offer within six months that will resolve the dilemma?

What you should use:

The forty Minor cards, Aces to Tens.

When:

The end of a working month.

408
IF YOU LIVE IN A CITY APARTMENT AND DO NOT HAVE A GARDEN, BUT WANT ONE

Purpose and background information:
When not having a garden is seriously bothering you.

CARD 1: Should you contemplate moving to a place with a garden, even if this involves a longer commute/less desirable premises? **CARD 2:** Can you adapt your balcony/window ledges even more to create an indoor garden/herb bed? **CARD 3:** Should you join a gardening club/rent an allotment/find a wilderness space you can visit, even in the city? **CARD 4:** Should/can you spend weekends and vacations where possible in the wilderness/rural places? **CARD 5:** Should you change your location/career/lifestyle so you can live in an area of natural beauty?

What you should use:
The twenty-two Major cards and the sixteen Court cards.

When:
A Friday, the day of nature.

409
IF YOUR HOUSEMATE LEAVES YOUR HOME LIKE A GARBAGE DUMP AND WILL NOT CONTRIBUTE THEIR FAIR SHARE

Purpose and background information:
When you are being forced to act like a parent to an overgrown selfish child.

CARD 1: Should you go on strike, buying your own food/keeping only your part of the apartment clean and tidy to see if your housemate gets the message? **CARD 2:** If you are responsible for paying the rent/utility bills, should you give a warning/then advertise for a replacement housemate if necessary? **CARD 3:** If the apartment isn't in your name, should you contemplate moving on to find a more considerate housemate? **CARD 4:** Have you been brought up to be the responsible one? Do others generally take advantage of this? Should this change? **CARD 5:** Would you be happier living in a smaller place by yourself?

What you should use:
The twenty-two Major cards and the sixteen Court cards.

When:
When subsidizing your housemate is making you broke and resentful.

410
IF YOU OR FAMILY MEMBERS OFTEN HAVE ACCIDENTS OR BREAK ITEMS IN THE HOME

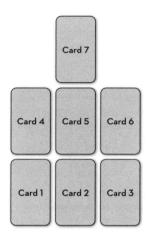

Purpose and background information:
If you are wondering if the home is unlucky.

CARD 1: Are you and family members always in a hurry or stressed? **CARD 2:** Are you naturally a clumsy/accident-prone family, or is it mainly one or two members? **CARD 3:** Are there lots of potential accidents waiting to happen around the home because things need fixing/securing? **CARD 4:** Should you have a family conference to discuss strategies for taking better care of the home? **CARD 5:** Should you invite safety officers to identify potential problem areas? **CARD 6:** Are family tensions/unexpressed resentments/jealousy creating negative energies in which accidents are more likely? **CARD 7:** Should you create an area of tranquility within the home using crystals, etc., to bring about a more harmonious atmosphere?

What you should use:
The whole deck.

When:
A Friday the 13th, or any period when a lot has gone wrong.

CHAPTER 24

SPREADS FOR FRIENDSHIPS AND YOUR SOCIAL LIFE

Lucky cards for Friendship Spreads:

Major Arcana: The Fool, the Magician, the Lovers, the Chariot, Strength, Temperance, the Moon, the Sun, the Star, the World.

Minor Cards: Aces of Cups and Wands, Three of Pentacles, Two and Three of Cups and Wands, Five of Pentacles and Wands, Six of Cups and Wands, Eight of Cups, Ten of Cups.

Court Cards: The Pages/Princesses and Princes/Knights of Pentacles, Cups, and Wands.

About Friendship Spreads:

Ones, twos, and three-carders for new and growing friendship; fives for questions about loyalty and conflict; sixes for happy friendships and making new friends; sevens for choices; eights and above for major questions and traveling with friends.

411
WHY DOES IT SEEM SO HARD TO MAKE FRIENDS?

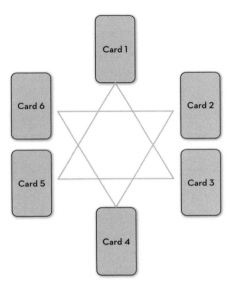

Purpose and background information:

If you never seem to get asked to parties or social events.

CARD 1: Are you naturally a loner who doesn't want company, but feel you ought to? **CARD 2:** Would you like a few like-minded friends? How/where can you meet them? **CARD 3:** If you want to socialize more, what deep down holds you back? **CARD 4:** Should you seek friends online, enjoying online friendships rather than face-to-face? **CARD 5:** Where should you go/what should you join/new activities to try to meet more people directly? **CARD 6:** Are you in the wrong place/ should you change jobs/relocate?

What you should use:

The full deck.

When:

The beginning of a new week or month.

412
DEALING WITH SOCIAL LIFE CONFLICTS

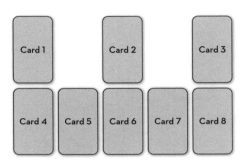

Purpose and background information:

When friendships are proving troublesome.

CARD 1: Who or what is causing problems in your social life? **CARD 2:** Is there a person/clique working to exclude you? **CARD 3:** What allies or friends do you have/could you develop within the social circle? **CARD 4:** Should you ignore the problem/hope the troublemakers lose interest? **CARD 5:** Do you need to tackle the difficult people head-on? **CARD 6:** Should you move on? **CARD 7:** What can be gained by staying in the same social circle, with or without resolution? **CARD 8:** What is the best outcome for you?

What you should use:

The forty Minor cards, Aces to Tens, and the sixteen Court cards.

When:

A Wednesday, to protect against human snakes.

413

IF A FRIEND BORROWS MONEY, CLOTHES, AND POSSESSIONS AND NEVER RETURNS THEM

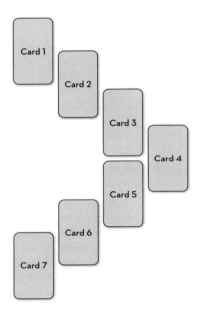

Purpose and background information:

When you are tired of acting as a bank and clothing store.

CARD 1: Are you naturally generous, frequently lending to others? **CARD 2:** Are you made to feel guilty/mean if you ask for money/property lent to your friend to be returned? **CARD 3:** Why do you feel guilty/obliged to help out your friend? **CARD 4:** Is your friend generally a user of people, or is this behavior reserved for you? **CARD 5:** Should you impose conditions for future lending, at the risk of damaging the friendship? **CARD 6:** Should you refuse, even if there is a hard-luck story attached? **CARD 7:** Do you really want a friend who takes and never gives? Will this friend ever change?

What you should use:

The twenty-two Major cards and the sixteen Court cards.

When:

When pay/allowance day is approaching.

414

IF A FRIEND NEVER PAYS THEIR SHARE ON OUTINGS OR RETURNS FAVORS FOR HELP GIVEN

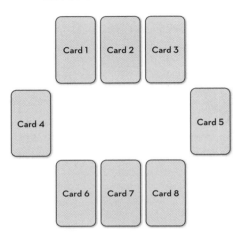

Purpose and background information:

If you are the one always doing the giving/helping out in crises.

CARD 1: Is your friend just thoughtless, or deliberately selfish/mean? **CARD 2:** Is there always an excuse your friend cannot pay/help out? **CARD 3:** Are you becoming increasingly resentful, or do you generally offer to pay for others anyway? **CARD 4:** Why do you feel you shouldn't ask for contributions/assistance when you need it? **CARD 5:** Should you say *no* more often, or split every bill/draw up a roster for mutual help? **CARD 6:** Have other friends noticed that this friend never contributes, or are you the only one taken advantage of? **CARD 7:** Should you change the ground rules so help/payments are mutual or not at all? **CARD 8:** Should you spend time with more generous/helpful friends who are there for you in a crisis?

What you should use:

The forty Minor cards, Aces to Tens, and the sixteen Court cards.

When:

A Saturday, day of financial caution.

415
IF YOUR PARTNER SPENDS MORE TIME WITH FRIENDS THAN WITH YOU

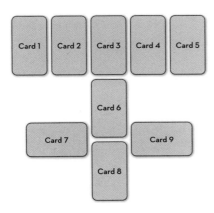

Purpose and background information:
When this is putting a strain on your relationship.

CARD 1: Are you excluded from your partner's group of friends, or do you have nothing in common with them?
CARD 2: Has your partner known these friends forever/ are they connected with a particular social activity/work?
CARD 3: Are they bad influences/monopolize your partner's time even when you are together, with constant texting/ calls? **CARD 4:** Does your partner need these friends as an ego boost/to maintain connections with an unattached life?
CARD 5: Do any of your partner's friends have partners you could get to know so you could go out together? **CARD 6:** Do you feel insecure about the influence of any particular friend?
CARD 7: Can you negotiate more time as a couple/plan new activities together that do not involve the friends? **CARD 8:** Would it help to spend more time with your own friends when your partner isn't around? **CARD 9:** Are there underlying relationship issues that need resolving, of which the friend issue is a symptom?

What you should use:
The full deck.

When:
At the waning moon.

416
IF YOU HAVE MOVED TO A NEW AREA AND LEFT ALL YOUR FRIENDS BEHIND

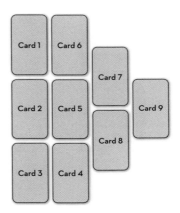

Purpose and background information:
When you don't know anybody and feel lonely.

CARD 1: Can you ease the transition by Skyping/using social media/arranging visits by the folks you have left behind?
CARD 2: Can you use your workplace/the children's school to find a new social network? **CARD 3:** Should you explore neighborhood groups/issue invitations to neighbors?
CARD 4: Should you join community groups and activities?
CARD 5: Should you volunteer for local fundraising/local branches of charities you are already involved with? **CARD 6:** Should you join a sports club/gym even if you are not sporty/ social club to meet locals in a relaxed environment? **CARD 7:** Should you join online forums/social media to find local people to meet face to face? **CARD 8:** Would you welcome some time to find your feet exploring the area and its facilities before commencing any social life? **CARD 9:** Will you soon meet new friends?

What you should use:
The whole deck.

When:
Once you are settled in your new home.

417
IF YOUR BEST FRIEND IS POSSESSIVE AND RESENTS YOUR SPENDING TIME WITH OTHER FRIENDS

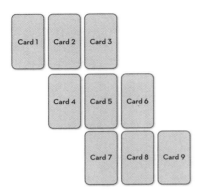

Purpose and background information:

When you are starting to feel stifled.

CARD 1: Has your friend always been possessive, or has a recent break up/betrayal made them insecure? **CARD 2:** Can/should you help your friend to find other interests/ activities that do not involve you? **CARD 3:** Should you introduce your friend to different people who could offer friendship? **CARD 4:** Should you invite them along more, so they can get to know your friends? **CARD 5:** Can you avoid feeling guilty/emotional blackmail/manipulation if you do not always invite them along? **CARD 6:** If your friend is making your life stressful, should you start to distance yourself? **CARD 7:** If your friend constantly uses you as an agony aunt/ uncle, can you steer them toward counseling/a self-help group? **CARD 8:** Were you raised to feel responsible for the happiness of others? Has this happened before with friends? **CARD 9:** If the situation becomes too stifling, should you walk away (you can be reasonably sure they'll soon find someone else).

What you should use:

The forty Minor cards, Aces to tens, and the sixteen Court cards.

When:

The end of a month/year.

418
IF YOUR BEST FRIEND IS BECOMING MORE THAN A FRIEND

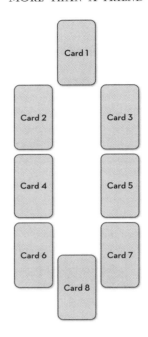

Purpose and background information:

When you sense friendship turning into love.

CARD 1: Are you totally on the same wavelength/twin souls without the romance? **CARD 2:** Is there more than friendship growing from your side? **CARD 3:** Do you get signs/are you sensing that the feelings are reciprocal? **CARD 4:** Should you up the love stakes a notch or two? **CARD 5:** Should you take it more slowly so as not to damage the friendship? **CARD 6:** Should you/when should you express your feelings? **CARD 7:** Will it work? **CARD 8:** Even if it doesn't, do you still want to/ can you still be friends?

What you should use:

The twenty-two major cards and the sixteen Court cards.

When:

Any significant date in your friendship/Valentine's Day.

419
IF YOUR BEST FRIEND IS JEALOUS OF YOUR NEW PARTNER

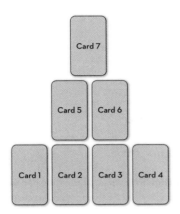

Purpose and background information:
When you are tired of having to choose.

CARD 1: Why does your friend dislike your partner: because you are less available, or because s/he worries you'll be hurt as you have been in the past? **CARD 2:** Is the bad feeling mutual between partner and friend? Why? **CARD 3:** Since being in your new relationship, have you had less time for the friendship? **CARD 4:** Can you/should you spend more time with your friend without your partner? **CARD 5:** Should your partner be a priority? **CARD 6:** Can you balance life to keep the friendship going? **CARD 7:** If your friend cannot accept your new partner, should you let the friendship go?

What you should use:
The twenty-two Major cards and the sixteen Court cards.

When:
A Tuesday, day of choices.

420
SHOULD YOU ATTEND AN OLD SCHOOL OR COLLEGE REUNION?

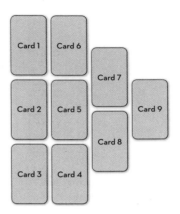

Purpose and background information:
If you have received an invitation but are in two minds about attending.

CARD 1: What are the potential advantages of attending? **CARD 2:** What are the potential drawbacks of attending? **CARD 3:** Should you make contact with old classmates on social media before the event? **CARD 4:** Are you hoping an old flame may be there to maybe reconnect? **CARD 5:** If an old adversary will probably be there, do you want to make peace, or show how well you have done? **CARD 6:** Do you hope to reconnect with old friends on a more permanent basis? **CARD 7:** Are you happy to accept the occasion for whatever it brings, good and bad memories alike? **CARD 8:** If you were unhappy at school/college, will this lay old ghosts to rest/prove a few people wrong about you? **CARD 9:** Is the past best left in the past?

What you should use:
The whole deck.

When:
Before deciding whether to accept.

IF YOU HAVE BEEN FRIENDS FOREVER, BUT ONE OF YOU HAS HAD A BABY AND IT HAS SHAKEN THE FRIENDSHIP

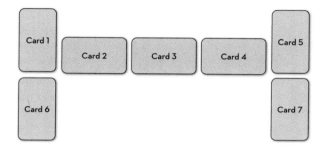

Purpose and background information:

When you have done everything together but suddenly are in different worlds.

CARD 1: Have you been friends through different life stages and adapted before to changing circumstances? **CARD 2:** Is this a sensitive issue, because of fertility problems/a decision by one of you to not have babies? **CARD 3:** Would you/your friend like to be an honorary aunt/uncle and share their upbringing? **CARD 4:** Should you still plan child-free meetings/conversations? **CARD 5:** Can/should you/your friend accept that children bring different priorities? **CARD 6:** Do you want/will the friendship survive this change? **CARD 7:** Were you growing apart anyway?

What you should use:

The whole deck.

When:

When it's getting harder to arrange getting together.

Example:

Meg had recently had a baby who has colic and rarely sleeps. Her best friend Esther hasn't been at all sympathetic and makes Meg feel inadequate, because right now her days inevitably revolve around the baby. Is the friendship doomed?

CARD 1: The High Priestess. When Meg had been ill some years before, Esther had been annoyed because they had to cancel a holiday. Generally, Meg has been the one to adapt; she actually turned down a prestigious college admission so she could be near Esther. **CARD 2: The Star.** Esther is dedicated to her career and had made it clear that children were not part of her future. Meg had been a high flyer, but has taken a step back to raise her children herself. **CARD 3: The Hermit.** Meg had asked Esther to be a godparent, but she had refused and sent an expensive gift instead. **CARD 4: Eight of Swords.** They have met a few times, but Meg is too exhausted to stay out late and finds it hard to avoid mentioning her baby, which Esther hates her to do. **CARD 5: The Five of Cups.** Walking away. Esther wanted Meg to commit to two weeks overseas, just the two of them, which just isn't possible. **CARD 6: Six of Cups.** Meg knows if the friendship is to survive, she will have to make the sacrifices. **CARD 7: Eight of Cups.** Meg walking to her new life, deciding this time that if Esther wants to stay friends, she will have to make some of the effort.

Esther was promoted shortly after the reading, met a lot of new people, and dropped Meg.

422
IF YOU MAKE FRIENDS EASILY, BUT THE FRIENDSHIPS DO NOT LAST

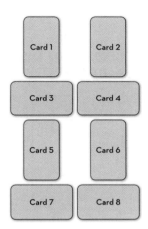

Purpose and background information:

When you wonder why friends come and go in your life.

Card 1: Do you outgrow friendships linked to a particular life stage setting or interest, such as workplace/gym/college? **Card 2:** Do you have high hopes for a new friendship but get rapidly disillusioned? **Card 3:** Should you cultivate one or two lasting friendships, rather than a wide social circle? **Card 4:** Do you give/offer too much, so attracting users who take and move on? **Card 5:** Are you attracted to fun/exciting people who are more superficial? **Card 6:** Should you reconnect with former good friends with whom you have lost touch? **Card 7:** Should you avoid seeking new friendships at the expense of developing existing if less exciting friendships where you have a lot in common? **Card 8:** Have you temporarily lost faith in people and need time alone learning to value yourself?

What you should use:

The forty Minor cards, Aces to Tens, and the sixteen Court cards.

When:

Before a social event where you will meet new people.

423
IF YOU MEET SOMEONE WITH WHOM YOU INSTANTLY CLICK

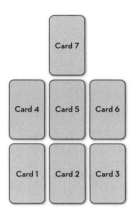

Purpose and background information:

If you feel you have known a new friend forever.

Card 1: Could there be a past life connection? (Study the card to link with an old world.) **Card 2:** Do you believe you have met at this time for an unfolding purpose? Any clues in the card? **Card 3:** Do you have a telepathic connection that makes you feel you have known each other forever? **Card 4:** Will/how will this new friendship fit in with your existing friendship base? **Card 5:** Will this friendship enhance your present life? **Card 6:** Are you able, as you know each other longer, to incorporate differences between you without spoiling the closeness? **Card 7:** Will this friendship grow over the years, or will it burn itself out if circumstances change?

What you will use:

The twenty-two major cards and the sixteen Court cards.

When:

At a full moon.

424
IF YOUR NEIGHBOR IS A CLOSE FRIEND, AND YOU HAVE A FALLING-OUT

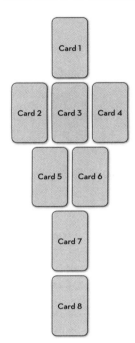

Purpose and background information:
When a falling-out affects your everyday life.

CARD 1: Were you too closely knit in your daily lives and needed some breathing space? **CARD 2:** Is there a competitive edge, connected with home/partner/family, that needs rebalancing? **CARD 3:** Was it a quarrel between neighbors about children/boundary disputes/noise, rather than a friendship issue? **CARD 4:** Do you value your neighbor's friendship? **CARD 5:** Are you prepared to compromise/forget hurtful words? **CARD 6:** If you cannot compromise friendship-wise, can you still live in harmony as neighbors? **CARD 7:** Will the new dealings between you be more workable, even if not personally as close as before? **CARD 8:** Will the friendship be revived, given time?

What you should use:
The full deck.

When:
A Friday, day of mending quarrels.

425
IF YOUR BEST FRIEND LIVES IN OR MOVES TO ANOTHER STATE OR COUNTRY

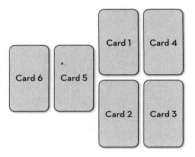

Purpose and background information:
When you miss your friend and do not want to lose the friendship.

CARD 1: Is the friendship strong enough to survive the distance? **CARD 2:** Can you fix regular chat times via social media/Skype, etc., to bridge the miles to share important life changes/exchange advice and everyday events? **CARD 3:** Can you meet halfway, visit each other on vacation to keep the friendship strong? **CARD 4:** Should you develop new friendships locally for daily interactions? **CARD 5:** Will you be able to move nearer to one another in the foreseeable future? **CARD 6:** Will you always be best friends in spite of obstacles?

What you should use:
The forty Minor cards and the sixteen Court cards.

When:
A significant time or day that you used to spend together.

426
IF YOUR CHILDREN AND YOUR FRIEND'S CHILDREN DO NOT GET ALONG

Purpose and background information:
When family get-togethers prove a nightmare.

CARD 1: Can you/how can you fix activities where both families meet and the children do their own thing? **CARD 2:** Should you both acknowledge the problem and develop strategies/ground rules for more harmonious gatherings? **CARD 3:** Should you invite the most amenable/closest in age child from each family for a fun treat so they bond? **CARD 4:** Should you see your friend without the family/just with partners? **CARD 5:** Will the situation improve spontaneously with time?

What you should use:
The forty Minor cards, Aces to Tens, and the sixteen Court cards.

When:
The day before a planned get-together.

427
IF YOU WANT TO GO ON VACATION WITH YOUR FRIEND, BUT YOUR PARTNER OR FAMILY OBJECTS

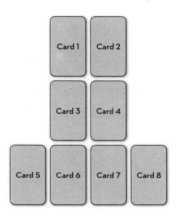

Purpose and background information:
When a vacation plan is becoming a three-act drama.

CARD 1: Should you go ahead with plans and present a fait accompli? **CARD 2:** Why should/do your partner or your partner's family try to make you feel guilty for wanting to spend time with a friend? **CARD 3:** Why do you/should you allow them to make you feel guilty/neglecting their needs? **CARD 4:** Should you suggest a family holiday/vacation with your partner later in the year? **CARD 5:** Are there underlying tensions in the relationship with your partner that make independent actions a threat? **CARD 6:** If your partner is needy/possessive, should you encourage them to develop friendships/go on vacations connected with their interests? **CARD 7:** Should you change plans to include partners/families? **CARD 8:** Should you give up and tell your friend you cannot go?

What you should use:
The whole deck.

When:
When your plan is in danger of derailment.

428
IF YOUR PARTNER'S BEST FRIEND ALWAYS TAGS ALONG

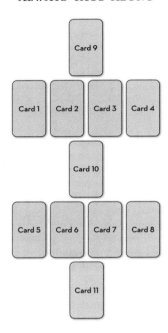

Purpose and background information:
When your partner's best friend seems to come first.

CARD 1: Is your partner's friend thoughtless/insensitive to hints, or genuinely possessive? **CARD 2:** Is your partner so used to having his/her best friend as a part of life, it's not an issue for them? **CARD 3:** Are you excluded from the friendship/do you experience resentment from the friend at your presence? **CARD 4:** Should you explain to your partner that you want more time together? Would this work? **CARD 5:** Should you issue specific invitations when the best friend is included? Would this work? **CARD 6:** Should you fix weekends/vacations away with only two tickets? **CARD 7:** Why does your partner need the best friend tagging along? Habit/immaturity/insecurity? **CARD 8:** Should/can you compromise/accept the situation? **CARD 9:** Will your partner grow out of this dependency? **CARD 10:** If your partner still encourages the friend to be part of your lives, should you consider relocating/setting new ground rules? **CARD 11:** Is this the right relationship for you?

What you should use:
The full deck.

When:
When you are made to feel like the outsider.

429
IF YOUR BEST FRIEND FLIRTS WITH YOUR PARTNER

Purpose and background information:
When you are competing for your partner's attention.

CARD 1: Is your friend a natural attention-seeker who uses good looks/charisma to seek admiration? **CARD 2:** Is your partner annoyed, or flattered, by the attention? **CARD 3:** Should you encourage your friend to bring along a partner/set up dates so s/he has a ready audience? **CARD 4:** Should you explain to your friend this flirting must stop, even if this damages your friendship? **CARD 5:** If your partner encourages/reciprocates with flirting, should you take a stand, or just ignore it? **CARD 6:** Is your friend seriously making a play for your partner? **CARD 7:** Time to dump your friend? **CARD 8:** Is this a weakness in your partnership/relationship that needs addressing?

What you should use:
The twenty-two Major cards and the sixteen Court cards.

When:
When you are feeling insecure.

430
IF YOUR PARTNER'S OR CHILDREN'S FRIENDS ARE BAD INFLUENCES

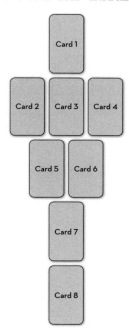

Purpose and background information:

When you are aware that your partner/children are being led astray.

CARD 1: Are these people deliberately leading your partner/children astray, or is it thoughtlessness/immaturity? **CARD 2:** Are the problems getting worse/causing anti-social behavior/bad habits/financial strains? **CARD 3:** Can you/how can you best steer your partner/children toward more suitable friends? **CARD 4:** How far are you prepared/need to go to break the hold? **CARD 5:** Do you need outside support/counseling for your partner/child? **CARD 6:** Should you consider moving to a new location/changing schools/encouraging a new workplace for your partner? **CARD 7:** What do they get from this association that keeps the connection going? **CARD 8:** Should you get tough, or do you think hoping the association will end will do the trick?

What you should use:

The full deck.

When:

At the waning moon.

431
SHOULD YOU RECONNECT WITH AN OLD FRIEND ON SOCIAL MEDIA IF YOU PARTED BADLY AND NOW REGRET THAT YOU ARE NO LONGER ON SPEAKING TERMS?

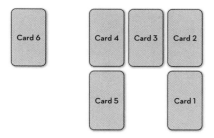

Purpose and background information:

When you see a social media entry that makes you regret that you are no longer on speaking terms.

CARD 1: Should you initially make a new friend request/remove any blocks on your side? **CARD 2:** Should you make positive comments/like posts/via any social media platform which you share? **CARD 3:** Should you send a private message/friendly email not referring to the split? **CARD 4:** Should you use a friend as an intermediary to reconnect? **CARD 5:** How would you ideally like the reconnection to develop? **CARD 6:** If underlying issues are still there, would it be better to leave matters as they are?

What you should use:

The twenty-two Major cards and the sixteen Court cards.

When:

At a crescent/waxing moon.

432

WILL YOU MAKE FRIENDS IN YOUR NEW WORKPLACE?

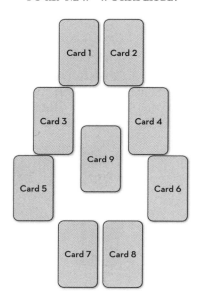

Purpose and background information:

When you are the newbie and everyone seems to know everybody else.

CARD 1: Should you leap straight in socially, or stand back and watch—or a bit of both? **CARD 2:** Are there any major cliques to avoid? **CARD 3:** Can you quickly work out the power structure/unspoken rules to avoid treading on toes? **CARD 4:** Is anyone especially unwelcoming/anti-newcomer/ friends with the person you are replacing? **CARD 5:** Are there leisure facilities/after-work wine bar/gym everyone goes to where you can get to know colleagues better? **CARD 6:** Are there mixed messages about coffee-making/buying schedule/favored workspace you need to be aware/wary of? **CARD 7:** Will you soon settle? **CARD 8:** Anything to watch out for positive or challenging about workplace politics/ underlying power structure? **CARD 9:** Is there anyone who could become a good after-work friend?

What you should use:

The forty Minor cards, Aces to Tens, and the sixteen Court cards.

When:

Any time during your first week on the job.

433

TO PUT RIGHT COLDNESS OR ESTRANGEMENT IN A FRIENDSHIP CAUSED BY A STUPID MISUNDERSTANDING

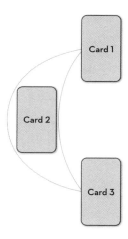

Purpose and background information:

When you regret losing a friendship, but neither of you will make the first move.

CARD 1: Is it worth making the first move in order to restore what was and could be a good friendship? **CARD 2:** Are you prepared to persist if the other person proves stubborn? **CARD 3:** Will the friendship be restored?

What you should use:

The twenty-two major cards and the sixteen Court cards.

When:

A Sunday morning for new beginnings.

434
TO OVERCOME A HURTFUL EXPERIENCE IN AN OTHERWISE GOOD FRIENDSHIP

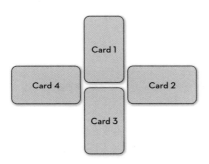

Purpose and background information:
When you have every reason to be angry, but miss your friend.

CARD 1: Should you forgive this betrayal/nastiness as totally out of character/provoked by a setback in your friend's life? **CARD 2:** Should you make the first move, as you suspect your friend will not? **CARD 3:** Should you, for your self-esteem, discuss what happened/ask for an apology? **CARD 4:** Should you not refer to the incident/start again?

What you should use:
The twenty-two Major cards.

When:
A day/evening when you would normally meet.

435
WHEN A FRIEND CONSTANTLY LIES TO YOU

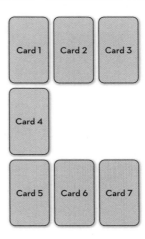

Purpose and background information:
When your friend's lies are damaging your trust.

CARD 1: Does your friend always say what they think you want to hear to please you/out of fear of losing your friendship? **CARD 2:** Is your friend a liar in other parts of their life/ to other people as well? **CARD 3:** Is the inability to trust your friend damaging the relationship, even if the lies are harmless? **CARD 4:** Do you suspect your friend lies about you to other people? **CARD 5:** Should you confront your friend at the risk of damaging the friendship? **CARD 6:** Can/will your friend change/become more truthful? **CARD 7:** If not, should you end the friendship?

What you should use:
The forty Minor cards, Aces to Tens, and the sixteen Court cards.

When:
A Wednesday, for overcoming deception.

436
BREAKING AN ONLINE FRIENDSHIP THAT YOU FEAR MAY EXPLOIT YOU

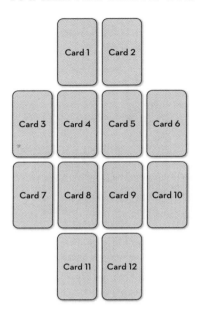

Purpose and background information:

When you are becoming increasingly dependent on the online connection.

CARD 1: Does your online friend anticipate your moods/feelings and spend hours talking over your problems? **CARD 2:** Is the nature of the friendship changing/becoming more intense/moving toward love? **CARD 3:** Does your online friend always have a plausible reason for not meeting, but continues to promise? **CARD 4:** If overseas, does your friend need financial support for a major family crisis/help with an airfare/work permit? **CARD 5:** What is making you suspicious: extra pressure to send money, or withdrawal of affection if you ask too many probing questions? **CARD 6:** Are you keeping the friendship secret from friends and family for fear of disapproval? **CARD 7:** Should you insist on a meeting in a safe environment rather than traveling overseas? **CARD 8:**

Should you check other sites for the same photo with a different name/a number of clearly romantic attachments? **CARD 9:** If no meeting is forthcoming, should you reduce/cut connection? **CARD 10:** Should you seek new friends offline, as well as online? **CARD 11:** Is this encounter genuine? **CARD 12:** Is it going anywhere?

What you should use:

The whole deck.

When:

After another broken promise of a meeting.

437
IF YOUR FRIEND CRITICIZES YOU OR PUTS YOU DOWN IN PUBLIC

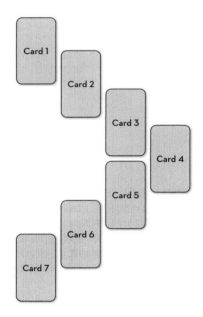

Purpose and background information:

When you are seriously losing confidence in yourself as a result of the put-downs.

CARD 1: Is it only when you go out socially that your friend makes fun of you, or does this occur when you are alone as well? **CARD 2:** Is your friend naturally sarcastic at the expense of others, or are you the sole target? **CARD 3:** Should you get tough, explaining that you will not put up with this? **CARD 4:** Should you reply in a similar way in public so people laugh *with* you? **CARD 5:** Are you/why are you afraid of losing this friendship which makes you feel bad? **CARD 6:** Should you go out without your friend, with people who make you feel good? **CARD 7:** Should you find a new friend who is more loyal?

What you should use:
The twenty-two Major cards and the sixteen Court cards.

When:
The evening before you go to a social gathering with your friend.

438
WHEN TWO FRIENDS ARE PULLING
YOU IN OPPOSITE DIRECTIONS

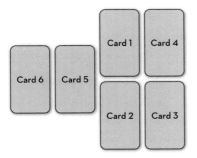

Purpose and background information:
If you are being asked to choose between two friends or their strongly held opinions, which you fear will damage your friendship with the one you do not choose.

CARD 1: Has there been conflict between the two friends before, or is this a major issue that has suddenly flared up? **CARD 2:** Is there any chance that you could mediate/bring about a compromise? **CARD 3:** Do you strongly agree with one of them, or can you see both sides? **CARD 4:** Should you refuse to make the choice and maybe upset both? **CARD 5:** Is it possible to remain friends with either/both of them if you

refuse to choose? **CARD 6:** Does the stress caused make it not worth being friends with either?

What you should use:
The forty Minor cards and the sixteen Court cards.

When:
A Saturday, day of wise caution.

439
IF YOU ARE NATURALLY NOT VERY
SOCIABLE, BUT PEOPLE TELL YOU THAT
YOU SHOULD MAKE MORE FRIENDS

Purpose and background information:
If you feel pressured to make an effort when you are not sure you want to.

CARD 1: Are you/should you be happy with your social life the way it is? **CARD 2:** Do you dislike parties and large noisy gatherings? **CARD 3:** Would you sooner chat to people online/through computer games than face-to-face? **CARD 4:** Do you have one or two good friends who respect your personal space and time? **CARD 5:** Should you ignore those telling you what you *should do* and follow your own rules?

What you should use:
The twenty-two Major cards and the sixteen Court cards.

When:
When you feel unhurried.

440
IF YOUR PARTNER OBJECTS TO ALL YOUR FRIENDS

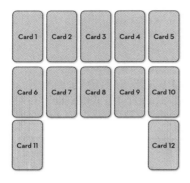

Purpose and background information:

When you feel increasingly cut off from your former social life and new people you meet.

CARD 1: Is this inclusiveness connected with the first flush of being a couple, or has this gone on rather too long? **CARD 2:** Why does your partner say they do not like your friends? **CARD 3:** What is the real reason your partner is cutting you off from your friends? **CARD 4:** Should you insist on seeing them/talking to them, even if your partner makes a fuss? **CARD 5:** Do you have/should you make joint friends so it's not always just the two of you? **CARD 6:** Is your partner solitary, enjoying their own company for much of the time? **CARD 7:** Is your partner over-possessive/insecure/jealous because you are giving your attention elsewhere? **CARD 8:** Should you both go for counseling to see if there are relationship issues your partner is denying? **CARD 9:** Can/should you compromise so you see your friends away from the home once or twice a week? **CARD 10:** Does this restrictive attitude intrude on other aspects of your life? What can fix it? **CARD 11:** Will you gain more freedom within the relationship? **CARD 12:** If not, should you reassess the relationship?

What you should use:

The whole deck.

When:

When the moon passes through Aquarius.

CHAPTER 25

SPREADS FOR FERTILITY, CONCEPTION, PREGNANCY, AND BABIES

Lucky cards for fertility, pregnancy, and babies:

Major Cards: The Fool/Inner Child, the Empress, Emperor, the Lovers, Wheel of Fortune, Strength, Temperance, the Star, Moon, and Sun.

Minor Cards: All Aces (Swords for successful medical intervention). Three of Cups and Three of Wands, Six of Cups, Seven of Cups, Eight of Wands, Nine of Wands, Ten of Cups, and Ten of Pentacles.

Court Cards: All Pages/Princesses and Knights/Princes; Queens and Kings of Cups and Wands.

About fertility Spreads:

Three-card Spreads represent two becoming three; and if you already have children, you can use the same number of cards as you have children plus yourself and your partner plus one card for the new baby; you want four cards for security vs. freedom and five for choices or medical intervention. Six is for the happy family and fertility; seven cards especially for fertility, conception, pregnancy, and safe delivery; and eight cards and above for any major questions.

441
ARE YOU BOTH READY FOR THE LIFE CHANGES A BABY WILL BRING?

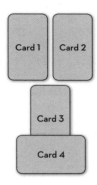

Purpose and background information:
When you are discussing having a family.

CARD 1: What does your partner really feel? **CARD 2:** What do you really feel? **CARD 3:** Is this the right time/ do you still have things to do as a couple first? **CARD 4:** Are the advantages of having a family greater than the disadvantages?

What you should use:
The Major twenty-two cards.

When:
At the full moon, folklorically the traditional time for conception.

442
IS MY PARTNER THE RIGHT PERSON TO BE THE PARENT OF MY CHILD?

Purpose and background information:
When you aren't 100% sure the person you love is good parent material.

CARD 1: Is s/he sufficiently mature, or does s/he need more time to grow up? **CARD 2:** Would s/he be a loving supportive co-parent? **CARD 3:** Should I go ahead and try for a baby with him/her, or move on to another relationship/go it alone?

What you should use:
The twenty-two Major cards.

When:
When the talk turns to babies.

443
IF YOU ARE TRYING TO CONCEIVE BUT ARE HAVING DIFFICULTY

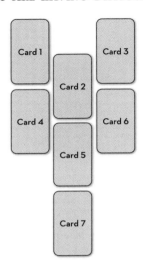

Purpose and background information:

When you are getting anxious and you know anxiety is not helping.

CARD 1: Are you both fit and well, or is there more you could do to improve your lifestyle? **CARD 2:** Do emotional issues around having a baby need resolving? **CARD 3:** Should you try extra alternative methods, meditation/ yoga, energy therapies/relax more? **CARD 4:** Is now the time to seek advice, or should you wait a few more months? **CARD 5:** Are you/should you be enjoying life more as a couple/spontaneous lovemaking/holidays/fun outings, etc.? **CARD 6:** Is it just a matter of time before you conceive? **CARD 7:** Should/can you arrange more time so you are always together at peak ovulation, or do you trust to nature to take her course?

What you should use:

The forty Minor cards, Aces to Tens, plus the Court Cards.

When:

A Friday, the day of fertility.

444
IF YOU DO NOT HAVE A PARTNER WITH WHOM TO HAVE A BABY, AND YOUR BIOLOGICAL CLOCK IS TICKING AWAY

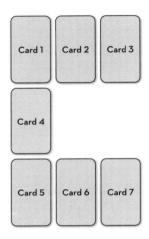

Purpose and background information:

When you want a baby and do not feel you can wait forever.

CARD 1: Should you freeze your eggs now, or wait a year or two? **CARD 2:** Do you want to find a partner with whom to have a baby before conceiving? **CARD 3:** Should you go it alone now, or wait a while? **CARD 4:** If you go it alone, will you find a partner who will welcome a ready-made family? **CARD 5:** What are the advantages of going it alone? **CARD 6:** What are the drawbacks of going it alone? **CARD 7:** What friends and family will offer you support if you decide to go ahead?

What you should use:

The twenty-two Major cards and the sixteen Court cards.

When:

When you need to consider all your options before making a decision.

445
SHOULD YOU TRY ONE MORE IVF IF NONE HAS SO FAR BEEN SUCCESSFUL?

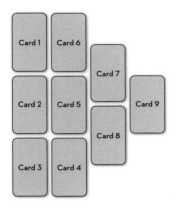

Purpose and background information:

When you feel like giving up, but something stops you.

CARD 1: Does this time feel different/more hopeful? **CARD 2:** Should you have a break before trying/go on holiday/get to know each other as lovers again? **CARD 3:** Are you/should you strive for peak fitness before trying again, not only physically but if the whole process has proven stressful? **CARD 4:** Should you use alternative methods, such as meditation/visualization of your infant/crystals before and during treatment to give yourself a calm approach? **CARD 5:** Should you go for IVF this time without expectation, opening yourself to nature and destiny, letting the baby come if it will? **CARD 6:** Can/should you keep trying, regardless of whether this attempt succeeds or fails? **CARD 7:** Are you happy with your treatment/clinic, or should you seek a new center of excellence? **CARD 8:** Should you stop trying altogether now and open yourself to the cosmos/destiny and nature if the child is meant to be (miracles do happen)? **CARD 9:** Do you have a good chance this time?

What you should use:

The full deck.

When:

The beginning of a month.

446
IF PREGNANCY IS TAKING A WHILE TO OCCUR, SHOULD YOU GO FOR TESTS, TRY INTERVENTION, OR LET NATURE TAKE ITS COURSE?

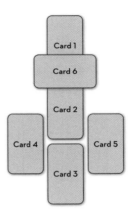

Purpose and background information:

When you are increasingly anxious because pregnancy did not occur straight away.

CARD 1: If you are getting anxious each month that you are not pregnant, would tests/intervention reassure you/identify any issues that needed resolving? **CARD 2:** Is this the right time to seek advice, or should you wait a while? **CARD 3:** Should you deliberately focus on being a twosome/go on a special vacation to get in tune with yourselves again? **CARD 4:** Should you increase your pre-conception care/extra supplements/relaxation/exercise, etc.? **CARD 5:** Do you have a good chance of getting pregnant if you are patient and let nature take her course? **CARD 6:** Do you need to rearrange your lifestyle so you are both less stressed and can make love regularly at ovulation times and also spontaneously?

What you should use:

The forty Minor cards, Aces to Tens, and the sixteen Court cards.

When:

The day after your most recent menstrual cycle began.

447
IF YOU WANT A BABY BUT WORRY ABOUT FERTILITY AND HEALTH ISSUES, AS YOU WILL BE AN OLDER PARENT

Purpose and background information:

When you and your partner are trying for your first baby late in life.

Card 1: Are you both fit and healthy, or do you need to change your lifestyles? **Card 2:** Are you both equally committed to the realities of a baby changing your lives? **Card 3:** Would you be prepared to seek medical advice/ intervention if necessary? **Card 4:** Do you have a good chance of a healthy baby? **Card 5:** Is trying it a now-or-never proposition?

What you should use:

The twenty-two Major cards and the sixteen Court cards.

When:

At a full moon.

448
IF, AFTER HAVING A CHILD OR CHILDREN TOGETHER, YOU ARE HAVING DIFFICULTY CONCEIVING ANOTHER BABY

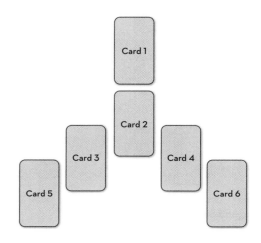

Purpose and background information:

When there seems no medical reason you cannot conceive.

Card 1: Are either or both of you under stress, never having time for each other? **Card 2:** Is it a practical logistics problem that you are always busy and tired, and lovemaking to conceive has become a chore? **Card 3:** Should you give yourselves more time and let it happen on its own schedule? **Card 4:** Has there been a drop in fertility/hormone levels since your first baby that warrants some medical advice? **Card 5:** Do you both *really* want another baby at this time, or would you sooner delay trying/decide you do not want another baby? **Card 6:** Will you get pregnant with or without intervention?

What you should use:

The forty Minor cards, Aces to Tens, and the sixteen Court cards.

When:

At a crescent or waxing moon.

449
WHEN THERE IS A LATE UNEXPECTED PREGNANCY AND YOUR OTHER CHILDREN ARE TEENAGERS OR ADULTS

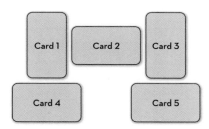

Purpose and background information:
When you thought your child-rearing days were over.

CARD 1: What are the advantages of the new baby? **CARD 2:** What are the drawbacks for you/your partner becoming pregnant at this stage of your lives? **CARD 3:** What strategies will prepare the other children to welcome the new arrival? **CARD 4:** Will the pregnancy and birth go well? **CARD 5:** Will/how will the new baby unite the family and prove a blessing in disguise?

What you should use:
The twenty-two Major cards and the sixteen Court cards.

When:
A Monday, the day of the moon and pregnancy.

450
IF YOUR PARTNER ALREADY HAS CHILDREN AND YOU DO NOT, AND S/HE IS RELUCTANT TO START AGAIN

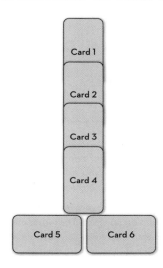

Purpose and background information:
When you want to have a child to unite the families.

CARD 1: Does the reluctance lie in bad experiences your partner had/has with their ex? **CARD 2:** Has your partner been told by the ex that they are a bad father/mother—and believes it? **CARD 3:** Are the existing children manipulative, perhaps influenced by the ex, causing trouble between you? **CARD 4:** If you wait, will your partner's attitude soften? **CARD 5:** If your partner will not agree, can you accept the situation? **CARD 6:** If not, what is your best action if you really want a child?

What you should use:
The full deck.

When:
When you are aware that the issue is driving a wedge between you.

451
IF THE MEDICAL PROFESSION IS DISMISSIVE OR NEGATIVE ABOUT YOU AND YOUR PARTNER'S CHANCES OF CONCEIVING

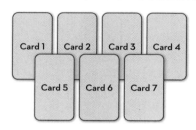

Purpose and background information:
When you are told by medics you are too old, not fertile, but you believe you/your partner still can have a child.

CARD 1: Are there new interventions/treatments you can try that you are not being offered to overcome the problem? **CARD 2:** Should you/where should you find more positive doctors who do not defeat you with their negativity? **CARD 3:** Should you find a center of excellence interstate or overseas that specializes in the kind of problems you are experiencing? **CARD 4:** Should you consider alternative methods/artificial insemination/a donor egg/a surrogate? **CARD 5:** Should you leave it to nature, no matter how bad the odds? **CARD 6:** Should you explore a lifestyle without a child? **CARD 7:** Do you have a good chance of conceiving in spite of the gloomy prognosis?

What you should use:
The twenty-two Major cards and the sixteen Court cards.

When:
A Sunday, for hope and new beginnings.

452
IF YOU HAVE SUFFERED PREVIOUS MISCARRIAGES AND ARE ANXIOUS ABOUT YOUR LATEST PREGNANCY GOING TO FULL TERM

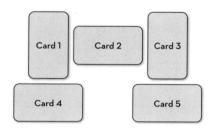

Purpose and background information:
When you are understandably worried.

CARD 1: Does/how does this pregnancy feel different? **CARD 2:** Are you/should you be cherishing yourself/insisting and demanding that others cherish you? **CARD 3:** Are you getting the best medical care at key times in the pregnancy? **CARD 4:** Are your chances better of going full-term this time? **CARD 5:** Will you have a healthy baby one day?

What you should use:
The forty Minor cards, Aces to Tens. Remember, swords indicate fears, not disasters.

When:
Any early morning or crescent moon.

453
WILL YOUR PREGNANCY AND DELIVERY BE SAFE AND HAPPY?

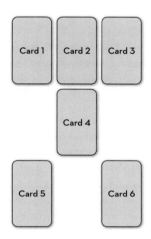

Purpose and background information:
When medically you are fine, but you are anxious, especially if it's your first baby.

CARD 1: Will you have a good pregnancy and healthy baby?
CARD 2: Even if you have a definite birth plan, do you have backup plans if circumstances around the delivery change?
CARD 3: Do you have confidence in those who will be/are caring for you? If not, should you address the worries now?
CARD 4: How can you help yourself/get those around you to help best in the pregnancy/as birth partners? **CARD 5:** Are you and your partner on the same page over the baby? If not, how can this be resolved? **CARD 6:** Are you getting enough relaxation/exploring hypnobirthing, etc., whatever feels right for you to put yourself in a calm frame of mind for pregnancy/birth?

What you should use:
The full deck.

When:
As early in the pregnancy as you wish.

454
IF YOUR PARTNER HAS LEFT YOU DURING PREGNANCY AFTER BEING INFORMED THAT YOU WERE PREGNANT

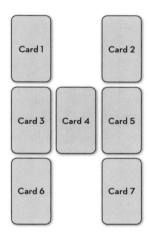

Purpose and background information:
If you are left to deal with pregnancy alone.

CARD 1: Do you believe this is cold feet/unresolved issues around mothers and babies, and is it resolvable? **CARD 2:** Were there deeper relationship issues/insecurities that the pregnancy has brought to a head? **CARD 3:** Will s/he come back for the birth/after the baby is born? **CARD 4:** Do you want them back after this desertion? **CARD 5:** Should you get together all the legal matters of financial support for the baby now, rather than after the birth? **CARD 6:** Who will be most helpful to you in the months ahead, maybe unexpected? **CARD 7:** Will it all end happily, with or without your partner?

What you should use:
The forty Minor cards, Aces to Tens, and the sixteen Court cards.

When:
A Tuesday, the day of personal power and independence.

IF CLOSE RELATIVES ARE INTERFERING TOO MUCH
IN YOUR PREGNANCY AND THE BABY'S FUTURE LIFE

Example:

Elspeth's partner Joel came from a long tradition of farmers, although he became a social worker. Whenever they went to see Joel's parents, he was constantly pressured to return to the land, as he was their only son. Since Elspeth was pregnant with a boy, his parents saw this as a chance to continue the family line. They were renovating a house on the land for Joel, although he said he wanted to stay in the city where Elspeth had a good job as a teacher. Joel had always been pressured by his mother, as the farm had been in the family for generations. Joel was wavering, but there was no way Elspeth was moving onto the land.

CARD 1: The Chariot. Elspeth was panicking as she watched her whole future being mapped out, even down to his parents buying furniture for the nursery at the newly renovated house. **CARD 2: The Empress.** Joel's mother was talking about how she would look after the baby while Elspeth went to work at a local school. Joel's mother, who was very unfulfilled, saw this baby as a second chance at motherhood for herself. **CARD 3: The Page of Pentacles,** not the new baby but Joel who allowed his parents to treat him like a child. **CARD 4: Seven of Wands.** Elspeth knew that unless she stuck to what she wanted, she and her new baby would be swallowed up in her in-laws' dream. **CARD 5: The Two of Cups.** Hard though it was, Elspeth had to get Joel on her side, say the renovated house was great for vacations but they were not ready to move onto the land. **CARD 6: The Eight of Cups:** Joel had been offered a major promotion in another state and Elspeth could stay home, care for her baby without interference, while studying psychology. Moving was a very viable option with promises of lots of visits to the farm once they were settled.

Purpose and background information:

When you feel that the pregnancy and birth are spiraling out of your partner's and your hands.

CARD 1: Is this interference seriously affecting your life and well-being? **CARD 2:** What are the motives behind it? **CARD 3:** Are/should you and your partner be 100% united, or is this divisive? **CARD 4:** Should you ignore this as over-involvement, or stick to your guns? **CARD 5:** Should you confront the issue head-on? **CARD 6:** If it is really bad, should you move away from the negative influence?

What you should use:

The whole deck.

When:

When you fear that you may lose your temper with the perpetrators.

456
IF YOU ARE EXPECTING TWINS OR HAVING A MULTIPLE INFANT PREGNANCY

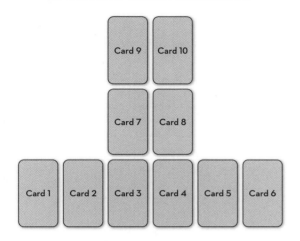

Purpose and background information:
When you are excited but a little overwhelmed.

Card 1: What is the best aspect of having more than one child at once? **Card 2:** What are your actual fears about coping? **Card 3:** What are your hidden fears? **Card 4:** What extra help/support can/should you call on now and after the birth? **Card 5:** What adjustments to your home/working life will now be necessary for you/your partner? **Card 6:** How best should you care for yourself/the babies during pregnancy and after the birth? **Card 7:** What financial strategies can you put in place to ease the extra costs? **Card 8:** What do *you* want in later pregnancy and for the delivery in terms of professional care? **Card 9:** What are your contingency plans if you need to change the birth plan at the last minute? **Card 10:** Will you have a healthy pregnancy and good delivery?

What you should use:
The forty Minor cards, Aces to Tens, and the sixteen Court cards.

When:
Any time during the pregnancy.

457
IF YOU KNOW YOU ARE HAVING A CAESAREAN BIRTH, AND YOU WANTED A NATURAL ONE

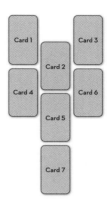

Purpose and background information:
When you find out you cannot have the birth plan you wanted.

Card 1: Can any of the original birth plans be adapted, especially if you stay awake for the caesarean? **Card 2:** Should you research as much as possible about caesarean birth, from experts and mothers who made it a special experience, so you create a new plan? **Card 3:** Can you plan quiet time with your partner immediately before and after the birth/prepare yourself with meditation so it becomes a spiritual, not just a medical, experience? **Card 4:** Can you make your hospital room pre- and post-birth homey and reassuring so you create an oasis of calm? **Card 5:** Can you aim for bonding experiences with your baby and partner, even if you are not so mobile for a day or two? **Card 6:** Will you have a beautiful healthy baby who will more than compensate for your original disappointment? **Card 7:** Will the birth of your next baby be more as you want it?

What you should use:
The whole deck.

When:
When your plans are changed.

458
IF IT'S YOUR FIRST BABY AND YOU ARE SCARED YOU WILL NOT BE A GOOD PARENT

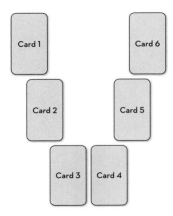

Purpose and background information:
When you become aware that you lack confidence and as a result feel you will not be a good parent.

Card 1: Do you know/can you spend time with other expectant/new parents to realize everyone has to adjust? **Card 2:** If you/your partner didn't have loving homes as children, should/can you accept that you are not your parents and have learned from their mistakes? **Card 3:** Are there trusted relatives/friends who will give you a break/allow you to rest when you go home, without taking over? **Card 4:** If you are a perfectionist, should you accept in advance that you will not have time for house chores/social life/major decisions, that it will for a time be all about the baby? **Card 5:** Should you join online pregnancy and parenting groups and local groups to share experiences and to network? **Card 6:** Will this be a wonderful life-changing experience once you accept you are the best person to parent your own child?

What you should use
The whole deck.

When:
Once the baby starts kicking in the womb.

459
IF YOU ARE GOING IT ALONE AND WILL BE HAVING ARTIFICIAL INSEMINATION

Purpose and background information:

Card 1: Should you choose someone you know who will take an interest in the child? **Card 2:** Is it better to use an unknown donor to make it easier on future relationships? **Card 3:** Would you prefer to do this informally, or go to an accredited clinic? **Card 4:** Are you prepared to try several times if it doesn't work the first time? **Card 5:** Are you ready for the responsibility of bringing up a child alone? **Card 6:** Who will encourage/support you in this? **Card 7:** Who will be critical/unhelpful, and should/can you avoid them? **Card 8:** What/when will you tell your child in the future? **Card 9:** Will/should you worry about this when the time comes? **Card 10:** Will this birth bring the happiness you desire? **Card 11:** Is now the right time, or should you wait a while?

What you should use:
The whole deck.

When:
When your biological clock is ticking and the right partner is not on the horizon.

460
IF YOUR PARTNER SHOWS NO INTEREST IN THE NEW BABY AND RESENTS THE TIME YOU SPEND WITH THE LITTLE ONE

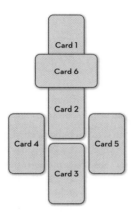

Purpose and background information:
When you feel totally unsupported at what should be the happiest time of your life.

CARD 1: Was this lack of interest/resentment visible during the pregnancy, or only since the birth? **CARD 2:** Is your partner depressed/overwhelmed by the responsibility of parenthood and needs counseling/medical support? **CARD 3:** Is this pure jealousy, perhaps stemming from childhood of being rejected by parents in favor of a sibling? **CARD 4:** Should you try to get help with the baby so you can spend more non-baby time with your partner? **CARD 5:** Can you accept this behavior if it continues? **CARD 6:** Should you/do you want to get tough with your partner and say *shape up or ship out*?

What you should use:
The forty Minor cards, Aces to Tens, and the sixteen Court cards.

When:
When your partner is acting like a spoiled child instead of a responsible parent.

461
WILL YOUR PARTNER, WHO IS NOT THE BIOLOGICAL FATHER OR MOTHER OF YOUR BABY, BOND WITH THE NEW INFANT?

Purpose and background information:
If you or your partner used a sperm donor, a donor egg from another woman, surrogacy, or the baby is from a previous relationship.

CARD 1: Did you discuss all the implications before you began the process? Were there still unresolved issues? **CARD 2:** Is the reality of the baby different from what was imagined? **CARD 3:** Can you talk through and resolve any problems? **CARD 4:** Do you need joint counseling? **CARD 5:** Should you involve your partner in hands-on care for the baby from day 1, even if at first unwilling? **CARD 6:** Will the situation improve naturally as the baby becomes a little person? **CARD 7:** Can you find a compromise if the resentment continues? **CARD 8:** Do you plan to tell the baby when s/he is old enough to understand, or will you consider that you are both the true parents anyway, even if not 100% biologically?

What you should use:
The full deck.

When:
After you/your partner bring the baby home.

462
IF YOU ARE A FEMALE COUPLE AND WANT CHILDREN

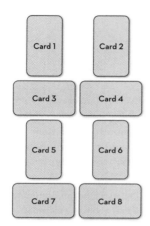

Purpose and background information:

When you are balancing the emotions and logistics.

CARD 1: Do you both want to give birth, or will one of you keep things going while the other is pregnant? **CARD 2:** If you are both going to be biological mothers, do you want to give birth at approximately the same time, or with a gap between the pregnancies? **CARD 3:** Do you want a male friend to act as donor and honorary uncle to the child/ren, using artificial insemination at home? **CARD 4:** Should you try artificial insemination/IVF with an unknown donor? **CARD 5:** Are you ready now, or do you want to wait a while? **CARD 6:** Do you have good friends and family/a positive local community to support you and your new family? **CARD 7:** What obstacles do you anticipate and the strategies to resolve them? **CARD 8:** Will one, or both, of you have children?

What you should use:

The twenty-two Major cards and the sixteen Court cards.

When:

At the full moon.

463
IF YOU ARE A MALE COUPLE AND WANT CHILDREN

Purpose and background information:

If you would like a child or children to complete your family.

CARD 1: Do you both want to father a child through donor sperm, or just one of you? **CARD 2:** If you want more than one child, would you seek the same surrogate mother, with a gap between the children? **CARD 3:** Would you ask a friend/family member to carry your child? **CARD 4:** Would you select someone you did not know from an organization, or choose two different women if you wanted your children very close? **CARD 5:** Would you prefer adoption of slightly older children? **CARD 6:** Have you/should you work out the logistics/financial aspects of incorporating children into your present life? **CARD 7:** Are you ready now/soon, or would you prefer to wait until you have done all the "couple" things? **CARD 8:** Will you have beautiful children?

What you should use:

The forty Minor cards, Aces to Tens, and the sixteen Court cards.

When:

When planning your next few years.

464
IF YOUR YOUNG TEENAGE
DAUGHTER IS PREGNANT

Purpose and background information:

When you have to guide your daughter through a minefield.

CARD 1: Does she need more impartial counseling, or is she better talking with you so she can find a positive way forward? **CARD 2:** How much are you prepared/able to do for the baby in the months and years ahead? **CARD 3:** Does she want a permanent relationship with the father of her baby, and is this realistic/desirable? **CARD 4:** How can you help the rest of the family to accept the addition to the family, especially her father? **CARD 5:** Are there any ways your daughter could continue her education after the baby is born/college nursery/home study, etc.? **CARD 6:** How much does the baby's father intend to be/will in practice be involved in her life/the baby? **CARD 7:** What support can/should his family offer, and will this be helpful? **CARD 8:** How will this new life bring blessings upon your family?

What you should use:

The whole deck.

When:

Once the initial shock has passed and you are able to discuss the situation in a calm rational manner.

465
IF YOUR TEENAGE SON FATHERS A CHILD
AND DOESN'T KNOW HOW TO COPE

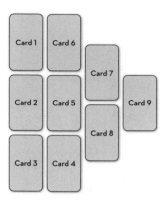

Purpose and background information:

When your son is totally out of his depth.

CARD 1: Is he in a serious relationship with the girl, or was it a casual encounter—in which case, is it definitely his? **CARD 2:** Does he want to be part of the baby's life, or should these details be left to emerge as the pregnancy progresses? **CARD 3:** Are her parents happy for you and your son's father to be part of her baby's life/involved in discussions? **CARD 4:** Can you and her father find a way your son can continue his education/planned training? **CARD 5:** Does the mother-to-be want your son to be part of the pregnancy/birth experience? **CARD 6:** Do they have a future together now/later? **CARD 7:** Can you/the other parents come to some financial arrangement, with your son taking a vacation/weekend job to help? **CARD 8:** Can regular access be arranged so you and your son can be part of the baby's life if they do not stay together? **CARD 9:** Will this turn out well after all/your son surprise everyone with his new maturity?

What you should use:

The full deck.

When:

Before any major planning meetings with the other parents.

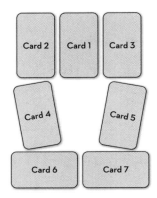

Purpose and background information:

When you have bought up the local baby store, but invitations are not forthcoming.

Card 1: Could/should you offer practical help cooking/shopping taking the baby for a walk while the mother has a rest? **Card 2:** Could you suggest very short visits, giving a choice of days and times, taking a small gift for the new mother who often gets forgotten? **Card 3:** Are the parents just exhausted/run off their feet, in which case they will not want visitors? **Card 4:** Is the mother depressed/how can you help without saying anything which will be construed as criticism? **Card 5:** Is the other grandmother very pushy and dominant? What's your best strategy? **Card 6:** Has there been any tension between you and the parents, perhaps due to insecurity/possessiveness by one of the couple, that will involve treading slowly and carefully? **Card 7:** Will things get better naturally when the baby is older and the new parents relax?

What you should use:

The forty Minor cards, Aces to Tens, and the sixteen Court Cards.

When:

At the crescent or early waxing moon.

CHAPTER 26

SPREADS FOR JUSTICE, TRUTH, COMPENSATION, AND INHERITANCE

Lucky Cards for justice, truth, compensation, and inheritance:

Major Arcana: The Hierophant, Justice, the Wheel of Fortune, Strength, Temperance, the Sun, Judgment. Justice and Judgment together in a Spread are particularly lucky.

Minor Cards: Aces of Pentacles, Wands, and Swords, Three of Pentacles, Three of Wands, Four of Pentacles, Four of Wands, Four of Swords (what you fear will not happen), Five of Pentacles, Six of Wands, Six of Swords, Seven of Pentacles, Seven of Wands, Eight of Cups, Nine of Pentacles, Nine of Wands, Ten of Pentacles.

Court Cards: Queen of Pentacles, King of Pentacles.

About Justice Spreads:

One- and two-card Spreads for basic questions or options, three-carders for truth, four for securing uncertain financial and property matters, five-carders for overcoming dishonesty and corruption, sixes for amicably resolving family matters, sevens for hidden matters, eights for major court cases, nines and above for overcoming injustice.

467
WILL YOU WIN YOUR COURT CASE?

Card 1

Purpose and background information:
For a basic answer.

CARD 1: Will judgment go in your favor?

What you should use:
The twenty-two Major cards.

When:
When deciding whether to proceed or not.

468
IS IT MORE ADVANTAGEOUS TO ACCEPT AN OUT-OF-COURT SETTLEMENT OR TO GO AHEAD WITH THE COURT CASE?

Card 1   Card 2

Purpose and background information:
When you are tempted to settle out of court to avoid further lawyers' bills.

CARD 1: What are the advantages of settling out of court?
CARD 2: What are the disadvantages of settling out of court?

What you should use:
The twenty-two Major cards.

When:
When you have received your final out-of-court offer.

469
FOR ALL KINDS OF INJUSTICE

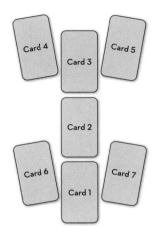

Card 4   Card 3   Card 5
Card 2
Card 6   Card 1   Card 7

Purpose and background information:
An all-purpose Spread for any injustice, whether personal, family, or legal.

CARD 1: What are the implications of this injustice, hidden as well as visible? **CARD 2:** What is the full extent of the injustice, present and future implications? **CARD 3:** Who is/are the true perpetrator/s? **CARD 4:** Strategies to overcome the injustice. **CARD 5:** Truths to be revealed. **CARD 6:** Lies to be unmasked. **CARD 7:** What will be the outcome?

What you should use:
The whole deck.

When:
When you are aware that there is a lot of behind-the-scenes dishonesty.

470
TO UNCOVER THE TRUTH THAT IS BEING DELIBERATELY CONCEALED

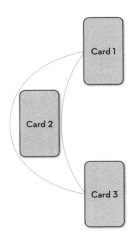

Purpose and background information:
When you need to know the truth but are being denied this.

CARD 1: What is the real situation about which you doubt you are being told the whole truth? **CARD 2:** Who or what is concealing the truth, and why? **CARD 3:** What is coming into the light of day, the truth revealed.

What you should use:
The twenty-two Major cards.

When:
At a crescent or waxing moon.

Example:
Trisha knew things were going on behind the scenes in the hospital where she was a radiologist, but there was a complete wall of silence by the managers. **CARD 1: The Chariot** suggested there was to be a change of direction that fit with rumors of a major takeover by government or a major trust.

CARD 2: The Hierophant, authority/organizational figures, probably higher up even than her managers, preventing the truth being revealed. But Trisha needed to know whether her job was secure, as she was taking on a sizable home loan.

CARD 3: The Five of Cups, three Cups spilled but two

upright, showing the person (Trisha) moving on. This Trisha took to represent job insecurity, so she applied for a position in a private hospital and got it. Three months later, her original hospital was amalgamated with a larger trust. Half of her former department was axed.

471
SHOULD YOU KEEP THIS SECRET?

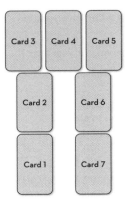

Purpose and background information:
When you have been told something that you would rather not have known.

CARD 1: Why should you keep this secret? **CARD 2:** For how long should/must you keep this secret? **CARD 3:** Is there anyone you can trust to share the secret? **CARD 4:** Is there anyone for whom it would be disastrous to find out? **CARD 5:** Will the secret matter naturally be resolved, or will it continue to be a problem? **CARD 6:** Is there any advantage in knowing the secret to avoid a personal minefield? **CARD 7:** Is there any way you can work behind the scenes to resolve the matter so it no longer needs to be a secret?

What you should use:
The twenty-two Major cards and the sixteen Court cards.

When:
Right at the end of the moon cycle when the moon no longer appears in the sky.

472
FOR COMPENSATION OR RECOMPENSE

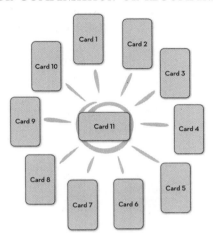

Purpose and background information:
An all-purpose Spread, whether for actual compensation or someone needing to put right a situation where you have suffered loss or a damaged reputation.

Card 1: What compensation is being sought and why, underlying as well as actual causes? **Card 2:** By whom is it owed? If a big organization, is anyone taking responsibility or hiding? **Card 3:** Why is it being withheld, official and underlying reasons? **Card 4:** Is there behind-the-scenes dishonesty/lies/corruption? **Card 5:** Do you have the right representation, especially if you are fighting a big powerful organization? **Card 6:** Who/what can move the situation along? **Card 7:** Unknown factors at play. **Card 8:** Will you/should you settle for partial compensation? **Card 9:** Will you get all you are asking for? **Card 10:** What is your plan when you receive compensation/new career/lifestyle change? **Card 11:** Will all you have been through prove worthwhile in getting justice as well as compensation?

What you should use:
The whole deck.

When:
At any key stage in the proceedings.

473
THE DAVID-VERSUS-GOLIATH ATTEMPT TO CLEAR YOUR NAME AT WORK

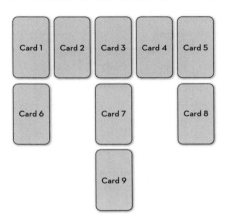

Purpose and background information:
When you are being blamed as part of a major cover-up.

Card 1: Do you have any allies/support/witnesses within the organization who would speak out on your behalf? **Card 2:** Do you have written evidence/files/emails/texts to back up your word? **Card 3:** Is there a union/industrial tribunal you could contact to offer you support/official representation? **Card 4:** If you are being offered a deal to go quietly, would you do better to accept and fight the organization from the outside? **Card 5:** Do you know any previous employees who suddenly left who would back up what you are experiencing as it happened to them? **Card 6:** Should you take stress leave rather than face the daily battle? **Card 7:** Should you cut your losses, take the opportunity to go into a different field, or study to start a business where you do not need a reference? **Card 8:** Should you take legal advice? **Card 9:** Will you win, David against Goliath?

What you should use:
The whole deck.

When:
A Tuesday, for protection against intimidation.

474

TO LEAVE BEHIND THE PAIN AND BITTERNESS OF AN INJUSTICE THAT CANNOT BE PUT RIGHT

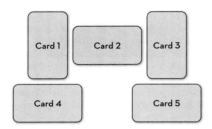

Purpose and background information:

When past unfairness is eating away at you and stopping your moving forward.

CARD 1: Is there any way you can get at least an acknowledgment of wrongdoing by the perpetrator? **CARD 2:** Have you been able to express your anger and hurt in counseling, a self-help group, or to a trusted friend or mentor? **CARD 3:** Is there any way you can prevent anyone else from experiencing the same injustice by campaigning/ telling your story in the media/on social media? **CARD 4:** What strategies will help you to move forward? **CARD 5:** Will you be happy again?

What you should use:

The forty Minor cards, Aces to Tens, and the 16 Court cards.

When:

New Year's, the anniversary of the bad event, or the beginning of any new month.

475

IF YOUR FAMILY HAS TURNED AGAINST YOU BECAUSE IT DOESN'T APPROVE OF YOUR PARTNER

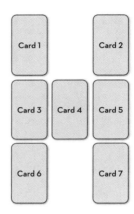

Purpose and background information:

When you have been given an ultimatum, "choose us or your partner."

CARD 1: Is this an ingrained prejudice based on ethnic background/gender/religion/culture, or simply a personal dislike? **CARD 2:** Is there anyone who could mediate for you/ family friend or counselor? Would your family listen? **CARD 3:** Do you want to/can you still see any less prejudiced members of the family with your partner? **CARD 4:** Would/should you consider seeing your family without your partner on special family occasions? **CARD 5:** Would you/should you keep the door open through birthday cards/emails/text messages, even if the family doesn't respond? **CARD 6:** Is it *love you and accept your partner* or lose you? **CARD 7:** Will your family soften their attitude in the future if you stick to your guns, perhaps if you have children/a major family anniversary?

What you should use:

The twenty-two Major cards and the sixteen Court cards.

When:

A Friday, the day of family reconciliation.

476

IF YOU KNOW THAT A PLAUSIBLE EX-PARTNER WILL LIE IN COURT IN A CUSTODY DISPUTE OR FINANCIAL SETTLEMENT

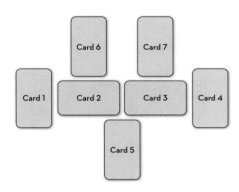

Purpose and background information:
If you are afraid you will not be believed.

CARD 1: Is your ex-partner using a tactic that was ingrained in your relationship, intimidating you by making you doubt yourself? **CARD 2:** What strategies can you use to keep cool and calm and not get upset by the lies and false impressions s/he tries to create? **CARD 3:** Are you well represented by someone whom you trust to speak on your behalf to shield you from your ex-partner's power ploys in court? **CARD 4:** If your legal representative has already made concessions you aren't happy with/seems to have sympathy with your partner's charm, should you change to someone who is there for you 100%? **CARD 5:** Is there a trusted friend/family member/counselor who will boost your self-confidence before and during the court appearance? **CARD 6:** Will the judge/arbitrator be sympathetic toward you and see through your partner's false charisma? **CARD 7:** Will you get what you want/need?

What you should use:
The full deck.

When:
When you have a court date/the latest court date.

477

IF YOU ARE ACCUSED OF A CRIME OR OFFENSE THAT YOU DID NOT COMMIT

Purpose and background information:
If you feel helpless and scared.

CARD 1: Do you have/should you urgently obtain a good representative to explain the precise charge and the basis of the charge to you? **CARD 2:** Is there anyone you haven't thought of who might have witnessed you at the crucial time/CCTV evidence, etc.? **Alternative CARD 2:** If a fraud matter, have you been through every piece of relevant paperwork that might prove your innocence/is there anything you may have missed? **CARD 3:** Is there anyone who has an interest in framing/blaming you who has been left out of the picture by the accusers? **CARD 4:** Will the matter be dropped for lack of evidence? **CARD 5:** If it goes ahead, will you be found innocent?

What you should use:
The full deck.

When:
Once there is a strong possibility of being formally charged.

478

TO CLEAR YOUR NAME WHEN AN ANONYMOUS ACCUSER HAS CONTACTED AN OFFICIAL AGENCY, SUCH AS THE IRS, WITH UNFAIR ACCUSATIONS OF MALPRACTICE

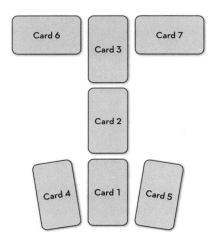

Purpose and background information:

When you are suddenly under scrutiny by officialdom.

CARD 1: Do you strongly suspect the identity of your accuser/maybe a business rival, and their motive? **CARD 2:** Can/should you demand to know the precise nature and basis of the accusations, especially dates? **CARD 3:** Do you have the right accountant who will back you/check for any genuine mistakes? **CARD 4:** Have you/can you collect all the relevant paperwork to disprove the allegations? **CARD 5:** Will the case be dropped with any re-adjustment for genuine mistakes? **CARD 6:** If it goes ahead, will you be vindicated? **CARD 7:** As a result of this, will/should you be extra vigilant with recording details in the future?

What you should use:

The full deck.

When:

A Saturday, for official matters.

479

TO CLEAR YOUR NAME WHEN YOUR EX-PARTNER HAS CONTACTED SOCIAL SERVICES OR THE COURTS, TELLING THEM THAT YOU ARE AN UNFIT PARENT

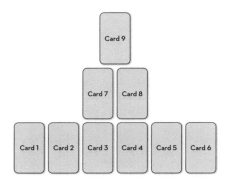

Purpose and background information:

When you are being accused of being an unfit mother/father.

CARD 1: Do you know the motive behind the accusation/s? **CARD 2:** If your child recently had an accident in your care, do you have relevant medical backup/witnesses to assist in verifying that you were not liable? **CARD 3:** Do you have a personal case worker/GP/a professional who knows you, who will support you? **CARD 4:** Do you have good legal representation? **CARD 5:** Should you/can you collect character-witness statements/people whose children interact regularly with you? **CARD 6:** If there is talk of *no smoke without fire,* should you ignore it, or should you deal with the perpetrators calmly and factually? **CARD 7:** Will this be disproven/blow over? **CARD 8:** Should you be more wary of your ex-partner in the future if you have been too trusting? **CARD 9:** In spite of this, can you avoid criticizing your partner to the children for their sakes (really hard)?

What you should use:

The forty Minor cards, Aces to Tens, and the sixteen Court cards.

When:

A Thursday, day of truth and justice.

480
FOR CHALLENGING A CHILD-CUSTODY OR ACCESS DECISION WHEN YOU KNOW THE OTHER PARENT IS A DANGER TO THE CHILDREN, BUT NO ONE BELIEVES YOU.

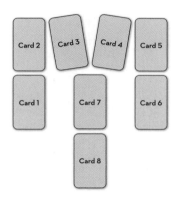

Purpose and background information:
When your children come back from an access visit neglected, afraid, and with alarming accounts of events.

CARD 1: If you know that prior to your divorce, your partner was involved in drugs or heavy alcohol consumption or with dubious connections, can you persist in pressing the authorities so access is more supervised? **CARD 2:** Does your ex have a trustworthy relative whom you could insist be present on visits? **CARD 3:** If old enough, should a visit be arranged to a play therapist/child psychologist so the children can express their worries in a relaxed situation? **CARD 4:** Should you hire a lawyer experienced in child-custody cases to act on your behalf? **CARD 5:** Should you be more forceful and—at the risk of looking over-anxious—insist that the authorities investigate/pay surprise visits and don't simply take your ex-partner's word? **CARD 6:** If the children are unwilling to see your ex, should you demand that their worries be taken into account? **CARD 7:** If nothing is done, should you stop the children from going and hope your ex loses interest/makes a mistake in their own life that cannot be ignored? **CARD 8:** Will this be resolved soon so the children will be safe and happy?

What you should use:
The full deck.

When:
When a visit is due.

481
IF YOU ARE RECEIVING UNPLEASANT WRITS, NASTY PHONE CALLS, OR THREATS OF LEGAL ACTION FROM RUTHLESS FINANCE COMPANIES

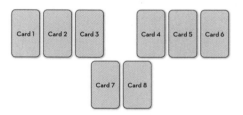

Purpose and background information:
When your life is being made a misery by unscrupulous debt collectors.

CARD 1: Are you getting/should you get urgent help from a debt charity rather than an expensive financial adviser, to negotiate on your behalf? **CARD 2:** Should you offer reasonable repayment, so everyone gets something, however small? **CARD 3:** Should you avoid getting into further debt by trying to consolidate through unscrupulous moneylenders? **CARD 4:** Should you change to a new mobile number for friends and family/not answer the number the lenders use, to avoid harassment? **CARD 5:** If possible, should you stay with friends or family for a while to give yourself a break while things are sorted out? **CARD 6:** Should you consider a legal solution/an official repayment scheme through the courts? **CARD 7:** Should you, as a last resort, consider bankruptcy? **CARD 8:** Will you get through this and have a good future life free from worry?

What you should use:
The full deck.

When:
When the moon is just past full, or a Monday for changing energies for the better.

482
IF YOU ARE GOING FOR ARBITRATION OR AN OFFICIAL JUDGMENT

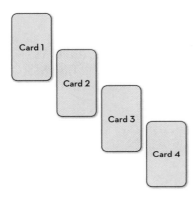

Purpose and background information:
If official matters scare you and you are afraid you'll say the wrong thing or get upset.

CARD 1: What is your ideal outcome? **CARD 2:** Do you have all the facts and figures at your fingertips and well-rehearsed in case you're questioned? **CARD 3:** Are you/should you use legal representation, or is it okay to go it alone? **CARD 4:** Will you get judgment in your favor?

What you should use:
The twenty-two Major cards.

When:
Once you have a date for the arbitration.

483
TO OVERCOME INTIMIDATION BY DEVELOPERS WHO ARE THREATENING TO EVICT YOU FROM YOUR HOME OR CLOSE YOUR BUSINESS DOWN

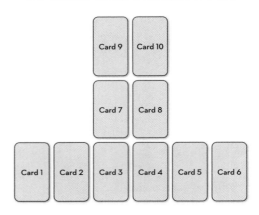

Purpose and background information:
When you are under threat by people whose actions verge on being illegal.

CARD 1: Have you talked/should you talk to the police so they are aware that there is a problem? **CARD 2:** Are there any support/legal advice centers which can give you advice on your rights? **CARD 3:** Do you need urgent legal representation? **CARD 4:** What is the minimum offer you would accept to move on if you do have rights over the premises? **CARD 5:** Do you want to stay regardless? **CARD 6:** Are there other local homes/businesses under similar threat who would join you in official resistance/a class action? **CARD 7:** Can you/should you involve the media, especially if there is an environmental threat? **CARD 8:** Are there any clauses in your lease/restrictions on the area that would prevent this action against you? **CARD 9:** Will you win? **CARD 10:** Have you had enough of the fight and want to go?

What you should use:
The full deck.

When:
After an intimidatory encounter.

484
IF A COURT CASE OR COMPENSATION CLAIM IS HELD UP FROM RESOLUTION BY CONSTANT DELAYS

Purpose and background information:
When a legal or official matter has been dragging on for months or even years.

CARD 1: Is there a particular person or department causing the delay/general inefficiency? **CARD 2:** Are there any people/departments you need to contact again in case you have been forgotten/lost in the system? **CARD 3:** Is there anyone official/a support organization/a super-efficient lawyer who can intervene on your behalf? **CARD 4:** Will the matter be resolved with intervention within three to six months? **CARD 5:** Will it be resolved, even without intervention, within the year?

What you should use:
The twenty-two Major cards and the sixteen Court cards.

When:
After yet another postponement.

485
IF YOU NEED A FAST DECISION, PERMISSION, OR VISA AND YOU HAVE BEEN CAUGHT UP IN RED TAPE

Purpose and background information:
If your life has been put on hold until you get results.

CARD 1: Has your application been lost somewhere in the system/put to one side and forgotten? **CARD 2:** Who/which department should you put polite pressure on to hasten the decision? **CARD 3:** Should you keep pressing until things move, or be patient? **CARD 4:** Will your application be successful in the near future?

What you should use:
The twenty-two Major cards and the sixteen Court cards.

When:
A Wednesday, the day of rapid movement.

IF YOU ARE TAKING YOUR WORKPLACE TO AN INDUSTRIAL TRIBUNAL OR COURT FOR UNFAIR DISMISSAL

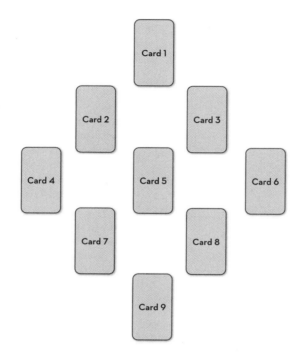

Purpose and background information:
If you know you have a good case but are nevertheless anxious.

CARD 1: Under what circumstances would you accept an out-of-court settlement/compensation or a good reference in lieu of payment? **CARD 2:** Is it a matter of principle to get an official verdict? **CARD 3:** Are you happy with your representation/union/lawyer, or would you sooner go it alone? **CARD 4:** Either way, are you ready to answer calmly and factually *any* question/any accusations, however hostile? **CARD 5:** Can/should you avoid getting emotional, however provoked? **CARD 6:** Are you confident in your witnesses,

especially if they still work for the same company, or would ex-employees with similar grievances be better? **CARD 7:** Will you win? **CARD 8:** Will you get the full compensation you deserve? **CARD 9:** If you are denied victory, will you appeal/carry on the fight through the media, or cut your losses?

What you will use:
The full deck.

When:
When you have a definite date for the tribunal/hearing.

487

TO FIND THE RIGHT LEGAL REPRESENTATION IF YOUR LAWYER IS NOT ACTING EFFECTIVELY ON YOUR BEHALF

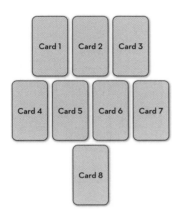

Purpose and background information:

When you are paying fees and nothing useful is happening.

CARD 1: Do you feel you are being fobbed off with excuses and blinded with legal jargon? **CARD 2:** Should you be become more assertive and proactive, asking for deadlines and regular updates of progress? **CARD 3:** Does the amount you pay seem out of proportion to actual results? **CARD 4:** Should you inquire around/look at legal-association websites/visit different firms that specialize in your need to find a lawyer who gets results? **CARD 5:** Would you be better with a small firm, not necessarily in the most expensive-looking offices, where the lawyer as opposed to a junior is dedicated to you? **CARD 6:** With a new lawyer or even your current one, should you ask for an assessment of future fees based on the anticipated time to be taken, with regular reviews/updates built in? **CARD 7:** Even if your current lawyer is good, is there a mismatch in personality/priorities that makes them not the best for you to work with? **CARD 8:** Should you consider changing to a *no win, no fee* lawyer even if it works out being more expensive in the end?

What you should use:

The full deck.

When:

When another demand for fees arrives.

488

TO WIN A COMPENSATION CLAIM FOR ANY PURPOSE WHEN PEOPLE ARE LYING, COVERING UP, OR TRYING TO DISCREDIT YOU

Purpose and background information:

When you are rightly entitled to compensation but are being denied it.

CARD 1: Do you have in your mind—and recorded—the precise order of events from any witnesses/medical records/police who took statements? **CARD 2:** Can/should you go above those who are obstructing you to someone in whose interest it is to settle quickly and quietly? **CARD 3:** If you make it clear that you will not be silenced, would the people responsible/their employers want to avoid publicity about malpractice? **CARD 4:** Will those who are lying tie themselves in knots when closely questioned by a tribunal/court? **CARD 5:** Is there already dissension among those involved in discrediting you/disputing your claim? **CARD 6:** Will they settle out of court? **CARD 7:** Will you win? **CARD 8:** If not, should you persist with your claim through a higher tribunal/court?

What you should use:

The full deck.

When:

When you receive a derisory offer or another denial of responsibility.

489

IF YOU HAD A TRAFFIC OR SPORTS ACCIDENT AND YOUR INSURANCE IS DISPUTING YOUR CLAIM

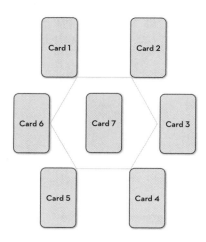

Purpose and background information:
When you are told you are not entitled to medical expenses/compensation.

Card 1: Have you/should you insist on medical assessment by an independent source as well as the insurer's doctors? **Card 2:** Do you have dashcam evidence/witnesses of the accident who will testify if necessary? **Card 3:** If the insurers are trying to get out of paying through an unreasonable minor exclusion, should you appeal through an insurers' association/ombudsman? **Card 4:** Can you successfully push for an interim payment for immediate expenses/losses? **Card 5:** Should you get expert advice/representation to deal with the insurance company if they are causing you extra stress? **Card 6:** Will you get your full claim? **Card 7:** If partial, should you/will you accept that, or appeal?

What you should use:
The full deck.

When:
A Tuesday for courage and victory.

490

IF YOU HAVE BEEN SOLD A FAULTY EXPENSIVE ITEM AND YOU AREN'T GETTING YOUR RIGHTS

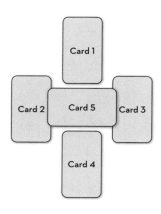

Purpose and background information:
If you hate making a fuss, but the item is useless.

Card 1: Have you/should you check your legal rights to a replacement/refund so you can argue from a position of strength? **Card 2:** Even if the store from which you bought it says you must contact the manufacturer, should you insist on dealing with the most senior manager in the store? **Card 3:** Will you get more satisfaction by phoning/mailing the store's head office with details of the person with whom you have been dealing and explain their response so far? **Alternative Card 3:** If an online purchase, will you be more successful by complaining via PayPal/Amazon rather than trying to get satisfaction out of an indifferent unresponsive seller directly? **Card 4:** Will it benefit you to contact a consumer group/media program dealing with unsatisfactory service, to raise the fear of negative publicity? **Card 5:** Will you get your refund/replacement in the near future?

What you should use:
The forty Minor cards, Aces to Tens, and the sixteen Court cards.

When:
When your first complaint has been dismissed or ignored.

491

IF YOUR FAMILY IS DIVIDED OVER AN INHERITANCE IF THERE WAS NO WILL

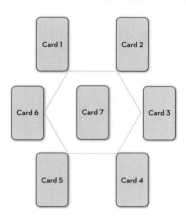

Purpose and background information:

When the family is in dispute about what the deceased relative intended.

Card 1: Did your deceased relative express any witnessed views about their wishes? **Card 2:** Who is causing the most dissension/demanding more than anyone else? Have they always been acquisitive? **Card 3:** Should you take the initiative/negotiate with the more reasonable family members for an equal split of assets? **Card 4:** Can you persuade the more avaricious family member/s that it will waste the inheritance in lawyers' and court fees if the family takes the dispute to court? **Card 5:** Should you contact everyone, separately, saying that to honor the memory of the loved one, there should be an amicable settlement? **Card 6:** Should you walk away and leave them to their squabbles for your own peace of mind? **Card 7:** Will the family resolve this peacefully and find unity again?

What you should use:

The forty Minor cards, Aces to Tens, and the sixteen Court cards.

When:

A Saturday, day of resolving inheritance matters.

492

IF YOU CARED FOR A RELATIVE, AND UPON THEIR DEATH THE FAMILY INSISTS YOU GET OUT OF THE HOME YOU SHARED SO THE PROPERTY CAN BE SOLD

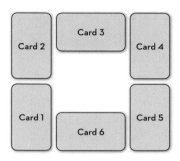

Purpose and background information:

When you had been promised that the property was your home for life.

Card 1: If not in the will, is there any written confirmation or close family friends who heard the intention that might strengthen your case? **Card 2:** Should you consult a lawyer to see if you have any sitting tenant/long-term residency rights to at least postpone the sale? **Card 3:** Could you offer the other claimants a realistic rent/your share of other assets such as the deceased relative's savings/insurance policies? **Card 4:** Is there a sympathetic relative who could persuade the others to give you time to grieve/plan your future? **Card 5:** Should you consider if maybe you do want to move on, in return for sufficient assets from the estate, putting a deposit on your own place? **Card 6:** Will you be able to stay in your former home as long as you want?

What you should use:

The twenty-two Major cards and the sixteen Court cards.

When:

Once serious discussions begin.

CHAPTER 27

SPREADS FOR PETS LARGE AND SMALL

Lucky Cards for Spreads about pets:

Major Cards: The Fool (Inner child, often showing a dog), Strength, Temperance, the Moon, the Sun, and the World.

Minor Cards: Any cards showing animals or birds, such as the Six of Wands with a horse and the Nine of Pentacles with a hawk in many decks.

The Court Cards: All the Knights/Princes who are on horseback; the Queen of Wands, pictured with a black cat.

About Pets' Spreads:

Any one- or two-card readings for basic choices, threes for growth of health and adding to your animal family, fours for domestic animals and security, fives for helping difficult or distressed animals, sixes for pets in the family, sevens for choices, uncertainty, and losing a pet (also eights), eights and above for any major questions.

493
SHOULD YOU BUY A PET?

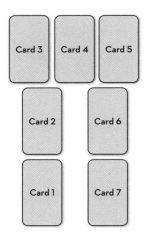

Purpose and background information:
When you want a pet but need to consider whether it is practical, given your lifestyle.

CARD 1: Will it/how will a pet fit in with your lifestyle?
CARD 2: What kind of pet would best fit your living arrangements? **CARD 3:** If you share your home, will your partner/family/housemates welcome/accept, or dislike, a pet? **CARD 4:** Who will care for the pet when you are on vacation/away working? Or will it be able to go with you to most places? **CARD 5:** Will a young animal, or an older animal from a rescue center, fit best with your lifestyle? **CARD 6:** Will your new pet fit well in your current home, or will you need to adapt/move? **CARD 7:** Do you want a pet so much that you are willing to find a way around any difficulty?

What you should use:
The full deck.

When:
A Saturday, the day of animals.

494
CHOOSING THE RIGHT PET

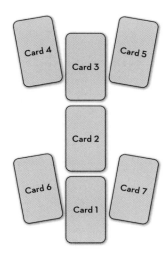

Purpose and background information:
When you want to be sure your new pet is right for you and you for your chosen pet.

CARD 1: Are you definite as to the right kind of pet, the species and age, or do you need more time to decide? **CARD 2:** Do you want more than one pet, to be company for the other? Or is this impractical? **CARD 3:** Have you narrowed down your choice to a particular breeder/rescue center, or should you explore more widely? **CARD 4:** Will you instantly know the pet is right for you as soon as you see him/her? **CARD 5:** Will your pet/s give you a sign that they are the right one? **CARD 6:** Do you suspect that this will be a former deceased pet returned/a past life connection/a new but lovely connection? **CARD 7:** Are you going to be happy together?

What you should use:
The forty Minor cards, Aces to Tens.

When:
Before you make your final choice.

495
FOR ADOPTING A RESCUE-CENTER PET OR A STRAY

Purpose and background information:
If you want to give an abandoned animal a loving home.

CARD 1: Do you generally attract the waifs and strays of the animal kingdom? **CARD 2:** Is there a special rescue center you know of/visit/support? **Alternative CARD 2:** Is there a stray you have been feeding without a microchip/collar and nobody locally knows where s/he came from? **CARD 3:** Have you experienced a special affinity with a particular stray, or will you be instantly drawn to a rescue-center pet even if it is not at all the species you would normally choose? **CARD 4:** Do you have the time and patience to help the possibly distressed animal to settle? **CARD 5:** Will this be for now your only pet, or will you have to be extra-patient with other pets who will have to accommodate a possibly difficult newcomer? **CARD 6:** Will this adoption work well?

What you should use:
The full deck.

When:
A day or two before you adopt.

496
WILL A NEW YOUNG PET SETTLE EASILY IN YOUR HOME, ESPECIALLY IF THERE ARE OTHER ANIMALS THERE?

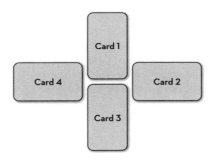

Purpose and background information:
If you are worried that a new pet will be missing its mother.

CARD 1: If an only pet, should you devote a day or two to settling the pet in? **Alternative CARD 1:** If there is another or other pets, is one of them maternal/good with young creatures, or do you need to be careful before introducing them to each other? **CARD 2:** Either way, should you allow the baby to sleep in your bedroom for the first few nights, at the risk of creating a habit? **CARD 3:** Should you protect the new addition from boisterous family members/visitors/other pets who may show jealousy, or can you let the puppy/kitten free under supervision? **CARD 4:** Will the new addition easily fit in?

What you should use:
The forty Minor cards, Aces to Tens.

When:
Before you bring the new pet home.

497
WHEN YOU SUSPECT YOU HAVE A SPECIAL TELEPATHIC BOND WITH YOUR PET

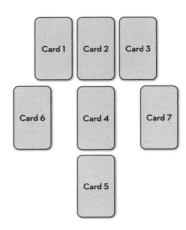

Purpose and background information:
When you and your pet seem to have a psychic connection.

CARD 1: Did you feel instinctively connected to the pet when you first saw them? Did they settle instantly? **CARD 2:** Does your pet know when you are sad or unwell and, even if normally boisterous, sit quietly by you? **CARD 3:** Do you know when your pet is sad, distressed, or nervous even if there are no physical signs or you are away from them? **CARD 4:** Does your partner/a family member comment that five minutes before you get home, your pet will sit by the door waiting, even if you return at a different time every day? **CARD 5:** Does your pet anticipate when you are going out/were thinking of taking them for a walk at an unusual time, even if you haven't yet given any indication of your intention to go out? **CARD 6:** Has your pet been with you as a deceased pet or in a past world? **CARD 7:** Does your pet act hostilely toward an untrustworthy visitor or stranger who comes too near, even if normally docile?

What you should use:
The twenty-two Major cards and the forty Minor cards, Aces to Tens.

When:
When your pet does something uncanny.

IF YOUR FUR BABIES ARE YOUR WHOLE WORLD, AND PEOPLE DO NOT UNDERSTAND

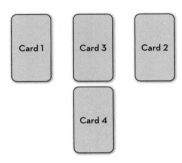

Purpose and background information:

If your pet/s are the center of your life.

CARD 1: Does your pet/s have distinct personalities and bring you a huge amount of joy? **CARD 2:** If you have a partner, do you both share the deep love of your pet/s? **CARD 3:** Do you include your pet/s in your life whenever possible? **CARD 4:** Should you ignore people who criticize you for devoting your love to animals, rather than trying to explain it to them?

What you should use:

The twenty-two Major cards and the sixteen Court cards.

When:

A Friday or Saturday, for loving animals.

SHOULD YOU GIVE IN TO PRESSURE FROM YOUR CHILDREN TO ALLOW THEM TO HAVE A PET?

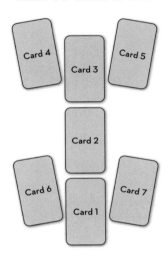

Purpose and background information:

If your children promise anything if you will buy them a pet or pets.

CARD 1: Are your children sufficiently responsible, as well as old enough, to take on the bulk of animal care (with prompting)? **CARD 2:** If these intentions do not last, do you have the time/inclination to provide backup? **CARD 3:** What kind of pet/s would fit in with your home space/lifestyle? **CARD 4:** If you do not buy the pet/s, will your child/ren forget and go on to another craze? **CARD 5:** If they are genuine animal lovers, will this be a lost opportunity? **CARD 6:** Should you go ahead now? **CARD 7:** Should you wait a couple of months and see if your children have changed their minds?

What you should use:

The forty Minor cards, Aces to Tens, and the sixteen Court cards.

When:

When you are being nagged for a decision.

500
IF YOU PLAN TO TRAVEL OR VACATION WITH YOUR PET FOR THE FIRST TIME OR AFTER PREVIOUS PROBLEMS

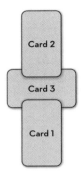

Purpose and background information:
When your pet is part of the family, but you could make alternative arrangements for its care while you vacation.

CARD 1: What are the advantages of taking your pet along?
CARD 2: What are the disadvantages, hidden as well as visible? **CARD 3:** To take your pet or not, depending partly on the relative strengths and challenges of the previous two cards?

What you should use:
The twenty-two Major cards and the sixteen Court cards.

When:
Before making your final decision.

501
IF YOUR PET IS VERY TIMID OR ANXIOUS AROUND PEOPLE AND OTHER ANIMALS

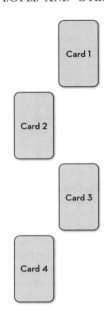

Purpose and background information:
When in spite of size and breed, your animal is a mouse at heart.

CARD 1: Has this always been your pet's basic nature, or did a bad experience bring it on? **CARD 2:** Are there any people/animals your pet feels safe with who could introduce unfamiliar places and so broaden its horizons? **CARD 3:** Should you allow your pet to stay within their parameters of what is safe rather than forcing change? **CARD 4:** Are there any natural remedies such as flower essences, crystals, or animal reiki healing that might alleviate the worst anxieties?

What you should use:
The twenty-two Major cards.

When:
A Monday, the day of the moon and sensitivity.

502
WOULD YOUR DOG BENEFIT FROM OBEDIENCE TRAINING?

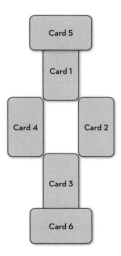

Purpose and background information:
If your dog is affectionate but out of control in public and overly boisterous within the home.

CARD 1: Does your dog need more exercise/longer walks/outdoor games to run off some excess energy? **CARD 2:** Would your dog benefit from actual classes to learn more controlled behavior? **CARD 3:** Would you benefit from the classes to share experiences with other owners/learn strategies for coping as soon as out-of-control behavior begins? **CARD 4:** Has your dog become too close to humans and considers him/herself as leader of the pack, including the owner? **CARD 5:** Would you rather devise your own training program using the love between you to improve behavior? **CARD 6:** Will your pet's behavior improve, whatever method you use?

What you should use:
The full deck.

When:
When your dog's behavior is making life difficult for you.

503
WHEN YOUR PET IS SICK OR HAS NO ENERGY

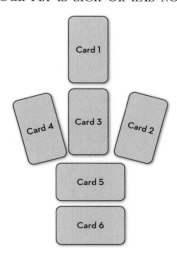

Purpose and background information:
When the vet cannot work out what's wrong.

CARD 1: Is something stressing/distressing your pet that can be traced to a traumatic incident with another animal/a nasty neighbor? **CARD 2:** Does your animal need more connection with the natural world outdoors? **CARD 3:** Should you explore a more natural diet, especially if your pet loves human treats a little too much? **CARD 4:** Should you explore natural health supplements/use only natural products for everything? **CARD 5:** Does your pet need less noise/less stimulation/a quiet place away from the family if wanted? **CARD 6:** Will your animal get better soon, with or without treatment?

What you should use:
The full deck.

When:
A Wednesday, day of health regeneration.

504
IF YOUR VET DOESN'T SEEM TO BE HELPING YOUR PET

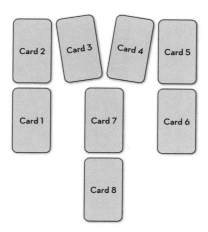

Purpose and background information:
When tests are inconclusive, your pet hates going to the vet, and treatment is expensive and ineffective.

CARD 1: Have you previously been happy with your veterinary practice/has there been a change of personnel/are you new to it? **CARD 2:** Should you make one more visit and ask why the treatment isn't working, what alternatives there are, and the length of time anticipated until recovery? **CARD 3:** Should you try a new vet, perhaps one who is recognized as an expert in the condition your animal seems to have? **CARD 4:** Should you explore alternative animal practitioners and healers as the answer? **CARD 5:** Should you find out about animal health supplements, both conventional and natural? **CARD 6:** Should you rely more on a very plain natural diet and peace and quiet? **CARD 7:** Will time be the healer? **CARD 8:** Will your animal soon recover?

What you should use:
The full deck.

When:
When yet another invoice from the vet arrives in your mailbox.

505
WILL YOUR INJURED ANIMAL, WHETHER HURT IN A FIGHT OR ACCIDENT, RECOVER SOON?

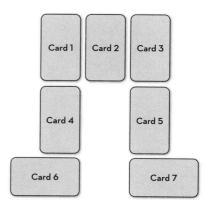

Purpose and background information:
When you are worried because your pet isn't his/her old self, even though the wound is healing.

CARD 1: Is the wound healing as it should, or is there an undiscovered infection that is making the animal lethargic or unwell? **CARD 2:** If the incident was very traumatic, is your pet still suffering from shock? **CARD 3:** Does your pet needs extra supplements/a rich natural diet to boost the self-healing system? **CARD 4:** Should you take your pet to a pet healer to stimulate their own self-healing system? **CARD 5:** Should you be patient/accept that healing of your pet's psyche may take longer than healing the actual physical injury? **CARD 6:** Will your pet get better within the next three months? **CARD 7:** Will your pet recover, even if it takes longer?

What you should use:
The full deck.

When:
At the crescent or waxing moon, or on any Monday.

506
IF YOUR PET HATES ALL VETS

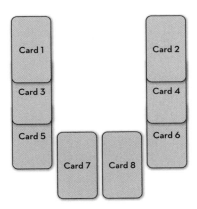

Purpose and background information:
When your pet gets distressed and terrified, even during routine visits.

CARD 1: Was there a specific incident/unsympathetic vet when the trouble started? Is the pet a rescue animal with early bad experiences of strangers? **CARD 2:** Does your pet not like being touched by strangers/is naturally timid? **CARD 3:** Is it worth paying extra for home visits, so the atmosphere is more relaxed? **CARD 4:** Should you familiarize yourself with one particularly gentle vet who the animal could learn to trust? **CARD 5:** Can you limit veterinary visits to medical essentials, using dog washers, etc., visiting your home for routine care? **CARD 6:** When visits are necessary, could you give your animal a mild sedative in advance? **CARD 7:** Would alternative practitioners in more homey settings familiarize your pet with non-invasive treatments, such as massage? **CARD 8:** Will the problem be overcome with patience and a sympathetic practitioner?

What you should use:
The full deck.

When:
If you have a veterinary appointment due and are dreading it.

507
IF YOUR PET IS JEALOUS OF A NEW ANIMAL OR BABY

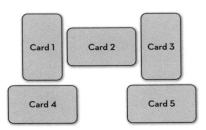

Purpose and background information:
If you are worried that your normally placid pet will be aggressive to the new arrival.

CARD 1: Has your pet previously been the center of attention and suddenly feels displaced? **CARD 2:** Do you need to re-assert that you are the leader of the pack? **CARD 3:** While protecting a vulnerable baby or small child, can you gradually introduce the newcomer to the pet with plenty of physical reassurance? **CARD 4:** Will the problem settle down, given reassurance and vigilance? **CARD 5:** Is it just a matter of time before a new pecking order is established?

What you will use:
The forty Minor cards, Aces to Tens, and the sixteen Court cards.

When:
When you strongly suspect that your pet will become aggressive toward the new arrival.

IF YOUR PET IS JEALOUS OF A NEW PARTNER, OR YOUR NEW PARTNER'S ANIMAL IS HOSTILE TOWARD YOU

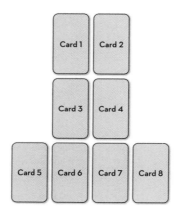

Purpose and background information:

If a normally friendly pet sees a new partner as a rival.

CARD 1: Does the pet fear that they are no longer the center of attention, and thus try to oust the rival? **CARD 2:** Is the owner determined to show the pet their place in the pecking order by supporting the human/refusing to hide their affectionate behavior? **CARD 3:** If the owner is ambivalent about this, is there something that needs to be resolved in the human relationship? **CARD 4:** Is the dislike two-way and not all the animal's fault? If so, how can this be resolved? **CARD 5:** Should the human rival resort to bribery of treats, etc., to win over the pet? **CARD 6:** If safe, should the pet be left with the human rival, so the pet will learn to trust him/her? **CARD 7:** Will this be resolved with patience and determination? **CARD 8:** Will you/your partner choose human love over the animal if necessary?

What you should use:

The forty Minor cards, Aces to Tens, and the sixteen Court cards.

When:

When romantic evenings at home are wrecked by a jealous pet.

Example:

Linda was very much in love with Peter but found it strange that his huge dog slept on the bed and growled at her whenever she moved, putting a major damper on their love life. Peter has asked Linda to move in.

CARD 1: The Nine of Cups. Peter had lived alone with the dog since he left home five years ago, and so they had their routine. **CARD 2: The Page of Cups.** Peter thinks of the dog as his child and indulges it 100%. **CARD 3: The Two of Swords.** None of Peter's relationships have worked out, as he has made *love me, love my dog* clear. **CARD 4: The Three of Pentacles.** Linda has been patient and done everything to make the dog accept her, as she loves Peter very much. **CARD 5: The Six of Pentacles.** The dog accepts offered treats, then snarls at Linda and runs behind Peter. **CARD 6: The Five of Swords.** When she stayed alone with the dog, it backed her into a corner until Peter returned. Peter said she must have upset the dog. **CARD 7: The Eight of Cups.** Linda walking away, as it was clear to her that if she moved in, it would only get worse. **CARD 8: The Ten of Swords.** Endings. No contest: Pete chose the dog.

509
IF YOU ARE MOVING OR GOING AWAY FOR A LENGTHY PERIOD AND CANNOT TAKE YOUR PET

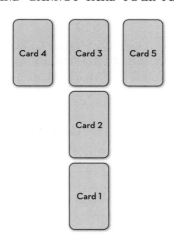

Purpose and background information:

When you are facing a dilemma about the future of your pet.

CARD 1: Is there any way you can cancel/avoid the trip so you can stay? Do you want to stay with your pet at all costs? **CARD 2:** Is there any way, however difficult, you could take the pet along? **CARD 3:** If you are returning, could you find a reliable house-sitter who would take care of your pet until you come back? **Alternative CARD 3:** if you are moving away permanently, is there a close friend/family member who would adopt your pet so you can still see them on visits? **CARD 4:** Could you ask among friends and family, well before the move, if they know of anyone reliable who would adopt your pet, so the pet could get to know their new owner before you go? **CARD 5:** Will you find a good safe home where your pet will be happy?

What you should use:

The twenty-two Major cards and the sixteen Court cards.

When:

As soon as possible after the move/major travel becomes likely.

510
IF YOUR PET IS THREATENED BY AN AGGRESSIVE HUMAN OR ANIMAL

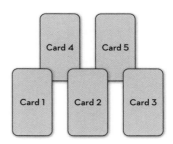

Purpose and background information:

When you are worried about your pet going out alone.

CARD 1: Should you keep your pet indoors for a while and then proceed cautiously? **CARD 2:** If your pet goes out alone, should you restrict them for even longer? **Alternative CARD 2:** If you walk or exercise your pet, should you change your route to avoid the aggressor/s? **CARD 3:** If the danger comes from a neighbor or their animal, should you deal with the matter directly without getting into a major confrontation? **CARD 4:** If the person/owner of the aggressive animal is hostile/threatening at your approach, should you take legal advice/complain to the police? **CARD 5:** Will the matter resolve soon so you can continue your normal routine?

What you should use:

The twenty-two Major cards and the sixteen Court cards.

When:

A Tuesday, day of courageous action and standing up to bullies.

511
IF YOU ARE MOVING, WILL YOUR PET SETTLE INTO YOUR NEW HOME?

Purpose and background information:
When you are moving into a new home with your pet.

Card 1: If a dog or horse, should you take them to visit/walk around the neighborhood/visit their paddock well before the move, so it becomes familiar? **Alternative Card 1:** If a bird, cat, or other small animal, should you familiarize them with their carrying box so it becomes part of their life? **Card 2:** Is there a safe quiet sanctuary in the new home so the animal can settle in? **Card 3:** Should you leave your pet/s with friends/family until you are settled and can spend time getting them adjusted? **Card 4:** Should you keep your pet/s indoors at the new home for a few days so they don't try to find their way back to the old home? **Card 5:** Should you check out the new area/neighbors for possible hazards/aggressive animals/people, especially if your pet goes out alone? **Card 6:** Will your pet settle in easily/quickly? **Card 7:** If not a good pet environment, would they be happier staying permanently with friends/family they know?

What you should use:
The full deck.

When:
A few weeks before the move.

512
IF YOUR NEIGHBOR'S DOG CONSTANTLY BARKS WHEN ITS OWNERS ARE AT WORK OR AWAY ALL DAY.

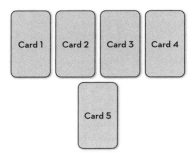

Purpose and background information:
When you are being driven to distraction by the noise.

Card 1: Assuming the owner doesn't know, should you inform them tactfully? **Card 2:** If the neighbors are nice and you have time, should you offer to take the dog for an occasional walk during the day? **Card 3:** If there is no/a hostile response, should you contact the local authority anti-noise department so they can take action? **Card 4:** If you suspect that the dog is neglected, should you contact the local animal welfare? **Card 5:** Will the situation unexpectedly improve over time?

What you should use:
The twenty-two Major cards and the sixteen Court cards.

When:
At the waning moon.

513

IF YOU ARE NOT HAPPY WHERE YOU ARE STABLING OR GRAZING YOUR HORSE

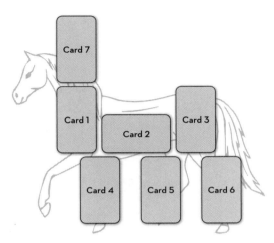

Purpose and background information:

When you are unsure your horse/s is/are safe and cared for if they are stabled away from your home.

Card 1: Has there been a change in conditions/an event that has caused you to lose confidence, or were you always uncertain? **Card 2:** Will raising concerns/suggesting strategies/offering practical help improve the situation? **Card 3:** Is it only a temporary glitch that will improve naturally in the next few weeks? **Card 4:** Should you consider finding an alternative place for your horse/s sooner rather than later? **Card 5:** Is it possible to obtain grazing land nearer where you live so you can be on hand to check? **Card 6:** If the situation cannot be resolved, should you find an individual to care for your horse/s in return for being allowed to ride them? **Card 7:** Is this maybe a time to think about selling your horse/s until you can have them with you full-time?

What you should use:

The forty Minor cards and the sixteen Court cards.

When:

As soon as you are aware of a problem.

514

IF YOU WANT AN UNUSUAL PET

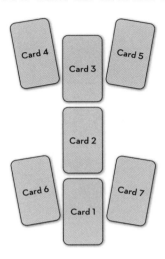

Purpose and background information:

When you have a desire for an exotic species.

Card 1: Are you 100% sure your exotic pet will fit into your home/lifestyle? **Card 2:** Are you certain that your pet comes from a reputable and healthy source/breeding stock? **Card 3:** Will your local vet take on the care, or do you need a specialist: one, for example, who is attached to a zoo? **Card 4:** Will the fascinating aspects of your pet compensate for a lack of close companionship/interaction? **Card 5:** Will your pet be securely housed in the right habitat so it will thrive? **Card 6:** Any unexpected hazards? **Card 7:** Would you do better to adopt one and visit it regularly in a local wildlife sanctuary/reptilarium?

What you should use:

The twenty-two Major cards.

When:

Before purchasing.

515

WILL YOUR MISSING PET RETURN?

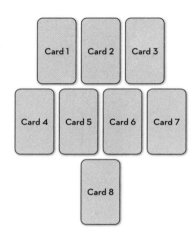

Purpose and background information:
When you have advertised widely and inquired at all the local refuges.

CARD 1: Should you make another major push on social media/widen the area even more, as missing animals can stray a long way? **CARD 2:** Did something or someone frighten your pet so it bolted? Was s/he restless? **CARD 3:** Has your pet strayed before and returned? **CARD 4:** If you recently moved, has your pet returned, as many do, to your old home area even if a long way away? **Alternative CARD 4:** Did your pet just decide to move on, especially if a rescue animal? **CARD 5:** Has s/he been taken in by someone who believed s/he was a stray? **CARD 6:** Could there be someone local who took an undue interest in your pet and may have lured it away? **CARD 7:** Is it just a matter of time before someone sees your advertisement and responds? **CARD 8:** Will your pet come back in the next month? A little longer?

What you should use:
The full deck.

When:
A Monday, the moon day, to call home your pet.

516

HAS YOUR MISSING PET BEEN ADOPTED BY SOMEONE ELSE, OR DIED?

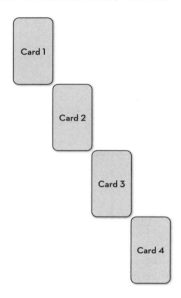

Purpose and background information:
If a long time has elapsed since your pet disappeared.

CARD 1: Do you sense that your pet is still alive, or do you feel just an emptiness when you think of them? **CARD 2:** Do you feel that your pet is happy and settled? **CARD 3:** Should you give up waiting, even considering a new pet? **CARD 4:** Will they still come home?

What you should use:
The twenty-two Major cards.

When:
The anniversary day, a month or even a year since your pet went missing.

517
OVERCOMING GRIEF FROM THE LOSS OF A PET

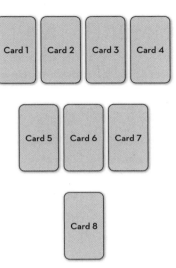

518
SHOULD YOU LET A VERY OLD OR SICK PET GO?

Purpose and background information:
When a pet dies, and people do not seem to understand how deeply this has affected you.

CARD 1: What you feel inside, the process of grief you need to allow yourself to work through over weeks and months. **CARD 2:** How can you best remember your pet: a grave in the garden/a pet cemetery/scattering the ashes in a favorite place/keeping the ashes at home/planting a tree? **CARD 3:** Do you sense your pet still around? **CARD 4:** How can you best recall the happy memories? In photos/a memorial in the burial place if appropriate/a picture by the urn? **CARD 5:** How long should you take off work/allow yourself to grieve before you are ready to move forward, regardless of what others say? **CARD 6:** How are any other pets/family members taking the loss? Can they comfort you? **CARD 7:** If people are unsympathetic, should you ignore them, try to explain, or realize maybe they're people you do not want to be around right now? **CARD 8:** When the grief eases, would you consider a new pet in honor of the old one?

Purpose and background information:
When you know your pet is fading, but saying good-bye seems so hard.

CARD 1: Have you/should you stop any treatment/ways of artificially prolonging your pet's life? **CARD 2:** If your pet is comfortable, are you prepared to let it go in its own time and way, regardless of the prognosis/pressures from others? **CARD 3:** Will you know/be ready to act mercifully if/when intervention is necessary?

What you should use:
The twenty-two Major cards.

When:
As the sun sets.

519
HAS YOUR DECEASED PET RETURNED TO YOUR HOME?

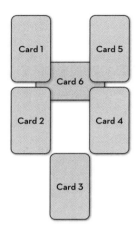

Purpose and background information:
When you can sense your pet, but others tell you it is your imagination.

CARD 1: Do you sense your pet around in the same places s/he loved in life/see a flash of light out of the corner of your eye? **CARD 2:** Do you feel your pet's fur brushing against you? **CARD 3:** When you wake, is there a dent on the bed where s/he used to sleep? **CARD 4:** Do the other animals/a small child look into the corner and see the deceased pet? **ALTERNATIVE CARD 4:** Does another family member who was especially close to the animal also still experience it around? **CARD 5:** Do you just *know* your pet has returned? **CARD 6:** Will it return in the form of another animal when the time is right, behaving in a way that you will recognize as being them?

What you should use:
The full deck.

When:
You need confirmation from the cards that it's not all in your mind.

CHAPTER 28

NEIGHBORS, NEIGHBORHOOD, AND COMMUNITY SPREADS

Lucky cards for Spreads about Neighbors:

Major Cards: The Hierophant, the Chariot, Justice, Strength, Temperance, the Sun, Judgment.

Minor Cards: Aces of Pentacles, Cups, and Wands; Threes of Cups and Wands; Fours of Pentacles and Wands; Five of Pentacles, Sixes of Wands and Swords; Seven of Wands; Eight of Wands; Nines of Pentacles and Wands; Tens of Pentacles and Cups.

Court Cards: Queens and Kings of Pentacles, Cups, and Wands.

About Spreads for Neighbors:

Ones and Twos for quick answers and choices; threes for increasing good will and coming together; fours for property, security, and general neighborhood safety; fives for dealing with difficult neighbors; sixes for neighbors as friends and peacemaking; sevens for choices such as where to live; eights and above for major issues.

520
SHOULD YOU MOVE TO A PARTICULAR NEIGHBORHOOD?

Purpose and background information:
When you have found the right house but are not sure about the neighborhood.

CARD 1: Is this the right neighborhood for you? (answer depends on the strength of the positive feeling you get from the card).

What you should use:
The twenty-two Major cards.

When:
Before you put in an offer on the property.

521
WHEN YOU MOVE INTO A NEW NEIGHBORHOOD AND NO ONE COMES TO GREET YOU

Purpose and background information:
If you come from a friendly neighborhood and aren't sure if people here are just busy or do not mix.

CARD 1: Should you knock on a few doors to say *hi*? **CARD 2:** Should you wait for them to contact you?

What you should use:
The forty Minor cards, Aces to Tens.

When:
Once you are settled, if contact is not forthcoming.

522
IF YOUR NEIGHBOR IS PUTTING UP A NEW EXTENSION OR FENCE THAT WILL BLOCK YOUR LIGHT/VIEW

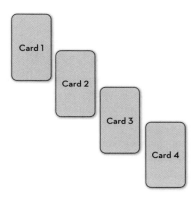

Purpose and background information:
When you haven't been consulted and work is starting.

CARD 1: Is your neighbor just thoughtless and will adapt plans when you explain the problem? **CARD 2:** If they ignore you/turn hostile, do they have planning permission? If not, get straight on to the planning department. **CARD 3:** Should you threaten legal action? **CARD 4:** Should you accept it as not worth the trouble fighting?

What you should use:
The twenty-two Major cards.

When:
As soon as you discover what is happening.

523
IS YOUR NEIGHBOR FRIGHTENING YOUR CAT?

Purpose and background information:

When your cat has suddenly become very nervous about going out in the garden or beyond, and you know your neighbor doesn't like animals.

CARD 1: Is your neighbor responsible? **CARD 2:** Is it someone else/an aggressive animal in the vicinity?

What you should use:

The twenty-two Major cards and the sixteen Court cards.

When:

At the full moon, or any Monday.

524
IF TWO NEIGHBORS ARE SAYING HORRIBLE THINGS TO YOU ABOUT EACH OTHER

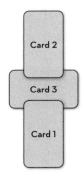

Purpose and background information:

When you feel you are being asked to take sides in a dispute between neighbors.

CARD 1: Should you try to discover the real facts? **CARD 2:** Should you refuse to get involved and remain friendly toward them both? **CARD 3:** Should you stay away from both of them until the quarrel is mended?

What you should use:

The forty Minor cards, Aces to Tens, and the sixteen Court cards.

When:

When you are being asked to choose.

525
SHOULD YOU STAY IN YOUR CURRENT NEIGHBORHOOD OR MOVE AWAY?

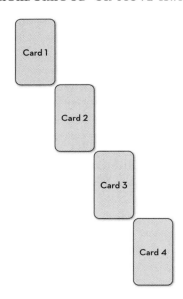

Purpose and background information:

When you are deciding whether to move on and, if so, locally or further afield.

CARD 1: Should you stay in your current neighborhood? **CARD 2:** Should you buy/rent something new in your current location? **CARD 3:** Should you move to a new neighborhood in the same town/area? **CARD 4:** Should you move to an entirely new location?

What you should use:
The forty Minor cards, Aces to Tens.

When:
The start of a new month.

526
IF YOU HAVE A HOSTILE NEIGHBOR

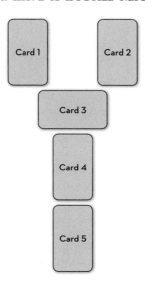

Purpose and background information:
When reason and negotiation have failed.

CARD 1: What you can no longer tolerate. **CARD 2:** What is infuriating you but can be ignored. **CARD 3:** Is there a weak link/a reasonable person in the house/apartment who could be persuaded to see sense? **CARD 4:** Should you take legal/official action? **CARD 5:** Should you move on as soon as possible?

What you should use:
The forty Minor cards, Aces to Tens, and the sixteen Court cards.

When:
At a time when you are expecting confrontation.

527
IF YOU HAVE A NOISY NEIGHBOR

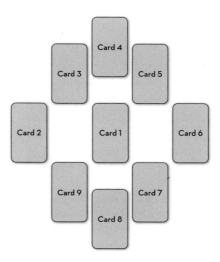

Purpose and background information:
When your neighbor constantly plays loud music/slams doors/runs a used-car lot outside your front door/has screaming children or barking dogs.

CARD 1: Is this noise seriously affecting your peace/your sleep, or is it just an irritant but intermittent? **CARD 2:** What is tolerable? **CARD 3:** What is not tolerable? **CARD 4:** Is it worth talking again reasonably to the neighbor about the worst aspects? **CARD 5:** If your neighbor is/is still unresponsive or hostile, should you make a recording and send it to the local noise abatement department? **CARD 6:** If no results, should you consult a lawyer? **CARD 7:** As a last resort, should you consider moving? **CARD 8:** Will the problem be resolved soon? **CARD 9:** Is it going to take time, determination, and persistence to resolve it?

What you should use:
The full deck.

When:
At the waning moon.

528
OVERCOMING NEIGHBORHOOD GOSSIP ABOUT YOU OR YOUR FAMILY

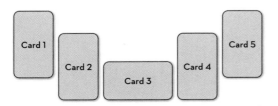

Purpose and background information:
If you are at the center of a whispering campaign and it is making you unwilling to go out.

Card 1: What/who is the source of the gossip? **Card 2:** Who is a/are false friend/s to avoid/be careful what you say? **Card 3:** Whom can you trust? **Card 4:** Can you silence the gossip by confrontation whenever you hear it? **Card 5:** Should you ignore the gossip/hold your head high and wait for it to blow over?

What you should use:
The twenty-two Major cards and the sixteen Court cards.

When:
A Wednesday, the day for overcoming lies and gossip.

529
IF YOU DO NOT KNOW ANY OF YOUR NEIGHBORS

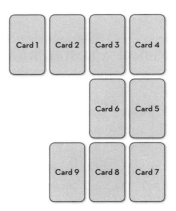

Purpose and background information:
If you are at work all day or work unsociable hours.

Card 1: Would you like to know any particular neighbors better, maybe your age or with similar families? **Card 2:** Would you like to socialize with your neighbors, or just be on speaking terms? **Card 3:** Is your neighborhood an established area with established social connections, or is mostly transient people or those who seem to be away a lot? **Card 4:** Should you send invitations for a get-together at your home/organize an event for a particular occasion? **Card 5:** Should you join a community group/a neighborhood watch and get to know the neighbors through that? **Card 6:** Should you wait for an organized event in the immediate vicinity as a way of introducing yourself? **Card 7:** Is there anyone who seems unfriendly who you would wish to avoid, or would you give them another chance? **Card 8:** Will you make one or two new good friends? **Card 9:** Would you sooner not bother, as you are out/away a lot?

What you should use:
The full deck.

When:
At a waxing moon.

530
COULD YOUR NEIGHBOR BECOME MORE THAN A NEIGHBOR?

Purpose and background information:
When there is definitely a spark between you.

CARD 1: Are you/is your neighbor free from another romantic attachment? **CARD 2:** Does s/he go out of their way to talk for longer than necessary and seem reluctant to part? **CARD 3:** Do you share common interests where you could meet casually at local venues? **CARD 4:** Should you make a subtle invitation to come in for coffee? **CARD 5:** Should you be more obvious and suggest you go somewhere together? **CARD 6:** Should you leave your neighbor to make the first move? **CARD 7:** Will romance develop? **CARD 8:** If it doesn't, can you still become friends?

What you should use:
The full deck.

When:
A full moon.

531
IF YOUR NEIGHBORS HAVE CHILDREN, BUT YOURS DO NOT WANT TO PLAY WITH THEM

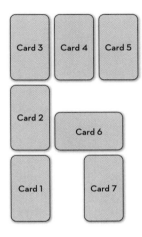

Purpose and background information:
When your children prefer school friends or their own family, in spite of your trying to persuade them.

CARD 1: Should you plan more barbecues/family get-togethers and invite the neighbors? **CARD 2:** Is/are your child/ren naturally home-lovers, or are they shy with people they do not know well? **CARD 3:** Should you invite neighbors' children of a similar age along to outings so they can get to know each other in a relaxing environment? **CARD 4:** Do any belong to the same school/local sports teams where contact could include sharing lifts? **CARD 5:** Should you allow your child/children to get to know the neighbors/children on their own terms, at their own pace without your intervention? **CARD 6:** Are there cliques/any bullies among them who you maybe don't see? **CARD 7:** Will there eventually be friendship among the neighboring families?

What you should use:
The forty Minor cards, Aces to Tens, and the sixteen Court cards.

When:
Friday.

532
FOR ESTABLISHING A MUTUAL-HELP NETWORK WITH NEIGHBORS

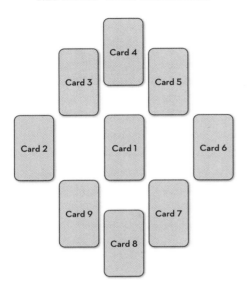

What you should use:
The full deck.

When:
When you have needed help, but not known whom to ask.

533
CAN YOU PRESERVE AMICABLE RELATIONS WITH NEIGHBORS WHEN RESOLVING ISSUES SUCH AS OVERHANGING TREES, PETS, TEMPORARY BUILDING WORKS, OR PARKING?

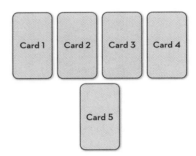

Purpose and background information:
If friends and family are far away and you know it's similar for some neighbors.

Card 1: Would it be best to establish informal connections, or to organize a more formal network? **Card 2:** Should you invite interested neighbors to a meeting to discuss the idea/ how it could work? **Card 3:** Do you have a variety of age groups to offer different skills/mutual babysitting/shopping for the elderly/DIY, etc.? **Card 4:** What are the practicalities/ advantages of developing a neighborhood exchange system? **Card 5:** How can you organize it so some people aren't left with all the work and one or two dominant personalities taking over? **Card 6:** How can you help single parents/the elderly or disabled people so they can share the benefits and contribute their gifts? **Card 7:** Would you sooner suggest the idea and let someone who enjoys organization set it up? **Card 8:** How can disputes be resolved amicably? **Card 9:** Will it be a huge benefit, or more trouble than it's worth?

Purpose and background information:
When your perfectly nice neighbors constantly overstep the bounds and impose on your better nature.

Card 1: Do your neighbors consciously or thoughtlessly take advantage of your easy-going nature? **Card 2:** Should you choose your battles to protest about and politely stick to your guns? **Card 3:** Is it more important to be thought the nice guy/gal and put up with inconvenience? Why? **Card 4:** If your *nice* neighbors turn difficult when crossed, even politely, should you sacrifice goodwill for getting what you need? **Card 5:** Would you prefer a quiet life and ignore it when they step over the bounds?

What you should use:
The full deck.

When:
When your neighbors say *you don't mind, do you?* and you realize that you *do* mind.

FOR GETTING THE BALANCE RIGHT BETWEEN FRIENDLINESS AND PRIVACY IF YOUR NEIGHBOR IS NICE BUT INTRUSIVE

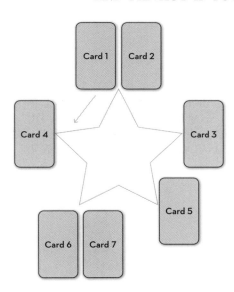

Purpose and background information:

When your neighbor is always dropping in at inconvenient moments and stays for ages when you need to do your own thing.

CARD 1: Are you too readily available, perhaps because you work from home/generally stay home in the evenings with partner/family? **CARD 2:** Are you naturally a welcoming person and haven't made clear what is working/family time and thus sacrosanct? **CARD 3:** Is your neighbor lonely and relies too much on you for company? **CARD 4:** Is your neighbor thick-skinned/an emotional drain and takes advantage of your good nature? **CARD 5:** Should you make it clear when a visit/phone call is not the right time/cut short the same politely but firmly? **CARD 6:** Are you prepared if necessary to be blunt and risk what may be a one-sided friendship? **CARD 7:** Do you feel guilty for putting your own needs/priorities first? Is this a deeply ingrained reaction you need to break generally?

What you should use:
The full deck.

When:
When you dread yet another visit/phone call.

Example:
Alan was a single dad and worked from home. Paul lived next door and had retired. Paul came over two or three times a day and would phone at all hours, or arrive when Alan was cooking and stay for the meal—which the children hated, as he monopolized Alan.

CARD 1: The Empress. Paul regarded Alan as someone who would care for him and even resented the presence of Alan's children when they got home from school. **CARD 2: The Two of Pentacles.** Alan had tight deadlines and often had to work late into the night because he hadn't been able to work during the day. **CARD 3: The Page of Cups.** Though retired, Paul was needy rather than lonely, as there were lots of local community activities he could join. **CARD 4: The Six of Pentacles.** Paul usually came with a lot of problems to talk over with Alan, though in fact he was healthy and had plenty of money. **CARD 5: The Page of Pentacles.** Paul was immune to hints; and although Alan didn't want to hurt his feelings, he was seriously affecting Alan's work and family life. **CARD 6: The Five of Wands.** Alan knew he had to spell it out that Paul wasn't welcome, except by invitation. **CARD 7: The Five of Pentacles.** A strange card, help from another source. Alan said he had been brought up to put others first. The meaning became clear after Alan told Paul he had to cut down the visits. Paul stormed off but within a week had established himself with another neighbor across the street and spent all his time there. Sometimes a meaning will become clear after the suggested action is taken; but if in doubt, draw another card.

535
IF A NEWLY DIVORCED NEIGHBOR IS ALWAYS ASKING YOUR PARTNER TO GO FIX THINGS AND HELP OUT

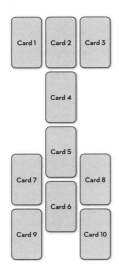

Purpose and background information:

When what started as a favor is turning into full-blown agony-aunt/uncle sessions and an ongoing DIY/catering service.

CARD 1: Has the number and lengths of requests for visits by your partner been increasing? **CARD 2:** Are you increasingly excluded from the visits/discussions of what was said? **CARD 3:** Is your partner becoming secretive/defensive and eager to dash next door? **CARD 4:** Is it unusual for you to feel insecure and jealous in your relationship? **CARD 5:** Should you tell your neighbor that your husband has major work/home projects, but *you* are happy to drop around sometimes? **CARD 6:** Should you point your neighbor in the direction of professional counseling/lists of local DIY specialists? **CARD 7:** Is it better to be subtle and divert your partner by fixing evenings out/weekends away? **CARD 8:** If your partner/your neighbor do not take the hint, should you be direct at the risk of being the unsympathetic guy/gal? **CARD 9:** Is your partner just flattered by the attention/easily falling for sob stories

but devoted to you? **CARD 10:** Are there any parts of your relationship you need resolving?

What you should use:
The full deck.

When:
When you are feeling resentful of being neglected in favor of your neighbor.

536
SHOULD YOU BUY A HOME IN A NEIGHBORHOOD WHERE THE SCHOOLS ARE GOOD, EVEN IF IT WILL INVOLVE DISRUPTION FOR YOU?

Purpose and background information:

When you feel the education of your family has to take priority.

CARD 1: Is there a particular area in which you need to live where there are suitable homes to buy/rent? **CARD 2:** Before you move, have you double-checked that there are no schools near where you now live that are good, even if they aren't so highly rated? **CARD 3:** Are you sure the school you are moving for would be right for your child, even if it's a recommended one? **CARD 4:** Will the disruption/uprooting be worth it in terms of giving the family a better new living environment in other ways too? **CARD 5:** If necessary, are you/your partner prepared to commute longer distances/ stay away overnight in order to live in the chosen location? **Card 6:** What will be the positive results of the move? **Card 7:** What will be the drawbacks? **Card 8:** On balance, will this decision bring the required success and happiness?

What you should use:
The full deck.

When:
When you have to decide whether to move to be in the right area in plenty of time for the desired school admission.

nearby neighborhood schools and, if there is one you like, consider moving? **Card 4:** Do the overall benefits of where you live now for the whole family outweigh the education question? **Card 5:** Will it all work out for the best by the time the new term/school year begins?

What you should use:
The forty Minor cards, Aces to Tens, and the sixteen Court cards.

When:
When you have to rethink your plans fast.

537
FOR FINDING THE RIGHT NEIGHBORHOOD SCHOOL FOR YOUR CHILDREN IF THE MOST POPULAR CHOICE IS FULL

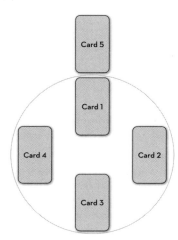

Purpose and background information:
When you are worried if you are in the right place to give your child/ren the best education?

Card 1: If you have been denied a place at the school you wanted, is there an appeals process? Is this sufficiently effective to be worth trying? **Card 2:** Should you visit all the other neighborhood schools with an open mind to see if one suits the personality/needs of your child/ren better than the originally desired one? **Card 3:** Should you explore other

538
FOR CAMPAIGNING FOR BETTER FACILITIES IN THE COMMUNITY

Purpose and background information:
If there is a need for better play areas and facilities for older people/green spaces, etc.

Card 1: Should you/why should you get involved personally? **Card 2:** Do you want to be/are you best as an ideas person, or as a campaigning/backroom organizer? **Card 3:** Could/ would you want to organize fundraising ventures/lead a committee of action/contact the right bodies for grants, etc.? **Card 4:** Would you sooner let other people set it up and join in if you do not like the limelight? **Card 5:** Can you deal with those who are all about ego and personal glory, inevitable in organized efforts? **Card 6:** Will your efforts spearhead the right results?

What you should use
The forty Minor cards, Aces to Tens, and the sixteen Court cards.

When:
A Sunday for major group endeavors.

539
FOR DEALING WITH VANDALS, THIEVES, AND MUGGERS WHO ARE RUINING THE COMMUNITY

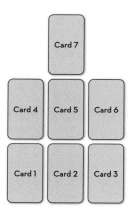

Purpose and background information:
When your neighborhood is unsafe because of vandalism, break-ins, and muggings.

CARD 1: Has the situation recently deteriorated? Why?
CARD 2: Is your home/personal security as good as you can make it, or do you need professional advice? **CARD 3:** Is there a good neighborhood watch, or can you organize/suggest one? **CARD 4:** Can you enlist others to put pressure on local politicians/lawmakers to clean up the neighborhood? **Card 5**: Can you use a press release/write on social media to highlight issues/attract extra resources by highlighting the problems? **CARD 6:** Can you campaign for/join an existing organization for facilities to get young people off the streets? **CARD 7:** Should you accept that the problem is too great and move?

What you should use:
The full deck.

When:
After a spate of particularly violent criminal behavior.

540
FOR A SUCCESSFUL COMMUNITY PARTY OR EVENT

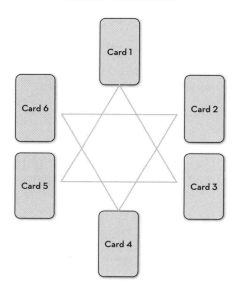

Purpose and background information:
When you would like to see the community coming together.

CARD 1: Is there a local/state/national/international event that would act as a focus? **CARD 2:** Is there an existing committee/organization that fixes events but might need new blood to add an original spin? **CARD 3:** Either way, do you want a major role, a supporting role, or to suggest ideas and let others put them in practice? **CARD 4:** Can you attract/suggest ways of attracting/raising funding? **CARD 5:** Can you overcome the inevitable pettiness that accompanies the organization of events, and simply focus on the results? **CARD 6:** Will the event be a resounding success?

What you should use:
The full deck.

When:
When an appropriate event is a month or two away.

541
FOR RELIGIOUS, SOCIAL, AND CULTURAL HARMONY IN A MULTICULTURAL COMMUNITY

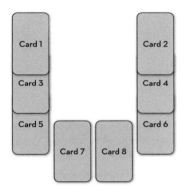

Purpose and background information:
When you would like to see different sectors of the community coming together more.

CARD 1: Are there multi-faith group events you can get involved in organizing? **CARD 2:** Would you sooner just go along/join online groups? **CARD 3:** Can you/would you want to help welcome newcomers from different areas/lands to settle in your neighborhood? **CARD 4:** If you meet hostility, should you step back, or try to find more moderate members of the community? **CARD 5:** Are there any local schools/youth organizations, local businesses, sporting activities, and workplaces for getting to know a variety of people better? **CARD 6:** Should you/do you want to learn more about different faiths/languages in order to promote integration? **CARD 7:** Could you invite immediate neighbors from different cultures to a get-together, for food and entertainment, to meet socially more rigid residents? **CARD 8:** Would you want to wait to integrate more until you are approached?

What you should use:
The full deck.

When:
At a waxing moon, or a special event in the local calendar.

542
IF YOU DO NOT WANT A MODERN SHOPPING MALL/FAST-FOOD CHAIN IN YOUR TRADITIONAL CHARACTERFUL COMMUNITY

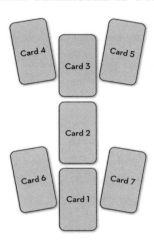

Purpose and background information:
When there are media reports of major changes in your vicinity.

CARD 1: Are there any unconsidered advantages of this unwelcome appearance of the 21st century? **CARD 2:** Will the new development change the infrastructure of local life/put a strain on existing facilities? **CARD 3:** Would you wish to organize/be a participant, but not a leader, in local resistance? **CARD 4:** Is there a local lawyer who would explore restrictions, such as environmental damage/heritage buildings that could halt the development? **CARD 5:** Can you involve local media/galvanize local/state representatives who may be apathetic? **CARD 6:** If it goes ahead, would you consider moving to another unspoiled area? **CARD 7:** Can/will the proposed development application be rejected?

What you should use:
The forty Minor cards and the sixteen Court cards.

When:
When the rumors prove to have a sound basis.

CHAPTER 29

SPREADS FOR CELEBRATIONS

Lucky cards for celebrations

Major Cards: The Magician, the Empress, the Lovers, the Wheel of Fortune, the Moon, the Sun, the Star, Temperance, the World.

Minor Cards: Ace and Two of Cups, Ace of Wands, Three of Cups, Four of Wands, Six of Wands, Ten of Pentacles, and Ten of Cups.

The Court Cards: Page/Princess, Knight/Prince, King, and Queen of Cups.

About Celebration Spreads:

One-carders for basic answers; twos for choices; threes for celebrations of all kinds, especially births; fours for family and close friend events; fives for naming ceremonies, graduations, and study successes, also conflicts; sixes for reconciliation through celebrations and love and marriage; sevens for anything special like a wedding or anniversary; eights and above for anything more complicated.

543
SHOULD YOU AND YOUR PARTNER CALL YOUR BABY THE NAME YOU WANT, OR THE ONE YOUR FAMILIES WANT?

Purpose and background information:
When you are being pressured to name your baby after an elderly relative or a traditional family name that you dislike.

CARD 1: Should you call your baby by the name you want, one that will fit into the modern world? **CARD 2:** Would it be possible/practical to use the desired family choice as a middle name to honor the family (and keep the peace)?

What you should use:
The forty Minor cards and the twenty-two Major cards.

When:
A Monday, the day of all matters concerning babies.

544
HOW CAN YOU DECIDE THE RIGHT NAME FOR YOUR BABY?

Purpose and background information:
When you have several names but are having difficulty making a decision.

CARD 1: Will you know once your baby is born/comes home which names fit the personality? **CARD 2:** Are the most likely names ones that will sound as good with a forty-year-old as a four-year-old? **CARD 3:** Can you resist pressure from family to select a name that is traditional to the family but not suitable for the modern world?

Now add a card for each name/combination of names you like, as many as you wish, to the right of **Card 3**. See which cards have the strongest positive meaning. If you need further guidance, see the Numerology Spread (page 428).

What you should use:
The full deck.

When:
A Sunday, a good naming day.

545
FOR A SUCCESSFUL BABY SHOWER

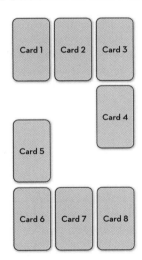

Purpose and background information:
When a friend or family member is getting near their due date.

CARD 1: Would the expectant mother welcome a baby shower, or prefer to see people separately? **CARD 2:** Would she welcome a surprise party, or want advance notice? **CARD 3:** Should you organize the party earlier rather than too close to the due date, in case the expectant mother goes into labor early/gets very tired? **CARD 4:** Should you leave everyone to bring whatever gifts they choose, or suggest that vouchers might be welcome to avoid too many small-size clothes/teethers/duplications? **CARD 5:** Who will help you organize the shower? Should there be a group of you arranging different aspects, especially if you are busy? **CARD 6:** Would the mother-to-be feel happier in someone's home/an outside venue? **CARD 7:** Should it be informal/a potluck buffet and chat, or with games like identifying people from their own baby photos that they are asked to bring along? **CARD 8:** Will the event prove a great source of joy to everyone?

What you should use:
The full deck.

When:
A few weeks before the anticipated birth.

546
IF YOUR FAMILY IS ORGANIZING A BIG WELCOME-HOME PARTY FOR THE NEW BABY, BUT IT'S THE LAST THING YOU, AS NEW PARENTS, WANT

Purpose and background information:
When your family means well, but you need peace and quiet.

CARD 1: Is there an older relative who can explain to excited but unaware family members that you/your partner and the baby need rest/promising regular updates/photos? **CARD 2:** Should you plan a celebration for the closest relatives in a month or two at one of your parents' homes, plus invites to the wider family later to a christening/naming ceremony?

What you should use:
The forty Minor cards, Aces to Tens.

When:
As soon as possible after the birth/homecoming.

547
DO YOU WANT A CHRISTENING OR NAMING DAY FOR YOUR NEW BABY?

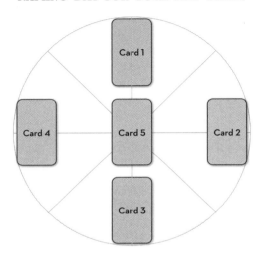

Purpose and background information:
When people start asking when the christening/naming day is, and you are not what you want or when.

CARD 1: Would you like to formally name your new baby at a celebration with family and friends? **CARD 2:** Even if you are not conventionally religious, should you consider a traditional blessing ceremony to welcome your child into the world? **CARD 3:** Alternatively, should you hold a naming ceremony, either informal or more formal, in your garden/an open space? **CARD 4:** Either way, would you choose/whom would you choose as god/goddess parents/mentors to guide and protect your baby through life? **CARD 5:** Is/should naming your child be a private event between you and your partner and any other children, in a special family place you love?

What you should use:
The full deck.

When:
When friends and relatives are asking for a date.

548
WHEN YOUR CHILD GRADUATES FROM COLLEGE OR HAS A MAJOR EDUCATIONAL SUCCESS

Purpose and background information:
When you want to celebrate your child's hard work and want the celebration to be a surprise.

CARD 1: Would your child welcome a big party for friends/family? **CARD 2:** Would they prefer money for a celebration/weekend away with their peers? **CARD 3:** Would they sooner have a quiet family dinner and a tangible gift or the money to buy whatever they want? **CARD 4:** Does your child hate surprises and would prefer you to ask?

What you should use:
The full deck.

When:
Once you receive the good news.

Example:
Jim was so excited that his son James had qualified with honors as a doctor and was going to join the family practice, he planned a big congratulatory party inviting everyone he knew and all his son's college friends. But Jenna, who knew her son better, realized James would hate being in the limelight, exclaimed over by adoring relatives while his friends watched.

CARD 1: The Hermit. James was naturally shy in his private life and mainly spent time with his girlfriend, who was equally shy. **CARD 2: The Eight of Wands.** James had wanted to go swimming with turtles in the ocean and to spend a few days at a turtle sanctuary, and so a trip with his girlfriend there would be a perfect gift. **CARD 3: The Ten of Pentacles,** showing the three generations of family, and Jenna knew nothing pleased James more than a quiet family dinner with his grandparents, an ideal time to give James the travel tickets and accommodation voucher for the turtles. **CARD 4: The Prince of Pentacles.** James enjoyed predictability and reliability, thus making an ideal, thorough, and reassuring future doctor. Had it been a Prince of Wands, a surprise party would have been fine.

Jenna persuaded her husband that the party would have been more for him and, as well as the ticket, they gave James a top-flight camera so he could record his experiences.

549
FOR A MILESTONE BIRTHDAY

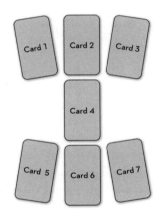

Purpose and background information:
Whether an 18th, 21st, 40th, 50th, 60th, and above right up to 100 years old and beyond.

CARD 1: Should this be a surprise, or planned by the person whose birthday it is? **CARD 2:** Depending on the age, who would be most welcome to attend/peers for the young/ friends and family for older people? **CARD 3:** Should you book a favorite venue, bring in caterers, or make it a family affair? **CARD 4:** Would the birthday boy/girl prefer to go away on vacation and celebrate there? **Alternative CARD 4:** If in the very senior age bracket, would a "happy reminiscences through the ages" party with longstanding friends and family be more appreciated? **CARD 5:** Will there be a joint present, or people left to bring gifts if they will? **Card 6:**

Is the person saving for something special, in which case money/vouchers might be more appropriate for those who wish to bring a present? **CARD 7:** Does the person really not want to celebrate their birthday, or are they just saying that and secretly would love it? (a crucial card, pick an extra one if unsure)

What you should use:
The full deck.

When:
A few weeks before the birthday.

550
IF YOU WANT A QUIET WEDDING, NOT A FULL-BLOWN CIRCUS

Purpose and background information:
When your wedding has been hijacked by overenthusiastic relatives.

CARD 1: Should you state once and for all that it is your day, and it's got to be the way you want it? **CARD 2:** If you face resistance (and maybe you are used to being steamrolled over big decisions by the family), should you be prepared to go off with your partner, without relatives if necessary, and do it your way?

What you should use:
The twenty-two Major cards.

When:
As soon as you notice that there's dissension in the ranks.

551
DO YOU WANT AN ENGAGEMENT PARTY?

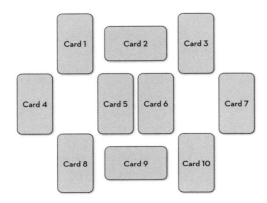

Purpose and background information:
Just before you tell close family and friends about your engagement.

CARD 1: Do you want to celebrate quietly with friends and family? **CARD 2:** Do you want a big party to share the good news with the world? **CARD 3:** Who will organize the party, you and your fiancé/e, or a family member who volunteers? **CARD 4:** Should you have a formal party at a venue, or a barbecue/potluck? **CARD 5:** Are you happy for friends to bring gifts if they wish? **CARD 6:** Would you sooner ask for a donation to a favorite charity or a small fun gift if guests want to give anything? **CARD 7:** Is the engagement for you and your fiancé/e to celebrate privately, perhaps with a weekend away or a meal at your favorite restaurant? **CARD 8:** Can/should you resist family pressure for a big circus, even if they really want this? **CARD 9:** Would/should you go along with family wishes to make them happy? **CARD 10:** Do you want only a few people to know and ask them to keep it quiet for now, especially if you do not yet have/want a ring?

What you should use:
The full deck.

When:
Before you agree to make any party plans.

552
FOR A POSITIVELY MEMORABLE BACHELORETTE OR BACHELOR PARTY

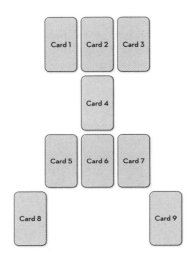

Purpose and background information:
When friends are making lots of plans, but you are not sure.

CARD 1: Revolutionary though it sounds, would you not want a bachelorette/bachelor party with just a few friends and family around for a quiet evening? **CARD 2:** If you are having a party, do you want to organize it yourself, perhaps a weekend away to avoid more extreme elements creeping in who would embarrass you? **CARD 3:** If not, are there trusted friends who will organize a fun event that stays within limits? **CARD 4:** If you have friends/siblings who you know will go too far, should you exclude them even at the risk of causing offense? **CARD 5:** Who can you trust to look out for you during the party, to keep you safe and unembarrassed? **CARD 6:** How should you finance the evening/weekend? Through equal shares by participants except the bride/groom, to be collected by a friend who is tough on freeloaders? **CARD 7:** If you suspect your friends are planning a surprise, do you want this? **CARD 8:** If it is to be a surprise, will you enjoy it? **CARD 9:** Will the party be a great success?

What you should use:
The full deck.

When friends are hinting that you may be in for a surprise before your wedding.

553
SHOULD YOU ORGANIZE A SURPRISE PARTY FOR YOUR PARTNER OR A CLOSE RELATIVE?

Purpose and background information:
When it is suggested to you that a surprise party would be fun.

CARD 1: Is there a milestone occasion you would like to celebrate by secretly getting together friends and family? **CARD 2:** Does your partner like surprises, or is it you who will get the pleasure? **CARD 3:** Would s/he prefer a small intimate event to a whole crowd of people? **CARD 4:** Would your partner prefer a home-based/venue/restaurant/pub/wine bar setting for the surprise party? **CARD 5:** Will this be an occasion that will bring great joy to your partner as a way of knowing that they are appreciated? **CARD 6:** Is the whole idea a recipe for disaster? **CARD 7:** Should you consult them anyway beforehand, so they can invite who they want/choose the venue, unless you are 100% sure of your partner's preferences?

What you should use:
The full deck.

When:
When you first get the idea/someone suggests it.

554
IF YOU OR YOUR PARTNER'S FATHER AND STEPFATHER BOTH INSIST ON ESCORTING THE BRIDE

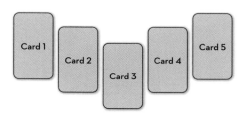

Purpose and background information:
When this is a symptom of the underlying/open rivalry between the two families.

CARD 1: Is there an obvious choice, with an important role—for example, making a speech at the wedding breakfast—for the other father? **CARD 2:** If there is jostling for first place between the mother and new partner/father and new partner on either side, what strategies for the practical organization can get around this? **CARD 3:** Should/can the birth mother/s and father/s be told that their partners need to take a back seat for this day, unless the stepfather has played the main role in the bride or groom's life? **CARD 4:** Would it be a good idea to get someone else to escort the bride/give major speeches: the mother/sister/brother/old family friend/grandfather/grandmother? **CARD 5:** If key players will not put differences aside for one day, should they be told to stay away?

What you should use:
The forty Minor cards, Aces to Tens, and the sixteen Court cards.

When:
When the key players are being stubborn and pressuring you/your partner to choose.

555
FOR A HAPPY WEDDING

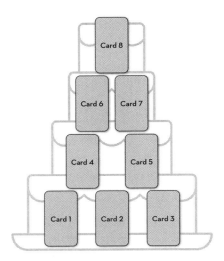

Purpose and background information:
When you want the best day ever.

CARD 1: Are the wedding venue and ceremony what you and your partner really want? **CARD 2:** Can/should you make compromises, but not at the cost of your dreams? **CARD 3:** Are you happy, or worried, about costs? If the latter, can you cut down on unnecessary extras and still have the wedding *you* want? **CARD 4:** Have you arranged for the bridesmaids/best man/person escorting the bride you would like, even if this choice ruffles a few family feathers? **CARD 5:** If you feel the wedding is being hijacked by parents and relatives, how can you take back control? **CARD 6:** Have you/should you arrange the guest list/seating/invitations to avoid petty quarrels that can break out even in the best organized event? **CARD 7:** Do you have a wingman/woman watching your back during the arrangement phase? **CARD 8:** Will it be the best day ever, whatever the weather?

What you should use:
The full deck.

When:
Before major planning becomes set in stone.

556
WHEN YOU HAVE BEEN EXCLUDED FROM THE GUEST LIST OF A CLOSE FRIEND OR FAMILY MEMBER'S WEDDING

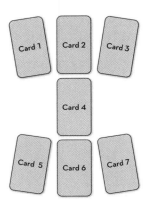

Purpose and background information:
When you feel hurt, as you cannot understand why you have not been invited.

CARD 1: Is there a quarrel or estrangement, even if not your fault, that could be mended, whether or not you go to the wedding? **CARD 2:** Regardless, should you send a gift/good wishes to the couple getting married? **CARD 3:** Should you write to the person you are closest to in the family, expressing hurt and asking for the reason? **CARD 4:** Is there a limit on numbers/children not being invited/internal family obligation decisions that may have excluded you, rather than ill will? **CARD 5:** Does this reflect the way you are taken for granted by the family in other ways/a sign to be less generous in the future? **CARD 6:** Even if the decision were reversed, would you exclude the family from your own invitations in the future? **CARD 7:** Should you let go and make sure you have a really good time elsewhere on the day of the wedding?

What you should use:
The twenty-two Major cards and the sixteen Court cards.

When:
When you hear that others have been invited who seem less close to the family than you.

557
FOR A SECOND OR THIRD WEDDING, OR A WEDDING LATER IN LIFE

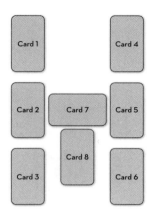

Purpose and background information:
When you want a very special day, even though it's not your first wedding.

CARD 1: Do you want/should you go for a full-blown wedding, dresses, bridesmaids/pages (even if grandchildren), big reception/lovely venue? **CARD 2:** Would you prefer a small event, but one with great significance to your romance? **CARD 3:** Should you combine the wedding with a vacation, perhaps overseas to a romantic setting? **CARD 4:** Do you want all your family and friends present, or just special ones and maybe a party for everyone later? **CARD 5:** Are there people who will be unhelpful/resentful of the wedding who should be excluded? **CARD 6:** What strategies can you use to make sure it is a harmonious day? **CARD 7:** Would you and your partner be happier getting married with just a couple of key witnesses, or even to elope and announce it later? **CARD 8:** Will it be a wonderful, memorable occasion?

What you should use:
The forty Minor cards, Aces to Tens, and the sixteen Court cards.

When:
A Thursday for wise mature love.

558
FOR A HAPPY HANDFASTING

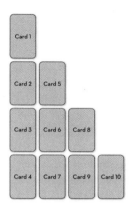

Purpose and background information:
When you do not want a traditional wedding.

CARD 1: Will you later regret not having a formal ceremony? Is a personal dedication right for you? **CARD 2:** Do you want an official pagan celebrant, or will you ask a friend/family member to lead the ceremony? **CARD 3:** Where would be the best place for your ceremony, a forest/seashore/ancient site? **CARD 4:** Do you plan to/should you write an order of service, or should you let the ceremony emerge spontaneously? **CARD 5:** What strategies can you use to overcome opposition from more conventional/religious family members? **CARD 6:** Will there be official invitations, notifying friends/family of the place and time, and/or inviting anyone who wants to come along? **CARD 7:** What kind of reception would be best: picnic/barbecue according to weather/home/an informal gathering at a restaurant/pub afterwards? **CARD 8:** Should you ask everyone to bring a plant or crystals in lieu of a gift, afterwards exchanging them among the guests? **CARD 9:** Any hidden challenges? **CARD 10:** Will this be a wonderful experience for you?

What you should use:
The forty Minor cards, Aces to Tens, and the sixteen Court cards.

When:
When you are exploring different options for a wedding.

559
WHEN THE WEDDING GIFT LIST IS PROVING A PROBLEM

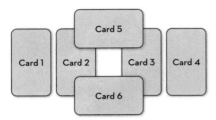

Purpose and background information:
When you do not want a conventional wedding list, which makes people feel obliged to send a gift in return for an invitation or spend more than they can afford.

CARD 1: Should you give a list of items of all kinds, none very expensive, to a trusted relative so only if people ask, you can refer them to that? **CARD 2:** Would you prefer to not have a list at all, just tell people whatever they choose will be wonderful and it is their presence/good wishes that are important? **CARD 3:** Should you avoid a display of presents at the wedding and say you'll open them afterward? **CARD 4:** Should you make sure, however big the wedding, you send personalized thanks to everyone, not just for the gift but for their presence/good wishes? **CARD 5:** In the weeks following the wedding, should you ensure that you have all the gifts, including duplicates (however hideous) on display in your home for when people visit—and never take any rejects to a local charity store? **CARD 6:** Can you get around the problem by asking everyone to donate to a chosen charity in lieu of a gift if they wish?

What you should use:
The forty Minor cards, Aces to Tens, and the sixteen Court cards.

When:
You are making the final arrangements for the wedding.

560
A MILESTONE WEDDING ANNIVERSARY, WHETHER SILVER, GOLD, RUBY, OR DIAMOND

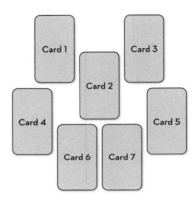

Purpose and background information:
When you are planning a milestone anniversary celebration for your parents or grandparents.

CARD 1: Can you get family and friends to club together to present something made of the gem or similar, such as ruby wine glasses for a ruby wedding? **CARD 2:** Would the couple *really* like to celebrate the anniversary with a party? **CARD 3:** Would they welcome a surprise event, or prefer to say what kind of celebration they would like? **CARD 4:** Should it be an elaborate party for old friends and family/former bridesmaids, or just a quiet family occasion? **CARD 5:** Would it be better to buy tickets/book a hotel in the place they first met/have happy memories? **CARD 6:** If they are still very much in love, should you go all-out for an occasion to remember forever? **Alternative CARD 6:** If they aren't happy together, should you keep celebrations low-key? **CARD 7:** Are there any people who shouldn't be invited/watched closely if the occasion is to remain harmonious?

What you should use:
The forty Minor cards and the sixteen Court cards.

When:
A Thursday for mature love.

561
FOR AN ENJOYABLE OFFICE PARTY WITHOUT ANY EMBARRASSING INCIDENTS

Purpose and background information:

When you want to have a great time and remember the evening with pleasure, not horror, the next day.

Card 1: Do you have bad memories of previous office parties, or are you just worried you might let your hair down too much? **Card 2:** What strategies can you adopt to avoid being offered and accepting too much drink? **Card 3:** Should you plan in advance to avoid anyone with whom you might loosen your tongue too much and say something you are likely to regret the following day? **Card 4:** Can/should you keep potential passion under wraps, given the fraught nature of instant—and maybe equally instantly regretted—workplace party liaisons? **Card 5:** Will the party be a happy occasion and good for positive networking?

What you should use:

The forty Minor cards and the sixteen Court cards.

When:

The evening before the party.

562
WILL YOUR WEDDING DAY BE ALL YOU HOPE?

Purpose and background information:

If there seem to be a thousand and one obstacles in the way right now.

Card 1: Will you have the best day ever?

What you should use:

The forty Minor cards, Aces to Tens. Remember, swords are fears, not predicting disaster.

When:

When you get last-minute nerves.

563
IF YOUR TEENAGERS WANT TO HOLD A PARTY

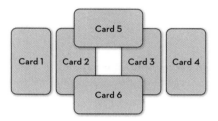

Purpose and background information:

When you know your teenagers are responsible, but you are worried about the other guests and gate-crashers.

Card 1: Will your teenagers listen to your worries/accept your precautions/conditions, albeit reluctantly? **Card 2:** At the risk of being unpopular, should you ask exactly who is being invited/insist it not be on social media so as to avoid attracting undesirables? **Card 3:** At the risk of being unpopular, should you at the beginning vet partygoers for uninvited guests/illicit drink if people are underage? **Card 4:** If you go out, should you stay local, leave emergency numbers, explaining to teens there will be no blame if help is needed? **Card 5:** Should you return home/stay upstairs later in the evening so you can see there is no drug-taking/drunkenness going on? **Card 6:** Should you take the risk as a token of trust, having removed breakables/valuables?

What you should use:

The forty Minor cards, Aces to Tens, and the sixteen Court cards.

When:

Before you agree.

564
FOR A RETIREMENT PARTY

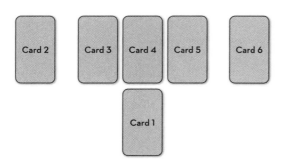

Purpose and background information:
When you do not know whether to celebrate or close the door fast on your working life.

CARD 1: If you would sooner do without a party on your last day of work, where you'll have to mix with insincere people as well as genuine friends, should you let it be known? **CARD 2:** Would you rather go for a quiet drink with people you will be genuinely sorry to leave? **CARD 3:** Would you be happier heading home fast and going out for a celebratory meal with immediate family/friends? **CARD 4:** Would it be better to head straight off to the airport/train station for a vacation or to your holiday home? **CARD 5:** Do you want to let what may be mixed emotions on the last day settle/put your retirement plans in motion before meeting with former colleagues socially/go back to visit the workplace? **CARD 6:** Will you be pleased, or disappointed, if there is a surprise party?

What you should use:
The twenty-two Major cards and the sixteen Court cards.

When:
At least two weeks before retirement.

565
FOR A RENEWAL OF VOWS

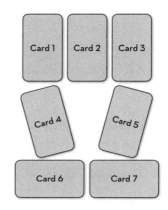

Purpose and background information:
When you have been together or married for a while and want to renew the promises you made to each other.

CARD 1: Would it be a good idea/possible to return to the place you originally exchanged your vows? **CARD 2:** Do you want a religious ceremony, or a less formal one? **CARD 3:** Would you like to renew your vows, either informally or with a celebrant, in a happy vacation location? **CARD 4:** Would you like family/old friends, if possible people from the original ceremony, along, or do you want a more private event? **CARD 5:** Will the vows you make now be different from the original vows in order to reflect your life experiences, or will they be the same? **CARD 6:** Are the vows intended to strengthen what is good, overcome challenges, or both? **CARD 7:** Will the ceremony start a lovely new lasting phase of happiness with all the challenges left behind?

What you should use:
The twenty-two Major cards and the sixteen Court cards.

When:
A Thursday for lasting fidelity.

CHAPTER 30

SPREADS FOR TRAVEL AND VACATIONS

Lucky cards for travel and vacation

Major Cards: The Chariot, the Hermit (for solo travel), the Wheel of Fortune, the Moon, the Sun, the World.

Minor Cards: Ace of Wands, Three of Wands, Six of Wands, Six of Swords, Seven of Wands, Eight of Cups, Eight of Wands.

Court Cards: All Wands Court cards.

About Travel and Vacation cards:

Ones for yes/no, twos for simple choices, threes for travel plans and choices between three options, fours for finances and safety, fives for short-term/distance trips and decisions about where to go and stay, sixes for happy vacations and traveling with loved ones, sevens for travel overseas and more detailed choices, dream holidays, and solo travel, eights and above for more complex questions.

566
WHERE SHOULD YOU GO ON VACATION?

Purpose and background information:
When you have several options but aren't sure which is best.

CARD 1: What do you hope to gain most from your vacation?
CARD 2: What are the drawbacks of going on vacation, if any? **CARD 3:** Is this/when is the right time to go on vacation?
CARD 4: Do you want to go far or near, or even vacation at home? **CARD 5:** Will you have a happy vacation?

Now choose one extra card for each location option. According to the strength and positivity of each card, this will help you make a choice. If two are of equal strength, pick an additional card for each. If one seems negative but you know it is one of your favorite locations, pick another card to ask why and if/how problems could be fixed.

What you should use:
The full deck.

When:
A Thursday, for serious planning.

567

WHERE TO STAY WHEN THERE'S A CHOICE BETWEEN TWO IN ANY QUESTION ABOUT TRAVELING OR VACATIONS

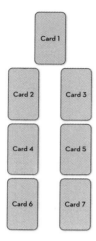

Purpose and background information:

For absolutely anything where you have a choice between two different dates, hotels, locations, between two family members or friends to stay/travel with, two airlines with similar prices, two similar cruises, two city breaks, whether to go for seven or fourteen days, expensive or budget range.

CARD 1: What factors aren't yet known that might influence the benefits and drawbacks of each choice? **CARDS 2 AND 3:** The positive benefits of each form of travel/accommodation under question. **CARDS 4 AND 5:** The negative aspects of each travel/accommodation under question. **CARDS 6 AND 7:** The best outcome for each choice. If there is a third choice, add three more cards.

What you should use:

The whole deck.

When:

When you have exhausted logic and the information available and need to look over the horizon.

568

FOR SAFE AND PLEASURABLE TRAVELING, OR GOING ON VACATION ALONE

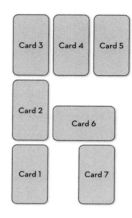

Purpose and background information:

To assess the benefits and pitfalls of traveling or vacationing alone.

CARD 1: Whether or not you have a choice, do you feel happy/accepting, or scared, of traveling alone? **CARD 2:** What are the advantages of traveling/vacationing alone? **CARD 3:** If on a solo vacation, do you want to go with an organized singles group/people of similar age, or go it alone/meet other solos informally on vacation to share trips with? **Alternative CARD 3:** If traveling alone on a long journey, can/should you arrange transit hotels/transport to and from overseas airports in advance, so you feel safe and not stressed at any stage? **CARD 4:** Are there any possible difficult challenges of going it alone? **CARD 5:** Will you make new friends/romance, if desired, on your travels? **CARD 6:** What knowledge/memorable experiences/new confidence will you bring home with you? **CARD 7:** Will your solo trip be so successful that you cannot wait for the next one?

What you should use:

The forty Minor cards, Aces to Tens.

When:

When planning your solo trip.

569
WHEN YOU HAVE BEEN ASKED ON TWO SEPARATE VACATIONS AT THE SAME TIME AND DON'T KNOW WHICH TO CHOOSE

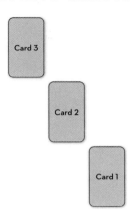

Purpose and background information:

When it's hard to choose for fear of hurting someone's feelings.

Card 1: The first option. **Card 2:** The second option.
Card 3: Is there a compromise/third option?

What you should use:

The forty Minor cards, Aces to tens.

When:

Early morning when you wake, for clarity.

Example:

Joe is planning a month-long pre-university wilderness and adventure trip with a group of guys from his high school. But his parents have offered to take him on a special vacation to Europe as a reward for passing his examinations. What should he do?

Card 1: Going with his friends. **The Three of Wands,** suggesting, as the leaves are growing and Wands are a fast suit, that the adventure trip will open new horizons for Joe. He is quite shy and pleased to be invited by a group he has always wanted to be part of. **Card 2:** For his parents' trip. **The Three of Cups.** His parents have sacrificed a lot so Joe could go to this university. He is their only child, and they want to spend this family time with him.

Card 3: The Eight of Wands. Joe is going to a university several hundred miles away that has lots of adventure-focused societies he can join. He will not be able to see his parents very often. He also suspects that the group was only inviting him to make up the numbers as someone had dropped out at the last minute. Joe decided to keep his parents happy and go to Europe.

570
WHAT IS THE BEST SHORT-BREAK OPTION?

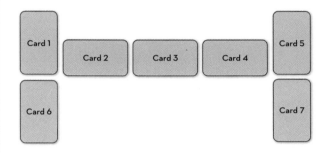

Purpose and background information:

You want to get away, but you only have a few days.

Card 1: What do you most want from this vacation, relaxation/pampering/adventure/luxury/wilderness/ocean/city break? **Card 2:** What type of vacation do you *really need* right now (if different from **Card 1,** why?) **Card 3:** Will a short break put you on track, or do you need more time away if at all possible? **Card 4:** Are you prepared to sacrifice some of the vacation traveling to go where you really want? Will it be worth it? **Card 5:** Do you want to/should you go alone/take a friend/a group of friends/family? **Card 6:** Should you economize? Go all out? Save elsewhere in your life? **Card 7:** Will the vacation be as good as you hope/even better?

What you should use:

The full deck.

When:

Any Wednesday for short vacations.

571
RESOLVING TRAVEL PLAN CONFLICTS

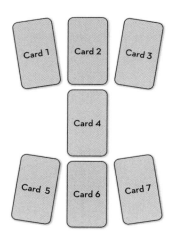

When you and your partner or traveling companion or family cannot agree on travel plans.

Purpose and background information:

CARD 1: What is the main difference in opinion/difficulty with agreeing on plans? **CARD 2:** Can differences be overcome with compromise? **CARD 3:** Would you sooner go alone if you cannot agree? **CARD 4:** Is there an alternative arrangement/ trip that both/all of you would enjoy? If so, what? **CARD 5:** Is this just a travel-plan difference, or are there underlying emotional issues you need to overcome? **CARD 6:** Would you consider abandoning the trip if you cannot agree? **CARD 7:** Will it all be resolved satisfactorily?

What you should use:

The full deck.

When:

Before making any bookings.

572
COPING WITH TROUBLESOME TRAVELING COMPANIONS

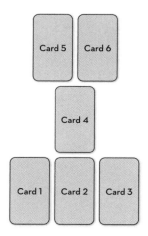

Purpose and background information:

Whether you are having to include a difficult person among the people you are vacationing with, or you meet them on a group holiday/a cruise or at your vacation hotel.

CARD 1: What is the underlying tension between you and the traveling companion/the guest whose company you share on vacation? **CARD 2:** If you are naturally accommodating, how can you protect yourself from being railroaded into what you do not want to do? **CARD 3:** Are there any people with you/ around you to dilute the difficult person? **CARD 4:** Should you plan trips/activities you know the other person will not share? **CARD 5:** If hints and subtle distancing do not work, should you be blunt in order to salvage your vacation? **CARD 6:** Will you have a good vacation in spite of this problem?

What you should use:

The forty Minor cards and the sixteen Court cards.

When:

Friday for harmonious relations.

573
IF IT'S YOUR FIRST VACATION WITHOUT THE CHILDREN

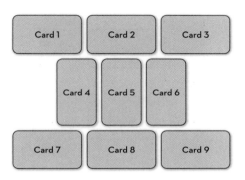

Purpose and background information:

When you are excited but uncertain, because you haven't been away together alone for years.

CARD 1: Should you go to an adult-only venue/would "away-from-it-all" spontaneous travel be better for this first time away? **CARD 2:** Have you left near-to-home contacts for older teens so you will not be getting texts every five minutes telling you they've run out of bread? **CARD 3:** Should you agree to not phone home/relatives too often, to avoid being caught up with domestic/family worries? **CARD 4:** Should you agree not to discuss children/relatives/contentious subjects, so you can devote this time to pleasure? **CARD 5:** If you have gotten out of the habit of talking/spending uninterrupted time together, should you plan lots of trips/activities to build new non-child centered memories? **CARD 6:** Are there underlying relationship issues best left till you are in tune again, or that may resolve naturally away from daily pressures/interference? **CARD 7:** If you have drifted apart, should you return to where you first romanced/a place with happy memories to rekindle the spark? **CARD 8:** Will this vacation be the first of many twosome travel plans for the future? **CARD 9:** Will it open up a more couple-focused aspect of your relationship?

What you should use:

The whole deck.

When:

The evening before booking your trip or fine-tuning details.

574
IF YOU ARE TRAVELING BY PLANE WITH YOUNG, DISABLED, OR MUCH OLDER FAMILY MEMBERS

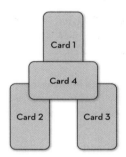

Purpose and background information:

When travel becomes more complicated in order to ensure good care.

CARD 1: Have you double/triple-checked all advance requirements/strollers to and from the plane/special meals/help for less mobile passengers? Will these actually happen on the day? **CARD 2:** For young children long-haul, does the airline offer accessible seats with space to move and for a bassinet, children's in-flight entertainment/special meals? Will they materialize? **Alternative CARD 2:** If there are mobility issues with a much older and/or disabled person, have you double-checked priority boarding/accessible seats/assisted transfers in transit, etc.? Are these arrangements going to work in practice on the day? **CARD 3:** Any unexpected hazards/aspects you have overlooked? **CARD 4:** Is the journey going to be pleasurable for all of you?

What you should use:

The forty Minor cards, Aces to Tens.

When:

When you think you have covered all eventualities but would like confirmation.

575
IF YOU ARE PLANNING A VACATION TO BRING YOURSELF AND YOUR PARTNER CLOSER TOGETHER

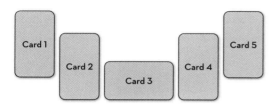

Purpose and background information:
If you have been so busy that you never talk, or you have had problems distancing yourself from each other physically and emotionally.

CARD 1: What do you most want to achieve by the trip away: romance/time out to relax/time to talk/recapturing a shared interest? **CARD 2:** Whether this is a make-or-break time or to overcome stagnation, what is the least potentially controversial/most harmonious setting? **CARD 3:** If your partner is reluctant to go on the trip, should you push for it regardless in the hope it will make things better between you? **CARD 4:** Should you focus on creating new good memories, whether through fun activities or chilling out, rather than worrying about rekindling romance? **CARD 5:** Will this trip make a positive difference to your relationship?

What you should use:
The twenty-two Major cards and the sixteen Court cards.

When:
Sunday for new beginnings.

576
IF IT'S A FIRST TRIP AWAY WITH A NEW PARTNER OR SOMEONE YOU LIKE A LOT

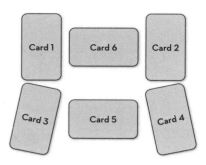

Purpose and background information:
When you are anxious for everything to go well.

CARD 1: Should you relax, accepting that any hitches/glitches will become memories to laugh about in the future? **CARD 2:** Should you find a location where there's lots to see and do, to overcome initial self-consciousness? **CARD 3:** Should you plan to spend some time on separate interests/activities to create space? **CARD 4:** Even if you do not live together, can/should you study your travel companion's quirks/likes/dislikes in advance to avoid nasty surprises? **CARD 5:** Will this trip be a success? **CARD 6:** Is it the beginning of future good times together?

What you should use:
The full deck.

When:
A Friday, for relationship harmony.

577
IF IT'S YOUR HONEYMOON

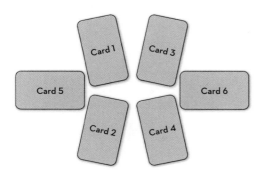

Purpose and background information:
If you want a stress-free memorable time together after the excitement of the wedding.

CARD 1: Do you want/should you have a honeymoon immediately after the wedding, or does it sound better to spend time at home relaxing and go later? **CARD 2:** Do you want an exotic trip-of-a-lifetime/holiday in a familiar setting using the money saved for something useful? **CARD 3:** Will your honeymoon mix fun, excitement, and relaxation to avoid the anticlimax after the big day turning into irritability, tiredness, or boredom? **CARD 4:** Would you prefer that the hotel/other holidaymakers not know you are on your honeymoon/avoid the champagne/rose petals razzmatazz, or would you welcome the trimmings? **CARD 5:** Should you take each day without expectations of perfection, so hitches in your days in paradise can be laughed through? **CARD 6:** Will your honeymoon happiness last into the days, weeks, months, and years ahead?

What you should use:
The full deck.

When:
At the planning stage.

578
IF YOU ARE A SINGLE PARENT AND TAKING YOUR CHILDREN ON VACATION FOR THE FIRST TIME WITHOUT YOUR PARTNER

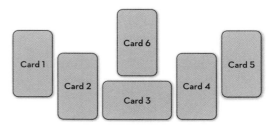

Purpose and background information:
When you are going on a solo family holiday and want it to be enjoyable.

CARD 1: Should you go just with the children, or also with a relative or friend who also has children and no partner? **CARD 2:** Should you go to a family-friendly resort to meet other single parents, or have a spontaneous adventure in a motorhome or camping? **CARD 3:** What do you want for yourself from the holiday? To meet new friends/potential romance? **CARD 4:** Even if your relationship was awful, what strategies do you have when you and the children miss the absent parent? **CARD 5:** Will the vacation go brilliantly/inspire you to have more breaks? **CARD 6:** What will you discover about yourself and your abilities to take on the world?

What you should use:
The twenty-two Major cards and the sixteen Court cards.

When:
School will soon be out.

579
IF YOU WANT TO FOLLOW AN ANCIENT PILGRIM ROUTE OR MAJOR HIKING TRAIL TO FIND YOURSELF

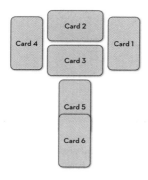

Purpose and background information:

When you want a meaningful vacation, such as hiking the Sierra Nevada cross-state route or the European St James de Compostela route. Maybe pick extra cards for all three alternatives in **Card 2** to see which seems best.

Card 1: Do you want to go alone, or with a friend/partner/family member/in an organized group? **Card 2(a):** If alone, are you prepared for any personal security/emergencies/being self-sufficient on a wilderness trail/booking ahead on a popular route so you have a hostel place when needed? **Alternative Card 2(b):** If going with a friend/relative/partner, are they sufficiently resourceful and enthusiastic if you hit snags en route? **Alternative Card 2(c):** If you join a group, will this make arrangements easier, or make you feel constrained by the needs of the group? **Card 3:** How to record your adventure/photographs and a diary for future generations/keep a blog/sell an article on it to a journal? **Card 4:** What do you most hope to gain from your pilgrimage? **Card 5:** Will you attain these goals? **Card 6:** As a result, will there be future similar journeys?

What you should use:

The full deck.

When:

Once you are determined to go.

580
IF YOU WANT TO GO BACKPACKING OVERSEAS, AND EVERYONE SAYS YOU ARE TOO OLD

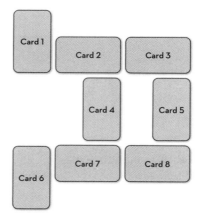

Purpose and background information:

If you know it's now or never.

Card 1: Are there particular places you want to visit and meet locals, or do you want to go wherever your fancy takes you? **Card 2:** Have you backpacked before? If not, should you get expert advice on what you will need to take, especially if you are going to remote places? **Card 3:** Should you allow for the fact that whatever you pack, you have to carry it everywhere? **Card 4:** Do you want to go alone and make friends as you travel, or is a trusted friend partner eager to go with you? **Card 5:** Especially if alone, have you planned security measures/emergency contacts/anything you have missed? **Card 6:** How can you reassure those who worry about you that you can take care of yourself? **Card 7:** Can you profit from media interest if your journey is unusual, or is it a personal quest for you to share with those you choose? **Card 8:** Will you be so glad you went?

What you should use:

The full deck.

When:

When you are determined to make the dream a reality.

581

IF YOU WANT TO SPEND TIME IN AN ASHRAM, BUDDHIST RETREAT, OR SPIRITUAL SANCTUARY

Purpose and background information:

When you want to step off the world for a while.

CARD 1: Does a particular form of Hinduism, Buddhism, or any other spiritual philosophy fascinate you, or do you just want to immerse yourself in any sincere spirituality? **CARD 2:** If you are uncertain as to the kind of spirituality you wish to follow, should you go along to different centers in your own state/country for a short time to see what resonates with you? **CARD 3:** If you want to go overseas for your retreat, how can you find the best/most genuine sanctuary/the authentic guru for you? **CARD 4:** Do you want/would you be best staying in a Westernized or traditional Far Eastern center? **CARD 5:** Do you want to pay for more comfortable accommodations, or a closer-to-grassroots basic experience? **CARD 6:** Especially if going alone, are you happy about the security, and are you prepared medically, especially if there is some political unrest/an increase in local diseases/viruses? **CARD 7:** What do you hope to find there that will positively change your life? **CARD 8:** Will it be all you want and need?

What you should use:

The full deck.

When:

Crescent or early waxing moon.

582

IF YOU ARE A NERVOUS TRAVELER

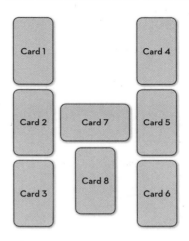

Purpose and background information:

If travel makes you nervous, but you have to—or want to—go on a journey.

CARD 1: Is there any aspect of the trip that worries you, so you can plan ahead to avoid possible hazards? **CARD 2:** Does all travel make you nervous, or just flying/ferries/countries where you cannot speak the language? **CARD 3:** What strategies can best help you to resolve these to enjoy this trip? **CARD 4:** Would you prefer to travel with someone else/in a group/with a travel guide, or do you want to do things at your own pace? **CARD 5:** If you have made this or similar trips before, did they work out well/what have you learned from them to plan for/avoid? **CARD 6:** Would counseling/relaxation/meditation/crystal therapy/cognitive behavioral therapy bring about a reduction in anxiety? **CARD 7:** Will it all turn out well? **CARD 8:** If you cannot face it, should/can you bail out without major loss, and would the loss be worth it?

What you should use:

The full deck.

When:

When you are starting to get anxious as the trip approaches.

583

IF YOU ARE WORRIED ABOUT TRAVELING OVERSEAS, ESPECIALLY IF THERE IS UNREST IN THE HOLIDAY AREA YOU HAVE BOOKED

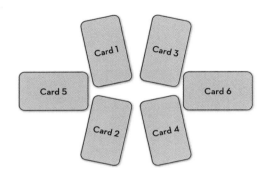

Purpose and background information:

When you have booked and there are no official foreign office warnings definitely not to go, just media reports.

CARD 1: Even if your insurance/travel agent will not give you a refund, is it worth trying/again for a change of date/voucher for when things settle? **CARD 2:** Should you keep updating on foreign office advice/a reliable international news agency, rather than relying on more sensational media reports? **CARD 3:** If you are unbearably anxious, would your physician give you a medical certificate for your insurance? **CARD 4:** Can you plan in advance to spend your holiday away from crowded places/entertainment venues/popular tourist sites? **CARD 5:** Will you be safe if you travel? **CARD 6:** Will you have a splendid holiday, in spite of everything?

What you should use:

The forty Minor cards, Aces to Tens, and the sixteen Court cards.

When:

As soon as you hear of security problems in your planned holiday destination.

584

IF YOU ARE WORRIED ABOUT GETTING SICK ON VACATION WHILE OVERSEAS

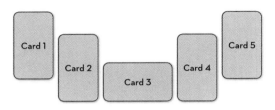

Purpose and background information:

When you are traveling to an exotic location but are worried about getting ill, especially if there are warnings about an epidemic or potential diseases.

CARD 1: Has the situation deteriorated since booking? How serious and long-lasting does it seem? **Alternative CARD 1:** If it is just generally a country with poor hygiene, have you taken every pre-trip precaution, inoculations/medicines/mosquito creams you may not be able to buy there? **CARD 2:** If there are warnings, should you change your holiday destination/change the date, especially if you have children or vulnerable older members in your party? **Alternative CARD 2:** If just a remote country, should you find out in advance what potential hazards there are: for example, street food/local water supply so you can be careful? **CARD 3:** Should you pre-check hotel hygiene standards/hazards before booking, and also pre-check popular tourist spots to avoid? **CARD 4:** Should you relax, once all precautions are taken, using meditation/relaxation massages, etc.? **CARD 5:** Will you be safe and have fun?

What you should use:

The forty Minor cards, Aces to Tens, and the sixteen Court cards.

When:

Once you have definite dates.

585
IF YOU ARE SCARED OF FLYING BUT NEED TO

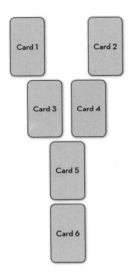

586
IF YOUR DREAM HOLIDAY PLANS NEVER SEEM TO MATERIALIZE

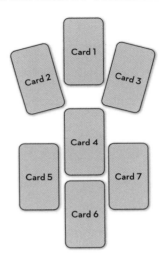

Purpose and background information:
When fear interferes with travel plans.

CARD 1: Is your fear based on a near-miss/bad turbulence on a previous flight/a recently reported air crash, or just free-floating anxiety? **CARD 2:** Should you book a desensitizer program/a second one if you tried before, which some airlines run? **CARD 3:** If you suspect this fear comes from a past-life/childhood trauma, will a hypnotherapist/counselor/past-life therapist be able to take away the fear? **CARD 4:** Should you try cognitive behavioral strategies/meditation/relaxation well in advance, to adopt pre- and during flight? **CARD 5:** Can you successfully distract yourself during the flight, especially takeoff and landing, by talking to your companion—or, if alone, reading/reciting mantras? **CARD 6:** Will the flight be better than you expect, thus increasing confidence for future flights?

What you should use:
The forty Minor cards, Aces to Tens.

When:
Before booking your flight.

Purpose and background information:
When you have been planning your dream holiday forever.

CARD 1: Is the dream holiday still what you want, or has your dream changed? **CARD 2:** What obstacles, known and underlying, stand in the way of its happening? **CARD 3:** What strategies can overcome these obstacles? **CARD 4:** Given a supreme effort, what is the earliest you can realistically go? **CARD 5:** Should you put a deposit down, make as much money as possible until the holiday date, or take an affordable loan on the assumption that if you do not, the date moves further away? **CARD 6:** If money is the issue, should you go on a more modest holiday now? **CARD 7:** Would you regret it if you didn't follow your dream?

What you should use:
The twenty-two Major cards and the sixteen Court cards.

When:
When you decide it's now or never.

587
IF YOU ARE PLANNING TO SPEND YOUR SAVINGS ON A WORLD CRUISE

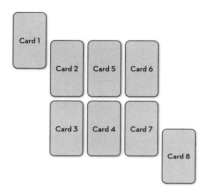

Purpose and background information:
When you long to see the world from the comfort of an ocean liner.

CARD 1: Would it be best/is it possible to take several months to sail around the whole world, or would you want/need to fly part of the way? **CARD 2:** If you haven't been on a cruise before, should you try a shorter one first to see if you enjoy shipboard life? **CARD 3:** Would you be better on a smaller, more personalized vessel, a floating city with every amenity, or something in between? **CARD 4:** Have you found the perfect cruise that goes to all the places you want to see? If not, should you keep looking until you find exactly what you want? **CARD 5:** Are you prepared to barter, especially nearer the cruise date, for upgrades/Internet special deals? Will you get a bargain by doing so? **CARD 6:** What strategies are best for the cruise to get the right mix among self-time, making new friends, avoiding difficult people, and getting cabin fever? **CARD 7:** Will your world cruise be worth the money? **CARD 8:** Will this trip satisfy your travel bug, or will you want to start saving for your next cruise?

What you should use:
The full deck.

When:
A full Moon, or a Monday, day of the moon and the sea.

588
IF YOU WANT A LUXURY, FITNESS, OR HEALTH-CLUB BREAK

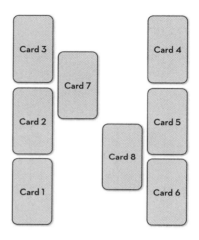

Purpose and background information:
If you need some pampering but feel guilty and selfish indulging yourself.

CARD 1: Should this be all about putting yourself in the center of the picture for once? **CARD 2:** Do you want to go alone, or with a like-minded friend? **CARD 3:** Is there anyone you feel you should invite but who would take away from the self-time? **CARD 4:** What do you seek from your break/luxury/exercise and fitness/pampering/spiritual arts such as yoga/Tai Chi/or just doing nothing? **CARD 5:** Is it better to go within the state to avoid unnecessary travel, or should you go to a beautiful location in another state or overseas to get away from it all? **CARD 6:** Can/should you avoid being influenced by anyone who accuses you of wasting your money/being selfish? **CARD 7:** Will you come back rejuvenated/relaxed and ready for anything? **CARD 8:** Should you try to build pampering/fitness breaks into your life?

What you should use:
The twenty-two major cards and the sixteen Court cards.

When:
When you are feeling frazzled.

589
IF YOU WANT TO TAKE A TRIP TO FIND OR RETURN TO YOUR FAMILY ROOTS

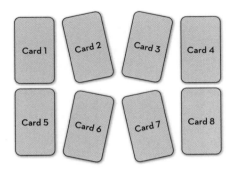

Purpose and background information:
When you are fascinated by family history and want to see where your ancestors lived.

CARD 1: Is there a particular place, perhaps in Europe, to which you are drawn and have old connections? **CARD 2:** Have you examined local modern records there to see if any people with the family name still live in the area? **CARD 3:** Are there any heritage sites/if not, a local museum to get a feel for the old world? **CARD 4:** Are there gaps in the known/online history of your family that you can solve by doing detective work in the locality? **CARD 5:** Will you meet relatives you didn't know about/be able to go inside an old house where your family once lived? **CARD 6:** Will you get information you can make into a book for future generations to enjoy? **CARD 7:** Will you find what you are really looking for/the missing link? **CARD 8:** Do you want to share your pilgrimage with your partner/children/parents/siblings, or do you want to go alone the first time?

What you should use:
The forty Minor cards and the sixteen Court cards.

When:
When you come across a mystery in the family tree that ends in the chosen place.

590
IF YOU DO NOT KNOW WHETHER TO BUY A MOTORHOME OR A PERMANENT HOLIDAY HOME

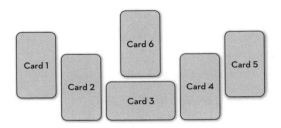

Purpose and background information:
When vacations are becoming increasingly important in your life.

CARD 1: The advantages of a motorhome. **CARD 2:** The disadvantages of a motorhome. **CARD 3:** The advantages of a permanent holiday home, close/interstate or overseas. **CARD 4:** The drawbacks of a permanent holiday home. **CARD 5:** Can/should you compromise/buy a cheaper version of both? **CARD 6:** Should you keep renting until you make up your mind?

What you should use:
The forty Minor cards, Aces to Tens.

When:
The beginning of a month or year.

CHAPTER 31

SPREADS FOR LIFE CHANGES AND TRANSITIONS, BOTH NATURAL AND PLANNED

Lucky cards for life changes:

Major Cards: The Fool, the Magician, the High Priestess, the Lovers, the Chariot, the Wheel of Fortune, the Moon, the Sun, the Star, the World.

Minor Cards: All the Aces, the Two of Cups, the Threes except for Swords, the Four of Wands, the Five of Pentacles, the Sixes of Cups and Wands, the Seven of Cups, the Eights of Pentacles, Cups, and Wands, the Nines of Pentacles and Wands, the Tens of Pentacles and Cups.

The Court Cards: All the Pages/Princesses and Knights/Princes.

About Spreads for life changes:

One card for yes/no variations, two cards for two options, three for natural transitions, fours for stability, fives for swift chosen changes, sixes for relationship and family transitions, sevens where matters aren't clear and more complex choices, eights and above for exploring changes and transitions in detail.

591
IF YOU FACE CHALLENGES AND OBSTACLES TO OVERCOME IN ORDER TO ACHIEVE DESIRED CHANGE

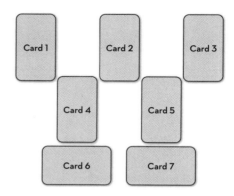

Purpose and background information:
If people or situations are getting in the way of desired change.

CARD 1: Who or what is challenging you? **CARD 2:** If you ignore the situation, will it pass/the person give up? **CARD 3:** Can/should you face the challenge head-on? **CARD 4:** What is in your favor if you take the challenge head-on? **CARD 5:** What are your main fears in facing the challenge? **CARD 6:** Desired or required action? **CARD 7:** Will the action open the way to the change you want?

What you should use:
The full deck.

When:
The beginning of any month, or New Year's Day.

592
FOR MAJOR LIFE-PATH CHOICES AND TRANSITIONS

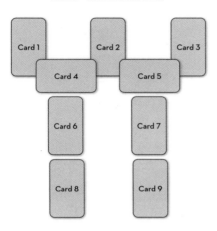

Purpose and background information:
For a major reassessment of where you are and what changes you seek.

CARD 1: Where you are in life right now generally. Are you happy with this? **CARD 2:** Have you met the person you want to share your future life path with? Will you meet them soon, or do you prefer to stay independent? **CARD 3:** Is your career path as you want it? If not, how should it progress/change? **CARD 4:** Are your leisure activities making you happy? Do you want to leave some/add new ones? **CARD 5:** Are you as fit and healthy as you would like to be? If not, how can you improve this? **CARD 6:** Where do you want to be/what do you want to do at this time next year? **CARD 7:** Where do you want to be/what do you want to do/be in five years' time? **CARD 8:** Where do you want to be/what do you want to do in ten years' time? **CARD 9:** What is your secret dream, and can you/how can you achieve it?

What you should use:
The full deck.

When:
When you have plenty of time to cast and interpret this Spread and consider the full implications.

593
IF YOU WANT TO MAKE A MAJOR LIFE CHANGE BUT FEEL STUCK

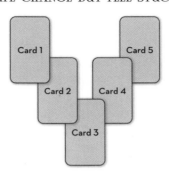

Purpose and background information:
When no matter how hard you try to initiate change in whatever part of your life you seek it, you're unable to progress.

CARD 1: What practical and underlying factors are holding you back from making those changes? **CARD 2:** Do you really want change, or do you just feel you ought to? **CARD 3:** Is now the right time for change? Do you have unfinished business? Are you not quite ready? **CARD 4:** If you are patient, will outside circumstances bring the desired change? **CARD 5:** If you go all out for change and do not let anyone or anything stand in your way, will you succeed?

What you should use:
The twenty-two Major cards and the sixteen Court cards.

When:
At a full moon, or when Mercury has just moved out of retrograde.

594
SHOULD YOUR CHILD GO TO CHILDCARE IF YOU NEED TO GO BACK TO WORK?

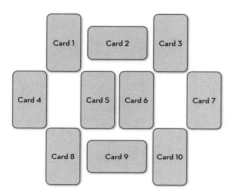

Purpose and background information:

When you need to make decisions about the care of your child.

CARD 1: Do you have to go/want to go back to outside work/could you do your present job from home? **CARD 2:** Could/should you do a staged return to work part-time at first, so you are away less while your child settles with alternative care? **CARD 3:** Is this a time to study for a career change if economically viable/go freelance/start a home-based business? **CARD 4:** Are there relatives who would help out/split care with your partner if you do not want to leave your child in childcare? **CARD 5:** Would your little one enjoy childcare? **CARD 6:** Will you find a facility with a good reputation, where your child would feel at home? **CARD 7:** Would you consider live-in help/find the right person? **CARD 8:** What emergency arrangements will you need if your child is ill on a working day/you are delayed? **CARD 9:** In spite of financial issues, do you want to stay home until your child is slightly older? **CARD 10:** Can you successfully juggle caring for your child and a career at the same time?

What you should use:

The full deck.

When:

When you have only a few weeks left of the paternity/maternity leave owed to you.

595
HELPING YOUR CHILD THROUGH THE TRANSITIONS IN EDUCATION

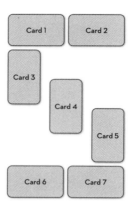

Purpose and background information:

When you want education to be a smooth path from kindergarten to college.

CARD 1: Whatever the transition, have you explored all the options in every educational sector open to you and made sure you fit the criteria of the school where your child will be happy and well educated? **CARD 2:** Should you/do you need to adapt your lifestyle/location/make economic sacrifices to find this right education? **CARD 3:** As far and as long as possible, can you keep your child/children's friendship groups together so changes of school have consistency? **CARD 4:** If your child has special educational needs/academic/sporting/musical gifts, will you obtain the right support/resources? **CARD 5:** Will the current transition be a smooth one for your child? **CARD 6:** Will there be any temporary initial teething troubles if your child is particularly sensitive? **CARD 7:** Will your child be able to fulfill his/her potential within the educational system, not just academically or in sporting success but emotionally?

What you should use:

The full deck.

When:

The beginning of any month, or New Year's Day.

596
WHEN YOUR CHILD MOVES AWAY FROM HOME FOR THE FIRST TIME

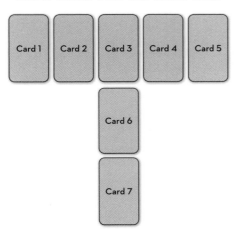

Purpose and background information:
When your child is going to college/work or study far away from home.

CARD 1: Is this what your child really wants/the right placement/the right facilities for their gifts? **CARD 2:** Are peers fueling the belief in a more exciting lifestyle far away from home? **CARD 3:** How are the practicalities, such as finances, going to work/your contribution plus any they need to make? **CARD 4:** If your child is particularly dependent/needy, would a crash course in self-sufficiency prepare them/make them decide they would like to stay closer? **CARD 5:** If they do not know the location, should you vacation there before they apply, especially if overseas? **CARD 6:** Will they be happy in their new life? **CARD 7:** Will it give them a new appreciation of family when they come home?

What you should use:
The full deck.

When:
When the future location is under discussion.

597
WHEN YOUR TEEN WANTS TO MOVE IN WITH THEIR BOY/GIRLFRIEND AND YOU THINK THEY ARE TOO YOUNG

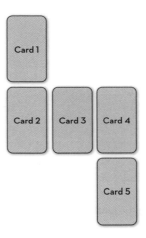

Purpose and background information:
When your teen is in love and will not listen to reason.

CARD 1: Is this their first big love, and whatever you say against the romance just makes it worse? **CARD 2:** Should you focus on the practicalities to inject reality? **CARD 3:** Whether or not you approve of the partner, can you successfully bring about a postponement for completion of vital education? **CARD 4:** Should you invite them to live with you, to minimize potential harm if you do not trust the partner? **CARD 5:** Will your child grow out of this passion if you let him/her evolve and diminish naturally?

What you should use:
The forty Minor cards, Aces to Tens, and the sixteen Court cards.

When:
A Saturday, day of wise caution.

598
IF YOUR CHILD IS DETERMINED TO JOIN THE MILITARY

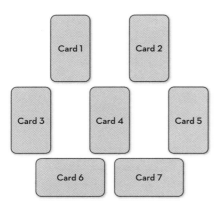

Purpose and background information:
When your child has always been interested in the military and has expressed interest in enlisting.

CARD 1: Is this a long-standing desire, family connections/being dedicated to the military cadets? **CARD 2:** Is your child naturally active and fearless? **CARD 3:** Would your child enjoy military training and travel? **CARD 4:** Will it be best for your child to apply for a university scholarship first, or go directly into the military to train? **CARD 5:** What are your actual/underlying fears for your child? Are these valid? **CARD 6:** Is this to be a lifelong career, or a step to training for an eventual civilian job/business? **CARD 7:** Will your child be safe in the military, in spite of your perfectly understandable fears?

What you will use:
The twenty-two Major cards and the sixteen Court cards.

When:
When you realize that whatever you say only makes your child more determined to join.

599
WHEN YOU ARE GOING FOR YOUR FIRST REAL JOB OR INTERNSHIP?

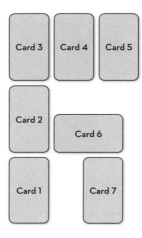

Purpose and background information:
When you know you are ready but are fearful of the competition.

CARD 1: Is it better, even if you have applied for the post you really want, to apply at the same time for alternatives? **CARD 2:** Should you be prepared to relocate if a similar opportunity arises in a more distant area? **CARD 3:** Are you confident that you are qualified/experienced in every way for the post, or is there anything you need to improve upon? **CARD 4:** Do you have financial backing/can you raise extra money to support yourself until you get established? **CARD 5:** Is this the right permanent field for you/a stepping-stone, or will you take any job to get on the ladder of employment? **CARD 6:** Will you be offered your first choice/something close to the ideal? **CARD 7:** If not, will you follow the new path you have been offered, or keep applying for what you really want?

What you should use:
The forty Minor cards, Aces to Tens, and the sixteen Court cards.

When:
Just before applying for your ideal position?

600
WHEN YOU PLAN TO MOVE IN WITH YOUR PARTNER

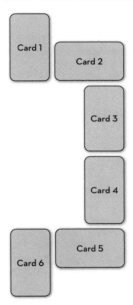

Purpose and background information:
When you feel ready for this major step but worry whether it is the right move.

Card 1: Should your partner move in with you, you with your partner, or both find a new place together? **Card 2:** Is this the right time, or should you wait a while? **Card 3:** Are you buying/planning to buy a joint property, or should you initially rent to see how it goes? **Card 4:** What are the advantages of living together? **Card 5:** What are the anticipated/unforeseen drawbacks, and what strategies need to be overcome? **Card 6:** Is this the beginning of a long and happy future together?

What you should use:
The whole deck.

When:
Once you start to make definite plans.

601
IF YOU WANT YOUR PARTNER TO PROPOSE

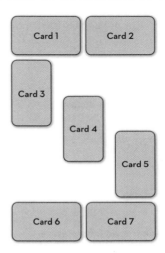

Purpose and background information:
When your partner is slow in the romance stakes.

Card 1: Have you dropped hints, and the idea has not been rejected? **Card 2:** Is there a romantic setting you both love and a time when you will not be interrupted? **Card 3:** Should you initiate a romantic weekend/vacation to build up to the big moment? **Card 4:** Should you drop lots of *forevers* into the everyday conversation? **Card 5:** Should you forget subtlety and propose yourself? **Card 6:** If s/he doesn't get the idea, should you accept the status quo? **Card 7:** Should you contemplate moving on?

What you should use:
The forty Minor cards and the sixteen Court cards.

When:
When you are tired of waiting.

602

IN AN ON/OFF RELATIONSHIP WHERE YOU HAVE FREQUENTLY BEEN LET DOWN, SHOULD YOU GIVE YOUR PARTNER ONE LAST CHANCE?

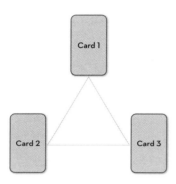

Purpose and background information:
When you love your partner but fear they will never change.

CARD 1: Should you give your partner just one more chance?
CARD 2: Are the problems that have caused the differences still there? **CARD 3:** Should you go forward to a new life and close that old door once and for all?

What you should use:
The forty Minor cards, Aces to Tens, and the sixteen Court cards.

When:
When your heart says *yes* and your head says *no*.

Example:
Jess separated from her partner Adam because he was frequently unfaithful. She became tired of his coming back promising it will be different, then betraying her again.

Now she has started a new life and career in another state and is dating again. But suddenly Adam turns up at her door, promising it would be different and he would move interstate to live with her. Can she trust him?

CARD 1: The Ten of Wands, showing the person staggering along carrying lots of wands with leaves on them. Does Jess want to pick up the burden she has just shed, represented by the wands blocking her view?

CARD 2: Prince of Wands, a fun, dashing, charming prince who isn't reliable. The prince represents Adam. Jess decides she wants a King, not a charismatic overgrown adolescent.

CARD 3: The Eight of Cups, the person shown walking away to happiness with all their personal cups the right way up. Having done that already, Jess realizes she would be taking a backward step to take Adam back.

So Jess refused and has started her own business, no longer wasting her energies on Adam.

603

WHEN A CHILD ENTERS ADOLESCENCE

Purpose and background information:
When you realize your child is no longer a child.

CARD 1: No matter how sophisticated and knowledgeable your child seems, what emotional support should you offer? **CARD 2:** Are there potential hazards/excess anxiety/depression/undue secrecy/body image problems, especially from peers, that you need to be aware of? **CARD 3:** If your child enters adolescence earlier/later than his/her peers/what extra support/reassurance/unobtrusive medical advice would help? **CARD 4:** What strategies will you need to balance hormonally induced moods with family life and boundaries? **CARD 5:** Will this be a smooth adolescence, or stormy waters that you will nevertheless negotiate successfully?

What you should use:

The twenty-two Major cards and the sixteen Court cards.

When:

At the waxing moon.

604
IF YOUR PARTNER HITS A MID-LIFE CRISIS

Purpose and background information:

When there is need for a major positive life reassessment to avoid destructive/self-destructive behavior by your partner.

Card 1: Are there warning signs you shouldn't ignore, sudden excessive interest in appearance/fitness/discontent with work and family/lack of interest in sex/staying out late/ being secretive even when there is no reason? **Card 2:** Will you succeed in reassuring your partner if s/he is worried about getting older/maybe being overtaken at work? **Card 3:** Can you successfully move to the next phase of life together/planning fun vacations/evenings/getting fit together? **Card 4:** If your partner wants a life change/career change, can you plan one together? **Card 5:** Should you nip in the bud any hints of seeking the company of younger people out for thrills? **Card 6:** Will your partner overcome this phase and move to a new future with you?

What you should use:

The twenty-two Major cards and sixteen Court cards.

When:

When you detect in your partner warning signs of discontent.

605
IF YOU ARE HAVING A BAD TIME DURING MENOPAUSE

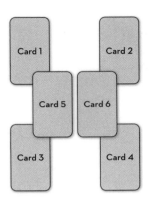

Purpose and background information:

When your life and health are out of balance.

Card 1: Are you getting the best medical care, conventional, and/or alternative treatment for physical symptoms? **Card 2:** Can you flow with the restlessness/desire for change by making good choices in your lifestyle/relationships? **Card 3:** Can you ride the mood swings/intense emotions by shaping a powerful spiritual life/shedding what you no longer want? **Card 4:** Can you use times you feel exhausted to relax/ meditate/enjoy quiet pursuits/rearrange work schedules to fit with your energy levels? **Card 5:** Will you come out of menopause a far more powerful person, maybe on a new more fulfilling life path? **Card 6:** Spiritually, can you use this life transition as a rite of passage to become a truly wise woman?

What you should use:

The twenty-two Major cards.

When:

When you feel at the mercy of your hormones.

606
FACING REDUNDANCY

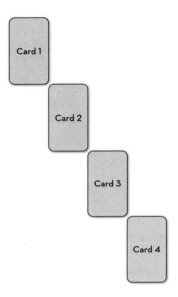

Purpose and background information:

When a once seemingly secure career proves not to be so.

Card 1: Whether you are offered redundancy/made compulsorily redundant, what advantages can be found? **Card 2:** If you have an option to refuse/want to fight the decision, should you resist, or would you succeed? **Card 3:** If you refuse offered redundancy/claim unfair or constructive dismissal if compulsory, will legal/union support reverse the decision? **Card 4:** Do you want to stay, or to go now on the best terms possible?

What you should use:

The full deck.

When:

When the matter of redundancy is raised.

607
WHEN YOU REALIZE YOU ARE NO LONGER AS YOUNG AS YOU WERE

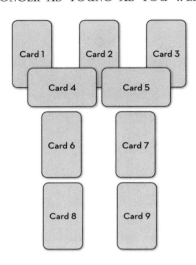

Purpose and background information:

When life seems more of an effort.

Card 1: Should you have a medical checkup in case of any undiscovered minor health conditions, such as anemia making you feel tired/lethargic? **Card 2:** Should you revise working/family life if you feel like you are overdoing it? **Card 3:** Is there underlying depression/anxiety/money worries/an over-competitive workplace? What strategies would help? **Card 4:** Should you plan how to develop a better quality of life? **Card 5:** Should you ask others to do more if you always do your best by everyone? **Card 6:** Should you make more time for travel/fun/love? **Card 7:** Should you find new activities you enjoy and shed those that are a burden? **Card 8:** Will you get your enthusiasm for life back again? **Card 9:** Should you move toward the role of wise man/woman/adviser instead of striving to succeed?

What you should use:

The whole deck.

When:

When each day becomes a chore, not an adventure.

608
TAKING RETIREMENT OR EARLY RETIREMENT

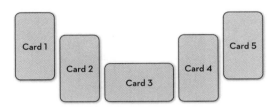

Purpose and background information:

When you are ready for the next phase of your life.

CARD 1: Is it economically possible to give up work totally, or will you need to supplement your income/economize/work for longer even if you have reached the statutory retirement age? **CARD 2:** Will you downsize/change location/stay put? **CARD 3:** Do you and/or your partner have talents to turn into a business/money-spinner? **CARD 4:** Do you want/will you travel extensively in the years ahead? **CARD 5:** Is now the time to give up work and worry about how you'll manage once you are free?

What you should use:

The forty Minor cards, Aces to Tens, and the sixteen Court cards.

When:

When you feel the urge to seriously consider retirement.

609
IF YOU WANT TO HOMESCHOOL THE CHILDREN WHILE YOU TAKE A YEAR DRIVING AROUND THE CONTINENT

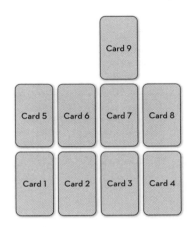

Purpose and background information:

When you feel you are missing out on family adventure and togetherness.

CARD 1: Is this a good time to take children out of school, or should you wait a while? **CARD 2:** Are the practicalities of homeschooling/income/savings in place so you will not run out of money/can deal with emergencies? **CARD 3:** Are there ways to supplement your income/work remotely while on the road? **CARD 4:** Will the great outdoors compensate for cramped living accommodations? **CARD 5:** Are the children 100% behind the decision, or can you at least convince them of the advantages? **CARD 6:** If an older teen doesn't want to come, can they stay with a relative/close friend, joining you during vacations? **CARD 7:** Is this the best plan ever? **CARD 8:** Should you try longer vacation trips first to see how/if it will work? **CARD 9:** Is it a recipe for disaster/best postponed until you are child-free?

What you should use:

The full deck.

When:

At the discussion stage.

610
IF YOU WANT TO LEAVE A SECURE JOB AND TRAVEL THE WORLD

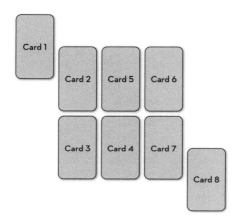

Purpose and background information:

When you are considering sacrificing security for adventure.

Card 1: Can you take a sabbatical/unpaid leave from your job to travel? **Card 2:** If not, will you get another job in your field when you return? Or will you simply worry about that when you return, not now? **Card 3:** Will you/can you cash in assets to have sufficient money, or can you find work as you travel? **Card 4:** Do you/should you have a definite itinerary/timescale, or leave it totally open? **Card 5:** Will you go solo/with a friend/find love en route, or are you going to discover long-sought independence? **Alternative Card 5:** Will you travel with your partner/meet your partner at regular intervals if they cannot/do not want to come, or will you just go anyway? **Card 6:** Are you/should you be prepared for any eventuality before you go, or will you improvise en route? **Card 7:** Should/will you go soon, or will you postpone the trip for a few months/a year? **Card 8:** Will the trip both be safe and fulfill your dreams?

What you should use:

The full deck.

When:

When the desire becomes stronger than the doubts.

611
IF YOU WANT TO BUY A BOAT TO SAIL AROUND THE WORLD

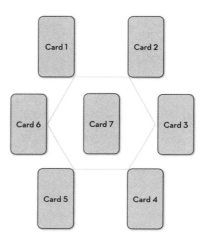

Purpose and background information:

When you are ready to reach for your dream.

Card 1: Do you share your dream with a partner, or will you go solo? **Card 2:** If your partner is unwilling, can you agree to meet at different ports, or will you go anyway and hope they wait? **Alternative Card 2:** If traveling solo, will you find the right crew you could live with in a confined space, or would it be totally solo? **Card 3:** Are you totally prepared for a worldwide trip, or do you need more long trips to become used to every eventuality? **Card 4:** Will you spend all your free money on the best vessel possible, keep your land base for when you return, or buy a smaller base if you do not have a partner? **Card 5:** Is this the first of many trips/a prelude to living on the boat permanently? **Card 6:** Could/will you find a sponsor/publish articles/blogs/a book, or just enjoy the experience? **Card 7:** Could this trip be the beginning of a new sailing-related career, even if you are retired?

What you should use:

The full deck.

When:

When the dream dominates everything else in your mind.

612
IF YOU ARE RELOCATING OVERSEAS OR EMIGRATING

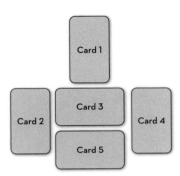

Purpose and background information:

When your future is to some degree unknown.

CARD 1: Whether this move is your choice or caused by circumstances, what are the actual and hidden opportunities of relocating/emigrating? **CARD 2:** What are the actual/hidden disadvantages of the move? **CARD 3:** If relocating, is this for a set time? Will this lead to a permanent life in the new location? **Alternative CARD 3:** If emigration/relocation doesn't work out, can you afford/will you be able to afford to come back? What are the alternatives? **CARD 4:** Are there regrets/worries about anyone left behind? Are they resolvable? **Alternative CARD 4:** If you have no ties, will you meet love/good friends in the new location? **CARD 5:** Will this move be successful and fulfilling?

What you should use:

The forty Minor cards, Aces to Tens, and the sixteen Court cards.

When:

Once you have been offered the overseas posting/been accepted for immigration.

613
DISCOVERING YOUR FAMILY HERITAGE

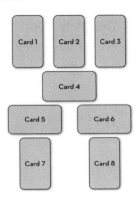

Purpose and background information:

When you are fascinated by where your family roots are, especially if they emigrated centuries ago from the Old World.

CARD 1: Would a DNA test or the services of an online ancestry service work for you, or do you prefer to do your own research via census/parish records, etc.? **CARD 2:** Are there any fascinating family legends/mysteries to investigate? **CARD 3:** Should/will you return to the place your family emigrated from to explore actual records/museums, etc.? **CARD 4:** Do you want to contact distant relatives from other branches of the family, or do you just want the information? **CARD 5:** Will you be/are you prepared to find skeletons in the family cupboard? **CARD 6:** If any relatives would be opposed to your investigating, will you go ahead/not tell them, or insist it's your right to know? **CARD 7:** Should you collect old photos to remaster/family recipes and remedies/talk to old relatives, to create a family record for future generations? **CARD 8:** Is there a particular ancestor you will feel close to who you will find had a very similar life path to yourself, even hundreds of years ago?

What you should use:

The forty Minor cards, Aces to Tens, and the sixteen Court cards.

When:

When you discover a fascinating fact about your family that arouses your interest.

614

TO CONNECT WITH A BIRTH PARENT OR CHILD FOR THE FIRST TIME, AFTER MANY YEARS OF BEING SEPARATED

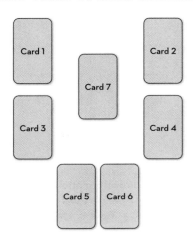

Purpose and background information:

When you are planning to phone or visit and have gotten cold feet.

CARD 1: If you are not quite ready, should you go for counseling/more counseling to be emotionally prepared? **CARD 2:** Is there an intermediary/a birth family relative who could ease the way? **CARD 3:** Would the birth family/your partner and children/adoptive family be best initially kept out of the equation, or best involved even if hostile? **CARD 4:** Should you meet on neutral territory/in a public place so you can extend or cut short the first meeting more easily, should it be necessary? **CARD 5:** Will it go well and grow into a positive relationship? **CARD 6:** Has too much water gone under the bridge, so best left unexplored? **CARD 7:** On reflection, would it be better to go ahead, or not go ahead, with the meeting?

What you should use:

The twenty-two Major cards and sixteen Court cards.

When:

When you feel you just *have* to learn about your family tree.

615

WHEN YOU DISCOVER YOUR PARTNER HAS BEEN LIVING A DOUBLE LIFE OR A LIE

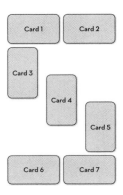

Purpose and background information:

When you discover your partner is married to someone else/has another partner and family/a secret child.

CARD 1: Is this deliberate deception, or was your partner already committed when you met and didn't have the courage to tell you? **CARD 2:** Are you 100% certain of the reliability of the source, or should you do some detective work to find out the full story? **CARD 3:** Should you confront your partner/visit the other family, who may not know about you, or should you step back until you feel calm enough to make rational logical decisions? **CARD 4:** If you give your partner a choice, will s/he choose you and your family? **Alternative CARD 4:** If a secret child, can you agree upon arrangements so the child doesn't suffer from the revelations? **CARD 5:** Would you never trust your partner again/no longer want him/her in your life? **CARD 6:** If children/property are involved, should you get legal advice at once, or let things settle before acting? **CARD 7:** Will there be happiness with your partner in the future, or for you without him/her?

What you should use:

The twenty-two Major cards and sixteen Court cards.

When:

When inexplicable absences and excuses of working away fall into place.

616
WHEN YOUR PARTNER IS CONVICTED OF AN OFFENSE YOU KNEW NOTHING ABOUT

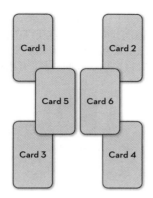

Purpose and background information:

When your world collapses following revelations of your partner's offense.

CARD 1: Do you believe in your partner's innocence and are ready to fight for it? **CARD 2:** Has s/he been in trouble with the law before and had really tried to change? **CARD 3:** Should you/do you want to stick by your partner regardless/prison visit and be there on release? **CARD 4:** Is this/should this be the end of the relationship? **CARD 5:** Should you move away for your sake/the sake of any children, to avoid gossip/prejudice regardless of whether you are willing to wait? **CARD 6:** Will your partner really change this time so there could be a future for you?

What you should use:

The full deck.

When:

At a waning moon.

617
IF YOU WANT TO LEAVE THE FRANTIC DASH OF LIFE CITY AND LIVE OFF THE GRID IN THE WILDERNESS

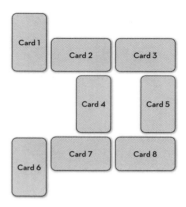

Purpose and background information:

When you have had enough of city chaos.

CARD 1: Has this desire become urgent to fulfill, or is it just a vague future plan? **CARD 2:** Do you share this dream with your partner/family, or is it a solo enterprise? **CARD 3:** Are you experienced in self-sufficiency and wilderness living, or will you learn as you go? **CARD 4:** If you want to go to a remote area in another country, will you get the necessary visas/land rights, or is it better to stay in your own state/another state nearer to civilization? **CARD 5:** Can/will you self-build, if necessary clearing land you have bought, or renovate an existing building/farmstead? **CARD 6:** Do you have sufficient money to get established, or are there assets you can sell in an emergency? **CARD 7:** Will your new life prove the dream you hoped it would? If not, is there a backup life plan? **CARD 8:** Should you satisfy your desires for freedom in less dramatic ways/stop watching away-from-it-all movies?

What you should use:

The forty Minor cards, Aces to Tens.

When:

The beginning of a month.

618

IF ONE OF YOUR FAMILY JOINS A CULT AND SEVERS ALL TIES WITH YOU

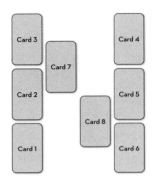

Purpose and background information:

When you fear your family member has been brainwashed.

CARD 1: If you have advance warning, can you give your family member emergency numbers, including a pre-paid cab firm, and say you will come day or night/urging them to hide this info? **CARD 2:** Is there anyone/an organization for former cult members/online information/a counselor or medic who can have some influence if they will not listen to you? **CARD 3:** If your family member is a minor or has special educational or social needs, will you be able to get effective help from the authorities? **Alternative CARD 3:** Will you be able to keep/fight for any contact via phone or Internet/supervised visits even if monitored, avoiding any open criticism to keep the connection? **CARD 4:** Should you go for/can you get power of attorney/temporarily freezing finances if the family member has a lot of assets being donated to the cult? **CARD 5:** Can you get help from an organization that works to free cult members? **CARD 6:** Will your family member leave by choice/run away if desperate or within the year? **CARD 7:** Is there a safe place your family member can go to right away for a few weeks to break contact/get professional debriefing? **CARD 8:** Will you get your family member back relatively unscathed, even if you have to wait?

What you should use:

The whole deck.

When:

When you discover that your family member is attending cult meetings.

619

IF YOU SUDDENLY REALIZE THAT YOUR LIFE HAS LOST ITS PURPOSE AND YOU NEED A TOTAL LIFE CHANGE

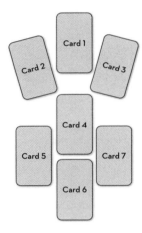

Purpose and background information:

When you are living to work, not working to live.

CARD 1: Can you start a staged changeover to new work that has meaning, even if it pays less? **CARD 2:** Do you want to retrain/study something new, ready for a major life change? **CARD 3:** Would relocating to an area you love make you feel better about life? **CARD 4:** Does your relationship need improving/do you want to find love, or do you want to be alone? **CARD 5:** Do you need to change all/some of these to find fulfillment? **CARD 6:** What sacrifices should/must you make to find fulfillment? **CARD 7:** What advantages will make the sacrifices worthwhile?

What you should use:

The twenty-two Major cards and the sixteen Court cards.

When:

The evening before the start of the work week.

620
IF YOU HAVE SURVIVED A MAJOR ILLNESS AND YOUR PRIORITIES CHANGE

Purpose and background information:
When each day becomes precious.

CARD 1: What do you treasure most? If you don't have it, how can you attain it? **CARD 2:** Do you want to scale down your perhaps previously hectic lifestyle? **CARD 3:** Do you want to travel/relocate, or stay where you are and enjoy it? **CARD 4:** Can you manage with less money than you used to make, in order to enjoy a better quality of life? **CARD 5:** Do you want to become closer to certain friends and family members, letting them know how much you value them? **CARD 6:** Do you want to let certain people/old grievances and redundant activities go? **CARD 7:** Should you give those family heirlooms/money gifts *now* to those who would appreciate them and enjoy their pleasure? **CARD 8:** Will each day be precious, whether your life will be long or short? **CARD 9:** Do you nevertheless see a long and happy future ahead for yourself?

What you should use:
The full deck.

When:
When you are given back the gift of health.

621
IF THERE IS A MAJOR PANDEMIC, AND SUDDENLY LIFE IS NO LONGER SAFE

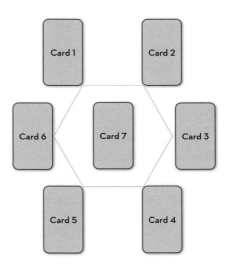

Purpose and background information:
When the world shakes on its axis.

CARD 1: Have your personal priorities changed so health and loved ones are at the top of the list? **CARD 2:** Can/will you adapt to food and financial shortages/realize that what seemed necessities were luxuries? **CARD 3:** Do you and your loved ones have a good chance of surviving this? **CARD 4:** Has quarantining/self-isolating taken you away from your creative and spiritual gifts? Should you continue to develop them afterward? **CARD 5:** Should you speak the words of love, appreciation, and forgiveness by Skype and other online communication that you never said face to face? **CARD 6:** Afterward, will you reassess your life path? **CARD 7:** Will you as a result live a happier, more thoughtful, and more fulfilling life when the pandemic passes?

What you should use:
The forty Minor cards, Aces to Tens.

When:
When we are lucky enough to wake healthy for another day.

CHAPTER 32

ASTROLOGICAL SPREADS, PART 1

Lucky Astrological Cards:

Some of the astrological Spreads center around the Major Arcana cards representing personal Zodiac signs, or Sun signs as they are often referred to, and more generally the Zodiac sign we are passing through at the time of the reading. Your personal zodiac card appearing in any astrological Spread, or indeed in any Spread, represents immense good fortune for you in the area of life described by the card position where it appears.

About Zodiac/Sun sign Spreads:

All you need to know for astrological Spreads is the Sun sign under which you were born. I have changed the ordering of some Spreads slightly, so you have the relevant information on how to deal the cards and interpret the Spreads before beginning. Zodiac meanings are given in the individual Zodiac spreads below, one for each sign.

The Major cards I have used in this chapter linked with particular zodiac signs are associations I have used with success for many years. If you look online and in books, you'll see that other authors and Tarot readers have made different associations. There aren't any definitive one-size-fits-all associations between specific Major cards and the zodiac signs; so if mine don't feel right, you can make your own associations between the twelve zodiac signs and the Major Tarot cards. As Libra has two distinct aspects, justice and love, you might like to pick a different Major card for each area of Libra, and the same with Aquarius where you have independence and friendship, two different areas.

The Associations

Following are the astrological Major Arcana cards and what they represent:

Aries the Magician

Taurus Temperance

Gemini the Chariot

Cancer the Moon *or* the Empress (your choice)

Leo the Emperor

Virgo the High Priestess

Libra Justice and the Lovers, for its two aspects, justice and love

Scorpio the Wheel of Fortune

Sagittarius the World

Capricorn Judgment *or* the Hierophant (your choice)

Aquarius the Hermit (independence)/Strength (friendship) for its two aspects

Pisces the Inner Child (Fool)

622
A FAST-ANSWER SUN SIGN SPREAD

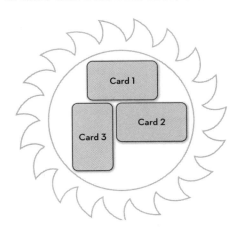

Purpose and background information:

If you have a specific question that is of great significance, but you want a fast answer. Check back for Major card zodiac associations.

CARD 1: The advantages of going ahead with what you are asking about. **CARD 2:** The disadvantages of what you are asking about. **CARD 3:** The outcome of acting/going forward.

What you should use, and how:

Pick out the 12 astrological Major Arcana cards listed on page 331. Shuffle them well. Pick three from anywhere in your mini-deck to answer any question. If your special Sun/Zodiac card appears, it indicates that this issue is going to work out especially well for you with very little effort.

When:

At a full moon.

For each of the following 14 zodiac spreads, use the Tarot card formation above. Note that the opposing card represents the challenging qualities of the opposing sun sign.

623
THE ARIES SPREAD OF ACTION

Aries, the Ram (March 21–April 20)
· drive and passion · reaching goals · courage ·
unblocking energies · action · assertiveness

Purpose and background information:

For anyone born under Aries, anyone asking the question during the Star sign period or if you need an Arian quality in your life.

CARD 1: Where in your life do you most need action? **CARD 2:** How can you best assert yourself in this matter? **CARD 3:** What advantages/opportunities will make this possible? **CARD 4:** How can you avoid/overcome the *wanting to please everyone* influence of Libra that blocks personal harmony? **CARD 5:** The unexpected factor. **CARD 6:** The key to positive action. **CARD 7:** The desired outcome. **CARD 8:** The actual outcome.

What you should use:

The full deck.

When:

During the Star sign period, or when the moon enters Aries during each month (for about two and a half days).

624
THE TAURUS SPREAD OF HARMONY

Taurus, the Bull (April 21–May 21)
· beauty · harmony · all material matters and
security · patience and persistence

Purpose and background information:

For anyone born under Taurus, anyone asking the question during the Star sign period, or if you need a Taurean quality in your life.

CARD 1: Where in your life is persistence most needed to achieve harmony? **CARD 2:** Where or how do you need to be patient? **CARD 3:** What advantages/opportunities will this persistence/patience bring about? **CARD 4:** How can you

overcome the intensity of Scorpio in others that stands in the way of harmony? **CARD 5:** The unexpected factor. **CARD 6:** The key to seeking a practical solution. **CARD 7:** The desired outcome. **CARD 8:** The actual outcome.

What you should use:

The full deck.

When:

During the Star sign period, or when the moon enters Taurus during each month (for about two and a half days).

625
THE GEMINI SPREAD OF CHANGE

Gemini the Heavenly Twins (May 22–June 21)
· communication · learning · choices · logic
· technology · medicine · versatility · short-
distance travel · house moves · speculation

Purpose and background information:

For anyone born under Gemini, anyone asking the question during the Star sign period, or if you need a Gemini quality in your life.

CARD 1: Where or how do you most need change? **CARD 2:** How will logic and persuasion be most useful in this matter? **CARD 3:** What advantages/opportunities will make change possible at the right time? **CARD 4:** How can you avoid/overcome the *aiming-for-too-much-too-soon* influence of Sagittarius and as a result failing. **CARD 5:** The unexpected factor. **CARD 6:** The key to introducing new things and places into your life, following your head, not your heart. **CARD 7:** The desired outcome. **CARD 8:** The actual outcome.

What you should use:

The full deck.

When:

During the Star sign period, or when the moon enters Gemini during each month (for about two and a half days).

626
THE CANCERIAN SPREAD OF THE HOME AND FAMILY

Cancer the Crab (June 22–July 22)
• home and family • fertility • mothering • protection
• gentle love and nurturing • wishes

Purpose and background information:
For anyone born under Cancer, anyone asking the question during the Star sign period, or if you need a Cancerian quality in your life.

CARD 1: What do you most need to know about home or family matters? **CARD 2:** What or who is causing the problem/question? **CARD 3:** What advantages/opportunities will make happiness/resolution possible? **CARD 4:** How can you avoid/overcome the rigid conventional attitudes due to the influence of Capricorn? **CARD 5:** The unexpected factor. **CARD 6:** The key to resolving any dissension. **CARD 7:** The desired outcome. **CARD 8:** The actual outcome.

What you should use:
The full deck.

When:
During the Star sign period, or when the moon enters Cancer during each month (for about two and a half days).

627
THE LEO SPREAD OF AMBITIONS ACHIEVED

Leo the Lion (July 23–August 23)
• fame and fortune • leadership • power • fathering
• sensual pleasures • the arts • love affairs

Purpose and background information:
For anyone born under Leo, anyone asking the question during the Star sign period, or if you need a Leonine quality in your life.

CARD 1: Where do you want or need to take the lead or achieve an ambition in your life? **CARD 2:** How can you best reveal your talents/reach to attain your ambition? **CARD 3:** What advantages/opportunities will make this possible? **CARD 4:** How can you avoid/overcome the doubts that make you hold back, influenced by Aquarius? **CARD 5:** The unexpected factor. **CARD 6:** The key to launching or developing your gifts in a major way. **CARD 7:** The ideal outcome. **CARD 8:** The actual outcome.

What you should use:
The full deck.

When:
During the Star sign period, or when the moon enters Leo during each month (for about two and a half days).

628
THE VIRGO SPREAD OF HEALTH AND HEALING

Virgo the Maiden (August 24–September 22)
• efficiency • bringing order to chaos • self-improvement
• fitness • attention to detail • health and healing

Purpose and background information:
For anyone born under Virgo, anyone asking the question during the Star sign period, or if you need a Virgoan quality in your life.

CARD 1: What worries you about your health or that of a loved one? **CARD 2:** What are the actual and hidden obstacles to good/better health? **CARD 3:** What advantages/opportunities will make good/better health possible? **CARD 4:** What alternatives need to be considered or choices made, in view of the uncertainties caused by the opposition of Pisces? **CARD 5:** The unexpected factor. **CARD 6:** The key to a new approach. **CARD 7:** The ideal outcome. **CARD 8:** The actual outcome.

What you should use:
The full deck.

When:
During the Star sign period, or when the moon enters Virgo during each month (for about two and a half days).

629
THE JUSTICE SPREAD OF LIBRA

Libra the Scales (September 23–October 23)
• justice and the law • balancing options and
priorities • harmony and reconciliation •
charisma • romance • love • twin souls

Purpose and background information:
For anyone born under Libra, anyone asking a justice question
during the Star sign period, or if you need Libran justice in your
life.

CARD 1: The injustice or need for compensation. **CARD 2:**
Who or what opposes justice or compensation? **CARD 3:**
What advantages/opportunities will make this possible?
CARD 4: How can you avoid/overcome the aggressive or
intimidating influence of Aries in others? **CARD 5:** The
unexpected factor. **CARD 6:** The key to truth revealed.
CARD 7: The ideal outcome. **CARD 8:** The actual outcome.

What you should use:
The full deck.

When:
During the Star sign period, or when the moon enters Libra
during each month (for about two and a half days).

630
THE LOVE SPREAD OF LIBRA

Purpose and background information:
For anyone born under Libra, anyone asking a love question
during the Star sign period, or if you need Libran love in your life.

CARD 1: The love question. **CARD 2:** The obstacles to
love. **CARD 3:** That advantages/opportunities will make
this love possible? **CARD 4:** How can you avoid/overcome
the interfering or over-dominant opposition from Aries?
CARD 5: The unexpected factor. **CARD 6:** The key to finding/
keeping love. **CARD 7:** The ideal outcome. **CARD 8:** The actual
outcome.

What you should use:
The full deck.

When:
During the Star sign period, or when the moon enters Libra
during each month (for about two and a half days).

631
THE SCORPIO TRANSFORMATION SPREAD

Scorpio the Scorpion (October 24–November 22)
• transformation • increasing second sight • passion
and sex • keeping secrets • any burning ambition •
claiming what is rightfully yours in any area of life

Purpose and background information:
For anyone born under Scorpio, anyone asking a question during
the Star sign period, or if you need a Scorpio quality in your life.

CARD 1: What needs reviving or transforming in your life?
CARD 2: What or who keeps you emotionally from being able
to make the transformation in a relationship or situation?
CARD 3: What advantages/opportunities will make this
possible? **CARD 4:** How can you avoid/overcome the material
or practical issues from holding you back every time you try,
through the opposition of Taurus? **CARD 5:** The unexpected
factor. **CARD 6:** The key to making the transformation/revival.
CARD 7: The ideal outcome. **CARD 8:** The actual outcome.

What you should use:
The full deck.

When:
During the Star sign period, or when the moon enters Scorpio
during each month (for about two and a half days).

632
THE TRAVEL OR WIDENING HORIZONS SPREAD OF SAGITTARIUS

Sagittarius the Archer (November 23–December 21)
· optimism · fresh perspectives · long-distance travel ·
house moves · all creative ventures · expanding horizons

Purpose and background information:
For anyone born under Sagittarius, anyone asking a question
during the Star sign period, or if you need a Sagittarian quality in
your life.

Card 1: What travel, widening horizons, or location/house
moves do you want or need? **Card 2:** Who or what makes
this hard to fulfill? **Card 3:** What advantages/opportunities
will make this possible? **Card 4:** How can you overcome/
avoid the conflicting advice of others influenced by Gemini?
Card 5: The unexpected factor. **Card 6:** The key to
widening your horizons. **Card 7:** The ideal outcome. **Card 8:**
The actual outcome.

What you should use:
The full deck.

When:
During the star sign period, or when the moon enters Sagittarius
during each month (for about two and a half days).

633
THE STEADY FINANCIAL OR CAREER ADVANCEMENT OF CAPRICORN

Capricorn, the Goat (December 22–January 20)
· wise caution · achieving career ambitions through
perseverance · officialdom · loyalty · the acquisition
and preservation of money and property

Purpose and background information:
For anyone born under Capricorn, anyone asking a question during
the Star sign period, or if you need a Capricorn quality in your life.

Card 1: What additional security or advancement do
you desire/need? **Card 2:** Who or what opposes this?
Card 3: What advantages/opportunities will make this
possible? **Card 4:** The emotional and manipulative factors
of others caused by the opposition of Cancer. **Card 5:**
The unexpected factor. **Card 6:** The key to gaining your
objective. **Card 7:** The ideal outcome. **Card 8:** The actual
outcome.

What you should use:
The full deck.

When:
During the star sign period, or when the moon enters Capricorn
during each month (for about two and a half days).

634
THE INDEPENDENCE SPREAD OF AQUARIUS

Aquarius, the Water Carrier (January 21–February 18)
· independence · friendship · ingenuity ·
original perspectives · transitions · detachment
from emotional pressures · altruism

Purpose and background information:
For anyone born under Aquarius, anyone asking a question about
independence during the Star sign period, or if you need an
Aquarian quality in your life.

Card 1: How or from whom do you seek/need
independence? **Card 2:** Who or what ties your hands?
Card 3: What advantages/opportunities will make freedom
possible? **Card 4:** How to avoid/overcome the pressure to
accept what others say is best in the form of the opposition
of Leo. **Card 5:** The unexpected factor. **Card 6:** The key
to independence. **Card 7:** The ideal outcome. **Card 8:** The
actual outcome.

What you should use:
The full deck.

When:
During the Star sign period, or when the moon enters Aquarius
during each month (for about two and a half days).

635
THE FRIENDSHIP SPREAD OF AQUARIUS

Purpose and background information:

For anyone born under Aquarius, anyone asking a question about friendship during the Star sign period, or if you need an Aquarian quality in your life.

CARD 1: What concerns you most about a friendship/friendships in your life? **CARD 2:** By whom/how are you feeling stifled or pressurized? **CARD 3:** What advantages/opportunities will make this possible? **CARD 4:** Are you being dominated or excluded from a friendship or by a friend or clique by the influence of Leo? **CARD 5:** The unexpected factor. **CARD 6:** The key to good friendship. **CARD 7:** The ideal outcome. **CARD 8:** The actual outcome.

What you should use:

The full deck.

When:

During the star sign period, or when the moon enters Aquarius during each month (for about two and a half days).

636
THE PISCES SPREAD OF BEING ASKED TO CHOOSE BETWEEN TWO PEOPLE OR OPTIONS

Pisces the Fish (February 19–March 29)
• increased spiritual awareness and intuition •
imagination • spiritual gifts • fulfilling hidden dreams
• the need to choose if being pulled two ways

Purpose and background information:

For anyone born under Pisces, anyone asking a question about friendship during the Star sign period, or if you need a Piscean quality in your life.

CARD 1: What are the main and hidden pressures or choices being imposed upon you? **CARD 2:** Who or what stands in the way of free choice? **CARD 3:** What advantages/opportunities, maybe a third option, that will make a free choice possible? **CARD 4:** Can you resist the guilt trip and obligations being imposed on you through the opposition of Virgo? **CARD 5:** The unexpected factor. **CARD 6:** The key to stepping back and making up your own mind, or maybe accepting neither choice. **CARD 7:** The ideal outcome. **CARD 8:** The actual outcome.

What you should use:

The full deck.

When:

During the star sign period, or when the moon enters Pisces during each month (for about two and a half days).

637
THE ZODIAC THREE-STEPS SPREAD

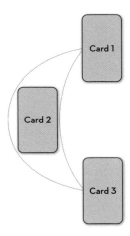

Purpose and background information:

What you should use and how:

Work with the fourteen Major cards representing the zodiac signs, shuffling them (see list on pages 338–339 in this chapter). Pick a question about what you want or need most in your life, and then see the three steps toward it. Focus on both the meaning of the card and its astrological significance. The combination will give you the answer.

CARD 1: Step 1 to initiate. **CARD 2:** Step 2 to consolidate. **CARD 3:** Step 3 to achievement.

When:

When you need forward planning.

638
GETTING IT TOGETHER

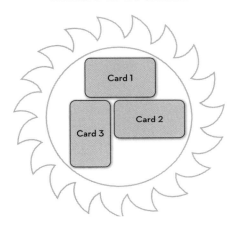

Purpose and background information:

To make a significant decision where there is no clear answer.

What you should use and how:

Use all 78 cards. The first card you deal represents the real essential you (symbolized in the Spread as the Sun zodiac sign) and the second the persona you show to the world (symbolized by the Ascendant sign, the zodiac sign that is rising into/is in the First House at your birth).

You do not need to know your actual Ascendant sign, but if you do draw your actual personal Sun sign card and Ascendant zodiac sign card (the same one as your zodiac card), that of course is extra lucky.

CARD 1: The Sun sign aspect, what you know in your heart is right, whatever others say or do. **CARD 2:** The Ascendant sign aspect, the action you need to take to maintain your position in the world. **CARD 3:** Putting them together for an integrated response.

When:

When people have totally confused you.

THE TWELVE HOUSES SPREAD

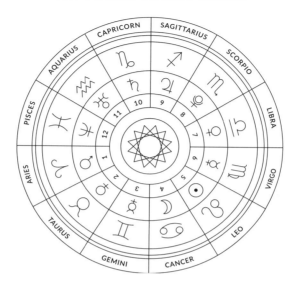

Purpose and background information:

This Spread is especially good for a major decision or life review; it helps you to draw together all the aspects of your life over any chosen period from one to five years.

Scan or trace the Spread Layout. You will use the Layout for this and the next Spread.

Each of the Houses shares the qualities of its ruling zodiac sign, though of course house and zodiac signs are not the same, and indeed the sun passes through each house during the 24-hour period.

Which cards you should use, when, and how:

Shuffle the full deck of seventy-eight cards. Pick two cards for each house, the first symbolizing the Sun sign, your real self; the second symbolizing the Ascendant card, your outer responses and actions.

Start with House 1, then travel counterclockwise until each house has its two cards. Read each house as you add the cards.

If you pick your own Sun card or the one that belongs to the house you are focusing on, that is positively significant (check back to page OO for these).

CARD 1:

The First House: Aries, March 21–April 20

• the self • individuals and core personality •
new beginnings • change and renewal

CARD 2:

The Second House: Taurus, April 21–May 21

• possessions • financial matters • material
concerns and security of all kinds

CARD 3:

The Third House: Gemini, May 22–June 21

• relationships with equals, whether brothers and
sisters, neighbors, and interaction with others • travel
and communication • learning, study, and memory

CARD 4:

The Fourth House: Cancer, June 22–July 22

• the home and private world of the individual •
the mother • older people, especially relations
and all the issues involved in aging

CARD 5:

The Fifth House: Leo, July 23–August 23
• love, emotions, and passions • emotional issues • strong feelings • the father, children, and younger relations

CARD 6:

The Sixth House: Virgo, August 24–September 23
• health, physical matters, and anything where detail is concerned • work relationships, especially those you care for professionally or as subordinates

CARD 7:

The Seventh House: Libra, September 24–October 23
• close relationships and partnerships, whether marriage or business • aspects and the actions of rivals • justice and balance

CARD 8:

The Eighth House: Scorpio, October 24–November 22
• endings that form the seed of new beginnings • inheritance, taxes, and debts • psychic and mystical matters • revenge

CARD 9:

The Ninth House: Sagittarius, November 23–December 21
• philosophy and far-reaching ideas • distant travel • far-reaching communication • new educational fields • religion and new ideas

CARD 10:

The Tenth House: Capricorn, December 22–January 20
outward public and social image • career matters • convention • tradition • officialdom

CARD 11:

The Eleventh House: Aquarius, January 21–February 18
• influence of friends and organizations • social activities • friendships • detachment • individualism • hopes, principles, and ideals

CARD 12:

The Twelfth House: Pisces, February 19–March 20
• overcoming limitations • conflicting sorrows and difficulties • intuitive insights • anything regarding choices or options

640
THE ZODIAC WHEEL OF FORTUNE SPREAD

Purpose and Background information:
A quick assessment of your future twelve months' destiny, using four cards.

What you should use, how, and when:
This time, disregard the house meanings, as this is a slower twelve-month assessment, the time the sun takes to pass through all the signs. Use *only* the fourteen Major cards chosen associated with the zodiac signs (see page 00).

Cast a round clear quartz crystal (about the size of a small coin) or pure white stone onto the zodiacal chart four times, to show in which segment the card should be placed.

Shuffle the cards for each cast, and once after each crystal cast. Consider both the zodiac meaning of the segment and the actual card meaning.

If the crystal falls more than once in a single segment, this zodiac meaning is dominant. If your Sun Sign card appears in a reading in any position, then that is very lucky. If a card appears in its own zodiac sign, this is also a good omen.

CARD 1: Your current strengths. **CARD 2:** Your current weaknesses. **CARD 3:** The area in your life you need to develop. **CARD 4:** The card of fate, where future success lies.

When:
When you need an overview of significant periods.

CHAPTER 33

ASTROLOGICAL SPREADS, PART 2: THE PLANETARY SPREADS

Lucky planetary cards

Though there are twelve zodiac signs, there are only ten ruling planets, since Mercury controls Gemini and Virgo and Venus, Taurus and Libra. Like the Sun Sign Major Arcana cards in the previous chapter, there are Major Arcana cards associated with each of the planets. If you pick a Major Arcana card linked with the planet that rules your Sun or zodiac sign, that is extremely lucky in a Spread.

Astrologically, the following planets traditionally include the luminaries the Sun and Moon. There are many different suggestions online and in books as to which Major card is associated with which planet. This system I use is the one that has worked well for me for over forty years, and so I share it with you. In common with a lot of similar systems, for consistency I have stayed with the traditional Westernized astrological associations. I have therefore included Pluto but not Chiron, because of Pluto's association with a zodiac sign.

• **Sun** the Sun • **Moon** the Moon • **Mercury** the Magician • **Venus** the Lovers/the Star (your choice) • **Mars** the Chariot/the Emperor (your choice) • **Jupite**r Justice/the Wheel of Fortune (your choice) • **Saturn** the Hierophant/the Hermit (your choice) • **Uranus** The Tower of Freedom/the World (your choice) • **Neptune** The Fool/the Inner Child (your choice) • **Pluto** Judgment (Rebirth)/the Hanged Man (your choice)

About Tarot cards and the planets

The planetary Major cards refer to the effect the world has on us, whether in personal relationships, work, or social situations, and indicate possible strategies to deal with the situation.

The planets in these Tarot spreads are not related to the actual positions of the planets in the sky but, like the Zodiac card signs in the previous chapter, reflect our psychic resonances with the different planets.

641
THE SEVEN-DAY PLANET SPREAD

| Card 1 | Card 2 | Card 3 | Card 4 | Card 5 | Card 6 | Card 7 |

Purpose and background information:
Because each of the original seven planets (prior to the discoveries of Uranus, Neptune, and Pluto), including the Sun and Moon, is associated with a day of the week, this is a perfect Spread for a mini-life review. If you get a planet Tarot card on its own day. it is especially lucky.

What you should use, how and when?
The full deck, one card chosen each day for seven days starting on Sunday. Interpret and leave cards in position until you finish the Spread on Saturday and have all seven in place. Then look for the overall message.

CARD 1: Sunday, day of the Sun. What is your greatest potential or talent/how can you manifest it? **CARD 2:** Monday, day of the Moon. What is your current/long-term dream/is it attainable? **CARD 3:** Tuesday, the day of Mars. What is your greatest challenge/obstacle to success? **CARD 4:** Wednesday, the day of Mercury. What do you need to learn or initiate? **CARD 5:** Thursday, the day of Jupiter. How can you most advance your cause/impress others/will you get your lucky break? **CARD 6:** Friday, the day of Venus. What is your future in love/a significant relationship you are thinking about? **CARD 7:** Saturday, the day of Saturn. What is your greatest source of security/stability/your greatest limitation to overcome?

642
THE SUN SPREAD FOR GOING FOR A MAJOR ACHIEVEMENT EVEN IF YOU SUSPECT YOU MAY BE OUT OF YOUR LEAGUE

Purpose and background information:
Sun:

The Sun rules Leo.

The Sun represents the essential self, identity, personality, and unique qualities.

It spends approximately a month in each sign. The Sun is associated with power, creativity, vision, health and the life force, but also arrogance.

CARD 1: Is it *the trying* that matters to you, to let everyone know you are ready for a higher league? **CARD 2:** What unique qualities do you have that make you stand out? **CARD 3:** Will you succeed this time? **CARD 4:** If not, will you know how to succeed next time you try?

What you should use:
The twenty-two Major cards.

When:
A Sunday.

643
THE MOON SPREAD, WHEN YOUR LIFE FEELS OUT OF BALANCE AND NO ONE UNDERSTANDS

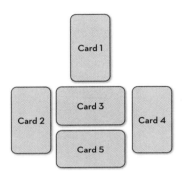

Purpose and background information:
Moon:

The Moon rules Cancer

The Moon represents the emotional and unconscious aspects of the personality.

The Moon spends only two and a half days in each sign per month. The Moon is associated with the home, emotional security, relationships with family and mothering, and, less positively, our fears and illusions.

CARD 1: Who/what external factors have thrown your life out of balance? **ALTERNATIVE CARD 1:** Are you feeling out of balance inside because you cannot let go of the past/ have fears for the future? **CARD 2:** Should you withdraw from life for a while until you feel better, or keep going and hope you get over it? **CARD 3:** What if any action can/should you take to make yourself feel better? **CARD 4:** Should you seek someone who does understand your feelings, or keep your angst to yourself? **CARD 5:** Do you need a life/relationship change, so you live/work/socialize with people who are in tune with you?

What you should use:
The twenty-two major Tarot cards and the sixteen Court cards.

When:
A Monday.

644
A MERCURY SPREAD WHEN YOU ARE NOT PREPARED FOR AN IMMINENT EXAMINATION, TEST, PRESENTATION, OR INTERVIEW

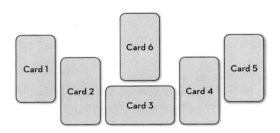

Purpose and background information:
Mercury:

Mercury rules Gemini and Virgo

Mercury represents the way our basic character is communicated or expressed in the everyday world. Mercury takes about 88 days to complete its orbit of the Sun and so is a swift-moving planet. Mercury is associated with the mind, science, technological abilities—especially computers, logic, communication, and with healing—but also with sharp practice, especially relating to money matters.

CARD 1: If you pulled out all stops now, is it possible to adequately prepare yourself? **CARD 2:** What stands in the way of this last-minute effort? **CARD 3:** What strategies can you use to overcome obstacles caused by lack of time? **CARD 4:** Will this single-minded effort bring desired results? **CARD 5:** Should you cancel/postpone to allow more time? **CARD 6:** Will luck be on your side?

What you should use:
The forty Minor cards, Aces to Tens, and the sixteen Court cards.

When:
A Wednesday, or any morning.

645
A MERCURY RETROGRADE
SPREAD TO AVOID PITFALLS

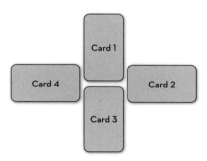

Purpose and background information:
Occurring about three times a year and lasting from around eighteen to twenty-four days when Mercury appears to move backward through the zodiac, causing delays and glitches especially in travel, communication, technology, and decision-making.

CARD 1: Are there major travel plans/uncertainties during this period where delays would be serious? **CARD 2:** What strategies can/should be inbuilt to avoid glitches? **CARD 3:** Will any retrograde delays/postponements/delayed or lost communication prove advantageous in the longer term? **CARD 4:** Do you make your own luck and destiny, or do you just need to double-check details more during this period?

What you should use:
The twenty-two Major cards.

When:
When Mercury retrograde is approaching or in retrograde.

646
A VENUS IN HER MORNING STAR
ASPECT SPREAD FOR MOVING
ON FROM A BROKEN HEART

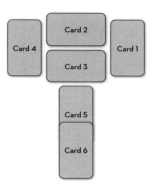

Purpose and background information:
Venus:

Venus rules Taurus and Libra

Venus represents the way an individual interacts with significant others, such as lovers, parents, family members, business partners, and friends. Venus is sometimes known as the Morning or Evening Star, because she shines with brilliant silvery hue. Venus is associated with love, beauty, the arts, all relationships, friendship, and possessions, but also with excesses of love and romance. Venus takes 225 days to travel around the Sun.

CARD 1: Have you been able to/should you cut all contact with your former love, in order to heal? **CARD 2:** Do you still believe there is hope for the relationship to be mended? **CARD 3:** Would it be in your best interest to revive the love, or should you move on? **CARD 4:** What positive steps can you take to move on to new love and life? **CARD 5:** Do you need a period of independence to clearly see your future with or without your former love? **CARD 6:** Will you be happy again?

What you should use:
The full deck.

When:
You are stuck in limbo.

647

A VENUS IN HER EVENING STAR ASPECT FOR LEAVING AN ABUSIVE OR UNKIND LOVER

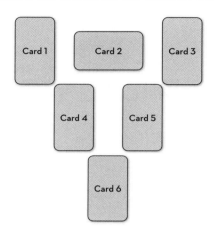

Purpose and background information:

When you know a relationship is destructive but cannot break and stay away.

CARD 1: What are the practical/financial problems of moving on and can/how can you resolve these? **CARD 2:** What makes you most afraid about leaving/keeps drawing you back? Is this a valid fear? **CARD 3:** What legal/official support do you have/can you get, to help you move away/start a new life? **CARD 4:** What strategies can you put in place to ease your leaving and stop you from going back? **CARD 5:** Will you succeed in leaving/making a new good life? **CARD 6:** Can/will you resist the temptation to stay/return if your lover promises yet again to change/tells you it's all your fault?

What you should use:

The forty Minor cards and the sixteen Court cards.

When:

The start of a new month.

648

A URANUS SPREAD TO PERSUADE A CONSERVATIVE BUSINESS OR MARITAL PARTNER THAT CHANGE IS LONG OVERDUE

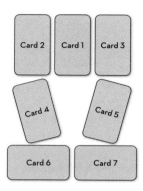

Purpose and background information:
Uranus:

Uranus rules Aquarius

Uranus represents liberation from the past and the striving of individuals and organizations toward positive collective change. It takes Uranus eighty-four years to complete its trip around the zodiac. Uranus is associated with sudden or necessary changes, originality, inventiveness and inventions, especially concerning telecommunications; also linked with sexuality and with impulsiveness.

CARD 1: In what area of your life or work do you most need change? **CARD 2:** In return, where are you prepared to accept the status quo even if you do not agree? **CARD 3:** Can you use persuasion/facts and figures, or are you limited to insisting? **CARD 4:** If your partner will not change, can you continue as things are? **CARD 5:** Could you subtly introduce the changes over time? **CARD 6:** Will s/he change eventually, even if you do nothing? **CARD 7:** Do you have a time limit for the changes to occur? If not, what then?

What you should use:

The twenty-two Major cards.

When:

New Year's Day or a full moon.

649
A SATURN SPREAD FOR SLOWING THE OUTFLOW OF MONEY TO ENABLE SAVINGS TO BUILD UP

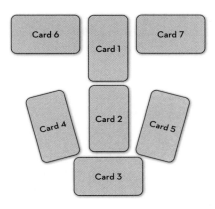

Purpose and background information:
Saturn:

Saturn rules Capricorn and is co-ruler of Aquarius

Saturn represents the expression of the individual's personality and interactions within the restrictions and boundaries imposed by society and the constraints of space and time. It takes Saturn twenty-eight to thirty years to complete its orbit of the zodiac.

Saturn is associated with limitation, slow progress and difficulties, and the reality factor, but turns challenge into opportunity through effort and perseverance, offers strength in overcoming debt, dealing with officialdom, and bringing security and stability, especially financial, through caution.

CARD 1: Are there areas of your life where expenditure can be cut without sacrificing the quality of life? **CARD 2:** What sacrifices can be made in order to stop the drain of money, painful but necessary? **CARD 3:** Are there assets that can be realized/debts called in/expensive items replaced with cheaper but serviceable ones? **CARD 4:** Are there ways of increasing the inflow of money each month? **CARD 5:** What is a realistic target for saving for a special purpose or to increase security in the long term? **CARD 6:** Can you turn

your finances around within twelve months? **CARD 7:** Are your long-term finances promising if you can get through the short term?

What you should use:
The forty Minor cards Aces to Tens.

When:
A Saturday, or during a waning moon.

650
A PLANET EARTH SPREAD IF YOU ARE FIGHTING FRACKING OR OTHER MAJOR EXPLORATION IN YOUR AREA THAT WILL DAMAGE THE ENVIRONMENT

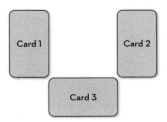

Purpose and background information:
When you can no longer stand by and watch the destruction of your environment.

What to use, and how:
Shuffle the ten Major planet cards listed at the beginning of the chapter and deal three cards, to see three steps toward stopping the intrusion. **CARD 1:** What initial approach should you use, for example the head-on approach of Mars? **CARD 2:** If that doesn't work, what is your next step? **CARD 3:** The ultimate strength you have.

When:
Before a major planning meeting.

651
A MARS SPREAD TO OVERCOME
A BULLY IN THE WORKPLACE

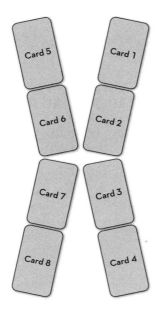

Purpose and background information:
Mars:

Mars rules Aries and is the co-ruler of Scorpio

Mars represents initiative, independent action, and maintaining a sense of separation from other people, at home or work in a small group situation.

It takes nearly two years for Mars to complete its orbit through the Zodiac.

The planet is associated with aggression, speed in action, ambition, competitiveness, sexual qualities, and passion, as well as warlike qualities. To this quality of courage is added a nobility of spirit when the anger and warlike impulses are directed against injustice and inertia.

CARD 1: Are you the sole victim/the main victim of the bullying, or are other workers subject to the intimidation? **CARD 2:** Does the bully use rank/sarcasm/isolating you from others? **CARD 3:** Should you ignore this or confront? What would be the likely consequences of either? **CARD 4:** Is there an effective Human Resources department/trade union/senior manager who will back you, or is this a non-starter? **CARD 5:** Should you get another job as soon as possible? **CARD 6:** Should you take stress leave in the meantime while you sort out your future? **CARD 7:** Is it worth leaving, even without another job, for your own health and well-being? **CARD 8:** Do you want to/is it worth fighting for compensation once you leave, or should you just let it go?

What you should use:

The full deck.

When:

When you dread going to work.

652
A JUPITER SPREAD FOR STICKING WITH
A SEEMINGLY ENDLESS PROGRESSION TO
QUALIFY IN A DESIRED PROFESSION

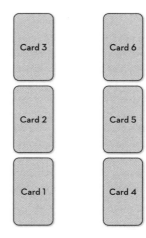

Purpose and background information:
Jupiter:

Jupiter rules Sagittarius and is co-ruler of Pisces

Jupiter represents expression of the personality in the context of wider society and culture. Jupiter takes about twelve years to circle the Zodiac.

Jupiter is known as the Joy-bringer and is associated with all forms of good fortune and prosperity. The planet is also associated with compassion, ideals and altruism, higher values, wisdom and learning for a long-term career, expansiveness and increase, long-distance travel and house moves, but also with extravagance and being autocratic.

CARD 1: Are you seeing results/incentives as you progress, or does it seem hard work with no reward in sight? **CARD 2:** What are the advantages of persisting? **CARD 3:** What are the drawbacks of persisting? **CARD 4:** If you give up now, will what you have learned qualify/give you enough experience to build a different career? **CARD 5:** Should you keep going? **CARD 6:** Should you step back for a while, or make the life changes you want regardless?

What you should use:
The full deck.

When:
At a transition point in your studies or training.

653
A NEPTUNE SPREAD IF YOU WANT TO LEARN HEALING OR AN ESOTERIC SUBJECT, BUT YOUR FRIENDS AND FAMILY SAY YOU HAVE LOST THE PLOT

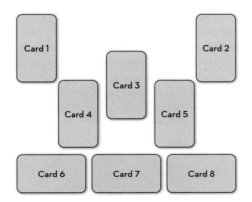

Purpose and background information:
Neptune:

Neptune rules Pisces

Neptune represents the search of the soul to find spiritual and mystical enlightenment. It takes Neptune 165 years to complete its cycle, with about fourteen years in each sign. Neptune is associated with all emotions, sensitivity, intuition, hidden potential, and with the unknown and mysterious, but also with indecisiveness.

CARD 1: Is this spiritual desire connected with a recent life-changing experience/a growing awareness that there is much more to life? **CARD 2:** Do you sometimes feel like you already have spiritual knowledge, explicable only by a past-life connection? **CARD 3:** Is this the beginning of a personal spiritual journey? Do you want it to become a new career/life path? **CARD 4:** Have you always felt different from family and friends? Is this a new dividing of the ways? **CARD 5:** Can you agree to differ and enjoy what you do still have in common? **CARD 6:** Will you meet new like-minded friends and separate your spiritual and family worlds? **CARD 7:** Will you find it difficult to carry on spiritually if your family/friends make it hard for you? **CARD 8:** Can you bring both parts of your life together/influence your family and friends to become more spiritual?

What you should use:
The full deck.

When:
When you feel that you are being asked to choose between worlds.

A GETTING-IT-ALL-TOGETHER INNER PLANET SPREAD

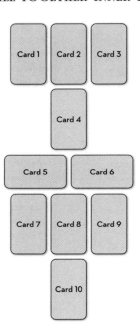

Purpose and background information:

When you feel at the mercy of fate rather than making the world as you most want it.

CARD 1: How can you best express your inner Sun unique qualities to get the recognition you deserve? **CARD 2:** How can you trust your Moon intuitive feelings as to the truth, rather than allowing others to emotionally pressure you? **CARD 3:** How can you utilize your inner Mercury logic to state clearly what you want—and get it? **CARD 4:** How can you unhesitatingly follow your inner Venus to attain a fulfilling, lasting emotional/love life? **CARD 5:** How can you best use your inner Fire of Mars to overcome obstacles and opposition? **CARD 6:** How can you show in the best light your natural inner Jupiter expertise to reveal your authority and

leadership qualities in the outer world? **CARD 7:** How can you build on the stability of your inner Saturn to provide your dreams with a solid basis in the world? **CARD 8:** How can you best adopt the right inner changes of Uranus to get the outer life changes you desire? **CARD 9:** How can you discover the secret magickal ingredient/unexpected quality of your inner Neptune to blend your life together? **CARD 10:** How can you transform all your inner planetary powers through your Pluto persona to likewise transform your life?

What you should use:

The full deck.

When:

When you have time to fully contemplate the cards.

655
A PLUTO SPREAD WHEN YOU HAVE A HIGH-POWERED JOB BUT ARE DISILLUSIONED BY THE ETHICS OF YOUR COMPANY.

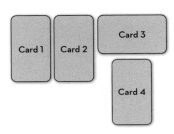

Purpose and background information:

Pluto:

Pluto rules Scorpio

Pluto represents the search for ultimate truth and for moving toward perfection on all levels of existence through refinement of what is imperfect and the desire for mastery over self and the world. Pluto takes 248 years to go around the Sun and spends, according to its irregular orbit, between twelve and twenty years in each sign.

The planet is associated with endings, removing what is redundant to herald a new beginning; with hidden and unconscious powers, especially psychic abilities; with the ability to start again even in difficult circumstances; and with financial astuteness and business acumen but occasionally with a seedy lifestyle.

CARD 1: Has dissatisfaction been growing/is it due to a major unethical decision you couldn't stop? **CARD 2:** How much influence can you exert over company policy if you work to rise higher? **CARD 3:** Should you be prepared to take a pay cut to work for a more ethical company? **CARD 4:** Should you change your career path entirely to focus on fulfillment rather than success?

What you should use:

The twenty-two Major cards.

When:

A Thursday, day of ethics.

656
A FULL 24-HOUR SUN SPREAD

Purpose and background information:

Maximizing your opportunities and achievements for an entire day or a whole week.

What you should use, how, and when:

From the full deck, pick two cards at each of the four solar transitions of the day. If the Sun card appears, that is extra lucky. This will enable you to keep track of your day to assess how you handle the opportunities and challenges. If you wish, you could do this for a whole seven days. You may find some startling insights telling you that what appears blind fate, you actually initiated or didn't resist.

CARDS 1 AND 2: Dawn, or when you wake. **CARD 1:** What is your greatest opportunity today? **CARD 2:** What is your greatest challenge for the day ahead?

CARDS 3 AND 4: Noon, or when you stop for lunch. **CARD 3:** What is your goal for the rest of the day that you haven't yet achieved? **CARD 4:** What or who stands in the way? How can you overcome this?

CARDS 5 AND 6: Sunset, or when you reach home. **CARD 5:** What is worthwhile that you have achieved today? **CARD 6:** What do you want/need from the rest of the day?

CARDS 7 AND 8: Midnight, or when you go to bed: **CARD 7:** What didn't work out that you need to fix or continue tomorrow? **CARD 8:** What do you need to abandon, including worries, so you can enjoy peaceful sleep?

CHAPTER 34

MOON SPREADS

Lucky Cards for Moon Spreads

Major Cards: The High Priestess, the Empress, the Moon, the Star, the World.

Minor Cards: Any Minor card showing water or the moon on its picture.

Court Cards: The Page/Princess and Queen of Cups.

About Moon Spreads

This chapter is divided into spreads for the Waxing (increasing) Moon, the Crescent Moon, the Full Moon, the Waning (decreasing) Moon, and the Dark of the Moon/New Moon when the moon is not visible in the sky.

Timings

When choosing the right Moon Spread, you can generally observe what is going on in the sky with the moon, and time your moon Spreads accordingly. However, if you want to pinpoint a moon phase, buy a diary for your region that gives, for each day, the current phase and which zodiac sign the moon is passing through. There are also numerous online sites and apps for your smartphone. One of the best is https://www.timeanddate.com/

Waxing Moon Spreads

From Day 3 or 4 in the monthly moon cycle, when you see the crescent in the sky until the night before the full moon. For questions about new beginnings in any area (crescent) and attracting or increasing anything from love to prosperity during the waxing phase.

657
A CRESCENT MOON SPREAD IF YOU ARE STARTING A NEW PHASE OF YOUR LIFE

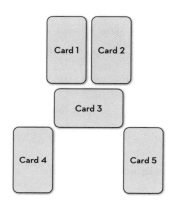

Purpose and background information:
For a major location, career or study move or new beginning after loss or betrayal in love.

CARD 1: What do you hope for most from this new beginning, not just outwardly? **CARD 2:** What are the outer and inner disadvantages/worries about this new phase? **CARD 3:** Are you fully prepared for this new phase? What have you overlooked? **CARD 4:** Is there anything/anyone you would like/need to take with you/leave behind? **CARD 5:** Will your new beginning bring happiness soon, or take months?

What you should use:
The forty Minor cards, Aces to Tens.

When:
The crescent moon, or as close as possible afterward.

658
A CRESCENT MOON SPREAD FOR A NEW SOURCE OF MONEY IN YOUR LIFE WITHIN A MONTH

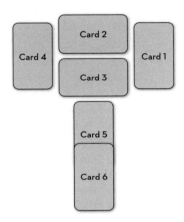

Purpose and background information:

When you have a shortfall or need to find extra money fast.

CARD 1: Could any of your existing sources of money offer short-term increase through extra hours/input? **CARD 2:** Are there any sources/assets from which you could borrow extra money/sell to make up the shortfall? **CARD 3:** Are/how are negotiations possible to take the immediate pressure off you? **CARD 4:** Will this shortfall continue unless you find a more permanent/lucrative source of income/input? **CARD 5:** Will there be unexpected help? **CARD 6:** Will you get the money by the time of the next crescent moon?

What you should use:

The forty Minor cards and the sixteen Court cards.

When:

As close to the crescent moon as possible.

659
A WAXING MOON SPREAD FOR DEVELOPING A NEW ROMANCE INTO SOMETHING MORE

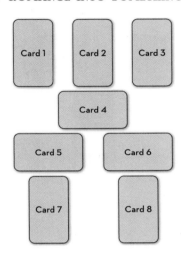

Purpose and background information:

When you meet or date someone you really like, but nothing's happening.

CARD 1: Was/is there a definite spark between you? **CARD 2:** Is there a genuine reason for the person not contacting you/if you are patient it will happen? **CARD 3:** Should you make the first move to say how much you enjoyed meeting/would love to get together again? **CARD 4:** What keeps you from getting in touch? **CARD 5:** What is the worst thing that could happen if s/he said no or ignored you? **CARD 6:** What is the best outcome that would encourage you to take a risk? **CARD 7:** Will you meet again? **CARD 8:** Is this a short-term romance/could it be forever?

What you should use:

The forty Major cards, Aces to Tens, and the sixteen Court cards.

When:

The waxing or increasing moon.

660
A WAXING MOON SPREAD FOR MAKING A GOOD IMPRESSION IN A NEW JOB/PLACE OF STUDY

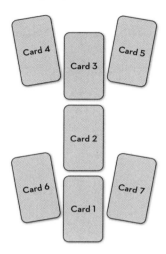

Purpose and background information:

If there are lots of mixed message signals in the new workplace.

Card 1: Should you take it slowly/keep quiet while you work out the dynamics of the workplace? **Card 2:** Is there any extra work/preparation you can do at home to master unfamiliar systems/avoid mistakes? **Card 3:** Is there a mentor/sympathetic person you can ask if you get stuck? **Card 4:** If you sense hostility, is this just general wariness/loyalty to your predecessor, or is it a generally unfriendly place, not just toward you? **Card 5:** Should you be patient/gradually make yourself useful/avoid overshadowing those with big egos? **Card 6:** Will you settle/feel part of the team by the end of the month? **Card 7:** Will it take more time and perseverance?

What you should use:

The twenty-two Major cards and the sixteen Court cards.

When:

At the waxing moon.

661
A WAXING MOON SPREAD FOR GETTING YOUR HEALTH UP AND RUNNING AFTER AN ILLNESS OR VIRUS

Purpose and background information:

When you want to get back into life but just do not have the energy.

Card 1: Should you be patient and let your body recover to catch up with your desire to get back into life? **Card 2:** Are you trying to do too much too quickly and not nurturing yourself? **Card 3:** Are there extra supplements/medical advice/alternative therapies to get your body back to fitness? **Card 4:** Are there unresolved/unacknowledged worries about your long-term health that need talking through/resolving/accepting? **Card 5:** Will you recover your old strength/be well in a different way?

What you should use:

The forty Minor cards, Aces to Tens, and the sixteen Court cards.

When:

At the waxing moon.

Full-Moon Spreads

The full moon is strictly the very second the moon is full, but also the twenty-four hours on either side of the full-moon moment. The day of the full moon represents full power, but it also represents instability and can be used for spreads for urgent needs, power, success, changing luck, fertility, and justice.

662
A FULL MOON SPREAD FOR CONSUMMATING LOVE

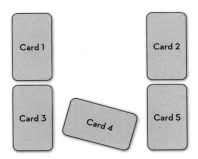

Purpose and background information:
When you have been waiting because you know that this will be a major emotional as well as physical step.

CARD 1: Should you wait for this to happen spontaneously at the right place and time? **CARD 2:** Do you want it to happen on a special occasion/a romantic vacation/the honeymoon, so it is right for you and your partner? **CARD 3:** If you are still hesitating, is this a natural fear, or is there something in the relationship that makes you hold back until you are sure your partner feels the same way as you? **CARD 4:** If you are not ready, should you wait? **CARD 5:** Will lovemaking be the next stage to a lasting happiness?

What you should use:
The twenty-two Major cards.

When:
Around the full moon.

663
A FULL-MOON SPREAD FOR MARRIAGE OR MAKING A PERMANENT COMMITMENT IN LOVE

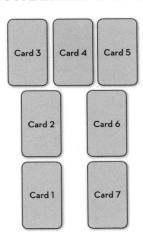

Purpose and background information:
When you feel that the relationship needs to go forward.

CARD 1: Are you both at the same stage of wanting commitment, or is one of you more hesitant than the other? **CARD 2:** Is anything slowing this commitment practical/financial/a deeper relationship issue? **CARD 3:** Should you initiate this if you feel ready? **CARD 4:** Should you set a time scale for the future of your relationship? **CARD 5:** Is it better to wait/are you prepared to wait if necessary? **CARD 6:** If there is no immediate prospect of commitment, are you willing to accept the status quo, or will you give an ultimatum? **CARD 7:** Will commitment happen and bring lasting happiness?

What you should use:
The full deck.

When:
You become tired of the uncertainty.

664
A FULL-MOON SPREAD FOR A MAKE-OR-BREAK STEP OR DECISION

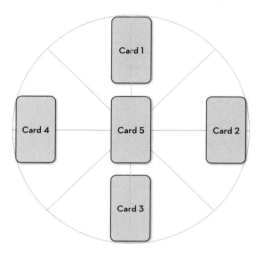

Purpose and background information:
When you have been putting off a decision or action because you know what you do will have major consequences.

CARD 1: What has held you back from deciding/acting/still holds you back? Hurting others/fear of being alone/having to leave behind your comfort zone? **CARD 2:** Are the sacrifices you will have to make worthwhile, to give you freedom from doubt? **CARD 3:** Will it be "make"? **CARD 4:** Will it be "break"? **CARD 5:** Would you prefer/would it be better to live with indecision rather than the stark choice?

What you should use:
The full deck.

When:
A full moon.

665
A FULL-MOON SPREAD IF YOU FEEL SPOOKED BY A PSYCHOLOGICAL OR PSYCHIC ATTACK

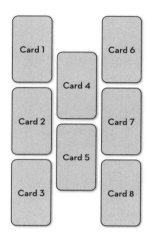

Purpose and background information:
When you can feel negativity coming toward you.

CARD 1: Do you know/suspect the source of the attack, and the reason? **CARD 2:** Does this occur when you are together, or when you are alone—especially at night? **CARD 3:** Can you block this mind manipulation/actual emotional draining by using psychological/psychic blocking techniques/mantras? **CARD 4:** Would it be better to use psychic/spiritual banishing techniques/calling on angels/powers of light/returning negativity to source? **CARD 5:** Should you, where possible, avoid the person/keep necessary communication to a minimum, never using their name or looking into their eyes? **CARD 6:** Should you ask a priest/medium/spiritual counselor to rid you of this influence? **CARD 7:** Should you confront the person, if they are being openly negative as well? **CARD 8:** Will it stop when the attacker realizes it's not working anymore?

What you should use:
The full deck.

When:
At a full moon.

A FULL-MOON SPREAD FOR CONCEIVING A BABY IF THE FUN AND PASSION HAS GONE OUT OF YOUR RELATIONSHIP

Purpose and background information:
When ovulation charts and fertility times have replaced spontaneous lovemaking.

CARD 1: Should you take a break from trying for a baby and let it happen naturally at the right time? **CARD 2:** Should you focus on having fun and emotional and physical intimacy in general and take the emphasis off lovemaking unless you both want to? **CARD 3:** Is conceiving a baby so important to both of you right now that you are prepared to accept the loss of spontaneity? **CARD 4:** Is one of you more focused on conceiving soon? If so, how can you reconcile this difference of opinion? **CARD 5:** Do you have a good chance of conceiving in the next few months?

What you should use:
The twenty-two Major cards.

When:
At a full moon.

A FULL-MOON SPREAD FOR GOING AHEAD WITH A COURT CASE OR AN UNFAIR DISMISSAL OR COMPENSATION TRIBUNAL

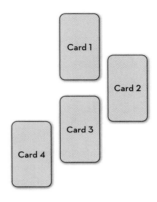

Purpose and background information:
When you have been advised to go quietly and not make a fuss, but the injustice bothers you.

CARD 1: Is this about the principles and corruption involved, just as much as the financial claims? **CARD 2:** If you go ahead, will you face opposition/dishonesty and maybe even intimidation? **CARD 3:** If you do not go ahead, will you always regret that you didn't fight for what was right? **CARD 4:** Will you win if you go ahead with the court case?

What you should use:
The twenty-two Major cards.

When:
At a full moon.

668
A FULL-MOON SPREAD IF YOU ARE DUE TO HAVE SURGERY OR A MAJOR MEDICAL INTERVENTION

Purpose and background information:

If you are feeling very uncertain about the outcome, though you have been assured by your doctors it is safe, but of course there are risks.

CARD 1: Do you have a lot of questions you need answering realistically before you will feel relaxed? And who can/will answer them? **CARD 2:** Will your quality of life be sufficiently enhanced by the procedure going ahead in spite of your worries? **CARD 3:** What are the consequences of delaying/ not going ahead, and are these worse than the possible drawbacks of going ahead? **CARD 4:** Will the procedure go well?

What you should use:

The forty Minor cards, Aces to Tens.

When:

At a full moon.

Waning-Moon Spreads

From a day or two after the full moon, depending on how powerfully a full moon is felt, till the waning-moon crescent disappears from the sky.

Waning-moon spreads are good for the need to banish what is no longer wanted or is destructive, from pain to negative people and situations.

669
A WANING-MOON SPREAD IF YOU ARE TROUBLED BY A CHRONIC ILLNESS OR PERSISTENT PAIN

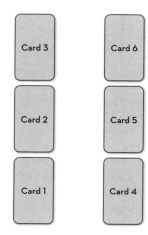

Purpose and background information:

When you have tried everything, and nothing works.

CARD 1: Should you blitz the Internet to find the latest research and centers of excellence and, if necessary, fundraise/sell assets to take yourself there? **CARD 2:** In the meantime, should you refuse to be fobbed off/made to feel a nuisance and insist on proper pain relief/the most effective treatment to alleviate symptoms, even if there is yet no cure? **CARD 3:** Are there any reputable trials you could apply for/ push for a place on? **CARD 4:** Have you explored/should you explore further alternative therapies/learn self-healing/ meditation strategies to relieve the worst symptoms? **CARD 5:** Are there any areas of your life where there is additional stress where you can ask for resources/help? **CARD 6:** Will things get better?

What you should use:

The full deck.

When:

At a waning moon.

670

A WANING-MOON SPREAD WHEN YOU CANNOT LET GO OF BETRAYAL AND IT PREVENTS YOU FROM LOVING AGAIN

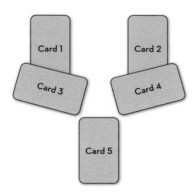

Purpose and background information:

When you are in a new relationship but are aware that you are anticipating something going wrong.

CARD 1: Should you give yourself time to get over the anger/injustice before you go fully into another deep relationship?
CARD 2: Should you talk/talk more to a counselor/a trusted friend so you can express negativity toward your ex that you have kept inside because you unfairly accepted blame?
CARD 3: Has your new partner done or said anything to make you doubt/are you constantly testing him/her out of fear?
CARD 4: Is this new relationship a step on the road for you to learn to trust again? **CARD 5:** Will it bring lasting happiness to you?

What you should use:

The twenty-two Major cards and the sixteen Court cards.

When:

At a waning moon.

671

A WANING-MOON SPREAD IF YOU HAVE FALLEN OUT OF LOVE WITH YOUR PARTNER

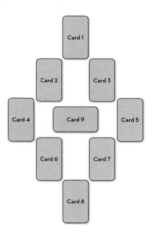

Purpose and background information:

When your partner is a lovely person, but you just do not want to be with them anymore.

CARD 1: Have you gradually fallen out of love over time, or was there a major setback that started the rift? **CARD 2:** Does your partner still want to be with you, or has it just become a habit? **CARD 3:** Do you want/is there any hope of reviving the love and passion, or is it too late? **CARD 4:** Is there anyone else you are interested in, or do you just want to be independent? **CARD 5:** What would be the most negative consequences of asking for/making a split with your partner? Is there any gentle way? **CARD 6:** Who would turn against you/blame you/cause trouble? Could you deal with this? **CARD 7:** What are the positive aspects of the split for you/your partner? **CARD 8:** Would it be best if you moved out suddenly, or stayed away more and more, or created a separate life at first within the relationship? **CARD 9:** Will leaving be worth it in the end, in terms of your future happiness?

What you should use:

The full deck.

When:

At a waning moon.

672
A WANING-MOON SPREAD TO REMOVE MAJOR OBSTACLES TO YOUR SUCCESS AND HAPPINESS

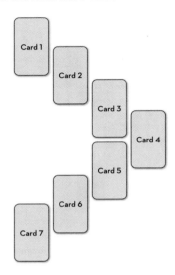

Purpose and background information:
When you find your future constantly blocked by a series of obstacles.

CARD 1: Do you believe you are unlucky, or that you sometimes create obstacles yourself through reacting too slowly/fear/half and half? **CARD 2:** What is the main current obstacle to what you want/need? **CARD 3:** How much power/opportunity do you have to overcome this? **CARD 4:** How much are you dependent right now on circumstances changing? Can you hasten this? **CARD 5:** Who will help you overcome the obstacle/s? **CARD 6:** What unexpected luck/change in luck can you expect in the next three to six months? **CARD 7:** This time, will you overcome the obstacle/s and succeed/find happiness?

What you should use:
The full deck.

When:
At a waning moon.

673
A WANING-MOON SPREAD WHEN NO MATTER HOW HARD YOU TRY, YOU CANNOT LOSE WEIGHT PERMANENTLY

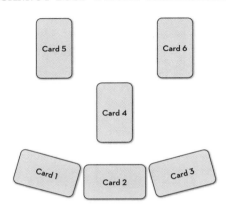

Purpose and background information:
When yet another diet has failed.

CARD 1: Do you actually need to lose weight, or just get fitter and more toned? **CARD 2:** Do you have major guilt issues over food, maybe after years of dieting? **CARD 3:** Are these issues just to do with food, or do you have other relationship/image issues/childhood hang-ups that make food a bigger issue than it deserves to be? **CARD 4:** Should you forget dieting if it is making you feel on trial/a failure, focusing instead on eating healthily and for pleasure? **CARD 5:** Do you need support, a fitness trainer/counselor, or a good slimming club that works on building confidence and self-esteem, not just losing weight? **CARD 6:** Will you succeed this time and make a good lasting relationship between yourself and food?

What you should use:
The full deck.

When:
At a waning moon.

The Dark-of-the-Moon or New-Moon Spreads

The intervening two and a half to three days after the waning moon are called the dark of the moon, when the moon is so close to the sun that it is invisible.

New-moon spreads are good for discovering the right detoxing programs, for sexuality, transformation, and reducing the hold of addictions and compulsions, and for secrets.

674
A NEW-MOON SPREAD IF YOU ARE OVERSTRESSED AND NEED TO DETOX

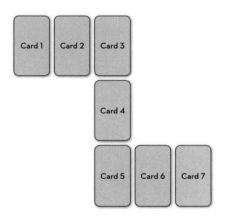

Purpose and background information:

When you are not certain how to de-stress yourself but know you need something.

CARD 1: Should you stay home for a while and see no one, letting all the pressures of life drain away as you take a total technological break? **CARD 2:** Do you need to physically detox by fasting for a short time and then introducing a diet of only health supplements, water, and raw or plain cooked fruit and vegetables? **CARD 3:** Would you do better with an organized program of detoxing at a health spa/healing sanctuary? **CARD 4:** Would you benefit from a sanctuary with basic accommodations/a beautiful environment? **CARD 5:**

Would you be better splashing out, where you can have lots of beauty/therapeutic treatments? **CARD 6:** Will you go back to the world with a different life perspective, rather than leaping back into the 24/7 dash? **CARD 7:** Will your spiritual detox make you think about adopting a less stressful lifestyle, if not now then in the future?

What you should use:

The full deck.

When:

At a dark of the moon/new moon.

675
A NEW-MOON SPREAD IF YOU OR YOUR PARTNER IS HAVING SEXUAL PROBLEMS

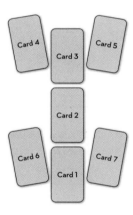

Purpose and background information:

When a formerly passionate love life comes to a halt.

CARD 1: Can you think of any recent physical illness/exhaustion that would benefit from a general medical checkup that might solve the problem? **CARD 2:** If there has been stress in work life/family troubles that has made physical contact less welcome, should this be resolved first? **CARD 3:** If life becomes routine/filled with money and practical considerations/children, can you spend time alone just to get back in tune emotionally with each other/have fun? **CARD 4:** Is there a difference in your sexual desires that maybe you can compromise/show affection and caring, not just in the bedroom? **CARD 5:** Should you talk to a sexual counselor/relationship counselor to resolve any hidden worries? **CARD 6:** If you relax and get on with life, will the problem resolve naturally? **CARD 7:** Is this just a temporary blip in an otherwise happy life together?

What you should use:
The full deck.

When:
At a dark of the moon/new moon.

676
A NEW-MOON SPREAD IF YOU ARE TAKING TOO MANY PAINKILLERS OR PRESCRIPTION DRUGS AND IT IS AFFECTING YOUR LIFE

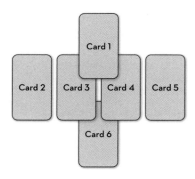

Purpose and background information:
If you find it hard to do without what at one time was essential medication.

CARD 1: Is your physician/alternative practitioner helpful in weaning you off/changing medication, or does s/he just sign another prescription? Should you question your medication? **CARD 2:** Are there alternative treatments, both conventional and spiritual/natural therapies and remedies that can help you reduce your dependency? **CARD 3:** Is there stress/worry in your life that needs resolving in order to feel in control of your life again? **CARD 4:** Are you/should you be gradually reducing, with advice, if a prescribed remedy, the medication step by step rather than attempting drastic measures?

CARD 5: Are you as physically healthy/spiritually in harmony as possible/following good nutrition so your body can take over your welfare? **CARD 6:** Will you overcome this issue and feel good again?

What you should use:
The forty Minor cards, Aces to Tens.

When:
At a dark of the moon/new moon.

677
IF YOU WANT TO COMPLETELY TRANSFORM YOUR IMAGE

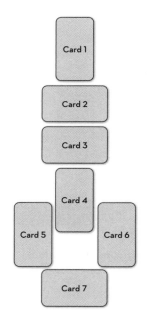

Purpose and background information:
When you realize you are totally stuck in a rut and want radical change.

CARD 1: Do you want/need an outward change/new look/new clothes, or is this a deeper change you are seeking? **CARD 2:** Do you want a fast change, or a step by step transformation? Which would work best? **CARD 3:** Do you need advice/style and hair expertise/a new fitness/ diet regime, or do you want to make changes regardless of trends? **CARD 4:** Does this image change coincide with the end of a relationship/career setback, or a personal inner change that will be reflected in outer expression? **CARD 5:** What/who do you want to keep and what throw out? Are these sound choices, or should you reassess? **CARD 6:** What new factors do you want/need in your life as a result of the image change: new love/a better social life/recognition in your career/freedom from redundant emotional patterns? **CARD 7:** Will the new image bring happiness as well as success?

What you should use:
The full deck.

When:
At a dark of the moon/new moon.

678
IF YOU HAVE TO KEEP YOUR LOVE SECRET

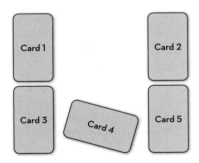

Purpose and background information:
When you aren't free to show the love you feel without negative consequences.

CARD 1: Whether your love is forbidden within your family community/religion or not allowed in your workplace, are you prepared to take risks to be together? **CARD 2:** Are you prepared to move/move away to be together? **CARD 3:** Would you prefer to carry on with your secret love in the hope that things change? **CARD 4:** Is there anyone you can trust with your secret who will help you/keep you safe?

CARD 5: Will you be together one day?

What you should use:
The twenty-two Major cards and the sixteen Court cards.

When:
At a dark of the moon/new moon.

Moon Void-of-Course Spreads
The void of course occurs as the moon leaves one astrological sign and travels to another. The moon spends about two and a half days each month in each zodiac sign. The void of course can last from a few minutes to almost a day.

This is a time when meetings or projects tend to get stuck and travel plans can go haywire. It is a good time to cast a Spread asking about possible delays in the area of the zodiac that the moon is leaving (see Chapter 32). But you can, regardless of the zodiac sign it is leaving or entering, use that interim period for spreads about any anticipated delays or potential setbacks to plans, which can be useful if you have difficult or unreliable people in your life.

679
A VOID-OF-COURSE SPREAD TO SEE IF AN UNRELIABLE FRIEND OR POTENTIAL LOVE MATCH WILL LET YOU DOWN OVER AN IMPORTANT EVENT

Purpose and background information:

When you need the support or presence of a particular friend but worry about whether they'll turn up or offer the help you need.

CARD 1: Is their unreliability an issue in your friendship, but they have other good qualities that make you want to keep the friendship? **CARD 2:** Is this an occasion when they may let you down? **CARD 3:** Should you have a backup plan on this occasion? **CARD 4:** Should you stop relying on them? **CARD 5:** Even if they do have good qualities, should you seek friends on whom you can depend?

What you should use:

The twenty-two Major cards and the sixteen Court cards.

When:

Any time you need the help of a friend.

680
SHOULD YOU INBUILD, IN A COMPLICATED TRAVEL SCHEDULE, MORE TIME THAN USUAL FOR TRANSITS?

Purpose and background information:

If timings are crucial for a particular trip or journey.

CARD 1: Even if you are not usually anxious, do you intuitively feel there may be delays? **CARD 2:** Should you revise your schedule so, even if overall traveling time is longer than usual, you have inbuilt any delays? **CARD 3:** Will the journey go well and be stress-free since you aren't working to a tight timetable?

What you should use:

The twenty-two Major cards.

When:

Any time you are going on a trip.

Blue-Moon Spread

A seasonal blue moon, which isn't really blue but refers to its rarity, occurs as the third full moon in an astronomical season when there are four instead of three full moons between solstices and equinoxes. A moon is also called blue when a month has two full moons, one at the beginning and one at the end. A blue moon occurs on average every 2.7 years. This is a Spread you will not do very often.

681
A BLUE-MOON SPREAD FOR BRINGING A MUCH-DESIRED OPPORTUNITY INTO YOUR LIFE

Purpose and background information:

When you have put in the hard work but need the good luck.

CARD 1: Is this the time to risk all and go for what you want? **CARD 2:** Is Lady Luck with you? **CARD 3:** Even if you do not get the 100% result you want, will it prove worthwhile in terms of raising your profile/showing you the missing ingredient to success?

What you should use:

The twenty-two Major cards.

When:

At a blue-moon time or during the month when it occurs.

Lunar-Eclipse Spread

A lunar eclipse, which can be partial or complete, occurs when the moon passes on the opposite side of the earth from the sun, and so is in earth's shadow. It only occurs during a full moon. Most years have two, though occasionally there may be more. They are good for initiating changes, especially after getting rid of any fears or obstacles.

682
A LUNAR-ECLIPSE SPREAD FOR MAKING A CHANGE THAT SCARES YOU

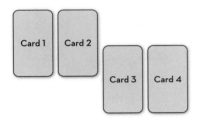

Purpose and background information:

CARD 1: What is the unacknowledged fear that holds you back? **CARD 2:** What would be the worst that can happen? **CARD 3:** What is the best that could happen? **CARD 4:** What is most likely to be the result of making the change?

What you should use:

The twenty-two Major cards.

When:

Any time within two days of a lunar eclipse.

Solar-Eclipse Spread

A solar eclipse occurs generally twice yearly during new moons, but occasionally up to five times, and can be total—or more—usually partial. You can use this Spread during any solar eclipse, even if it's not visible in your area. Solar-eclipse Spreads are good for very major decisions or changes and for going for your dreams.

683
A SOLAR-ECLIPSE SPREAD FOR GETTING THE OPPORTUNITY OF A LIFETIME

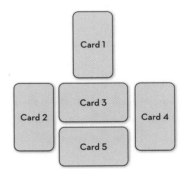

Purpose and background information:

When everything is in place, but you have to put yourself out there and risk failing.

CARD 1: Have you done everything possible to make this opportunity materialize? Any last-minute additions to make? **CARD 2:** Are you in the right place? If not, where must you be to seize the moment? **CARD 3:** If you do not try, will you regret it? **CARD 4:** If you try and don't succeed, will you regret it? **CARD 5:** Should you go for it regardless, and use whatever happens as a major step on the way to the ultimate dream?

What you should use:

The twenty-two Major cards.

When:

Any time within two days of a solar eclipse.

CHAPTER 35

MOON ZODIAC SPREADS

Lucky full-moon zodiac cards

If a Major card appears in a Spread associated with one of the zodiac signs in which the moon is full (see Chapter 32), that is especially lucky; so too is when your own zodiac card appears in a reading for any of the full moons. As with the previous moon-Spread chapter, any cards showing the moon or water are also good omens.

About the Zodiac and the Moon

The moon stays for about two and a half days each month in each zodiac sign. You can work with the waxing or waning energies according to how it falls each month within a particular sign.

For Spreads for major decisions or events, choose a Spread focused on the full moon. This combines the full-moon power with the zodiac energies of the sign in which it falls. Since the full moon only appears in each zodiac sign about once a year, if a matter is urgent, cast your full-moon Spread toward the height of the waxing moon in the desired sign as it occurs during each month. Check your moon diary. Online at https://mooncalendar.astro-seek.com/full-moons-new-moons is also a good site and updates each year.

ARIES

Waxing Moon in Aries
• courage • independence • self-reliance • self-employment • action • health • assertiveness • launching major ventures or life changes • energy and passion

684
A WAXING MOON IN ARIES SPREAD FOR LAUNCHING A SELF-EMPLOYED VENTURE

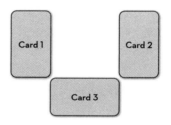

Purpose and background information:
When you are wondering if you can make a go of it.

CARD 1: What advantages are there in your going for self-employment now? CARD 2: What disadvantages are there in launching now? CARD 3: Go for it, wait, or abandon the idea?

What you should use:
The forty Minor cards, Aces to Tens, and the sixteen Court cards.

When:
Any time during the two and a half days of the month that the moon is waxing as it moves through Aries.

Full moon in Aries
• for an all-out effort for independence • survival
• a major leap to overcome a huge obstacle

685
A FULL MOON IN ARIES SPREAD FOR INDEPENDENCE FROM AN OVER-POSSESSIVE OR DOMINANT FAMILY

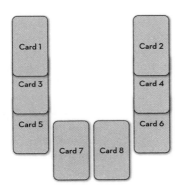

Purpose and background information:
If you are feeling stifled by your family's constant interference in your lifestyle/decisions.

Card 1: Do I/how do I get the strength to follow my own path? **Card 2:** What is the worst aspect of the interference/domination? **Card 3:** Are there/what are the positive benefits such as financial support/security that makes me allow this behavior to continue? **Card 4:** Should I speak out and not be shouted down? **Card 5:** Should I/do I want to physically move away/have reduced contact until I am more confident? **Card 6:** Can I overcome the problem and still retain the love of the family? **Card 7:** What will I have achieved toward my independence by the time the full moon is in the sky again? **Card 8:** What will I have achieved by the next full moon in Aries?

What you should use:
The full deck.

When:
When the full moon is in Aries, about once a year.

Waning moon in Aries
• anti-bullying and aggressiveness • to reduce hyperactivity

686
A WANING-MOON-IN-ARIES SPREAD IF YOUR CHILD OR TEENAGER HAS BEEN DIAGNOSED WITH HYPERACTIVITY

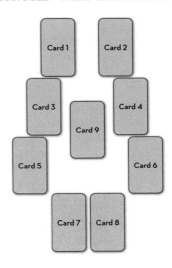

Purpose and background information:
When you doubt the diagnosis but are pressured to accept it.

Card 1: If your child is very active but can focus when interested, should you demand a second opinion/if necessary a private assessment to answer your concerns? **Card 2:** If you are being offered medication and you are not happy, should you insist on exploring alternatives such as cognitive behavioral therapy? **Card 3:** If the school is very formal, large, and academically focused and highly structured, would your child benefit from a different, quieter, more child-centered school so your child can develop their gifts? **Card 4:** Have you/should you explore further for possible allergies/dyslexia (often undiagnosed)/suppressed anger/fear that could be causing problems? **Card 5:** Should you consider alternative therapies and arts such as meditation, yoga, tai chi, reiki, or martial arts in order to restore control, balance, and harmony? **Card 6:** Can you find the right support/resources within the education system so your child can maximize their gifts? **Card 7:** Are there non-structured physical sports so your child can channel excess energy?

Card 8: Will your child/teenager grow out of the problems?

Card 9: Will your child/teenager have a fulfilling and successful life ahead?

What you should use:

The full deck.

When:

Any time during the two and a half days of the month that the moon is waning as it moves through Aries.

TAURUS

Waxing Moon in Taurus

· fertility · love · radiance · money · material security · to acquire beautiful things

687
A WAXING-MOON-IN-TAURUS SPREAD TO INCREASE YOUR CHARISMA IF YOU LACK SELF-CONFIDENCE

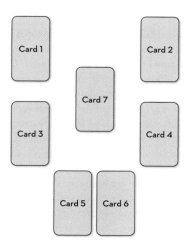

Purpose and background information:

If you lack confidence at social gatherings.

Card 1: Is it all social gatherings, or large ones, or ones where you do not know many people that you find hardest? **Card 2:** Should you accept that you are happiest with a small number of people, and go to events with one or two people you know well to gradually increase your confidence? **Card 3:** Should you practice meditation, yoga, singing, or gentle dance to allow yourself to harmonize your body, mind, and soul? **Card 4:** Are there certain people you should avoid who shake your confidence/deliberately make you feel inferior? **Card 5:** Should you go to events based around your interests, so the people are like-minded/you are confident on the main topics? **Card 6:** Should you make friends online/join forums to increase your confidence? **Card 7:** Should you love yourself as you are, and so project the real lovely self and not worry about being charismatic?

What you should use:

The forty Minor cards, Aces to Tens.

When:

Any time during the two and a half days of the month that the moon is waxing as it moves through Taurus.

Full moon in Taurus

· for conception of a child · getting a lover to commit · for creating a home of beauty and harmony · for peacemaking where there has been major quarrels or estrangement · for a major money venture

688
A TAURUS-FULL-MOON SPREAD TO MEND A MAJOR FAMILY QUARREL

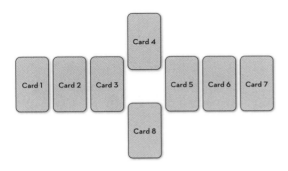

Purpose and background information:
Where there is ongoing hostility or estrangement and a major family celebration is coming up.

CARD 1: Are you the person to make peace, or is there another family member the combatants will listen to?
CARD 2: Does the rift and rivalry go back to childhood, or is it a more recent breakdown caused by a bereavement/divorce and people taking sides? **CARD 3:** Is it possible/will it work to use the family celebration as a neutral zone in which everyone makes an effort, whatever their personal grievances?
CARD 4: Can you build on this to mend bridges for future get-togethers? **CARD 5:** If one or two family members are prolonging the enmity, should they be told to behave or stay away from the event? **CARD 6:** Should you give up hope of peace/invite only those you know are friendly? **CARD 7:** Should you organize separate events and see the factions separately? **CARD 8:** Will the family be reconciled, if not by the event then in the months afterwards?

What you should use.
The twenty-two Major cards and the sixteen Court cards.

When:
When the full moon is in Taurus, about once a year.

Waning moon in Taurus
• for losing weight • overcoming possessiveness and emotional blackmail • anti-debt • to protect possessions

689
A TAURUS WANING-MOON SPREAD IF YOU ARE BEING EMOTIONALLY BLACKMAILED BY A FRIEND, FAMILY MEMBER OR COLLEAGUE

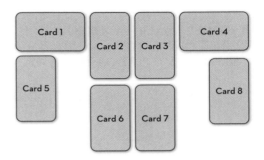

Purpose and background information:
If someone constantly makes you feel guilty for not helping them but never helps themselves.

CARD 1: Are you the only person being emotionally blackmailed, or is this the person's normal way of dealing with the world? **CARD 2:** Why do you feel guilty/obliged to help? **CARD 3:** Does the emotional vampire refuse to take any of your suggestions for improving their life/should you stop wasting your breath? **CARD 4:** Would/do suggestions they might benefit from counseling fall on deaf ears, or meet with indignation? **CARD 5:** If constant contact is emotionally draining/takes excess time you cannot spare, should you step back? **CARD 6:** Should you/how can you gradually step back? **CARD 7:** Will you need to completely withdraw at the risk of causing offense? **CARD 8:** Will they find someone else to emotionally drain if you are not around?

What you should use:
The twenty-two Major cards and the sixteen Court cards.

When:
Any time during the two and a half days of the month that the moon is waning as it moves through Taurus.

Waxing moon in Gemini

690

A GEMINI WAXING-MOON SPREAD IF YOU HAVE BEEN OFFERED AN APARTMENT SHARE IN A LOCATION YOU LOVE

• for speculation and games of chance • for passing examinations and tests • for healing using surgery or medical intervention • for communication • travel • moves of all kinds • for good luck

Purpose and background information:
When you are used to living on your own and do not know the other people in the apartment very well.

CARD 1: Will there be space in the new apartment where you can be private/entertain friends? **CARD 2:** Will the advantages of living in your chosen location outweigh the disadvantages of sharing? **CARD 3:** Would you prefer to share with people you know better? Could you organize this? **CARD 4:** Would you prefer to stay solo? **CARD 5:** Can you find a smaller apartment where you would like to live?

What you should use:
The forty Minor cards, Aces to Tens, and the sixteen Court cards.

When:
Any time during the two and a half days of the month that the moon is waxing as it moves through Gemini.

Full Moon in Gemini
• for taking a necessary risk • for unresponsive health problems • for successful dealings with the media • for backing the right person or cause • for changing careers if it is in a totally new field

691

A GEMINI FULL-MOON SPREAD FOR EMBARKING ON A TOTALLY NEW CAREER MIDWAY THROUGH LIFE

Purpose and background information:
When you know you are doing well, but you have lost your enthusiasm for your career and want to move on.

CARD 1: Can I/how can I incorporate my new career into my present life? **CARD 2:** What do I need to remove from my life to make room for this new direction? **CARD 3:** Do I want to balance the two, or will the new career eventually take over? **CARD 4:** How and when do I launch this new career? **CARD 5:** Do I already have/do I need to obtain new resources/knowledge to succeed in my new career? **CARD 6:** What/who might cause conflict between the two careers? **CARD 7:** Should I totally quit my old career first, or keep it as security in case I don't succeed? **CARD 8:** Will I succeed totally/partially in my new direction?

What you should use:
The full deck.

When:
When the full moon is in Gemini, about once a year.

Waning Moon in Gemini
• protection against deceit, gossip, lies, and spite • to reverse bad luck

692
A GEMINI WANING-MOON SPREAD WHEN THERE IS UNTRUE GOSSIP ABOUT YOU IN THE WORKPLACE

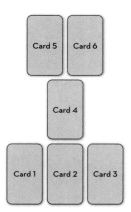

Purpose and background information:

When it's hard to concentrate on your work with a constant whispering campaign against you.

CARD 1: What is the underlying reason for the attack: jealousy over potential promotion/praise, or new opportunities by management? **CARD 2:** What is your best way of dealing with this: confrontation of the ringleader, or ignoring it? **CARD 3:** Would an official complaint be counter-productive/could it even make things worse? **CARD 4:** Can/should you get a transfer within the organization, or contemplate finding a new job? **CARD 5:** If this is a common problem with a particular clique, can you get support from previous victims/create a counter-group of those afraid of being picked on themselves? **CARD 6:** Will the problem resolve itself in time?

What you should use:

The forty Minor cards, Aces to Tens, and the sixteen Court cards.

When:

Any time during the two and a half days of the month that the moon is waning as it moves through Gemini.

Waxing Moon in Cancer

• for the home • family • mothers • children • fidelity

693
A CANCER WAXING-MOON SPREAD IF YOU WANT TO KNOW IF YOUR PARTNER IS FAITHFUL DESPITE BEING FLIRTATIOUS

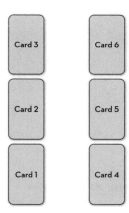

Purpose and background information:

If your partner is a serial flirt and it's starting to bug you.

CARD 1: Is your partner totally up front about flirting/doesn't try to hide anything/so innocent but annoying? **CARD 2:** Is the flirting simply part of your partner's expansive/sociable nature? How far can/should you accept it? **CARD 3:** Do you worry when your partner's not with you that s/he may let flirting go a bit far? **CARD 4:** Do you have any actual reason to distrust your partner? **CARD 5:** Is it time to tell your partner to reserve the flirting for you? **CARD 6:** If not, will you find a non-serial flirt as your partner?

What you should use:

The forty Minor cards, Aces to Tens, and the sixteen Court cards.

When:

Any time during the two and a half days of the month that the moon is waxing as it moves through Cancer.

Full Moon in Cancer

• for conceiving a baby, especially if you have been trying for a while • for overcoming relationship problems or betrayal • for answering questions about your mother or grandmother • major family issues • major home projects

694
A CANCER FULL-MOON SPREAD IF YOU WANT TO GIVE YOUR HOME A TOTAL MAKEOVER

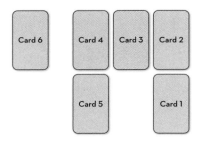

Purpose and background information:

When you want to change absolutely everything.

Card 1: Do you have a master plan/a general restlessness because you want to make major alterations? **Card 2:** Do you want structural changes/redecoration/new fixtures and fittings/all of these? **Card 3:** Would you be better off to move and start over again? **Card 4:** Should you take it a project at a time, or make major changes all at once? **Card 5:** Will it all be completed quickly/by the time the full moon is in Cancer again? **Card 6:** Will you then settle for the foreseeable future, or get a taste for renovating future houses?

What you should use:

The full deck.

When:

When the full moon is in Cancer, about once a year.

Waning Moon in Cancer

• for protection of the home and family • spreads about accidents • hostile neighbors

695
A CANCER WANING-MOON SPREAD IF YOUR LOVELY NEIGHBORS MOVE OUT AND HOSTILE ONES MOVE IN

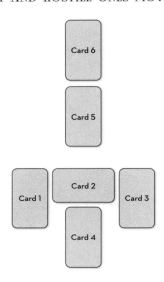

Purpose and background information:

If you are overwhelmed by the noise/mess and undesirable visitors.

Card 1: What is acceptable/what is not? Should you focus on protesting about the latter? **Card 2:** Should you try the *softly, softly* approach, be welcoming, or subtly slip into the conversation what's bothering you? **Card 3:** Should you go head-on to re-establish your territory? Will you make inroads? Will this succeed? **Card 4:** Will complaints to noise abatement/council/other local authorities help, or just make the situation worse? **Card 5:** Will the neighbors move on before too long? **Card 6:** If not, should you?

What you should use:

The twenty-two Major cards and the sixteen Court cards.

When:

Any time during the two and a half days of the month that the moon is waning as it moves through Cancer.

LEO

Waxing Moon in Leo
• for growing success • power • leadership • fame • prosperity
• career and abundance • potency and safe childbirth

Full Moon in Leo
• for applying for or being offered a leadership role
• for a chance to shine if you have previously been
overlooked • for overcoming a challenge to your authority
or expertise • for major success in a competition,
talent show, or any creative or performing venture

696
A LEO WAXING-MOON SPREAD IF YOU ARE GOING FOR A PRESTIGIOUS COLLEGE PLACE, OR AN INTERNSHIP OR JOB WITH A MAJOR COMPANY

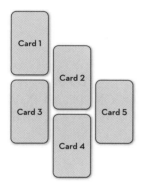

697
A LEO FULL-MOON SPREAD IF YOU HAVE A NEW MANAGER OR COLLEAGUE WHO IS CONSTANTLY TRYING TO UNDERMINE YOU

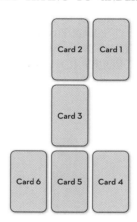

Purpose and background information:
When you want the best training or career opening possible.

Card 1: Will the most prestigious establishment actually be the best for you? **Card 2:** Have you missed anything in your preparations for your interview/presentation/examination? **Card 3:** Will you get a fair chance, or are certain people more likely to be accepted because of family connections/previous educational establishments? **Card 4:** Will your special qualities/qualifications/experience overcome any obstacles? **Card 5:** Will you obtain your desired place?

What you should use:
The full deck.

When:
Any time during the two and a half days of the month that the moon is waxing as it moves through Leo.

Purpose and background information:
When you are losing confidence and making mistakes because your authority is being undermined.

Card 1: Are you 100% confident in your own expertise, or do you need to get one step ahead? **Card 2:** What is the motive of the person undermining you? Insecurity/jealousy? Should you see them as a weak person? **Card 3:** What is your best strategy? Ignoring criticism/confronting/banding together to complain along with others experiencing similar problems? **Card 4:** if a personal attack, should you complain to a senior manager who knows your work/union? Would that make it worse? **Card 5:** Will the perpetrator move on/get transferred, especially if others complain? **Card 6:** Should you leave?

What you should use:
The twenty-two Major cards and the sixteen Court cards.

When:
When the full moon is in Cancer, about once a year.

Waning Moon in Leo
• for letting go of situations you aren't going to win • for banishing fears that hold you back from success or happiness • for making the best of what is on offer • for clearing the decks for future success

---

698
A WANING-MOON-IN-LEO SPREAD FOR DECIDING IF IT'S WORTH PURSUING A PATH SEEMINGLY GOING NOWHERE, OR MODIFYING PLANS ACCORDING TO WHAT IS ON OFFER

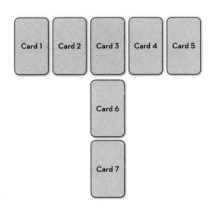

Purpose and background information:
If a long-held plan or ambition is not materializing.

CARD 1: Should you wait longer? How long is realistic? **CARD 2:** What is causing the delay? A person/people/circumstances/finances/hidden factors? **CARD 3:** If you change tactic/make a supreme effort, is your original plan still possible? **CARD 4:** Should you compromise, or accept what is on offer right now? **CARD 5:** If you compromise, could you still achieve a modified version of your dream? **CARD 6:** Should

you just give up? **CARD 7:** Could it still happen against the odds?

What you should use:
The full deck.

When:
Any time during the two and a half days of the month that the moon is waning as it moves through Leo.

VIRGO

Waxing Moon in Virgo
• for all health and healing matters • for animals • for any detailed matters • for craftsperson skills • for gardening and the environment • for keeping to diets

---

699
A WAXING-MOON SPREAD IN VIRGO WHEN YOU WANT TO WORK WITH NATURE

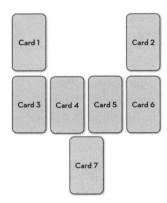

Purpose and background information:
When you want to make your living with plants or the land.

CARD 1: Do you have the knowledge/expertise/experience to start your own plant/crop growing business? **CARD 2:** Do you need to gain more expertise by working in someone else's business for a time? **Card 3:** Do you want/need to go to agricultural/horticultural college, or learn as you go, maybe employing experienced staff? **Card 4:** Do you want/need to move to a place with land to cultivate/lease/buy an existing plant business? **Card 5:** How will you support yourself financially while getting established? **Card 6:** Will you succeed? **Card 7:** Would you prefer to keep this as a hobby/sideline?

What you should use:
The forty Minor cards, Aces to Tens, and the sixteen Court cards.

When:
Any time during the two and a half days of the month that the moon is waxing as it moves through Virgo.

Full Moon in Virgo
• for striving to be the best in your field • for seeking perfection whether in love or career • overcoming a major health setback • urgently putting your financial affairs in order

---

700
A FULL-MOON-IN-VIRGO SPREAD WHEN YOUR TAX AFFAIRS ARE IN CHAOS AND YOUR PAPERS ARE DUE FOR INSPECTION

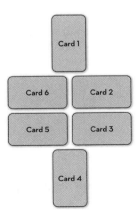

Purpose and background information:
When you have been putting off sorting out your financial affairs, and the deadline is looming.

Card 1: If you can shut yourself away with all your papers, can you sort it out yourself, however painful, or is it too chaotic? **Card 2:** Will you find a reliable accountant/bookkeeper who will makes sense of it all to meet the deadline? **Card 3:** If you know you will not be able to pay, will you be able to negotiate a delay/installments? **Card 4:** Will this get sorted out in time to avoid penalties? **Card 5:** Will you be able to prevent future chaos and panic by fixing earlier intervention/an ongoing system of record-keeping? **Card 6:** Will you worry about next year when it comes?

What you should use:
The twenty-two Major cards.

When:
When the full moon is in Cancer, about once a year.

Waning Moon in Virgo
• for lingering and progressive illnesses • sorting out the details of a complicated matter • any form of phobia, addiction, or compulsion • for clumsy children or adults • overcoming unemployment later in life • for personal safety

A WANING-MOON SPREAD IN VIRGO IF YOU HAVE A DEBILITATING OR PROGRESSIVE CONDITION AND THERE SEEMS LITTLE GOOD NEWS

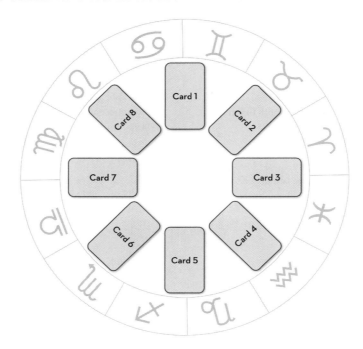

Purpose and background information:

When you are trying to find a way to have a good quality of life.

CARD 1: How can you maximize the strength/mobility you have now? **CARD 2:** How can you maximize your emotional well-being so you have as a good quality of life as possible? **CARD 3:** What new research/treatments can you explore to get the best help possible, if necessary seeking group funding for travel to a center of excellence? **CARD 4:** Would natural/energy therapies/healing give you relief, or at least delay symptoms from worsening? How to find them? **CARD 5:** Should you forward-plan so you can work/live in different ways if your health/mobility deteriorates? **CARD 6:** Should you change your lifestyle, or plan things you want to do and see now? **CARD 7:** If you persist with your current treatment, will you see good results? **CARD 8:** Should you be realistically hopeful about your future?

What you should use:

The full deck.

When:

Any time during the two and a half days of the month that the moon is waning as it moves through Virgo.

NOTE: Scan or copy the Spread wheel and place the Tarot cards exactly according to the picture.

LIBRA

Waxing Moon in Libra
• for engagements and weddings • for establishing a business partnership with your love partner • for peace and harmony • for popularity issues • for compromise

702
A WAXING-MOON-IN-LIBRA SPREAD IF YOU ARE CONTEMPLATING SETTING UP A BUSINESS WITH YOUR LOVE PARTNER

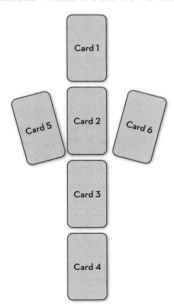

Purpose and background information:
When the idea of living and working together seems idyllic, but . . .

CARD 1: Can you separate your work from your home life and not bring work/work disagreements home? **CARD 2:** If one of you is more assertive than the other, can you arrange the business so you each have your own areas of control? **CARD 3:** Do you have similar ideas on money management/priorities? If not, how can you compromise to avoid disagreements? **CARD 4:** Can you still make your own time and space to avoid 24/7 claustrophobia? **CARD 5:** Will it provide a new and even better dimension to your relationship? **CARD 6:** Is working together a non-starter for now?

What you should use:
The forty Minor cards, Aces to Tens, and the sixteen Court cards.

When:
Any time during the two and a half days of the month that the moon is waxing as it moves through Libra.

Full Moon in Libra
• for righting a major injustice • for the successful outcome of court cases • for resolving or restoring balance to a partnership or marriage crisis • for finding the perfect match in love or business

703
A FULL-MOON-IN-LIBRA SPREAD FOR RESOLVING A COURT CASE AGAINST A MAJOR ORGANIZATION WHICH HAS TRIED TO DESTROY YOUR REPUTATION

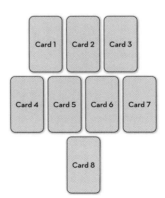

CARD 1: What is the best result I seek? CARD 2: Who/what is opposing me? CARD 3: How will an individual standing against a big organization favor me? CARD 4: Will these slurs against me be disproved? CARD 5: What recompense will I receive for the loss of my reputation and the fallout? CARD 6: What will be the results of my being vindicated in the short term? CARD 7: What will be the results of my being vindicated in the long term? CARD 8: Will justice be done in every way?

What you should use:
The full deck.

When:
When the full moon is in Libra, about once a year.

Waning Moon in Libra
• where lack of commitment is an issue • when a partner has been unfaithful • when someone is sitting on the fence and will not decide • when a court case or an official decision is constantly delayed

704
A WANING-MOON-IN-LIBRA SPREAD WHEN YOUR PARTNER IS TRYING TO PLEASE EVERYONE

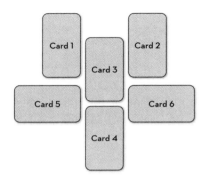

Purpose and background information:
When your partner will never back you in a family dispute, whether concerning the children or his/her parents.

CARD 1: Is your partner generally a nice person who hates confrontation? CARD 2: Does this attitude leave you in the line of fire as the bad guy/gal? CARD 3: Should you step back/disappear when trouble looms so s/he is forced to decide/act? CARD 4: Will your partner change if you explain your dilemma? CARD 5: If your partner cannot/will not change, can you accept this as the downside of his/her good nature? CARD 6: Will it become an increasing problem if not resolved, one that may affect the relationship and so force your partner to act or you to deliver a few ultimatums?

What you should use:
The twenty-two Major cards and the sixteen Court cards.

When:
Any time during the two and a half days of the month that the moon is waning as it moves through Libra.

SCORPIO

Waxing Moon in Scorpio
• for Spreads on life transformation • increasing psychic powers • for the best way to fulfill strongly felt desires or needs • for Spreads on recovering what has been lost or stolen

705
A WAXING-MOON-IN-SCORPIO SPREAD FOR DISCOVERING THE LOCATION OF SOMETHING YOU HAVE LOST OR MISPLACED

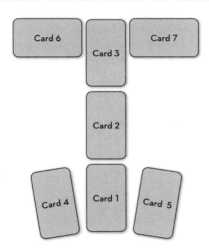

Purpose and background information:
When you have exhausted logic and backtracking and need a little psychic help.

CARD 1: Is the missing item in the home? **CARD 2:** Is it in a totally unexpected place/hidden beneath what you were carrying when you were interrupted? **CARD 3:** Is it outside the home, such as at your workplace/a vehicle you used the day it went missing/the garden? **CARD 4:** Has it been stolen? If so, whom do you suspect? **CARD 5:** Will it turn up when you aren't looking for it? **CARD 6:** Will someone else find it and return it as a result of advertising on social media/reporting to the police/transport/venue for lost properties you frequent? **CARD 7:** Is it gone forever?

What you should use:
The forty Minor cards, Aces to Tens.

When:
Any time during the two and a half days of the month that the moon is waxing as it moves through Scorpio.

Full Moon in Scorpio
• for love affairs and the temptation to stray
• for passion • for dealing with overpowering feelings of jealousy or desire for revenge

706
A FULL-MOON-IN-SCORPIO SPREAD IF YOU ARE IN LOVE WITH TWO PEOPLE AT THE SAME TIME

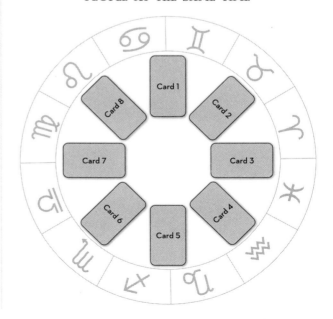

Purpose and background information:
When you are in a settled relationship but suddenly fall madly in love with someone else.

CARD 1: What practical, as well as emotional, consequences will result if you follow your passion? **CARD 2:** Have underlying issues in your existing relationship made you seek/be responsive to other love? **CARD 3:** If you follow your heart, will your new love last? **CARD 4:** Can you have both relationships without major damage to yourself/others affected? Is it worth it? **CARD 5:** If you gave up your new love, would you regret it forever? **CARD 6:** Should you be alone if neither relationship will ultimately make you happy? **CARD 7:** Should you risk all? **CARD 8:** Should you play it safe?

What you should use:
The full deck.

When:
When the full moon is in Scorpio, about once a year.

NOTE: Scan or copy the Spread wheel and place the Tarot cards exactly according to the picture

Waning Moon in Scorpio
• spreads for obtaining protection against physical, emotional, or psychic attack • for when you have been the victim of criminal activity • for when theft or vandalism is a problem where you live

707
A WANING-MOON-IN-SCORPIO SPREAD IF YOU HAVE BEEN THE VICTIM OF A PHYSICAL ATTACK, MUGGING, OR BURGLARY

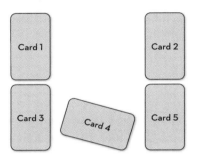

Purpose and background information:
If you have suffered an attack and the fears remain.

CARD 1: Are you safe from further attack? What extra security can you ask for/receive? **CARD 2:** Has the perpetrator been caught? If not, what justice can you expect? **CARD 3:** Are you getting sufficient support/counseling, or should you ask for more? **CARD 4:** Do you want/should you stay away temporarily/permanently until the trauma fades? **CARD 5:** Will you ever feel safe again?

What you should use:
The twenty-two Major cards.

When:
Any time during the two and a half days of the month that the moon is waning as it moves through Scorpio.

SAGITTARIUS

Waxing moon in Sagittarius
• for travel • adventures • house moves • horses • publishing and creative ventures • for happiness and optimism • for good ideas • sports • finding lost pets

708
A WAXING-MOON-IN-SAGITTARIUS SPREAD IF YOU CANNOT GET YOUR BOOK PUBLISHED

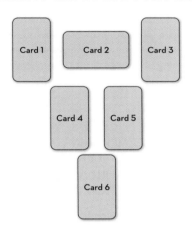

Purpose and background information:
When you know what you have created is good, but you have a pile of rejections.

CARD 1: Should you keep trying, especially smaller publishers/who print books in your field? Should you expand overseas? **CARD 2:** Should you keep trying for a reputable literary agent to open doors? **CARD 3:** Should you create a website for your books? **CARD 4:** If publication matters more than financial gain, should you self-publish? **CARD 5:** Should you write your next book/a trilogy in readiness? **CARD 6:** Will you succeed?

What you should use:
The twenty-two Major cards and the sixteen Court cards.

When:
Any time during the two and a half days of the month that the moon is waxing as it moves through Sagittarius.

Full moon in Sagittarius
• for major travel or relocation plans, especially overseas career moves • for long-distance holidays • for urgent house moves

709
A FULL-MOON-IN-SAGITTARIUS SPREAD IF YOU ARE OFFERED A MAJOR CAREER MOVE OVERSEAS, BUT YOUR PARTNER OR FAMILY DOESN'T WANT TO GO

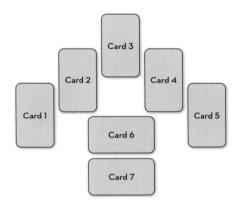

Purpose and background information:
When you are torn between family and dream job.

CARD 1: Would the move benefit your partner/family financially/a successful future that leans you toward accepting it? **CARD 2:** If you postpone acceptance, will the chance come again? **CARD 3:** If you give up the opportunity, will you always regret/resent it? **CARD 4:** If you accept, would your family come for long vacations/possibly eventually move there? **CARD 5:** Could/should you negotiate terms so you can frequently fly home? **CARD 6:** Should/must your family come first? **CARD 7:** Can you ultimately have both?

What you should use:
The forty Minor cards, Aces to Tens, and the sixteen Court cards.

When:
When the full moon is in Sagittarius, about once a year.

Waning Moon in Sagittarius
• spreads for protection on journeys and against getting lost • for preventing pets straying or being stolen • for training or competing difficulties, especially with horses • for slowing or reversing money losses

710
A WANING-MOON-IN-SAGITTARIUS SPREAD IF YOU ARE COMPETING WITH YOUR HORSE BUT SUFFERING FROM OPPOSITION TO YOUR JOINING THE CIRCUIT

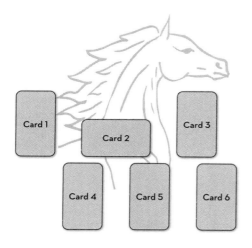

Purpose and background information:
When there's an unofficial cartel of privilege excluding you.

CARD 1: Should you insist on your rights to compete/ignore the prejudice? **CARD 2:** Should you confront the perpetrators, making it clear that you are here to stay? **CARD 3:** Should/can you go out there and win/make them acknowledge you? **CARD 4:** Is there a weak link in the chain of command to bypass opposition? **CARD 5:** Should you deal directly with the national/international chain of command/bypass local prejudice? **CARD 6:** Will you succeed in competing as and where you want?

What you should use:
The whole deck.

When:
Any time during the two and a half days of the month that the moon is waning as it moves through Sagittarius.

CAPRICORN

Waxing moon in Capricorn
• for loyalty in love and business • for financial security • for all official matters • for wise caution • for steady promotion and career success • for stable business ventures • for perseverance and overcoming obstacles through persistent effort

711
A WAXING-MOON-IN-CAPRICORN SPREAD TO TELL YOU IF YOU SHOULD TRUST A COLLEAGUE WHO SEEMS VERY FRIENDLY BUT YOU ARE NOT SURE

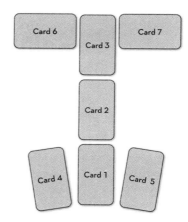

Purpose and background information:
When you need to make a decision as to whether or not to trust a colleague.

CARD 1: What is your intuition telling you? **CARD 2:** Do you suspect they are passing on things you've said in confidence? **CARD 3:** Do they have an interest in discrediting you to further their own career? **CARD 4:** Are they friendly to everyone but gossip about them behind their back? **CARD 5:** Should you be careful what you say/let them know until you are sure they are reliable? **Card 6:** Should you watch your back for what they say about you? **Card 7:** Should you generally be more careful about whom you trust with confidences?

What you should use:

The twenty-two Major cards and the sixteen Court cards.

When:

Any time during the two and a half days of the month that the moon is waxing as it moves through Capricorn.

Full moon in Capricorn
• for overcoming a seemingly insurmountable object or opposition • operating within limitations • starting again after failure or major setback

712
A FULL-MOON-IN-CAPRICORN SPREAD FOR STARTING AGAIN AFTER BANKRUPTCY

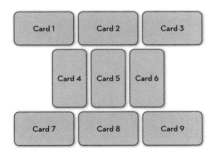

Purpose and background information:

When you have lost your lifestyle and don't know how to rebuild.

Card 1: How can you best adapt to/live within the restrictions imposed by bankruptcy? **Card 2:** What are the advantages of being free of debt to make long-desired changes? **Card 3:** Who has disappointed you in their response whom you now have lost/must leave behind? **Card 4:** What loyalty, expected and unexpected, can you draw around you as you make your new life? **Card 5:** Should you relocate to start again? **Card 6:** What existing skills/ expertise can you build on? **Card 7:** Is this a good time to begin a new career/lifestyle? **Card 8:** What is the most

valuable lesson you have learned? **Card 9:** Will you have a good life after bankruptcy?

What you should use:

The full deck.

When:

When the full moon is in Capricorn, about once a year.

Waning moon in Capricorn
• for overcoming depression and self-doubt • for the release of money that is tied up or disputed

713
A WANING-MOON-IN-CAPRICORN SPREAD IF MONEY IS TIED UP IN AN INHERITANCE DISPUTE

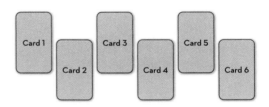

Purpose and background information:

If a case is dragging through the courts with no sign of resolution.

Card 1: Should you shortcut the proceedings and make an offer to those disputing, even though it's less than you might get legally? **Card 2:** Can you talk to anyone in the disputing party's family to bring reason and compromise? **Card 3:** Should you go all-out with an enthusiastic lawyer? **Card 4:** Have you spent enough on lawyers/prefer to leave everything to resolve in its own time? **Card 5:** Will you eventually win what you are entitled to? **Card 6:** Is it worth the stress to continue, or should you quit?

What you should use:

The twenty-two Major cards and the sixteen Court cards.

When:

Any time during the two and a half days of the month that the moon is waning as it moves through Capricorn.

AQUARIUS

Waxing moon in Aquarius

• for original ventures • the success of inventions • for any intellectual matters • for humanitarian issues • for friendships • for developing unique gifts and talents • for complementary medicine

Full moon in Aquarius

• for an original solution to a long-standing problem • for major world aid or peace needs • for launching a second career based on an innate but previously undeveloped talent • for going against the crowd

714
A WAXING-MOON-IN-AQUARIUS SPREAD IF YOU HAVE INVENTED SOMETHING YOU ARE SURE WILL BE A MONEY-SPINNER

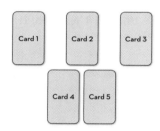

715
AN AQUARIUS-FULL-MOON SPREAD IF YOU FEEL STRONGLY ABOUT A CAUSE OR ISSUE, BUT NO ONE ELSE SEEMS TO CARE

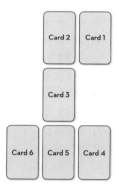

Purpose and background information:
When you have invested a lot of time and money in your creation.

CARD 1: Have you/should you patent your idea to avoid its being copied? **CARD 2:** Can you/will you find a sponsor, whether an individual to come into partnership or a company to invest in the idea? **CARD 3:** Would you be happy to sell the idea, or do you want to stay involved? **CARD 4:** Is it the first part of a series of inventions that could be developed as a second career/become your main earner, or is it a one-off? **CARD 5:** Is this the invention that will be the money-spinner, or just a step on the way?

What you should use:
The forty Minor cards, Aces to Tens.

When:
Any time during the two and a half days of the month that the moon is waxing as it moves through Aquarius.

Purpose and background information:
If you are hitting a blank wall in raising enthusiasm locally or among friends.

CARD 1: Is there generally a lack of information about the cause locally/do you need to let people know more about it? **CARD 2:** Is there an online organization/national or international organization which could help with local publicity? **CARD 3:** Can you attract local media interest for an eye-catching fundraising event in your vicinity? **CARD 4:** Could you join/create a website with first-person accounts to make the cause more relevant to others? **CARD 5:** Should you accept local indifference and focus your efforts to work nationally/internationally? **CARD 6:** Will you eventually raise awareness locally if you keep trying?

What you should use:
The forty Minor cards, Aces to Tens.

When:

When the full moon is in Aquarius, about once a year.

Waning moon in Aquarius

• for overcoming intolerance • for quitting bad habits • for overcoming prejudice and inequality • for banishing loneliness and isolation

716
A WANING-MOON-IN-AQUARIUS SPREAD IF YOU ALWAYS FEEL ALONE, EVEN IN A CROWD

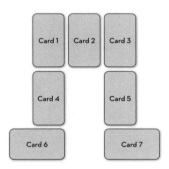

Purpose and background information:

Card 1: Have you always felt like this? Has it been since you moved/divorced? **Card 2:** Are you happy in yourself, or are there changes to lifestyle/career/location that isolate you? **Card 3:** Do you find a lot of people superficial/should you aim to make a few like-minded friends? **Card 4:** Should you avoid big gatherings/parties/social chatter/focus on meeting people through your interests? **Card 5:** Should you get to know people through social media/online chat rooms where you can talk in depth? **Card 6:** Will you find your twin soul/a best friend totally on your wavelength? **Card 7:** Will you gain harmony within yourself and with chosen others?

What you should use:

The twenty-two Major cards and the sixteen Court cards.

When:

Any time during the two and a half days of the month that the moon is waning as it moves through Aquarius.

PISCES

Waxing moon in Pisces

• for new love or love after a loss • for developing talents in music and the performing arts • for balancing two commitments or having two careers • for adaptability • for merging two families • for telepathic powers

717
A WAXING-MOON-IN-PISCES SPREAD IF YOU WANT TO LEARN MUSIC AT ANY AGE

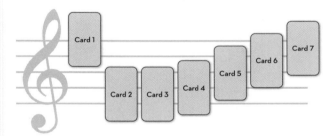

Purpose and background information:

When you regret not learning music but fear it's too late.

Card 1: Have you always loved singing/dancing but never had the time/opportunity to develop your gifts? **Card 2:** Should you start by using online singing/music teaching lessons to gain confidence? **Card 3:** Would you prefer/ should you afterwards take lessons/join a choir/a music jamming session? **Card 4:** Would you like to develop your gifts to perform publicly, whether for fun or to enter competitions? **Card 5:** Will it remain a fun hobby? **Card 6:** Do you want to go further/music college/producing You Tube videos/online downloadable songs? **Card 7:** Do you believe you could still have a career in music if you choose?

What you should use:

The forty Minor cards, Aces to Tens, and the sixteen Court cards.

When:

Any time during the two and a half days of the month that the moon is waxing as it moves through Pisces.

• for making an intuitive leap • for proof of
psychic abilities • for doing two things or
successfully following two careers at once.

• for overcoming rivalries and people pulling you
in different directions • for reconciling quarrels
and custody or divorce disputes • for overcoming
excesses or imbalances of any kind

718
A FULL-MOON-IN-PISCES SPREAD FOR STARTING A BUSINESS WHILE HAVING A FULL-TIME JOB

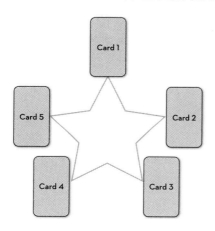

719
A WANING-MOON-IN-PISCES SPREAD IF YOU ARE A FEAST-OR-FAMINE YO-YO DIETER

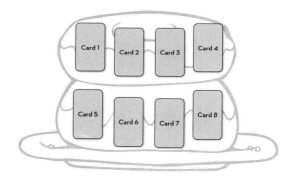

Purpose and Background Information:

When you're wondering if you have the time and energy to push ahead with a second venture but know you'll regret it if you don't.

CARD 1: What non-priorities/demands of others can you shed to give yourself extra time and energy? **CARD 2:** Do you want this business so much that you are prepared to put in all the time and effort needed? **CARD 3:** Who/what will help this venture? **CARD 4:** Who/what will hinder it? **CARD 5:** By the time the full moon is in Pisces again, will you be able to quit your full-time job?

What you should use:

The forty Minor cards, Aces to Tens, and the sixteen Court cards.

When:

When the full moon is in Pisces, about once a year.

Background and purpose information:

When for years you've alternated between dieting and bingeing and want to find balance in body and peace of mind.

CARD 1: Is *all or nothing* true of your life generally? **CARD 2:** Is it due to your lifestyle/your nature, or are you pushing yourself too hard toward perfection? **CARD 3:** How can you generally gain more balance in your life, so food is part of your growing harmony? **CARD 4:** Do certain people or triggers set off the cycle? How can you avoid these? **CARD 5:** Should you love yourself more as you are now? **CARD 6:** Should you eat what you want when you want, to get back in touch with your natural body rhythm? **CARD 7:** Will food balance come naturally once you let go of the unrealistic expectations of others/yourself? **CARD 8:** Will food become your friend, or at least not your enemy?

What you will use:

The twenty-two Major cards.

When:

Any time during the two and a half days of the month that the moon is waning as it moves through Pisces.

CHAPTER 36

MOON-ANGEL SPREADS

Lucky Cards for Moon-Angel Spreads

Major Cards: Temperance (the angel of the rainbow), the Moon, the Star, the World.

Minor Cards: Any moon and water card, Aces to Tens in the Cups suit.

Court Cards: The Cups cards, but especially the Queen of Cups.

About Moon-Angel Spreads

Each of the 29 days of the lunar month is ruled by a specific angel. These are traditionally grouped into the eight main moon phases. In the previous chapters were Spreads for the broader waxing, full, waning, and new moon phases.

Moon-angel Spreads combine angelic and lunar energies and are good for personal issues, questions about children, mothers and mothering, fertility, health and healing, love and romance, and for moving between phases of our life. Though the angels are grouped in threes or fours according to the moon phase, a few have additional roles and areas they assist with, and so have their own Spreads. Count Day 1 of the moon cycle as the first day after the waning moon crescent, marked as a black circle in a moon diary as Day 1. You can use a diary listing the daily moon phase or an online lunar calendar such as https://www.timeand-date.com/moon/phases/

720
A NEW MOON-ANGEL SPREAD FOR RETURNING TO LIFE AFTER HURT, BETRAYAL, LOSS, OR ILLNESS

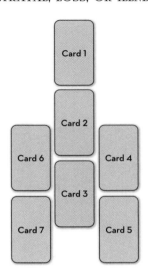

Purpose and background information:
Under the protection of angels Geniel, Enediel, and Anixiel, angels described with pale silver wings and a pale silver halo.

CARD 1: What should you temporarily withdraw from or take a step back from until you feel stronger? **CARD 2:** What should you permanently withdraw from or not return to?
CARD 3: What plans/hopes do you have for the month ahead to start to enter life again? **CARD 4:** What worries you about putting them in practice? **CARD 5:** Can you/should you take advice/seek help, or would you sooner work to achieve these plans alone? **CARD 6:** Is it realistic to have made progress by the time of the next new moon, or should you take as long as you need? **CARD 7:** Will you find peace and harmony again?

What you should use:
The twenty-two Major cards.

When:
Days 1, 2, and 3 from when the waning moon disappears from the sky until the night of the crescent.

721

A CRESCENT-MOON ANGEL SPREAD FOR NEW BEGINNINGS IN ANY PART OF YOUR LIFE IF YOU ARE UNSURE

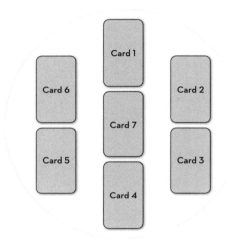

Purpose and background information:
Under the protection of Azariel, Gabriel, and Dirachiel, crescent-moon angels with the exception of Gabriel (see page 393) described with crescent-moon haloes and a soft shimmering light all around them.

CARD 1: Is your new beginning in the right direction for you? **CARD 2:** Should you begin slowly and build up, or start decisively? **CARD 3:** What resources/help can you call on to support you in these early days? **CARD 4:** Are there practical steps you can take to hasten your new beginning? **CARD 5:** Must you first/at the same time initiate an inner new beginning? **CARD 6:** Who/what do you fear might hold it back? **CARD 7:** How far will you have progressed by the next crescent moon?

What you should use:
The forty Minor cards, Aces to Tens, and the sixteen Court cards.

When:
Crescent moon days 4–7.

722

A FIRST-MOON-QUARTER ANGEL SPREAD FOR A NEW FITNESS REGIME IF YOU ARE ALWAYS SHORT OF TIME

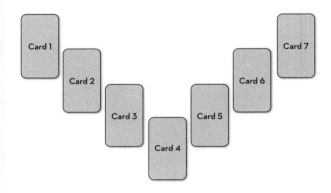

Purpose and background information:
Under the protection of Amnediel, Barbiel, Ardifiel, and Neciel, angels described as surrounded by radiant silver moonbeams with glowing golden wings.

CARD 1: So you feel out of sorts/stressed/get minor illnesses/know you are not taking care of yourself? **CARD 2:** Is it lack of time, energy, or both that holds you back from being fit? **CARD 3:** Do you need gym/membership/a personal trainer/exercise programs, or is this out of the question, given your lifestyle? **CARD 4:** Could you take up an unstructured solitary/family activity such as walking/cycling/swimming? **CARD 5:** Do you first need to improve nutrition/rest/relax/ meditate/stop the whirling mind? **CARD 6:** Can/should you cut down on the 24/7 dash/demands of others so your well-being is center stage? **CARD 7:** Will you get fit/feel better once you refocus your life?

What you should use:
The full deck.

When:
Days 8–11 of the waxing moon cycle.

723

AN AMNEDIEL ANGEL OF THE FIRST MOON QUARTER SPREAD FOR LEARNING COMPLEMENTARY MEDICINE AND THERAPIES

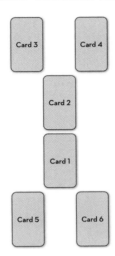

Purpose and background information:
Amnediel and his moon day are especially helpful for health and healing, particularly all-natural methods.

CARD 1: Do you want to learn complementary methods for your own health/for family and friends/to work as a health professional, or all of these? **CARD 2:** Are you especially drawn to natural living and nutrition as a lifestyle/particular natural medicine therapies? **CARD 3:** Do you intend to study professionally, attend classes run by a therapist, or mainly teach yourself? **CARD 4:** Do you sense/recall a past life connection with natural methods/sometimes know something spontaneously and find it is correct? **CARD 5:** What drawbacks/safeguards should/will you adopt against potentially fraudulent/unreliable information/false gurus? **CARD 6:** Is this the way forward for you?

What you should use:
The twenty-two Major cards.

When:
Day 8 of the moon cycle.

724

AN ARDIFIEL FIRST-MOON-QUARTER-ANGEL SPREAD FOR FINDING THE SOLUTION TO A SEEMINGLY INSOLUBLE PROBLEM

Purpose and background information:
Ardifiel is especially useful for Spreads for visions, brainstorming, and spiritual insights.

CARD 1: Should you go through all the options and alternative solutions once more, in case you have missed something? **CARD 2:** Should you step away from the problem for a while, to allow your brain to clear? **CARD 3:** Will the answer come in an unmistakable sign/new contact if you are patient? **CARD 4:** If you pray/meditate, will the angels, especially Ardifiel, bring the answer? **CARD 5:** If expert advice isn't helping, should you brainstorm with friends/family, no holds barred/no suggestion dismissed out of hand? **CARD 6:** Should you search the Internet daily/relevant websites/centers of excellence/forums/ask in chat rooms? **CARD 7:** What does this card tell you about an unconsidered option? **CARD 8:** Will you solve the seemingly unsolvable in time?

What you should use:
The full deck.

When:
Day 10 of the Moon cycle

725
A GIBBOUS (ALMOST-FULL-MOON) ANGEL SPREAD FOR FINDING A LASTING LOVE IF YOU HAVE NO LUCK

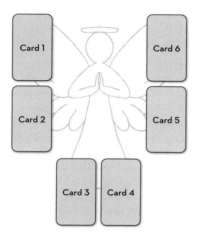

Purpose and background information:
Protected by Abdizuel, Jazeriel, and Ergediel, pictured in flowing robes of silver and gold with long white gold flowing hair.

CARD 1: Do you go to the wrong places to meet reliable, sincere people and widen your social circle? **CARD 2:** If you don't meet many people, should you go for an online dating site based on interests rather than appearances? **CARD 3:** Should you go along to singles groups based on shared interests/travel rather than romance? **CARD 4:** Should you be more open to getting to know people in depth than looking for the ideal partner? **CARD 5:** Should you relax, enjoy yourself, and let lasting love happen as and when it will? **CARD 6:** Will you meet the right person in the next twelve months/a little longer?

What you should use:
The forty Minor cards, Aces to Tens, and the sixteen Court cards.

When:
Days 12–14 of the Moon cycle.

726
AN ATLIEL FULL-MOON-ANGEL SPREAD FOR FINDING HIDDEN TREASURE AT A MARKET OR ANTIQUE SHOW

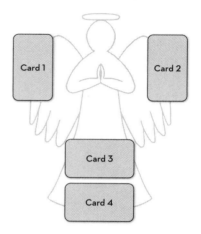

Purpose and background information:
Atliel is very helpful, whether you are looking for fossils, prospecting, or simply developing an eye for a bargain.

CARD 1: Do you generally have good intuition to back up knowledge where a hidden treasure is to be found? **CARD 2:** Will you find your treasure in one of your usual haunts, especially if you always get there early? **CARD 3:** Should you go somewhere entirely different to find your treasure? **CARD 4:** Will it be the next market you are drawn to? Should you repeat this Spread in a month's time?

What you should use:
The twenty-two Major cards.

When:
Day 15 of the moon cycle, if necessary repeated monthly.

727

A FULL MOON ANGELS SPREAD FOR CREATIVE AND ARTISTIC SUCCESS

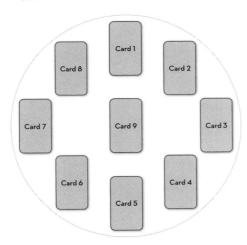

Purpose and background information:

Empowered by Atliel, Azeruel and Adriel, glorious silver and gold angels studded with stars and with huge full starry haloes.

CARD 1 do you have a ready sales outlet for your creative ventures/do you need to find extra markets? **CARD 2** do you have sufficient creative products to launch an exhibition/a stall? **CARD 3** should you offer samples on and offline and take commissions? **CARD 4** do you need/will you find a mentor/agent to publicize/exhibit your creations/prefer to keep sole control? **CARD 5** what is the extra magic ingredient you need to stand out from similar products? **CARD 6** can you successfully use local media/social media publicity to raise your profile? **CARD 7** can you be everywhere so you get known both in and beyond your field? **CARD 8** will you succeed sufficiently to make a living from your creations soon? **CARD 9** will you get a big break/have a steady path to success?

What you should use:

The full pack.

When:

Days 15-17 of the moon cycle.

728

A DISSEMINATING (WANING-FULL-MOON) ANGELS SPREAD IF YOU STILL REGULARLY SEE A PERSON WHO HAS CAUSED YOU MUCH UNHAPPINESS

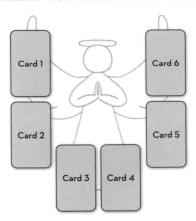

Purpose and background information:

Protected by Egibiel, Amutiel, Kyriel, and Bethnael, mature angels with pure white robes and pale shimmering blue haloes and wings.

CARD 1: However you feel inside, can you keep the communication cool and businesslike, outwardly amicable if children are involved? **CARD 2:** Can you refuse to be provoked/manipulated by the other person so in time the encounters lose their power? **CARD 3:** Can you develop tactics so you are in control of any interaction, especially if you were formerly emotionally manipulated? **CARD 4:** Can you focus on building your self-confidence so you become emotionally insulated? **CARD 5:** If there is ongoing injustice, can you deal with it through a third party, or will you avoid direct confrontation which would arouse negative feelings/increase personal connection? **CARD 6:** Will this situation positively reduce/cease even sooner than anticipated?

What you should use:

The twenty-two Major cards.

When:

Days 18–21 in the moon cycle.

729

A JAZERIEL AND ERGEDIEL GIBBOUS-MOON-ANGEL SPREAD FOR GETTING RID OF FEARS OF MAKING A FOOL OF YOURSELF IN PUBLIC

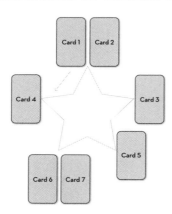

Purpose and background information:

These two angels are also especially helpful for taking away fears, especially where we doubt ourselves.

Card 1: Have you always felt uneasy in a group of people/when attention is on you? Was this caused by a specific incident where you were made to feel foolish? **Card 2:** Have there been/are there still people who make you feel self-conscious/bad about yourself? How can this be avoided? **Card 3:** If this is spoiling your social/work life, would counseling/cognitive behavioral therapy help? **Card 4:** Should you go for/learn Reiki/another energy therapy/adopt relaxation techniques to get in tune with yourself? **Card 5:** Should you consider acting/singing classes/joining a choir where you can adopt a public persona, or learn coping techniques? **Card 6:** Should you limit social/work events to where there are people you are comfortable with, or make yourself useful in the background to gain confidence? **Card 7:** Will you overcome this?

What you should use:

The twenty-two Major cards and the sixteen Court cards.

When:

Day 13 or 14 of the moon cycle.

730

A BALSAMIC OR WANING CRESCENT MOON ANGEL SPREAD IF YOU JUST CANNOT SLEEP OR ARE TROUBLED WITH NIGHTMARES

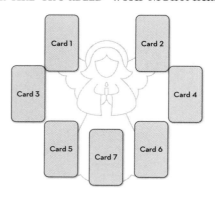

Purpose and background information:

Protected by Tagriel, Atheniel, and Amnixiel who are almost transparent with a single star on their headdress and silver-gray hair.

Card 1 have you always had sleep problems/is this recent due to extra pressure at work/relationship problem/worries about money? **Card 2** have you been working too hard/not looking after yourself properly/maybe should have a health checkup to eliminate minor physical issues/allergies? **Card 3** are you bringing work home/watching movies to relax late into the night/should you deliberately switch off activity for a couple of hours before sleep (get up early if necessary)? **Card 4** do you need to resolve the stresses in your life however caused? **Card 5** will it help to use oils/massage/relaxation/natural sleep remedies in a bedtime routine? **Card 6** should you visit a natural health practitioner/a sleep clinic/a counselor to get back in balance with yourself/establish a good sleep routine/? **Card 7** will peaceful sleep be soon restored?

What you should use:

The 22 Major cards and the 16 Court cards.

When:

Days 27, 28, and 29 (if needed) of the moon cycle.

731
A WANING HALF-MOON-ANGELS SPREAD FOR FINDING YOURSELF SOME PRIVACY AT HOME IF YOU HAVE A FULL HOUSE

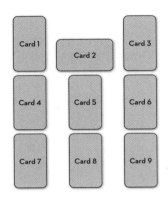

Purpose and background information:
Protected by Geliel, Requiel, Abrinael, and Aziel, mistier but still shimmering silver and gold from their wings and haloes.

Card 1: Can you create, for yourself/self and partner, private living space within your bedroom, if necessary, that is off limits? **Card 2:** Is there space for an extension to your house, whether upward or outward, to create more room? **Card 3:** If sharing with teenagers/older generations, can you give them some self-contained facilities/limit interference in your organization? **Card 4:** Should you create a timetable for family times/meals/bathroom use/chores so frustrations are minimized/you aren't providing 24/7 room service? **Card 5:** Should there be a neutral weekly time when differences can be peacefully aired? **Card 6:** Can you/your partner get away for weekends/buy a fun vehicle to escape? **Card 7:** What advantages are there of having a shared home? **Card 8:** Is there/must there be a time limit/should overgrown baby birds be helped to get their own places? **Card 9:** Will you one day have an empty nest/look back with fondness on crowded times?

What you should use:
The forty Minor cards, Aces to Tens, and the sixteen Court cards.

When:
Days 22–25 of the moon cycle.

732
A HAURVATAT ANGEL-OF-GATHERINGS SPREAD FOR A HARMONIOUS FAMILY CELEBRATION

Purpose and background information:
Originally a Zoroastrian deity of plants and drink and creation, described as an angel carrying a full-moon sphere.

Card 1: If you have difficult people coming, can you dilute them with more benign relatives to keep the peace? **Card 2:** Is it important that everyone gather together, or could any potential adversaries or sharp-tongued folk be invited to an alternative mini-celebration? **Card 3:** What activities/entertainment/buffet seating, etc., do you have available to keep everyone occupied and out of mischief? **Card 4:** Will the occasion flow harmoniously and pleasurably?

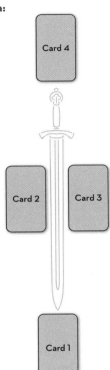

What you should use:
The twenty-two Major cards and the sixteen Court cards.

When:
Any full moon during the month of the occasion, or the Monday nearest to the celebration.

733

A REQUIEL WANING-HALF-MOON-ANGEL SPREAD FOR PERSUADING A STUBBORN PARTNER TO MOVE BACK HOME AFTER THEY STORMED OUT

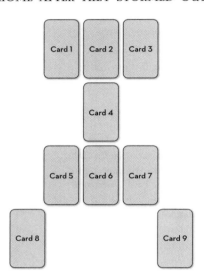

Purpose and background information:

Requiel is helpful for softening histrionics or volatile people and behavior.

CARD 1: Is this your partner's general reaction to problems, or was this a one-off overreaction because s/he was stressed? **CARD 2:** Do you generally have to make peace, or wait for calm to be restored? **CARD 3:** Do you want your partner back, even if the separation wasn't caused by you? **CARD 4:** Is it best that you meet on neutral ground, or act as if nothing has happened, or make online/text overtures/turn up where you know s/he will be? **CARD 5:** Is there anyone who stirs the pot/offers refuge/knows how to deal with this? **CARD 6:** Will your partner return if you just wait? **CARD 7:** Are there good times ahead, or will this recur at the next crisis? **CARD 8:** Does your partner need to/will they grow up? **CARD 9:** If not, will you get tired of this/next time maybe not invite them back?

What you should use:

The twenty-two Major cards and the sixteen Court cards.

When:

Day 23 of the moon cycle.

734

AN AZIEL WANING-HALF-MOON-ANGEL SPREAD FOR PROTECTING A RELATIVE YOU KNOW IS BEING ABUSED BUT DENIES IT

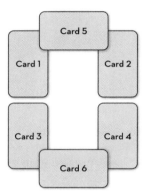

Purpose and background information:

Aziel is very protective of all in danger or sorrow.

CARD 1: Should/can you give your relative plenty of time without pressure to talk/emphasizing that you are always there, whatever the need? **CARD 2:** However unwilling s/he may be, can you set up a code conversation so s/he can always call for help/the number of a prepaid taxi? **CARD 3:** Can you offer a helpline number/phone a helpline yourself for advice on how best to help your relative? **CARD 4:** If any children are in danger, should this override your relative's right to confidentiality? **CARD 5:** Will s/he get away and start a new life? **CARD 6:** In the meantime, will s/he be safe?

What you should use:

The twenty-two Major cards and the sixteen Court cards.

When:

Day 25 of the moon cycle.

735
A GABRIEL ARCHANGEL-OF-THE-MOON SPREAD IF YOU OR YOUR PARTNER ARE VERY ANXIOUS DURING PREGNANCY

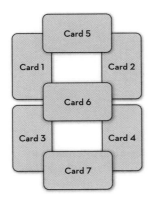

Purpose and background information:
Gabriel is the supreme Archangel of fertility, pregnancy, mothers, children, and psychic powers, described as clothed in silver or dark blue with a mantle of stars and a crescent moon for her halo.

CARD 1: Is this your first child/a baby after a difficult birth, or free-floating anxiety? **CARD 2:** Are there underlying anxieties/of the baby's health in spite of scan/unanswered relationship/career/financial issues? **CARD 3:** Should you go alone/go together to every possible class on relaxation/massage/different birthing techniques? **CARD 4:** Should you decide what is right for you/ignore unwanted advice? **CARD 5:** Should you be open to alternative birth plans if your chosen method isn't possible at the time? **CARD 6:** Should you cut back trying to be super-efficient during pregnancy/go with your body more? **CARD 7:** Will it all be 100% worthwhile?

What you should use:
The forty Minor cards, Aces to Tens, and the sixteen Court cards.

When:
The fifth day after the new moon (counting the new moon day), or any Monday, her special day.

736
A QAPHSIEL MOON ANGEL SPREAD IF YOU KEEP LOSING OR BREAKING THINGS OF IMPORTANCE

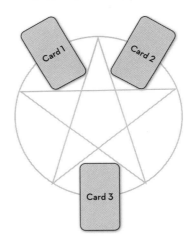

Purpose and background information:
Qaphsiel, a burgundy-robed stately waning-moon angel, who cares for our possessions and guards against accidents.

CARD 1: Have you always lost/mislaid/dropped things? Is it getting worse? **CARD 2:** Are you especially stressed/overworked/always rushing? Should you slow down and check more to avoid mishaps? **CARD 3:** Once you have adopted a more leisurely, thoughtful attitude to life, will this problem cease/greatly diminish?

What you should use:
The twenty-two Major cards.

When:
At a waning moon.

737

AN UWULA, ANGEL OF ECLIPSES OF THE SUN AND MOON SPREAD FOR LETTING GO OF OLD GUILT

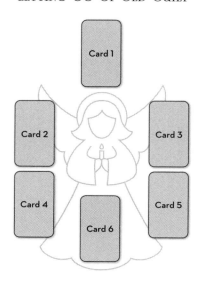

Purpose and background information:

The angel who helps us to make a transition, shedding what is redundant so we can go forward. She has a silver veil.

CARD 1: Is there any way you can repair the damage now, or was it long ago and so unfixable? **CARD 2:** Was it all your fault, or were you made to feel guilty/responsible when you weren't? **CARD 3:** Can you accept that you view your mistake/omission/commission with the wisdom of present hindsight/knowledge that you didn't have then? **CARD 4:** Can you do a good deed in your present world to assuage the guilt? **CARD 5:** Is holding on to the guilt counterproductive, preventing you learning from past mistakes? **CARD 6:** Is it time to let go?

What you should use:

The twenty-two Major cards and the sixteen Court cards.

When:

Any eclipse, or the night before the crescent moon.

738

A YAHRIEL, ANGEL-OF-THE-CHANGING-MOON-PHASES SPREAD FOR A MUCH-NEEDED VACATION OR SABBATICAL

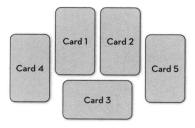

Purpose and background information:

When you feel burned out but feel guilty about slowing down.

Yahriel shimmers with different intensity according to the moon phase.

CARD 1: Is there any way you can take leave/have unused holiday soon? **CARD 2:** Why are you afraid of stepping back? That the world will not/will manage without you? **CARD 3:** Should you/partner/family plan a spontaneous easy travel/stay where you have a vacation, as opposed to organized activities involving complex traveling? **CARD 4:** If you do this, will you get a taste for vacations? **CARD 5:** Could this be the beginning of a better quality of lifestyle/relationships?

What you should use:

The forty Minor cards, Aces to Tens.

When:

Any day as the moon moves into a new phase.

739

A PHUEL MOON SPREAD IF YOU ARE PLANNING A SAILING/WATER SPORTS HOLIDAY BUT ARE NERVOUS AROUND WATER

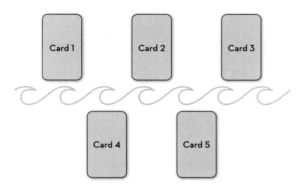

Purpose and background information:

When you really want to go on the vacation because of the person/people who have invited you. Phuel is often called Lord of the Moon and shines blue, green, and silver, especially in full moonlight.

Card 1: Is it possible to choose a location by a lake or river where there are also land-based activities? **Card 2:** Is there time for a crash course in swimming/lifesaving for nervous beginners, so you know you are safe? **Card 3:** Can you have a weekend before you go, watching and trying out one or two water-based activities so you are not self-conscious? **Card 4:** Should you check out the company providing equipment for reliability, to allay worries? **Card 5:** Will you have a brilliant time even if not 100% converted to life on the water?

What you should use:

The forty Minor cards and the sixteen Court cards.

When:

A Monday, day of the moon.

740

AN OFANIEL ARCHANGEL-OF-THE-MOON WHEEL FOR GETTING BACK IN TOUCH WITH YOUR NATURAL FERTILITY RHYTHMS IF YOU HAVE HAD MEDICAL INTERVENTION

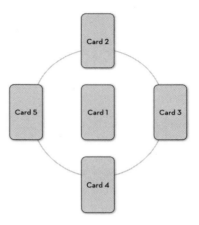

Purpose and background information:

Ofaniel turns the Moon wheel through the months of the year. He has been described as having 100 pairs of silver wings and being able to see everywhere at once. He also regulates the stars as the wheel of the year brings each new constellation into focus.

Card 1: Does your body need a rest to get back its natural rhythms before any more attempts at conception? **Card 2:** Should you take a month or two to watch the moon in the sky and link it with your moods and the ebbs and flows of your body? **Card 3:** Should you restore a spontaneous and joyous element to lovemaking as far as possible, in order to make the process an act of love and creation even if further intervention is needed? **Card 4:** Should you and your partner use relaxation, massage, meditation, and visualization techniques in order to flow with any treatment? **Card 5:** Do you have a good chance of having that beautiful family?

What you should use:

The full deck.

When:

At the crescent, waxing, or full moon.

CHAPTER 37

ANGEL AND ARCHANGEL SPREADS

Lucky Cards for Angel and Archangel Spreads

Major Cards: The High Priestess, The Hierophant, The Wheel of Fortune, Temperance.

Minor Cards: Ace, Two, and Three of Cups, Seven of Cups, Ten of Cups.

Court Cards: Princess and Queen of Cups.

About the Angel and Archangel Spreads

Each angel and Archangel offers assistance and guidance in different areas of our lives, not just in spiritual matters but also in practical needs. Since these are very special Spreads, you should allow plenty of time to contemplate not only the outer but inner meaning of the selected cards. Angel Spreads are especially good for personal readings. You can light a white candle and floral incense to add extra atmosphere. Angel Spreads not only answer questions, but connect us with the help and protection of the angel of the Spread.

741
A GUARDIAN-ANGEL SPREAD IF YOU ARE FEELING ALONE OR AFRAID

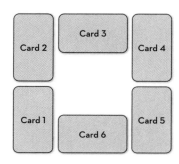

Purpose and background information:
Whether or not you know your guardian angel, to gain strength and support when life seems bleak. Picture your guardian angel as shimmering light.

Card 1: How can you feel the presence of your guardian angel in your life at this time? **Card 2:** What sign in the everyday world can your angel reveal so you know you are not alone? **Card 3:** What is the help you most need from your angel, rather than what you think you need? **Card 4:** Will earthly help/support come to you? **Card 5:** How can you most help yourself? **Card 6:** What special blessings will your angel bring into your life?

What you should use:
The twenty-two Major cards and the sixteen Court cards.

When:
As twilight falls.

742
AN ARCHANGEL SACHIEL SPREAD FOR A PERMANENT JOB IF YOU CAN ONLY GET TEMPORARY WORK

Purpose and background information:

When you need job security. Sachiel is pictured with a rich purple and golden halo and blue and purple wings. He is the Archangel of Jupiter.

Card 1: Will your current workplace offer more permanent employment if you ask? **Card 2:** Is there one particular place you have recently worked where you did especially well that would put you on a future vacancy list? **Card 3:** Is there an extra qualification/expertise that would make it easier to get a permanent job? **Card 4:** What special help would you ask of Archangel Sachiel to open the right doors to permanent employment? **Card 5:** Will you succeed?

What you should use:

The forty Minor cards, Aces to Tens, and the sixteen Court cards.

When:

Thursday, Sachiel's special day.

743
A BARIEL ANGEL-OF-SMALL-MIRACLES SPREAD IF YOU NEED A SMALL MIRACLE TO SAVE YOUR HOME FROM REPOSSESSION OR YOUR BUSINESS FROM CLOSURE

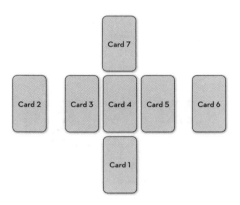

Purpose and background information:

When you know that if you had more time, you would have a chance of saving everything. Bariel is pictured in indigo/burgundy robes.

Card 1: How long a stay of execution would give you a fighting chance? **Card 2:** Can you successfully renegotiate a last-minute deal through a debt charity/business association/direct appeal to the creditors? **Card 3:** What will change to enable you to make a more permanent rescue plan? **Card 4:** Is there anybody/an unrealized asset, an overdue expected incoming payment due to you that would buy you time? **Card 5:** What small miracle from Bariel would enable you to carry on/recover in the longer term? **Card 6:** Have you had enough fighting and want to give up? **Card 7:** Will you win through?

What you should use:

The full deck.

When:

Any time during the Scorpio star period that Bariel rules, October 24–November 22, October his month; or any urgent time, especially when the moon is waning in Scorpio during any month.

744

A HAMIED ANGEL-OF-BIG-MIRACLES SPREAD WHEN A CLOSE FRIEND OR RELATIVE IS GIVEN A POOR FUTURE PROGNOSIS

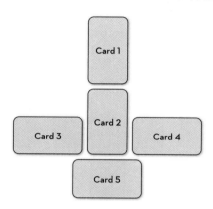

Purpose and background information:

If someone you care for is told there is no further treatment and it is just a matter of time. Hamied is described as dazzling white.

Card 1: Is a miracle or at least a major remission possible? **Card 2:** What is the most helpful way you can make the remaining days, long or short, happy and fulfilling? **Card 3:** Do you know what the person really wants in terms of end-of-life care? **Card 4:** Are they refusing to give up/determined to beat this/want to visit special places you could make possible? **Card 5:** What blessing can Hamied most bring in terms of a miracle, either of remission or a good remaining quality of life?

What you should use:

The twenty-two Major cards.

When:

A Sunday, or the beginning of a month.

745

AN ARCHANGEL CASSIEL SPREAD FOR THE RETURN OF GOOD FORTUNE IF YOU ARE IN A DOWN PERIOD OF YOUR LIFE

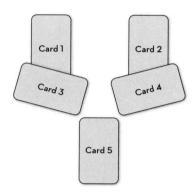

Purpose and background information:

When you are doing all you can, but life isn't giving you the breaks. Cassiel is described as riding a dragon, wearing dark burgundy or indigo robes with indigo flames sparking from his halo. He is the Archangel of Saturn.

Card 1: Is there a specific person or situation that stands in the way of the changing of your fortunes? **Card 2:** Can you/how can you remove this obstacle/do you need help? **Card 3:** Would a fresh approach/a new start/a new location change your fortune? **Card 4:** What blessings can Cassiel bring to create that change in fortunes? **Card 5:** If you persevere, will you have good fortune again?

What you should use:

The forty Minor cards, Aces to Tens, and the 26 Court cards.

When:

A Saturday, day of Cassiel.

746
A SUIEL ANGEL-OF-PROTECTION-AGAINST-VOLCANOES-AND-EARTHQUAKES SPREAD FOR A PERMANENTLY ANGRY PARTNER

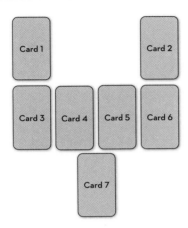

Purpose and background information:

When whatever you say or do, your partner veers between irritability and anger. Suiel is a deep-red and golden-brown angel.

Card 1: Has your partner always been angry, or did s/he learn it from a family member in childhood? **Card 2:** Is it triggered by work stress/financial worries/children, or reaction whatever the circumstances? **Card 3:** Is your partner different/charming with other people/outside the home? **Card 4:** Are you afraid of the anger/potential violence tipping over into violence, in which case what support/refuge are you/should you urgently be seeking? **Card 5:** Will your partner acknowledge the problem and seek anger management/psychological help, or does s/he blame you for provoking him/her? **Card 6:** What protection and courage do you most seek from Suiel? **Card 7:** Should you leave until you know your partner has changed, or is it too late for that?

What you should use:

The twenty-two Major cards and the sixteen Court cards.

When:

The end of the waning moon.

747
A DERDEKEA HOUSEHOLD-ANGEL SPREAD IF YOU HAVE MOVED INTO YOUR OWN PLACE AFTER AN ACRIMONIOUS DIVORCE

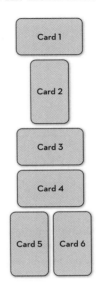

Purpose and background information:

When it's not what you hoped for but it's yours. Derdekea wears green robes and baskets of herbs.

Card 1: Can/will you make this home just as you want because it's yours? **Card 2:** Financially, is there more you are entitled to, or are you tired of fighting? **Card 3:** Do you need time to settle/shake off the past and make a sanctuary for yourself (and children if they are living with you?) **Card 4:** Is this/do you want this to be your permanent home, or just an interim base until you get on your feet again? **Card 5:** What do you miss most about your old home/can you restore here what you have left behind? **Card 6:** What blessings do you ask Derdekea for most to make this a truly happy home?

What you should use:

The twenty-two Major cards and the sixteen Court cards.

When:

A Sunday, or the beginning of a month.

748

A MIHAEL ANGEL-OF-THE-REGROWTH-OF-TRUST SPREAD FOR THE RESTORATION OF LOVE AFTER A BETRAYAL

Purpose and background information:

When you are trying again to make your relationship work, but it's hard to forget. Mihael has deep green wings and a halo.

Card 1: Are you confident that your partner has given up all contact with the person who came between you/will not see them again except if necessary in a work setting? **Card 2:** If you have doubts, are these based on new suspicious behavior, or natural fears because of broken trust? **Card 3:** Should you move on right away from all the bad memories or rebuild in a familiar setting? **Card 4:** If you are distrustful, can/should you talk over anger/resentment with a counselor/trusted friend, rather than let it eat away or repress it? **Card 5:** Do you both want to be together, not because of finances/children, etc., but to forge a new, stronger relationship out of the ashes of the old? **Card 6:** What blessings do you seek from Mihael on your restored relationship? **Card 7:** Can you accept that it will not be the same, but stronger, as a result of the determination to make it work? **Card 8:** Will trust regrow?

What you should use:

The twenty-two major cards and the sixteen Court cards.

When:

A Thursday, Mihael's day.

749

A SAMAEL ARCHANGEL-OF-CLEANSING-FIRE SPREAD FOR SHAKING UP INERTIA IN YOUR WORKPLACE WHERE YOU DO ALL THE WORK

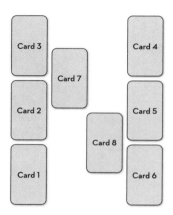

Purpose and background information:

When you are constantly stressed and exhausted and nobody else is bothered. Samael, the Archangel of Mars, is described with blue and red flames in his halo and midnight-blue wings, with a huge gleaming dark-gold sword.

Card 1: Has your workplace always been lackadaisical, or have there been recent staff changes with a different work ethic? **Card 2:** If you do not do the work, will clients/customers suffer? Are you supporting an indifferent organization? **Card 3:** Why do you feel responsible for the efficient running? What would happen if you stepped back? **Card 4:** Do you have the necessary salary/status/authority to change working practices/insist others do their share? **Card 5:** If not, should you demand it/will you be given it/insist that the person with the kudos act to sort the situation out? **Card 6:** Should you take all leave owing to you as a block, so the organization has to cope without you or it falls apart? **Card 7:** What special help do you need from Samael to right the situation? **Card 8:** Do you want to stay, or is it time to move on where you'll be paid and properly valued?

What you should use:

The full deck.

750
A ZADKIEL ARCHANGEL-OF-TRUTH-AND-INTEGRITY SPREAD IF A FRIEND ASKS YOU IF THEIR PARTNER IS HAVING AN AFFAIR

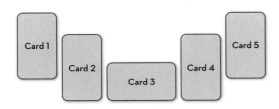

Purpose and background information:
When you know the truth but do not want to cause further hurt. Zadkiel is described as surrounded by pale blue light with sky-blue wings, with a white standard bearing the white background and red cross of Michael, whom he defends.

CARD 1: Can/should you sidestep the issue by asking what is making them doubt their partner? **CARD 2:** Should you lie to save your friend's feelings/risk being blamed if the affair comes out? **CARD 3:** Should you confront the guilty party/insist they deal with it? **CARD 4:** What help should you seek from Zadkiel so your response causes the least hurt? **CARD 5:** Should you keep right out of it?

What you should use:
The twenty-two Major cards.

When:
A Thursday, day of Zadkiel.

751
A HARIEL ANGEL-OF-ANIMALS SPREAD IF YOU WANT TO RUN AN ANIMAL SANCTUARY

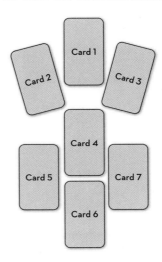

Purpose and background information:
If you love animals of all kinds and want to help them.

CARD 1: Do you see your sanctuary as a hobby on land attached to your home, allowing people to come and visit on weekends in return for a donation for animal feed? **CARD 2:** Do you want to set up an animal charity/make it your full-time living? **CARD 3:** Do you want your sanctuary to become profitable, focusing on rare species/regular events/a center for animal study/research? **CARD 4:** Do you have/can you acquire land/resources to set up initially/will you need to do paid work as well? **CARD 5:** Do you need/want any special training/working at an existing animal sanctuary/rescue center, or will you learn as you go? **CARD 6:** What blessings would you seek from Hariel? **CARD 7:** Is this a viable idea that can be developed into something bigger?

What you should use:
The full deck.

When:
A Friday, Hariel's day.

752
A MICHAEL ARCHANGEL-OF-THE-SUN SPREAD FOR INDEPENDENT LIVING AT ANY AGE

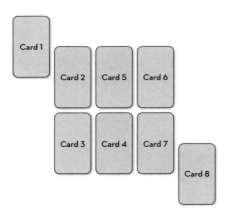

Purpose and background information:
When you have decided you are happy with independent living, but others keep trying to marry you off. Michael has a golden shield and sword.

Card 1: Are you enjoying/aiming for living by yourself in your own way and space? **Card 2:** When friends try to set you up on blind dates at dinner parties, should you explain once and for all that you would love to meet them for dinner/meet their friends, but not to be matched up? **Card 3:** Should you resist offers to tag along on other people's holidays, especially as babysitter/book yourself on trips to exciting non-child-friendly locations? **Card 4:** Should you avoid going on singles holidays to meet other unattached people where the idea is matching you up? **Card 5:** Have you rehearsed your polite refusal for unhappy husbands/wives who assume you are desperate for a bit on the side/explain to their spouses you do not do second-hand? **Card 6:** What blessing do you seek for Michael to make a happy life even happier? **Card 7:** Should you rejoice in your single life/ignore pitying comments if you love your fur babies, or avoid the company of those who have babies/sprinkle every conversation *with my better half*? **Card 8:** should you keep an open mind in case you ever change your mind?

What you should use:
The forty Minor cards and the sixteen Court cards

When:
At the end of any month.

753
A RAPHAEL ARCHANGEL-OF-TRAVELERS SPREAD IF YOU NEED TO LEARN ANOTHER LANGUAGE FAST

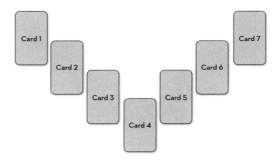

Purpose and background information:
When you find that your brain seizes up at the thought, but time is running out. Raphael is described as radiating the colors of early morning sunlight, a green healing ray emanating from his halo.

Card 1: Should you use an online program that you build into your day, every day? **Card 2:** Should you use downloads/recorded classes that you carry with you for any spare moments? **Card 3:** Should you book a face-to-face class fast? **Card 4:** Should you start to think in your new language whenever possible? **Card 5:** What help do you most need from Raphael in increasing your fluency? **Card 6:** Should you learn from the locals in everyday situations when you arrive? **Card 7:** Should you aim to meet people who speak your language when you arrive?

What you should use:
The forty Minor cards, Aces to Tens.

When:
A Wednesday, the day of Raphael.

754
AN ANAEL ARCHANGEL-OF-LASTING-LOVE SPREAD IF YOU ADMIRE SOMEONE FROM AFAR

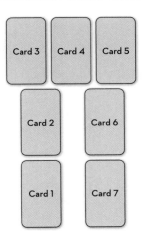

Purpose and background information:

When you are suffering from an unrequited love that is holding you back from finding other love. Anael is described as being surrounded by rose and green light, with silver wings.

Card 1: Is this a long-standing attraction, or have you recently encountered them and fallen instantly in love? **Card 2:** Is this person free to love/someone you could get to know within your present world? **Card 3:** Have you ever indicated your interest? Would this be possible? **Card 4:** Has the other person ever shown interest in you/is shy but aware of you? **Card 5:** What would be gained by a friendly approach/conversation? **Card 6:** What would be the worst that could happen? **Card 7:** Should you seek other love, or let this unrequited love develop if it is meant?

What you should use:

The twenty-two Major cards and the sixteen Court cards.

When:

A Friday, the day of Anael.

755
AN ARIEL ARCHANGEL-OF-FREEDOM SPREAD IF YOU HAVE BEEN HAVING AN AFFAIR FOR YEARS, BUT YOUR LOVER WILL NOT LEAVE THEIR PARTNER

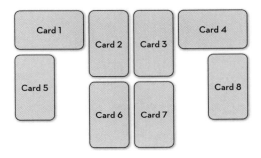

Purpose and background information:

When you are getting tired of promises and spending every holiday alone. Ariel is described with long silver hair, with a cloak of radiant white with rainbows at the hem.

Card 1: Were the reasons your lover could not leave their partner/young children, etc., valid when you were first together? **Card 2:** Have they been replaced by other reasons that seem to have no end in sight? **Card 3:** Should you ask your partner for a definite time you will be openly together? **Card 4:** If your lover will not/cannot commit, should you widen your own social circle so you are not always waiting for the call? **Card 5:** Should you issue an ultimatum, even if you suspect what the answer will be? **Card 6:** Is there more benefit to staying in the relationship than leaving? **Card 7:** How can Ariel best bring you the freedom to be with your love/the courage to move on? **Card 8:** Should/will you find a love who is there for you 24/7?

What you should use:

The twenty-two Major cards and the sixteen Court cards.

When:

A Friday, Ariel's day.

756

A JOPHIEL ARCHANGEL-OF-JOY SPREAD IF YOU FEEL UNHAPPY BUT DO NOT KNOW WHY

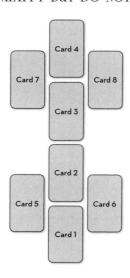

Purpose and background information:

When life is not as good as it might be. Jophiel is described as with an orange sun-like halo, radiating sunbeams.

Card 1: Have you felt unhappy for a while, or is it a recent setback/loss? **Card 2:** Does a particular person/people/situation/environment make you unhappy? Can you change this? **Card 3:** Do you constantly feel under the weather/exhausted trying to do too much? Should you take a step back? **Card 4:** Do you spend too much time making other people happy at the expense of yourself? **Card 5:** Do you always appear happy instead of flowing with the down times? **Card 6:** What can you do for yourself to make your life happier? **Card 7:** What form of happiness can Jophiel bring into your life? **Card 8:** What can you ask others to do to make you happy? Will they?

What you should use:

The whole deck.

When:

A Sunday, Jophiel's day.

757

A METATRON ARCHANGEL-OF-ADVANCEMENT SPREAD IF YOU DIDN'T GET THE PROMOTION YOU WANTED

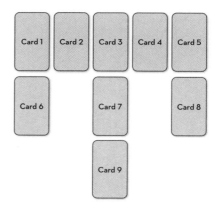

Purpose and background information:

When the interview and assessment went well, but the results were not what you wanted. Metatron is described as a pillar of light from which sparks flash, with thirty-six wings and eyes as brilliant as the sun.

Card 1: Did the promoted candidate have unfair personal connections within the organization? **Card 2:** Can you appeal without creating more problems for yourself? **Card 3:** Can you work under the new person? Will resentment show? **Card 4:** Can/should you transfer within the organization/apply for a different role not controlled by the person? **Card 5:** Should you leave the organization if there is a glass-ceiling policy? **Card 6:** Should you focus on a better quality of life outside work/start your own business? **Card 7:** What strengths can Metatron give you to rise above this? **Card 8:** Will the promoted candidate not stay in the new post long? **Card 9:** Will you get a promotion next time, here or elsewhere?

What you should use:

The forty Minor cards, Aces to Tens, and the sixteen Court cards.

When:

A Saturday.

758
A URIEL ARCHANGEL-OF-FIRE-AND-PROTECTION SPREAD WHEN YOU ARE TIRED OF BEING TREATED BADLY OR DISREGARDED

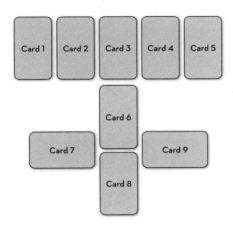

Purpose and background information:

When you feel you are going to lose your temper and walk out. Uriel is described with a bright flame-like halo blazing in the darkness and a fiery sword, flashes of lightning.

Card 1: Is showing your anger the best way to shock the perpetrator/s? **Card 2:** Has a long-standing situation become worse, or is it a new situation you have walked into? **Card 3:** Why do you accept the role of fall guy/gal? Do you have a choice? **Card 4:** Have you always done your best for others? How has this kindness become abused? **Card 5:** Is the perpetrator/s thoughtless/selfish/has a deliberate disregard for your needs? **Card 6:** Should you temporarily stop doing more than your share until you are appreciated? **Card 7:** Should you speak out calmly but firmly/state future conditions? **Card 8:** What fire of Uriel will make you be taken seriously/respected? **Card 9:** If it will not change, is it time to move on?

What you should use:

The full deck.

When:

A Tuesday or Saturday, Uriel's days.

759
AN IRIS ANGEL-OF-THE-RAINBOW SPREAD FOR FORGIVING A WRONG DONE TO YOU BY A FRIEND

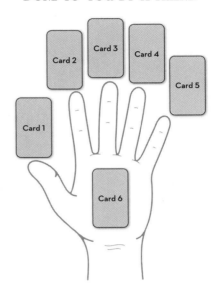

Purpose and background information:

When it hurts twice as much because you have been friends for years. Iris is pictured with rainbow wings and carrying a purple-and-yellow iris and a golden lily.

Card 1: Can you understand what went wrong/someone interfering in the friendship/great stress in your friend's life/impulse? **Card 2:** Has your friend expressed regret/tried to put it right, or is s/he too ashamed to approach you? **Card 3:** Can you make the first move/talk about what went wrong/ignore it and start again? **Card 4:** Will it take time to regain trust/will you always be more wary around your friend? **Card 5:** Can you be sure it will not happen again? **Card 6:** Even if you can forgive, is the friendship best let go?

What you should use:

The twenty-two Major cards and the sixteen Court cards.

When:

A Friday, Iris's day.

AN AZRAEL ARCHANGEL OF COMFORT IN LOSS IF YOUR LOVER HAS DIED BUT YOU CANNOT SHARE YOUR GRIEF

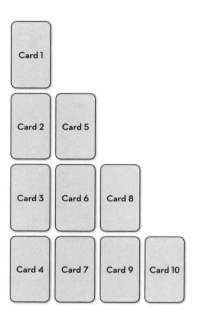

Purpose and background information:

If your lover's family does not know anything about you. Azrael is described with a halo of dark purple flames, huge, dark wings, and a deep red and purple enfolding cloak.

CARD 1: Can/should you go to the funeral as an old friend without arousing suspicion? **CARD 2:** If not, should you have your own private memorial/planting a tree/returning to a place with happy memories? **CARD 3:** Do you have close friends/a member of your own family who knew your lover to support you? **CARD 4:** Should you resist the temptation to go and see/go where the family will be? **CARD 5:** If there is going to be fallout from a will, especially if the family doesn't know of your existence, should you avoid any direct contact if possible? **CARD 6:** Should you take as much time as you need to grieve/take time off work until you can face the world, even if you cannot explain the real reason? **CARD 7:** Should you avoid major decisions regarding joint property/inheritances until you feel stronger? **CARD 8:** If your lover left you nothing tangible, should you let it go even if you were together for years? **CARD 9:** What consolation can you seek from Azrael that you most need? **CARD 10:** Will you find happiness again?

What you should use:

The twenty-two Major cards and the sixteen Court cards.

When:

A Tuesday, Azrael's day.

ZODIAC ANGEL SPREADS

Purpose and background information for all 12 Spreads:
Each zodiac sign has its own ruling angel that answers a special question in your life.

When and how:
You can pick the appropriate Spread when the moon enters a particular zodiac sign during the month, during the actual zodiac period, and especially on your birthday. The mini-Spreads can also give you a quick insight into different areas of your life as needed, any time during the month or year.

Use the full deck for each Spread.

761
THE MACHIDIEL OR MICHIDIEL ARIES WARRIOR-ANGEL SPREAD FOR ACTING OR SPEAKING OUT

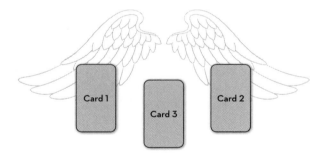

March 21–April 20. Machidiel has a sparkling golden-red halo and wings.

CARD 1: Where and how do you need to assert yourself? **CARD 2:** What challenges/pitfalls to success should you be aware of? **CARD 3:** How will Machidiel help you attain the results you want?

762
ASMODEL OR ASHMODEL, THE TAURUS ANGEL OF HARMONY, FOR BRINGING HARMONY TO YOURSELF IF OTHERS ARE CAUSING STRESS

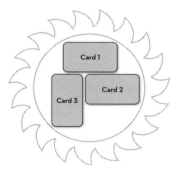

April 21–May 21. Asmodel is surrounded by pink rays.

CARD 1: How can you restore more harmony into your life if others are creating chaos/causing trouble? **CARD 2:** What challenges/pitfalls to finding harmony should you be aware of? **CARD 3:** How will Asmodel smooth your path so you feel at peace?

763

THE AMBRIEL OR AMBIEL GEMINI-MESSENGER-AND-TRAVEL-ANGEL SPREAD FOR PERSUADING OTHERS TO ACCEPT YOUR POINT OF VIEW

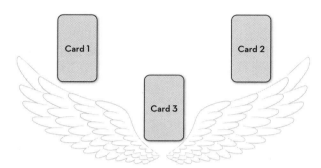

May 22–June 21. Ambriel wears the colors of early-morning sunlight.

CARD 1: How can you get others to see that yours is the best way forward/the right solution to a problem? **CARD 2:** If there is dissension, what challenges/pitfalls to getting your words heard should you be aware of? **CARD 3:** How will Ambriel create a receptive atmosphere so you will succeed?

764

A MURIEL CANCERIAN ANGEL-OF-THE-HAPPY-FAMILY SPREAD TO UNITE THE FAMILY IF EVERYONE IS ALWAYS TOO BUSY

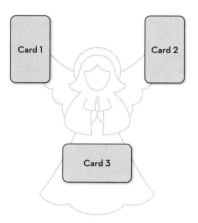

June 22–July 22. Muriel is described as a silvery and pearl-robed healing angel with her magic carpet of dreams.

CARD 1: How can you preserve/improve happy family life when everyone is going in their own direction and rarely meet? **CARD 2:** What challenges/pitfalls that stand in the way of togetherness should you be aware of? **CARD 3:** How will Muriel draw the family together in unity?

765

A VERCHIEL LEO ANGEL OF ACHIEVEMENT AND FULFILMENT TO DECIDE BETWEEN GOING FOR THE BIG TIME OR ENJOYING LIFE AS IT IS

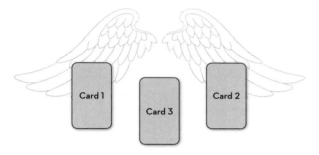

July 23–August 23. Verchiel, the golden joy bringer, is surrounded by sunbeams.

CARD 1: Should you strive for success/fame and fortune? **CARD 2:** What challenges/pitfalls would result from going for broke that you should be aware of? **CARD 3:** How will Verchiel help you find the fulfillment that is right for you, both short- and long-term?

766

A HAMALIEL OR HAMAIEL VIRGOAN ANGEL-OF-PERFECTION SPREAD FOR WHEN YOU ARE STRUGGLING TO FINISH A PROJECT OR ASSIGNMENT

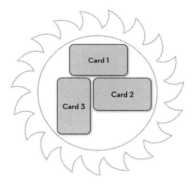

August 24–September 22. Hamaliel is described as surrounded by misty forest green.

CARD 1: Should you/how can you accept that what you have achieved is good enough and doesn't need constant revising for 100% perfection? **CARD 2:** What challenges/pitfalls stop you from accepting the assessment of others that you have done well? **CARD 3:** How will Hamaliel help you attain/send/hand in your work without worry?

767
A ZURIEL ANGEL-OF-LIBRA SPREAD OF CALM AND REASON IF YOU KEEP WAVERING REGARDING AN URGENT DECISION

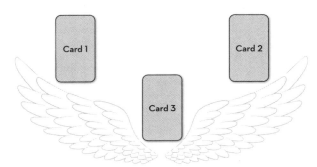

September 23–October 23. Zuriel is described as a pale blue angel who brings calm and reason to any situation.

CARD 1: Do you know the right decision? What is it? **CARD 2:** What challenges/pitfalls such as fear of causing unavoidable hurt or criticism are causing unnecessary delays? **CARD 3:** How will Zuriel give you the quiet confidence to say what must be said?

768
A BARIEL ANGEL-OF-SCORPIO SPREAD OF LEARNING FROM LIFE TO AVOID MAKING THE SAME MISTAKES AGAIN

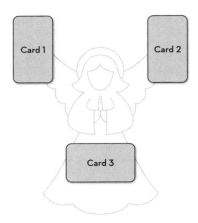

October 24–November 22. We have already met Bariel in another role, as angel of small miracles. He wears indigo/burgundy robes but is sometimes pictured in the colors of sunset.

CARD 1: What old patterns should you avoid/mistakes you should not make again? **CARD 2:** What is drawing you back to an old pattern in the belief that it will be different this time? **CARD 3:** What insights and wisdom will Bariel offer to guide you on a new better path?

769

AN ADNACHIEL OR ADVACHIEL THE SAGITTARIAN ANGEL-OF-LEARNING-AND-EXPLORATION SPREAD TO TAKE A MAJOR DEGREE OR LEARNING PROGRAM LATER IN LIFE

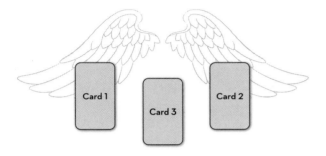

November 23–December 21. Adnachiel has bright yellow robes and carries a golden bow and arrow.

CARD 1: Will you succeed in this new study/program?
CARD 2: What challenges/pitfalls caused by others and other demands might hold you back? **CARD 3:** What encouragement when you have doubt will Adnachiel bring to your new venture?

770

A HANAEL OR HANIEL ANGEL-OF-CAPRICORN SPREAD TO EXERCISE WISE CAUTION TOWARD A FINANCIAL OFFER TO MAKE FAST MONEY

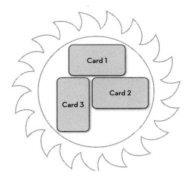

December 22–January 20. Hanael is often linked with Anael, Archangel of love. In his Capricorn role, he is described as a golden brown-robed angel with brown wings.

CARD 1: Is it best to examine the offer in detail/ask for reliable financial advice/only proceed if it is proved safe?
CARD 2: What pressures do you need to resist to make a quick decision so you will not be tempted by seemingly instant riches? **CARD 3:** What wise restraints can Hanael offer to ensure that your money remains safe, whatever you decide?

771

A CAMBIEL GUARDIAN-ARCHANGEL-OF-DETACHMENT SPREAD TO PROTECT YOU FROM BEING SWAYED BY ONE TOO MANY HARD-LUCK STORIES

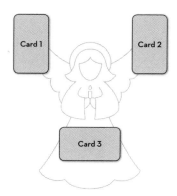

January 21–February 18. Cambiel is described as a tall, shadowy Archangel.

CARD 1: Should you make the decision to help with your head and common sense rather than your heart, especially if the same person asks time and again? **CARD 2:** What pressures will you encounter from the person in need? Your own guilt and obligation to fall for this ploy for money? **CARD 3:** What emotional detachment can Cambiel offer you to persuade the person to help themselves?

772

A PISCES BARAKIEL OR BARKIEL ARCHANGEL SPREAD TO BRING GOOD LUCK WHEN AND WHERE MOST NEEDED

February 19–March 20. Barakiel is described as a blue and gold Archangel with lightning flashing from his halo.

CARD 1: What can you do to accelerate good fortune? **CARD 2:** Who or what might hinder or hold you back from reaching for that opportunity? **CARD 3:** How can Barakiel bring unexpected factors into play to hasten good fortune?

CHAPTER 38

CRYSTAL TAROT SPREADS

Each of the twenty-two Major Tarot cards has an associated crystal. These Tarot crystal links I have found especially useful in adding an extra dimension to Tarot reading. Tarot spreads using crystals are especially powerful because they combine the meaning of each Major Tarot card associated with the crystal with the energies of the crystal. Each crystal shares the same qualities as its card.

However, below I've listed an extra quality for each crystal that complements its Tarot card.

If the associations I suggest between crystal and tarot card do not feel right, substitute your own. The authenticity of a system is whether it works for you.

The crystals you will need are all easily obtainable and cheap.

If you want to know more about the individual crystals, my *A Little Bit of Crystals* (Sterling Ethos) describes each in detail.

Table of Tarot Crystal Meanings:

Tarot Card	Associated Crystal	Crystal Meaning
The Fool/Inner Child/the essential self	Clear crystal quartz	Optimism
The Magician	Yellow citrine or brown tiger eye	Money-making gifts
The High Priestess	Purple amethyst or fluorite	Perfect inner balance
The Empress	Pink rose quartz	Nurturing gifts
The Emperor	Turquoise or blue howlite	Leadership
The Hierophant	Gray smoky quartz or deep blue sodalite	Spiritual wisdom
The Lovers	Green jade	Fidelity
The Chariot	Golden rutilated quartz or rainbow shining laboradite	Adventurous nature
Justice	Gray or brown/fawn banded agate	Truth/freedom from corruption
The Hermit	Brown glinting desert rose	Following inner promptings
The Wheel of Fortune	Green aventurine	Good luck, especially in speculation
Strength	Green and black malachite	Perseverance
The Hanged Man	Red and green bloodstone/heliotrope	Releasing fear
Death	Apache tear or jet	Light at the end of the tunnel
Temperance	Blue lace agate or mid blue and white angelite	Inner harmony and outer peace
The Devil	Red jasper	Courage to overcome any obstacles
The Tower of Freedom	Leopardskin jasper or turritella agate	The end of restrictions
The Star	Lapis lazuli	Fame and fortune through talents
The Moon	Shimmering translucent moonstone or selenite	Psychic powers
The Sun	Orange amber or carnelian	Joy, especially after sorrow/success
Judgment	Gray shining hematite or polished gold/silver iron pyrites	New growth through abandoning wha is no longer needed
The World	Aquamarine	Limitless horizons physically and in new opportunities

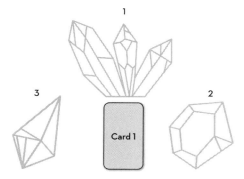

Reading your Crystal Tarot

◆ Make sure the twenty-two crystals are of similar size and shape.

◆ Choose the Tarot Crystal Spread from the twenty-two listed that is closest to your question or need. For casting each of the twenty-two Spreads, place the twenty-two stones in a drawstring bag or purse. Shake the bag and pick out of it three crystals, one at a time, purely by feel.

◆ Now set the three crystals in a triangle with the first at the apex, moving clockwise.

◆ Next shuffle the twenty-two Major cards and pick one without looking to set in the center of the triangle.

◆ Hold each of your crystals in order of picking and interpret it, firstly by its associated Tarot card meaning (for example rose quartz with the Lovers). Then as you hold the crystal, take time to feel impressions and ideas that come to you as you hold it. As I said, its basic meaning is close to its associated card, but you will receive a lot of extra information through your fingertips.

◆ Now read your chosen Tarot card and see what it says about the outcome of your question.

◆ If the Tarot card chosen is either the same as the name of the Spread or represents one of the crystals chosen, you know it is especially lucky.

Use the following three-crystal, one-card Layout for the next twenty-two Spreads (Spread numbers 773 to 795).

773
SPREAD OF THE FOOL/INNER CHILD IF YOU SEEK A NEW BEGINNING

Purpose and background information:
- Lucky card: The Fool
- Lucky crystal: clear quartz

CRYSTAL 1: Are you ready to take a chance? **CRYSTAL 2:** How can you remain true to yourself in spite of pressures to conform? **CRYSTAL 3:** What action should you take to initiate that new beginning? **CARD 1:** What will be the results of your new beginning?

774
SPREAD OF THE MAGICIAN FOR THE SUCCESS OF AN ENTREPRENEURIAL VENTURE

Purpose and background information:
- Lucky card: The Magician
- Lucky crystal: citrine or brown tiger eye.

CRYSTAL 1: Are you totally ready to launch your idea/anything missing? **CRYSTAL 2:** What difficulties will you have to overcome initially? **CRYSTAL 3:** What opportunities should you look for? **CARD 1:** Will your venture succeed immediately/take longer to evolve?

775
SPREAD OF THE HIGH PRIESTESS FOR DEVELOPING YOUR UNIQUE TALENTS IN YOUR OWN WAY

Purpose and background information:
- Lucky card: The High Priestess
- Lucky crystal: amethyst or purple fluorite

CRYSTAL 1: If you feel different, is it time to benefit from your uniqueness? **CRYSTAL 2:** Who/what stands in the way of your expressing your unique talents? **CRYSTAL 3:** What opportunities will arise from following your own rules and ethics? **CARD 1:** What will be the results of openly using your special talents and life vision?

776
SPREAD OF THE EMPRESS FOR A HAPPY PREGNANCY AND GOOD BIRTH OF A HEALTHY CHILD

Purpose and background information:
- Lucky card: The Empress
- Lucky crystal: rose quartz

CRYSTAL 1: Is it time to slow down and care for yourself more? **CRYSTAL 2:** What anxieties do you have and need to talk over to get reassurance? **CRYSTAL 3:** What are you most looking forward to with the birth of your first/new infant? **CARD 1:** Will you find that any doubts/fears were groundless once the baby is born?

777
THE SPREAD OF THE EMPEROR FOR HOLDING YOUR OWN IN AN OVERLY COMPETITIVE WORKPLACE

Purpose and background information:
- Lucky card: The Emperor
- Lucky crystal: turquoise or dyed blue howlite

CRYSTAL 1: Can you project confidence, even if you do not feel it inside? **CRYSTAL 2:** What tactics do rivals use to undermine you? **CRYSTAL 3:** What strategies can you use to get credit for all you do? **CARD 1:** Will you succeed/get the promotion/recognition/salary you deserve?

778
THE SPREAD OF THE HIEROPHANT FOR BREAKING WITH FAMILY TRADITION AND FOLLOWING THE CAREER YOU WANT

Purpose and background information:
- Lucky card: The Hierophant
- Lucky crystal: smoky quartz or sodalite

CRYSTAL 1: Are you set on your future career without personal doubt/ready/already training for it? **CRYSTAL 2:** If it's not for you, can/should you avoid following the traditional profession practiced by generations of your family in spite of pressure? **CRYSTAL 3:** Are you prepared to help your family overcome its disappointment/reservations about your career path? **CARD 1:** Will you succeed and your family realize you were right in your chosen path?

779
THE SPREAD OF THE LOVERS TO RESIST TEMPTATION TO STRAY

Purpose and background information:
- Lucky card: The Lovers
- Lucky crystal: jade

CRYSTAL 1: Should you try to improve your present relationship before looking elsewhere? **CRYSTAL 2:** What is at stake if you take the flirtation further? **CRYSTAL 3:** Can/should you keep the new relationship just as harmless flirting to make you feel better about yourself/more able to make an effort with your partner? **CARD 4:** Can you find happiness within your present relationship if you give up the fun of flirting?

780
THE SPREAD OF THE CHARIOT FOR PLANNING A MAJOR ADVENTURE IF YOUR PARTNER'S NOT ENTHUSIASTIC

Purpose and background information:
- Lucky card: The Chariot
- Lucky crystal: rutilated quartz or laboradite

CRYSTAL 1: Do you have your master plan ready to the last detail, to show your partner the benefits of the trip? **CRYSTAL 2:** Can you resolve in advance the fears/drawbacks your partner has, in order to give reassurance? **CRYSTAL 3:** Are you ready to go, with or without your partner if necessary? **CARD 1:** Will your partner come and enjoy every minute?

781
THE SPREAD OF JUSTICE IF YOUR OLDER PARENTS IGNORE ALL YOU DO FOR THEM AND CONSTANTLY PRAISE YOUR ABSENT OR NEGLECTFUL SIBLING

Purpose and background information:
- Lucky card: Justice
- Lucky crystal: gray, brown, or fawn banded agate

CRYSTAL 1: Should you withdraw from offering help/insist the other family member/s does more to help? **CRYSTAL 2:** If your sibling has always been favored, is it worth trying to get justice, or is it worth carrying on? **CRYSTAL 3:** Can you accept that what you do is out of love and that injustice is the price you pay for knowing that your parents are cared for? **CARD 1:** Will your parents become more appreciative over time/as the absent sibling increasingly shows their true colors?

782
THE SPREAD OF THE HERMIT FOR STEPPING BACK FROM AN ONGOING FAMILY OR WORKPLACE CONFLICT

Purpose and background information:
- Lucky card: The Hermit
- Lucky crystal: desert rose

Crystal 1: Are you usually the peacemaker in any situation/ is this always in your best interest? **Crystal 2:** If you intervene, do you usually end up having to choose/getting blamed by both sides? **Crystal 3:** If disputes are frequent, should you suggest counseling/workplace mediation? **Card 1:** If you step back, will this give you inner harmony/ allow you to relate to both parties on a social, not advisory, level?

783
THE SPREAD OF THE WHEEL OF FORTUNE IF YOU WANT TO KNOW IF THIS IS A GOOD TIME TO SPECULATE OR GAMBLE

Purpose and background information:
- Lucky card: The Wheel of Fortune
- Lucky crystal: green aventurine

Crystal 1: Have you explored the practical and financial implications of this speculation/gambling and applied limits? **Crystal 2:** What as-yet unknown/unrecognized factors might make this a bad choice? **Crystal 3:** Is Lady Luck with you in this venture? **Card 1:** Will the overall result be good/ break-even/a loss?

784
THE SPREAD OF STRENGTH IF YOU FEEL LIKE GIVING UP ON A RELATIONSHIP OR SITUATION

Purpose and background information:
- Lucky card: Strength
- Lucky crystal: malachite

Crystal 1: Should you persevere for now/seek support for yourself? **Crystal 2:** Who/what is proving resistant to resolution/will this change? **Crystal 3:** What new input/ favorable factors may move the impasse? **Card 1:** Will you succeed eventually if you do not give up?

785
THE SPREAD OF THE HANGED MAN FOR LETTING GO OF A RELATIONSHIP OR SITUATION THAT WILL NEVER WORK

Purpose and background information:
- Lucky card: The Hanged Man
- Lucky crystal: bloodstone/heliotrope

Crystal 1: Have you tried absolutely everything, but nothing's working? **Crystal 2:** What worries/scares you most about walking away? **Crystal 3:** What good things lie just over the horizon if you move on? **Card 1:** If you are not yet ready, should you wait until you are/something radically positive occurs?

786
THE SPREAD OF THE DEATH CARD FOR STARTING AGAIN AFTER A MAJOR LOSS OR SETBACK

Purpose and background information:
- Lucky card: Death
- Lucky crystal: Apache tear or jet

CRYSTAL 1: What light at the end of the tunnel will soon appear? **CRYSTAL 2:** What grief/fears do you still need time and space to deal with? **CRYSTAL 3:** Who/what will help you the most at this time/can you reach out? **CARD 1:** What/who will lead the way back to happiness and that new beginning when you are ready?

787
THE SPREAD OF TEMPERANCE FOR BLESSINGS AND WISHES FULFILLED

Purpose and background information:
- Lucky card: Temperance
- Lucky crystal: blue lace agate or angelite

CRYSTAL 1: What blessing or wish do you most need fulfilled right now? **CRYSTAL 2:** What burdens must you shed in order to be open to receive blessings? **CRYSTAL 3:** What opportunities will open so you can maximize these blessings? **CARD 1:** What will be the long-term benefits in your life?

788
THE SPREAD OF THE DEVIL FOR USING YOUR ANGER OR RESENTMENT FOR POSITIVE CHANGE

Purpose and background information:
- Lucky card: The Devil
- Lucky crystal: red jasper

CRYSTAL 1: What area of your life do you feel most resentful about? **CRYSTAL 2:** Why do you feel guilty/not entitled to protest? **CRYSTAL 3:** How can you transform your negative feelings by expressing/acting to right the injustice calmly and firmly? **CARD 1:** What will be the positive outcome of your new resolve/actions?

789
THE SPREAD OF THE TOWER OF FREEDOM TO REMOVE A RESTRICTIVE SITUATION THAT HOLDS YOU BACK

Purpose and background information:
- Lucky card: The Tower
- Lucky crystal: leopardskin jasper or turritella agate

CRYSTAL 1: Should you be/are you ready to break the restrictive hold on your life/leave the restrictive situation? **CRYSTAL 2:** What potential disruption/fear of disruption holds you back from acting? **CRYSTAL 3:** What benefits await, once you have acted? **CARD 1:** Will you be free sooner than anticipated?

790
THE SPREAD OF THE STAR FOR GETTING THAT LUCKY BREAK

Purpose and background information:
· Lucky card: The Star
· Lucky crystal: lapis lazuli

CRYSTAL 1: Are you trying every avenue for that lucky break/anything missing? **CRYSTAL 2:** Should you avoid/ignore people who try to deter you/laugh at your dream? **CRYSTAL 3:** How and when will your lucky break come? **CARD 1:** Will this open those doors to future success/recognition if you persevere?

791
THE SPREAD OF THE MOON FOR INJECTING REALISM INTO ROMANCE

Purpose and background information:
· Lucky card: The Moon
· Lucky crystal: moonstone or selenite

CRYSTAL 1: Do you have a lovely romance, but want more than flowers and poems? **CRYSTAL 2:** Do you fear/suspect your lover isn't offering commitment or anything permanent? **CRYSTAL 3:** Is this enough for you now/in the future? If not, will you move on? **CARD 1:** Can/will this romance develop into lasting committed love?

792
THE SPREAD OF THE SUN FOR ENJOYING LIFE AS IT IS NOW IF YOU ARE ALWAYS WORRYING ABOUT THE FUTURE

Purpose and background information:
· Lucky card: The Sun
· Lucky crystal: amber or carnelian

CRYSTAL 1: If life, relationships, and career are good, should you maximize every minute and build on those happy experiences? **CRYSTAL 2:** Is there anything worrying you, or are you just afraid happiness will suddenly be taken from you/that you are too happy? **CRYSTAL 3:** What can you do to build a secure future on these happy times? **CARD 1:** Will happiness continue (allowing for the down times everyone experiences) in your life?

793
THE SPREAD OF JUDGMENT IF YOU WORRY ABOUT THE APPROVAL OF OTHERS FOR YOUR ACHIEVEMENTS AND LIFESTYLE

Purpose and background information:
· Lucky card: Judgment
· Lucky crystal: hematite or polished iron pyrites

CRYSTAL 1: Are you satisfied with your life choices and style, but worry others may not approve? **CRYSTAL 2:** Do you have critical people in your life/come from a judgmental family that makes you doubt yourself? **CRYSTAL 3:** Should you rely on those you trust and respect to affirm your achievements/avoid/ignore the detractors? **CARD 1:** Will you gradually gain confidence in your own judgment and decisions and not care what others think?

794
THE SPREAD OF THE WORLD IF YOU KNOW THERE'S SO MUCH MORE TO LIFE

Purpose and background information:

- Lucky card: The World
- Lucky crystal: aquamarine

CRYSTAL 1: Do you have a specific dream that is calling? Is this a growing dissatisfaction with your life as it is at present? **CRYSTAL 2:** What holds you in your familiar world: finances/familiarity/commitments? Can these be resolved to free you? **CRYSTAL 3:** Would travel/a change of location satisfy this restlessness, or do you need a complete life change? **CARD 1:** Will your new life bring you satisfaction, or should you make inner changes first?

795
A SIX-CRYSTAL-AND-TAROT-CARD SPREAD IF YOUR PROMOTION OR JOB CHANGE ISN'T WORKING OUT

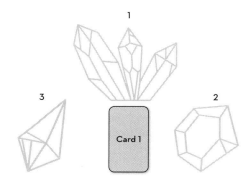

Purpose and background information:

This is a good way of combining card and crystal energies, and it can also be used for a six-month life review or any question where you need to use your intuition if the answers aren't immediately clear.

This time, choose your six crystals from the bag one at a time by feel.

Put the chosen crystals in a circle clockwise. Then set beneath each crystal the specific Major Tarot card to which it relates by choosing it from the deck quite deliberately as you look at the pictures. For example, you would put the Lovers card under the jade crystal in the circle (if you had picked the jade crystal from the bag without looking).

Your six crystals/cards will not have specific position meanings. Read them in the order you pulled them out of the bag.

Let the answer unfold by first considering the card's meaning and then holding the crystal. Do not only use its special meaning, but what you feel as you hold it, images that come into your mind and words you hear.

What you will use:
Your twenty-two crystals and your twenty-two Major cards, from which you will select six of each.

When:
Take your time over this Spread so you can let the crystals' significance gradually emerge. Light your favorite-colored candle and an incense or oil to burn that relaxes you. Make notes in your journal. I have given an example so you can see how this method works

Example:
Jill is twenty and has recently been promoted to a junior managerial position in the fashion store where she has worked since leaving high school. There are no questions about her ability, experience, or qualifications. However, staff who have been at the store for years resent someone so young being senior to them. Although Jill loves her job, the gossip and back-biting have made her consider asking for her old position back.

Jill selects:
CRYSTAL 1: Apache Tear (Death, endings leading to beginnings). Can Jill realistically go back to her life as it was before? What she is really asking is whether she can become the person she was before her promotion, carefree, not only at work but in her social life, which she says has suffered. She sees the image of the light flooding through the dark but semi-transparent crystal as a doorway through which she must pass into a new world. She is hesitating on the threshold.

CRYSTAL 2: Leopardskin Jasper (the Tower, freedom from restrictions). Leopardskin Jasper (The Tower) conjures up in Jill's mind an image of a leopard running through the jungle in a storm with the lightning illuminating his fur. He is running so fast that before long, he has left the jungle behind and is all alone.

Jill says that she has moved on even in the few months since her promotion, and has wanted to leave her loving but restrictive home and get her own place. Often, when you introduce Tarot crystals, a Tarot reading will widen to other life issues that affect/are affected by the specific question or problem.

CRYSTAL 3: Desert Rose (The Hermit, following your own star). Jill *saw* in her mind a lizard on a rock in the desert. He moved inside the rock—which is a treasure house of glittering gems—and she suddenly sees the riches within herself.

Before her promotion, Jill had tried to be "one of the girls," socializing even when she did not want to. Now that she has joined the management team, she realizes she will have to remain a little more aloof. Jill admits that she has tried to have the best of both worlds, but it has not been possible. But the change goes deeper. Jill recognizes that she is now looking for a different kind of life that will develop her inner potential.

CRYSTAL 4: Bloodstone (The Hanged Man, letting go of what holds us back). She pictures travelers on a pilgrimage, on a stony path. Jill realizes that she needs to give up the comfort—and the financial incentives—of remaining at home. Jill's greatest fear is being alone; but without living independently, she knows she will stagnate and stay as the little girl.

CRYSTAL 5: Amber (The Sun, success through developing our unique talents). This is the Good Fairy crystal. Jill sees an orange ball in the sky rising over a wide plain and an endless horizon. The Sun assures success and happiness. There is a chance for her to work at the head office for six months. Jill had turned down this offer, as it would involve moving a hundred miles away and her being entirely self-sufficient.

CRYSTAL 6: Aquamarine (The World, the opening of horizons in every way). As she held the aquamarine, Jill pictured a boat sailing across the sea, taking her to the other side of the world. She is suddenly afraid and, when the pilot boat returns to the harbor, she goes with it. Yet she stands, watching the big ships filled with longing, and knows that one day she will make her journey. Can Jill really move on? This seems a very different question from the original inquiry that she had framed as to whether she should give up her promotion to avoid the petty spite at work. Even if Jill does not move away now, within her is stirring the impetus for change and maybe that move to the head office.

CHAPTER 39

SPREADS FOR FORETELLING YOUR DESTINY

Lucky cards for your destiny spreads

Major Cards: The Chariot, the Wheel of Fortune, the Star, the Moon, the Sun, the World.

Minor Cards: The Aces of Pentacles, Cups, and Wands; the Threes of Cups and Wands; the Six of Wands; the Eights of Pentacles and Wands; the Tens of Pentacles and Wands.

Court Cards: The Princes/Knights of Pentacles and Wands, the Queens of Pentacles and Wands; the Kings of Pentacles and Wands.

About Spreads for foretelling your destiny

A variety of spreads involving oracles, karmic/past-life links, pendulums, and numerology that are more predictive and focus more on the unknown and seeing over the horizon for clues as to the best decisions and actions.

796
A FOUR-WINDS SPREAD OF FATE

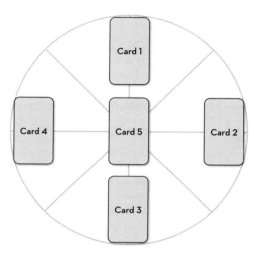

Purpose and background information:
If matters feel out of your control, to see what the likely results will be and what, if anything, you can do to make things better/right.

CARD 1: Boreas, the North Wind, the actual situation/ the most likely effects if nothing changes/you do nothing. **CARD 2:** Eurus, the East Wind, logically what can be done to positively affect matters. **CARD 3:** Notus, the South Wind, what unexpected boost or mitigation exists of the situation from outside sources. **CARD 4:** Zephyrus, the West Wind, what might blow you off course? **CARD 5:** The result of all these factors coming together.

What you should use:
The full deck.

When:
A windy day if possible, otherwise when it is cloudy.

797

THE RING-OF-FATE PENDULUM SPREAD FOR ASKING A SPECIFIC QUESTION ABOUT AN UNKNOWN ASPECT OF YOUR FUTURE

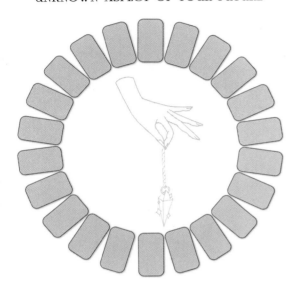

Purpose and background information:

Using a pendulum, a crystal on a chain, or a favorite pendant with the chain twisted to form a single chain.

Shuffle the twenty-two Major cards and place them in a facedown circle.

Pass the pendulum over each card slowly as you ask your question. You will feel it pulling down quite strongly, vibrating through your fingers or swinging clockwise over the card to answer your question (the response varies).

Turn your card over and read it.

What you should use:

The twenty-two Major cards.

When:

When the answer cannot be deduced logically or from what is known.

798

WILL A DESIRED EVENT HAPPEN WITHIN A YEAR?

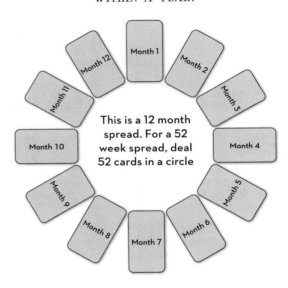

This is a 12 month spread. For a 52 week spread, deal 52 cards in a circle

Purpose and background information:

This Spread pinpoints the number of weeks/months till the event will occur, according to the position of the card the pendulum indicates. By the meaning of the card selected, information emerges about the event/advantages/pitfalls.

Decide in advance whether to use weeks or, if you need to be more specific, months.

Shuffle the full deck and select either twelve cards for months or fifty-two cards for weeks of the year. Place them in a facedown circle.

Pass a pendulum slowly over the circle clockwise until it pulls down/vibrates/circles.

The position of the chosen card in the circle will indicate the correct number of weeks/months, counting the first card set as week/month 1.

If the pendulum doesn't indicate any card, the event will be delayed/not occur. Use the previous Spread to ask which.

When:

The beginning of the earliest likely month the event might occur.

799
WHICH SHOULD I CHOOSE?

Purpose and background information:

An all-purpose pendulum Spread for choosing between different options/hotels or locations for a vacation, healing oils, or therapies/colleges or potential workplaces: nothing is too bizarre or important.

Not only does the pendulum intuitively choose the best, but the card gives extra information that will be useful in understanding your final choice. The method works best with six or fewer choices.

Shuffle the deck and select a card for each option set in a left-to-right row, plus an extra card for the unknown factor.

Hold the pendulum over each card in turn.

If you get a strong reaction, it's a definite yes; if not very strong, see if there is a second option that the pendulum reacts more strongly to. Your extra card will provide extra information.

What you should use:

The full deck initially, from which the number of choices will be selected.

When:

The information isn't helping a clear choice.

800
A THREE-STEP TAROT-AND-DICE SPREAD FOR COMPLETING A BORING NECESSARY TASK OR PAPERWORK

Purpose and background information:

Shuffle the forty Minor cards.

Cast three dice. Pick the first card in the facedown deck that corresponds to the total number on the dice.

Do the same for the next two cards.

Card 1: When is the best time to tackle the paperwork when you will not be disturbed? **Card 2:** Where is the best place to do the paperwork where you will not be distracted? **Card 3:** Have you got everything you need to hand so you can complete the task quickly and easily/anything missing?

When:

When the deadline is looming.

801
A TAROT-CARD-AND-DICE SPREAD WHEN YOU WANT TO KNOW WHICH IS THE MOST PROMISING COURSE OF ACTION

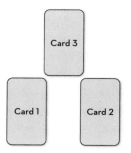

Purpose and background information:

A way of tapping into the unknown factors.

Shuffle your full deck and then throw your three dice.

Pick the card from the facedown deck that corresponds with the number shaken by all three dice as you deal the deck, so if you rolled three sixes you would pick Card 18 from the facedown deck.

Continue until you have picked two or three cards, according to the number of options. Leave the chosen cards in position.

Card 1: Option 1, Card 2: Option 2, Card 3: Option 3

If you have more than three options, shake the dice and choose a card for each option and read them.

Shake the three dice a final time to give yourself a card to offer you an overall view.

When:

Just before deciding.

802

A KARMIC SPREAD TO UNDERSTAND WHAT YOU HAVE BROUGHT INTO THIS LIFE AND HOW YOU CAN OVERCOME OR DEVELOP IT

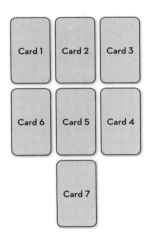

Purpose and background information

A powerful Spread if you are wondering why certain situations of the same kind recur throughout your life.

CARD 1: What strengths do you carry from past worlds?

CARD 2: What challenges do you carry from past worlds?

CARD 3: Who is your soul mate, and have you met them yet in this lifetime? **CARD 4:** Who is your soul adversary/enemy, and have you yet met them? **CARD 5:** What burdens/weaknesses should you leave behind in past worlds? **CARD 6:** What strengths/qualities should you bring forward to develop in this current lifetime? **CARD 7:** What is your karmic/soul purpose to fulfill in this lifetime?

What should you use:

The twenty-two Major cards and the sixteen Court cards.

When:

Whenever you have an uninterrupted evening, as this is not a Spread to hurry.

803

THE ORACLE SPREAD

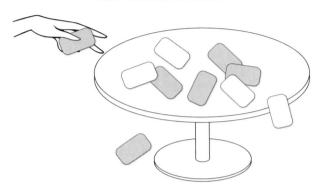

Purpose and background information:

In the ancient tradition of Oracles, where you are given the information that's right for you at a particular time.

Take ten cards from your shuffled facedown deck.

Throw the cards one at a time onto the table from a distance without trying to control which side they fall on. Read only the ones that fall picture-uppermost. Some might fall on the floor: leave them where they land.

Do not read the facedown cards, whether on the table or floor, but collect them in a mini-deck.

Each day, continue to cast those remaining cards daily until all are picture-side uppermost.

Each day, your deck of unread cards will get smaller as more of them fall right-side up.

If a card is particularly unwilling to appear by day 5, read it anyway and discover what challenge it offers to you.

What you should use:

The full deck from which to select your ten Oracle cards.

When:

Each morning until you have read them all, up to five days.

804
IN SEARCH OF WISDOM

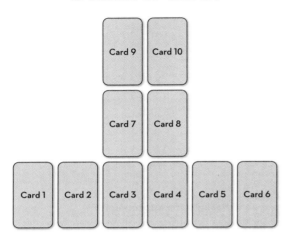

Purpose and background information:

A nine-card Spread when you do not have a specific question but want to see markers of the best action ahead so that you make the right choices and decisions.

Nine is traditionally the number of perfection and completion, so there are nine main questions to answer. **Card 10** represents the hidden message to unify the other nine cards.

CARD 1: What is most important for you to know at this time? **CARD 2:** What do you need to reach out for before you can move forward? **CARD 3:** Who or what, either right now or coming into your life soon, will help you to gain the necessary knowledge/wisdom to move forward? **CARD 4:** Who or what stands in the way of your acquiring the necessary knowledge/wisdom? **CARD 5:** What actions do you need to make/say? **CARD 6:** Who/what should you avoid doing/saying? **CARD 7:** Do you need to change anything in your present life/attitudes? **CARD 8:** What should you preserve/develop in your present life? **CARD 9:** What must you give up/leave behind? **CARD 10:** The hidden message/key to the necessary knowledge/wisdom to bring your life together and show the future way.

What you should use:

The twenty-two major cards and the sixteen Court cards.

When:

An unhurried time to consider your cards. After you finish, sleep with Card 10 under your pillow.

805
THE CROSS OF DESTINY

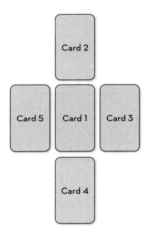

Purpose and background information:

A briefer overview in order to make a fast but necessary decision by getting advance knowledge of what is not yet revealed.

CARD 1: The situation as it seems. **CARD 2:** The situation as it really is. **CARD 3:** What you should/can change. **CARD 4:** What you cannot/should not change. **CARD 5:** The best outcome, putting known and unknown factors together.

What you should use:

The forty Minor cards.

When:

When you wake.

806
THE NUMEROLOGY MONTH-BY-MONTH-DESTINY SPREAD

Card 1

Card 2

Card 3

Card 4

Purpose and background information:

A method using Tarot cards to pinpoint the most relevant information each month, based on your birthdate.

Use the full shuffled deck.

Write your birthdate in full: day number, month number, full year number. Do not worry about your birth time in this Spread.

Reduce each number to a single digit by adding the digits together (example: 58 = 5+8 = 13 = 4), except for 11 and 22, special Master numbers.

Deal from the top, turning cards until you reach the number of the day of your birth. **CARD 1** will show you the opportunities in the month ahead.

Remove that card and reshuffle the rest of the deck.

Continue counting the cards from the top of the deck till you reach the number of the month of your birth. **CARD 2** will give you the challenges to overcome in the month ahead.

Remove that card from the deck. Reshuffle the remainder, dealing again till you reach the combined number of your birth year, so 1948 would be 22 and therefore the 22nd card, whereas 1947 would be 21, which further reduces to 3.

CARD 3 will give you the strengths to overcome the

challenges in the month ahead.

Remove that card. Reshuffle. Deal from the top until you reach the combined single digit of day, month, and year, so 03-08-1948—which adds up to six—means your 4th card would be the 6th card dealt.

Card 4 gives you the card of unexpected good luck in the month.

When:

The first day of the month under question. You can repeat the Spread monthly if you wish to see what new cards/influences lie ahead.

807
A ONE-CARD NUMEROLOGY BIRTH-TIME SPREAD TO SHOW THE UNEXPECTED FEATURE OF THE DAY AHEAD

Purpose and background information:

You can do this in addition to your Card of the Day reading, or instead if you are expecting an unusually challenging day ahead. If using the Card of the Day as well, return this card to the deck and reshuffle before Spread 808.

As before, reduce your birth time to a single digit unless 11 or 22. Shuffle the full deck and count your cards as you deal (as described in the previous Spread) until you come to the card in the same number position as your birth time digit, so if 7 the 7th card dealt.

CARD 1: What unexpected or unusual opportunity/challenge lies ahead today. Whether opportunity or challenge will depend on the card.

What should you use:

The full shuffled deck.

When:

First thing in the morning.

808
THE SPREAD OF THE WISE ONES

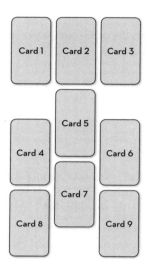

Purpose and background information:

A Spread in which you use the pictures on the cards plus your intuition to better understand which Spirit guides are guarding your Destiny. If this isn't working, hold each individual card and let the scene on the card appear in your mind and expand like a story.

CARD 1: Which Spirit Guide/guardian is with me now? **CARD 2:** Which of my ancestors is with me? **CARD 3:** Which angel is with me? **CARD 4:** What is my soul purpose? **CARD 5:** What is my greatest challenge that keeps me from my soul purpose? **CARD 6:** How can I best achieve my soul purpose? **CARD 7:** What signs should I look for in my daily life to show that my guides are with me? **CARD 8:** Who in the everyday world will act as my mentor/wise friend or teacher? **CARD 9:** What is the overall message of this reading?

What you should use:

The twenty-two Major cards and the sixteen Court cards.

When:

When you need guidance. A Spread for which to allow time and silence.

809
A ONE-CARD NUMEROLOGY SPREAD FOR THE FULFILLMENT OF YOUR INNER DESIRE FOR THE WEEK/MONTH AHEAD

Purpose and background information:

This Spread uses the vowels in your full name added together and reduced to a single digit unless 11 or 22. Again, use the full deck, shuffle, and, as you deal, pick one card that is for example 9th in the deck if the vowels in your name reduce to 9. This number/letter correspondence is the old Pythagorean system

1	2	3	4	5	6	7	8	9
A	B	C	D	E	F	G	H	I
J	K	L	M	N	O	P	Q	R
S	T	U	V	W	X	Y	Z	

CARD 1: How your secret hope/desire for the week/month ahead can be partly/totally fulfilled/delayed.

When:

If you do this weekly or monthly, you may find that your dream changes/if any are the same how the manifestation of the original dream is growing/temporarily held back in your life.

810
THE NUMEROLOGY FOR THE OUTSIDE EVENT ONE-CARD SPREAD, FOR INPUT OR CHALLENGE THAT WILL MOSTLY AFFECT YOUR WEEK OR MONTH AHEAD

Purpose and background information:

Calculate the number values of your name/s and reduce to a single digit except for 11 and 2. Use the Pythagorean values in Spread 809. Using the full deck, shuffle and deal each card from the top, stopping and turning over at the card corresponding with your outer number (example: for 7, stop at the 7th card).

Card 1: The major external influence that will affect you most in the week or month ahead. From the nature of the card, you will see whether it's a benefit or a challenge.

When:
The first day of each week or month about which you are asking.

811
THE SPREAD OF NUMBER 1 FOR INITIATING A DIFFICULT CONVERSATION

Purpose and background information:
Lucky Card: Any Ace or card with a 1 in the number. Pages or Princesses, except for Swords, count as one for this purpose as the first of the Court cards.
Shuffle the full deck and take the top card.

Card 1: How can you get your point over/the result you need without causing offense or hurt?

When:
The first day of the week or month.

812
THE SPREAD OF NUMBER 2 FOR WEIGHING UP THE ODDS ON WHETHER TO ACT OR WAIT IN ANY SITUATION

Purpose and background information:
Lucky Card: Any two card or with two anywhere in the number. Princes or Knights, except for Swords, count as twos as the second of the Court cards.
Shuffle the full deck and take the top two cards.

Card 1: The consequences of acting. **Card 2:** The consequences of waiting.

What you should use:
The full deck.

When:
The second day of the week or month.

813
THE SPREAD OF NUMBER 3 IF YOU ARE DECIDING WHETHER TO TRY FOR A BABY

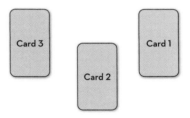

Purpose and background information:
Lucky Card: Any three card or card with the three in the number. Queens, except for Swords, count as three cards, as they are the third Court card.
Shuffle the full deck and take the top three cards.

Card 1: Is now the right time? **Card 2:** Should you wait a while? **Card 3:** If you try soon, will you be lucky?

What you should use:
The full deck.

When:
The third day of the week or month.

814
THE SPREAD OF 4 IF YOU NEED TO ECONOMIZE

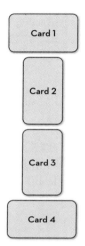

Purpose and background information:
Lucky Card: Any four card or card with the four in the number. Kings, except for Swords, count as four cards, as they are the fourth Court card.

Shuffle the full deck and take the top four cards.

CARD 1: Will a short-term or small economy be sufficient to resolve finances? **CARD 2:** Do you need longer-term or a more major economy? **CARD 3:** Is it/how is it possible to add to incoming money/resources? **CARD 4:** Is it/how is it possible to reduce/remove causes of the unnecessary outflow of money?

What you should use:
The full deck.

When:
The fourth day of the week or month.

815
THE SPREAD OF 5 IF YOU ARE HAVING PROBLEMS COMMUTING

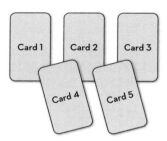

Purpose and background information:
Lucky Card: Any five card or card with a five in the number. Shuffle the full deck and take the top five cards.

CARD 1: Can I change my actual commuting times by altering my working hours? **CARD 2:** Is there an alternative means of transport/a lift share I could use? **CARD 3:** Can I work from home more/consolidate my hours so I travel on fewer days? **CARD 4:** Are there ways I can make my commute more pleasant/new music/talking books? **CARD 5:** Should I change my job?

What you should use:
The full deck.

When:
The fifth day of the week or month.

816
THE SPREAD OF 7 IF YOUR WORKPLACE DISCOURAGES RELATIONSHIPS BETWEEN EMPLOYEES

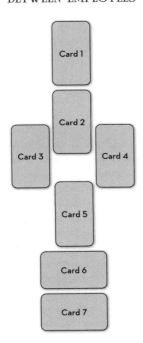

Purpose and background information:
Lucky Card: Any seven card or card with a seven in the number. Shuffle the full deck and take the top seven cards.

Card 1: Are you finding it increasingly hard to hide your relationship? **Card 2:** Are colleagues getting suspicious/gossiping? **Card 3:** Could/should either of you move to a different department if a large organization/change your place of work? **Card 4:** Do you want to move to a workplace where you are allowed to be together? **Card 5:** Is it possible now or in the not-too-distant future to start a business together? **Card 6:** Is hiding your relationship putting too much strain on it, in and out of work? **Card 7:** Should you speak out to someone sympathetic/try to get policy changed, or is this too risky?

What you should use:
The full deck.

When:
The seventh day of the week or month.

817
THE SPREAD OF 6 IF YOU WANT MORE ROMANCE IN YOUR RELATIONSHIP

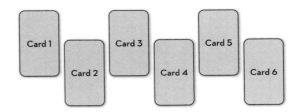

Purpose and background information:
Lucky Card: Any six card or card with a six in the number. Shuffle the full deck and take the top six cards.

Card 1: Has your partner always been unromantic, or is this a habit s/he has developed? **Card 2:** Are the circumstances of your present lives not conducive to romance/working long hours/small children/money worries? **Card 3:** How can you increase the time/atmosphere for romance so it feels natural, not forced? **Card 4:** Are there underlying relationship issues standing in the way of romance that need resolving? **Card 5:** Are there special places you can go/recreate memories of when you were first in love? **Card 6:** Can/will the increase in romance enhance your life together/bring you closer in many ways?

What you should use:
The full deck.

When:
The sixth day of the week or month.

818
THE SPREAD OF 8 IF YOU WANT TO PUBLISH YOUR POETRY BUT PEOPLE SAY YOU ARE WASTING YOUR TIME

Purpose and background information:

Lucky Card: Any eight card or card with an eight in the number.

Shuffle the full deck and take the top eight cards.

CARD 1: Do you want your poetry published for fulfillment and not just money? **CARD 2:** Do/should you belong to poetry societies with journals on and offline/enter poetry competitions to create recognition for your work? **CARD 3:** Could you organize/participate in poetry social evenings at libraries/schools for live audience feedback? **CARD 4:** Is there a niche market for your work, humorous poems for comedy clubs/poetry for children? **CARD 5:** Would you be successful in producing online poetry books/self-financed works for local outlets/small publishers? **CARD 6:** Can/should you find an illustrator/photographer to produce word and picture books for children/greeting cards? **CARD 7:** Should you persevere and aim for wider audiences/even Poet Laureate league? **CARD 8:** Do you want to write for pleasure/family/friends and future generations?

What you should use:
The full deck.

When:
The eighth day of the month, or a date in the week under consideration with an 8 in it.

819
THE SPREAD OF 9 IF YOU WANT TO PROTEST AGAINST A DECISION THAT IS WRONG AND AFFECTS YOUR COMMUNITY

Purpose and background information:

Lucky Card: Any nine card or card with a nine in the number.

Shuffle the full deck and take the top nine cards.

CARD 1: Is there similar unhappiness with the decision in the community, or is there too much inertia? **CARD 2:** Can/should you organize a powerful peaceful protest, or would you sooner join one organized by others? **CARD 3:** What vested commercial/organizational interests are behind the decision/open and hidden? **CARD 4:** Are there serious environmental/social consequences if the decision is upheld? **CARD 5:** Can you effectively use local/national media for support/are there any unique features/eye-catching publicity to create wider interest? **CARD 6:** Can you win a protection/staying order while a wider inquiry is held? **CARD 7:** What are the negative financial implications on the area? **CARD 8:** For how long are you prepared to carry on the fight, even if work on the project starts? **CARD 9:** Will you win?

What you should use:
The full deck.

When:
The ninth day of the month, or a date in the week under consideration with a 9 in it.

CHAPTER 40

SPREADS FOR SELF-AWARENESS AND KNOWLEDGE AND PLANNING YOUR LIFE PATH

Lucky cards for self-awareness and life-path planning

Major Cards: The Magician, the High Priestess, the Hierophant, the Hermit, the Wheel of Fortune, Temperance, the Star, the Moon, the Sun, Judgment/Rebirth, the World.

Minor Cards: All Aces including Swords; Two of Cups; Threes of Pentacles, Cups, and Wands; Fours of Cups and Wands; Five of Pentacles; Sixes of Cups, Wands, and Swords; Sevens of Pentacles and Cups; Eights of Pentacles, Cups, and Wands; Nine of Pentacles; Tens of Pentacles and Cups.

Court Cards: Any Princess/Page if its own Queen is present in the Spread, except for Swords; any Prince/Knight if its own King is present except for Swords.

About Self-Awareness spreads:

Spreads vary in the number of cards, according to how-in depth the Spread is. Self-awareness and life-path Spreads help us to understand our thoughts, dreams, and true selves and offer ways of considering our inner world. They also consider how we can avoid being affected adversely by others' demands or chaos. Therefore, this is a chapter not to be hurried through. The next chapter, Chapter 41, develops the theme with spreads that use the Tarot as a powerful way of working with the psychic powers we all possess.

820
THE COMING-INTO-BALANCE SPREAD

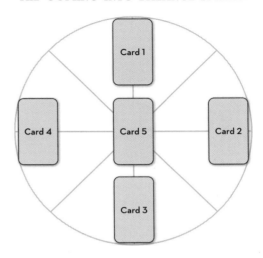

Purpose and background information:
When external events or relationships are proving chaotic and you want normality restored in your own life.

> **CARD 1:** What/who really caused/is causing the chaos?
> **CARD 2:** Should you intervene, or wait for things to settle?
> **CARD 3:** Who/what will prove most helpful in bringing peace to the situation? **CARD 4:** How can you restore your own balance if others' behaviors are shaking it? **CARD 5:** How can you prevent others' future chaos affecting your lasting harmony?

What you should use:
The twenty-two Major cards.

When:
A Friday, the day of finding peace.

821
THE HIDDEN-SELF SPREAD

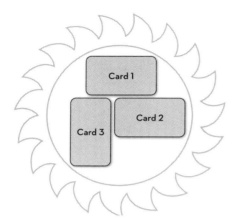

Purpose and background information:
When you feel that the image you present to the world is holding you back from revealing your true self.

CARD 1: How you are seen by the world. **CARD 2:** The hidden self the world never sees. **CARD 3:** How you can combine the two, so you feel at home in the world without becoming too vulnerable.

What you should use:
The twenty-two Major cards and the sixteen Court cards.

When:
At a crescent moon, or early in the waxing cycle

822
THE FOUR-STEPS-TO-NEW-HAPPINESS SPREAD

Purpose and background information:
When life didn't work out the way you thought it would, and you are wondering *what next?*

CARD 1: What can be salvaged in terms of experience/knowledge of self, life, and people to take forward to the future? **CARD 2:** What new things/places are open to you that were not possible before? **CARD 3:** How will your new happiness be manifested? **CARD 4:** What/who should you avoid in order to avoid falling back into the old patterns and in order to make the happiness last?

What you should use:
The full deck.

When:
At the beginning of a month.

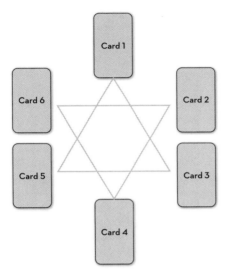

823
THE PAST, PRESENT, AND FUTURE KARMIC SPREAD

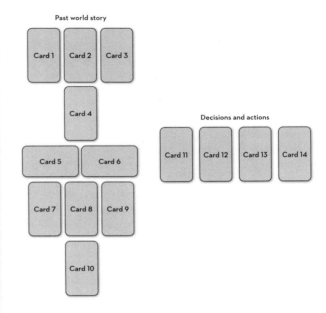

824
TEN-STEPS-TO-PAST-WORLDS SPREAD

Purpose and background information:

When you are trying to move forward to a new way of living, free from the past.

CARD 1: What you have brought forward from past lives that you no longer need. **CARD 2:** The strengths you have forgotten from past worlds that can help you to start a new pattern. **CARD 3:** The past in this lifetime, including childhood and previous relationships that may contribute to any negative repeated patterns or feelings. **CARD 4:** The present/the key to breaking negative patterns and establishing positive new ones. **CARD 5:** The future years in this life, and the results of following a positive new path. **CARD 6:** The positive lessons you can/will carry into future incarnations.

What you should use:

The twenty-two Major Arcana cards and the sixteen Court cards.

When:

Any transition time, such as sunset, the end of a month.

Purpose and background information:

A quiet way of working with past worlds. Ask before picking from the full shuffled deck to see a particular world you are drawn to, a specific fear you do not understand, or let the card images unfold as a story. Look for yourself and loved ones in the card images.

Hold each card one after the other, closing your eyes, experiencing in your mind images, words, and impressions.

If you wish, after you have studied each card, write whatever you feel. **CARDS 1 TO 10:** Your past world story. **CARD 11:** What strengths can you bring from your old worlds? **CARD 12:** What should you leave behind? **CARD 13:** Who is your soul mate? How can you meet them? **CARD 14:** Who is your soul adversary/enemy? How can you overcome them?

What you should use:

The full deck.

When:

Repeat Spread monthly or more/less frequently as the need arises.

825
ARE YOU PSYCHIC?

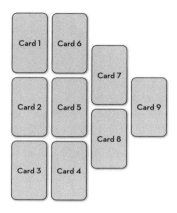

Purpose and background information:

When you are having lots of strange experiences and wonder what's going on.

Card 1: Were you psychic as a child/teenager? **Card 2:** Has any major change occurred in your life to bring those psychic powers back to the fore? Is it a natural awakening? **Card 3:** Do you know that things are going to happen/see ghosts and find out that what you saw can be verified? **Card 4:** Do these powers, especially premonitions of disaster, randomly appear? Is that worrying you? **Card 5:** Should you channel your powers through classes/courses/joining a circle? **Card 6:** Would it be better to work alone through books/ online courses, or just let it evolve naturally? **Card 7:** Should you block your psychic powers/divert them into everyday life/develop at a later time? **Card 8:** Do you want to train as a medium or clairvoyant, or just use your powers informally in your own life and to help others? **Card 9:** Should you dismiss your premonitions that come to fruition as coincidence/ imagination?

What you should use:

The full deck.

When:

At any transition time or date, sunset, or when the seasons or clocks change.

826
ARE YOU A HEALER?

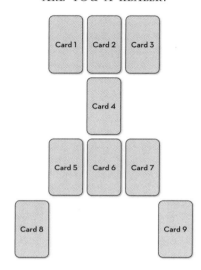

Purpose and background information:

When people tell you that you have healing hands.

Card 1: Do people say they feel better just by talking to you? **Card 2:** Do you feel a tingling in your fingers/especially when you touch people/are very receptive to static electricity? **Card 3:** Have animals always been soothed by you and wild birds/animals are inclined to come close? **Card 4:** Do you have a natural feeling for crystals/sense energy pulsating through them? **Card 5:** Should you/would you like to learn an energy therapy such as reiki/kinesiology/crystal work/ spiritual massage? **Card 6:** Would you like to train as a healer/sit in a healing circle? **Card 7:** Would it be better to let your healing develop in its own way? **Card 8:** Do you want to carry on making people feel better in the everyday world? **Card 9:** Would you consider, if not already, working in a conventional profession with people or animals?

What you should use:

The twenty-two Lucky and the twenty-two Court cards.

When:

A Wednesday, the day of healers and healing.

827
ARE YOU AN OLD OR A NEW SOUL?

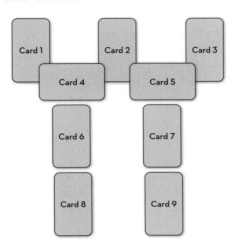

Purpose and background information:
When you feel you have lived many times before.

CARD 1: Are you attracted to particular ancient cultures such as Ancient Egypt or Greece/if you visit these places, do you feel you have come home? **CARD 2:** Do you watch a historical movie or read historical novels and know the details are wrong? **CARD 3:** Do you feel connections with indigenous cultures and old traditions wherever you go in the world? **CARD 4:** Have you experienced past life dreams or daydreams that remain with you all day? **CARD 5:** Do you have an inexplicable irrational fear or scar? **CARD 6:** Have you instantly felt that you know a total stranger, and the connection is mutual? **CARD 7:** Do you take a seemingly irrational mutual dislike with a stranger without knowing why? **CARD 8:** Do you believe past life experiences are imagination/coincidence? **CARD 9:** Are you an old soul?

What you should use:
The full deck.

When:
Saturdays or Halloween.

828
ARE YOU A STAR PERSON?

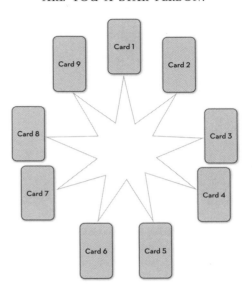

Purpose and background information:
When you feel the stars are special to you.

CARD 1: Did you/do you always feel different from your birth family? **CARD 2:** Have you always been fascinated by the stars/star-watching? **CARD 3:** Are you eager to know more about astronomy/astrology? **CARD 4:** Do you experience a sense of wanting to go home/do not know where home is? **CARD 5:** Are you interested in literature/movies about other dimensions but feel something's missing? **CARD 6:** Do you sense you are here for a special purpose/not sure what it is? **CARD 7:** Do you occasionally meet someone totally on your wavelength? **CARD 8:** Should you research more the possibility of life in other galaxies, maybe study mind travel? **CARD 9:** Does being a Star soul and one day returning feel authentic even though you cannot prove it?

What you should use:
The full deck.

When:
Within two days of any full moon.

829
WHY HAVE YOU ALWAYS FELT DIFFERENT FROM OTHER PEOPLE?

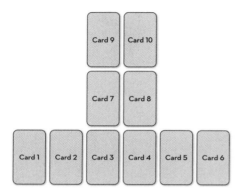

Purpose and Background Information:
When you try to fit in with others and life but always feel you are on the outside looking in, no matter what you say or do.

CARD 1: Have you always felt alone, even in a crowd or with friends? **CARD 2:** Do you have different values/dreams from your family and peers? **CARD 3:** Do you believe you are a Star Soul, a very old soul among younger souls, or just that you work from the heart and soul? **CARD 4:** Have you been rejected/labeled with a syndrome for being different/forced to conform? **CARD 5:** Are you very sensitive to/physically and emotionally affected by toxic people and hostile atmospheres? **CARD 6:** Should you rejoice in your uniqueness/original talents? **CARD 7:** Would you be best running your own business/working creatively? **CARD 8:** Should you/can you use your sense of isolation helping others who are different? **CARD 9:** If you persist, will you find the twin soul/special friends who value you? **CARD 10:** Can you use your unique perspectives to make a difference in the world?

What you should use:
The full deck.

When:
A full moon, or any unusual day like February 29 or a Friday the Thirteenth.

830
DO YOU BELIEVE YOU HAVE EXPERIENCED AN EXTRATERRESTRIAL ENCOUNTER?

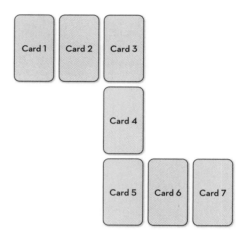

Purpose and background information:
If people laugh and say you have watched too many movies.

CARD 1: Is it more likely than not that we are not alone in the universe/other beings may be more advanced, communication/travel-wise? **CARD 2:** Have you experienced an extraterrestrial dream that seemed more than a dream where you traveled in a craft/talked to other beings? **CARD 3:** Do you wake with a halo of light around your vison/a sense of sadness to return? **CARD 4:** Have you experienced an extraterrestrial encounter where you traveled in your mind as an out-of-body experience? **CARD 5:** Have you seen craft in the sky, witnessed by others that authorities cannot explain away? **CARD 6:** Should you find sensible online groups/extraterrestrial research organizations to contribute your own experiences? **CARD 7:** Do you believe you will have other experiences in your lifetime?

What you should use:
The forty Minor cards, Aces to Tens, and the sixteen Court cards.

When:
The last day of any month.

831
THE VICTIM, DRAGON, AND RESCUER SPREAD

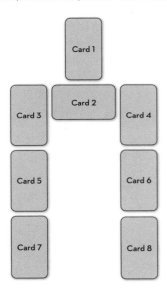

Purpose and background information:
A semi-mythological way of working out your role in a relationship quandary. For example, involving your partner and parents-in-law when you are always cast as the bad guy/gal.

CARD 1: Are you generally cast as the dragon, attacking the victim who is defended by the rescuer in this situation? Why?
CARD 2: Do you take on this role, or are you pushed into it?
CARD 3: Is there an unspoken agreement between the victim and rescuer to take on these roles to deal with any conflict?
CARD 4: Do you go along with the dragon role out of guilt, or because you do not want to upset anyone? **CARD 5:** Who do you *want* to be in the scenario? **CARD 6:** Can you/how can you change your role? **CARD 7:** Will this change be resisted by the other players? **CARD 8:** Should you refuse to play the game anymore?

What you should use:
The twenty-two Major cards and the sixteen Court cards.

When:
When yet again you have apologized for what was not your fault.

832
THE PRINCE/PRINCESS-IN-THE-TOWER SPREAD

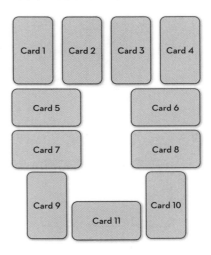

Purpose and background information:
Another semi-mythological Spread where you feel trapped by a situation, whether a job, family commitments, or a destructive relationship. If the Tower card is turned over, it is of immense significance, saying freedom will come soon.

CARD 1: Who/what keeps you helpless/locked in your tower? **CARD 2:** What is the freedom you most need/want? **CARD 3:** Do you have more power than you realize? What is it? **CARD 4:** Should you wait for rescue/circumstances to change? **CARD 5:** Who will rescue you? (The answer might be yourself.) **CARD 6:** By what means can you escape from the tower/do you have these means? **CARD 7:** Where do you want to be when you escape? **CARD 8:** First step to escape. **CARD 9:** Second step to escape. **CARD 10:** How best to use your freedom. **CARD 11:** How to avoid being captured again.

What you should use:
The full deck.

When:
At the waning Moon.

833
THE FAIRY-TALE LOVE SPREAD

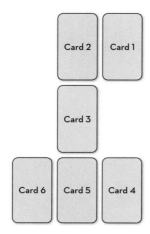

Purpose and background information:

When you are in what you thought was a perfect relationship, but you find that your prince or princess has turned into the wicked wizard or witch.

CARD 1: What false enchantment holds you? **CARD 2:** Will a new love rescue you, or will your wizard/witch turn back into the lovely prince/ess if you wait? **CARD 3:** What is the dark wood of fear you must find your way through to break the enchantment? **CARD 4:** Can you/must you rescue yourself? **CARD 5:** Can you resist falling under the spell again if the witch/wizard, dressed up as the prince/princess, comes after you? **CARD 6:** Do you need to make your own magick for a while before seeking another happy-ever-after?

What you should use:

The twenty-two Major cards and the sixteen Court cards.

When:

When you want to go, but you are scared.

834
THE TRIPLE-MOON SPREAD FOR A WOMAN INTEGRATING THE DIFFERENT PARTS OF HERSELF

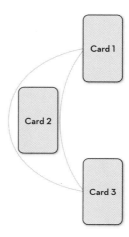

Purpose and background information:

For women of any age to discover their three inner moon phases that correspond with the main cycles of the moon. Each quality can be felt most easily during the relevant moon phase leading the way. Men can use this Spread to get in touch with the cycles of their anima gentle self.

CARD 1: The waxing proactive maiden moon: What do you most anticipate and plan for right now? **CARD 2:** The creative full moon mother (whether a biological mother or not): How can you best express your power and passion for life? **CARD 3:** The waning wise grandmother moon: What can you let go to flow with the tides of life?

What you should use:

The twenty-two Major cards.

When:

At a crescent moon.

(You can check in the cards each month for your triple-moon message for the month ahead.)

835
THE MAN-IN-THE-MOON SPREAD FOR A GUY INTEGRATING THE DIFFERENT PARTS OF HIMSELF

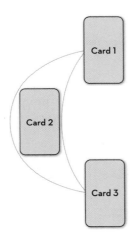

Purpose and background information:

For men of any age to discover their three inner moon phases that correspond with the main cycles of the moon. Each quality can be felt most easily during the relevant moon phase, leading the way. Women can use this Spread to get in touch with the cycles of their animus assertive self.

CARD 1: The adventurous waxing moon youth: What challenges are you setting yourself to achieve? **CARD 2:** The warrior king full-moon self: What principles do you need to defend? **CARD 3:** The priest healer waning moon: What can be accepted and compromised?

What you should use:

The twenty-two Major cards.

When:

At a crescent moon.

(You can check in the cards each month for your triple-moon message for the month ahead.)

836
OVERCOMING THE UNFAIR POWER OF THE WEAK OVER THE STRONG

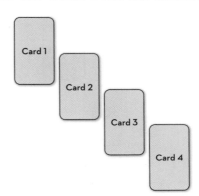

Purpose and background information:

When a person manipulates you by acting helpless and using guilt and obligation to control you, whether financially or in constantly listening to their problems.

CARD 1: What makes you feel obliged to try to put right/compensate for this person's never-ending troubles? **CARD 2:** How can you weaken the stranglehold of guilt that drains your energies/finances? **CARD 3:** Is it time to move away/limit time/energy/money before resentment boils over? **CARD 4:** Will they soon find another person to leech off of?

What you should use:

The twenty-two Major cards and the sixteen Court cards.

When:

The moon disappears from the sky.

837
THE HERO OR HEROINE'S QUEST FOR REALIZING YOUR FULL POTENTIAL

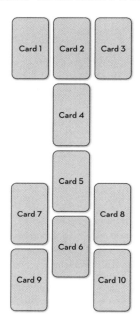

Purpose and background information:

Based on the traditional myths that underlie the Major Tarot cards of the journey to personal enlightenment and fulfillment of life purpose. I have listed by each card the Major card that would be especially lucky if it turned up in that position.

CARD 1: What is your ultimate mission in life, if you choose to embrace it? (the Fool/inner child). **CARD 2:** Will you go with your love/is finding love part of the quest/must you find yourself first? (the Lovers). **CARD 3:** Will you need to physically move/make an inner shift/learn new things? (the Chariot). **CARD 4:** Who will help/advise you? (the High Priestess/Hierophant). **CARD 5:** What unexpected luck will you have on the way? (the Wheel of Fortune). **CARD 6:** Will you persist in spite of obstacles? (Strength). **CARD 7:** What will you have to give up to reach your goal? (the Hanged Man). **CARD 8:** Who will oppose you/what could tempt you to give up? (the Devil). **CARD 9:** Will you get the chance you need if you persist? (the Star). **CARD 10:** Will you find what you are looking for and take your unique place in the world? (the World).

What you should use:

The twenty-two Major cards.

When:

On your birthday or New Year's Day.

838
REPLACING YOUR GREATEST FEAR WITH YOUR GREATEST DREAM

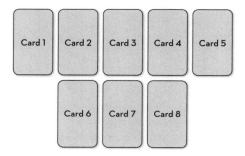

Purpose and background information:

When a fear is holding you back from attaining your dream.

CARD 1: What is the fear that holds you back? **CARD 2:** What do you want most in the world? **CARD 3:** Is your fear likely to happen? **CARD 4:** Is your dream realistic? **CARD 5:** Should you ignore your fear and press ahead with your dream? **CARD 6:** Should you confront/deal with your fear before reaching for your dream? **CARD 7:** Will you overcome your fear by succeeding with your dream? **CARD 8:** Will you succeed with your dream in spite of your fear?

What you should use:

The forty Minor cards, Aces to Tens.

When:

When you wake, best of all on the first day of the month.

839
A JUNGIAN PSYCHOLOGICAL SPREAD TO UNDERSTAND WHAT HIDDEN FACTORS ARE INFLUENCING RECURRING EVENTS AND REPEATING PATTERNS

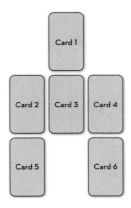

Purpose and background information:
This method of reading, inspired by Swiss psychologist Carl Jung, is useful for looking at why you find yourself in the same position through the years but with different people and different scenarios—and how this can be changed once recognized.

CARD 1: Your *key or predominant pattern* card, the situation that has occurred before in your life. **CARD 2:** Your *animus card,* your competitive, assertive, logical side/the forceful arguments of others. **CARD 3:** Your *anima card,* your caring, nurturing side/the influences of nurturing, mothering, or smothering people that can lead to guilt around others' unreasonable demands. **CARD 4:** Your *shadow side,* the hidden fears or buried resentment toward people in your life—once recognized, this releases hidden strengths and the power to overcome your fears. **CARD 5:** Your *Inner Child,* the real essential you, what you really want and feel free from the expectations and demands of others. **CARD 6:** Is the key.

What you should use:
The twenty-two Major and sixteen Court cards.

When:
When you have plenty of time.

840
A THIRTY-TWO-CARD SPREAD FOR PAST, PRESENT, AND FUTURE

Purpose and background information:
To see the interconnections in your life. A more detailed version of Spread 85.

Stage 1: The first twenty-four cards
Row 1: The Past
What has passed and is passing out of your life, including unresolved issues and situations and people who have brought success or happiness.

Row 2: The Present
Present influences, relationships, home and work influences, personal current goals and achievements.

Row 3: The Future
Potential paths. The immediate future is to the left of the row, moving right to reveal the next ten years.

Stage 2: The eight strategy cards
Strategies to move from the present to the future in the most positive way.

Reshuffle the remaining cards, dealing eight cards from left to right, on top of the middle line of cards so each one covers one of the present cards.

Each strategy card reveals how to get from the present to the future, connected with the meaning of the card it covers.

841
EARTH, AIR, FIRE, AND WATER
WHICH STRATEGY SHOULD YOU USE TODAY?

Purpose and background information:

Use the forty Minor cards (Aces to Tens) and the sixteen Court cards in the four suits.

Each suit also carries an inbuilt strategy:

Pentacles or Discs (Earth): Find a practical solution; approach an issue slowly and cautiously, trusting ears, eyes, and common sense rather than the words of others.

Cups or Chalices (Water): Use your natural empathy with others to see what they mean and feel. If in doubt, listen to your heart and your gut feelings. Be prepared to go with the flow and cooperate with others.

Wands or Staves (Fire): Rely on intuition and inspiration. Seek a new or unusual approach to an existing problem or challenge, and be prepared to explain and sell your ideas.

Swords (Air): Believe in yourself and use your head, not your heart. Be prepared for opposition, but if you are logical and ignore critics, not least the old voices in your head, you will succeed.

How and when:

In the morning before work.

Shuffle the cards.

Deal from the top. Your aim is to see which of the four suits is completed first.

You must begin with an Ace and cannot begin to lay out a new suit until you have its Ace.

Keep to strict card order, each suit rising vertically from Ace to Ten.

You can build up a number row in the suit of any Ace/Aces dealt, before all four Aces are turned.

If a card cannot be placed in one of the four rows, place it facedown on a new pile to be reshuffled and used.

After the Tens, the order is Page, Knight, Queen, King.

If you have not completed one of the rows before you run out of cards, shuffle the discard pile and continue to deal.

The first suit to be completed gives you the elemental strength, which will give you the correct strategy to follow.

842
AN INSTANT "WHAT IS MY BEST STRATEGY RIGHT NOW?" SPREAD

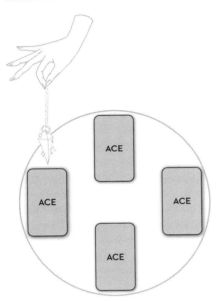

Purpose and background information:

An instant version of the previous Spread to do any time when there is an urgent need to know how best to tackle a situation, using just the four Aces.

Shuffle the four Aces nine times, place them face-down in a circle.

Hold the index finger of your writing hand (or your pendulum if you prefer) a few centimeters above each card, moving clockwise.

The card where you feel strongest vibrations will give you the correct strategy.

If you get no response, try to postpone the meeting/decision for now.

What you should use:

The four aces.

When:

You are desperate to find the answer—*now*.

843
THE FOUR-ELEMENTS SPREAD

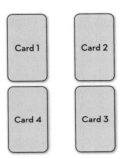

Purpose and background information:

Using the forty Minor cards, make four shuffled piles, one for each suit.

Ask any question when you've gotten no clear pointers.

Deal one card from each suit for each position.

The highest number card out of all four suits will give you the main tactic to use—and, by the card's meaning, how best to apply that tactic.

The next highest number is a backup approach, the third not to bother with, the fourth you should avoid at all costs.

CARD 1: Should you deal with the matter practically and step by step? (Use your Pentacles pile.) **CARD 2:** Should you deal with the matter using facts and figures, calmly but firmly? (The Swords pile.) **CARD 3:** Should you act swiftly, using persuasion and charm to resolve the matter? (The Wands pile.) **CARD 4:** Should you use your intuition as to the right words and action and try to flow with the prevailing mood? (The Cups pile.)

844

AN EARTH-ELEMENT SPREAD FOR WHEN YOU NEED TO BE PRACTICAL WHEN ARRANGEMENTS HAVE GONE WRONG

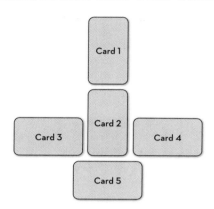

Purpose and background information:
When arrangements for a celebration or vacation have been canceled at the last minute.

CARD 1: What can be done practically to salvage arrangements/find alternatives so the celebration/vacation can still go ahead? **CARD 2:** Can/should you rebook for another time? **CARD 3:** Will you be able to rally others around to contribute in a practical way to the necessary rearrangements so it's not all left up to you? **CARD 4:** Should you ask for/will you get out-of-pocket expenses/ compensation if the cancellation wasn't your fault? **CARD 5:** Will the new arrangements be just as good as/better than the original?

What you should use:
The twenty-two Major cards, the 10 Pentacles cards, Aces to Tens, and the four Pentacles Court cards.

When:
When everybody is panicking and complaining.

845

AN AIR-ELEMENT SPREAD FOR WHEN YOUR HEAD NEEDS TO RULE YOUR HEART

Purpose and background information:
When you have to be calm and be tough with someone who you like a lot or is a family member in business.

CARD 1: If this were a stranger, would you be firm and take necessary steps to deal with the matter? **CARD 2:** Can you do this without diminishing the person's self-esteem, but not be emotionally manipulated? **CARD 3:** Do you have the necessary dates, facts, and figures to keep matters impersonal? **CARD 4:** Is it possible/desirable for someone else to deal with the matter who isn't emotionally involved? **CARD 5:** Can the matter be resolved to everyone's satisfaction?

What you should use:
The twenty-two Major cards, the 10 Swords cards, Aces to Tens, and the four Swords Court cards.

When:
A Wednesday for logical thought and communication.

846
A FIRE-ELEMENT SPREAD FOR GOING ALL OUT FOR WHAT YOU WANT

Purpose and background information:

If you have always lived to make others happy, and suddenly it's about you.

CARD 1: Has a major change/setback in your life prompted this/a growing awareness that time is passing? **CARD 2:** Do you want gradual changes to put yourself at center stage/a major life makeover? **CARD 3:** Who will be supportive/join you in your new lifestyle, or is this about independence? **CARD 4:** Who will oppose you/criticize the changes? Should you ignore/avoid them? **CARD 5:** Will you find your inner fire again/maybe for the first time?

What you should use:

The twenty-two Major cards, the 10 Wands cards, Aces to Tens, and the four Wands Court cards.

When:

A Tuesday for determination.

847
A WATER-ELEMENT SPREAD FOR FOLLOWING YOUR HEART, NOT YOUR HEAD

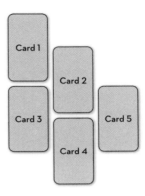

Purpose and background information:

If you want to give up a promising career and play with your grandchildren or grow roses, and everyone says you are crazy.

CARD 1: Is money and success no longer the prime mover of your life? **CARD 2:** Will you have sufficient money to live in a way that is authentic for you, or will you need to get a part-time but enjoyable job for a while? **CARD 3:** Are you closing the door on your career forever, or should you leave a way back if you change your mind? **CARD 4:** Is this the first of more sweeping life changes, or is this everything you dreamed of? **CARD 5:** Will you be happy and fulfilled by following your heart into your new life?

What you should use:

The twenty-two Major cards, the 10 Cups cards, Aces to Tens, and the four Cups Court cards.

When:

At a waxing moon.

CHAPTER 41

COMBINING TAROT SPREADS AND PSYCHIC POWERS

Lucky cards

Major Cards: The Magician, the High Priestess, the Hierophant, the Wheel of Fortune, Temperance, the Star, the Moon.

Minor Cards: Aces of Cups and Wands, Seven of Cups.

Court Cards: All Cups royalty.

About Combining Tarot Spreads and Psychic Powers

You may have met these psychic arts in other forms, but following are some ways that I have found work well in enhancing Tarot card readings.

848

VISUALIZING YOUR CHOSEN CARD IN YOUR MIND'S EYE FOR AN IN-DEPTH UNDERSTANDING INTO THE CARD'S RELEVANCE TO YOUR LIFE

Purpose and background information:
Expanding the meaning of the card using clairvoyant or psychic vision through your Third or mind's eye.

Ask a question, then choose a card from the deck. Study the card to memorize its details. Close your eyes and picture the card in your mind. Follow any pathways in the card or across water. You may identify with one of the figures. Allow words or impressions to add to your visions.

What you should use:
Twenty-two Major cards and thirty-six Minor cards, Twos to Tens (Aces aren't detailed enough).

When:
An evening by candlelight when you will not be disturbed.

849

A TAROT SPREAD USING AUTOMATIC WRITING

Purpose and background information:
Choose a card from the deck as you ask a question. Hold the card in the hand you do not write with. Allow your hand to write without consciously formulating words. When your hand slows, read what you have written. If you wish, choose another card and repeat the process, using up to five cards, one at a time. The information reveals what was not known about the question.

What you should use:
The full deck.

When:
When a matter has hidden factors.

850
PAST LIFE VISUALIZATION WITH A PARTNER OR CLOSE FRIEND YOU FEEL YOU HAVE KNOWN IN OTHER WORLDS

Purpose and background information:
Sitting side by side in candlelight, burning rose or lavender incense or oil.

From the facedown cards, pick the top card. Look at it, saying *Where was it we were first together in this place?* Still looking at the card, start speaking spontaneously about how the image links with a joint past world. Hand it to your partner to do the same. Keep talking so logic does not intrude. Continue turning cards until you have shared six cards, each adding to the vision. Any well-illustrated deck will take you to past worlds. If there is a special world you both feel a connection with, use a deck linked to that tradition.

What you should use:
Forty shuffled Minor cards, Aces to Tens.

When:
When you know you will not be disturbed.

851
A TAROT SPREAD USING A PENDULUM AND AUTOMATIC WRITING

Purpose and background information:
To tune into your inner wisdom, externalized through the pendulum.

Ask a question. Randomly pick five cards, placing them facedown in a circle. Slowly pass a pendulum over each card in turn, a few centimeters above each, until the pendulum vibrates or spirals over one. Using the hand you write with, hold the pendulum over the chosen card. See what information comes in the form of pictures in your mind, words, or impressions.

Transfer the pendulum to the other hand. Use automatic writing, as in the previous Spread, to get an answer. Pick a second card if you need more clarity.

What you should use:
The full deck.

When:
When you are getting conflicting information.

852
A TAROT SPREAD TO RECEIVE MESSAGES FROM YOUR SPIRIT GUIDES, ANCESTORS, OR ANGELS

Purpose and background information:
To discover if your chosen guide, angel, or ancestor has a message for you.

Set the cards in a circle and pass the index finger of your writing hand, or a pendulum, over each, asking your guide which card has the message. Look at the card and see what comes into your mind; then, holding it in the hand with which you do not write, ask your guardian to guide your hand as you write. As before, let your hand write; you may feel the gentle pressure of your guardian helping you.

When your hand slows, put down the card and read the message your hand has written. Look at the card once more and see the new insights in the picture.

What you should use:
The twenty-two Major cards.

When:
When you are alone so that you will not be disturbed.

853
AN EIDETIC IMAGING SPREAD WHEN YOU NEED DEEPER INSIGHT INTO THE RELEVANCE OF A CARD

(Eidetic means mental images that have unusual vividness, detail, and retention.)

Purpose and background information

This is a follow-on from visualization Spreads 846 and 847. Ask a question. Sit facing a well-lit white wall. Choose just one card from the deck. Focus on your card for about three minutes to absorb detail. Close your eyes and picture the card's details in your mind's eye. Open your eyes, blink, and project the image onto the wall, as if you are throwing paint at the wall. Even if you see the card on the wall for only a few seconds, the process will trigger remarkable insights about the future in the area of life that relates to the question. If it doesn't work, try again in a few weeks.

What you should use:

The full deck.

When:

When the answer depends on several variables.

854
A TAROT SPREAD AND DREAMS

Purpose and background information:

When we sleep, our conscious mind loosens its hold and we can receive psychic insights in dreams.

In your bedroom, light a scented candle (in a safe container) and put some lavender oil on your pillow. Ask a question. Choose a card facedown from the deck. Put the rest by your bedside. If the card doesn't feel right, pick a substitute.

Look at your card, weaving a story around it relating to your question. When you are ready, put the card under your pillow, blow out the candle, and close your eyes. Picture the card in your mind as you drift into sleep. A similar scene may appear in your dreams. Whatever you dream, write it all down as soon as you wake.

If you cannot recall your dream, write whatever comes into your mind as soon as you wake.

What you should use:

Forty Minor cards, Aces to Tens.

When:

The last thing at night, immediately before you go to sleep.

855
A TAROT SPREAD AND LUCID DREAMING

Purpose and background information:

When you are aware, you are dreaming and so can control and change your dreams while asleep.

As in the previous Spread, choose your card at bedtime. Hold it. You do not need a question.

Weave your bedtime story incorporating a feature of the card, for example the rainbow in the Ten of Cups. Say *When I see the rainbow in my dream, I will know I am dreaming and can go anywhere and do anything.*

Put the card under your pillow. Close your eyes, filling your mind with the rainbow. Say the words as a soft mantra till you sleep. If nothing happens, repeat with the same card, symbol, and words until you see the rainbow in your dreams.

Use this method any night thereafter to enter different cards, using their symbol.

What you should use:

Forty Minor cards, Aces to Tens.

When:

Before sleep.

856
A TAROT SPREAD FOR HOW WELL A SPECIFIC EVENT, CELEBRATION, OR MEETING WILL GO

Purpose and background information:

Pick cards to predict how a job interview, meeting, or event will go by focusing on the specific date, to maximize opportunity and minimize potential conflict—or make an excuse and opt out. Write day and month numerically. Deal cards from the top.

CARD 1: Corresponds in the deck position to the day number, showing your opportunities on that day: if the 12th of the month, **CARD 12** in the dealt deck. **CARD 2:** Represents the month number, the challenges: so if September, the ninth month, this will be **Card 9** in the deck as you deal. Focus on each card for one or two minutes and weigh up whether advantages outweigh potential problems so you are prepared either way, or consider changing the date if negative.

What you should use:
A full deck.

When:
As soon as the meeting/event is given a date.

857
TO DECIDE THE BEST DATE FOR AN EVENT, CELEBRATION, OR MEETING

Purpose and background information:
Choose up to six different dates for a special event. Add together the total number for both day and month for each possible date. Reduce this number to a single digit 1–9, except for 11 and 22.

Starting at the top of the card pile, deal until you reach the card position in the deck corresponding with the first date under consideration. If a date number came to 7, for example 06-01, June 1st, you would deal the seventh card to represent that date.

Do the same for each date.

Choose which date is most favorable according to the meaning of the cards. The Seven of Swords (a sneaky card) wouldn't be as good as the Six of Swords. which means moving into calmer waters.

What you should use:
The forty Minor cards, Aces to Tens, and the twenty-two Major cards.

When:
Whenever needed.

858
A TAROT SPREAD FOR A PREDICTION USING BIBLIOMANCY OR STICHOMANCY

Purpose and background information:
Stichomancy involves choosing, at random, lines from books of wisdom such as the I Ching, the Hindu scriptures, the works of Shakespeare, or classical poetry. Using the Bible is called Bibliomancy. Combining this with Tarot cards offers a powerful prediction about a situation whose outcome is uncertain.

Pick a single card. Open your chosen book anywhere that feels right. Starting at the top of the left-hand page, read the first complete paragraph. Apply the words to the card meaning to shape the prediction. If unclear, repeat with a second card and a second passage from the book.

What you should use:
The twenty-two Major cards.

When:
When you need an in-depth prediction.

859
A TAROT SPREAD AND MEDITATION

Purpose and background information:
Scan and print a large copy of your chosen card, attached to a plain wall between two white lighted candles. Burn your favorite incense or oil. Play soft music and totally relax.

As you inhale and exhale slowly and gently, allow the Tarot image to draw around you so that you move within the card. You may pass through a doorway within the card to other realms.

Let the card world continue to expand and fill your mind. Allow words and impressions to come and go freely. When you are ready, gradually tune in to the world again. Your Tarot meditation is complete.

What you will need:
Your Card of the Day, or one randomly picked from the shuffled Major and forty Minor cards.

When:
When you feel the need to relax.

860
A TAROT SPREAD USING THE FOOL CARD FOR ASTRAL PROJECTION

Purpose and background information:
Astral projection, mind travel, or out-of-body experience can occur in dreams, spontaneously or through using Tarot cards.

Light a frankincense, jasmine, or sandalwood incense and a semicircle of pure white candles or a large circular white lamp to stand behind your card or an enlarged card copy. Study the Fool card and memorize it. Close your eyes. In your mind, follow the direction the Fool is leaping or stepping. A flying or floating sensation begins as you leave the cliff of certainty and restriction. Fly or float wherever you wish, holding the hand of the Fool. You cannot fall. Travel to magickal lands, across the world, to past worlds or across the universe. Be open to what the Fool can teach you, for the Fool is the real true inner person we can become.

Gradually the Fool will take you back to the cliff, landing effortlessly. Before you go, look into his/her eyes and ask what you most want to know. Open your eyes slowly and sit in the candlelight for a while.

What you will need:
The Fool card.

When:
After dark.

861
FOLLOWING THE STAR CARD IN ASTRAL PROJECTION

Purpose and background information:
Use incense and candles and the Star card, enlarged and propped up. Memorize the Star card. Closing your eyes, focus on the star, seeing a stairway of thirteen steps of shimmering light, which you will then walk up until, on step thirteen, you are among the stars. Walk among the stars, noticing windows of light in the shape of stars. Look through any of them, seeing worlds that are familiar from dreams, reminding you of who you are and what you can achieve.

When you are ready, catch one small falling star, holding a talent you need to follow: your life star. You will see the stairs of light ahead: walk down them again and open your eyes, knowing the shimmer is within you.

What you will need:
The Star card.

When:
Your dream seems hard to attain.

862
THE TAROT AND ASTRAL PROJECTION TO FIND YOUR POWER ANIMAL

Purpose and background information:
Use a card with a horse or animal to act as your steed, such as the Six of Wands or one of the Knights on horseback or the Chariot pulled by sphinxes.

Light incense and candles and prop up your picture as in Spread 861. Play soft drum music to establish the rhythm of movement.

Memorize your card and, closing your eyes, the horseman/woman will allow you to take their place on the horse. Move slowly, then faster and faster as you pass through an arch of trees into a grassy clearing. You may experience a slight sensation of whirling wind as you pass through the arch.

You will see a creature waiting for you in the clearing who is, at this time in your life, the power animal you most need. This is your protector and, however fierce, it will not hurt you.

The nature of the animal or bird, maybe even a magickal creature, will represent the powers you need most right now: the courage of a lion, the fierce focus of the eagle. Let your animal tell or show you what you most need.

Next time, when you return, you can take the power of your creature with you.

863
A TAROT WHEEL-OF-FORTUNE CARD FOR PAST-LIFE EXPLORATION USING A MIRROR AND CANDLES

Purpose and background information:
Very similar to astral projection, except you specify that you want to explore a past world.

Prop a large mirror on a table and, in front of the mirror, angle three lighted tea lights in total darkness so they make a pathway into the mirror and are reflected within the mirror, extending the pathway. Hold your Wheel of Fortune card as your talisman to enter the past, and walk along the pathway of light through the mirror and along the pathway within it. Ahead is the Wheel of Fortune as a carousel of light. Ride on it; when it stops, you will be in a different place and time. Though only an observer, you may see yourself as part of that world, with people you recognize, and understand what you need to know from that time to help your present life.

Once you become aware of the Wheel, you will know it is time to retrace your way to the carousel, down the pathway of light out of the mirror.

Blow out the candles. In the afterglow in the mirror, you will see the image of your own future fortune and where you are on the wheel.

864
USING THE TAROT PAST-LIFE MIRROR WORLD TO EXPLORE A CERTAIN FEAR THAT YOU HAVE

Purpose and background information:
If you have a special fear—for example, food issues or a fear of enclosed spaces; whatever it is—you can go back to the past world where it first occurred and overcome it.

Repeat the previous Spread (Spread 863) using the Wheel of Fortune card again and ask to be taken to when you were first afraid. This time see yourself in the fear situation, perhaps with no food for your family or locked away in the dark.

Now, give that past self the key and lead yourself out of the dungeon, or fill a basket with food and say it will never happen again. Just as with a dream, you can change the past because it is on the thought plane.

Look for your wheel/carousel of light and return to your present world. As you blow out the candles, blink and visualize/see your past-world self, happy and free in the mirror afterglow.

When:
The end of the moon cycle.

865
A TAROT SPREAD FOR EXPLORING
YOUR AURA STRENGTHS AND CHALLENGES

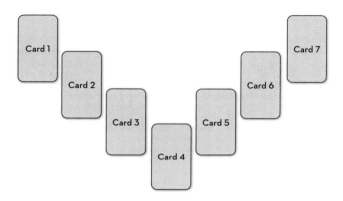

Purpose and background information:

Using the Tarot to assess the relative strengths and challenges within each of the seven aura bands, and seeing how your Aura strength cards can offer power to overcome the challenges. The aura is made up of the seven rainbow bands of energy, invisible to the physical eye, that we radiate into the world and by which we absorb positive and negative effects from the world. Whether a card is positive or challenging, according to its meaning, you will know where you need to strengthen a particular band to overcome its challenges. The most powerfully positive card shows which of your aura bands is predominant right now.

CARD 1: Red innermost layer of the aura. Positive: physical strength and energy, sharp instincts, awareness of opportunity and danger. Challenging: irritability, impulsiveness.

CARD 2: Orange second layer. Positive: awareness of own needs, dreams, intuition. Challenging: unrealistic expectations, illusions, physical excesses.

CARD 3: Yellow third layer. Positive: confidence, determination, unique qualities. Challenging: perfectionism, workaholic tendencies.

CARD 4: Green fourth layer. Positive: for balanced committed love, good relationships. Challenging: guilt, possessiveness.

CARD 5: Blue fifth aura. Positive: creativity, clear communication, ideas, ideals. Challenging: dogmatic, overbearing, wanting to be center stage.

CARD 6: Indigo sixth layer. Positive: imagination, spiritual gifts, wisdom. Challenging: living in dream world, indecision, not getting things done.

CARD 7: White/violet/gold seventh/outer layer. Positive: balanced mind, body, spirit, clear vision. Challenging: detached emotions, intolerance of weakness.

What you should use:

The forty Minor cards, Aces to Tens.

When:

Monthly, or whenever you feel out of sorts.

866
A PAST, PRESENT, AND FUTURE TAROT SPREAD USING YOUR BIRTH NAME, CURRENT NAME, AND MAGICKAL NAME

Purpose and background information:

To understand how the names we use/are called by reflect our evolving psyche.

From the full deck as you deal, pick a card in the same position in the deck as the number of each of the different name forms listed below.

Pythagorean system

1	2	3	4	5	6	7	8	9
A	B	C	D	E	F	G	H	I
J	K	L	M	N	O	P	Q	R
S	T	U	V	W	X	Y	Z	

Card 1: Your birth-certificate name in full, all the letters added together and reduced to a single digit except for 11 and 22. Reveals what you have learned so far in life, maybe also in past lives. **Card 2:** The current name that friends and colleagues call you by (maybe a single nickname; maybe different for friends and family, in which case add them together and reduce) to reveal the current persona that you show to the world. **Card 3:** The magickal name you would give yourself as you see your real inner self (can be one or more to add together and reduce), to show yourself your potential. **Card 4:** Add all three numbers together and reduce to a single digit or 11 or 22 to give you the card of your future.

What you should use:

The full deck.

When:

When you are not sure of your identity. Whenever name 2 or 3 changes.

867
A TAROT SPREAD FOR DISCOVERING MORE ABOUT THE HEART, HEAD, LIFE, AND FATE OR DESTINY LINES ON YOUR PALM

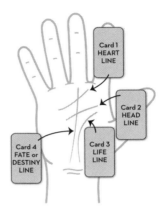

Purpose and background information:

Using Tarot to discover more about the energies reflected in your palms.

Hold the deck of Major Arcana cards between your hands to pick up the psychic impressions imprinted there. Pick four cards. Hold each in turn between your palms before reading it.

Card 1: Your Heart line impressions: what you need to know most now in the area of your emotional life, relationships of all kinds, and using your heart as a wise guide for these. **Card 2:** Your Head line impressions: what you need to know about your career, learning processes, and using your logic and knowledge right now for these. **Card 3:** Your Life line impressions: your energy, physical strength, enthusiasm, and sense of/need for adventure and the need to go all out for what you want in life. **Card 4:** Your Fate or Destiny line impressions: who controls your Destiny right now, your life plan, obstacles, and making the changes you want and need right now.

What you should use:

All Major cards.

When:

For a quick assessment whenever you want to tune in to yourself as the cards and energies will change.

868
A TAROT SPREAD FOR UNDERSTANDING YOUR MOTIVATING FORCES FROM YOUR PALM

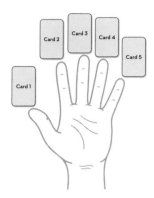

Purpose and background information:
Matching Tarot cards with the energy of your fingers and thumb to tap into what motivates you and the way you see the world right now.

Hold the full deck in your non-writing hand and run your fingers and thumb over the cards to imprint them with your psychic energies. Pick five cards. Press your thumb on Card 1, your index finger on Card 2, your middle finger on Card 3, your ring finger on Card 4, your little finger on Card 5.

CARD 1: Your thumb tells you the strength of your willpower, motivation, and perseverance right now; what you want and need most. **CARD 2:** Your Jupiter (index) finger tells you how you can best make your mark on the world. **CARD 3:** Your Saturn (middle) finger tells you how you can overcome/adapt to the restrictions being imposed by life and authority figures. **CARD 4:** Your Apollo (ring) finger tells us how you can use your creativity and ingenuity to turn any challenges into advantages. **CARD 5:** Your Mercury (little) finger tells you how you can best persuade others to see things your way and benefit financially.

What you should use:
The full deck.

When:
When you want to check in on life.

869
DEVELOPING YOUR PSYCHIC GIFTS

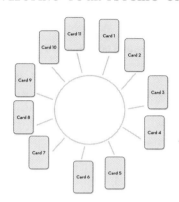

Purpose and background information:
When you are ready to develop or expand your psychic work, how do you choose a path? See which cards are strongest and most positive. If you are not already following that psychic path, explore it. If one path seems negative, ask yourself if there is anything that worries you, that could be addressed—or is best left for another time. You may find that, by combining several spiritual paths, you can work holistically to resolve clients' life problems.

CARD 1: Should you focus on healing and energy therapies? **CARD 2:** Are you gifted with cards, runes, or another traditional divinatory art? **CARD 3:** Are you gifted with the pendulum/dowsing rods/earth energies generally? **CARD 4:** Are you a natural palm reader? **CARD 5:** Do you have gifts with nature, herbs, oils/essences? **CARD 6:** Are you gifted in magick? **CARD 7:** Are you good at psychometry/psychic touch/receiving information from people's possessions/old artifacts? **CARD 8:** Are you a natural medium/spirit communicator? **CARD 9:** Do you have talents in psychic artistry, drawing people's ancestors/spirit guides/guardian angels? **CARD 10:** Do you work best with angels/spirit guides? **CARD 11:** Are you a natural aura reader?

What you should use:
The full deck.

When:
At the full moon.

1001 TAROT SPREADS

CHAPTER 42

SPREADS FOR FESTIVALS AND SEASONS

Lucky Cards

Major Cards: The Fool (inner child), the Magician, the Empress, the Chariot, the Sun, the World.

Minor Cards: All the Aces; Threes of Pentacles, Cups and Wands; Eights of Pentacles and Wands; Ten of Cups.

Court Ctards: Princesses/Pages of Cups and Wands; Princes/Knights of Cups and Wands.

About Festival and Seasons Spreads

Each Spread taps into the energies of its own festival and season and reveals how those energies link with the inner energies of the reader/person having the reading. On the whole, odd numbers of cards or eight-card Spreads seem to work best, and twelves for Spreads looking at the whole year. Specific festivals are often empowered by one of the ancient earth-energy change points, and so are natural times for a reading linked with that theme. This chapter contains Spreads linked with festivals from different cultures that have moved into wider society as they become increasingly multicultural.

870
A FOUR-SEASONS SPREAD

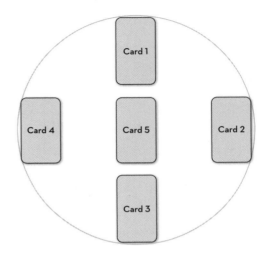

Purpose and background information:

To link your inner changing energies with the changing energy flows of the year.

CARD 1: Spring: What is growing/needs to grow in your life? **CARD 2:** Summer: How can you best gain recognition/rewards for your efforts? **CARD 3:** Fall: What has worked well and will continue to flourish in your life? **CARD 4:** Winter: What needs preserving for longer-term results, and what to let go? **CARD 5:** Which will be my best season in the year ahead?

What you should use:

The forty Minor cards, Aces to Tens.

When:

Start at any seasonal change points, or at any time during the current season.

A MONTH-BY-MONTH SPREAD FOR TAKING ADVANTAGE
OF THE UNDERLYING ENERGIES OF EACH MONTH

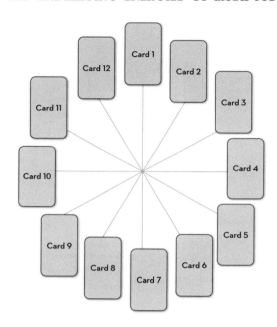

Purpose and background information:

Discovering what the cards say about how you should take advantage/avoid pitfalls each month. According to the meaning of the card, you will know whether following the month trend will bring a positive result, or a challenge you will need to win through in order to succeed.

Card 1: January: How can you make a wise investment/financial decision? **Card 2:** February: How can you improve your social life? **Card 3:** March: How can you successfully divide your time between two people who both need you? **Card 4:** April: Should you compete in an event even if you do not think you will win? **Card 5:** May: Should you invest in a new health or fitness regime, major beauty treatment, or cosmetic surgery? **Card 6:** June: Should you take up a completely new interest that has always fascinated you? **Card 7:** July: Should you spend more quality time with your partner/family/friends

if you work 24/7? **Card 8:** August: Should you take center stage/seek extra recognition/reward for what you do? **Card 9:** September: Should you relax more and slow down in order to enjoy life and avoid making careless mistakes? **Card 10:** October: Should you avoid being involved in other people's quarrels/trying to keep everyone around you happy? **Card 11:** November: Should you focus on your spiritual self/explore your psychic abilities to keep you one step ahead? **Card 12:** December: Should you enroll to learn something new/take an opportunity to extend your skills when the New Year begins?

What you should use:

The full deck.

When:

Start the reading in the current month, or the first day of the following month.

872
THE NEW YEAR'S EVE GOOD-RESOLUTION SPREAD

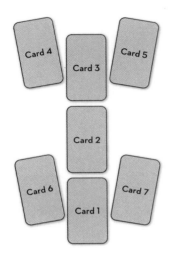

Purpose and background information:
To make plans and resolutions for what you most want for the New Year.

CARD 1: What do you want to take forward from the year just ending? **CARD 2:** What do you want to leave behind in the old year? **CARD 3:** What should be your New Year's resolution? **CARD 4:** What will be hardest about keeping it? **CARD 5:** How does your heart advise you to have a good year ahead? **CARD 6:** How does your head advise you? **CARD 7:** (optional time at midnight) What is your as-yet-unknown future?

What you should use:
The full deck.

When:
During a New Year's Eve celebration, or privately any time before midnight on New Year's Eve.

873
A CANDLEMAS OR EARLY SPRINGTIME SPREAD, CALLED IMBOLC IN THE OLD CELTIC-INSPIRED MAGICKAL CALENDAR

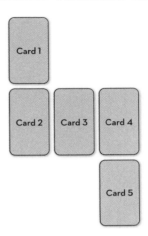

Purpose and background information:
For melting opposition to a plan you want to fulfill, or healing a relationship where there is coldness or estrangement.

CARD 1: What has caused this coldness/estrangement, and is there any justification? **CARD 2:** How far are you prepared to go to gain/regain approval, even if not your fault? **CARD 3:** How far is the other person/people prepared to meet you halfway? **CARD 4:** If it cannot be resolved, will or can you go on without this approval/reconciliation? **CARD 5:** Will the opposition or estrangement soften naturally, given time and patience?

What you should use:
The Major cards.

When:
Between January 31 and February 2 in the Northern hemisphere, July 31 and August 2 in the Southern hemisphere, early evening. All dates go from early evening on the first day to early evening on the last.

874

A VALENTINE'S EVE SPREAD IF THERE'S SOMEONE YOU REALLY LIKE BUT ARE TOO SCARED TO SEND A CARD

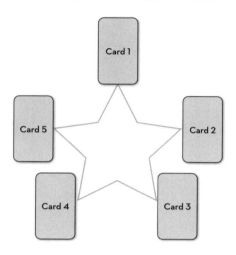

Purpose and background information:

When you have been talking to someone at work, at the gym, or socially but nothing romantic has happened.

CARD 1: What stands in the way of this romance progressing? Another person in his/her life/shyness? **CARD 2:** Should I send an anonymous card in the hope that I will receive one back from him/her? **CARD 3:** Will s/he send a card? If not, should I make a joke about Valentine's Day, or just ignore the subject? **CARD 4:** Should I ask him/her out casually just for a coffee/drink after work/after the gym? **CARD 5:** If s/he refuses, should I find someone who will make more of an effort?

What you should use:

The forty Minor cards and the sixteen Court cards.

When:

A few days before Valentine's Day.

875

A VALENTINE'S DAY SPREAD IF YOU ARE WITH YOUR LOVE AND WANT TO KNOW IF YOUR RELATIONSHIP WILL LAST FOREVER

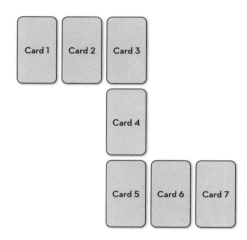

Purpose and background information:

If Valentine's Day was wonderful but you still worry whether you are with your forever love.

CARD 1: What is special about this love that makes it different from other relationships/if it's the first, what is the magickal spark? **CARD 2:** What worries you about the relationship? Are these real worries, or just fears/lack of confidence? **CARD 3:** What unites you? **CARD 4:** Who/what divides you, if anything? How to resolve it? **CARD 5:** Is this forever? **CARD 6:** Do you want it to be? **CARD 7:** Is this your twin soul, or is there another?

What you should use:

The forty Minor cards, Aces to Tens, and the sixteen Court cards.

When:

Valentine's night before bed, or the 15th day of the ancient Roman day of love, known as Lupercalia, which was an ancient pagan festival held in Rome each year on February 15.

876

A VALENTINE DAY'S SPREAD IF YOUR PARTNER DIDN'T EVEN BUY YOU A CARD OR TAKE YOU OUT FOR DINNER

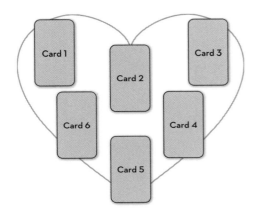

Purpose and background information:

When you made a huge effort for Valentine's Day with little or no result.

Card 1: Is your partner not romantic at all, or does s/he just hate commercial festivals? **Card 2:** Does your partner show love by what s/he does rather than what s/he says? **Card 3:** Should you talk it over to explain how hurt you were, or just forget the whole thing? **Card 4:** Should you rethink if your partner has a point but was just thoughtless, and maybe love shouldn't just be for one day? **Card 5:** Are there underlying issues in your relationship that you need to resolve? **Card 6:** Can you teach your partner to be more romantic, in readiness for next Valentine's Day?

What you should use:

The forty Minor cards, Aces to tens, and the sixteen Court cards.

When:

February 15, when you are calmer.

877

AN INTERNATIONAL WOMEN'S DAY SPREAD IF YOU ARE SUFFERING FROM PREJUDICE OR DISCRIMINATION IN THE ARMED FORCES, SECURITY SERVICES, OR THE WORKPLACE

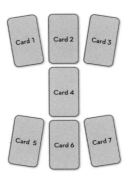

Purpose and background information:

This prejudice can come from other women as well as men. International Men's Day is on November 19 (see Spread 885)

Card 1: Are you being discriminated against because of gender or ethnicity, or is this just bullying with an outward excuse? **Card 2:** Are there others being similarly treated who would join with you to give your complaint weight, or are others too scared to speak out? **Card 3:** Is this subtle but insidious pressure, or exclusion from privileges/opportunities? Can you collate evidence to make a reasoned case if you know there will be major denial? **Card 4:** Is there any department within the organization which deals with/is forced to sympathetically deal with such matters? **Card 5:** If you have suffered physical attacks and/or psychological trauma, can you get impartial medical backup? **Card 6:** Can you use your experiences to help others? **Card 7:** If you transfer away from the problem or leave, can/should you fight this from the outside and get justice/compensation?

What you should use:

The twenty-two Major cards and the sixteen Court cards.

When:

March 8, International Women's Day; but also whenever urgently needed.

878

AN EASTER-MORNING SPREAD IF YOU DESPERATELY WANT ONE MORE BABY

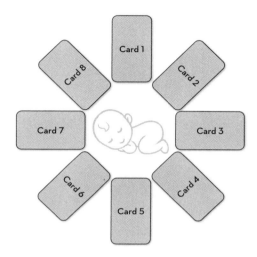

Purpose and background information:

If your family is growing up, but you want a baby you can enjoy.

CARD 1: Is this your decision? Is your partner on board/open to persuasion/definitely against? **CARD 2:** Is this a time in your life when you can step back from career/self-sufficient family and focus on a baby? **CARD 3:** Were you always busy when you had your other children? Did feel you missed out? **CARD 4:** Will inevitable changes/disruption be compensated for by the pleasure of a new baby? **CARD 5:** Can you adapt your life to fit in the hard work/inevitable restrictions? **CARD 6:** Is there another way you could feel fulfilled? Is there something missing in your life/relationship? **CARD 7:** Will you go ahead now, or get everyone on board when the baby arrives? **CARD 8:** Will a baby make you happy?

What you should use:

The forty Minor cards, Aces to Tens, and the sixteen Court cards.

When:

Easter morning, or the beginning of any week.

879

AN EASTER-DAY SPREAD FOR A MAJOR NEW START IN LIFE THAT YOU NEVER THOUGHT WOULD COME

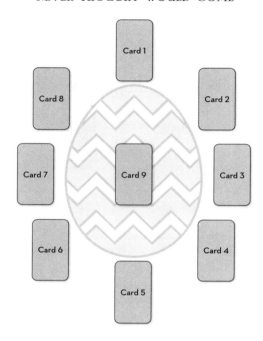

Purpose and background information:

When life opens up in a way you have wanted it to for ages.

CARD 1: How will this new phase first open up? **CARD 2:** Will anything hoped for be lost or temporarily delayed? **CARD 3:** What new opportunities will present themselves early on? **CARD 4:** What good new input will there be, and from where? **CARD 5:** What will quickly bear fruit? **CARD 6:** What will take longer to fulfill? **CARD 7:** What/who will try to waste time? **CARD 8:** Where will you be/what will you be doing by next Easter/12 months from the reading? **CARD 9:** The surprise.

What you should use:

The full deck.

When:

Easter Sunday, or a Sunday at/near the beginning of a month.

880

A SPRINGTIME SPREAD, OFTEN CALLED OSTARA AFTER THE NORSE GODDESS OF SPRINGTIME, FOR CLEARING OUT THE CLUTTER IN YOUR LIFE

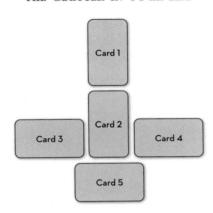

Purpose and background information:
When you feel weighed down and unable to move because of clutter and obligations in your life.

Card 1: What actual clutter in your life is slowing you down/frustrating you that needs to be cleared? **Card 2:** What activities do you no longer enjoy that could free up time? **Card 3:** What people no longer make you happy/bring you down that clutter your harmony? **Card 4:** Do you want/need a step-by-step decluttering of your life, or an all-at-once spring clean of your life? **Card 5:** How will you fill the free space and time? Or will you leave it clear to see what comes along?

What you should use:
The twenty-two Major cards and the sixteen Court cards.

When:
Between March 21 and 23, the Spring Equinox in the Northern hemisphere and September 21–23, the Spring Equinox in the Southern hemisphere, when day and night are equal and afterward days get longer.

881

AN EARTH-DAY OR EARTH-HEALING-DAY SPREAD IF YOU LIVE IN A POLLUTED OR GARBAGE-STREWN PART OF TOWN

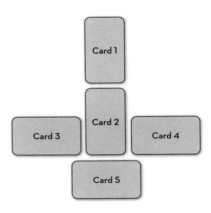

Purpose and background information:
When you care about the environment but where you live has been neglected and polluted and no one seems to care.

Card 1: Is there a community/environmental organization to pressure local authorities/arrange regular cleanups? If not, could you organize one? **Card 2:** Is the mess caused by people passing through/a local takeaway restaurant/local youngsters? Can you liaise with local schools/stores/youth groups to tackle the problem? **Card 3:** Can you make your own special space of beauty/window boxes/deck garden to inspire others? **Card 4:** Is there a local wildlife/nature area/green space to work with? If not, is there unused land that, with media interest, could become a center of beauty/family picnic area? **Card 5:** Could/should you relocate, even if this involves a longer commute?

What you should use:
The forty minor cards.

When:
Earth Day, March 21 or April 22; World Earth Healing Day, in mid-August around the 17th; or the fourth Sunday of every month.

882
A LATE-SUMMER OR EARLY-FALL/AUTUMN LUGHNASADH SPREAD IF YOU ARE ALWAYS THE GIVING ONE IN THE FAMILY

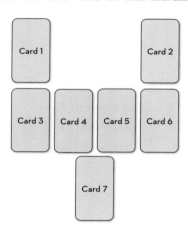

Purpose and background information:

This Lughnasadh festival centers around the first bread that is baked from the last sheaf of grain cut down, as an offering and so of mutual exchange. If you are always the one to remember birthdays, and no one remembers yours.

CARD 1: Are you/have you always been the person at the hub of the family wheel/arranging celebrations/inviting everyone? Does this make you happy? **CARD 2:** Do one or two family members take advantage, or do most people take you for granted? **CARD 3:** How, without going against your natural generous giving nature, can you ask others to do their share? **CARD 4:** Should you remind everyone in advance of your birthday/how Christmas, etc., can be shared, not delivered ready-served? **CARD 5:** If necessary, are you prepared to show tough love to those one or two selfish individuals? **CARD 6:** Can you overcome your natural sense of guilt/responsibility and step back? **CARD 7:** Will a happy balance be achieved so family events become a shared pleasure, not a burden?

What you should use:

The forty Minor cards and the sixteen Court cards.

When:

Between July 31 and August 2 in the Northern hemisphere and January 31 and February 2 in the Southern hemisphere, a festival of the first grain harvest, called Lughnasadh, a name inspired by the Celtic magickal tradition, and Lammas in the Christian calendar.

883
A MAY 1 SPREAD FOR BEAUTY AND CHARISMA

Purpose and background information:

The day when, traditionally at dawn, young maidens would wash their faces in the morning dew in order to become even lovelier.

CARD 1: Are you fine the way you are, just lacking self-confidence, or do you let others make you feel bad out of jealousy? **CARD 2:** Is this a good time to begin a new healthful eating/fitness regime in order to feel good about yourself? **CARD 3:** Have you considered having a makeover in order to feel better about yourself? **CARD 4:** Would major outer changes enhance your appearance? Is the look you want realistically attainable? **CARD 5:** Do you need an inner change/a new lifestyle, or to avoid the people who try to make you feel bad?

What you should use:

The twenty-two Major cards and the sixteen Court cards.

When:

The early summer festival of flowers, between April 30 and May 2 in the Northern hemisphere and October 31 and November 2 in the Southern hemisphere, often called Beltain or Beltane in honor of the Celtic-inspired magickal tradition.

AN INDEPENDENCE-DAY SPREAD WHEN THERE IS A MAJOR SAFETY ISSUE, OR CORRUPTION EXISTS WHERE YOU WORK

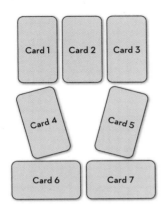

Purpose and background information:

If you are told that if you officially complain you will lose your job, but it's hard to remain silent.

CARD 1: Is there an official impartial regulatory body which would take you seriously? What are the risks of speaking to them? **CARD 2:** Would you need to find another job/relocate right away before you spoke out? **CARD 3:** Is there anyone else within the workplace who would support you? **CARD 4:** Before you complain/if you cannot, should you keep careful notes of your own involvement in case you are implicated? **CARD 5:** Should you tip off the local media/a current-affairs investigative program in return for anonymity? **CARD 6:** Are there legal implications of speaking out/would you get justice or a cover-up response? **CARD 7:** Should you speak out before something really dangerous happens, regardless of consequences?

What you should use:

The full deck.

When:

July 4, or any time around the Independence Day Holiday; or any Thursday, day of justice.

A SCANDINAVIAN MIDSUMMER SPREAD IF YOU HAVE BEEN DATING SOMEONE FOR YEARS BUT THEY ARE HAPPY LIVING ALONE

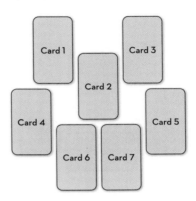

Purpose and background information:

When you do not want to spend the rest of your life in limbo, neither committed nor free.

CARD 1: What hidden—as well as given—reasons hold your partner back from commitment? **CARD 2:** What stops you from giving an ultimatum/meaning it? **CARD 3:** What keeps you in the relationship? **CARD 4:** What can blossom in the relationship with effort on your part? **CARD 5:** Can you accept the status quo if that is all that is on offer? **CARD 6:** Would you ultimately be happier alone, or finding someone else? **CARD 7:** If you are patient and persist, will you be together forever?

What you should use:

The twenty-two Major cards and the sixteen Court cards.

When:

From June 21 to 23 (St John's Eve, the eve of Midsummer); or June 24 (Midsummer Day) in the Northern hemisphere and December 21–23/24 in the Southern hemisphere, often called Litha, or the sun at its height, after the old Anglo-Saxon calendar, thus the Summer Solstice, when days are longest and nights shortest.

886
A FALL/AUTUMN SPREAD FOR BALANCING WHAT HAS BEEN OR IS TO BE GAINED OR LOST IN A PARTICULAR SITUATION

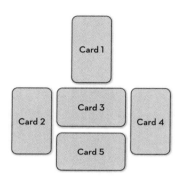

Purpose and background information:

When you are weighing up a course of action to see whether to go ahead or, if you have started, whether you should continue.

CARD 1: What are/will be the immediate advantages of going ahead/continuing with a course? **CARD 2:** What are/will be the immediate disadvantages of going ahead/continuing with a course? **CARD 3:** What are/will be the longer-term advantages of going ahead/continuing with a course? **CARD 4:** What are/will be the longer-term disadvantages of going ahead/continuing with a course? **CARD 5:** Overall, will gains exceed losses, or losses exceed gains?

What you should use:

The twenty-two Major cards.

When:

September 21–23 in the Northern hemisphere and March 21–23 in the Southern hemisphere, the festival of the second harvest, often named Mabon in honor of the Celtic magickal tradition. This is the Autumnal Equinox, equal day and night, after which nights get longer.

887
AN INTERNATIONAL MEN'S-DAY SPREAD FOR MEN WHO SUFFER DOMESTIC VIOLENCE

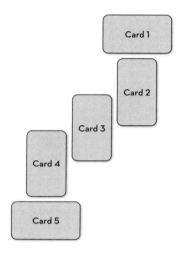

Purpose and background information:

If someone you love is being physically and/or emotionally abused by a parent or partner.

CARD 1: Can you/how can you help the person to overcome the embarrassment and shame, especially if the abuse is at the hands of a woman, to seek urgent help? **CARD 2:** Can you, even if there is denial of the seriousness, offer helpline contacts/domestic abuse victims' group that helps men/refuges/temporary refuge with you if appropriate so everything is in place if the situation becomes dangerous? **CARD 3:** Can you talk/set up counseling so the person can work through guilt and a feeling that it's their fault? **CARD 4:** Will the person accept help in time? **CARD 5:** Is there happiness/peace for him on the other side of this?

What you should use:

The twenty-two Major cards and the sixteen Court cards.

When:

November 19 preferably, but any time when help is urgently needed.

888
A DIWALI SPREAD FOR GOOD FORTUNE AND ABUNDANCE

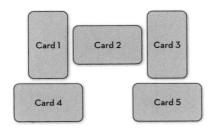

Purpose and background information:

Divali, Diwali, or Deepawali which is celebrated also in the Sikh tradition, is an autumnal Hindu festival of lights. Diwali is celebrated twenty days after Dussehra, on the thirteenth day of the dark fortnight of the month of Asvin (October–November). The date varies each year. The festival is sacred to the Goddess Sri Lakshmi, who is invoked at this time for wealth and prosperity, fertility, and abundant crops, and to bring good fortune in the coming year.

This Spread can be used by anyone of any faith or no faith around the festival to ask at this festival of light about good fortune and abundance.

CARD 1: What do you need to clear from your life/old attitudes/redundant activities/negative feelings that hold you back from good fortune and abundance? **CARD 2:** How can you best open yourself to new opportunities through positive thoughts and actions? **CARD 3:** What/who will best bring you the most joy and fill your life with light? **CARD 4:** How can you make your home/home life, whether alone or with others, a source of strength and good fortune? **CARD 5:** From where/how will new good fortune and abundance enter your life?

What you should use:

The forty Minor cards and the sixteen Court cards.

When:

Any of the days around Diwali.

889
A HALLOWEEN CONNECTING-WITH-THE-ANCESTORS SPREAD

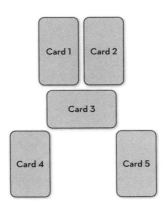

Purpose and background information:

Traditionally an evening when the dimensions part and we can access our ancestors who draw near.

CARD 1: What unfinished business with living and deceased relatives haunts you most? How can it best be resolved? **CARD 2:** Which ancestor is closest to you right now? **CARD 3:** What message do the ancestors have for you about love/family relationships/home? **CARD 4:** What do the ancestors have to tell you about your present life path/career? **CARD 5:** Which of your ancestors, living or deceased, who is most like you will best guide you in the months ahead?

What you will use:

The twenty-two Major cards.

When:

The evening of October 31, the beginning of the traditional early winter ritual called Samhain, in honor of the Celtic magickal tradition that runs between October 31 and November 2 in the Northern hemisphere and April 30 and May 2 in the Southern hemisphere.

890
A HALLOWEEN PAST-LIVES SPREAD

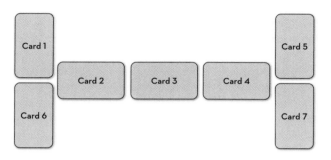

Purpose and background information:
Halloween is a natural magickal change point when past worlds move close.

CARD 1: Which past life most resembles your present world?
CARD 2: What past world explains an unusual talent not shared by your present family? **CARD 3:** From where do your seemingly inexplicable fears or strong dislikes originate?
CARD 4: Who is the soulmate/s most with you in past worlds? Are they in your current world yet? **CARD 5:** What was your earliest past life? **CARD 6:** What is your most recent past world whose Soul purpose you now carry? **CARD 7:** What is your next incarnation if you decide to return?

What you should use:
The full deck.

When:
The evening of October 31. Take your time with this Spread by candlelight to allow impressions to emerge–and record it. Follow up any special insights in private meditation or in dreams.

891
A THANKSGIVING DAY SPREAD

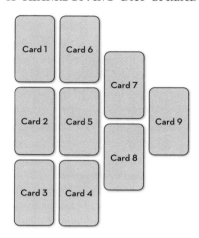

Purpose and background information:
For focusing on what is good in our lives.

CARD 1: Who is/has been the most positive living influence/inspiration in your present life? **CARD 2:** Which of your ancestors/a historical figure has been the most positive influence on your life? **CARD 3:** For what should you most give thanks in your life? **CARD 4:** Who/what is missing from your life? How can you find/replace them/it by next Thanksgiving Day? **CARD 5:** How can you attain abundance/prosperity by next Thanksgiving Day? **CARD 6:** How can you most share your abundance/prosperity? **CARD 7:** What do most you seek health-wise between now and next Thanksgiving Day? **CARD 8:** What good fortune can you expect? **CARD 9:** What gifts will you be most grateful for by next Thanksgiving Day?

What you should use:
The full deck.

When:
The fourth Sunday in November, or early morning on Thanksgiving Day.

892
A HANUKKAH SPREAD FOR BRINGING LIGHT AND HOPE INTO YOUR LIFE

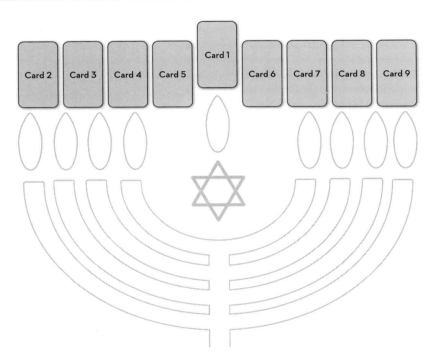

Purpose and background information:

Chanukah or Hanukkah is the Jewish Festival of Light, beginning on the twenty-fifth day of Kislev, which falls during November and December on the conventional calendar. On the eve of Hannukah, the Shamash central candle is lit first and is used to light all the other candles on the special festival Menorah (candelabra). One candle is added on each of the eight nights of the festival until all eight candles are alight (nine including the Shamash). The candles are lit left to right.

Card 1 (the Shamash, central card): How do you most need light in your life? **Card 2** (far left, representing the first candle to be lit from the Shamash candle): How can you reach out for happiness if things seem dark? **Card 3** (moving right): Who/what will help you? **Card 4:** Who/what doubts/obstacles hold you back? **Card 5:** What should be your first action? **Card 6:** How can you keep up the momentum? **Card 7:** What unexpected boost of opportunity will come into your life to show that you are on the right track? **Card 8:** How can you maximize this opportunity? **Card 9:** How/when will resulting fulfillment come?

What to use:

The twenty-two major cards.

When:

Early in the Festival of Light, the date of which varies each year.

893
A SCANDINAVIAN ADVENT-CANDLE SPREAD TO ATTAIN THE BLESSINGS OF THE SEASON

Purpose and background information:
A Spread for each of the four Sundays of Advent. Traditionally, four red candles of ascending height are lit, one on Advent Sunday, two the following Sunday, until on the fourth Sunday of Advent or Christmas Eve all four candles are alight. On the first Sunday, pick one card, on the second Sunday two, on the third Sunday three, and on the fourth Sunday of Advent (or Christmas Eve) four.

Record the earlier cards so you can see how the message of the earlier cards has evolved/changed by the fourth Sunday.

CARD 1: The blessings that are most being sought at this time. **CARD 2:** Ways these blessings will be manifested by Christmas. **CARD 3:** What you need to give/forgive at this time. **CARD 4:** Your personal/family message for this Christmas.

What you should use:
The full deck.

When:
Beginning on the Sunday nearest to St. Andrew's Day, November 30, and the next three Sundays or the fourth on Christmas Eve.

894
A PRE-CHRISTMAS SPREAD IF YOU ARE FEELING DISTINCTLY UNFESTIVE

Purpose and background information:
Around the shortest and darkest day of the year when everyone seems to be having fun except you.

CARD 1: If you do not want to participate in the workplace Christmas party/drinks with neighbors, do you have a good excuse or can you create one now? **CARD 2:** If you are organizing Christmas, is it time to issue lists/divide chores/accept that you have probably overbought anyway? **CARD 3:** Time to lay down ground rules about putting rivalries aside for one day/who does what to make the occasion restful for you. **CARD 4:** What do you hope from Christmas for yourself in any and every way? How can you get it, even at this late date? **CARD 5:** Is it time to plan next Christmas, maybe on a tropical island/a hotel/cruise where it's gift-wrapped for you?

What you should use:
The forty Minor cards and the sixteen Court cards.

When:
The prelude to Christmas, especially between December 21 and 23 in the Northern hemisphere and June 21 and 23 in the Southern hemisphere, the Midwinter Solstice, often called Yule from the old Norse calendar.

Card 1

Card 2

Card 3

Card 4

Card 5

THE TWELVE-DAYS-OF-CHRISTMAS SPREAD

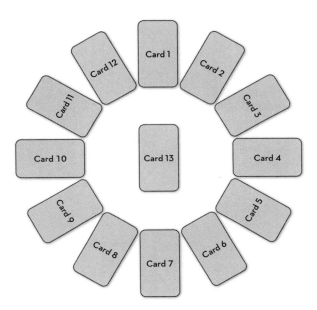

Purpose and background information:

Originally linked to a time when work could not be carried out in Northern Europe because of the bad weather. A good Spread for settling plans for the New Year.

CARD 1, DECEMBER 25: What gift or benefit (not necessarily material) do you seek for a good year ahead? **CARD 2, DECEMBER 26:** Who can grant this/how can you give it to yourself? **CARD 3, DECEMBER 27:** What most is there to celebrate in the year ahead? **CARD 4, DECEMBER 28:** Where must you look location-, career-, or love-wise to find what you most seek? **CARD 5, DECEMBER 29:** Who will you meet, or what will you find of greatest help in shaping your year ahead? **CARD 6, DECEMBER 30:** What/who will settle/stabilize in your life in the year ahead? **CARD 7, DECEMBER 31:** What will be most unexpected in the year ahead? **CARD 8, JANUARY 1:** What is your New Year plan/resolution? **CARD 9, JANUARY 2:** Can you achieve your resolution within your present lifestyle? Do you need to change things? **CARD 10, JANUARY 3:** What new/exciting opportunities are waiting for you to discover? **CARD 11, JANUARY 4:** are there any major unplanned movements physically/career-wise? **CARD 12, JANUARY 5:** How can you most ensure good health in the year ahead? **CARD 13:** For your personal year ahead, unique energies.

What you should use:

The full deck.

When:

Any time around the Twelve days of Christmas. If you prefer, you can pick one card for each of the thirteen days, returning the card to the deck, as repetitions would be positively significant.

CHAPTER 43

TAROT SPREADS AND THE SAINTS

Lucky Cards

Major Cards: The High Priestess, the Hierophant, Strength, Temperance, the Star, the Moon, the Sun.

Minor Cards: The Aces of Cups and Wands; the Two and Three of Wands; the Eight of Cups; the Nines of Pentacles and Cups.

Court Cards: The Queen of Cups, and the King of Cups.

About the Saints Tarot Spreads:

These are based on the particular strengths and qualities associated with different Saints. As well as their religious significance, Saints have come to symbolize in wider folk tradition those qualities as manifest in everyday life and needs, as well as more spiritual matters. Three, four, five, six, and seven-card spreads seem to work particularly well.

896
A ST.-JOAN-OF-ARC SPREAD FOR DECIDING WHETHER TO CONTINUE TO SEEK JUSTICE OR ACCEPT A COMPROMISE

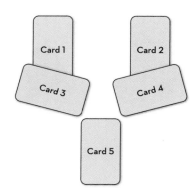

Purpose and background information:

The warrior Saint. If you are running out of money for a court case, but fear that to give way now would be to condone injustice.

CARD 1: If you carry on to the bitter end and win, will you recoup your expenses and more and be vindicated? **CARD 2:** If you lose the case, will you suffer a severe financial loss because of court costs? **CARD 3:** Should you transfer to a no-win/no-fee lawyer (also known as a contingency fee agreement), or do you want to stay with the lawyer you know and trust even if they do not work on a no-win/no-fee arrangement? **CARD 4:** If partial compensation can be negotiated outside court, would that be enough to prove to the world that you were in the right? **CARD 5:** Should you risk all?

What you should use:

The twenty-two Major cards and the sixteen Court cards.

When:

A Tuesday for courage, or a Thursday for justice.

897

A ST.-MARTHA-DRAGON-SLAYING SPREAD FOR DEALING WITH A DIFFICULT RELATIVE WITHOUT CAUSING A MAJOR FAMILY RIFT

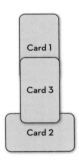

Purpose and background information:
The motherly St. Martha slayed a dragon because it was threatening the people of Tarascon, an ancient fortified town on the Rhône, between Avignon and Arles in France, not with a sword but by sprinkling holy water over it. When you know the difficult relative is just unhappy, rather than malicious.

CARD 1: Can/should you deal with the underlying unhappiness that is causing the problem, or try to resolve it once and for all? **CARD 2:** Is anybody causing trouble behind the scenes and offloading the blame? **CARD 3:** Is this a long-standing problem that can only have a temporary fix to avoid immediate disruption?

What you should use:
The twenty-two Major cards and the sixteen Court cards.

When:
Traditionally, St. Martha is asked for help on a Tuesday.

898

A ST.-JOSEPH-THE-CARPENTER SPREAD IF YOU ARE LOOKING FOR WORK IN AN AREA OF HIGH UNEMPLOYMENT OR A FIELD WHERE THERE ARE FEW VACANCIES

Purpose and background information:
St. Joseph is traditionally asked to bring employment of all kinds, especially when there have been difficulties or a long period of unemployment.

CARD 1: Are there extra skills you should acquire to make you stand out? **CARD 2:** Should you think about relocating to where there are more opportunities? **CARD 3:** Should you take any kind of job for now, if necessary retraining or in an unfamiliar field to get into/back into the job market? **CARD 4:** If you are patient and persevere, will you find a job within a few weeks/months?

What you should use:
The forty Minor cards, Aces to Tens.

When
A Wednesday, the day people traditionally ask St. Joseph for help.

899
A ST. JUDE PATRON-SAINT-OF-HOPELESS-CAUSES SPREAD TO TURN AROUND A BUSINESS IN TROUBLE

Purpose and background information:

St. Jude was said to never have turned away from any challenge during his lifetime, and he is called on to bring relief in the most difficult situations.

CARD 1: Is it worth one more try to see if you can get a stay of execution to get on your feet again? **CARD 2:** Will a source of help/resources appear at the last minute? **CARD 3:** Is there still hope? **CARD 4:** Can you turn it around/come up with a compromise so you do not lose everything?

What you should use:

The twenty-two Major cards.

When:

October 28, St. Jude's special day, or any Saturday for damage limitation.

900
A ST.-ANTHONY-OF-PADUA SPREAD IF YOU HAVE LOST AN IMPORTANT DOCUMENT AND NEED IT URGENTLY

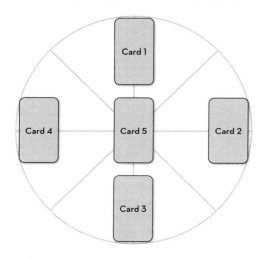

Purpose and background information:

St. Anthony is traditionally asked for help with anything that is missing, whether mislaid or stolen.

CARD 1: Is there another copy filed anywhere or with an official body that you can locate quickly? **CARD 2:** Can you retrace your actions to when you were putting the document away and became diverted? **CARD 3:** Did you give it to someone you trust for safekeeping, and have forgotten? **CARD 4:** If you recheck the place it should be, will you find it the second time you look, stuck to another paper or in the wrong file? **CARD 5:** If you relax, will you suddenly remember where you put it?

What you should use:

The forty Minor cards, Aces to Tens.

When:

St. Anthony's special day on June 13, but any Monday is good for what is not known or is uncertain.

901

A ST. AGNES LOVE SPREAD IF YOU HAVE BEEN MARRIED BEFORE AND ARE HESITATING TO COMMIT A SECOND TIME

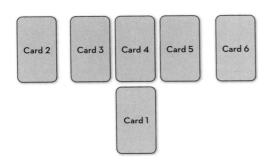

Purpose and background information:

St. Agnes was a Roman saint and represents all who are betrothed but uncertain in love. When you are afraid of making a mistake because of previous experiences.

CARD 1: What do you doubt, your future partner/yourself/ the state of marriage/all of these? **CARD 2:** Do you need longer to heal/to get to know yourself/to regain your confidence? **CARD 3:** Are there issues with/from your former relationship that need clearing up before you feel fully free to go forward? **CARD 4:** Are there any issues with the new relationship that need sorting out before you marry? **CARD 5:** Should you live together for a time to establish a new pattern for (maybe) both of you? **CARD 6:** If you go ahead, will you live happily ever after?

What you should use:

The full deck.

When:

St. Agnes Eve, on January 20 at 10 p.m. is traditionally the time for love divination; but any Friday is good for taking a chance on love.

902

A ST.-ANDREW-OF-SCOTLAND-EVE SPREAD FOR PINNING DOWN A LONG-DISTANCE ROMANCE

Purpose and background information:

If you have been together a while but rarely meet.

St. Andrew was said to draw your lover to your door at midnight on his evening.

CARD 1: Does a long-distance love suit one of you more than the other? Why? **CARD 2:** Do you find it hard to stay close emotionally with sporadic meetings, or do you like the idea of romantic reunions and partings? **CARD 3:** Are there/do you want definite plans for one or both of you to move closer together? **CARD 4:** What is the sticking point if this isn't happening? **CARD 5:** Can you accept the status quo if it's not going to change in the near future? **CARD 6:** If not, are you ready to move to a relationship where you see your partner regularly?

What you should use:

The forty Minor cards, Aces to Tens, and the sixteen Court cards.

When:

St. Andrew's Eve, November 29, or any Wednesday/Thursday for love over distance.

903

A ST.-CATHERINE-OF-ALEXANDRIA SPREAD IF YOU SUDDENLY FALL MADLY IN LOVE WITH SOMEONE WHO IS NOT AT ALL YOUR TYPE

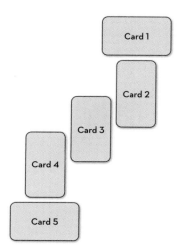

Purpose and background information:
The saint was traditionally invoked at one of her sacred springs for love on her feast day in the early morning, and so she is good as a focus for unexpected-love Spreads.

CARD 1: Could this be the attraction of opposites/a soul connection that completes you by supplying your missing qualities? **CARD 2:** Right now, are you looking for love and so are especially receptive to any romance and passion? **CARD 3:** Should you take it slowly/take a step back/get to know each other on an everyday level? **CARD 4:** Is this the real thing that defies all expectations and takes love into a new dimension? **CARD 5:** Will this last, or is it a stage on your journey?

What you should use:
The forty Minor cards, Aces to Tens, and the sixteen Court cards.

When:
November 25, St. Catherine's special day, or early morning at the beginning of any month.

904

A ST. HILDA OF WHITBY SPREAD IF YOU HAVE HUMAN SNAKES SPITTING VENOM AT YOU AT WORK OR IN YOUR NEIGHBORHOOD

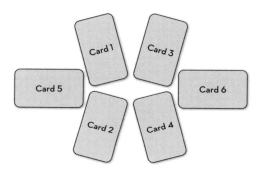

Purpose and background information:
St. Hilda, it is said, drove all the snakes over a cliff to clear the land for her abbey, and they turned into beautiful ammonites that are still found on the beach.

CARD 1: Are these particularly venomous people? Have they picked on you specifically? **CARD 2:** Should you confront the ringleader directly, who may back down without his/her cronies? **CARD 3:** Should you make friends with some of the fringe group/divide and conquer? **CARD 4:** Should you threaten to take official/legal action if the accusations are potentially damaging? **CARD 5:** Should you ignore them entirely, reasoning that those who matter will not listen anyway? **CARD 6:** If you refuse to react/defend yourself, will their vicious game lose its point?

What you should use:
The full deck.

When:
On November 17, her saint's day, or on any Wednesday to protect against spite.

905
A ST. ANNE, GRANDMOTHER OF JESUS, SPREAD IF YOU ARE OLDER THAN MOST OF THE PARENTS IN THE SCHOOLYARD

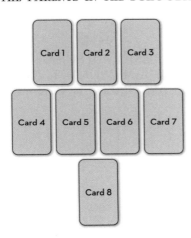

Purpose and background information:

When you are getting tired of being asked if you are the grandmother.

St. Anne was said to have conceived Mary when she was past her childbearing years.

CARD 1: What are the benefits of having a child later in life?
CARD 2: What are the drawbacks? How can you adapt/focus on the benefits? **CARD 3:** How can you best use your experience of life/more settled lifestyle to provide a stable environment for your child? **CARD 4:** Should you wait for other parents to get the idea that you are glad to be an older parent, rather than trying to justify your decision to have a child later in life? **CARD 5:** How can you make other parents welcome at your home/enjoy their homes without trying to fit in with younger parents' lifestyles unless you want to? **CARD 6:** If you chose to have a child alone later in life, can you find other parents in similar positions on- and offline to share experiences? **ALTERNATIVE CARD 6:** If you are an older couple/one of you is older, can you make friends with parents of different ages and stages/exchange ideas and learn from one another's lifestyle? **CARD 7:** When you get stressed out and/or when you get it wrong, can you accept that it's not because you are older, but that child-rearing is hard at any age? **CARD 8:** Should you enjoy the present and not worry what will happen in twenty years' time?

What you should use:
The full deck.

When:
On St. Anne's special day, July 26, or any Friday for family diversity.

906
A ST. EXPEDITE (ALSO KNOWN AS ST. EXPEDITUS) SPREAD IF YOU NEED MONEY FAST FOR AN EMERGENCY

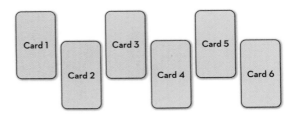

Purpose and background information:
The patron saint of all emergencies and sudden needs, especially financial and legal.

CARD 1: Will you be able to halt matters/postpone payments while you get funds together? **CARD 2:** Do you have accessible assets/salable goods that you can release to raise money fast? **CARD 3:** Is there someone official and reputable/friends or family who would temporarily bail you out?
CARD 4: Can you make money fast for a short period until you have made inroads into what you owe? **CARD 5:** If you cannot pay, how can you minimize consequences/negotiate longer-term manageable payments? **CARD 6:** How can you keep this problem/shortfall from recurring?

What you should use:
The forty Minor cards, Aces to Tens.

When:
A Wednesday evening.

907

A ST. BRIGID (OR BRIDE, BRIDGET) OF IRELAND, THE MIDWIFE SAINT, SPREAD IF YOU ARE TERRIFIED OF CHILDBIRTH BUT WANT TO HAVE A BABY

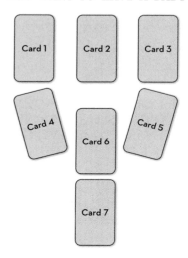

Purpose and background information:

When you have a total phobia about giving birth but desperately want a baby.

In legend (but not fact, since St. Brigid was a 5th-century saint), she was said to be the midwife of Jesus and has become associated with fertility, pregnancy, and safe childbirth.

CARD 1: What triggered off the original fear: seeing/hearing about childbirth when you were very young/a past life experience/one too many scary accounts? **CARD 2:** Would counseling/hypnotherapy/past-life regression lift the fear? **CARD 3:** Before getting pregnant, should you plan to talk with midwives about options for childbirth/pain relief/Caesareans/hypnobirthing during labor? **CARD 4:** Should you explore perhaps-hidden fears about pregnancy/the baby's early months, so labor is just part? **CARD 5:** Should you make sure you are fit before conception so you are prepared? **CARD 6:** Are there deeper issues/do you not want a baby yet/ever? **CARD 7:** If you go ahead, will all go well?

What you should use:

The twenty-two Major cards and the sixteen Court cards.

When:

On February 1 or 2, St. Brigid's Day, but you can use any Friday or Sunday, day of fertility.

908

A ST. CHRISTOPHER SPREAD IF YOU ARE THE FAMILY CAB DRIVER AND YOU ARE FINDING IT TOO MUCH

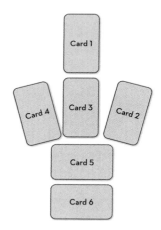

Purpose and background information:

St. Christopher is the patron saint of travelers, especially commuting and journeys for necessity. His medallions are still popularly worn for safety while traveling.

CARD 1: How did you become the family cab driver/has it remained a habit even though not needed, now that the family is older? **CARD 2:** Are you expected to drop everything/come out late at night in all weathers? **CARD 3:** Is it assumed that you always drive your partner home from parties? **CARD 4:** Should you start to be less available/ask for notice except in emergencies? **CARD 5:** Should you encourage family members to save for/get their own wheels/use a taxi or car service? **CARD 6:** Is this wider than a transport issue and a general lack of consideration for your needs that needs righting?

What you should use:
The forty Minor cards, Aces to Tens, and the sixteen Court cards.

When:
On July 25, St. Christopher's feast day; or any Wednesday, day of short-distance travel.

909
A ST. MARGARET OF ANTIOCH SPREAD FOR SINGLE-MINDEDLY ACHIEVING YOUR WISHES

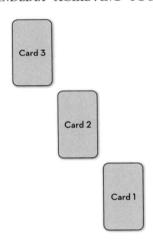

Purpose and background information:
Another dragon-slaying saint, said to be one of the inspirations many centuries later of St. Joan of Arc to fight for what she believed in.

CARD 1: What do you want most in the world for yourself? **CARD 2:** Are you prepared to sacrifice almost anything to attain it? **CARD 3:** Will you achieve this as long as you remain single-minded?

What you should use:
The twenty-two Major cards.

When:
During St. Margaret's festival, July 20, or July 13 in the Eastern world; or any Monday for fulfilling wishes.

910
A ST.-PATRICK-OF-IRELAND SPREAD FOR OVERCOMING THE PAST THAT HOLDS YOU BACK

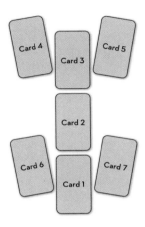

Purpose and background information:
Patrick overcame his own past as a slave to become Patron Saint of Ireland. He is a good focus if you find it hard to let go of a bad childhood or earlier abusive or destructive relationships.

CARD 1: Can you get justice for what happened in the past, whether legal, financial, or personal acknowledgment of wrongs done to you? **CARD 2:** Even if you cannot, should you shed your own sense of guilt and failure/look at what you *have* achieved? **CARD 3:** Do you need to talk over the past with a friend/counselor/express the pain creatively through music/writing/art? **CARD 4:** Can you go forward in new ways to prove to yourself that your life is of great worth? **CARD 5:** Can you mend the past through loving relationships with a partner/children/grandchildren? **CARD 6:** Can you help others with similarly sad lives, either informally, through a self-help group, or by training professionally? **CARD 7:** Do you have a happy, fulfilling life ahead?

What you should use:
The twenty-two Major cards and the 26 Court cards.

When:
On St. Patrick's Day, March 17; or any Sunday for new beginnings.

911

A ST.-JULIAN-THE-HOSPITALER SPREAD IF YOU ARE WORRIED BECAUSE YOU HAVEN'T HEARD FROM A YOUNG BACKPACKING RELATIVE FOR A WHILE

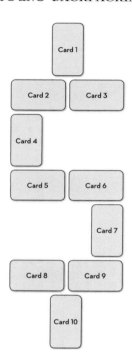

Purpose and background information:

If you are worried because there hasn't been any phone or Internet connection for a while.

Julian was an early 1st-century Belgian saint associated with travelers far from home finding safe shelter.

CARD 1: Is s/he safe? **CARD 2:** Is it quite common for your relative to not contact you for a while/not respond to calls/emails, assuming you would know they were fine? **CARD 3:** Were they heading somewhere remote, where any connection might be bad/non-existent? **CARD 4:** Is it typical for them to lose their phone/computer charger/ break or lose their phone so there's no connection when you try? **CARD 5:** Do you know their last stopping place, to track through their onward journey? **CARD 6:** Should you ask their friends back home if they've heard anything since your last contact? **CARD 7:** Should you put money on their travel card in case they've run out? **CARD 8:** Should you contact/check the embassy website where they last were, in case there have been any travel restrictions/updates? **CARD 9:** Will they contact you really soon, amazed that you were worried? **CARD 10:** In the future, can you set up some totally foolproof way they can touch base even if it costs you a lot?

What you should use:

The forty Minor cards, Aces to Tens.

When:

When you start to worry. St. Julian's day is February 12.

912

A ST.-BERNADETTE-OF-LOURDES SPREAD FOR HELPING A FAMILY MEMBER REGAIN INDEPENDENCE AFTER A LIFE-CHANGING ACCIDENT

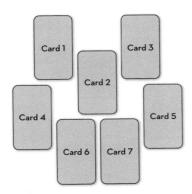

Purpose and background information:

In February 1858, Saint Bernadette experienced her first vision of the Virgin Mary that led to the healing grotto, site of many miracles at Lourdes.

CARD 1: How can you best help your family member to regain a new kind of independence? **CARD 2:** How can you assist him/her to find/if necessary fight for the required resources/financial allowances for conversion of living premises to allow independence? **CARD 3:** How can you assist with finding retraining opportunities/adaptation of the present workplace? **CARD 4:** What strategies/outside support/helping organizations are needed to cope with times of darkness/despair? **CARD 5:** What resources are available for social life/travel that will prevent isolation? **CARD 6:** Will your loved one find a new good quality of life? **CARD 7:** What support is there/can you find for yourself in these difficult times?

What you should use:

The full deck.

When:

On St. Bernadette's feast day, April 16, or February 18 (in some parts of France). Also, any Wednesday, the day of healing.

913

A ST. SARA-LA-KALI SPREAD IF LIFE IS GETTING TOO PREDICTABLE

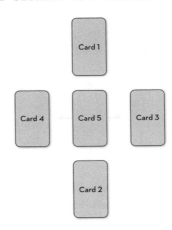

Purpose and background information:

Probably the most fascinating and mysterious of the saints, Saint Sara is the Romany saint who has her shrine at Saintes-Maries-de-la-Mer in southeastern France. She is in legend said to have rescued from the sea the boat carrying Marie-Salomé, Marie-Jacobé, Saint Martha, and Mary Magdalene, in some accounts carrying the child of Jesus, as they fled the persecution after the Crucifixion.

CARD 1: Do you seek small changes to make your life gradually more spontaneous if you are stuck in routine? **CARD 2:** Do you want/need some major changes to start to enjoy life/express your authentic self? **CARD 3:** What/who will welcome/share your freer lifestyle? **CARD 4:** Who will disapprove/stand in the way of your following your heart? **CARD 5:** Is now the time to pursue your desires/plan now for when you can put them into practice?

What you should use:

The full deck.

When:

On St. Sara's Day, May 24. Every year, there is a major Romany festival at her shrine. Also, on any Wednesday for spontaneous change.

914
A ST. PETER SPREAD FOR UNLOCKING DOORS IN THE WAY OF ADVANCEMENT

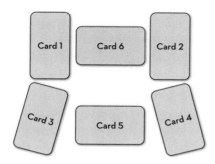

Purpose and background information:
The Apostle is said in the Bible to have been given the keys of Heaven and thus is a Saint associated with authority. When you seek to be given a position of authority.

CARD 1: Given no behind-the-scenes favoritism, should you be confident about being offered this new position? **CARD 2:** Will you effectively argue at interviews/presentations that you will make a positive difference in this role if given the chance? **CARD 3:** Who with influence/what factors are in your favor? **CARD 4:** Who/what stands in your way? **CARD 5:** Will you be offered this position/something with equal authority? **CARD 6:** Is this position the key to even greater future advancement/as far as you want to go?

What you should use:
The twenty-two Major cards and the sixteen Court cards.

When:
On June 29, St. Peter's Day, or any Thursday for leadership matters.

915
A ST. BARBARA SPREAD FOR SPEAKING YOUR MIND WHEN YOU HAVE REACHED THE LIMITS OF TOLERANCE

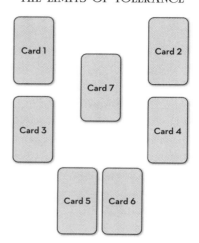

Purpose and background information:
The saint of lightning and of artillerymen and women/bomb defusion/engineers/fireworks and miners.

CARD 1: Are you generally patient and tolerant but have been pushed too far at home or work? **CARD 2:** How can you express your justifiable anger without totally losing it and putting yourself in the wrong? **CARD 3:** What specific grievances do you want put right, and what steps do you want to see toward this? **CARD 4:** Is it better to persist with the most urgent problems, rather than a general complaint about everything, which may be ignored? **CARD 5:** If your protest has no effect, are you prepared to impose sanctions and stick to them? **CARD 6:** If it doesn't change, do you want to walk away/accept the status quo? **CARD 7:** Will you get the results you need, even if you need to persist?

What you should use:
The forty Minor cards, Aces to Tens, and the sixteen Court cards.

When:
On December 4, St. Barbara's Day, or any Tuesday for action.

916

A ST.-GEORGE-THE-DRAGON-SLAYER SPREAD FOR FIGHTING AGAINST A COMPANY THAT MAKES IT HARD TO WORK BECAUSE YOU HAVE SPECIAL NEEDS

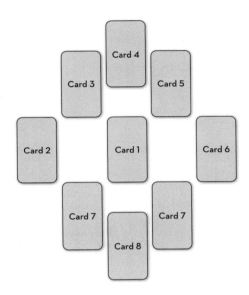

Purpose and background information:

St. George, the Patron Saint of England, was a soldier from what is now Turkey who served the Roman Emperor Constantine in England. Many centuries later, he became Patron of the Crusaders and was associated with dragon-slaying exploits. He stands against persecution and injustice.

Card 1: Are the problems due to thoughtlessness/inertia/budget considerations rather than malice? **Card 2:** Does the company avoid legislation by promising it is all in hand, but it never is? **Card 3:** Should you make a direct approach, along with other similarly disadvantaged workers, to the highest management? **Card 4:** If no response, should you contact the relevant discrimination authorities? **Card 5:** Is there discrimination in other more subtle ways/unspoken threats of job loss if you make a fuss? **Card 6:** Should you accept the status quo/look for a better employer? **Card 7:** Is this a matter of principle which must be fought? **Card 8:** Will you win through? **Card 9:** Will your efforts spearhead other workers to fight who are in similarly affected companies?

What you should use:

The full deck.

When:

On St. George's Day, April 23; or any Tuesday for courage and victory.

917
A ST. FRANCIS OF ASSISI SPREAD WHEN CONSIDERING WHETHER TO ADOPT A RESCUE ANIMAL THAT HAS BEEN BADLY ABUSED

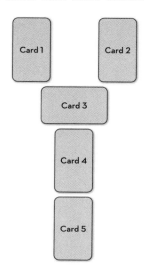

Purpose and background information:
St. Francis, an early 13th-century Italian saint, gave up a life of luxury to help the poor. He had a gift for healing animals and enticing even wild animals to come near, which he healed.

Card 1: Has this animal won your heart in the way an ordinary well-cared-for kitten or puppy would not? **Card 2:** Are you prepared/able to devote a lot of time to staying with the animal, maybe for weeks or months, until they recover? **Card 3:** Can you pay higher pet insurance/vet bills, as there may be many unresolved health issues? **Card 4:** Can you cope with antisocial behavior that cannot be changed/may limit you in some social situations? **Card 5:** Is it worth it to see this animal happy and safe?

What you should use:
The forty Minor cards, Aces to Tens.

When:
St. Francis's day on October 4; also any Friday or Saturday, days of animals of all kinds.

918
A ST. DUNSTAN SPREAD FOR FINALLY BEATING A BAD HABIT OR ADDICTION

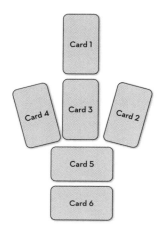

Purpose and background information:
This 10th-century UK Saint is often called the Blacksmith Saint because he was a skilled metalworker as well as a musician and artist and maker of church bells. His greatest claim to fame was nailing the Devil to his forge wall, some say catching his nose in red-hot tongs, according to the legend.

Card 1: What compels you to carry on with a habit/addiction you know is destructive to you? **Card 2:** Who/what will help you overcome this? **Card 3:** Is it a triggered/made worse by a deeper worry/problem for which you should seek help/relief? **Card 4:** Is it better to go all out for a fast, radical solution for the bad habit/addiction? **Card 5:** Would you succeed better with a slower, gentler detox system? **Card 6:** Will you overcome it this time, like St. Dunstan nailing your problem to the wall?

What you should use:
The full deck.

When:
On May 19, Dunstan's special day, or any Saturday for shedding what is destructive.

919
A ST.-TÉRÈSE-OF-LISIEUX SPREAD FOR DEALING WITH A VULNERABLE BUT OVER-DEMANDING ELDERLY RELATIVE

Purpose and background information:

Called Little Flower for her love of gardens, St. Térèse, who had a short life in the late 1800s, believed in gentleness and kindness as the way forward.

CARD 1: What is the biggest burden imposed on you by your over-demanding relative? **CARD 2:** Is there anyone professionally/in the voluntary sector/a local church/a member of the family who can offer outings/community centers/respite care? **CARD 3:** Is there anyone to whom you can offload the frustrations you cannot express to the perpetrator? **CARD 4:** Should you gently but firmly detach yourself from fulfilling the more unreasonable demands? **CARD 5:** Are there any strengths/talents that can be encouraged, perhaps shared with a local school/used creatively/recorded for future generations? **CARD 6:** Should you accept that *you are not* a saint and, as with a demanding child, draw boundaries/sometimes be less available?

What you should use:

The full deck.

When:

October 1, St. Térèse's Day, or any Friday for patience.

920
A ST. BRENDAN THE NAVIGATOR SPREAD IF YOU HAVE A LIMITED HOLIDAY BUDGET BUT WANT TO TRAVEL

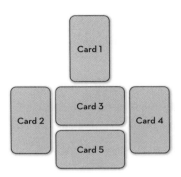

Purpose and background information:

St. Brendan, the Celtic saint, was a traveler often in his coracle (a small round boat made of wickerwork, covered with watertight material, propelled with a paddle) from Ireland to Scotland, the Hebrides, Brittany, and Wales and, in legend, on a fabled journey to the Island of Saints near the Azores.

CARD 1: What is your planned/ideal trip regardless of budget restrictions? **CARD 2:** Is it possible to go to those places using basic overland travel/accommodation where possible? **CARD 3:** Could you work along the way when you stay in different locations, to subsidize the trip? **CARD 4:** Do you want to wait until you can afford to travel more comfortably? **CARD 5:** Will you go, regardless of difficulties and budget restrictions?

What you should use:

The forty Minor cards, Aces to Tens.

When:

On May 16, St. Brendan's Day, or any Thursday for big adventures.

CHAPTER 44

THE GO-FOR-IT SPREADS: HEALTH, FITNESS, LEISURE, AND SPORTS

Lucky Cards

Major Cards: The Fool, the Magician, the Emperor, the Chariot, Strength, the Sun, the Star, the World.

Minor Cards: Ace, Two, and Three of Wands; Six of Wands; Eights of Pentacles and Wands; Nine of Wands.

Court Cards: Any Wands.

If water sports, water cards are lucky; if horses, cards showing a rider are lucky.

About fitness spreads:

These can vary according to the complexity of the question, especially if there are deep underlying feelings behind the basic question, as fitness and weight issues can be a minefield of hidden emotions and insecurity. Three-, four-, and five-card spreads answer straightforward planning questions, though more cards may be needed if the fitness issue involves life changes or overcoming major blocks. Eight- or nine-card spreads are especially good for decisive action.

921
THE SPORTS-AND-FITNESS SPREAD

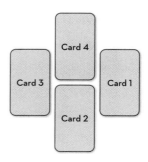

Purpose and background information:
When you are considering how far to push yourself in sports and fitness.

CARD 1: Should you undertake serious training with the aim of turning professional? **CARD 2:** Would you be happier just getting fit or joining a team for pleasure? **CARD 3:** Would gentle exercise for personal satisfaction and health be just one part of your many wider interests or occupations? **CARD 4:** If you go for the top, will you succeed totally/partly/be happy?

What you should use:
The full deck.

When:
A Wednesday for health and fitness, also for competitiveness.

Example:
Nicola had trained at swimming from when she was a small child, and through the years she had won many events. Her father, who was also her coach, encouraged her to train for several hours a day, even on weekends, but as a teenager she wanted to spend time with her friends. Nicola no longer enjoyed competitive swimming; but she didn't want to disappoint her father, who had dedicated his life to the dream of her becoming an international swimmer.

CARD 1: The Two of Pentacles, Nicola juggling different aspects of her life and feeling that she was not doing any of them properly, not a competitive card.

CARD 2: The Seven of Pentacles, showing how much Nicola

has achieved. However, this is not a going-for-the-top card. Nicola, who wanted to enjoy swimming for its own sake and has reached her limit, reflected in drawing the seven, not the ten, of Pentacles.

CARD 3: The Emperor: and so Nicola is no longer enjoying swimming but is fulfilling her father's dream. It's time, even at the risk of causing hurt, to speak out.

CARD 4: The Ten of Wands. Success if she wants it, but the person on the card is staggering beneath the weight of too many wands.

922
IF YOU ARE WORRIED ABOUT THE WAY OTHER PEOPLE PERCEIVE YOUR APPEARANCE AND FEEL GETTING FIT WILL HELP

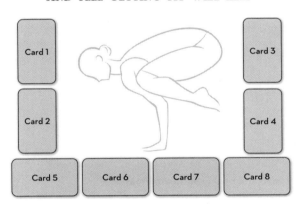

Purpose and background information:
When you are feeling negative about your body image and are looking for a way to improve your self-confidence.

CARD 1: How you see yourself right now/what you feel is wrong or unattractive. **CARD 2:** What, from the past/childhood/teenage years, made you doubt your attractiveness. **CARD 3:** Who in your present life/what airbrushed media images are making you feel insecure about yourself? **CARD 4:** Do others want/in the past wanted to unsettle you because of their own insecurities? Should you disregard this negativity? **CARD 5:** Is becoming fitter a first step to improving your feelings about yourself?

CARD 6: Who/what can help to make this happen? **CARD 7:** Will anyone perhaps implicated in **CARDS 2** and **3** want to discourage you? **CARD 8:** Will your becoming fitter improve your confidence in yourself and your life?

What you should use:
The forty Minor cards, Aces to Tens, and the sixteen Court cards.

When:
When you are contemplating taking action, such as joining a gym.

923
IF YOU WANT TO JOIN A GYM BUT ARE SELF-CONSCIOUS THAT YOU ARE NOT IN PERFECT SHAPE

Purpose and background information:
When you fear you would stand out from the fit-looking crowd.

CARD 1: Should you go along at a quiet time/go with a friend/ask for a tour/demonstration using the equipment? **CARD 2:** Should you find out if there are beginners' sessions/classes at different levels of expertise? **CARD 3:** Should you start with a gentler form of communal activity, such as water aerobics/yoga to gain confidence? **CARD 4:** Should you book a private session with a personal trainer to talk over worries/devise a program that includes nutrition? **CARD 5:** Should you go along anyway/focus on getting fit and not comparing yourself with anyone else?

What you should use:
The forty Minor cards, Aces to Tens.

When:
The beginning of a month.

924
WILL LOSING WEIGHT CHANGE YOUR LIFE FOR THE BETTER?

Purpose and background information:
When your clothes are too tight and you hate going out socially.

CARD 1: Is this an ongoing/lifelong issue, or weight gain due to an emotional setback/having a baby/illness? **CARD 2:** Do you need/want to join a self-help group/slimming club/a group of friends with similar problems/an online group, or to go it alone? **CARD 3:** Should you start with some gentle exercise/family activity to get motivated? **CARD 4:** Do you want a fast diet/reduce high calorie food intake, or better eating and nutrition changes to lose weight gradually? **CARD 5:** Are there people in your life who will make your weight loss easier? **CARD 6:** Are there people in your life who will make this harder? How can you lessen their influence? **CARD 7:** If there are underlying issues/grief/anger/relationship issues, should you consider counseling? **CARD 8:** If you usually self-sabotage your efforts, what frightens you about losing weight? **CARD 9:** Will you succeed in getting fitter/more confident and as a result want/make other lifestyle changes?

What you should use:
The full deck.

When:
The beginning of any month.

925
IF YOU NEED MORE THAN DIET AND EXERCISE TO PROMOTE A SENSE OF WELL-BEING

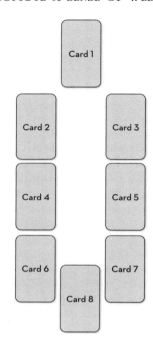

Purpose and background information:
When you want to move your whole self into harmony, but you are not sure where to start.

CARD 1: What needs to be let go, such as negative energies or people, in order to clear the spiritual, emotional, and physical space around you? **CARD 2:** Which is the easiest point of intervention, a detox/nutrition advice/exercise/spiritual balance such as meditation? **CARD 3:** Can/should you kick-start the process by staying at a health spa/healing sanctuary/learning yoga, Tai Chi, or regular energy therapy sessions such as massage or Reiki? **CARD 4:** Is anything hidden from you that may hinder your progress/cause you to give up/self-sabotage? **CARD 5:** How can you overcome both outward and hidden obstacles on the way to fulfilment? **CARD 6:** Where/how would you be the happiest living to maintain this sense of well-being? **CARD 7:** If your job is stressful, can/should you move on, or can you just compensate with extra relaxation? **CARD 8:** Will you achieve total well-being?

What you should use:
The whole deck.

When:
At the crescent or waxing moon.

926
FIVE STEPS TO SUCCESSFUL TRAINING IN YOUR CHOSEN SPORT

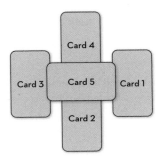

Purpose and background information:
When you want to train, whether professionally or for pleasure, but cannot find the right opportunities.

CARD 1: What is the main reason for not being able to obtain the right training? **CARD 2:** Will/where can you find what you are looking for, whether a weekly/daily training session/a residential school during vacations/a coaching academy? **CARD 3:** How far do you want to go through training/weekend participation/joining an amateur or professional team/competing/making a career of it? **CARD 4:** Can you/are you prepared to pay the required expenses/coaching fees to reach your desired level, even if they are high? **CARD 5:** Will you succeed in fulfilling your dream, however modest or ambitious, fully/partially?

What you should use:
The forty Minor cards, Aces to Tens, and the sixteen Court cards.

When:
A Wednesday for moving things along.

927
WHAT CHALLENGES STAND IN THE WAY OF YOUR GETTING A PLACE ON YOUR CHOSEN TEAM?

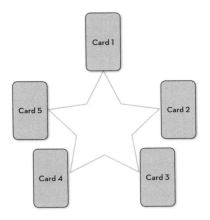

Purpose and background information:
When you know you are good enough but do not get a trial or an offer of a training place.

CARD 1: What is missing from the equation that means you get passed over? **CARD 2:** Are there special training schemes/venues where you would be spotted by scouts for your desired team? **CARD 3:** Is entry to the desired team a matter of who you know rather than what you can do? If so, can you find someone of influence to help you be accepted? **CARD 4:** Will you be accepted if you persist? **CARD 5:** In the meantime, will you get a better offer/apply for other teams as a stepping-stone/good substitute?

What you will use:
The twenty-two Major cards and sixteen Court cards.

When:
After a setback.

928
WILL YOU OVERCOME ALL COMPETITION WHEN YOU ARE UP AGAINST SOME TOP ATHLETES?

Purpose and background information:

CARD 1: Have you competed against all/some of these people before and didn't win, or is this a first attempt?
CARD 2: Are you totally prepared physically to have a good chance, or do you need extra last-minute training/input?
CARD 3: Is the problem lack of confidence/others making you doubt? **CARD 4:** Can/should you focus on doing your best, regardless of winning/do you thrive on the adrenalin of the competition? **CARD 5:** Would you be happy with second or third place, or will only a win do? **CARD 6:** Will you succeed this time? **CARD 7:** If you do not win this time, will that spur you on to win next time? **CARD 8:** Is victory the end in itself, or just the stepping-stone to your upward path to success?

What you should use:
The forty Minor cards, Aces to Tens.

When:
When you are doubting your power to win.

929
WORKING ON FITNESS IF YOU HAVEN'T DONE ANY FORMAL EXERCISE SINCE SCHOOL

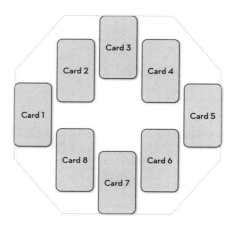

Purpose and background information:
If you decide it's time to get fit but do not know where to start.

CARD 1: What is motivating you: concerns about health/a partner or family members who follow exercise regimes/general desire to be more active if you have a sedentary job?
CARD 2: what activity used to/might still give you pleasure: dance/swimming/cycling/running? How can you reintroduce it into your life? **CARD 3:** Do you need classes/online videos/exercising with a friend/joining a group/sharing exercise with your family/solo? **CARD 4:** How can you clear unnecessary activities/demands on your time to enjoy your new sport, rather than cramming it in as an extra chore? **CARD 5:** Do you want to enjoy it at your own pace, set yourself targets, compete, or join a team? **CARD 6:** Is this/should it be all about yourself/your confidence/your new self-awareness? **CARD 7:** Will it lead to other activities/an interest in healthy living?
CARD 8: As well as greater fitness, will it improve your social life and relationships?

What you should use:
The forty Minor cards, Aces to Tens.

When:
As a New Year's resolution, or any Sunday, day of new beginnings.

930
IF YOU WANT TO TAKE UP SWIMMING BUT ARE TERRIFIED OF THE WATER

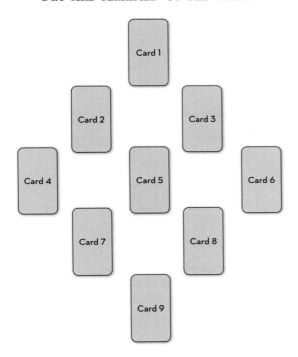

Purpose and background information:
When you realize that you are missing out on vacation fun or have a family and need to learn water safety.

Card 1: Can you trace your fear of water to childhood/a water accident earlier in your life/a past life memory? **Card 2:** Do you want help with this, such as hypnotherapy/counseling/past life regression, or do you prefer just to get on with it? **Card 3:** Should you go along to a water park with fun shallow pools so you can reassociate water with pleasure? **Card 4:** Should you book private lessons with a teacher who specializes in nervousness around water? **Card 5:** Should you supplement this with solo sessions when the local pool is quiet and there is shallow water at one end? **Card 6:** Once you are a bit more confident, should you try water aerobics/

go along with children who will enjoy playing around in water? **Card 7:** Should you indulge in spa treatments/luxury spas to be pampered around water? **Card 8:** Should you progress to learning basic water safety in case you ever panic? **Card 9:** Will you learn to love water/become more confident, even if always wary?

What you should use:
The forty Minor cards, Aces to Tens, and the sixteen Court cards.

When:
At a full moon, when the connection with water is strongest.

931
IF YOU HAVE ALWAYS WANTED TO TAKE UP JUGGLING AND OTHER CIRCUS PERFORMING ARTS

Purpose and background information:
When people laugh and tell you to grow up, but your dream is to be a circus performer.

Card 1: Should you first learn basic juggling and other circus tricks, including magic, from online videos? **Card 2:** Should you go along to circus workshops that are held in many big cities/depending on your level of fitness, learn anything from basic acrobatics to clowning? **Card 3:** Once you are proficient and have created a basic juggling/clowning act, should you hire yourself out to children's parties? **Card 4:** If you want more, should you find other people through circus schools who are equally interested in circus tricks, and enter talent shows?

What you should use:
The twenty-two Major cards and the sixteen Court cards.

When:
A Wednesday, the day of unusual arts.

932
IF YOU HAVE ALWAYS LOVED DANCING BUT FEEL VERY SELF-CONSCIOUS ABOUT DANCING IN PUBLIC

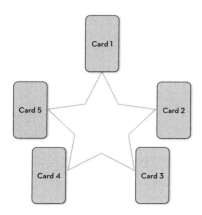

Purpose and background information:

When you were always dancing but, over the years, stopped.

CARD 1: Should you at first, to regain your confidence, dance to music when you are alone for the sheer joy? **CARD 2:** Would you feel more confident initially practicing steps of your favorite kind of dancing using YouTube videos before dancing in public? **CARD 3:** Should you go along to classes of your favorite kind of dance/go to tea dances/get involved in the local dance community events? **CARD 4:** If you would like to perform in a production, should you join a dance academy that provides dancers for local theaters/apply directly to a local amateur theater company putting on a musical? **CARD 5:** Should/could you learn choreography/perhaps get involved in a children's dance group/create your own dance troupe to enter talent contests/work on your own dance routines, if only for fun?

What you should use:

The forty Minor cards, Aces to Tens.

When:

A Thursday, day of the performing arts.

933
IF YOU ALWAYS WANTED A PONY AS A CHILD AND NEVER LOST YOUR LOVE OF HORSES

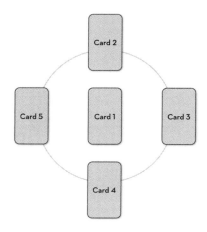

Purpose and background information:

When you can afford lessons/a horse of your own but wonder if it's too late to fulfill a childhood dream.

CARD 1: Should you try private riding lessons to see if the old magic is still there? **CARD 2:** Should you book a horseback vacation that caters to beginners, to assess how much you still enjoy being around horses? **CARD 3:** Should you explore the financial viability of owning/keeping/stabling a horse, or would you sooner ride a particular horse regularly at a local riding stable? **CARD 4:** If deciding to buy, should you get expert advice/find out beforehand where you would be happy stabling if you do not have facilities/time yourself? **CARD 5:** Would you sooner consign your dream to childhood/continue to go on riding vacations/visiting the local stables?

What you should use:

The forty Minor cards, Aces to Tens, and the sixteen Court cards.

When:

A Tuesday or Wednesday, both activity days.

IF YOU WOULD LOVE TO BE PART OF THE HORSE WORLD BUT DO NOT HAVE THE MONEY

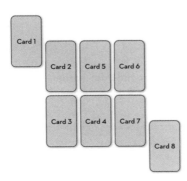

Purpose and background information:

When you were always the kid hanging around the competitors at horse shows and want to be part of that world.

CARD 1: Can you make yourself useful around riding stables in return for the chance to exercise the horses/learn eventing? **CARD 2:** If you are good at riding/eventing, will you find a sponsor/mentor who has horses as a status symbol but doesn't want the trouble of actually competing themselves? **CARD 3:** Should you learn absolutely everything about horses so you can apply for an equine scholarship? **CARD 4:** Alternatively, should you apply for work at a training stable/stud farm, no matter how hard or menial at first/work your way up/move on to more prestigious establishments step by step? **CARD 5:** Could you work at your local horse/animal rescue center to get experience/volunteer at a veterinary surgery where they do lots of work with horses? **CARD 6:** Should you train as a veterinary assistant/a vet/to enter the horse world via the back door by networking with the right people? **CARD 7:** Should you spend every spare cent on riding lessons, or find a well-paid job in any field till you are earning enough to get your own horse? **CARD 8:** Will you break into the horse world against all odds?

What you should use:

The full deck.

When:

At a waxing moon.

WOULD GOLF BE A GOOD SPORT FOR BUSINESS NETWORKING?

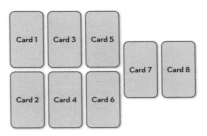

Purpose and background information:

If you have never played more than miniature golf in a fun park but realize a lot of business is done on the golf course.

CARD 1: Should you take lessons so you know what you are doing if you play golf with a business associate? **CARD 2:** Should you learn everything about golf through watching matches/online interviews/books so you know the right jargon and golf course etiquette? **CARD 3:** Should you enlist absolutely everyone you know to take you as a guest to different golf courses to meet the right people for your business? **CARD 4:** Should you get sponsored to the most expensive golf course you can afford without having to re-mortgage your home? **CARD 5:** Should you attend all social events/fundraisers to raise your profile? **CARD 6:** Will the outlay/hard work be worthwhile in terms of extra business contacts? **CARD 7:** Should you keep up with international golf tournaments/vacation to major events to be in the know? **CARD 8:** As a bonus, will you enjoy golf/establish a good handicap/even play for your club?

What you should use:

The forty Minor cards, Aces to Tens, and the sixteen Court cards.

When:

A Wednesday for business and socializing combined.

936
ARE YOU PREPARED TO SACRIFICE ALMOST EVERYTHING TO REACH THE TOP OF YOUR SPORT?

Card 4

Card 3

Card 7

Card 5

Card 8

Card 2

Card 9

Card 6

Card 1

Purpose and background information:
When you are doing well in your sport but still combining it with everyday life.

CARD 1: What is the ultimate price you must pay for reaching the top? **CARD 2:** What must you give up/leave behind if you go for the top? **CARD 3:** Are you prepared to be single-minded, or would you prefer to take it more slowly? **CARD 4:** What are the immediate advantages of wholeheartedly embracing opportunity? **CARD 5:** Who/what will ease your path/what new people share your experience? **CARD 6:** What choices/alternatives will emerge on the way? **CARD 7:** Will you make it? **CARD 8:** If you do not make it, will you regret trying? **CARD 9:** If you stay as you are, will you regret not trying?

What you should use:
The full deck.

When:
A Thursday, the day of major upward steps.

937
WHEN FITNESS SEEMS A CHORE

Purpose and background information:
When you feel you should get more exercise but aren't enthusiastic.

CARD 1: Do you really need to get fitter, or is this pressure from others toward activities you do not enjoy? **CARD 2:** What physical activities would give you pleasure, anything from salsa dancing to yoga to surfing? **CARD 3:** Can you fit exercise into your present life, or do you need to prioritize your life more so you can have this self-time without getting stressed out by conflicting demands? **CARD 4:** Are there other lifestyle changes you could make, a better diet/walking up the stairs at work instead of taking the elevator/going on activity-based vacations without working out? **CARD 5:** As a bonus, will new physical activities enhance your social life/help you meet new friends, even a partner?

What you should use:
The full deck.

When:
A non-working morning.

938
MAKING A MAJOR LEISURE EXPENDITURE

Purpose and background information:
When you have a chance to invest in your leisure time but there are options. You may have choices of your own and so can substitute your dreams for the suggestions here.

Card 1: Could be a fun camper van, **Card 2:** a boat, or **Card 3:** long-distance travel. If you have more choices, for example a retreat in the wilderness or by the shore, add extra cards to the right of the original three. The method is the same. See which card is the most promising. If it's not clear, add a second card to clarify a choice.

What you should use:
The full deck.

When:
Once you have priced your different options.

939
FOR MAKING YOUR MARK IN HORSE OR ANIMAL SHOWS, EVENTS, AND RACES

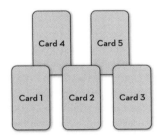

Purpose and background information:
When this is your lifelong dream.

Card 1: Do you have a game plan for winning particular events, or are you going to compete anywhere opportunities arise? **Card 2:** Are your animals in top condition, or do you need some more work/a special animal that will bring success? If so, have you located it? **Card 3:** Will you get the right sponsor/make enough from prize money for a fulltime business? **Card 4:** Would you prefer to keep this as a passionate interest, or fit the right employed job around it? **Card 5:** Do you have/will you achieve longer-term plans for expansion/opening your own training/breeding center?

What you should use:
The full deck.

When:
A Wednesday for succeeding in competitions.

940
IS IT TIME TO TAKE UP NEW INTERESTS AND SOCIAL GROUPS, OR SHOULD YOU STICK WITH WHAT IS FAMILIAR?

Purpose and background information:
When you feel vaguely bored and restless when it's time for a familiar leisure activity, but there's nothing you can put your finger on.

Card 1: Have you been doing the same things with the same people at the same time for ages, and there's never anything new to say? **Card 2:** Should you suggest to those people you still want in your life that you try new things/go to new places together? **Card 3:** If you have outgrown some of the friendships because you have moved on to a different life stage and they haven't, should you try some new leisure/sporting activities where you will meet new people? **Card 4:** Is it an internal restlessness that needs some wider life changes, rather than the external situation? **Card 5:** Will you get your enthusiasm back?

What you should use:
The twenty-two Major cards and the sixteen Court cards.

When:
The beginning of a month.

941
IF YOU ARE BECOMING OBSESSED WITH EXERCISING

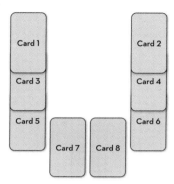

Purpose and background information:
When you feel that you have to push yourself to complete ever harder targets.

Card 1: Are you working out with a particularly fit/competitive group/gym where you feel pressured to keep up? **Card 2:** Do you have too many targets, given your lifestyle and other commitments? **Card 3:** Are there any underlying worries about the way others see you/your own self-image/underlying relationship issues that are pushing you beyond your reasonable limits? **Card 4:** Are you naturally a perfectionist in other areas of your life? **Card 5:** Should you step back from exercising for a while and focus on an activity you enjoy that doesn't have goals or targets? **Card 6:** If it's getting to be a real problem, should you talk to an impartial sports counselor to discuss your regime and the emotional as well as physical pressures you are putting yourself under? **Card 7:** Should you find a new personal trainer/a less competitive gym to regain the pleasure factor? **Card 8:** Will you resolve this and get your life back into perspective?

What you should use:
The twenty-two Major cards and the sixteen Court cards.

When:
The end of a month, or whenever you are getting exhausted.

942
FOR ADOPTING A FITNESS REGIME AFTER RETIREMENT WHEN YOUR PARTNER DOESN'T WANT TO KNOW

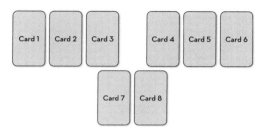

Purpose and background information:
If you are planning a fit retirement but cannot persuade your partner to join you.

Card 1: Is your partner adjusting to his/her retirement as well as yours and shouldn't be pressured into your fitness activities s/he isn't interested in? **Card 2:** Does s/he have plans for travel/relocating/starting a new creative activity so fitness isn't on the priority list right now? **Card 3:** Can you incorporate pleasurable activity into travel/weekends away, where there is dancing/tennis, etc., as optional activities without pushing the fitness aspect? **Card 4:** If your partner hasn't done a lot of activity recently, is s/he nervous about looking a like a fool/being overweight, especially if you are already very fit? **Card 5:** Are there other worries about retirement/the relationship that are tangled up with this that need resolving? **Card 6:** Does your partner have personal plans for retirement that you could share? **Card 7:** Should/could you enjoy preparing/going out for nutritious meals to subtly approach fitness? **Card 8:** Should you go it alone fitness-wise, or invite your partner along to social activities connected with your interests?

What you should use:
The forty Minor cards, Aces to Tens, and the sixteen Court cards.

When:
When you are arguing in circles.

943
FOR GAINING A PLACE ON A SPORTING TEAM OR TRAINING OPPORTUNITY OVERSEAS

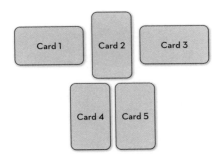

Purpose and background information:
When you want to train and compete overseas.

CARD 1: What facilities/opportunities can you not get interstate or nationally in your home country? **CARD 2:** Do you have the necessary skills/track record to get the desired training/team place/sponsorship/sports scholarship? **CARD 3:** Is it the training/career opportunities, or the location that attracts you most? Would you compromise on either? **CARD 4:** Will you get the place/sponsorship you desire? **CARD 5:** Will you return home in triumph to take up opportunities in your home country/stay overseas as long as possible?

What you should use:
The twenty-two Major cards and the sixteen Court cards.

When:
The morning before applying.

944
IF YOU WANT A SPORTS SCHOLARSHIP TO FUND YOUR WAY THROUGH HIGHER EDUCATION

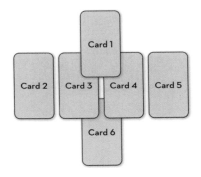

Purpose and background information:
When you are planning your long-term sporting future.

CARD 1: Do you know precisely where you want your sports scholarship? Are you open to others, so long as the establishment has a good sporting/educational reputation? **CARD 2:** Is there more than one area of sport in which you are expert, or is there only one lifetime sporting love for you? **CARD 3:** Are your academic achievements as good as your sporting attainments so you have a strong chance of being accepted? **CARD 4:** Do you want to study for a sports-related degree so you can work in sport even if you ultimately cannot get the full-time playing future you want? **CARD 5:** Do you have your future mapped out, or are you open to whatever opportunities come? **CARD 6:** Will you be offered your desired scholarship/one that will make you just as happy?

What you should use:
The forty Minor cards, Aces to Tens, and the sixteen Court cards.

When:
A day you generally play your favorite sport.

945
IF A PARTICULAR INSTRUCTOR OR TRAINER ALWAYS GIVES YOU A HARD TIME

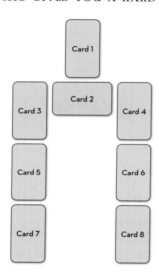

Purpose and background information:
When no matter how hard you try, you cannot get it right.

CARD 1: Is it a clash of personality, an attitude s/he displays to everyone, or a personal vendetta against you? **CARD 2:** Do others notice? If they do, how does that make you feel? **CARD 3:** What do you think/what is the underlying reason? **CARD 4:** Have you/should you tackle the issue head-on politely but firmly and was/will that be counter-productive? **CARD 5:** Will anyone senior intervene on your behalf? **CARD 6:** Will the situation improve as your talents become recognized by others/as you succeed in ways that cannot be ignored? **CARD 7:** Is the perpetrator going to bully others, or get transferred or fired? **CARD 8:** Should you apply for a transfer to another team/training facility where you will be appreciated?

What you should use:
The full deck.

When:
At the waning moon.

946
IF YOUR GYM OR SPORTS CLUB IS CLIQUEY

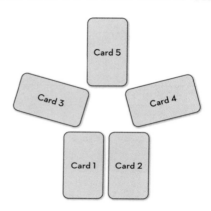

Purpose and background information:
If you are new to a gym or club and everyone excludes you from conversations/invitations.

CARD 1: Have the others known one another for a while, suggesting that new people do not stay because they feel unwelcome? **CARD 2:** Should you be patient/keep being friendly in the hope of a thaw? **CARD 3:** Should you ignore the atmosphere/get on with your own training if the facilities are good? **CARD 4:** Should you make a formal complaint to the owners if the instructors are part of the clique, or just ignore the problems? **CARD 5:** Should you move on, regardless, to somewhere more sociable, asking for a refund?

What you should use:
The forty Minor cards, Aces to Tens, and the sixteen Court cards.

When:
The end of a month.

947
WILL YOU FIND LOVE THROUGH SPORTS?

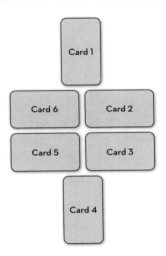

Purpose and background information:
When you are looking for a kindred spirit if you are sports-mad.

CARD 1: Is there someone you like in your present sporting activity who you could get to know better? **CARD 2:** Do you need to join a club/gym where there are lots of people of similar age who do not come with partners? **CARD 3:** If you meet someone promising jogging/carrying sports gear, should you find out where they train/buy a guest membership and take it from there? **CARD 4:** Should you go to lots of sporting events connected with your main sporting interests? **CARD 5:** If your locality draws a blank, should you connect with someone sporty online/arrange to meet? **CARD 6:** Will you find love through sports in the next six to twelve months?

What you should use:
The forty Minor cards, Aces to Tens.

When:
A Monday for good detective work.

948
DOES THE PERSON YOU LIKE AT THE GYM LIKE YOU TOO?

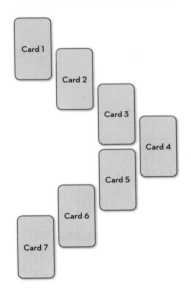

Purpose and background information:
When there is clearly interest but you need to speed things up.

CARD 1: Should you arrange to go at regular times when you know the subject of interest will be there? **CARD 2:** Should you find out all you can from casual conversation with instructors/social media if the person is reasonably free/your sort of person? **CARD 3:** Should you raise the conversation stakes/discover how much you have in common? **CARD 4:** Should you issue a direct invitation to coffee if you suspect s/he's lacking in confidence? **CARD 5:** Should you wait till there's a fundraising event/organize one and ask for their help? **CARD 6:** Will love work out? **CARD 7:** If not, will someone else join the gym who you like even more, who is more up-front interest-wise?

What you should use:
The twenty-two Major cards and the sixteen Court cards.

When:
As soon as possible.

949
IF YOU ARE USELESS AT SPORTS AND YOUR NEW PARTNER IS INTO SPORTS IN A BIG WAY

Purpose and background information:
When you are in love but the hobbies leave you cold.

CARD 1: Should you go along/cheer from the sidelines/ enjoy being together afterwards? **CARD 2:** Should you take secret lesson/a crash course in your partner's main interests so you can be surprisingly competent/knowledgeable when s/he tries to teach you? **CARD 3:** Should you do your own thing and meet up afterward? **CARD 4:** Should you negotiate a compromise, so your partner tries your interests too?
CARD 5: If sports occupy a disproportionate amount of your leisure time, maybe you should reconsider whether this is the person for you.

What you should use:
The forty Minor cards, Aces to Tens, and the sixteen Court cards.

When:
You dread another afternoon on the sidelines.

950
WHEN YOU WANT TO START AN ADVENTURE SCHOOL

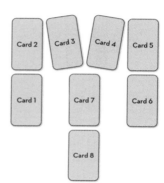

Purpose and background information:
When this is your ultimate lifetime dream.

CARD 1: Do you have the expertise necessary in extreme sports/wilderness training, or would you bring in others with special skills? **CARD 2:** If you haven't already, should you work at a similar center to get experience in the business side? **CARD 3:** Can you afford to buy/lease land/insurance/ starting modest with DIY equipment/basic accommodation/ even building shelters as part of the courses? **CARD 4:** Do you need/want a backer? Are there enterprise grants/ tax breaks you can obtain? **CARD 5:** Who will you aim to attract: bored city people/team building from companies/ bachelor/ette groups/individuals/groups of friends wanting to compete/all these and more? **CARD 6:** Will you be able to build up the business with more elaborate equipment within a year or two of launch, or do you want to stick with basic/ survival experiences? **CARD 7:** Will you wait until you have money behind you to start, or go for it as soon as you have the minimum? **CARD 8:** Will you succeed in a big way?

What you should use:
The whole deck.

When:
Your birthday/New Year's Day, or a personally significant date.

CHAPTER 45

SPREADS FOR ALTERNATIVE LIFESTYLES, DOING YOUR OWN THING, AND LIVING YOUR OWN WAY

Lucky cards:

Major Cards: The Fool, the Chariot, Temperance, the Moon, the World.

Minor Cards: All the Aces; all the Threes except the Swords; the Four of Wands; the Six and Seven of Cups; the Eights of Wands and Pentacles; the Nines of Pentacles and Cups; and the Ten of Cups.

Court cards: Princesses/Pages and Princess/Knights of Cups and Wands for freedom.

About Alternative Lifestyle Spreads:

You can use two- and three-card spreads as well as seven-carders for options, fours where finances are involved, sixes for happiness, fives for fulfilling dreams, and even larger spreads for exploring complex or emotionally charged issues.

951
BREAKING DOWN THE WALLS THAT STOP YOU SEEKING AN ALTERNATIVE LIFESTYLE

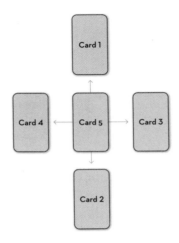

Purpose and background information:
For finding the freedom and independence you want and need. This is a more concise version of the earlier nine-card Tower of Freedom Spread for gaining clarity. Cards 1, 2, 3, and 4 each represent a wall; after you have read each one, remove it from the Spread.

CARD 1: The barriers of convention that may still hold you back through the disapproval of others and all those old voices from childhood. **CARD 2:** The wall of economic stability: How you would manage financially if you gave up your steady day job to earn money based on your initiative and ingenuity. **CARD 3:** The hidden fear: What has sometimes held you back because it hasn't been examined and faced or overcome. **CARD 4:** The practical organization, selling up and finding somewhere new to live, maybe not even a house but a boat or recreational vehicle, where to go, what if you fall ill. **CARD 5:** The way of freedom.

What you should use:
The full deck.

When:
When you change *if only* to *why not?*

952
IF YOU ARE OFFERED A RUN-DOWN ANIMAL SANCTUARY OR INDIGENOUS WILDLIFE CENTER

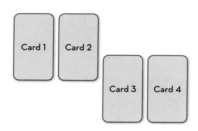

Purpose and background information:
When it would be a dream come true but would need a lot of financing and organizing.

CARD 1: Could/should you take it over even though it would need time and resources to get it up and running? **CARD 2:** Would it be better to turn the offer down and look for land/buildings suitable for conversion to fulfill your own blueprint? **CARD 3:** Should you accept but keep your day job/give yourself a time limit to make it a viable enterprise? **CARD 4:** Will your dreams of saving wildlife materialize?

What you should use:
The forty Minor cards, Aces to Tens.

When:
When you have looked at the finances and practicalities but hesitate in making a decision.

953
IF YOU HAVE STARTED YOUR DREAM ENTERPRISE AND IT IS FAILING

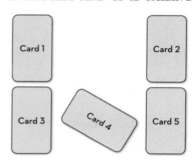

Purpose and background information:
When you know what you are doing is worthwhile but financially it's not proving viable.

CARD 1: Should you accept that you did your best and then cut your losses? **CARD 2:** Should you have one last push/taking a different, daring approach to fund-raising/attracting interest? **CARD 3:** Can you find urgent external help/grants/loans/a sponsor/appealing to a connected umbrella organization/joining with a similar enterprise? **CARD 4:** Should you/your partner get a salaried job for a while to tide yourselves over? **CARD 5:** Is there light at the end of the tunnel if you hold on?

What you should use:
The twenty-two Major cards and the sixteen Court cards.

When:
When the latest pile of bills appears.

954
IF YOU AND FRIENDS OR AN EXTENDED FAMILY WANT TO LIVE WITHIN THE SAME LARGE PROPERTY OR AREA OF LAND

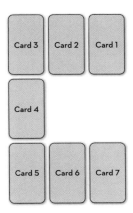

Purpose and background information:
If it seems a good idea to live close and share expenses and resources with people you know well.

CARD 1: Is there a shared enterprise, such as farming or a family business, that makes living close common sense? **CARD 2:** Do you get on well with your family all the time/ mainly, or might tensions increase at close quarters? **CARD 3:** What would be the advantages of having friends/family on hand for socializing/mutual practical and emotional support? **CARD 4:** What are the main drawbacks? Could you overcome/resolve these in advance/sort them as they arise? **CARD 5:** Would you have privacy/freedom to make your own personal decisions? **CARD 6:** Is there an easy exit strategy if things do not work out without major financial/property loss/ family disruption? **CARD 7:** Will it work out well?

What you should use:
The full deck.

When:
At the discussion stage.

955
IF YOU WANT TO JOIN AN EXISTING COMMUNE WITH PEOPLE YOU DO NOT KNOW WELL

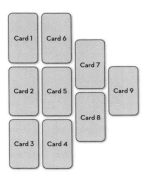

Purpose and background information:
When communal living is appealing.

CARD 1: What do you most want from a commune in terms of financial arrangements/closeness vs. independence/spiritual ethos? **CARD 2:** Do you have a commune in mind/a specific location/a beautiful rural setting? **CARD 3:** Do you want to work as well as live in a spiritual center, for example in a craft workshop collective/organic gardening? **CARD 4:** What safeguards do you need/legally/financially/property-wise in terms of purchasing/security of tenancy? **CARD 5:** Can you accept the way major decisions are made/disagreements resolved/privacy respected? **CARD 6:** Should you visit several times before moving in/attend social events/take a short tenancy to see how it works out/explore exit strategies in case you want to move on? **CARD 7:** What are the strongest drawbacks/advantages for you of communal living, both in principle/specific communes? **CARD 8:** Should you vacation in different communal settings to see if the life is for you? **CARD 9:** Is communal living for you now/in the future/not ever, once you consider the implications?

What you should use:
The forty Minor cards and the sixteen Court cards.

When:
A Friday, the day of sociability

956
IF YOU WANT TO ENTER A RELIGIOUS OR SPIRITUAL COMMUNITY

Purpose and background information:
If you feel you are ready to leave the everyday world and devote yourself to a religious or spiritual cause.

CARD 1: Have you always been ever more powerfully drawn to this faith/spirituality? Has there been recent trauma you need to resolve first that makes you want to quit the world to enter for the right reasons? **CARD 2:** Do you have a particular Order/religious house/temple/ashram you wish to join, or do you need to explore different options, especially regarding the continuing contact with or isolation from the world? **CARD 3:** After training, do you aim to work in and for the community/in your own existing profession but living within the Order/spend your life learning/in prayer and contemplation? **CARD 4:** Will you undertake training before dedicating yourself, or do you want options at every stage whether how far to proceed? **CARD 5:** Is this a lifelong commitment, or for a set/flexible number of years? **CARD 6:** Are you free to leave at any time without pressure if it doesn't work out, or does this not concern you? **CARD 7:** Before deciding, do you want to spend longer on retreats/spiritual journeys/vacations in ashrams/Buddhist orders, etc.? **CARD 8:** Is this new life what you want, or are there other ways within your current life to develop/express your spirituality?

What you should use:
The twenty-two major cards.

When:
The day of contemplation or religious celebration within your chosen faith.

957
WHEN TENSIONS ARISE WITHIN A COMMUNE

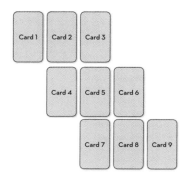

Purpose and background information:
When communal living is not as idyllic as you would have hoped.

CARD 1: Are there particular individuals/families making major decisions/arranging things to their advantage? **CARD 2:** Should/can you approach them directly? Will they listen/change their behavior? **CARD 3:** Is there a formal dispute procedure/informal ways of raising concerns? Is this the time to use them? **CARD 4:** Is there support for you, or are others going along with the status quo/forming cliques? **CARD 5:** Can you ignore tensions, or do problems interfere with your well-being? **CARD 6:** What is the best path forward to steer the commune into calmer waters? **CARD 7:** Will matters settle/be resolved amicably? **CARD 8:** If not, should you move on peaceably/leave but be prepared for a battle? **CARD 9:** Is living in the right commune still for you, or do you want independence?

What you should use:
The full deck.

When:
When the disadvantages of communal living appear to outweigh the positives.

958
IF YOU WANT TO DEDICATE YOUR LIFE TO HEALING

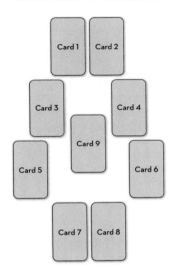

959
IF YOU WANT TO BECOME A PROFESSIONAL OVERSEAS AID WORKER

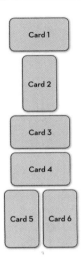

Purpose and background information:
When you feel you have a calling to become a healer.

CARD 1: Can you heal within your everyday world?
CARD 2: Do you believe you were a healer in past lives?
CARD 3: Do you want to use your healing gifts by training as a nurse/a doctor/veterinarian/heal within conventional medicine? **CARD 4:** Are you attracted to/gifted in specific complementary healing therapies? **CARD 5:** Do you want to join a healing circle within a particular faith group? **CARD 6:** Do you want to heal professionally, or to work without payment? **CARD 7:** What are the financial constraints of life devoted to freely offered healing? **CARD 8:** Do you need to leave your present life/become part of a residential healing community? **CARD 9:** Is healing for you an enrichment of your life, or a total life change?

What you should use:
The full deck.

When:
Any key date in your life.

Purpose and background information:
If your dream is to become an international aid worker

CARD 1: Do you have the right academic qualifications/language skills if you want to work for an international organization, or can you acquire them? **CARD 2:** Should you do voluntary aid work in your own state/country to get necessary experience? **CARD 3:** Should you offer to do online work/fundraising to get yourself known? **CARD 4:** Should you go to any and every conference/seminar connected with your desired area of aid/if possible speak at a small event/network wherever and whenever possible? **CARD 5:** Should you initially take a domestic-based charity post with your chosen organization/a less prestigious overseas post to get your foot in the door? **CARD 6:** Will you succeed in your dream if you persevere?

What you should use:
The forty Minor cards, Aces to Tens.

When:
New Year's Day; a day associated with your favorite aid charity; or on your birthday.

960
IF YOU HAVE ESCAPED FROM A CULT AND THEY ARE DENYING YOU ACCESS TO YOUR FUNDS AND ASSETS

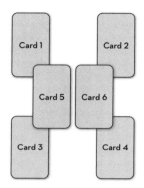

Purpose and background information:

When you are glad to get out, but the cult still controls your finances.

CARD 1: Are you being pressured to return to the cult/has all contact been cut off, including family within the cult? **CARD 2:** Are you offered protection by an organization for ex-cult members/can you find advice/support online? **CARD 3:** Have/will you get police help/protection if the cult is ruthless/find a lawyer experienced in cult coercion? **CARD 4:** Should you avoid any contact with the cult when claims are put in? **CARD 5:** Do you have/can you collect evidence from bank statements/credit card payments exactly what you handed over? **CARD 6:** Will you get what is rightfully yours?

What you should use:

The twenty-two Major cards.

When:

A Sunday, for transparency of actions and honesty.

961
CAN YOU BECOME PART OF LOCAL LIFE AND CULTURE IF YOU ARE MOVING TO A VERY DIFFERENT LAND?

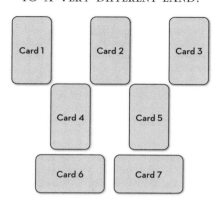

Purpose and background information:

When you want to experience living in a very different culture.

CARD 1: Do you have/can you acquire in advance good language skills/knowledge of customs/what is safe for overseas workers? **CARD 2:** Even if you are moving into an expat community, can/will you meet, through your work, local people/invite them/get them to invite you to their homes? **CARD 3:** Can you shop in local markets/participate in local festivals/sample local delicacies? **CARD 4:** Can you ignore disapproval from some fellow workers/parents at international schools who live the way they do back home? **CARD 5:** Can you, with local guides/accepting security restrictions, visit places off the normal tourist track to see the real country? **CARD 6:** Can/will you find like-minded expats to help arrange intercultural events/clubs? **CARD 7:** Will this experience open you to a desire to further explore the world?

IF YOU ARE MARRYING SOMEONE FROM THE OTHER SIDE OF THE WORLD AND GOING TO LIVE IN THEIR COUNTRY

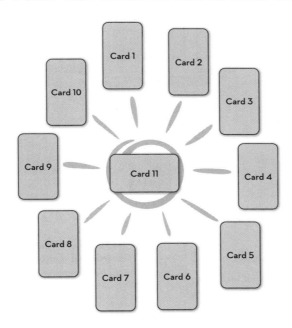

Purpose and background information:

If you have been for a few visits and realize it's a very different lifestyle.

CARD 1: How can you best prepare yourself for this change of lifestyle/learning a new language/maybe converting to a different religion/transferring your career? **CARD 2:** To what extent can you keep what is important of your present way of life? Will your partner adapt? **CARD 3:** Is there a different family structure you will be expected to adapt to? Can/will you keep your own family structure within your home if you are planning children/combine? **CARD 4:** Is this a permanent move, or will you be returning to your own country eventually, or divide your time between the two countries? **CARD 5:** What legal/actual safeguards are there if things go wrong,

especially if children are involved? **CARD 6:** Is this the right time to make this move? Should you wait? **CARD 7:** Are there any hidden obstacles/opposition to the move? **CARD 8:** Will there be support in the new land from people you already know/have yet to meet? **CARD 9:** Will you/how can you make this transition go smoothly? **CARD 10:** Should your partner live with you in *your* home country/visit their country for vacations? **CARD 11:** Should you go but not make permanent arrangements until you are sure?

What you should use:

The full deck.

When:

Before finalizing moving plans

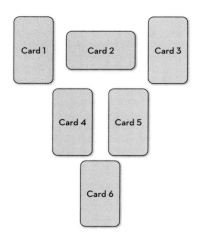

Purpose and background information:

If it has always been your dream to live on an island.

Card 1: Should you vacation on remote islands with basic facilities to see if it's the life for you? **Card 2:** Can/will you find a job as a warden on remote islands/seabird sanctuaries? **Card 3:** Do you have a career you could adapt to living on an island/sell articles/podcasts, etc., via satellite phone? **Card 4:** Do you have a partner to share the dream, or is it a solo venture? **Card 5:** Should you save until you have enough money to rent/buy a remote island/build your own accommodation/live self-sufficiently? **Card 6:** Is this a lovely dream, prompting maybe a more nature-based lifestyle?

What you should use:

The full deck.

When:

When the dream becomes as strong as everyday life.

Example:

Damien had a great interest in seabirds and longed for his own island where he could write books in peace away from his frantic city life.

Card 1: Temperance. Damien frequently spent vacations on an island where there was a single hut and loved it, but he had been too preoccupied recently. **Card 2: The Hermit.** Damien was on waiting lists for wardenships of remote islands round the world and had become an expert in seabird conservation. **Card 3: The Six of Cups.** Damien's other dream, to write nature-based adventure books for children, had interest from a publisher but he had never followed it up. **Card 4: The Lovers.** Damien had recently met a partner who shared his dreams/neither wanted children. **Card 5: The Ten of Pentacles.** Damien had accumulated enough money for five years on a deserted island while he studied self-sufficiency. **Card 6: The Star.** The island was Damien's ultimate dream, nothing less.

Not long after the reading, Damien was offered, along with his partner, a wardenship of an island tracking the migratory/nesting habits of endangered sea birds. He plans to use the initial three-year contract to practice self-sufficiency and eventually hopes to buy/lease his own desert island.

964
IF YOU FALL MADLY IN LOVE WITH A LOCAL ON VACATION AND S/HE ASKS YOU NOT TO GO HOME

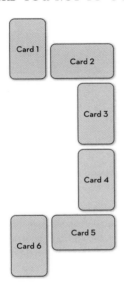

Purpose and background information:
When you are sensible and logical but love has swept you off your feet.

CARD 1: Is it possible to extend your vacation by a week or two to see if the feeling continues? **CARD 2:** Should you go home and sort everything out, visa/job-wise, so you can move? **CARD 3:** Practically and economically, how would you live if you remained in the vacation location? **CARD 4:** Have you met your lover's family/will there be language/cultural barriers to overcome? **CARD 5:** Should you return home/plan another vacation as soon as practical/arrange for your love to visit you/keep in touch on social media? **CARD 6:** Is this the love of your life, or just a lovely romance?

What you should use:
The twenty-two Major cards and the sixteen Court cards.

When:
Before making a life-changing decision.

965
IF YOU ARE RETURNING TO YOUR HOME COUNTRY AFTER MANY YEARS' ABSENCE TO CARE FOR A SICK OR AGING PARENT

Purpose and background information:
When you have been back for visits but have made a life in your adopted country.

CARD 1: Do you anticipate/is it possible to stay as long as necessary? **CARD 2:** Is there a time limit because of commitments in your adopted country? **CARD 3:** Should/will you return permanently to the home country? **CARD 4:** Are there people with whom you have remained in touch/need to reconnect/make new connections before you go/when you get there? **CARD 5:** Is it a place untouched by time/will there be huge changes and adjustments staying there longer term? **CARD 6:** Where are your true roots/where will you replant them?

What you should use:
The forty Minor cards, Aces to Tens.

When:
A Thursday, a day of safe travel.

966

IF YOU OR YOUR PARTNER ARE IN THE MILITARY OR A PROFESSION WHERE YOU MOVE INTERSTATE OR OVERSEAS AT REGULAR INTERVALS

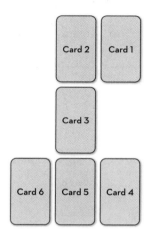

Purpose and background information:

If the excitement of new places is wearing off.

Card 1: Are you able to synchronize your careers/postings if one of you has a different profession/different commitments within the same profession? **Card 2:** Will this happy merging of interests increase? If not, can/how can you make it happen to minimize disruption? **Card 3:** If not already, should you buy a home base for vacations or between postings/where would you most like this to be? **Card 4:** Is this lifestyle indefinite, or is there an end date? Are you looking to settle regardless? **Card 5:** Is there a chosen location where you would like to/could seek more permanent postings/move there with different jobs? **Card 6:** Does one of you want permanence more than the other? If so, how can you best resolve this to maintain/restore a happy relationship?

What you should use:

The full deck.

When:

Near the end of a posting/contract.

967

IF YOU ARE BRINGING UP YOUR GRANDCHILDREN WITHOUT THEIR PARENTS BECAUSE OF A MARITAL BREAKUP OR FAMILY PROBLEMS

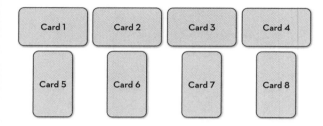

Purpose and background information:

When you are acting as a surrogate parent/s to a grandchild/ren

Card 1: Do the children see their parents/either parent regularly? If so, do you end up in the middle of conflict? **Card 2:** How can you best protect yourself as well as the children if one of the parents is using them as a pawn in the dispute/bleeding you financially? **Card 3:** Is this a long-term arrangement, or until one or other gets settled, or totally unknown? **Card 4:** What rights do you have/need to make decisions for the children as well as providing the care/finances? **Card 5:** Should/will you get help from social care/legally so you do not end up with the worst of both worlds? **Card 6:** What support/relief do you need/are you getting from other family members/the reliable parent, so you have life as well as a parent/s second-time round? **Card 7:** Are/will the children be happy/well balanced as a result of your intervention? **Card 8:** Will it be resolved satisfactorily so you can enjoy being just grandparents again?

What you should use:

The forty Minor cards, Aces to Tens, and the sixteen Court cards.

When:

The first Sunday in September after Labor Day; Grandparents' Day; or a Friday for loving families.

968
IF YOU ARE CONSIDERING USING A SURROGATE MOTHER

Purpose and background information:
When surrogacy seems the best way to have a much-wanted child.

CARD 1: Have you explored legal/financial factors in your state/country/emotional implications? **CARD 2:** Should you choose a more expensive agency setting/consider the cheaper way by finding your own surrogate option with maybe more risks/go interstate to avoid future post-natal accidental contact with the surrogate? **CARD 3:** Are you happy about the egg/sperm donor/especially if the surrogate's egg or sperm or an egg from a relative is used? **CARD 4:** How involved do you/both of you want to be in the pregnancy/scans/delivery/is the surrogate agreeable to dietary care? **CARD 5:** Is there the slightest risk, even with a good attorney, that the surrogate could change her mind after the birth? **CARD 6:** Will you be delighted with your baby, even though you/your partner did not bear it? **CARD 7:** If this doesn't feel right, have you considered adoption?

What you should use:
The full deck.

When:
When you are considering options.

969
IF YOU ARE A FOSTER CHILD OR ADOPTEE, AND YOUR BIRTH MOTHER HAS DIED BEFORE MEETING YOU

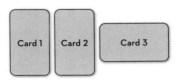

Purpose and background information:
When the connection came too late.

CARD 1: If you know where your birth family is, can you tactfully find out if they know who you are/would welcome contact? **CARD 2:** If you do not feel contact would be welcome (might rake up an unknown past), should you find out all you can about your mother's life after you parted/mourn her in your own way? **CARD 3:** Can/do you want to track down your birth father, or just let the past go and focus on your adoptive family?

What you should use:
The twenty-two Major cards.

When:
The end of a month, or when you discover the sad news.

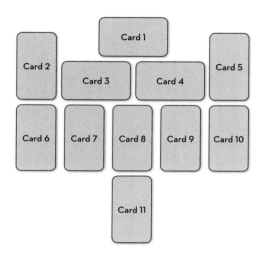

Purpose and background information:

CARD 1: Once you understand the regulations for international adoption, should you explore different agencies with children from your chosen countries to find one you feel comfortable with? **CARD 2:** Are there any particular countries you are drawn to/should you go on vacation there/use the time to visit orphanages through the chosen agency to experience the true situation? **CARD 3:** Are you prepared to endure intrusive examinations through the agency/immigration? **CARD 4:** When you are approved, should you spend time in a specific orphanage watching the children play/seeing if any of the children you are offered is drawn to you/you develop a bond with? **CARD 5:** During pre-adoption visits, must you put aside expectations since the babies/children may be understimulated/have minor ills? **CARD 6:** Should you learn the language before visiting, both for dealing with officials and communicating with the child? **CARD 7:** Can you go along with delays/obstructions/make health check inquiries so you know any problems/get the best attorney you can afford? **CARD 8:** Will homecoming be frightening for the child, as well as exciting for you and hopefully for the child once he/she meets the family? **CARD 9:** Will you make connections with people from your child's root culture/make the child bi-lingual so he/she grows up with a strong root identity? **CARD 10:** Will this be the best experience of your life? **CARD 11:** Do you think you will want to adopt more children?

What you should use:

The forty Minor cards and the sixteen Court cards.

When:

When you know this is the route for you.

971
SHOULD YOU BECOME A FOSTER PARENT?

Purpose and background information:

When you want to give a good home to a child/children in need.

CARD 1: Are you/is your home/any children of your own sufficiently secure to offer a home to children who may be afraid or challenging? **CARD 2:** Will your home remain stable with the arrival of possibly troubled child/children? **CARD 3:** If you want to foster children for short times/emergencies, could you deal with sudden arrivals/only to lose them just as they become settled in their new environment? **CARD 4:** Would you prefer longer-term fostering/welcoming a child for months/years? **CARD 5:** Could you let a child go without huge pain after many months/years/always keep in touch? **CARD 6:** Since the child has another family, could you cope with the effects of negative parental access/the child/children wanting their parents regardless? **CARD 7:** Would you feel confident with children with special needs? **CARD 8:** Is fostering for you/would you succeed as a foster parent/would you sooner work in childcare/adopt?

What you should use:

The full deck.

When:

You see an advertisement for foster careers and think *why not?*

972
IF YOU HAVE TRACED YOUR BIRTH MOTHER BUT WANT TO CONNECT WITH YOUR BIRTH FATHER

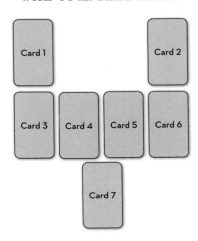

Purpose and background information:

When you have half the picture but want to discover your roots.

CARD 1: Will/can your birth mother share with you information she has, so you can find him? **CARD 2:** Does your birth father know about you? If not, do you still want to/should you still make contact? **CARD 3:** How far are you prepared to go in your quest to find him? **CARD 4:** Will you succeed? **CARD 5:** If you meet, will it be a happy event? **CARD 6:** If he will not meet you/if the meeting doesn't work out, will it be good to know your roots anyway? **CARD 7:** If signs of finding/meeting aren't good, should/will you mourn what never can be, or just let it go?

What you should use:

The twenty-two Major cards and the sixteen Court cards.

When:

The day of your birth or adoption, or any significant date for you personally.

IF YOU ARE ADOPTING AN OLDER CHILD, SIBLINGS, OR ONE WITH A LIFE-CHALLENGING CONDITION

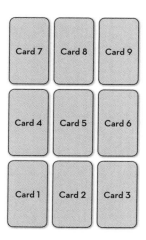

Purpose and background information:

When you want a child and know there are many children who need a home.

CARD 1: Are you totally clued up on home study/applications/adoption agencies/the ocean of paperwork and still want to go ahead? **CARD 2:** Are you open to adopting siblings/older children/those with life-challenging conditions who may have previously been fostered? **CARD 3:** Before you meet your chosen child/children, can you accept it's like any first date where you may all be nervous/on best behavior, and let go of expectations? **CARD 4:** What's the best way to prepare for the arrival day/if old enough, consulting on decorations for room/space for familiar comfort items? **CARD 5:** What challenges will you face/how do you think you will go about overcoming them in a nonconfrontational way? **CARD 6:** What support can you obtain in the early days, especially with any disabilities, interracial children who will need connection with their root culture/language? **CARD 7:** Do you want an open adoption where, although you make all the decisions, the birth parent has contact if wished, or would this be too intrusive for you/the child? Will you collect birth family mementoes for when the child is older? **CARD 8:** Does the child/children have any hidden issues/what/who can help you to help the child? **CARD 9:** What is the path to happiness for the family?

What you should use:

The full deck.

When:

The start of a new month.

974

IF YOU HAVE MOVED IN WITH A PARTNER OF THE SAME GENDER, AND YOUR CHILDREN FROM A PREVIOUS RELATIONSHIP WILL NOT ACCEPT IT

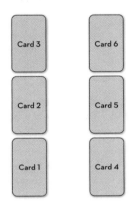

Purpose and background information:
When you have left a heterosexual marriage and want your children to understand.

CARD 1: Should you try for now to see your children on your own so you can get them used to the idea/deal with any fallout without hurting your new partner? **CARD 2:** Are your children influenced by the other parent and so, as in any split-up, have divided loyalties? **CARD 3:** Should you gradually introduce your partner/invite everyone for a day out/on vacation so they get to know your partner in a relaxed neutral situation? **CARD 4:** Should you go for family counseling to work through the underlying—and maybe not even acknowledged—issues? **CARD 5:** Will your children learn to like your new partner in the months and years ahead/become less judgmental as they mature? **CARD 6:** If not, then will you continue to see your children separately/say "love me, love my partner"?

What you should use:
The forty Minor cards, Aces to Tens, and the sixteen Court cards.

When:
At the crescent or waxing moon.

975

IF YOU FALL IN LOVE WITH SOMEONE YOUNG ENOUGH TO BE YOUR GRANDCHILD, AND EVERYONE SAYS YOU ARE BEING CONNED

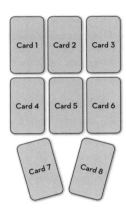

Purpose and background information:
When you feel like a million dollars and fifty years younger.

CARD 1: What worries your friends: the age gap itself/ the unsuitability of the person/if they will want children/ financial affairs in the future? **CARD 2:** Do any of these issues secretly worry you too/how can you and your new partner resolve these? **CARD 3:** Are you truly happy/having fun/ passion/feel young again/experiencing what you may have previously missed out on? **CARD 4:** Do you want/need to talk about the longer-term future, or let the future take care of itself? **CARD 5:** If you are marrying, should you see a good attorney about your finances/wills, etc./pre-nuptials in case it goes wrong? **CARD 6:** Should you take this slowly/gradually introduce your new partner to more receptive members of the family/present them with your marriage certificate? **CARD 7:** If folks cannot be glad for you, is that their problem? **CARD 8:** Will you be happy, whether forever after or for the foreseeable future?

What you should use:
The whole deck.

When:
A Thursday, for love in later years.

CHAPTER 46

PASSION AND TEMPTATION SPREADS

Lucky cards for Passion and Temptation Spreads

Major Cards: The Magician, the Lovers, The Wheel of Fortune.

Minor Cards: The Aces of Cups and Wands, the Two of Cups, the Threes of Cups and Wands, the Five of Cups, the Sixes of Cups and Wands, the Seven of Cups, the Eight of Wands, the Ten of Cups.

Court Cards: All Cups and Wands.

About Passion and Temptation spreads:

Sometimes a simple either-or *should I/shouldn't I, what are the risks?* can be resolved with two or three cards. Four cards recognize questions about emotional security. Often, however, since sex questions can conceal deep unresolved emotions and perhaps more fundamental problems in love and relationships, six, seven, or even more cards may be needed.

976
WHEN A RELATIONSHIP IS ALL ABOUT SEX AND NOT ABOUT LOVE

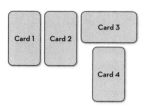

Purpose and background information:
If you regularly meet for a date followed by sex, but the relationship doesn't progress.

CARD 1: Are you happy with this arrangement for now/ for the foreseeable future? **CARD 2:** Do you want to spend time together/go on vacation, but your partner is not free? **CARD 3:** Are you ready to risk the relationship by asking for more? **CARD 4:** Are you outgrowing the relationship as fun but going nowhere?

What you should use:
The sixteen Court cards.

When:
When the excitement is waning.

977
IF YOUR NEW LOVE IS GIVING MIXED MESSAGES ABOUT LOVEMAKING

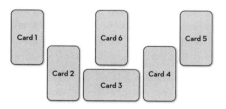

Purpose and background information:
If you have indicated that you are willing and your love seems keen, but nothing happens.

Card 1: Is your new love generally shy/finds it hard to show affection? **Card 2:** Has your love come out of a bad relationship/been betrayed by the affair of a previous partner? **Card 3:** Should you take the initiative? **Card 4:** Should you arrange a weekend vacation where it's obvious that you are sharing a room? **Card 5:** Should you talk about the subject generally, or would that send him/her heading for the hills fast? **Card 6:** If the relationship is otherwise good and sex is seen as a serious step to commitment by your partner, should you wait until your partner is ready?

What you should use:

The forty Minor cards, Aces to Tens, and the sixteen Court cards.

When:

Any evening before you meet.

978
IF YOUR LOVER NEVER STAYS THE NIGHT

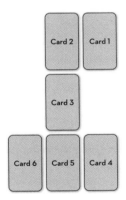

Purpose and background information:

If you are starting to feel used.

Card 1: If you know your lover is in a complicated relationship, can you accept the way things are as the price you have to pay? **Card 2:** If this is part of a more general need for secrecy, is there a time limit for you/limit on your patience? **Card 3:** Are you promised s/he will stay overnight soon/will that happen? **Card 4:** Does this relationship give you freedom and so works for you most of the time? **Card 5:**

Should you seek a new lover who is there day as well as night? **Card 6:** Is this your lasting love, or is this just a stage on the way to lasting happiness?

What you should use:

The forty Minor cards, Aces to Tens.

When:

New Year's Day, or a significant date of your meeting.

979
SHOULD YOU OR SHOULDN'T YOU?

Purpose and background information:

When you meet someone gorgeous when you are staying away from home, but you know it's for one night only.

Card 1: Even if you do not get found out, should you? **Card 2:** Even if you do get found out (and if you are free there are still colleagues, etc., who might discover and gossip), should you? **Card 3:** Will you regret it if you do? **Card 4:** Will you regret it if you do not?

What you should use:

The twenty-two Major cards and the sixteen Court cards.

When:

A fast decision in your hotel room.

IF YOUR PARTNER IS AWAY FOR WEEKS OR MONTHS AT A TIME, AND AN OLD FLAME OR EX OFFERS TO KEEP YOU COMPANY

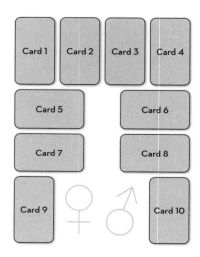

Purpose and background information:

You know you are playing with fire since you love your partner, but you are so lonely.

Card 1: Is there still a spark between you, but you know it didn't work before and so it's about excitement? **Card 2:** Do you value your relationship enough not to risk it by getting emotionally as well as sexually entangled? **Card 3:** If there are underlying problems with your relationship, can they be resolved? **Card 4:** Could you trust your ex/old flame/anyone else not to kiss and tell? **Card 5:** Is there any way you could move nearer your partner/visit more often/arrange vacations halfway? **Card 6:** Are there other ways you could fill your time/learning new things/home renovations/going out with friends/working on your own career? **Card 7:** What are the advantages of giving way to temptation? **Card 8:** What are the dangers to your existing relationship/your peace of mind in reconnecting with the old flame/ex? **Card 9:** Should you, yes or no? **Card 10:** If yes, should you end your existing relationship first/hope the affair improves it?

What you should use:

The full deck.

When:

When loneliness kicks in.

981
IF THE PASSION HAS GONE OUT OF A RELATIONSHIP

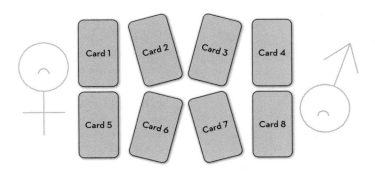

Purpose and background information:

If you have been together forever and have become Mom and Dad or passing strangers.

CARD 1: Is the lack of passion a symptom of a wider malaise in the relationship/circumstances such as children/work pressures/financial worries/care of elderly relatives? **CARD 2:** Is there still enough underlying love to be rekindled? **CARD 3:** Can you escape overnight/weekends to enjoy good times together that lead to spontaneous passion? **CARD 4:** If privacy is an issue at home, can/should you draw boundaries for exclusive couple time/space? **CARD 5:** Do you want/need outside help for minor health/sexual problems/counseling for underlying relationship problems? **CARD 6:** Should/do you want to rekindle the romance/passion in ways that are right for you? **CARD 7:** Will passion return spontaneously as the relationship regrows? **CARD 8:** Will your relationship endure on every level?

What you should use:

The full deck.

When:

Any significant date in your relationship.

982

IF YOU HAVE PASSIONATE FEELINGS FOR SOMEONE AT WORK, AND YOU ARE GOING ON A WEEKEND CONFERENCE TOGETHER

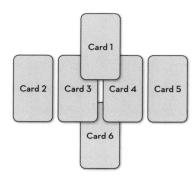

Purpose and background information:

A temptation too far, or an opportunity to find out if there really is a spark?

CARD 1: Will you find out if the other person feels the same about you/are you hopeful/excited/scared/all of these? **CARD 2:** Should you initiate the connection, or just let it happen if it will? **CARD 3:** Will anyone else be affected by your weekend of passion, relationship-wise? Will workplace gossip be an issue? Is it worth it? **CARD 4:** Do you want/anticipate an ongoing relationship, or just a weekend of passion to remember? **CARD 5:** Whatever happens if you go ahead, will it/how will it affect the dynamics of your working relationship for better/worse? **CARD 6:** Will it all happen as you hope?

What you should use:

The forty Minor cards, Aces to Tens, and the sixteen Court cards.

When:

The evening before you go away for the weekend.

983

WHEN THE OWNER OF THE BUSINESS OR SOMEONE IN SENIOR MANAGEMENT IS BEHAVING INAPPROPRIATELY TOWARD YOU AT WORK

Purpose and background information:

When you have heard of similar incidents, but no one will complain.

CARD 1: Should you make it clear to the perpetrator that such behavior will not be tolerated, even though you know the person will make life hard for you at work? **CARD 2:** Should you make an official complaint through your union/a women's organization as well as Human Resources, as you know you'll be branded a troublemaker if you complain to someone at work? **CARD 3:** Can you persuade anyone else to speak out? **CARD 4:** Should you get another job as soon as possible/pursue your complaint once you have moved? **CARD 5:** Should you keep your complaint on file/any video/audio evidence for when the matter finally is exposed, even if you have to wait months/years? **CARD 6:** Will justice be done?

What you should use:

The twenty-two Major cards and the sixteen Court cards.

When:

At a full moon.

984
IF YOU HAVE FEELINGS TOWARD A COLLEGE LECTURER, YOUR COUNSELOR, OR YOUR DOCTOR AND YOU BELIEVE THE FEELINGS ARE RECIPROCAL

Purpose and background information:

When you are sure this is more than a crush, but you are afraid to speak out.

CARD 1: If the constraints of the official setting are in the way of personal contact, are there events/places where you might meet them socially? **CARD 2:** Are they unconsciously blurring the barrier between personal and professional because you are on the same wavelength? **CARD 3:** Are they already in a relationship/can you find out from gossip/casual remarks/social media if their relationship is happy? **CARD 4:** Do you want an affair that might be problematic professionally/do you want more? **CARD 5:** If you speak up and the feelings aren't/cannot be reciprocated, will this damage the professional relationship? **CARD 6:** Should you find another doctor/counselor, or go on a different course so they can contact you if they wish without compromising your/their position? **CARD 7:** Are the qualities in them ones you may find in a future partner who is free to love you? **CARD 8:** Do you want to leave things as they are/enjoy your contact/hope they make their feelings known to you?

What you should use:

The full deck.

When:

When the moon is not in the sky.

985
IF THERE ARE DEFINITE SPARKS WITH YOUR PARTNER'S BEST FRIEND

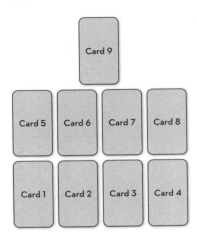

Purpose and background information:

When you are increasingly finding reasons why your partner should invite their best friend.

CARD 1: Has there always been an attraction, or has it grown over the years? **CARD 2:** Does the best friend share the best characteristics of your partner plus the excitement of unattainability? **CARD 3:** Should you meet in the company of other friends to dilute the intensity? **CARD 4:** Should/can you encourage your partner to go out alone with their best friend? **CARD 5:** Is this just a flirtation you and the best friend enjoy, or is there a risk of something more? **CARD 6:** Is your partner aware of the attraction/pleased you like their best friend so much? **CARD 7:** Can you spice up your own relationship to incorporate missing exciting qualities? **CARD 8:** What do you want to happen/what will happen if you do not draw back? **CARD 9:** Can you avoid hurting anyone involved, including yourself?

What you should use:

The forty Minor cards and the sixteen Court cards.

When:

The waning moon for damping down feelings best concealed.

986
IF YOU HAVE BEEN IN A HETEROSEXUAL MARRIAGE FOR YEARS
BUT REALIZE YOU HAVE SEXUAL FEELING FOR PEOPLE OF THE SAME GENDER AS YOURSELF

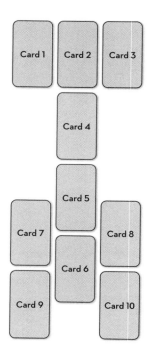

Purpose and background information:

When you feel you are living a lie.

Card 1: Has your partner noticed the emotional change in you, or are you concealing your true feelings at great cost to yourself? **Card 2:** Is it possible that you are bisexual/can stay married while enjoying deep friendship and spiritual connections with people of the same gender? **Card 3:** If you are sexually and emotionally attracted to one particular person/want to go to clubs/online to find new love, should you be honest with your partner? **Card 4:** If they want to keep the relationship going, especially if there are children, could this work if you had the freedom to discover your true self? **Card 5:** Do you need to move out/live alone for a while until you are sure of your future? **Card 6:** Can you/how

can you help children/your parents, if very conventional, to accept you as the same person who will always love them? **Card 7:** Are you prepared to accept condemnation from some people you have known for years as the price for revealing your authentic self? **Card 8:** Do you/your family need a helpline/face-to-face counseling to help you in the transition? **Card 9:** Did you always know deep down your true sexuality/were you coerced into following convention when you were young? **Card 10:** Will you find happiness and, if you want it, new love?

What you should use:

The full deck.

When:

As one season or month changes into another.

987

WHEN YOU ARE DATING SOMEONE WHO HAS HAD MANY PASSIONATE AFFAIRS BUT ASSURES YOU THAT YOU ARE DIFFERENT

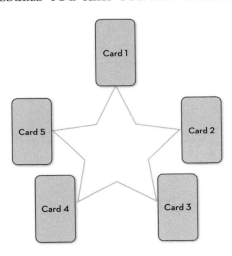

Purpose and background information:

When people warn you that your new partner is a serial flirt, but you believe you can tame her/him.

CARD 1: Is it the thrill of having attracted such a charismatic partner, or do you see a deeper more sensitive side? **CARD 2:** Do you have any reason to doubt? **CARD 3:** Do you have reason to trust? **CARD 4:** Will s/he break your heart? **CARD 5:** Has s/he really changed?

What you should use:

The twenty-two Major cards and the sixteen Court cards.

When:

When you have been together a month or more and it's going well.

988

WHEN YOUR FIRST PASSIONATE WEEKEND AWAY TOGETHER GOES WRONG

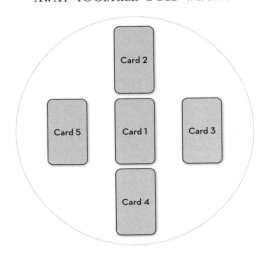

Purpose and background information:

When there was the champagne, the rose petals on the bed, the romantic setting, and it was a disaster.

CARD 1: Were the expectations too high? **CARD 2:** Was the weekend overly stage-managed? **CARD 3:** Will the relationship survive? **CARD 4:** Are you still speaking/can you talk about it without blame/can you/will you laugh about it some day? **CARD 5:** Should you make the next occasion really soon, and low-key, in which the passion is spontaneous, not the main event?

What you should use:

The twenty-two Major cards and the sixteen Court cards.

When:

The day after the disaster.

CHAPTER 47

SPREADS FOR GRIEF AND LOSS

Significant cards:

Major Cards: The High Priestess, the Hierophant, the Chariot, Justice, Strength, the Sun, Judgment.

Minor Cards: Any of the Aces for new beginnings, Five of Pentacles, Six of Swords, Seven of Pentacles, Nine of Pentacles, Ten of Pentacles.

Court Cards: The Queens and Kings of Pentacles and Cups.

About Spreads for grief and loss:

Since these tend to be emotive and take longer to unfold, Spreads with six and more cards seem to work especially well. Spreads linked to ancient traditions can also offer a pathway from loss to life, and I have suggested two of my favorites: an Ancient Egyptian Spread, and a Norse-inspired Spread for starting again. However, three- and four-card spreads can give clear answers where practical property and financial matters are concerned.

989
WHEN A RELATIVE OR CLOSE FRIEND DIES IN AN ACCIDENT

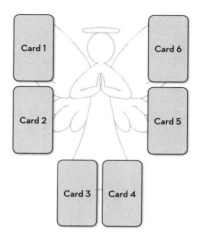

Purpose and background information:

When the loss makes no sense and seems such a waste of life.

CARD 1: Do you have closure why/how the accident happened/justice against anyone to blame? **CARD 2:** If not, can this/how can justice/closure be obtained, if necessary by increasing pressure for justice/an official inquiry? **CARD 3:** How can you best remember the person at their most vibrant/collect memories in recordings/videos/photographs or a memory book so younger and future family members will know them? **CARD 4:** What kind of a memorial would your relative have liked/at the place of the accident/in a favorite spot/a prize or trophy in their honor? **CARD 5:** What can be done to campaign to prevent similar accidents/if, for example, it was a dangerous stretch of road or lack of safety measures in the workplace? **CARD 6:** What can you do in your life that they planned to do in order to fulfill their wishes?

What you should use:

The twenty-two Major cards and the sixteen Court cards.

When:

A Sunday with the sun rising again.

990
WHEN A RELATIVE SUFFERS A MYSTERIOUS DEATH AND YOU CANNOT GET JUSTICE

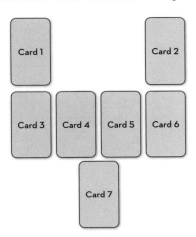

Purpose and background information:

When the police insist the death is suicide or an accident, but you know that there are unexplained facts.

CARD 1: Do the circumstances of the death go against your relative's pattern of behavior/where they would have been/had unexplained injuries? **CARD 2:** Was your relative worried but wouldn't explain why/was getting strange phone calls/had dubious friends/connections with drugs? **CARD 3:** Are the police so overwhelmed that they are going for the easiest explanation/if you live in a small community could there be a cover-up? **CARD 4:** Do you want justice/are prepared to hire a detective/go to an investigative journalist/a medium? **CARD 5:** Although people say let it rest, are you determined justice will be done? **CARD 6:** Do you just want to move away/let your relative rest in peace? **CARD 7:** Will you get justice if you persist?

What you should use:

The full deck.

When:

When no one will listen to you.

991
THE LOSS OF A CHILD IN THE FAMILY

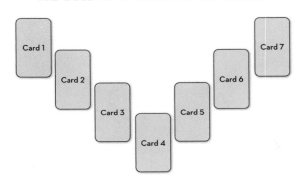

Purpose and background information:

When the ultimate tragedy occurs, whether it's a stillborn babe or a toddler, or a teenager passes away through illness or as a result of an accident.

CARD 1: What practical background help can/should you offer to make the parents' life easier/childcare for siblings/taking over household chores/doing their shopping? **CARD 2:** Can you tread on eggshells for many months if necessary/allowing the parent/s to talk about the child if, when, and how they want, dealing with their anger/frustration? **CARD 3:** Can you shield them from people who say the child was an angel taken back to heaven/other platitudes, however well-intentioned, that may pour salt into the wounds? **CARD 4:** If there was negligence connected with the death, can you assist with filing complaints that, even if not successful, ease the parents' sense of helplessness? **CARD 5:** Can you help reassure other children in the family that they aren't going to die? **CARD 6:** Will you always in future still talk of the child/remember their birthday and the anniversary of their death, when some may after a time pretend they never existed? **CARD 7:** Though there will always be sadness at the loss, can you help the parents when they're ready to move forward?

What you should use:

The twenty-two major cards and the sixteen Court cards.

When:

After the death.

992
THE LOSS OF A PARENT OR GRANDPARENT

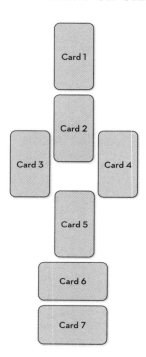

Purpose and background information:

When the matriarch or patriarch of the family is no longer there.

CARD 1: Did you get a chance to say good-bye? If not, is there a special place you can go to get closure? **CARD 2:** If the death was expected, was there a chance for your parent/grandparent to put things in order/make up any differences/disagreements with you/other family members? **Alternative CARD 2:** If unexpected, can everything be arranged as would have been wanted? **CARD 3:** Should you avoid all personal guilt/blame/refuse to allow reproaches from family members to sour the time of mourning? **CARD 4:** Do you dream or sense your deceased relative around you/protecting the family? If not, can you accept that the raw grief is, for now, obscuring the sense of presence? **CARD 5:** Should you collect a special memory box of mementos/a book of memories/sayings/recipes to keep good memories alive? **CARD 6:** Should you take all the time you need to grieve, rather than rushing back into life/being strong for everyone? **CARD 7:** Should you refuse to be hurried over property/financial settlements in the early days/insist everyone honor the memory of the grandparent/parent and put rivalries aside when settlement comes?

What you should use:

The full deck.

When:

After the funeral.

993

WHEN YOU ARE TOTALLY OVERWHELMED BY RESPONSIBILITY AND WORRY AND SEE NO WAY FORWARD

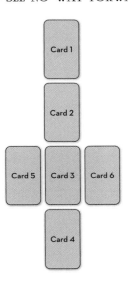

Purpose and background information:

When you cannot cope any more.

CARD 1: What/who is your greatest burden? **CARD 2:** What unnecessary burdens have you taken on out of kindness/guilt? **CARD 3:** What burdens can/must be most easily and urgently be shed? **CARD 4:** What burden/s cannot be put down? **CARD 5:** Who, whether individual or organization, can/must you ask for urgent help/respite now and insist you get it no matter how resistant they may be? **CARD 6:** How can you avoid becoming overwhelmed by responsibilities in the future/making sure others do their share?

What you should use:

The twenty-two Major cards and the sixteen Court cards.

When:

The end of the week or month.

994

WHEN YOUR PARTNER DIES AND YOU HAD SO MANY PLANS FOR RETIREMENT

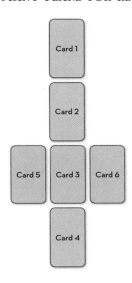

Purpose and background information:

When you waited so long for the freedom of traveling together and starting a new life, but it was never to be.

CARD 1: Should you resist pressure from family and friends, however well-meaning, to make irrevocable decisions about your future before you are ready? **CARD 2:** Which plans can still be salvaged, travel/moving to a much-desired location/moving nearer grandchildren? **CARD 3:** How can these plans be adapted to do solo? **CARD 4:** Are there things you always wanted to do/places to see that you put aside because of joint plans that now might be possible? **CARD 5:** Will your new life ultimately be fulfilling? **CARD 6:** Will you, as you travel/change location, eventually meet new friends and maybe even one day much further down the track, if you choose, new love?

What you should use:

The forty Minor cards, Aces to Tens.

When:

The start of a new month or year.

995

WHEN A PARTNER OR CLOSE RELATIVE IS LOSING A BATTLE FOR LIFE THAT IT SEEMED THEY WOULD WIN

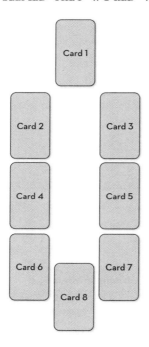

practitioner/spiritual healing/Reiki/massage/oils to maximize life quality? **Card 6:** Do you/can you find practical and emotional support for yourself if you are the one having to stay strong for everyone? **Card 7:** Can you/would you, when the time comes and if they wish, encourage your partner or relative to let go when they are ready/let them drift away in their own time and way/be there to the end in the way they want? **Card 8:** Afterward, can you give yourself time, space, and support when needed for what has been a life-changing journey for you?

What you should use:

The full deck.

When:

When it's clear that your partner or relative is unlikely to recover.

996

DEALING WITH A SUICIDE IN THE FAMILY

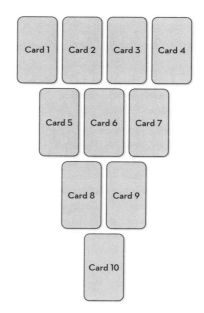

Purpose and background information:

When you are preparing a friend or relative for the last journey.

Card 1: Does the person want to know they're reaching the later stages of life, or do they prefer to keep up hope to the last, knowing miracles do happen? **Card 2:** Do they want to stop intrusive treatment/move into palliative care? How can you best support this decision? **Card 3:** Do they want to have home care/a hospice? How can you best help practically and emotionally so they get the best care? **Card 4:** Can you/will you, where possible, ensure that their wishes for their end-of-life care are followed, accepting that they may wish to change any legal instructions they made when healthy? **Card 5:** Do they want to see a religious minister/a spiritual

Purpose and background information:
When the death has the additional trauma of the person's choosing to take their own life.

CARD 1: Had the family member threatened or attempted suicide before, or was this totally unexpected? **CARD 2:** Do you know the reason/mental illness/depression/bullying, or a seemingly impossible situation to solve such as debt/threats/pressures for repayment? **CARD 3:** Can you feel that the person is at peace if they have lived a troubled existence/do you want to consult a sympathetic priest/a medium for reassurance? **CARD 4:** If there is to be/was an inquest, do you think it was fair/will uncover the truth? Are there friends/enemies who know the real reason for the desperate action? **CARD 5:** Was it a cry for help that went wrong/did the person not intend to die? **CARD 6:** If there was a suicide note, was it/did it reflect sudden anger/desperation and missed the love that was there? **CARD 7:** Can you deal with your own/family's tangled emotions to avoid unnecessary/pointless guilt at what-ifs to overshadow your lives? **CARD 8:** Can you celebrate the good things of the person's life, their gifts/happy moments in the way that seems most appropriate? **CARD 9:** Would counseling help, or are you better dealing with the emotions as a family/yourself? **CARD 10:** Will you find your way to happiness again?

What you should use:
The forty Minor cards, Aces to Tens, and the sixteen Court cards.

When:
A quiet evening for reflection.

997
WHEN YOUR FIANCÉ/FIANCÉE CALLS OFF THE WEDDING JUST WEEKS BEFORE THE CEREMONY WITHOUT EXPLANATION

Purpose and background information:
When your fiancé/fiancée sends a message to say he/she cannot marry you and they're going away.

CARD 1: Why has this happened/what went wrong pre-wedding? Nerves/something more? **CARD 2:** Can you/how can you get in touch with your fiancé/e urgently? **CARD 3:** If you talk, will he/she change their mind/agree to go ahead on this/another occasion? **CARD 4:** Could/should you ever trust them again, even if they agreed/what assurances would persuade you? **CARD 5:** Who will help you cancel/postpone the arrangements/how must your fiancé/e help, not just hide? **CARD 6:** Can anything be salvaged? Should you go away with a friend/relative to the honeymoon destination out of sheer defiance/to get your head straight? **CARD 7:** Can you see this not as a failure in you, but put the blame where it belongs, for pulling out at the last minute? **CARD 8:** If your fiancé/e doesn't come back/you do not want them, will you find love/happiness again with someone you can trust, and finally have the wedding you longed for?

What you should use:
The full deck.

When:
Soon after receiving the bad news so you can plan what best to do.

Card 8

Card 7

Card 6

Card 5

Card 4

Card 3

Card 2

Card 1

A PYRAMID SPREAD WHEN YOUR PARTNER OF MANY YEARS HAS DESERTED YOU FOR A NEW LIFE THAT THEY HAVE PLANNED FOR YEARS

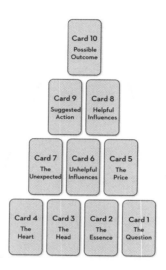

Purpose and background information:

The pyramid formation in Ancient Egypt is sometimes credited as being a repository of inexplicable physical phenomena and transformers of cosmic energy and, as such, is an excellent Spread for an upward path when life cannot get any worse.

CARD 1: The question, in this case: how could someone you trusted prove so devious and calculating? **CARD 2:** The essence, sometimes called the root of the matter, is the deeper, often unformed question, in this case: did you ignore warning signs/should you have been less trusting/looked out for yourself more? **CARD 3:** The head or logical considerations: how can you make sure that you are not left financially destitute, even if you have to be far more ruthless than you have ever been? **CARD 4:** The heart of the matter: did your partner ever love you/have they found a new love/was the other person always around? **CARD 5:** The price, not only monetary but emotional, of any decision: how far are

you prepared to legally pursue your partner to get what is rightfully yours? **CARD 6:** Unhelpful influences, those friends/family members who did know but kept quiet/those who will say it was your fault s/he left. **CARD 7:** The unexpected, seeing just over the next horizon as to what may happen in your partner's new life for good or ill. **CARD 8:** Helpful influences, friends/family/a good attorney who will help you through this crisis. **CARD 9:** Suggested action, what you can and should do to make a new life for yourself/if you would ever want them back if the new life didn't work out. **CARD 10:** Possible outcome, the happy future you can make once you have settled this crisis.

What you should use:

The full deck.

When:

Once you are over the initial shockwaves.

999
WHEN YOU HAVE BEEN CONNED OUT OF ALL YOUR SAVINGS AND YOUR RETIREMENT FUND AND FEAR THERE IS NO REDRESS

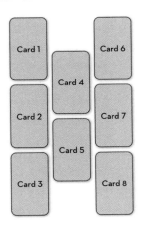

Purpose and background information:
When everything you have worked for is gone.

CARD 1: If you insist/if necessary going to an ombudsman, do you have any redress through your bank if your life savings were lost by someone claiming to be them, even though you agreed? **CARD 2:** Is there any legal/criminal redress if this is a scam scheme that has affected many others? **CARD 3:** Do you have any assets left you can realize/reinvest/downsize? **CARD 4:** If you are still working, can you extend your working life until you have built up some reserves? **CARD 5:** Do you have business ideas you could set up to make money for the future? **CARD 6:** Would family help, even temporarily, until you are back on your feet? **CARD 7:** Will you get through this and regain security even if the future is different from/more modestly funded than you planned? **CARD 8:** Will you get justice and at least part of your money back?

What you should use:
The full deck.

When:
When you discover the scam and financial institutions are proving unhelpful.

1,000
THE FOUR-PILLARS-OF-WISDOM SPREAD WHEN YOU HIT A MAJOR LOSS OF CONFIDENCE AND FEEL YOU HAVE WASTED YOUR LIFE

Purpose and background information:
When your career is going nowhere, your love life is non-existent, and all your dreams seem to have come to nothing.

CARD/PILLAR 1: The first change you can make career-wise based on a skill you aren't using. **CARD/PILLAR 2:** The second change you can make to improve your love/social life.
CARD/PILLAR 3: The dream you can still attain if you reach out.
CARD/PILLAR 4: The unexpected opportunity, once you set the wheels in motion.

What you should use:
The twenty-two Major cards.

When:
A Thursday, the day of traditional wisdom.

CHAPTER 48

SPREAD 1001

So far in this book I have suggested 1,000 different ways to read Tarot cards and many sample layouts that I have found work well, created or adapted by me over more than forty years.

You will no doubt have been scribbling in your Tarot journal or in the margins of the book your own ideas, alternatives, and improvements to my suggestions.

The book offers a basis for you to develop your own unique Tarot wisdom and maybe teach it to others, or write a book as well as helping and advising yourself and others using some of the Layouts I have described. Each Layout is based on an actual reading I have given as I travel the world; and as you have seen, I have divided the book into themes so you can select which is closest to a particular need.

Like you, I am still exploring and learning better ways of interpreting the Tarot in the years ahead; and I hope to be allowed to share with you, in subsequent books, my growing insights.

This is a special book written during my own lockdown resulting from the Coronavirus pandemic that has shaken so many certainties, lost so many unfinished lives, and has made me realize how precious life is. It has made me appreciate, too, that all wisdom—not just Tarot but in every area of life—must be shared, not set in stone, but freely offered as an evolving ever-swelling river of knowledge and experience. I hope that such knowledge I have acquired will enrich your own wisdom and traditions and inspire you to using your cards in new ways as you guide the lives of yourself and others.

You may find, if you have read my *1001 Spells*, that there are rituals with which you can increase the energy and manifest the possibilities uncovered in the Tarot spreads. Indeed in *1001 Spells* is a whole section dedicated to spells using Tarot cards as a focus. In this book too, *1001 Spreads*, I have suggested ways of using your Tarot cards for developing various psychic arts and using crystals and pendulums to enhance the wisdom of the cards.

Month 1	Month 2	Month 3	Month 4	Month 5	Month 6	Month 7	Month 8	Month 9	Month 10	Month 11	Month 12
Finances	Finances	Finances	Finances	Finances	Finances	Finances	Finances	Finances	Finances	Finances	Finances
Career, Business, Creative	Career, Business, Creative	Career, Business, Creative	Career, Business, Creative	Career, Business, Creative	Career, Business, Creative	Career, Business, Creative	Career, Business, Creative	Career, Business, Creative	Career, Business, Creative	Career, Business, Creative	Career, Business, Creative
Health	Health	Health	Health	Health	Health	Health	Health	Health	Health	Health	Health
Leisure-Friendships & Neighbors	Leisure-Friendships & Neighbors	Leisure/Friendships & Neighbors	Leisure/Friendships & Neighbors	Leisure/Friendships & Neighbors	Leisure/Friendships & Neighbors	Leisure/Friendships & Neighbors	Leisure/Friendships & Neighbors	Leisure/Friendships & Neighbors	Leisure/Friendships & Neighbors	Leisure/Friendships & Neighbors	Leisure/Friendships & Neighbors
Home Life	Home Life	Home Life	Home Life	Home Life	Home Life	Home Life	Home Life	Home Life	Home Life	Home Life	Home Life
Love & Relationships	Love & Relationships	Love & Relationships	Love & Relationships	Love & Relationships	Love & Relationships	Love & Relationships	Love & Relationships	Love & Relationships	Love & Relationships	Love & Relationships	Love & Relationships

Card 1

Overall Theme

Card 2

Unexpected

Card 3

Opportunity

Card 4

Challenges

SPREAD 1001
YOUR PERSONAL-YEAR-AHEAD SPREAD

Spread 1001 forms the template for a comprehensive Layout that looks at six different areas of your life for each month of the whole year ahead. You do not have to start in January. Both New Year's Day and the first day of the month after acquiring this book are ideal.

Record your insights for each of the six areas in each month and, as you enter that month, you can remind yourself of the key features highlighted by the six cards of that month. Use the full deck.

Each month has six cards: one for health; one for love and any relationships which can include parents and children; one for your home life; one for your career, business, or creative ventures; one for leisure, friendships, and neighbors; and the final one for finances.

As you hold each card after turning it over, allow any images, words, and impressions for each of the six cards to expand the meaning.

The cards will zoom in on each of those aspects. When the actual month begins, you can, if you wish, pick just one card again from the whole deck to see if there is any extra information to add to that which you discovered when you viewed the whole year.

How to organize the cards:

Since 6 times 12 equals 72, we have six cards left when we use the full deck of seventy-eight.

Before starting, remove the Death and Devil cards, as they aren't particularly helpful in twelve-month reviews; and do the same if you later pick an extra card at the beginning of a particular month. So that leaves you four cards.

Card 1 that remains is your overall year theme; **Card 2** is what is unexpected in the year ahead; **Card 3** is a particular opportunity the year will bring; and **Card 4** is the challenges to be overcome in the year ahead.

What if you know a certain day, or two, within the month will be especially significant?

In addition, during any month as you enter it, if a particular day is important, pick a single card for the actual day about which you want to know, selected from the whole deck.

This card will highlight what you need to know. You do not need to, but can if you wish, specify an area such as health if you are going for a check-up. If there are two significant areas such as career and finance, pick two cards from the whole deck.

Tarot and Magick Spells:

- If you pick an extra card at the beginning of a month or indeed for any significant day during any month, you can generate additional power and protection when you need special energy or good fortune in the area which the card indicates is most relevant to the day/month ahead.

- Choose a card or two if, for example, you are worried about career and finances, and set it/them in the center of a table.

- To the approximate North (furthest away from you as you face the table), set a dish of salt for the practical earth input. This corresponds with the Pentacles suit.

- To the approximate East, to your right hand, set an incense stick in a holder. You can check the appropriate fragrance and color of that day by looking in the Appendix of this book or use lavender or rose for every purpose. This represents the Air element to stir the energies, symbolized by Swords in the Tarot.

- To the approximate South, directly in front of you, set the candle in the color of the day, or use all-purpose white. This represents the element of Fire, to raise power, symbolized by Wands in the Tarot. Use a deep heatproof holder that you can carry safely.

- To the approximate West, to your left hand, set a small bowl of water or rose water, representing the element of Water, symbolized by Cups in the Tarot. This mixes together all the energies of the spell to create the fifth element, Aether or Akasha, the space in which magick occurs.

- Your four items form a circle around the card/s.

- Light your candle and, from it, your incense stick.

- Now sprinkle a clockwise circle of salt granules around the outside of the circle made by the four items starting in the North, saying nine times *I call* (whatever your card represents, for example a successful interview if you had picked the Sun card and you were focusing on career) *with the power of Earth.* Nine, the number of completion and perfection, is often used in magick.

- Return your salt to its place. Now take the incense stick from the holder and, holding it carefully like a smoke pen, starting in the East, make spirals clockwise around the circle saying nine times *I call* (the same as you did for Earth) *with the power of Air.*

- Return the incense to its holder. Take the candle and pass that around the outside of the circle saying nine times *I call* (---) *with the power of Fire.* Start in the South.

- Return the candle to its place. Finally taking the bowl of water, sprinkle water drops around the outside of the circle, starting in the West, saying nine times *I call* (--) *with the power of Water.*

- Return the water bowl to its place.

- Now circle the table nine times yourself, clapping and chanting faster and faster, saying the words faster and faster: *Earth, Air, Water, Fire, bring to me what I desire,* until you can clap and chant no faster.

- Then slow the words and the clapping and make them also quieter until you remain still and in silence.

- Now blow out the candle, saying *The Spell is done, the power is won, one two three, the power's in me.*

- Leave the incense to burn and tip the salt and the water away under a running tap.

- Carry the empowered Tarot card with you all day. You can do this with any Spread you use in this book, setting the most significant card of the Layout within the circle and adapting the chant to the theme of the reading.

May your Tarot readings and your life
be filled with beauty and significance.
Cassandra Eason, May 2020

INDEX